Small Business Fi...
All-in-One For Du...

C000171779

Can You Make Money?

Could your business idea leave you rolling in used tenners? You need to establish:

- Day-to-day operating costs
- How long it will take to reach break even
- How much start-up capital you need
- The likely sales volume
- The profit level required for the business not merely to survive, but also to thrive
- The retail price of your product or service

Calculating VAT

Calculating the VAT element of any transaction can be a confusing sum. Following these simple steps can help you get it right:

1. Take the gross amount of any sum (items you sell or buy) – that is, the total including any VAT – and divide it by 117.5, if the VAT rate is 17.5 per cent. (If the rate is different, add 100 to the VAT percentage rate and divide by that number.)
2. Multiply the result from Step 1 by 100 to get the pre-VAT total.
3. Multiply the result from Step 1 by 17.5 to arrive at the VAT element of the bill.

Tips for Controlling Your Business Cash

- **Separate cash handlers.** Be sure that the person who accepts cash isn't also recording the transaction.
- **Separate authorisation responsibilities.** Be sure that the person who authorises a payment isn't also signing the cheque or dispensing the cash.
- **Separate the duties of your bookkeeping function to ensure a good system of checks and balances.** Don't put too much trust in one person – unless it's yourself.
- **Separate operational responsibility (actual day-to-day transactions) from record-keeping responsibility (entering transactions in the books).**

Building Blocks of a Bookkeeping System

- **Chart of Accounts:** Lists all accounts in the books and is the road map of a business's financial transactions
- **Journals:** Place in the books where transactions are first entered
- **Nominal Ledger:** The book that summarises all a business's account transactions

Small Business Finance All-in-One For Dummies®

Your Best Sources of Help and Advice

- **Business Link** is the government's small business service with offices in most big towns and cities, and advisers with the whole range of business expertise. Visit www.business link.gov.uk or call 08456 009 006.

- **The Federation of Small Businesses** offers various services including a legal helpline. Call 01253 336 000 or visit www.fsb.org.uk.

- **The Advisory, Conciliation and Arbitration Service** (ACAS) is an invaluable source of help to business. Call 08457 474 747 or visit www.acas.org.uk.

- **Job Centre Plus** offices are helpful on recruitment and employing people with disabilities. Visit www.jobcentreplus.gov.uk or your local office.

- **The Disability Rights Commission Helpline**, call 08457 622 633.

- **The Women and Equality Unit** Web site at www.womenandequality.gov.uk can help on equal pay.

- **The Equal Opportunities Commission** is at www.eoc.org.uk.

- **The Commission for Racial Equality** is at www.cre.gov.uk.

- **Health and Safety Executive** is at www.hse.gov.uk or call the infoline on 08453 450 055.

- **HMRC** is at www.hmrc.gov.uk or call your local office.

- **The Information Commissioner** gives help on the Data Protection Act. Visit www.informationcommissioner.gov.uk or call 01625 545 745 (England), 0131 225 6341 (Scotland), 02920 894 929 (Wales), or 02890 511 270 (Northern Ireland).

Basic Financial Statements

- **Profit and loss account:** Your bottom line – subtracting costs from revenue to come up with net profit.

- **Balance sheet:** A financial snapshot that shows what you own, what you owe, and what your company is worth.

- **Cash-flow statement:** A cash monitor that follows the flow of cash in and out of your company.

- **Budget:** Your financial forecast that indicates where you plan to make and spend money.

For Dummies: Bestselling Book Series for Beginners

Small Business Finance

ALL-IN-ONE

FOR

DUMMIES®

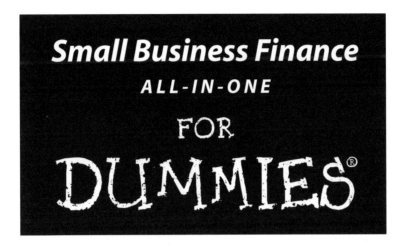

Small Business Finance
ALL-IN-ONE
FOR
DUMMIES®

by Liz Barclay, Colin Barrow, Paul Barrow,
Lita Epstein, Tony Levene, Steven Peterson,
Paul Tiffany, and John A. Tracy

Edited by Faith Glasgow

John Wiley & Sons, Ltd

Small Business Finance All-in-One For Dummies®
Published by
John Wiley & Sons, Ltd
The Atrium
Southern Gate
Chichester
West Sussex
PO19 8SQ
England

E-mail (for orders and customer service enquires): cs-books@wiley.co.uk

Visit our Home Page on www.wiley.com

For general information on our other products and services, please contact our Customer Care
Department within the U.S. at 800-762-2974, outside the U.S. at 317-572-3993, or fax 317-572-4002.

For technical support, please visit www.wiley.com/techsupport.

Wiley also publishes its books in a variety of electronic formats. Some content that appears in print may
not be available in electronic books.

British Library Cataloguing in Publication Data: A catalogue record for this book is available from the
British Library

ISBN: 978-0-470-99786-4

Printed and bound in Great Britain by Bell & Bain Ltd, Glasgow

10 9 8 7 6 5 4 3 2 1

WILEY

About the Authors

Faith Glasgow has been writing on finance, property, and more recently business for longer than she cares to remember, and has freelanced since 1998. She has contributed to a wide spectrum of publications during that time, including most of the broadsheets, a range of magazines from *Vogue* to *Investors Chronicle*, and Web sites such as www.iii.co.uk. In 2007, she edited *Personal Finance & Investing All-in-One* for Dummies. Faith lives in London with her husband, daughter and cat, and a large mortgage.

Liz Barclay is presenter of BBC Radio 4's daily consumer and social affairs programme *You and Yours*. Before joining the BBC she worked for Citizens Advice specialising in Employment and Family Law and Money Advice. She writes on business issues for *BBC Online* and has written on business and personal finance for various national newspapers, magazines, and Web sites over the past 10 years. Liz has also produced and presented 60 small business and 10 occupational health and safety programmes for BBC2 and written several booklets on work and personal finance to accompany BBC television and radio programmes. She chairs and speaks at conferences and seminars on work and business, is a trained counsellor, and lives in London.

Colin Barrow was, until recently, Head of the Enterprise Group at Cranfield School of Management, where he taught entrepreneurship on the MBA and other programmes. He is also a visiting professor at business schools in the US, Asia, France, and Austria. His books on entrepreneurship and small business have been translated into twenty languages including Russian and Chinese. He worked with Microsoft to incorporate the business planning model used in his teaching programmes into the software program, Microsoft Business Planner. He is a regular contributor to newspapers, periodicals and academic journals such as the *Financial Times*, *The Guardian*, *Management Today*, and the *International Small Business Journal*.

Thousands of students have passed through Colin's start-up and business growth programmes, going on to run successful and thriving enterprises, and raising millions in new capital. He is on the board of several small businesses, is a University Academic Governor, and has served on the boards of public companies, venture capital funds, and on Government Task Forces.

Paul Barrow trained and qualified as a Chartered Accountant with Deloitte & Touche before obtaining his MBA at Bradford University. As a senior consultant with Ernst & Young he was responsible for managing and delivering quality consulting assignments. During the mid-1980s, he was Investment Review Director for a UK venture capital business.

In 1998, as Group Finance Director of Adval Group plc, he was part of the team which took their software company on to the Alternative Investment Market. Adval specialises in providing multimedia training – both bespoke and generic. Paul has also been a director of several owner-managed businesses, and has started up and sold other businesses. He currently works with businesses as diverse as software, turkey farming, and food retailing.

Paul is a Visiting Fellow at Cranfield University where he teaches on the Business Growth Programme. This programme is designed specifically for owner managers who want to grow and improve their businesses. He also teaches at Warwick University and Oxford Brookes on similar programmes.

Paul has written several other business books: *The Business Plan Workbook* and *Raising Finance* (both Kogan Page/Sunday Times); *The Best Laid Business Plans* and *The Bottom Line* (both Virgin Books). All these books are aimed at owner managers trying to grow and improve their businesses.

Lita Epstein, who earned her MBA from Emory University's Goizueta Business School, enjoys helping people develop good financial, investing, and tax planning skills.

While getting her MBA, Lita worked as a teaching assistant for the financial accounting department and ran the accounting lab. After completing her MBA, she managed finances for a small nonprofit organisation and for the facilities management section of a large medical clinic.

She designs and teaches online courses on topics such as investing for retirement, getting ready for tax time, and finance and investing for women. She's written more than ten books, including *Streetwise Retirement Planning* and *Trading For Dummies*.

Lita was the content director for a financial services Web site, MostChoice. com, and managed the Web site Investing for Women. As a Congressional press secretary, Lita gained firsthand knowledge about how to work within and around the Federal bureaucracy, which gives her great insight into how government programmes work. In the past, Lita has been a daily newspaper reporter, magazine editor, and fundraiser for the international activities of former US President Jimmy Carter through The Carter Center.

Tony Levene is a member of *The Guardian* Money team where he writes on issues ranging from investment to consumer rights. He has been a financial journalist for over 30 years, after spending a year or so teaching French beforehand. Over his career, he has worked for newspapers including *The Sunday Times*, *Sunday Express*, *Daily Express, The Sun, Daily Star*, and *Sunday Mirror*. He has also published eight previous books on investment and financial issues. He lives in London with his wife Claudia, 'grown up' children Zoë and Oliver, and cats Plato, Pandora, and Pascal.

Steven Peterson is a senior partner and founder of Home Planet Technologies, a management training company specialising in hands-on software tools designed to enhance business strategy, business planning, and general management skills. He is the creator and designer of The Protean Strategist, a state of the art computer-based business simulation. The simulation creates a dynamic business environment where participants run companies and compete against each other in a fast-changing marketplace. Each management team in the simulation is responsible for developing its own strategy, business plan, and programme to make the plan work.

Steven has used The Protean Strategist to add excitement, hands-on experience, teamwork, and a competitive challenge to corporate training programmes around the world. He has worked with both large and small companies on products and services in industries ranging from telecommunications to financial services and from high technology to consumer goods and industrial equipment. He can be reached by e-mail at `peterson@HomePlanetTech.com`.

When he's not planning his own business, Steven is planning to remodel his 80-year old house or to redesign the garden. And he confesses that of the three, the garden proves to be the most difficult. Steven holds advanced degrees in mathematics and physics, receiving his doctorate from Cornell University. He teaches part-time at the Haas School of Business, University of California at Berkeley, and lives in the Bay Area with his long-time companion, Peter, and their long-lived canine, Jake.

Paul Tiffany is the managing director of Paul Tiffany & Associates, a Santa Rosa, California-based firm that has offered management training and consulting services to organizations throughout the world for the past fifteen years. In addition, he has taught business planning courses at some of the top business schools in the country, including Stanford, Wharton, and The Haas School of Business at the University of California, Berkeley, where he currently serves as adjunct professor. He holds an MBA from Harvard University and a PhD from Berkeley. He can be reached by e-mail at `tiffany@haas.berkeley.edu`.

John A. Tracy is Professor of Accounting, Emeritus, in the College of Business and Administration at the University of Colorado in Boulder. Before his 35-year tenure at Boulder he was on the business faculty for four years at the University of California in Berkeley. He has served as staff accountant at Ernst & Young and is the author of several books on accounting, including *The Fast Forward MBA in Finance* and *How To Read a Financial Report*. Dr Tracy received his MBA and PhD degrees from the University of Wisconsin and is a CPA in Colorado.

Publisher's Acknowledgements

We're proud of this book; please send us your comments through our Dummies online registration form located at www.dummies.com/register/.

Some of the people who helped bring this book to market include the following:

Acquisitions, Editorial, and Media Development

Project Editor: Steve Edwards

Content Editor: Nicole Burnett

Executive Editor: Samantha Spickernell

Compiled by: Faith Glasgow

Text Splicer: David Price

Publisher: Jason Dunne

Executive Project Editor: Daniel Mersey

Cover Photos: © Getty Images/Chemistry

Screenshots: © Sage (UK) Limited.

Cartoons: Ed McLachlan

Composition Services

Project Coordinator: Erin Smith

Layout and Graphics: Claudia Bell, Carl Byers, Stephanie D. Jumper, Ronald Terry, Christine Williams

Special Art:

Proofreaders: John Greenough

Indexer: Becky Hornyak

Special Help: Alissa D. Ellet

Contents at a Glance

Table of Contents

Introduction

*W*elcome to *Small Business Finance All-in-One For Dummies*, your one-stop shop for information about every aspect of managing small business finance.

Whether you're already set up in business and seek a greater knowledge about the finances, or you're looking to get started and need to understand the financial considerations of doing so, this book is here to help. Here, we bring together information on the key areas of small business finance, enabling you to understand the fundamentals of them all. From raising the money to put your business ideas into practice and the day-to-day running of your financial affairs, to the legalities of paying both your staff and the taxman and forecasting for growth, this book has it covered.

With help from *Small Business Finance All-in-One For Dummies*, you can get to grips with, and stay on top of, your business finances.

About This Book

If you're trying to get to grips with the ins and outs of payroll responsibilities, look ahead to the financial future of your business, gain an understanding of tax statuses, or work out which bookkeeping software package to invest in, this book provides an introduction to the most useful areas of financial advice.

You can read further details in other *For Dummies* books or see a financial adviser for more specific advice. If you've read all there is to read in this book but still want more, check out the extra information in these *For Dummies* titles (all published by Wiley):

- *Starting a Business For Dummies* (Colin Barrow)
- *Bookkeeping For Dummies* (Paul Barrow and Lita Epstein)
- *Paying Less Tax 2006/2007 For Dummies* (Tony Levene)
- *Small Business Employment Law For Dummies* (Liz Barclay)
- *Understanding Business Accounting For Dummies* (John A. Tracy and Colin Barrow)
- *Business Plans For Dummies* (Paul Tiffany, Steven Peterson, and Colin Barrow)

Conventions Used in This Book

To make your reading experience easier and to alert you to key words or points, we use certain conventions in this book:

- ✔ In This Chapter lists appear at the beginning of each chapter and are a kind of table of contents in miniature.

- ✔ Numbered lists indicate a series of steps that you need to take in order to accomplish a specific task.

- ✔ Bulleted lists (like this one) indicate things that you can do in any order, or list related bits of information.

- ✔ *Italics* introduce new terms and underscore key differences between words.

- ✔ **Bold** text is used to show the action part of bulleted and numbered lists.

- ✔ Monofont is used for web addresses.

- ✔ HMRC (you'll see this acronym a lot in this book!) means Her Majesty's Revenue and Customs – you might better know this organisation by it's old name of the Inland Revenue, or simply as 'the taxman' (regardless of gender). We stick to the technically correct term of HMRC.

It's also worth remembering that although we've included up-to-date financial and investment information at the time of writing, these things do change! Use the facts and figures within this All-in-One as a guide, but if in doubt, seek expert advice on the most up-to-date information.

What You're Not to Read

You can read this book cover to cover, or skip through just reading the sections that interest you the most. You can also glean plenty of information from this book without reading the sidebars (the grey boxes) – the detail in our sidebars is interesting but not crucial to understanding the rest of the book's content.

Foolish Assumptions

In writing this book we've made a number of assumptions about you. Perhaps you're one of the following:

- ✔ An owner or manager (or both) seeking a comprehensive reference guide to managing your small business.

🖊 Someone aspiring to owning your own business and considering the financial way ahead.

In addition, maybe some of the following apply to you.

🖊 You're not a financial expert, but you do want to feel secure in your knowledge.

🖊 You want to know the basics and essentials of small business finance and want access to tips and advice as and when you need them.

🖊 You're interested in some or all aspects of small business finance, for example:

- You want to know enough about to tax to make sure you are paying the right amounts.

- You know that you need money to ensure a continuous flow of customers, products, and services, as well as a place to work from, but want to know more about different places to source money from.

- You're feel you need to have a better understanding of the main financial statements used by accountants.

🖊 You're employing staff for the first time and want to know about your rights and responsibilities to them.

If any (or all) of these assumptions accurately describe you, you've come to the right book.

How This Book Is Organised

We've divided *Small Business Finance All-in-One For Dummies* into six separate books. This section explains what you can find in each of these books. Each book is broken into chapters tackling key aspects of small business finance. The table of contents gives you more detail of what's in each chapter, and we've even included a cartoon at the start of each part, just to keep you smiling!

Book 1: Getting Started

This is the place to head for if you're considering starting up a new business, or if you've recently arrived in the world of small businesses. Covering the ground from thinking through your business idea and researching the market to improving your business's performance after getting it off the ground, Book I helps you to get off to a flying start.

Book II: Accounting Basics

If you've ever thought of accounting and bookkeeping as daunting areas best left to the pros, Book II helps you to see the light. Clear and concise explanations enable you to master the essential basics of accounting and bookkeeping and use them to your business's advantage.

Book III: Reporting Results

Book III is your guide to the three primary financial statements prepared by accountants – the *profit and loss statement,* the *balance sheet,* and the *cash flow statement.* A good understanding of these statements is essential for reading into the financial health of your business, and Book III enables you to get to grips with them.

Book IV: Managing the Finances

As a business manager or owner, you rely heavily on financial statements to let you know what state of health your business is in. As well as knowing how to read the statements, you need to be able to use accounting tools and techniques to help keep your business in good financial health and meet your goals and targets. Book IV has the right advice.

Book V: Employing Staff

Unless you plan on working on your own, you're likely to employ staff as your business grows. Your staff are one of your biggest assets in business, so you need to keep them onside and to be aware of your rights and responsibilities as their employer. From wages and benefits through to pensions and redundancy, Book V helps you to get it right – first time.

Book VI: Keeping on Top of Tax

Tax is something we all wish we didn't have to deal with, but as a business-person you need to stay well informed. Covering the tax rules for the self-employed, business types and tax statuses, and the different types of taxation that businesses have to deal with, Book VI tells you what you need to know.

Icons Used in This Book

When you flick through this book, you'll notice little icons in the margins. These icons pick out certain key aspects of small business finance:

This icon highlights practical advice to get our investing and finance ideas working for you.

This icon is a friendly reminder of important points to take note of.

This icon highlights information that you might not need to know to sort the finances out immediately, but could stand you in good stead for the future or as background knowledge.

This icon marks things to avoid – they could be costly or drop you in deep water with HMRC, the government, or your bank.

This icon alerts you that we're using a practical example to illustrate and clarify an important financial point.

Where to Go from Here

We've designed this book as an easy-to-use reference tool that you can use comfortably, whether you already have some experience running or owning a small business, or if you're a complete newcomer. You can either read this book from cover to cover or as a reference tool to dip into when you need some information, skipping straight to the chapters that interest you.

If an idea for starting up a small business has been swimming around inside your head for a while but you don't know how to get the finances moving, head straight to Book I, or if your business has been up and running for some time and you're considering taking on employees for the first time, check out Book V. You can of course, read through each and every chapter of each and every book, but why not spend some time browsing through the detailed table of contents to see if anything of immediate interest springs out at you? Start at a place in the book that suits you, and come back later for more.

Book I
Getting Started

'In a previous life, before I became a lemming,
I was a small company without a business plan.'

In this book . . .

1f you're contemplating starting up a new business you've come to the right place! But before you can think seriously about starting your own business, you need to make sure that you're ready for the big step. This Book enables you to check out your skills and aptitude and see how they compare to the business idea you have in mind, and whether you can make the kind of money you're expecting from your idea. From researching the market and raising money to choosing your advisors and increasing sales when the business is up and running, this Book addresses the basic issues to consider when you begin your career in business.

Here are the contents of Book I at a glance:

Chapter 1

Preparing for Business

*W*ould you go into the jungle without carrying out some pretty rigorous preparation? You'd need to know something about the terrain and how to navigate it, as well as the temperature, rainfall, and food supply. You would also be keen to know what predators you might meet on the way and how to defend yourself against them.

When you're starting a business, particularly your first business, you need to carry out the same level of preparation as you would for crossing the Gobi desert or exploring the jungles of South America. You are entering hostile territory.

Your business idea may be good, it may even be great, but such ideas are two a penny. The patent office is stuffed full of great inventions that have never returned tuppence to the inventors who spent much time and money filing them. It's how you plan, how you prepare and how you implement your plan that makes the difference between success and failure. And failure is pretty much a norm for business start-ups. Tens of thousands of small firms fail, some disastrously, each and every year.

In this chapter the scene is set to make sure you are well prepared for the journey ahead.

Getting in Shape to Start Up

You need to be in great shape to start a business. You don't have to diet or exercise, at least not in the conventional sense of those words, but you do have to be sure you have the skills and knowledge you need for the business you have in mind, or know how to tap into sources of such expertise.

The following sections will help you through a pre-opening check-up so you can be absolutely certain that your abilities and interests are closely aligned to those needed by the business you have in mind. It will also help you to check that a profitable market exists for your products or services. You can use this section as a vehicle for sifting through your business ideas to see if they are worth devoting the time and energy that is needed to start up a business.

You may well not have all the expertise you need to do everything yourself. In Book I Chapter 6 you're introduced to the zillions of agencies and advisers who can fill in the gaps in your expertise.

Assessing your abilities

Business lore claims that for every ten people who want to start their own business only one finally does so. It follows that there are an awful lot of dreamers out there who, whilst liking the idea of starting their own business, never get around to taking action. For now, see whether you fit into one of the following entrepreneurial categories.

- ✔ **Nature**. If one of your parents or siblings runs his or her own business, successfully or otherwise, you are highly likely to start up your own business. No big surprise here as the rules and experiences of business are being discussed every day and some of it is bound to rub off. It also helps if you are a risk-taker who is comfortable with uncertainty.

- ✔ **Nurture**. For every entrepreneur whose parents or siblings have a business there are two who don't. If you can find a business idea that excites you, and has the prospect of providing personal satisfaction and wealth, then you can assemble all the skills and resources needed to succeed in your own business. You need to acquire good planning and organisational skills (Book I Chapter 4 covers all aspects of writing a business plan) and either develop a well-rounded knowledge of basic finance, people management, operational systems, business law, marketing, and selling, or get help and advice from people who have that knowledge.

- ✔ **Risk-taker**. If you crave certainty in everything you do, then running your own business may be something of a culture shock. By the time the demand for a product or service is an absolutely sure-fired thing, there may already be too many others in the market to leave much room for you. Don't confuse risk taking with a pure gamble. You need to be able to weigh things up and take a calculated risk.

✔ **Jack-of-all-trades.** You need to be prepared to do any business task at anytime. The buck definitely stops with you when you run your own business. You can't tell a customer her delivery will be late, just because a driver fails to show up. You will just have to put in a few more hours and do the job yourself.

Discovering a real need

You might be a great potential entrepreneur but you still need to spell out exactly what it is you plan to do, who needs it, and how it will make money. A good starting point is to look around and see if anyone is dissatisfied with their present suppliers. Unhappy customers are fertile ground for new businesses to work in.

One dissatisfied customer is not enough to start a business for. Check out and make sure that unhappiness is reasonably widespread, as that will give you a feel for how many customers might be prepared to defect. Once you have an idea of the size of the potential market you can quickly see if your business idea is a money making proposition.

The easiest way to fill an endurable need is to tap into one or more of these triggers:

✔ **Cost reduction and economy.** Anything that saves customers money is always an attractive proposition. Lastminute.com's appeal is that it acts as a 'warehouse' for unsold hotel rooms and airline tickets that you can have at a heavy discount.

✔ **Fear and security.** Products that protect customers from any danger, however obscure, are enduringly appealing. In 1998, two months after Long-Term Capital Management (LTCM), one of America's largest hedge funds, was rescued by the Federal Reserve at a cost of $2 billion, Ian and Susan Jenkins launched the first issue of their magazine, *EuroHedge*. In the aftermath of the collapse of LTCM, which nearly brought down the US financial system single-handedly, there were 35 hedge funds in Europe, about which little was known, and investors were rightly fearful for their investments. *EuroHedge* provided information and protection to a nervous market and five years after it was launched the Jenkins's sold the magazine for £16.5 million.

✔ **Greed**. Anything that offers the prospect of making exceptional returns is always a winner. *Competitors' Companion*, a magazine aimed at helping anyone become a regular competition winner, was an immediate success. The proposition was simple. Subscribe and you get your money back if you don't win a competition prize worth at least your subscription. The magazine provided details of every competition being run that week, details of how to enter, the factual answers to all the questions and pointers on how to answer any tiebreakers. They also provided the inspiration to ensure success with this sentence: You have to enter competitions in order to have a chance of winning them.

✔ **Niche markets.** Big markets are usually the habitat of big business – encroach on their territory at your peril. New businesses thrive in markets that are too small to even be an appetite wetter to established firms. These market niches are often easy prey to new entrants as they have usually been neglected, ignored or ill-served in the past.

✔ **Differentiation.** Consumers can be a pretty fickle bunch. Just dangle something, faster, brighter or just plain newer and you can usually grab their attention. Your difference doesn't have to be profound or even high-tech to capture a slice of the market. Book buyers rushed in droves to Waterstones' for no more profound a reason than that their doors remained open in the evenings and on Sundays, when most other established bookshops were firmly closed.

Checking the fit of the business

Having a great business idea and having the attributes and skills needed to successfully start your own business are two of the three legs needed to make your business stool balance. Without the third leg, though, your stool isn't stable at all. You need to be sure that the business you plan to start is right for you.

Before you go too far, make an inventory of the key things that you are looking for in a business. These may include working hours that suit your lifestyle; the opportunity to meet new people; minimal paperwork; a chance to travel. Then match those up with the proposition you are considering.

Checking Viability

An idea, however exciting, unique, revolutionary, and necessary is not a business. It's a great starting point, and an essential one, but there is a good deal more work to be done before you can sidle up to your boss and tell her exactly what you think of her.

The following sections explore the steps you need to take so that you won't have to go back to your boss in six months and plead for your old job back (and possibly eat a large piece of humble pie at the same time).

Researching the market

However passionate you are about your business idea, it is unlikely that you already have the answers to all the important questions concerning your market place. Before you can develop a successful business strategy, you have to understand as much as possible about your market and the competitors you are likely to face.

The main way to get to understand new business areas, or areas that are new to you at any rate, is to conduct market research. The purpose of that research is to ensure that you have sufficient information on customers, competitors, and markets so that your market entry strategy or expansion strategy is at least on the target, if not on the bull's-eye itself. In other words, you need to explore whether enough people are attracted to buy what you want to sell at a price that will give you a viable business. If you miss the target altogether, which you could well do without research, you may not have the necessary resources for a second shot.

The areas to research include:

- ✔ **Your customers:** Who will buy more of your existing goods and services and who will buy your new goods and services? How many such customers are there? What particular customer needs will you meet?

- ✔ **Your competitors:** Who will you be competing with in your product/market areas? What are those firms' strengths and weaknesses?

Inflated numbers on the Internet

If you plan to advertise on an Internet site it makes sense to check out the sites you're considering. Be aware that some sites publish a fair amount of gobbledygook about the high number of 'hits' (often millions) the site scores. Millions of hits doesn't mean the site has millions of visitors. Some Internet sites increase their hit rate by the simple expedient of adding the number of pages each viewer must download to view the page.

Another mildly meaningless measure of the advertising value of a site is the notion of a 'subscriber'. In Internet parlance anyone visiting a Web site and passing over her e-mail address becomes part of that company's share price! It is rather like suggesting that anyone passing a shop and glancing in the window will turn into hard cash tomorrow.

Any real analysis of Web site use starts with 'page impression', which is a measure of how many times an individual page has been viewed. The Audit Bureau of Circulations, which started its life measuring newspaper response, has now turned its attention to auditing Web sites (www.abce.org.uk).

- ✔ **Your product or service:** How should you tailor your product or service to meet customer needs and to give you an edge in the market?

- ✔ **The price:** What would be seen as giving value for money and so encourages both customer loyalty and referral?

- ✔ **The advertising and promotional material:** What newspapers, journals, and so forth do your potential customers read and what Web sites do they visit? Unglamorous as it is, analysing data on what messages actually influence people to buy, rather than just to click, holds the key to identifying where and how to promote your products and service.

- ✔ **Channels of distribution:** How will you get to your customers and who do you need to distribute your products or services? You may need to use retailers, wholesalers, mail order, or the Internet. They all have different costs and if you use one or more they all want a slice of the margin.

- ✔ **Your location:** Where do you need to be to reach your customers most easily at minimum cost? Sometimes you don't actually need to be anywhere near your market, particularly if you anticipate most of your sales will come from the Internet. If this is the case you need to have strategy to make sure potential customers can find your Web site.

Try to spend your advertising money wisely. Nationwide advertisements or blanketing the market with free disks may create huge short-term growth, but there is little evidence that the clients won by indiscriminate blunderbuss advertising works well. Certainly few people using such techniques made any money.

Doing the numbers

Your big idea looks as though it has a market. You have evaluated your skills and inclinations and you believe that you can run this business. The next crucial question is – will it make you money?

It's vital that you establish the financial viability of your idea before you invest money in it or approach outsiders for backing. You need to carry out a thorough appraisal of the business's financial requirements. If the numbers come out as unworkable you can then rethink your business proposition without having lost anything. If the figures look good, then you can go ahead and prepare cash flow projections, a profit and loss account and a balance sheet, and put together the all-important business plan. (These procedures are covered in Book I Chapter 4 and in Book III.)

You need to establish for your business:

- ✔ Day to day operating costs
- ✔ How long it will take to reach break-even

- ✔ How much start-up capital is needed
- ✔ The likely sales volume
- ✔ The profit level required for the business not just to survive, but also to thrive
- ✔ The retail price of your product or service

Many businesses have difficulty raising start-up capital. To compound this, one of the main reasons small businesses fail in the early stages is that too much start-up capital is used to buy fixed assets. While some equipment is clearly essential at the start, other purchases could be postponed. You may be better off borrowing or hiring 'desirable' and labour-saving devices for a specific period. This is obviously not as nice as having them to hand all the time but remember that you have to maintain every photocopier, electronic typewriter, word processor, micro-computer, and delivery van you buy and they become part of your fixed costs. The higher your fixed costs, the longer it usually takes to reach break-even point and profitability. And time is not usually on the side of the small, new business: it has to become profitable relatively quickly or it will simply run out of money and die.

Raising the money

Two fundamentally different types of money that a business can tap into are debt and equity.

- ✔ *Debt* is money borrowed, usually from a bank, and which you have to repay. While you are making use of borrowed money you also have to pay interest on the loan.
- ✔ *Equity* is the money put in by shareholders, including the proprietor, and money left in the business by way of retained profit. You do not have to give the shareholders their money back, but they do expect the directors to increase the value of their shares, and if you go public they will proba- bly expect a stream of dividends too.

  If you do not meet the shareholders' expectations, they will not be there when you need more money – or, if they are powerful enough, they will take steps to change the board.

Alternative financing methods include raising money from family and friends, applying for grants and awards, and entering business competitions.

Check out Book I Chapter 5 for a review of all these sources of financing.

Writing up the business plan

A *business plan* is a selling document that conveys the excitement and promise of your business to potential backers and stakeholders. These potential backers could include bankers, venture capital firms, family, friends, and others who could help you get your business launched if they only knew what you want to do. (See Book I Chapter 5 for how to find and approach sources of finance.)

Getting money is expensive, time-consuming, and hard work. Having said that, it is possible to get a quick decision. One recent start-up succeeded in raising £3 million in eight days, the founder having turned down an earlier offer of £1 million made just 40 minutes after his business plan was presented. Your business plan should cover what you expect to achieve over the next three years. (See Book I Chapter 4 for full details on how to write a winning business plan.)

Most business plans are dull, badly written, and frequently read only by the most junior of people in the financing organisations they're presented to. One venture capital firm in the US went on record to say that in one year they received 25,000 business plans asking for finance and invested in only 40. Follow these tips to make your business plan stand out from the crowd:

- ✔ **Hit them with the benefits:** You need to spell out exactly what it is you do, for whom, and why that matters. One such statement that has the ring of practical authority about it is: 'Our Web site makes ordering gardening products simple. It saves the average customer two hours a week browsing catalogues and £250 a year through discounts, not otherwise available from garden centres. We have surveyed 200 home gardeners, who rate efficient purchasing as a key priority.'

- ✔ **Make your projections believable:** Sales projections always look like a hockey stick: a straight line curving rapidly upwards towards the end. You have to explain exactly what drives growth, how you capture sales, and what the link between activity and results is. The profit margins will be key numbers in your projections, alongside sales forecasts. These will be probed hard, so show the build-up in detail.

- ✔ **Say how big the market is:** Financiers feel safer backing people in big markets. Capturing a fraction of a percentage of a massive market may be hard to achieve – but if you get it at least it's worth it. Going for 10 per cent of a market measured in millions rather than billions may come to the same number, but it won't be as interesting

- ✔ **Introduce you and your team:** You need to sound like winners with a track record of great accomplishments.

- ✔ **Include non-executive directors:** Sometimes a heavyweight outsider can lend extra credibility to a business proposition. If you know or have access to someone with a successful track record in your area of business who has time on her hands, you could invite her to help. If you plan to trade as a limited company (see Book I Chapter 2 for details on legal structures) you could ask her to be a director, without specific executive responsibilities beyond being on hand to offer her advice. But she needs to have relevant experience or be able to open doors and do deals.

✔ **Provide financial forecasts:** You need projected cash flows, profit and loss accounts, and balance sheets for at least three years out. No one believes them after Year One, but the thinking behind them is what's important.

✔ **Demonstrate the product or service:** Financiers need to see what the customer is going to get. A mock-up will do or, failing that, a picture or diagram. For a service, show how customers will gain from using it. That can help with improved production scheduling and so reduce stock holding.

✔ **Spell out the benefits to your potential investor:** Tell her that her money will be paid back within 'x' years, even on your most cautious projections. Or if you are speaking with an equity investor, tell her what return she will get on her investment when you sell the business on in three or five years time.

Banning Bad Reasons to Start a Business

You may have any number of good reasons to start a business, just make sure you're not starting a business for the wrong reasons – some of which we explore in the following sections.

Steering clear of bad assumptions

You need to be sure your business idea isn't a lemon. No one can be sure she has a winning idea on her hands, but you can take some steps to make sure you avoid obvious losers. Much as you want to start a business, it won't serve you if you get in over your head because you start from a bad premise, such as those in the following list:

✔ **The market needs educating.** A situation in which the market doesn't yet realise it can't live without your product or service. Many early Internet businesses fitted this description and look what happened to them. If you think customers have to be educated before they'll purchase your product, walk away from the idea and leave it to someone with deep pockets and a long time horizon; they'll need them.

Proving that small firms matter

One unusual thing to strike anyone thinking seriously about starting up her first business is just how many organisations there are around that have timely and valuable advice to offer and that appear willing and able to offer a helping hand. Enterprise Agencies, Business Link, The Small Business Service just seem to be busting a gut to help you get rich.

Whilst it would be good to believe that making sure that your venture succeeds is their only goal, it ain't necessarily so. Many of those organisations are either directly or indirectly linked to some government initiative. Apart from the obvious desire by the government types running those organisations to be seen in a favourable light by voters – and there are over 40 million owner managers with votes in the US and Europe alone – there are practical reasons to give small businesses a helping hand.

The most compelling reason why small firms matter so much was first brought to light by an American academic, David Birch, in the 1980s. Whilst conducting research at MIT (the Massachusetts Institute of Technology) Birch demonstrated that it was enterprises employing fewer than 20 workers that were responsible for over two-thirds of the increase in employment in the United States. This revealing statistic, which was shown to be valid for much of the developed world, was seized upon as the signal for governments and others to step up their efforts to stimulate and encourage enterprise.

Small firms had been neglected for most of the post-Second World War years. In the United Kingdom various studies, including the influential Bolton Committee Report commissioned in 1971 by the government to investigate the state of the small business sector, identified this sector as starved of equity capital and experienced management. But until Birch's paper no-one accepted quite how important new and small firms were to a country's economic well-being.

Alongside this recognition of the significance of small businesses, Birch's research also revealed their fragility. He estimated that roughly 8 million enterprises operating in America closed every year which means that 'every five to six years, we have to replace half of the entire US economy'. These findings on small firm failure rates have been repeated in study after study, throughout the world. Ultimately, only about half of all small firms survive more than five years.

In the years since Birch's research was first published, there has been a dramatic increase in new business creation. In the UK alone the small business population has more than doubled from 1.9 million in 1980 to nearly 4 million in 2000. However, the failure rates, though getting better, remain worryingly high. There is a general agreement that the two main reasons for small business failure are lack of management expertise and under-capitalisation, aside that is from the effects of macro-economic mismanagement.

Arising from these twin findings that new firms are both vital and fragile have come a plethora of government initiatives to both foster and protect small firms during their formative years.

✔ **We'll be first to market**. Gaining 'first mover advantage' is a concept used to justify a headlong rush into a new business. This principle is one of the most enduring in business theory and practice. Entrepreneurs and established giants are always in a race to be first. Research from the 1980s appeared to show that market pioneers have enduring advantages in distribution, product-line breadth, product quality and, especially, market share. Beguiling though the theory of first mover advantage is, it is probably wrong. A thorough review of the research studies that supported this theory, published in the *Sloan Management Review*, found the findings to be flawed. Amongst the many errors in the earlier research, the authors of the Sloan paper revealed that the questions used to gather much of the data were at best ambiguous, and perhaps dangerously so. In fact the only compelling evidence from all the research was that nearly half of all firms pursuing a first to market strategy were fated to fail, whilst those following fairly close behind were more likely to succeed.

✔ **If we can get just one per cent of the market we are onto a winner.** There are no markets with a vacant percentage or two just waiting to be filled. Entering almost any market involves displacing someone else, even if your product is new. Po Na Na, the chain of late night souk bars, failed despite being new and apparently without competitors. If they had captured just one per cent of the dining market instead of 100 per cent of the souk-eating student market they may have survived. But the dining market had Italian, Indian, Greek, and French competitors already in place. This, when combined with the vastly improved range of ready-to-eat meals from the supermarket means that every hundredth of a percent of this market is fought over bitterly.

Whilst every business begins with an idea, it does not necessarily have to be your own idea. It has to be a viable idea, which means there have to be customers out in the market who want to buy from you. And there have to be enough of them to make you the kind of living you want. It may be an idea you have nursed and investigated for years, or it may be someone else's great idea that is just too big for her to exploit on her own. A franchised business is one example of a business idea that has room for more than one would-be business starter to get involved with. Franchises can be run at many levels ranging from simply taking up a local franchise, through to running a small chain of two to five such franchises covering neighbouring areas.

Avoiding obvious mistakes

Your enthusiasm for starting a business is a valuable asset as long as you don't let it blind you to some practical realities. The following list contains some reasoning to resist:

✔ **Starting in a business sector about which you have little or no previous knowledge or experience.** The grass always looks greener, making business opportunities in distant lands or in technologies with which you have only a passing acquaintance seem disproportionately attractive. Going this route leads to disaster. Success in business depends on superior market knowledge from the outset and sustaining that knowledge in the face of relentless competition.

✔ **Putting in more money than you can afford to lose, especially if you have to pay up front.** You need time to learn how business works. If you have spent all your capital and exhausted your capacity for credit on the first spin of the wheel, then you are more a gambler than an entrepreneur. The true entrepreneur takes only a calculated risk. Freddie Laker, who started the first low-cost no-frills airline, bet everything he could raise on buying more planes than he could afford. To compound the risk he bet against the exchange rate between the pound and the dollar, and lost. You would be wise to learn from Mr Laker's mistake.

✔ **Pitting yourself against established businesses before you're strong enough to resist them.** Laker also broke the third taboo. He took on the big boys on their own ground. He upset the British and American national carriers on their most lucrative routes. There was no way that big entrenched businesses with deep pockets would yield territory to newcomers without a fight to the death. That's not to say Laker's business model was wrong. After all, RyanAir and EasyJet have proved it can work. But those businesses tackled the short haul market to and from new airfields, and, in the case of EasyJet, at least started out with tens of millions of pounds of family money that came from a lifetime in the transportation business.

Recognising that the Economy Matters

The state of the economy in general has an effect both on the propensity of people to start a business and their chances of survival.

In 1989–90 and 1996–97, both periods of strong economic growth in the UK, the quarterly business start-up rate was 130,000 and 140,000 new businesses, respectively. In 1991–92 and 1999–2000, both periods now seen as recession troughs, start-ups ran at around 80,000 per quarter. The business closure rates during the economic troughs were also about 15 per cent higher, so the small business population as a whole shrank.

There are two schools of thought on whether starting a business is more difficult when the economy is contracting – corresponding to whether you subscribe to the belief that a glass is half-full or half-empty. On the one hand there are fewer competitors in the market, as many will have failed, whilst on the other hand those remaining are both seasoned warriors and more desperate to keep what small amount of business there is to themselves.

In real life most people start a business when they want to and not at a favourable stage in the economic cycle. That, however, does not mean that you can just ignore the economy. In much the same way as a prudent sailor pays attention to the state of the tide, you need to see if the general trend of the economy is working with or against you.

If you have a choice of when to start-up it's usually best to have the current working for you rather than against, so choose to open your business during an economic upswing, if possible.

Preparing to Recognise Success

To be truly successful in running your own business you have to both make money and have fun. That's your pay-off for the long hours, the pressure of meeting tough deadlines, and the constant stream of problems that accompany most start-up ventures.

One measure of success for any business is just staying in business. That's not as trite a goal as it sounds, nor is it easily achieved, as you can see by looking at the number of businesses that fail each year.

But survival is not enough. Cash flow, which we talk about in Book I Chapter 5, is the key to survival, but becoming profitable and making a worthwhile use of the assets you employ determines whether staying in business is really worth all your hard work.

Measuring business success

No one in her right mind sets out to run an unsuccessful business, however that's exactly what millions of business founders end up doing. Answering the following questions can act as a check on your progress to keep you on track to success.

✔ Are you meeting your goals and objectives? In Book I Chapter 4, we talk about setting down business goals. Achieving those goals and objectives is both motivational and ultimately the reason you are in business.

✔ Are you making enough money? This sounds like a daft question, but it might well be the most important one you ask. The answer comes out of your reply to two subsidiary questions:

• Could you do better by investing your time and money elsewhere? If the answer to this question is yes, then it's time to go back to the drawing-board with your business idea.

• Can you make enough money to invest in growing your business? The answer to this question will only become clear when you work out your profit margins, which is covered in Book IV Chapter 1. But the evidence that many businesses do not make enough money to re-invest in themselves is pretty evident when you see scruffy run-down premises, and old worn-out equipment and the like.

Efficiency versus effectiveness

Effectiveness is often described as 'doing the right thing', whereas *efficiency* can be described as 'doing things right'. Doing the right thing has a great deal to do with choosing the right goals to pursue. For example, if your business's mission statement emphasises becoming customer-focused and market-driven, then to be effective you must set goals that encourage everyone who works for you to be in touch with your customers *first* and to be aware of market demands *before* they start, for example designing and creating new products.

Efficiency – doing things right – is concerned more with how well the business is applying resources in pursuit of its goals. To be efficient your employees must have objectives that ensure that the business can achieve its goals of becoming customer-focused and market-driven. Among other things, these objectives should lead to a proper allocation of the research budget among design, product development, and market testing. Resources are always scarce, and no business can afford to squander them.

Successful organisations are not just one or the other – either effective or efficient. The best businesses are both efficient and effective on a consistent basis. These businesses get that way by taking goal setting and the development of clear, measurable objectives seriously in the relentless pursuit of the business's mission.

Exploring the myth and reality of business survival rates

There is considerable misinformation in circulation about the number of failing businesses. The most persistent and wrong statistic is that 70 per cent (some even quote 90 per cent) of all new businesses fail. The failure rate is high, but not that high, and in any case the term 'failure' itself, if the word is used to mean a business closing down, has a number of subtly different nuances.

Whilst there are millions of small businesses starting up, many of these survive only a relatively short time. Over half of all independently-owned ventures cease trading within five years of starting up. However, if you can make it for five years, the chances of your business surviving increase dramatically from earlier years. The nearby sidebar 'Studying the Statistics' relates the results of a long-term study in the US.

The office of the Official Receiver lists the following causes for business failures:

✓ **Insufficient turnover:** This can happen if the fixed costs of your business are too high for the level of sales turnover achieved. See Book I Chapter 3, which shows how to calculate your break-even point and so keep sales levels sufficient to remain profitable.

✓ **Poor management and supervision:** You may well know how your business works, but sharing that knowledge and expertise with those who you employ is not always that easy.

✓ **Lack of proper accounting:** Often business founders are too busy in the start-up phase to keep track of the figures. Invoices and bills are often piled up to await a convenient moment when they can be entered in the accounts. But without timely financial information key signals are missed or wrong decisions made. In Book II you can read all about how to keep on top of the numbers.

✓ **Competition:** Without a sound strategy for winning and retaining customers your business will be at the mercy of the competition.

✓ **Not enough capital:** You, along with most business start-ups, may hope to get going on a shoestring. But you need to be realistic about how much cash is needed to get underway and stay in business until sales volumes build up. In Book I Chapter 5 you will see how to plan the cash flow so you can survive.

✓ **Bad debts:** Unfortunately having great products and services and customers keen to buy them is only half the problem. The other half is making sure those customers pay up on time. One or two late or non-payers can kill off a start-up venture.

 TECHNICAL STUFF

Studying the statistics

One comprehensive study of all 814,000 firms started up in the US in a particular year followed their destinies for eight years. That research indicated that only 18 per cent were failures, in that the founders had no real say in the final event. A higher proportion (28 per cent) opted for a voluntary closure, usually when they discovered that the business they had started was losing money, or that in some other way the venture was unsatisfactory. Of the remaining 54 per cent, about half sold out or in some other way changed their ownership, perhaps moving from a partnership to trading through a limited company.

Some of these ownership changes were no doubt symptoms of success brought about by business growth, but some would indubitably have been rescue operations in which a stronger competitor saved a drowning firm. Only 28 per cent of all the start-ups in this study survived as independent entities, which after all is the primary goal of most people starting a business.

The European Observatory study carried out a few years later using a smaller sample came to a similar conclusion on survival rates. However this study added one important extra fact: the failure rate in the early years is much higher than in later years and by year five of a firm's life the failure curve is flattening off.

✔ **Excessive remuneration to the owners:** Some business owners mistake the cash coming into the business for profit and take that money out as drawings. They forget that periodic bills for tax, VAT, insurance and replacement equipment have to be allowed for, before you can calculate the true profit, and hence what can be safely drawn out. In Book III Chapter 1 you can see how to tell profit from cash and how to allow for future bills.

Chapter 2

Structuring Your Business

In This Chapter

▶ Finding the right form

▶ Exploring working on your own

▶ Going into partnership with others

▶ Starting a larger company

*W*hen you start your business you will have to make a decision more or less from the outset on the legal structure you will use to trade. Whilst that is an important decision, luckily it is not an irrevocable one. You can change structures, though not without some cost and paperwork, as your business grows.

The simplest structure is to make all the business decisions yourself and take all the risk personally. You don't have to shoulder all the responsibilities when you start a business, though most people initially do so. It may be great doing everything your way, at last, after the frustrations of working for someone else. But it can be lonely, or even scary with no one to talk over the day-to-day problems and share the responsibility of decision-making with.

If your business requires substantial investment, or involves other people who will have a more or less equal hand in the venture alongside you then your decision as to the legal structure of the business is a bit more complicated. In this chapter you will see all the important factors to consider when deciding on the legal structure for your business.

Choosing the Right Structure

There are different legal frameworks for the ownership of a business and not all are equally appropriate for everyone.

Most small businesses in the UK trade as sole proprietorships, as the figures in Table 2-1 show. However, if the larger businesses are included, then you can see that limited companies and partnerships are very popular ways to structure a business.

Table 2-1	Popular Business Structures	
	All Businesses	**Businesses with Fewer Than 50 Employees**
Sole proprietorships	578,505	189,345
Partnerships	358,330	64,550
Limited companies	657,215	94,405

One of the many factors you have to consider when deciding on the legal structure of your business is the tax implications, and we talk about how to manage your tax position in Book VI Chapter 2.

But there may be even more compelling reasons than tax to choose one structure over another. Not all sources of finance are open to every type of business. When you know how much money you need either to start up or to grow a business and what that money is needed for, you're in a better position to make an informed choice as to the best way to structure your business. If you need to raise large sums of money from the outset for research and development, for example, then a limited company may be your only realistic option, with its access to risk capital. If you are nervous of embroiling your finances with other people's, a partnership isn't an attractive option.

In general, the more money required and the more risky the venture, the more likely it is that a limited company is the appropriate structure.

The good news is that you can change your legal structure at more or less any time. Even if you go the full distance and form a company and get it listed on the stock exchange you can de-list and go private. Richard Branson (Virgin) and Alan Sugar (Amstrad) have both done this. That's not to say it's easy to dissolve partnerships or shut down companies, but it can be done.

Both your accountant and your lawyer can help you with choosing your legal form. The types of business structures and some of their advantages and disadvantages are shown in Table 2-2.

Table 2-2	Pros and Cons of Various Organisational Structures	
Type of Entity	*Main Advantages*	*Main Drawbacks*
Sole proprietorship	Simple and inexpensive to create and operate.	Owner personally liable for business debts.
	Profit or loss reported on owner's personal tax return.	No access to outside capital.

Type of Entity	Main Advantages	Main Drawbacks
		Life of business restricted to life of owner.
		Limited potential for value creation.
General partnership	Simple and inexpensive to create and operate.	Partners personally liable for business debts.
	Partners' share of profit or loss reported on personal tax returns.	The business is dissolved when a partner dies.
	Potential for some value creation.	Only partners can raise outside capital.
Limited Partnership	Non-managing partners have limited personal liability for business debts.	General partners personally liable for business debts.
	General partners can raise cash without involvingoutside investors in management of business.	More expensive to create than general partnership.
	Wider access to outside capital than for a sole proprietor.	Life of business restricted to life of first partner to die.
	Potential for some value creation.	
Limited company	Owners have limited personal liability for business debts.	More expensive to create and run than partnership or sole proprietorship.
	Some benefits (such as pensions) can be deducted as a business expense.	Owners must meet legal requirements for stock regis- tration, account filing, and paperwork.
	Owners can share out the profit and could end up, paying less overall.	
	Access to full range of outside capital.	
	Business can live on after founder's death.	

(continued)

Table 2-2 (continued)

Type of Entity	Main Advantages	Main Drawbacks
	Potential for value creation.	
	Separate taxable entity.	
Co-operative	Owners have limited personal liability for business debts.	More expensive to create than a sole proprietorship.
	Owners' share of corporate profit or loss reported on personal tax returns.	Owners must meet legal requirements for account filing, registration, and paperwork.
	Owners can use corporate loss to offset income from other sources.	Restricted access to outside capital.
		Limited potential for value creation.

Going into Business by Yourself

You may want to develop your own unique ideas for a product or service, and if so setting up your own business from the drawing board may be your only option. You may want to start a home-based business that you can run in your time. You may want to start a business because you want to do things the right way, after working for an employer who goes about things in the wrong way.

It is much easier to do things your own way if you're working alone, rather than, say, buying someone else's business that already has its routines and working practices established.

Advantages

Working for and by yourself has several things going for it:

✔ It may be possible to start the business in your spare time. This will allow you to gain more confidence in the future success of your proposed venture before either giving up your job or pumping your life savings into the venture.

✔ If you have limited money to invest in your new venture, you may not need to spend it all at the start of the project. This also means that if things do start to go wrong, it will be easier to restrict the losses.

✔ Starting a business is not just about money. Setting up and running a successful business has the potential to give you a feeling of personal achievement which may not be there to quite the same extent if you buy someone else's business, for example.

Disadvantages

Going it alone isn't all fun and games. Some of the disadvantages are:

✔ Your business will take time to grow. It may not be able to support your current personal financial obligations for many months or years.

✔ There is a lot of one-off administration involved in setting up a new business such as registering for VAT and PAYE, getting business stationery, setting up phone, fax, and Internet connections at your trading premises, and registering your business name, in addition to actually trading.

These tasks can be very time-consuming and frustrating in the short term, and very costly in the long run if you get them wrong. Unfortunately, these tasks are often not easily delegated and can be expensive if you get other people to do them. If you buy a business or take up a franchise, these basic administrative tasks should have already been dealt with.

✔ There is no one to bounce ideas off, or to share responsibility with when things go wrong.

✔ As a result of this perceived riskiness it is generally more difficult to borrow money to fund a start-up than to borrow to invest in an established profitable business.

Settling on sole trader status

The vast majority of new businesses are essentially one-man (or woman) bands. As such they are free to choose the simplest legal structure, known by terms such as sole trader or sole proprietor. This structure has the merit of being relatively formality-free and having few rules about the records you have to keep. As a sole proprietor you don't have to have your accounts audited or file financial information on your business.

As a sole trader there is no legal distinction between you and your business. Your business is one of your personal assets, just as your house or car is. It follows from this that if your business should fail your creditors have a right not only to the assets of the business, but also to your personal assets, subject only to the provisions of local bankruptcy rules (these often allow you to keep only a few absolutely basic essentials for yourself and your family). It may be possible to avoid the worst of these consequences by distancing your assets.

The capital to start and run the business must come from you, or from loans. In return for these drawbacks you can have the pleasure of being your own boss immediately, subject only to declaring your profits on your tax return and if necessary applying for a trade licence. (In practice you would be wise to take professional advice before starting up.)

Often people who start up on their own do not have enough money to buy into an existing operation, so the do-it-yourself approach is the only alternative.

Building up to Network Marketing

Network marketing, multilevel marketing (MLM), and *referral marketing* are the names used to describe selling methods designed to replace the retail outlet as a route to market for certain products. Although referral marketing has been around since the early part of the last century, for many people it is still unfamiliar territory.

Network marketing is one way of starting a profitable, full-time business with little or no investment, and is also a method of starting a second or part-time business to run alongside your existing business or career. It is one of the fastest growing business sectors. Industry turnover has grown from £700 million ten years ago to £1,700 million today.

In most cases network marketing involves selling a product or service produced and supplied by a parent company. You take on the responsibilities of selling the products and introducing other people to the company. You get paid commission on the products/services you sell yourself and a smaller commission on the products/services sold by the people you have introduced to the company. In addition to this, you often get a percentage commission based on the sales of the people introduced to the company by the people you introduced to the company, and on and on.

Advocates of network marketing maintain that, when given identical products, the one sold face to face (without the cost of maintaining a shop and paying employees and paying insurance) is less expensive than the same product sold in a store. Additionally, network marketing fans believe that it makes more sense to buy a product from someone you know and trust than from a shop assistant behind a retail counter. There are a wide variety of good quality network marketing companies from all over the world to choose from. They offer products and services from a wide range of industries: health,

telecommunications, household products, technology, e-commerce, adult
industry etc. Household names include: Amway, Avon, Betterware, Herbalife,
Kleeneze, and Mary Kay Cosmetics. It would be advisable to choose a product or service that you are interested in because, when it comes to sales,
nothing beats enthusiasm and confidence in the product.

Evaluating the pros and cons

Like any other type of business, network marketing has its upside and its
downside. Some of the positives are:

- ✔ Little or no start-up costs: With most companies the investment in a
  business kit and a range of sample products rarely exceeds £100. The
  law governing MLM does not allow an investment of more than £200 in
  the first seven days.

- ✔ The potential to build a substantial business: By recruiting more and
  more people to join the company and by those people recruiting more
  people, your percentages of their sales grow and grow. And, of course,
  you're still selling at a high rate yourself.

- ✔ A proven business formula: Network marketing has been around since
  the early 1900s.

- ✔ Low risk: Unlike a brand new business idea that you may have uncovered, MLM products and services are usually tried and tested business
  concepts. That doesn't mean they can't fail, but if you follow the rules
  you are less likely to hit the buffers than you would on your own.

- ✔ A great deal of support and advice is often given: The parent company
  and the person who brought you into the company have a vested interest in helping you succeed because the more you sell, the more money
  they make.

- ✔ Flexible hours: You can sell on a full-time or part-time basis during the
  hours that suit you and your customers.

- ✔ Highly expandable: You don't have territory restrictions like conventional salespeople and with e-commerce capabilities, most parent companies can supply to many countries.

- ✔ Business can be run from your own home.

- ✔ Builds your confidence and increases your communication skills.

Again, as with any business, network marketing isn't all good. The following
lists some of the disadvantages:

- ✔ There may be restrictions on your business practices – for example,
  recruitment, advertising etc.

✔ Your business heavily relies on the success of one parent company and its ability to deliver its products/services on time.

✔ You may not feel comfortable selling to your friends or to strangers.

✔ Even the best network marketing companies may be thought of as pyramid schemes – see the next section.

One characteristic of network marketing that leads to its all-too-frequent excesses is that everyone can get in for very little money up front; thus, everyone does get in.

Distinguishing pyramids from networks

Pyramid selling schemes are sometimes disguised to look like network marketing schemes but commonly have the following characteristics:

✔ They encourage participants to make substantial investments in stocks of goods, by offering rewards to participants for getting others to do the same.

✔ They make little reference to direct selling, and the need to achieve consumer sales. Instead, they imply that the main source of rewards comes from getting others to make substantial initial investments.

✔ They do not offer contracts to participants, nor cancellation rights or the opportunity to buy back unsold goods – all of which are required under UK law.

Be sceptical of multilevel marketing systems, especially if the company promises outrageous incomes for very little work. Also, be wary if the company is a lot more interested in telling you how to sign up new recruits than how to sell its products. That's a red flag for a pyramid scheme.

Legitimate network marketing companies put as much emphasis, if not more, on the products or services they offer, and they don't claim that you'll make a killing without working hard to find new customers. Although not shy about advertising the big earnings its successful salespeople make, legitimate companies don't hype the income potential.

Quality network marketing companies make sense for people who really believe in a particular product and want to sell it but don't want to, or can't, tie up a lot of money buying a franchise or other business, or don't have a great idea of their own. Just remember to check out the network company using trade associations such as the Direct Selling Association (www.dsa.org.uk). You won't get rich in a hurry, or probably ever, but you probably won't lose your shirt either.

Working with a Limited Number of People

Unless you are the self-contained type, who prefers going it alone, you will have to work alongside other people to get your business going. Not just suppliers or employees and bankers and the like. Everyone in business has to do that to a greater or lesser extent.

The upside of going into business with others is that you have someone on your side to talk to when the going gets tough, and it will do from time to time. Two heads are very often better than one. Also, you will have the advantage of extra physical and mental resources, when they matter most, from the very outset.

However it is not a one-sided equation, unfortunately. With other people come other points of view, other agendas and the opportunity to disagree, argue, and to misunderstand.

Taking on an existing business

If you don't have a solid business idea of your own, with a clear vision and strategy, you could consider using someone else's wholly formed business. You could think of such ventures as virtually a business-in-a-box. Just buy it, take it home, open it up, and start trading. Of course it's not always quite that easy, but in broad principle that is what network marketing, franchising, and co-operative ventures are all about.

Forming a partnership

A *partnership* is effectively a collection of sole traders or proprietors. There are very few restrictions to setting up in business with another person (or persons) in partnership, and several definite advantages.

- ✓ Pooling your resources means you have more capital.
- ✓ You bring several sets of skills to the business, hopefully, instead of just one.
- ✓ If one of you is ill or disabled, the business can still carry on.

Partnerships are a common structure used by people who started out on their own, but want to expand.

The legal regulations governing partnerships in essence assume that competent businesspeople should know what they are doing. The law merely provides a framework of agreement, which applies 'in the absence of agreement to the contrary'. It follows from this that many partnerships are entered into without legal formalities and sometimes without the parties themselves being aware that they have entered a partnership! Just giving the impression that you are partners may be enough to create an implied partnership under the law.

In the absence of an agreement to the contrary these rules apply to partnerships:

✔ All partners contribute capital equally.

✔ All partners share profits and losses equally.

✔ No partner shall have interest paid on his capital.

✔ No partner shall be paid a salary.

✔ All partners have an equal say in the management of the business.

It is unlikely that all these provisions will suit you, so you would be well advised to get a partnership agreement drawn up in writing before opening for business.

Partnerships have three serious financial drawbacks that merit particular attention:

✔ If one partner makes a business mistake, perhaps by signing a disastrous contract without your knowledge or consent, every member of the partnership must shoulder the consequences. Under these circumstances your personal assets could be taken to pay the creditors even though the mistake was no fault of your own.

✔ If a partner faces personal bankruptcy, for whatever reason, his creditors can seize their share of the partnership. As a private individual you are not liable for your partner's private debts, but having to buy him out of the partnership at short notice rather than gain unwanted replacements could put you and the business in financial jeopardy.

✔ If one partner wants to quit the partnership, that partner will want to take the value of his part of the business with him. The remaining partner(s) will, in effect, have to buy out the partner that is leaving. The agreement you have on setting up the business should specify the procedure and how to value the leaver's share, otherwise resolving the situation will be costly. Several options for addressing this issue exist. A few are:

   • The traditional route to value the leaver's share is to ask an independent accountant. This is rarely cost-effective. The valuation costs money and worst of all it is not definite and consequently there is room for argument.

- Another way is to establish a formula, say eight times the last audited pre-tax profits, for example. This approach is simple but difficult to get right. A fast-growing business is undervalued by a formula using historic data unless the multiple is high; a high multiple may overvalue 'hope' or goodwill thus unreasonably profiting the leaver.

The multiplier can be arrived at by looking up the performance of a business, similar to the one in question that is listed on a stock market. Such a business will have a *P/E ratio* published in both its accounts and the financial sections of national newspapers. The P/E ratio is calculated by dividing the share price into the amount of profit earned for each share. For example, if a business makes £100,000 profit and has 1000 shares, the profit per share is £100. If the share price of that company is £10, then its P/E ratio is 10 (100/10). So much for the science, now for the art. As any business quoted on a stock market is big and its shares are liquid, that is, easy to buy and sell, it is considered more valuable than a small private company. In any event private firms don't have a published share price. To allow for that it is usual to discount the P/E ratio by a third to compensate. So in this example a private firm in the same line of work as the one listed on a stock market would be given a P/E of approximately seven (2/3 × 10).

- Under a third option, the assets of the business can be valued and that valuation could be used as a basis for dividing the spoils.

Even death may not release you from partnership obligations and in some circumstances your estate can remain liable for the partnerships' obligations. Unless you take public leave of your partnership by notifying your business contacts, and legally bringing your partnership to an end, you remain liable indefinitely.

Looking at limited partnerships

One option that can reduce the more painful consequences of entering a partnership is to have your involvement registered as a limited partnership. A limited partnership is very different from a general partnership. It is a legal animal that, in certain circumstances, combines the best attributes of a partnership and a corporation.

A limited partnership works like this: there must be one or more general partners with the same basic rights and responsibilities (including unlimited liability) as in any general partnership, and one or more limited partners who are usually passive investors. The big difference between a general partner and a limited partner is that the limited partner isn't personally liable for debts of the partnership. The most a limited partner can lose is the amount that he:

✔ paid or agreed to pay into the partnership as a capital contribution; or

✔ received from the partnership after it became insolvent.

To keep this limited liability, with very few exceptions a limited partner may not participate in the management of the business. A limited partner who becomes actively involved in the management of the business risks losing immunity from personal liability and having the same legal exposure as a general partner.

The advantage of a limited partnership as a business structure is that it provides a way for business owners to raise money (from the limited partners) without having to either take in new partners who will be active in the business, or having to form a limited company. Often, a general partnership that's been operating for years creates a limited partnership to finance expansion.

Checking out co-operatives

If making money is much lower on your list of priorities for starting up in business than being involved in the decisions of an ethical enterprise, then joining a co-operative or starting your own is an idea worth exploring.

A *co-operative* is an autonomous association of persons united voluntarily to meet their common economic, social, and cultural needs and aspirations through a jointly owned and democratically controlled enterprise.

You must have at least seven members at the outset, though they do not all have to be full-time workers at first.

Like a limited company, a registered co-operative has limited liability for its members and must file annual accounts.

Although the most visible co-operatives are the high street shops and supermarkets, pretty well any type of business can operate as a co-operative.

There are over 1,500 co-operatives in the UK, with over 40,000 people working in them. In the US there are 47,000 co-operatives, generating over $100 billion in sales output. There are co-ops that sell bicycles, furniture, camping equipment, appliances, carpeting, clothing, handicrafts, and books. There are co-operative wholesalers like those in the hardware, grocery, and natural foods businesses. There are co-operatives that disseminate news and co-operatives for artists. There are co-operative electric and telephone utilities.

There are co-operatively managed banks, credit unions, and community development corporations. There are thousands of farm co-ops, along with co-ops that provide financing to farm co-ops. There are subscriber-owned cable TV systems and parent-run day-care centres. There are co-operatively organised employee-owned companies, co-operative purchasing groups for fast food franchises, and, of course, various kinds of co-operative housing.

There are co-ops that provide healthcare, such as health maintenance organisations and community health clinics. There are co-operative insurance companies. There are co-operative food stores, food-buying clubs, and discount warehouses. You get the idea. There are co-ops in virtually every area of business you could possibly imagine.

If you choose to form a co-operative, you can pay from £90 to register with the Chief Registrar of Friendly Societies. Not all co-operatives bother to register as it is not mandatory, but if you don't register, your co-operative is regarded in law as a partnership with unlimited liability.

Finding Your Way to Franchising

Franchising can be a good first step into self-employment for those with business experience but no actual experience of running a business – often the case with those who are looking for something to do following a corporate career.

Franchising is a marketing technique used to improve and expand the distribution of a product or service. The franchiser supplies the product or teaches the service to you, the franchisee, who in turn sells it to the public. In return for this, you pay a fee and a continuing royalty, based usually on turnover. You may also be required to buy materials or ingredients from the franchiser, which gives them an additional income stream. The advantage to you is a relatively safe and quick way of getting into business for yourself, but with the support and advice of an experienced organisation close at hand.

The franchising company can expand its distribution with minimum strain on its own capital and have the services of a highly motivated team of owner managers. Franchising is not a path to great riches, nor is it for the truly independent spirit, as policy and profits will still come from on high.

Franchising in the UK and Europe is a relatively young industry. The whole franchise concept spread only slowly in the decades after the first really major British franchise, Wimpy, got going in the mid-1950s. Since then, however, development has been very rapid; more rapid, perhaps, than most people realise. Now there are few sectors of the economy be it babysitting, fast food, or knitwear that don't have a franchise operation working in them.

According to the latest annual franchise survey produced by the National Westminster Bank and the British Franchise Association (www.british-franchise.org), in 2007 34,000 franchised units operated through some 781 franchise chains (McDonald's, Domino's Pizzas, Kall-Kwik, and so on). The turnover of the industry in 2007 grew to £10.8 billion – up by 44 per cent over the past decade and rising twice as fast as the economy as a whole. The number of people employed in franchising, directly and indirectly, is estimated to be 371,600. London and the Southeast, the Southwest, Northwest, West and East Midlands are the main regions for franchising activity. London and the Southeast alone account for 30 per cent of all franchise units. Table 2-3 shows the sectors that are most popular for franchising, with the number of franchise chains operating in each sector.

Table 2-3	Popular Franchise Areas
Sector	*Number of Franchises*
Business and communication services	152
Hotel and catering	102
Personal services	113
Property services	124
Store retailing	125
Transport and vehicle services	71

Although franchising eliminates some of the more costly and at times disastrous bumps in the learning curve of working for yourself, it is not an easy way to riches. Whilst 93 per cent of franchisees report they are trading profitably, the number of those claiming high levels of profitability remains low at around 10 per cent.

Wild claims are made about how much safer a franchise is when compared to a conventional start-up. Whilst it is true that the long-established big franchise chains are relatively safe, though a few big names have got into trouble, the smaller and newer ones are as vulnerable as any other venture in their early formative years.

Looking at franchise types

Franchises can be clustered under these three main headings:

  ✔ **Job franchises:** This is where you are buying the rights to operate what is essentially a one-person business, such as plumbing, building services or a recruitment business. These require a financial investment in the

£7,000–£20,000 range and could be described as 'buying a job'. However, with back-up in the way of training, customer leads, advertising etc. from the franchiser these are suitable for someone with little capital but having a specific area of expertise or willing to be trained in it such as cleaning or vehicle repair and maintenance services.

✔ **Business franchises:** These businesses typically have premises and employees. These require a higher level of investment, typically in the range of £20,000–£120,000 in stock, equipment, and premises. There are large numbers of business franchises available in such areas as retailing, food services, and business services such as high street printing shops.

✔ **Investment franchises:** Here, you are talking about initial investments of over £120,000. Hotels and some of the larger and more established fast food outlets come into the top range of this category at around £750,000. The essence of this type of franchise is that the franchisee is unlikely to work in the business day to day. People operating investment franchises typically operate several similar franchises in nearby areas.

Defining a franchise

A franchise agreement is just like any business contract in that it sets out what each party is expected to do and what could happen if they don't.

The main ingredients of the franchise agreement are:

✔ Permission to use a business name and so be associated with that bigger enterprise.

✔ The right for the franchiser to set and enforce business and product standards, such as the use of ingredients, cooking processes, opening times, staff uniforms and so forth.

✔ An obligation for the franchiser to provide help, training and guidance in all aspects of operating the business.

✔ A definition of the way in which the rights to operate the franchise are to be paid for, for example, royalties on sales, initial purchase fee, marketing levy, mark-up on goods and services provided and so forth.

The British Franchise Association (BFA) agreement, though helpful, does not cover everything you need to know to make a sound decision. For example though running a pilot scheme is a condition of membership of the BFA, that in itself is no guarantee that the business model is fully tried and tested. Neither does the BFA standard contract mention that the business, once set up, is the property of the franchisee, nor does it warn him of the degree of control that he might be subjected to from the franchisor. Further, it gives no indication of the extent of the back-up services that the franchisee might reasonably expect to get for his money. In other words, the BFA definition is not a sufficient standard against which to check the franchise contract.

The British Franchise Association expects its members to follow its code of practice, and you can find out more on their Web site: www.thefba.org.

Whilst membership of the BFA and adhering to a code of practice is helpful it is not a guarantee of success for your franchise. You should be looking for a shortlist of as many as six opportunities, acquiring as much advice as you can get from franchisers, from franchisees, from your bank, and from other professional advisers.

Before deciding on a particular franchise it is essential that you consult your legal and financial advisers, as well as ask the franchiser some very searching questions:

> ✔ Has the franchiser operated at least one unit for a year or so as a pilot unit in the UK? This is an essential first step before selling franchises to third parties. Otherwise, how can they really know all the problems, and so put you on the right track?

> ✔ What training and support is included in the *franchise package,* the name given to the start-up kit provided by the franchiser? This package should extend to support staff over the launch period and give you access to back-up advice.

> ✔ How substantial is the franchise company? Ask to see the balance sheet (take it to your accountant if you cannot understand it). Ask for the track record of the directors (including their other directorships).

Sometimes a major clearing bank offers financial support to buy a particular franchise, which is an encouraging sign that the company is in good financial health. At least you know the concept is tried and tested and to some extent the business is reputable. However, as with everything to do with starting up a business, the buck stops with you.

You can meet franchisers and hear their pitches at one of the dozen or so franchise exhibitions held around the country each year. Details of dates and venues are available on the BFA Diary page at www.thebfa.org/diary.asp.

Founding a Larger Company

If your business looks like it will need a substantial amount of money from the outset and will be taking on the risk of customers owing money, as with any manufacturing venture, then the legal structures looked at so far may not be right for you.

In this section you can find out about the advantages and disadvantages of going for a limited company, or buying out a company already in business.

Opting for a limited company

As the name suggests, in this form of business your liability is limited to the amount you contribute by way of share capital.

Two shareholders, one of whom must be a director, can form a limited company. A company secretary must also be appointed, who can be a shareholder, director, or an outside person such as an accountant or lawyer.

The company can be bought 'off the shelf' from a registration agent, then adapted to suit your own purposes. This will involve changing the name, shareholders, and articles of association and take a couple of weeks to arrange. Alternatively, you can form your own company.

A limited company has a legal identity of its own, separate from the people who own or run it. This means that, in the event of failure, creditors' claims are restricted to the assets of the company. The shareholders of the business are not liable as individuals for the business debts beyond the paid-up value of their shares. This applies even if the shareholders are working directors, unless of course the company has been trading fraudulently. In practice, the ability to limit liability is restricted these days as most lenders, including the banks, often insist on personal guarantees from the directors. Other advantages include the freedom to raise capital by selling shares.

Disadvantages include the legal requirement for the company's accounts to be audited and filed for public inspection.

A *Ltd company* can be started with, say, an authorised share capital of £1,000. This is then divided into 1,000 £1 shares. You can then issue as few or as many of the shares as you want. As long as the shares you have issued are paid for in full, if the company liquidates, the shareholders have no further liabilities. If the shares have not been paid for, the shareholders are liable for the value; for example, if they have 100 £1 shares they only are liable for £100.

Limiting liability through the ages

The concept of limited liability, where the shareholders are not liable in the last resort for the debts of their business, can be traced back to the Romans. However it was rarely used, only being granted as a special favour to friends by those in power.

Some two thousand years later the idea was revived when in 1811 New York State brought in a general limited liability law for manufacturing companies. Most American states followed suit and eventually Britain caught up in 1854. Most countries have a legal structure incorporating the concept of limited liability.

A *PLC* (Public Limited Company) is a public company and may be listed on the Stock Exchange. Before a PLC can start to trade it must have at least £50,000 of shares issued and at least 25 per cent of the value must have been paid for. A PLC company has a better status due to its larger capital.

A company must have on its notepaper the company's full name, the address of its registered office, the fact that it's registered in England or Scotland etc., and the company number. However, the names of the directors need not be stated but, if any are (other than as signatory), all must be stated.

When a company is first registered it must send to Companies House, (www.companies-house.org.uk), the place where all business details and accounts are kept, a copy of its memorandum and articles of association and form 10, which contains the address of the company's registered office and details of its directors and company secretary. The directors' details are: current names, any former names, date of birth, usual residential address (currently under review), occupation, nationality, and other directorships. For the secretary only the names and address are required.

Companies House organises or attends a variety of seminars and exhibitions to support and advise businesses and to support new directors and secretaries. You can find details of these on the events section of the Companies House Web site at www.companies-house.org.uk/about/chevents.shtml.

Buying out a business

Buying out an existing business is particularly well suited to people who have extensive experience of general business management but lack detailed technical or product knowledge.

When you buy an established business, you not only pay for the basic assets of the business, but also the accumulated time and effort that the previous owner spent growing the business to its present state. This extra asset can be thought of as *goodwill*. The better the business, the more the 'goodwill' will cost you.

Advantages of buying a business include:

- ✔ You acquire some of the experience and expertise you do not have. It is much easier, and almost invariably less costly, to learn from the mistakes that other people have made in the past, rather than making all these mistakes yourself.
- ✔ You gain both access to your potential customers and the credibility of a trading history from the outset, which can save months if not years of hard work in building relationships.

✔ If the business you buy is already profitable, you could pay yourself a living wage from the outset.

✔ Bank financing may be easier to acquire for an established business than for a riskier start-up business.

Disadvantages of buying a business include:

✔ You run the risk of acquiring the existing unsolved problems and mistakes of the person who is selling it.

✔ Identifying the right potential acquisition and negotiating purchase can take a very long time, and there is no guarantee that you will succeed at your first attempt.

✔ The professional fees associated with buying a business can be a significant, though necessary, cost. If you buy a very small business, the total professional fees associated with the transaction will be a major percentage of the total cost of your investment, perhaps as much as 15 or 20 per cent. Experienced solicitors and accountants are vital to this process. They are your safeguards to ensure that you know exactly what you are buying.

Contact these organisations to find out more about buying a business and to see listings of businesses for sale:

✔ Christie & Co (www.christie.com, tel. 0207 227 0700) claims to have the largest database of businesses for sale in Europe. It is the recognised market leader in the hotel, catering, leisure, and retail markets and is also expanding into healthcare.

✔ Daltons (www.daltonsbusiness.com) has an online database of over 27,000 businesses for sale around the United Kingdom and some overseas countries.

✔ Grant Thornton, a major international accountancy firm, operates a service called Companies for Sale (www.companiesforsale.uk.com, tel. 0121 232 5219), where it lists companies for sale with turnover upwards of £1 million a year. Their Web site links through to a useful guide on how to buy a business.

Chapter 3

Testing Feasibility

· ·

In This Chapter

▶ Making sure you can find the product and people

▶ Doing market research

▶ Checking out business viability

▶ Seeing if you can make a profit

· ·

*Y*ou need to decide whether or not starting up your own business is for you. Maybe you have reached some tentative decision on whether to go it alone or to join forces with others with valuable resources or ideas to add to your own and now have the bones of an idea of what type of business you will start, buy into, franchise or in some other way get into.

So all you have to do now is wait for the customers to turn up and the cash to roll in. Right? Wrong, regrettably. Although you are beyond square one, there are still a good few miles to cover before you can be confident your big business idea will actually work and make money. This chapter gives you the right questions to ask to make you as sure as you can be that you have the best shot at success.

Finding Enough Product or People

The first test of feasibility is whether you can get enough goods to sell or enough people to provide the service you're offering. You need to be sure that you can get your product manufactured at the rate and quantity to meet your needs. Likewise, if you're starting a service business, you need to be sure that you can hire the people with the skills you need, whether you need housecleaners or web page designers.

Of course, if you're buying into a franchise or joining an existing business or co-operative, these issues are already addressed for the most part. Still, it never hurts to do your own assessment of the supply chain if only to familiarise yourself with the process.

How much is enough?

The amount of goods or services you need depends in part on the scale of your ambitions and also on what you believe the market will bear. If the restaurant you plan to open has a total population of 100 people within a fifty mile radius, that fact alone will limit the scale of your venture.

It makes sense to work backwards to answer this question. For example if you want to make at least as much money from your business as you have in wages in your job, then that figure can be used to work out the initial scale of your level of output. As a rough rule of thumb if you want to make £10,000 profit before tax, a business involved in manufacturing or processing materials will need to generate between £80,000 and £100,000 worth of orders. Taking away your anticipated profit from the sales target leaves you with the value of the goods and services you need to buy in.

Buying in equipment and supplies

In this area there are four main areas to check out:

- ✔ **Premises:** Finding the right premises can be the limiting factor for some businesses. If, for example you need to be in a particular type of area, as with restaurants, coffee shops, and night clubs, it could take months for the right place to come on the market and even longer to get planning or change of use consent if those are required. Once you have a clear idea of the type of premises you want, check out all the commercial estate agents in the area. It will make sense to have a few alternative locations in your plans too.

- ✔ **Equipment:** If you are going to make any or all of your products yourself then you need to check out suppliers, delivery times, payment terms and so forth for the equipment needed for the production processes. You will first need to check out the output levels and quality standards of any equipment you want, to make sure it will meet your needs. You can find equipment suppliers in either *Kelly's Directories* (www.kellys.co.uk) or *Kompass* (www.kompass.com). Between these two directories there is information on hundreds of thousands of branded products and services from suppliers in over 70 countries. These directories are available both in your local business library and, to a limited extent, online.

- ✔ **Finished goods:** It is usually a better use of scarce cash for a new business to buy in product in as close to finished state as possible, leaving you to complete only the high value-added tasks to complete. Few niche mail-order catalogue businesses make any of their own product; their key skills lie in merchandise selection, advertising copy, web design or buying in the right mailing lists. *Kelly's* and *Kompass* directories list almost every finished good supplier.

✓ **Consumable materials:** If you are making things yourself then you will need to check out suppliers of raw materials. Even if, like mail-order firms, you are buying in finished product you will need to check that out too. You can search in Google, Ask Jeeves or any of the major search engines for almost any product or service. However unless the quantities are large and significantly better terms can be had elsewhere it is better to stick to local suppliers for consumables. This is an inexpensive way to build up goodwill in the local community and may even create business for you. See *Kelly's* and *Kompass* directories for details of suppliers of consumables.

Hiring in help

Unless you plan to do everything yourself on day one, you will need to check out that people with the skills you need are available at wage rates you can afford in your area. Start by looking in the situations vacant section of your local newspaper under the appropriate headings. If you need kitchen staff for your new restaurant and the paper has 20 pages of advertisers desperately looking for staff, then you could well have a problem on your hands.

Sizing Up the Market

You need to ensure that there are enough customers out there, with sufficient money to spend, to create a viable marketplace for your products or services. You must also see who will be competing against you for their business. In other words, you need to research your market.

Market research is something that potential financial backers – be they banks or other institutions – will insist on. And in this they are doing you a favour. Many businesses started with private money fail because the founders don't thoroughly research the market at the outset.

Whatever your business idea, you must undertake some well-thought-out market research before you invest any money or approach anyone else to invest in your venture.

You don't have to pay professional companies to do your research, although sometimes it may make good sense to do so. You can often gather information effectively (and cheaply) yourself.

Market research has three main purposes:

- ✔ **To build credibility for your business idea:** You must prove, first to your own satisfaction and later to outside financiers, that you thoroughly understand the marketplace for your product or service. This proof is vital to attracting resources to build the new venture.

- ✔ **To develop a realistic market entry strategy:** A successful marketing strategy is based on a clear understanding of genuine customer needs and on the assurance that product quality, price, promotional and distribution methods are mutually supportive and clearly focused on target customers.

- ✔ **To gain understanding of the total market, both customers and competition:** You need sufficient information on your potential customers, competitors, and market to ensure that your market strategy is at least on the target, if not on the bull's-eye itself. If you miss the target altogether, which you could well do without research, you may not have the necessary cash resources for a second shot.

The military motto 'Time spent in reconnaissance is rarely time wasted' holds true for business as well.

Researching the market need not be a complex process, nor need it be very expensive. The amount of effort and expenditure needs to be related in some way to the costs and risks associated with the business. If all that is involved with your business is simply getting a handful of customers for products and services that cost little to put together, then you may spend less effort on market research than you would for, say, launching a completely new product or service into an unproven market that requires a large sum of money to be spent up front. However much or little market research you plan to carry out the process needs to be conducted systematically.

Before you start your research:

- ✔ **Define your objectives:** Figure out what you vitally need to know. For example, how often do people buy and how much?

- ✔ **Identify the customers to sample for this information:** Decide who you want to sample and how you can best reach them. For example, for DIY products, an Ideal Home Exhibition crowd might be best.

- ✔ **Decide how best to undertake the research:** Choose the research method best suited to getting the results you need. For example, face-to-face interviews in the street may allow you direct access to potential customers.

- ✔ **Think about how you will analyse the data:** If your research involves complex multi-choice questions, or a large sample size, you may need to plan in advance to use a computer and the appropriate software to help you process the data, which in turn means coding the questions. An even better idea is to keep it so simple you don't need a computer!

The raw market research data can be analysed and turned into information to guide your decisions on price, promotion, location, and the shape, design, and scope of the product or service itself.

The following sections cover the areas you need to consider to make sure you have properly sized up your business sector.

Figuring out what you need to know

Before embarking on your market research, set clear and precise objectives. You don't want just to find out interesting information about the market in general, and you don't want to spend the time and money to explore the whole market when your target is just a segment of that market. (I talk about segmenting the market in the 'Finding your segment of the market' section coming up in a bit.)

You have to figure out who your target customer is and what you need to know about her. For example, if you are planning to open a shop selling to young fashion-conscious women, your research objective could be to find out how many women between the ages of 18 and 28, who make at least £25,000 p.a., live or work within two miles of your chosen shop position. That would give you some idea if the market could support a venture such as this.

You also want to know what the existing market is for your product and how much money your potential customers spend on similar products. You can get a measure of such spending from Mintel reports (www.mintel.com). Mintel publishes over 400 reports every year examining nearly every consumer market from baby foods to youth holidays.

Figuring out the size of the market may require several different pieces of information. You may want to know the resident population of a given area, which may be fairly easy to find out, and also something about the type of people who come into your area for work, for leisure, on holiday, or for any other purpose. A nearby hospital, library, railway station, or school, for example, may pull potential customers into your particular area.

You also want to know as much as you can about your competitors – their share of the market, their marketing strategy, their customer profile, product pricing schemes, and so on.

You need to research in particular:

- **Your customers:** Who will buy your goods and services? What particular customer needs will your business meet? How many of them are there, are their numbers growing or contracting, how much do they spend and how often do they buy?

✔ **Your competitors:** Which established businesses are already meeting the needs of your potential customers? What are their strengths and weaknesses? Are they currently failing their customers in some way that you can improve on?

✔ **Your product or service:** Could, or should, it be tailored to meet the needs of particular groups of customers? For example if you are starting up a delivery business, professional clients may require a 'same day service', whilst members of the public at large would be happy to get goods in a day or two, provided it was less costly.

✔ **The price you should charge:** All too often small firms confine their research on pricing to seeing what the competition charges and either matching it or beating it. That may be a way to get business, but it is not the best route to profitable business. You need to know what price would be perceived as being too cheap, what would represent good 'value for money' and what would be seen as a rip off, so you can pitch in at the right price for your offering.

✔ **Which promotional material will reach your customers:** What newspapers and journals do they read and which of these is most likely to influence their buying decision?

✔ **Your location:** From where could you reach your customers most easily and at minimum cost?

✔ **Most effective sales method:** Can you use telesales, the Internet, or a catalogue, or will customers only buy face to face either from a salesperson or from a retail outlet?

Research is not just essential in starting a business but should become an integral part in the on-going life of the business. Customers and competitors change; products and services don't last forever. Once started, however, ongoing market research becomes easier, as you will have existing customers (and staff) to question. It is important that you regularly monitor their views on your business (as the sign in the barber shop stated: 'We need your head to run our business') and develop simple techniques for this purpose (for example, questionnaires for customers beside the till, suggestion boxes with rewards for employees).

Finding your segment of the market

Market segmentation is the process whereby customers and potential customers are organised into clusters of similar types, such as age, sex, education level or location.

The starting point for your business may be to sell clothes, but every person who buys clothes is too large and diverse a market to get a handle on. So you divide that market into different segments – clothes for men, women, and children, for example – and then further divide those segments into clothes for work, leisure, sports, and social occasions. You just segmented your market.

Most businesses end up selling to several different market segments, but when it comes to detailed market research you need to examine each of your main segments separately.

Above all it is customers who increasingly want products and services tailored to their needs and will pay for the privilege.

Grouping market segments

Some of the tried-and-tested ways by which markets can be segmented follow:

- ✔ **Demographic segmentation** groups customers together by such variables as age, sex, interest, education, and income. Some companies have made their whole proposition age-focused. Saga is only interested in those aged 50 and over, for example.

- ✔ **Psychographic segmentation** divides individual consumers into social groups such as Yuppie (young, upwardly mobile, professional), Bumps (borrowed-to-the-hilt upwardly mobile professional show-off) and Jollies (jet-setting oldies with lots of loot). These categories try to explain how social behaviour influences buyer behaviour.

- ✔ **Benefit segmentation** recognises that different people get different benefits from the same product or service. The Lastminute.com bargain travel site claims two quite distinctive benefits for its users. Initially it aims to offer people bargains, which appeals because of price and value. But lately the company has been laying more emphasis on the benefit of immediacy. The theory is rather akin to the impulse buy products placed at checkout tills that you never thought of buying until you bumped into them on your way out. Whether ten days on a beach in Goa, or a trip to Istanbul, is the type of thing people pop in their baskets before turning off their computer screens, time will tell.

- ✔ **Geographic segmentation** recognises that people in different locations have different needs. For example, an inner-city store might sell potatoes in 1kg bags, recognising its customers are likely to be on foot. An out of town shopping centre sells the same product in 20kg sacks, knowing their customers have cars.

- ✔ **Industrial segmentation** groups together commercial customers according to a combination of their geographic location, principal business activity, relative size, frequency of product use, urgency of need, loyalty, order size and buying policies. Using this approach a courier service would price its overnight delivery service higher than its 48-hour service.

- ✔ **Multivariant segmentation** uses a combination of segments to get a more precise picture of a market than using just one factor.

Use the following guidelines to help determine whether a market segment is worth trying to sell into:

- ✔ **Measurability:** Can you estimate how many customers are in the segment? Are there enough to make it worth offering something different for?

- ✔ **Accessibility:** Can you communicate with these customers, preferably in a way that reaches them alone? For example you could reach the over-50s through advertising in a specialist magazine, with reasonable confidence that young people will not read it. So if you are trying to promote a large-print edition of a game, you might prefer young people did not hear about it, so that they don't think of the game as strictly for old folks.

- ✔ **Open to profitable development:** The customers must have money to spend on the benefits you propose offering. Once upon a time oldies were poor, so that market wasn't a good target for upscale, expensive products. Then they became rich and everyone had products aimed at older markets.

Seeing natural market subsegments

Even after you determine your target market segments, your growth may not come through as fast as you were hoping. You have to realise that every market segment is itself made up of sub-segments. Everett M Rogers, in his book *Diffusion of Innovations* (New York: Free Press, 1962) broke markets into the following sub-segments:

- ✔ **Innovators**, the adventurous types who try out new things early on represent 2.5 per cent of the average market.

- ✔ **Early Adopters** make up 13.5 per cent of the average market. This type of customer only starts buying when the service has the seal of approval from the Innovators.

- ✔ **Early Majority and Late Majority buyers,** each 34 per cent of the market, follow on, after the Early Adopters have shown the way.

- ✔ **Laggards,** 16 per cent of the average market, follow well behind, perhaps taking years and some significant price drops before they can be tempted to put down their cash.

One further issue that has a profound effect on marketing strategy is that Innovators, Early Adopters, and all the other sub-segments don't necessarily read the same magazines or respond to the same images and messages. So they need to be marketed to in very different ways. This makes the blitz approach to market penetration taken by some new ventures look a bit suspect. Blitz marketing with a single message may work in stimulating a mature market, but how much use is it in a market that is still looking for the signal of approval from further up the chain?

You need to identify the innovators who will buy from you first. Whilst your product or service may not be earth shattering new, you and your business may well present a mature market with established competitors with a situation that looks much similar to a new innovation.

Budgeting for your research

Market research isn't free even if you do it yourself. At the very least, you have to consider your time. You may also spend money on journals, phone calls, letters, and field visits. And, if you employ a professional market research firm, your budgeting needs shoot to the top of the scale.

For example, a survey of 200 executives responsible for office equipment purchasing decisions cost one company £12,000. In-depth interviews with 20 banking consumers cost £8,000.

Doing the research in-house may save costs but limit the objectivity of the research. If time is your most valuable commodity, it may make sense to get an outside agency to do the work. Another argument for getting professional research is that it may carry more clout with investors.

Whatever the cost of research, you need to assess its value to you when you are setting your budget. So if getting it wrong will cost £100,000, then £5,000 spent on market research may be a good investment.

Doing the preliminary research

Research methods range from doing it all from your desk to getting out in the field yourself and asking questions – or hiring someone to do it for you. The following sections explore the various methods you can use to find out what you need to know.

If you are a member of a chamber of commerce, a trade association, small business association, or are or have taken a small business course, the chances are you can access some market data for free.

Even if it does cost something in time and money, getting the data you need helps you make better decisions. If you think knowledge is expensive, you should try ignorance!

Doing research behind your desk

Once you know the questions you want answers to, the next step is finding out if someone else has the answers already. Much of the information you need may well be published, so you can do at least some of your market research in a comfortable chair either in your home or in a good library.Even if you use other research methods, it is well worth doing a little desk research first.

Gathering information at the library

There are thousands of libraries in the UK and tens of thousands elsewhere in the world that between them contains more desk research data than any entrepreneur could ever require. Libraries offer any number of excellent information sources. You can either take yourself to your local library or bring the library's information to you via the Internet if you're dealing with one of the reference libraries in a larger city or town.

As well as the fairly conventional business books, libraries contain many hundreds of reference and research data bases. For example, the official Census of Population supplies demographic data on size, age, and sex of the local populace. You can also find a wealth of governmental and other statistics that enable you to work out the size and shape of the market nationwide and how much each person spends.

Details of every journal, paper, and magazines readership are to be found in *BRAD* (British Rate and Data) and every company has to file details of its profits, assets, liabilities, and directors at Companies House, the place where all business details and accounts are kept (www.companies-house.org.uk).

Sources of Unofficial UK Statistics published by Gower (www.gowerpub.com) gives details of almost 900 publications (including electronic publications) and services produced by trade associations, professional bodies, banks, consultants, employers' federations, forecasting organisations and others, together with statistics appearing in trade journals and periodicals. Titles and services are listed alphabetically by publisher and each entry contains information, where available, on subject, content, and source of statistics, together with frequency, availability and cost, and address, telephone, and fax details for further information.

Some market information data costs hundreds of pounds and some is available only to subscribers who pay thousands of pounds to have it on tap. Fortunately for you, your library (or an Internet link to a library) may have the relevant directory, publication, or research study on its shelves.

Librarians are trained, amongst other things, to archive and retrieve information and data from their own libraries and increasingly from Internet data sources as well. Thus, they represent an invaluable resource that you should tap into early in the research process. You can benefit many times from their knowledge at no cost, or you may want to make use of the research service some libraries offer to business users at fairly modest rates.

Apart from public libraries, there are hundreds of university libraries, specialist science and technology libraries, and government collections of data that can be accessed with little difficulty.

Using the Internet

The Internet can be a powerful research tool. However, it has some particular strengths and weaknesses that you need to keep in mind when using it.

Strengths of the Internet include:

✔ Access is cheap and information is often free

✔ Provides good background information

✔ Information is produced quickly

✔ Covers a wide geographic scope

Weaknesses of the Internet include:

✔ The bias is strongly toward the US

✔ Coverage of any given subject may be patchy

✔ Authority and credentials are often lacking

It would be a brave or foolhardy entrepreneur who started up in business or set out to launch new products or services without at least spending a day or two surfing the Internet. At the very least this will let you know if anyone else has taken your business idea to market. At best it might save you lots of leg-work around libraries, if the information you want is available online.

You can gather market research information on the Internet two main ways:

✔ Use directories, search engines, or telephone directories to research your market or product.

✔ Use bulletin or message boards, newsgroups, and chat rooms to elicit the data you require.

These three useful search engines can help get you started:

✔ **Business.com** (www.business.com)

✔ **Easy Searcher 2** (www.easysearcher.com)

✔ **The Small Business Research portal** (www.smallbusinessportal.co.uk/index.php)

Getting to the grass roots

If the market information you need is not already available, and the chances are that it won't be, then you need to find the answers yourself.

Going out into the marketplace to do market research is known as *field research*, or sometimes *primary research*, by marketing professionals.

Field research allows you to gather information directly related to your venture and to fine-tune results you get from other sources. For example, entrepreneurs interested in opening a classical music shop in Exeter aimed at young people were encouraged when desk research showed that of a total population of 250,000, 25 per cent were under 30. However, it did not tell them what percentage of this 25 per cent was interested in classical music nor how much money each potential customer might spend. Field research showed that 1 per cent was interested in classical music and would spend £2 a week, suggesting a potential market of only £65,000 a year (250,000 × 25% × 1% × £2 × 52)! The entrepreneurs sensibly decided to investigate Birmingham and London instead. But at least the cost had been only two damp afternoons spent in Exeter, rather than the horror of having to dispose of a lease of an unsuccessful shop.

Most field research consists of an interviewer putting questions to a respondent. No doubt you've become accustomed to being interviewed while travelling or resisting the attempts of an enthusiastic salesperson on your doorstep posing as a market researcher ('slugging' as this is known has been illegal since 1986).

The more popular forms of interviews are:

- ✔ personal (face-to-face) interview (especially for consumer markets)
- ✔ telephone (especially for surveying businesses)
- ✔ postal survey (especially for industrial markets)
- ✔ test and discussion groups
- ✔ Internet surveys

Personal interviews and postal surveys are clearly less expensive than getting together panels of interested parties or using expensive telephone time. Telephone interviewing requires a very positive attitude, courtesy, an ability not to talk too quickly and listening while sticking to a rigid questionnaire. Low response rates on postal surveys (normally less than 10 per cent) can be improved by including a letter explaining the purpose of the survey and why respondents should reply; by offering rewards for completed questionnaires (a small gift); by associating the survey with a charity donation based on the number of respondents; by sending reminder letters and, of course, by providing pre-paid reply envelopes.

Internet surveys using questionnaires similar to those conducted by post or on the telephone are growing in popularity. On the plus side, while the other survey methods involve having the data entered or transcribed at your expense, with an Internet survey, the respondent enters the data. Internet survey software also comes with the means to readily analyse the data turning it into useful tables and charts. Such software may also have a statistical package to check out the validity of the data itself and so give you some idea how much reliance to place on it.

Whilst buying the software to carry out Internet surveys may be expensive, you can rent it and pay per respondent for each survey you do.

Check out companies such as Free Online Surveys (`http://free-online-surveys.co.uk`) and Zoomerang (`www.zoomerang.com/web/signup/Basic.aspx`) who provide software that lets you carry out online surveys and analyse the data quickly. Most of these organisations offer free trials – Zoomerang, for example, lets you ask up to 30 questions, collect 100 responses, and analyse the data. After that unlimited surveys cost around £250 a year.

Once upon a time samples of Internet users were heavily biased towards students, big companies, and university academics. Not any more. With UK broadband access to the Internet at over 50 per cent of the population, you can canvas everyone's views.

Conducting the research

Field research means that you have to do the work yourself. Decide the questions, select the right people to ask those questions and then interpret the data once you have it. This is completely different from desk research where all that work has been done for you. But field research can be worth every ounce of sweat that goes into it. You get information that no one else is likely to have at their fingertips, and knowledge in the business start-up arena is definitely power. When you come to writing up your business plan (see Book I Chapter 4) you will have the evidence to support your belief in your business.

Setting up a sample

It is rarely possible or even desirable to include every potential customer or competitor in your research. Imagine trying to talk to all pet owners before launching petfeed.com! Instead you select a sample group to represent the whole population.

Sampling saves time and money and can be more accurate than surveying an entire population. Talking to every pet owner may take months. By the time you complete your survey, the first people questioned may have changed their opinions, or the whole environment may have changed in some way.

You need to take care and ensure you have included all the important customer segments that you have targeted as potential users or buyers of your products or services in your research sample.

The main sampling issue is how big a sample you need to give you a reliable indication of how the whole population behaves. The accuracy of your survey increases with the sample size, as Table 5-1 shows. There you'll see that a sample of 250 is generally (95% of the time) accurate only to between plus 6.2% to minus 6.2%. This means that 12.4% of the time it will generally be above or below the true figure. Up the sample to 6,000 and the error range drops to between plus 1.2% and minus 1.2%, a range of just 2.4%. You need to ensure that each of your main customer segments – for example the over-50s, people earning between £20,000 and £30,000 a year, or those without university degrees, if those are groups of people whose views are important to your strategy – are included in the sample in numbers sufficient to make your sample reasonably reliable.

Table 3-1	Sample Size and Accuracy
Number in Sample	*Percentage Accuracy of 95% of Surveys*
250	Accurate to a range of + to - 6.2% of true figure
500	Accurate to a range of + to - 4.4% of true figure
750	Accurate to a range of + to - 3.6% of true figure
1,000	Accurate to a range of + to - 3.1% of true figure
2,000	Accurate to a range of + to -2.2% of true figure
6,000	Accurate to a range of + to - 1.2% of true figure

For most basic research a small business will find the lower sample sizes accurate enough given the uncertainty surrounding the whole area of entering new markets and launching new products.

Andrews University in the United States has a free set of lecture notes explaining the subject of sample size comprehensively (www.andrews.edu/~calkins/math/webtexts/prod12.htm). At www.auditnet.org/docs/statsamp.xls you can find some great Excel spreadsheets that do the boring maths of calculating sample size and accuracy for you.

Asking the right questions

To make your field research pay off you have to ask the questions whose responses tell you what you need to know. Writing those questions is both an art and a science – both aspects of which you can master by using the follow-ing tips:

- ✔ Keep the number of questions to a minimum. A dozen or so should be enough – 25 is getting ridiculous.

- ✔ Keep the questions simple. Answers should be either Yes/No/Don't Know or somewhere on a scale such as Never/Once a Month/Three or Four Times a Month/Always.

- ✔ Avoid ambiguity. Make sure the respondent really understands the ques-tion by avoiding vague words such as 'generally', 'usually', 'regularly'. Seek factual answers; avoid opinions.

- ✔ Make sure you have a cut-out question at the beginning to eliminate unsuitable respondents. You don't want to waste time questioning people who would never use your product or service.

- ✔ Put an identifying question at the end so that you can make sure you get a suitable cross-section of respondents. For example, you may want to identify men from women, people living alone from those with children, or certain age groups.

The introduction to a face-to-face interview is important; make sure you are prepared, either carrying an identifying card (maybe a student card or watch-dog card) or with rehearsed introduction (such as 'Good morning, I'm from Cranfield University [show card] and we are conducting a survey and would be grateful for your help'). You may also need visuals of the product you are investigating (samples, photographs), to ensure the respondent understands. Make sure these are neat and accessible.

Try out the questionnaire and your technique on your friends prior to using them in the street. You may be surprised to find that questions that seem simple to you are incomprehensible at first to respondents!

Remember, above all, however, that questioning is by no means the only or most important form of fieldwork. Another form of fieldwork market research you should undertake is to get out and look at your competitors' premises, get their catalogues and price lists, go to exhibitions and trade fairs relevant to your chosen business sector, and get information on competitors' accounts and financial data. One would-be business starter found out from the company's accounts, obtained from Companies House (www.companies-house.gov.uk), that the 'small' competitor near to where she planned to locate was in fact owned by a giant public company that was testing out the market prior to a major launch itself.

All methods can be equally valid depending only on the type of market data you need to gather. The results of each piece of market research should be carefully recorded for subsequent use in presentations and business plans.

Once the primary market research (desk and field research) and market testing (stalls and exhibitions) are complete, if you are investing a substantial amount of money up front in your venture, then pilot testing of the business should take place in one location or customer segment before launching fully into business. Only then can you make a reasonably accurate prediction of sales and the cash flow implications for your business.

Finding test subjects

Now you need someone to ask your questions to. If you're doing a street survey then you will have to make do with whoever comes along. Otherwise to carry out a survey, your best bet is to buy or rent a mailing list. Typically, you'll pay a fee to the list owner, such as a magazine with its list of subscribers. You'll negotiate a fee for how many times you are allowed to use the list. Note that you are not the owner of the list.

There are several individual freelancers who specialise in brokering lists and building lists You may want to consider hiring an individual for a consultation or to manage the entire process. Marketing professionals claim there's a science to buying lists, but it's quite possible to master this science on your own, especially if you are trying to reach a local or regional market. Think of publications, organisations, and businesses whose lists would most likely contain people who could buy your product or service. Don't overlook trade magazines, regional magazines, or non-competing businesses with a similar customer base. You can then select and narrow your lists by looking at nearly any demographic variable to arrive at as close to your description of your target market as possible. Listbroker.com (www.listbroker.com) and Smart Lists (www.smartlists.co.uk) between them can provide lists of all types.

Determining whether you have enough information

Use Table 3-2 to check out whether you know enough about your market yet. Complete the questionnaire by entering the score in the box that most closely describes your knowledge. For example in the first question below if you don't know the likely age, sex or income group of your prospective or actual customers, put a zero in the left-hand column. Try to be honest and perhaps get someone else who knows your business area well to answer the questions also.

Table 3-2	Evaluating Your Results		
	No (0)	*Have some idea (1)*	*Yes, have detailed information (2)*
Do you know the likely age, sex, or income group of your prospective (or actual) customers?			
Do you know your customers' buying habits and preferences?			
Do know what other related products and services your customers buy?			
Do you know which of your competitors they also use?			
Do you know how much of your competitors' business you want or have?			
Do you know who else operates in this marketplace?			
Do you know how successful they are in terms of sales and profits?			
Do you know how they promote their goods and services?			
Do you know how satisfied their customers are with their service?			
Do you know how much your competitors charge?			
Do you know the overall size of your market?			
Do you know if your market is growing or contracting, and by how much?			
Do you know what papers, journals, and magazines your customers read?			
Do you know which other Web sites your customers are most likely to visit?			
Do you know how your competitors recruit their best staff?			

Add up all your scores and rate whether or not you know enough about your market yet.

- ✔ Less than 10: It seems unlikely that you know enough to start up yet.

- ✔ 10–15: You still have a lot more to find out, but at least you have made a start.

- ✔ 15–25: You have got a handle on the basic information, but there are still a few more important bits of data to research.

- ✔ Over 25: A high score is no guarantee of success, but you seem to have the right level of sector knowledge to start a business. Superior information can in itself be a source of competitive advantage, so keep up the good work.

Working Out Whether You Can Make Money

There isn't much point in trying to get a new business off the ground if it is going to take more money than you can raise or take longer to reach break-even and turn in a profit than you can possibly survive unaided. We look in more detail at financial matters such as profits and margins in Book III Chapter 1 and Book IV Chapter 1, but you can't start looking at the figures soon enough. Doing some rough figures at the outset can save you a lot of time pursuing unrealistic or unprofitable business opportunities.

Estimating start-up costs

Setting up a business requires money – there is no getting away from that. You have rent to pay, materials and equipment to purchase, and all before any income is received. Starting a business on the road to success involves ensuring that you have sufficient money to survive until the point where income continually exceeds expenditure.

Raising this initial money and the subsequent financial management of the business is therefore vital, and great care should be taken over it. Unfortunately, more businesses fail due to lack of sufficient day-to-day cash and financial management than for any other reason.

The first big question is to establish how much money you need. Look at every possible cost and divide them into one-off, fixed, or variable categories.

The *fixed costs* are those that you have to pay even if you make no sales (rent, rates, possibly some staff costs, repayments on any loans, and so on) as well as some *one-off costs,* or one-time purchases such as buying a vehicle or computer, which will not be repeated once the business is up and running. *Variable costs* are those that vary dependent on the level of your sales (raw materials, production and distribution costs, and so on).

Your finance requirements will be shown very clearly on your cash flow forecast, which is a table showing, usually on a monthly basis, the amount of money actually received into the business, and the amount of money paid out.

According to the Bank of England's report on small business finance, the average start-up cost for a new business in the UK is just over £18,000. However that average conceals some wide variations. Some start-ups, particularly those in technology or manufacturing, may require hundreds, thousands, or even millions of pounds, whilst others, such as those run from home may cost very little or nothing.

Six out of every ten people starting up a business use personal funds as their initial source of finance. Naturally, using your own money, your savings, your un-mortgaged property, your life insurance, and your other assets, is a logical starting point. You may not feel you can put all of your worth behind a business because of the risks involved, but whichever route you go down you will normally be expected to invest some of your own assets. Banks seek personal guarantees; venture capitalists like to see owners taking risks with their own money – why should they risk their clients' money if you will not risk yours?

If you can fund the project from your own resources there are attractions to doing so. Only in this way do all of the rewards of success flow to you. As soon as you bring in other sources of finance they slice off some of the reward, be it interest, share of the value on the sale of the business, or dividends. They may also constrain the business through the use of covenants, borrowing limits, and the placement of financial obligations on the business – potentially not only carving off part of your rewards but also capping them by restricting your operation.

Forecasting sales

While all forecasts may turn out to be wrong, it is important to demonstrate in your strategy that you have thought through the factors that will impact on performance. You should also show how you could deliver satisfactory results even when many of these factors work against you. Backers and employees alike will be measuring the downside risk, to evaluate the worst scenario and its likely effects, as well as looking towards an ultimate exit route.

Here are some guidelines to help you make an initial sales forecast:

- ✔ **Credible projections:** Your overall projections have to be believable. Most lenders and investors have an extensive experience of similar business proposals. Unlike you they have the benefit of hindsight, being able to look back several years at other ventures they have backed, and see how they fared in practice as compared with their initial forecasts.

  You could gather some useful knowledge on similar businesses yourself by researching company records (at the Companies House Web site, www.companies-house.gov.uk), or by talking with the founders of similar ventures, who will not be your direct competitors.

- ✔ **Market share:** How big is the market for your product or service? Is it growing or contracting and at what rate, percentage per annum? What is the economic and competitive position? These are all factors that can provide a market share basis for your forecasts. An entry market share of more than a few percent would be most unusual. But beware of turning this argument on its head. Unsubstantiated statements such as 'In a market of £1 billion per annum we can easily capture 1 per cent, which is £1 million a year', will impress no investor.

- ✔ **Customers:** How many customers and potential customers do you know who are likely to buy from you, and how much might they buy? Here you can use many types of data on which to base reasonable sales projections. You can interview a sample of prospective customers, issue a press release or advertisement to gauge response, and exhibit at trade shows to obtain customer reactions. If your product or service needs to be on an approved list before it can be bought, then your business plan should confirm that you have that approval, or less desirably, show how you will get it.

  You should also look at seasonal factors that might cause sales to be high or low at certain periods in the year. This will be particularly significant for cash flow projections. You should then relate your seasonal, customer-based, forecast to your capacity to make or sell at this rate. Sometimes your inability to recruit or increase capacity may limit your sales forecasts.

- ✔ **Market guidelines:** Some businesses have accepted formulas you can use to estimate sales. This is particularly true in retailing where location studies, traffic counts, and population density are known factors.

- ✔ **Desired income:** This approach to estimating sales embraces the concept that forecasts may also accommodate the realistic aims of the proprietor. Indeed, you could go further and state that the whole purpose of strategy is to ensure that certain forecasts are achieved. In a mature company with proven products and markets, this is more likely to be the case than with a start-up.

Nevertheless, an element of 'How much do we need to earn?' must play a part in forecasting, if only to signal when a business idea is not worth pursuing.

One extreme of the 'desired income' approach to forecasting comes from those entrepreneurs who think that the forecasts are the business plan. Such people cover the business plan with a mass of largely unconnected numbers. With reams of computer printout covering every variation possible in business, complete with sensitivity analysis, these people are invariably a big turn-off with financiers.

Calculating break-even

So far we've taken certain decisions for granted and ignored how to cost the product or service you're marketing, and indeed, how to set the selling price.

Your goal is to get past break even, the point at which you have covered all your costs, and into the realm of making profits as quickly as possible. So these decisions are clearly very important if you want to be sure of making a profit.

At first glance the problem is simple. You just add up all the costs and charge a bit more. The more you charge above your costs, provided the customers will keep on buying, the more profit you make. Unfortunately as soon as you start to do the sums the problem gets a little more complex. For a start, not all costs have the same characteristics. Some costs, for example, do not change however much you sell. If you are running a shop, the rent and rates are relatively constant figures, completely independent of the volume of your sales. On the other hand, the cost of the products sold from the shop is completely dependent on volume. The more you sell, the more it costs you to buy in stock. You can't really add up those two types of costs until you have made an assumption about how much you plan to sell.

Becoming lean and mean

Paradoxically, one of the main reasons small businesses fail in the early stages is that too much start-up capital is raised and used to buy fixed assets. While clearly some equipment is essential at the start, other purchases can be postponed until later in the day. This may mean that you rent or borrow desirable and labour-saving devices for a while. This is not quite as convenient but may mean the difference between surviving in business and going bust.

One other very good reason for keeping fixed costs as low as possible is that you may not know what you really need until you actually start trading. You may find that your suppliers are so reliable that you need only carry a couple of days' stock in hand rather than the month you anticipated that called for the extra space. In which case you will have spent the extra money for no gain whatsoever.

In any event, you need to keep your fixed costs low enough to break-even within six to nine months of starting up.

The University of Missouri (www.missouribusiness.net/docs/evalbus.pdf) has a tool that helps you examine your business idea and determine your potential for success before you invest too much time and money developing a business plan, the subject of our next chapter.

Chapter 4

Preparing the Business Plan

. . . .

In This Chapter

▶ Turning your ideas into plans

▶ Satisfying financiers' concerns

▶ Making your plan stand out

▶ Using software

▶ Preparing for an elevator pitch

. . . .

*P*erhaps the most important step in launching any new venture or expanding an existing one is the construction of a *business plan*. Such a plan must include your goals for the enterprise, both short and long term; a description of the products or services you offer and the market opportunities you anticipate; finally, an explanation of the resources and means you need to achieve your goals in the face of likely competition.

Preparing a comprehensive business plan along these lines takes time and effort – The Cranfield School of Management estimates anywhere between 200 and 400 hours, depending on the nature of your business and how much data you have already gathered. Nevertheless, such an effort is essential if you are both to crystallise and focus your ideas, and test your resolve about starting or expanding your business.

The core thinking behind business plans and their eventual implementation is strategic analysis. The strategic analysis refines or confirms your view of what is really unique about your proposition. Or to put it another way, 'why on earth would anyone want to pay enough for this to make me rich'.

Once completed, your business plan will serve as a blueprint to follow which, like any map, improves the user's chances of reaching their destination.

Finding a Reason to Write a Business Plan

There are a number of other important benefits you can anticipate arising from preparing a business plan. All these benefits add up to one compelling reason. Businesses that plan make more money than those that don't and they survive longer too.

The research on planning generally shows a positive relationship between planning and business performance. Businesses that follow a well-thought-out plan generally out perform businesses with no plans or informal plans in every relevant category. Businesses that continue to update their plans throughout the life of the business enjoy significantly more success than businesses that don't.

Key reasons for writing up your business plan are covered in the following sections.

Building confidence

Completing a business plan makes you feel confident in your ability to set up and operate the venture because you put together a plan to make it happen. It may even compensate for lack of capital and experience, provided of course you have other factors in your favour, such as a sound idea and a sizeable market opportunity for your product or service.

Testing your ideas

A systematic approach to planning enables you to make your mistakes on paper, rather than in the marketplace. One potential entrepreneur made the discovery while gathering data for his business plan that the local competitor he thought was a one-man band was in fact the pilot operation for a proposed national chain of franchised outlets. This had a profound effect on his market entry strategy!

Another entrepreneur found out that, at the price he proposed charging, he would never recover his overheads or break even. Indeed 'overheads' and 'break even' were themselves alien terms before he embarked on preparing a business plan. This naive perspective on costs is by no means unusual.

Showing how much money you need

Your business plan details how much money you need, what you need it for, and when and for how long you need it.

As under-capitalisation and early cash flow problems are two important reasons why new business activities fail, it follows that if you have a soundly prepared business plan, you can reduce these risks of failure. You can also experiment with a range of alternative viable strategies and so concentrate on options that make the most economic use of scarce financial resources.

It would be an exaggeration to say that your business plan is the passport to sources of finance. It will, however, help you to display your entrepreneurial flair and managerial talent to the full and to communicate your ideas to others in a way that will be easier for them to understand and to appreciate the reasoning behind your ideas. These outside parties could be bankers, potential investors, partners, or advisory agencies. Once they know what you are trying to do they will be better able to help you.

Providing planning experience

Preparing a business plan gives you an insight into the planning process. It is this process itself that is important to the long-term health of a business, and not simply the plan that comes out of it. Businesses are dynamic, as are the commercial and competitive environments in which they operate. No one expects every event as recorded on a business plan to occur as predicted, but the understanding and knowledge created by the process of business planning helps prepare the business for any changes that it may face, and so enables it to adjust quickly.

Satisfying financiers' concerns

If you need finance, it is important to examine what financiers expect from you if you are to succeed in raising those funds.

It is often said that there is no shortage of money for new and growing businesses, the only scarce commodities are good ideas and people with the ability to exploit them. From the potential entrepreneur's position this is often hard to believe. One major venture capital firm alone receives several thousand business plans a year. Only 500 or so are examined in any detail, less than 25 are pursued to the negotiating stage, and only six of those are invested in.

To a great extent the decision whether to proceed beyond an initial reading of the plan depends on the quality of the business plan used in supporting the investment proposal. The business plan is your ticket of admission, giving you your first and often only chance to impress prospective sources of finance with the quality of your proposal.

It follows from this that to have any chance at all of getting financial support, your business plan must be the best that can be written and it must be professionally packaged. The plans that succeed meet all of the following requirements.

Presenting evidence of market orientation and focus

You need to demonstrate that you recognise the needs of potential customers, rather than simply being infatuated with an innovative idea. Business plans that occupy more space with product descriptions and technical explanations than with explaining how products will be sold and to whom usually get cold-shouldered by financiers. They rightly suspect that these companies are more of an ego trip than an enterprise.

But market orientation is not in itself enough. Financiers want to sense that the entrepreneur knows the one or two things their business can do best and that they are prepared to concentrate on exploiting these opportunities.

Demonstrating customer acceptance

Financiers like to know that your new product or service will sell and is being used, even if only on a trial or demonstration basis.

The founder of Solicitec, a company selling software to solicitors to enable them to process relatively standard documents such as wills, had little trouble getting support for his house conveyancing package once his product had been tried and approved by a leading building society for their panel of solicitors.

If you are only at the prototype stage, financiers have no immediate indication that, once made, your product will appeal to the market. They have to assess your chances of succeeding without any concrete evidence that you will. Under these circumstances you have to show that the problem your innovation seeks to solve is a substantial one that a large number of people will pay for.

One inventor from the Royal College of Art came up with a revolutionary toilet system design that used 30 per cent less water per flush and had half the number of moving parts of a conventional product, all for no increase in price. Although he had only drawings to show, it was clear that with domestic metered water for all households a near certainty bearing in mind concerns about global warming, and a UK market alone for 500,000 new units per annum, a sizeable acceptance was reasonably certain.

As well as evidence of customer acceptance, you need to demonstrate that you know how and to whom your new product or service must be sold, and that you have a financially viable means of doing so.

Owning a proprietary position

Exclusive rights to a product through patents, copyright, trade mark protection, or a licence helps to reduce the apparent riskiness of a venture in the financiers' eyes, as these can limit competition, for a while at least.

One participant on a Cranfield enterprise programme held patents on a revolutionary folding bicycle he designed at college. While no financial institution was prepared to back him in manufacturing the bicycle, funds were readily available to enable him to make production prototypes and then license the design to established bicycle makers throughout the world.

However well protected legally a product is, marketability and marketing know-how generally outweigh 'patentability' in the success equation. A salutary observation made by an American Professor of Entrepreneurship revealed that less than 0.5 per cent of the best ideas contained in the *US Patent Gazette* in the last five years have returned a dime to the inventors.

Making believable forecasts

Entrepreneurs are naturally ebullient when explaining the future prospects for their businesses. They frequently believe that the sky's the limit when it comes to growth, and money (or rather the lack of it) is the only thing that stands between them and their success.

It is true that if you are looking for venture capital, then the providers are also looking for rapid growth in your business. However, it is as well to remember that financiers are dealing with thousands of investment proposals each year, and already have money tied up in hundreds of business sectors. It follows, therefore, that they already have a perception of what the accepted financial results and marketing approaches currently are for any sector. Any new company's business plan showing projections that are outside the ranges perceived as acceptable within an industry will raise questions in the investor's mind.

Make your growth forecasts believable; support them with hard facts where possible. If they are on the low side, then approach the more cautious lending banker, rather than venture capitalists. The former often see a modest forecast as a virtue, lending credibility to the business proposal as a whole.

Benefiting your business

Despite many valuable benefits, thousands of would-be entrepreneurs still attempt to start without a business plan. The most common among these are entrepreneurs who think that they need little or no capital at the outset, or those who have funds of their own. Both types of entrepreneurs may believe that they don't need a business plan because they don't need to expose their project to harsh financial appraisal.

The former type may believe the easily exploded myth that customers will all pay cash on the nail and suppliers will wait for months to be paid. In the meantime, the proprietor has the use of these funds to finance the business. Such model customers and suppliers are thinner on the ground than optimistic entrepreneurs think. In any event, two important market rules still apply: either the product or service on offer fails to sell like hot cakes and mountains of unpaid stocks build up, or the product or service does sell like hot cakes and more financially robust entrepreneurs are attracted into the market. Without the staying power that adequate financing provides these new competitors will rapidly kill the business off.

Those would-be entrepreneurs with funds of their own, or worse still borrowed from friends and relatives, tend to think that the time spent in preparing a business plan could be more usefully (and enjoyably) spent looking for premises, buying a new car, or installing a computer. In short, anything that inhibits them from immediate action is viewed as time wasting.

As most people's initial perception of their business venture is flawed in some important respect, it follows that jumping in at the deep end is risky, and unnecessarily so. You can often discover flaws cheaply and in advance when preparing a business plan.

Writing up Your Business Plan

In these sections, we give you some guidelines to make sure your plan attracts attention and succeeds in the face of some fierce competition. More than a thousand businesses start up in the UK each day, and many of those are looking for money or other resources that they are hoping their business plan will secure for them. Making your business plan the best it can be gives it a chance to stand out.

Defining your readership

Clearly, a business plan is more effective if you write it with your readers in mind. This involves some research into the particular interests, foibles, and idiosyncrasies of those readers. Bankers are more interested in hearing about certainties and steady growth, while venture capitalists are also interested in dreams of great things to come. *Business angels*, who put their own money at risk, like to know how their particular skills and talents can be deployed in the business.

You can benefit from carrying out your reader research before the final editing of your business plan, because you should incorporate something of this knowledge into the way you present it. You may find that you have to create slightly different versions of the business plan for different audiences. This makes the reader feel that you are addressing the proposal to them rather than them just being the recipient of a 'Dear Sir or Madam' type of missive. However, the fundamentals of the plan remain constant.

Choosing the right packaging

Appropriate packaging enhances every product and a business plan is no exception. Most experts prefer a simple spiral binding with a clear plastic cover front and back. This makes it easy for the reader to move from section to section, and it ensures the document will survive the frequent handling that every successful business plan is likely to get.

A letter quality printer, using size 12 typeface, double-spacing, and wide margins, results in a pleasing and easy to read plan.

Deciding on layout and content

There is no such thing as a universal business plan format. That being said, experience has taught us that certain styles have been more successful than others. Following these guidelines will result in an effective business plan, which covers most requirements. Not every sub-heading will be relevant, but the general format is robust.

The following list contains the elements of an effective business plan, one that covers most requirements. You may not need all of these sections, and you may need others to cover special requirements.

- ✔ The **cover** should show the name of your business, its address, phone and fax numbers, e-mail address, Web site, contact name, and the date on which this version of the plan was prepared. It should confirm that this is the current view on the business's position and financing needs.

- ✔ The **title page,** immediately behind the front cover, should repeat the above information and also give the founder's name, address, and phone number. A home phone number can be helpful, particularly for investors, who often work irregular hours too.

✔ The **executive summary** is ideally one page, but certainly no longer than two, and contains the highlights of your plan.

Writing this summary is a difficult task but it is the single most important part of your business plan. Done well it can favourably dispose the reader from the outset. Done badly, or not at all, then the plan may not get beyond the mail-room. This one page (or two pages) must explain:

- The current position of the company, including a summary of past trading results.

- A description of the products or services, together with details on any rights or patents and details on competitive advantage.

- The reasons why customers need this product or service, together with some indication of market size and growth.

- A summary of forecasts of sales and profits, together with short- and long-term aims and the strategies to be employed.

- How much money is needed to fund the growth and how and when the provider will benefit.

Write the executive summary only after you complete the business plan itself. Read the real-life example executive summary to get a feel for how this vital task can be successfully carried out.

✔ The **table of contents,** with page numbers, is the map that guides readers through the business plan. If that map is obscure, muddled, or even missing, then you are likely to end up with lost or irritated readers who are in no mind to back your proposal. Each main section should be listed, numbered, and given a page identity. Elements within each section should also be numbered: 1, 1.1, 1.2, and so on.

✔ Details of the **business and its management** should include a brief history of the business and its performance to date and details on key staff, current mission, legal entity, capital structure, and professional advisers.

✔ A description of **products and services,** their applications, competitive advantage, and proprietary position. Include details on state of readiness of new products and services and development cost estimates.

✔ The **marketing** section should provide a brief overview of the market by major segment showing size and growth. Explain the current and proposed marketing strategy for each major segment, covering price, promotion, distribution channels, selling methods, location requirements, and the need for acquisitions, mergers, or joint ventures, if any.

✔ Information on **management and staffing** should give details on current key staff and on any recruitment needs. Include information on staff retention strategies, reward systems, and training plans.

✔ The **operations** section describes how your products and services are made, how quality standards are assured, and how output can be met.

✔ A summary of the key **financial data,** including ratios together with a description of the key controls used to monitor and review performance.

✔ **Financing requirements** needed to achieve the planned goals, together with how long you will need the money for. You should also demonstrate how the business would proceed using only internal funding. The difference between these two positions is what the extra money will help to deliver.

✔ **E-commerce** isn't just about selling goods and services online, though that is important. It covers a range of activities that can be carried out online to make your business more efficient. These solutions extend across the supply chain from ordering your raw materials right through to after-sales service. It can incorporate market intelligence gathering, customer relationship management, and a whole range of back office procedures. Your business plan should show how you plan to tackle this area.

✔ Include **major milestones** with dates. For example: get prototype for testing by 20 December, file patents by 10 January, or locate suitable premises by such and such a date.

✔ **Risk assessment** features high on your reader's list of concerns, so it's best to anticipate as many as you can, together with your solution. For example: Our strategy is highly dependent on finding a warehouse with a cold store for stock. But if we can't find one by start date we will use space in the public cold store 10 miles away. Not as convenient but it will do.

✔ Detail an **exit route** for venture capitalists and business angels. Typically, they are looking to liquidate their investments within three to seven years, so your business plan should show them how much money they can make and how quickly.

If you think you need long-term investment (see Book I Chapter 5 for more about equity financing) then you need to say something about who might buy the business and when you might be able to launch it on a stock market.

✔ **Appendixes** include CVs of the key team members, technical data, patents, copyrights and designs, details on professional advisers, audited accounts, consultants' reports, abstracts of market surveys, details of orders on hand, and so on.

Writing and editing

The first draft of the business plan may have several authors and it can be written ignoring the niceties of grammar and style. The first draft is a good one to talk over the proposal with your legal adviser to keep you on the straight and narrow, and with a friendly banker or venture capitalist. This can give you an insider's view as to the strengths and weaknesses of your proposal.

When the first draft has been revised, then comes the task of editing. Here grammar, spelling, and a consistent style do matter. The end result must be a crisp, correct, clear, complete plan no more than 20 pages long. If you are not an expert writer you may need help with editing. Your local librarian or college may be able to help here.

Maintaining confidentiality

Finding an investor or a bank to lend to your business may take weeks or months. During that time, potential investors diligently gather information about the business so that they won't have surprises later about income, expenses, or undisclosed liabilities. The business plan is only the starting point for their investigations.

If you and the prospective financiers are strangers to one another, you may be reluctant to turn over sensitive business information until you are confident that they are serious. (This is not so sensitive an issue with banks as it is with business angels and venture capital providers.) To allay these fears, consider asking for a confidentiality letter, or agreement.

A confidentiality letter will suffice in most circumstances. But if substantial amounts of intellectual property are involved you may prefer a longer, more formal confidentiality agreement (also known as a non-disclosure agreement or NDA) drafted by a lawyer. That's OK, but you (and perhaps your lawyer as well) should make sure that the proposed document contains no binding commitment on you. The confidentiality letter should be limited to their agreement to treat the information as strictly confidential and to use the information only to investigate lending or investing in the business, and to the other terms set out in the letter. Figure 4-1 shows a sample confidentiality agreement.

Doing due diligence

Don't be surprised if the investor wants to learn about your personal financial status, job, or business history. They are interested in your financial stability, your reputation for integrity, and your general business savvy because they will, in effect, extend credit to you until you deliver them the interest or return they are expecting on their money. That is what the *due diligence* process is all about.

WHEREAS

1. The purpose of communication between the Parties to this Agreement is for the investor/lender to evaluate the suitability as an investment or lending proposition, the business proposition as set out in the business plan

2. The information to be communicated in strict confidence between the Parties to this Agreement includes the business plan, demonstrations, commercial and technical information, all forms of intellectual property and includes material for which patent or similar registration may have been filed.

THEREFORE THE PARTIES HEREBY UNDERTAKE AS FOLLOWS:

FIRST: Each Party hereto agrees to maintain as confidential and not to use any of the information directly or indirectly disclosed by the other Party until or unless such information becomes public knowledge through no fault of the recipient Party, or unless the Parties to the Agreement complete a further Agreement making provision for utilisation of information disclosed. Each Party undertakes to prevent the information disclosed from passing to other than those representatives who must be involved for the purpose of this Agreement.

SECOND: In the event that no further Agreement on utilisation or publication of information is concluded each Party hereto undertakes to return to the other all confidential items submitted and to furnish certification that no copies or other records of those items have been retained.

THIRD: In the event that either Party requires the assistance of a further party in pursuing the purposes of the Agreement the approval of the other Party to this Agreement shall be secured.

FOURTH: Any information which either Party can prove was in his possession prior to disclosure hereunder and was not acquired from the other Party or his representatives is excepted from this Agreement.

FIFTH: The construction, validity and performance of this Agreement shall be governed in all respects by Law and the Parties hereto submit to the jurisdiction of the Courts.

SIGNED for
First Party...

Position:...

For and on behalf of:

....

In the presence of:

....

SIGNED for
Second Party...

Position:...

For and on behalf of:

....

In the presence of:

....

Figure 4-1:
A con-
fidentiality
agreement.

Usually the due diligence process, which involves a thorough examination of both the business and its owners, takes several weeks, if not longer. But that depends on how much money your plan calls for and from whom you are trying to raise it. (We cover raising finance in Book I Chapter 5.)

Accountants and lawyers will usually subject your track record and the business plan to detailed scrutiny. You will then be required to warrant that you have provided *all* relevant information, under pain of financial penalties. The cost of this due diligence process, rarely less than a big five-figure sum and often running into six, will have to be borne by the firm raising the money, but will be paid out of the money raised, if that is any consolation.

Using Business Planning Software

You may consider taking some of the sweat out of writing your business plan by using one of the myriad of software programs on the market. You need to take some care in using such systems as the end result can be a bland plan that pleases no one and achieves nothing worthwhile.

Don't buy a package with several hundred business plans covering every type of business imaginable. The chances are that the person who wrote the plans knows far less than you do about your business sector and will add little or no value to your proposition. Worse still there is at least an even chance that the reader of your plan will have seen the fruits of these packaged plans before and may be less than enthusiastic to see yet another one.

You may well find it useful to use the test shown in Figure 4-2 as an uncomplicated form of self-assessment, before becoming bogged down in number-crunching software.

Recognising the limits of software

Good business planning software provides a useful structure to drop your plan in to and may provide a few helpful spreadsheets and templates for financial projections and market analysis. It also provides a valuable repository for your work-in-progress as you assemble the evidence to convince yourself and others that your business will succeed.

What software does not do is write a convincing business proposition by itself. The maxim, 'garbage in garbage out' applies to business planning software just as it does to everything to do with computers.

By answering the questions below you will get some idea of how well your business plan is progressing. Score 1, 2, or 3 following the key below for each of the questions. Mark the options closest to your instincts, and be honest. Then add up your scores and refer to the results at the end of the questionnaire to see how you scored and to check the potential of your plan.

Whatever your score, remember that this type of self-assessment test is broad brush. It is designed only to give an indication of whether you have the basic attitude, instincts, and capabilities to make a success of launching a home-based business.

If your score is low, the chances are that you do not. If it is high, the opposite is true.

1 = Made a start   2 = Some data only   3 = Comprehensive

Title page   ☐1 ☐2 ☐3

>   Name of business contact details, date of business plan, contents

Executive summary   ☐1 ☐2 ☐3

>   Your details; summary of key strategies; why you are better or different; summary of profit projections; summary of financial needs

The business and its management   ☐1 ☐2 ☐3

>   You and your team's relevant experience; business goals and objectives; legal structure of the business

The marketing strategy   ☐1 ☐2 ☐3

>   Market segment analysis; pricing strategy; promotion plans; product mix and range; e-commerce strategy; location; selling strategy

Management and staffing   ☐1 ☐2 ☐3

>   Staff numbers; roles and responsibilities; recruitment needs

Operations   ☐1 ☐2 ☐3

>   What facilities and equipment are needed; what services will be brought in?

Legal issues   ☐1 ☐2 ☐3

>   What intellectual protection do you have as a barrier to entry; what other legal issues affect your business?

Financial forecasts   ☐1 ☐2 ☐3

>   Summary of financial projections; monthly cash flows; profit and loss accounts; balance sheets; break-even analysis

Financing requirements   ☐1 ☐2 ☐3

>   How much money do you need; what is it needed for; how much money can you provide; how much do you need to raise from outside; what security is available?

Results:

9 points or less:
You still have a lot more information to gather or decisions to make. No serious plan can be drawn up at this stage.
Between 10 and 20 points:
You have made progress, but still have a few gaps to fill. Concentrate your efforts on completing your plan.
More than 20 points:
Your plan is now complete and ready for final editing.

Figure 4-2:
Assessing
the Content
of Your
Business
Plan.

The other danger is that you end up with spreadsheet solutions – numbers just pumped into the financials – without any evidence of the underlying logic to support them.

Use business planning software as an aid and not a crutch. Go beyond that and you may end up worse than if you had started with a blank sheet of paper.

Reviewing systems

This section provides reviews of some business planning software packages that have been used to good effect.

- ✔ **American Express** (`home3.americanexpress.com/smallbusiness/tool/biz_plan/index.asp`): American Express run something they call the Small Business Exchange Business Plan Workshop. This workshop will help you write a business plan using their 'Toolboxes' of samples, worksheets, and glossaries. You can experiment on someone else's business in the 'Try It Yourself' section by testing your skills on a fictional business plan and be rated on how prepared you are to create your own.

- ✔ **BizPlanit.Com** (Web site: `www.bizplanit.com`; e-mail: `biz@bizplanit.com`): BizPlanIt.Com's Web site has free resources offering information, advice, articled links to other useful sites and a free monthly newsletter, the *Virtual Business Plan* to pinpoint information. They also have an email service, providing answers to business plan questions within 24 hours.

- ✔ **National Federation of Enterprise Agencies (NFEA)** (`www.smallbusinessadvice.org.uk`): The Web site of NFEA has a step-by-step business planning guide with free downloads to help with the financial calculations.

- ✔ **Royal Bank of Canada** (`www.royalbank.com`): This site has a wide range of useful help for entrepreneurs. At `www.royalbank.com/sme/index.html` you can have access to their business plan writer package and three sample business plans.

- ✔ **Royal Bank of Scotland** (`www.rbs.co.uk/Small_Business`): This is the bank's small business Web site where you can find a number of free business guides as well as specialised support for certain business sectors such as franchising, healthcare, and agriculture. At `www.rbs.co.uk/Small_Business/Business_Plan_Software/default.htm` you can request a free copy of its Business Plan CD-Rom, or you can call 0800 521 607.

Presenting Your Plan

Anyone backing a business does so primarily because they believe in the management. They know from experience that things rarely go according to plan so they must be confident that the team involved can respond effectively to changing conditions. You can be sure that any financier you are presenting to will have read dozens of similar plans, and will be well rehearsed. They may even have taken the trouble to find out something of your business and financial history.

Starring in show time

When you present your business plan to financial backers, your goal is to create empathy between yourself and your listeners. Whilst you may not be able to change your personality you could take a few tips on presentation skills. Eye contact, tone of speech, enthusiasm, and body language all have a part to play in making a presentation go well.

Wearing a suit is never likely to upset anyone. Shorts and sandals just set the wrong tone! Serious money calls for serious people and even the Internet world is growing up.

Rehearse your presentation beforehand, having found out how much time you have. Explain your strategy in a business-like manner, demonstrating your grasp of the competitive market forces at work. Listen to comments and criticisms carefully, avoiding a defensive attitude when you respond.

Use visual aids and if possible bring and demonstrate your product or service. A video or computer-generated model is better than nothing.

Allow at least as much time for questions as you take in your talk. Make your replies to questions brief and to the point. If they want more information, they can ask. This approach allows time for the many different questions that must be asked either now or later, before an investment can proceed.

Making an 'elevator pitch'

You never know when the chance to present your business plan may occur – maybe even in a lift between floors (hence the term *elevator pitch*). You need to have every aspect of your business plan in your head and know your way around the plan backwards, forwards, and sideways. It's as well to have a five-, ten- and 20-minute presentation ready to run at a moment's notice.

One entrepreneur was given a chance to make a presentation of her business plan to the most powerful and influential person in her industry. This person could make or break new businesses and frequently did. The opportunity was a ten-minute ride in a chauffeur-driven car between the Dorchester hotel and Harrods. She had no room to demonstrate the product, set up flip charts or PowerPoint presentations or to involve the team. There was just enough space and time for a handful of powerful facts to be conveyed with passion, conviction, and authority. Fortunately the entrepreneur concerned had rehearsed her impromptu presentation and was completely prepared to seize the opportunity presented. She now has a £20 million business, barely a decade after taking that fateful car ride.

Chapter 5

Finding the Money

In This Chapter

▶ Working out how much outside money you need

▶ Looking at the different types of money available to you

▶ Choosing the best source of money for you

▶ Finding money to work with

*B*usinesses need a continuous flow of customers, products, or services to sell, and space to work from or store unsold goods. But they need money to make all of these events happen. The more the business actually does, the more money it needs. In fact, according to the Bank of England's report on the financing of small business (www.bankofengland.co.uk/publications/financeforsmallfirms/fin4sm11.pdf), owner-managed businesses have invested a colossal £51.8 billion to keep their show on the road. Starting a business on the road to success involves ensuring that you have sufficient money to survive until the point where income continually exceeds expenditure.

You need a steady flow of money from many different sources along the way. Karan Bilimoria, founder of Cobra Beer, and one of my former students, raised money from almost every source imaginable in the decade or so it took to get his business from start-up to £100 million annual turnover. (Check out www.startups.co.uk (click on How I Did It, Success Stories and then Cobra Beer) for his story.) This chapter helps you to find the right type of money for your business and avoid common pitfalls.

Assessing How Much Money You Need

You should work out from the outset how much money you will need to get your business off the ground. If your proposed venture needs more cash than you feel comfortable either putting up yourself or raising from others, then the sooner you know the better. Then you can start to revise your plans. The steps that lead to an accurate estimate of your financial needs start with the sales forecast, which you do as part of feasibility testing, which we cover in Book I Chapter 3, along with advice on estimating costs for initial expenditures such as retail or production space, equipment, staff, and so on.

Forecasting cash flow is the most reliable way to estimate the amount of money a business needs on a day-to-day basis.

Do's and don'ts for making a cash flow forecast:

- ✔ Do ensure your projections are believable. This means you need to show how your sales will be achieved.

- ✔ Do base projections on facts not conjecture.

- ✔ Do describe the main assumptions that underpin your projections.

- ✔ Do explain what the effect of these assumptions not happening to plan could be. For example, if your projections are based on recruiting three sales people by month three, what would happen if you could only find two suitable people by that date?

- ✔ Don't use data to support projections without saying where it came from.

- ✔ Don't forget to allow for seasonal factors. At certain times of the year most business are influenced by regular events. Sales of ice-cream are lower in winter than in summer, sales of toys peak in the lead up to Christmas and business-to-business sales dip in the summer and Christmas holiday periods. So rather than taking your projected annual sales figure and dividing by twelve to get a monthly figure, you need to consider what effect seasonal factors might have.

- ✔ Don't ignore economic factors such as an expanding (or shrinking) economy, rising (or falling) interest rates and an unemployment rate that is so low that it may influence your ability to recruit at the wage rate you would like to pay.

- ✔ Don't make projections without showing the specific actions that will get those results.

- ✔ Don't forget to get someone else to check your figures out – you may be blind to your own mistakes but someone else is more likely to spot the mistakes/flaws in your projections.

Projecting receipts

Receipts from sales come in different ways, depending on the range of products and services on offer. And aside from money coming in from paying customers, the business owner may, and in many cases almost certainly will, put in cash of her own. However not all the money will necessarily go in at the outset; you could budget so that £10,000 goes in at the start, followed by sums of £5,000 in months four, seven, and ten respectively.

There could be other sources of outside finance, say from a bank or investor, but these are best left out at this stage. In fact the point of the cash flow projection, as well as showing how much money the business needs, is to reveal the likely shortfall after the owner has put in what she can to the business and the customers have paid up.

You should total up the projected receipts for each month and for the year as a whole. You would be well advised to carry out this process using a spreadsheet program, which will save you the problems caused by faulty maths.

A sale made in one month may not result in any cash coming into the business bank account until the following month, if you are reasonably lucky, or much later if you are not.

Estimating expenses

Some expenses, such as rent, rates, and vehicle and equipment leases, you pay monthly. Others bills such as telephone, utilities, and bank charges come in quarterly.

If you haven't yet had to pay utilities, for example, you put in your best guesstimate of how much you'll spend and when. Marketing, promotion, travel, subsistence, and stationery are good examples of expenses you may have to estimate. You know you will have costs in these areas, but they may not be all that accurate as projections.

After you've been trading for a while, you can get a much better handle on the true costs likely to be incurred.

Total up the payments for each month and for the year as a whole.

Working out the closing cash balances

This is crunch time, when the real sums reveal the amount of money your great new business needs to get it off the ground. Working through the cash flow projections allows you to see exactly how much cash you have in hand, or in the bank, at the end of each month, or how much cash you need to raise. This is the closing cash balance for the month. It is also the opening cash balance for the following month as that is the position you are carrying forward.

The accounting convention is to show payments out and negative sums in brackets, rather than with minus signs in front.

Testing your assumptions

There is little that disturbs a financier more than a firm that has to go back cap-in-hand for more finance too soon after raising money, especially if the reason should have been seen and allowed for at the outset.

So in making projections you have to be ready for likely pitfalls and be prepared for the unexpected events that will knock your cash flow off target. Forecasts and projections rarely go to plan, but the most common pitfalls can be anticipated and to some extent allowed for.

You can't really protect yourself against freak disasters or unforeseen delays, which can hit large and small businesses alike. But some events are more likely than others to affect your cash flow, and it is against these that you need to guard by careful planning. Not all of the events listed here may be relevant to your business, but some, perhaps many, will at some stage be factors that could push you off course.

Getting the numbers wrong

It's called estimating for a reason. You can't know ahead of time how the future will pan out, so you have to guess, and sometimes you guess wrong. Some of the wrong guesses you can make about stock and costs are:

✔ **A flawed estimate:** There is no doubt that forecasting sales is difficult. The numbers of things that can and will go awry are many and varied. In the first place the entire premise on which the forecast is based may be flawed. Estimating the number of people who may come into a restaurant as passing trade, who will order from a catalogue mailing, or what proportion of Internet site hits will turn into paying customers, depends on performance ratios. For example a direct mail shot to a well-targeted list could produce anything from 0.5–3 per cent response. If you build your sales forecast using the higher figure and actually achieve the lower figure then your sales income could be barely a sixth of the figure in your cash flow projection. You can't avoid this problem, but you can allow for it by testing to destruction (see elsewhere in this checklist).

✔ **Carrying too much stock:** If your sales projections are too high, you will experience the double whammy of having less cash coming in and more going out than shown in your forecast. That is because in all probability you will have bought in supplies to meet anticipated demand. Your suppliers offering discounts for bulk purchases may have exacerbated the situation if you took up their offers.

✔ **Missed or wrong cost:** You may underestimate or completely leave out certain costs due to your inexperience. Business insurance and legal expenses are two often missed items. Even where a cost is not missed altogether it may be understated. So, for example, if you are including the cost of taking out a patent in your financing plan, it is safer to take it from a patent agent's Web site rather than from a friend who took out a patent a few years ago.

✔ **Testing to destruction:** Even events that have not been anticipated can be allowed for when estimating financing needs. 'What if' analysis using a cash flow spreadsheet will allow you to identify worst-case scenarios that could knock you off-course. After this you will end up with a realistic estimate of the financing requirements of the business or project.

✔ **Late deliveries:** If your suppliers deliver late, you may in turn find you have nothing to sell. Apart from causing ill will with your customers, you may have to wait weeks or months for another opportunity to supply. This problem can be minimised using online order tracking systems, if your suppliers have them, but some late deliveries will occur. Increasing your stocks is one way to insure against deficiencies in the supply chain, but that strategy too has an adverse impact on cash flow.

Settling on sales

Sales may be slow, pricing may be high – just two of the ways sales can make your projections look out of kilter. More ways follow:

✔ **Slower than expected sales:** Even if your forecasting premise is right, or nearly so, customers may take longer to make up their minds than you expect. A forecast may include an assumption that people will order within two weeks of receiving your mail-order catalogue. But until you start trading you will not know how accurate that assumption is likely to be. Even if you have been in business for years, buying patterns may change.

✔ **Not being able to sell at list price:** Selling price is an important factor in estimating the amount of cash coming into a business and hence the amount of finance needed.

Often the only way a new or small business can win certain customers is by matching a competitor's price. This may not be the price in your list, but it is the one you have to sell at.

Also the mix of products or services you actually sell may be very different from your projection and this can affect average prices. For example a restaurant owner has to forecast what wines her customers will buy. If the house wine is too good, then more customers might go for that rather than the more expensive and more profitable wines on the list.

✔ **Suppliers don't give credit:** Few suppliers are keen to give small and particularly new businesses any credit. So before you build in 30, 60, or even 90 days' credit into your financial projections, you need to confirm that normal terms of trade will apply to what a supplier may view as an abnormal customer.

You need to remember that whilst taking extended credit may help your cash flow in the short term, it could sour relationships in the long term. So in circumstances where a product is in short supply poor payers will be last on the list to get deliveries and the problems identified above may be further exacerbated.

Miscounting customers

Customers can confound your most well-thought-out projections. They pay late, they may rip you off, and they may not buy your goods as quickly as you'd like. Some of the ways customers can throw your estimates off are:

- **Paying slowly:** Whilst you set the terms and conditions under which you plan to do business, customers are a law unto themselves. If they can take extra credit they will. Unless you are in a cash-only business, you can expect a proportion of your customers to be late payers. Whilst with good systems you will keep this to an acceptable figure, you will never get every bill paid on time. You need to allow for this lag in your cash flow projections.

- **Bad debts:** Unfortunately late payers are not the only problem. Some customers never pay. Businesses fail each year and individuals go bankrupt, each leaving behind a trail of unpaid bills. You can take some steps to minimise this risk, but you can't eliminate the risk. You can try to get a feel for the rate of non-payment in your sector and allow for it in your plans. For example, the building and restaurant industries have a relatively high incidence of bad debts, whilst business services have a lower rate.

- **Fraud and theft:** Retailers claim they could knock 5 per cent off everything they sell if they could eliminate theft. But despite their best endeavours with security guards and cameras, theft continues.

- **Repeat orders take longer to come in than expected:** It is hard to know exactly what a customer's demand for your product or service is. The initial order may last them months, weeks, or days. For strategic reasons they may want to divide up their business between a number of suppliers. If, for example, they have three suppliers and they order a month's worth at a time, it may be some time before they order from you again. If your customer sales are sluggish or seasonal, then that timeframe could extend further still. So even delighted customers may not come back for quite some time.

You can check out potential customers by using a credit reference agency such as Snoop4 Companies (www.snoop4companies.co.uk) for businesses or Experian (www.experian.co.uk) for private individuals. Basic credit reports cost between £3 and £25 and may save you time and money if you have any reservations about a potential customer's ability to pay.

Reviewing Your Financing Options

Knowing how much money you need to get your business successfully started is an important first step, but it is only that: a first step. There are many sources of funds available to small firms. However not all are equally appropriate to all firms at all times. These different sources of finance carry very different obligations, responsibilities, and opportunities. The differences have to be understood to allow an informed choice.

Most small firms confine their financial strategy to long-term or short-term bank loans, viewing other financing methods as either too complex or too risky. In many respects the reverse is true. Almost every finance source other than banks shares some of the risks of doing business with you to a greater or lesser extent.

The great attraction of borrowing from a bank lies in the speed of the transaction. Most small businesses operate without a business plan so most events that require additional funds, such as sudden expansion or contraction, come as a surprise, either welcome or unwelcome, and with a sense of urgency. Basing financing choices on the fact that you need the money quickly may lead to more difficulties in the long run.

Deciding between debt capital and equity capital

At one end of the financing spectrum lie shareholders – either individual *business angels* who put their own money into a business, or corporate organisations such as *venture capital providers* – who provide equity capital which is used to buy a stake in a business. These investors share all the risks and vagaries of the business alongside you and expect a proportionate share in the rewards if things go well. They are less concerned with a stream of dividends, which is just as well as few small companies ever pay them, and instead hope for a radical increase in the value of their investment. They expect to realise this value from other investors who want to take their places for the next stage in the firm's growth cycle, rather than from any repayment by the founder. Investors in new or small businesses don't look for the security of buildings or other assets to underpin their investment. Rather they look to the founder's vision and the core management team's ability to deliver results.

At the other end of the financing spectrum are debt financiers – banks that try hard to take no risk and expect some return on their money irrespective of your business's performance. They want interest payments on money lent, usually from day one. Whilst they too hope the management is competent, they are more interested in making sure either you or the business has some type of asset such as a house that they can grab if things go wrong. At the end of the day, and that day can be sooner than the borrower expects, a bank wants all its money back, with interest. Think of bankers as people who help you turn part of an illiquid asset such as property into a more liquid asset such as cash – for a price.

Understanding the differences between lenders, who provide debt capital, and investors, who provide equity, or share, capital is central to a sound grasp of financial management.

In between the extremes of shareholders and the banks lie a myriad of other financing vehicles, which have a mixture of lending or investing criteria. You need to keep your business finances under constant review, choosing the most appropriate mix of funds for the risks you plan to take and the economic climate ahead. The more risky and volatile the road ahead, the more likely it is that taking a higher proportion of equity capital will be appropriate. In times of stability and low interest, higher borrowings may be more acceptable.

As a rule of thumb debt and equity should be used in equal amounts to finance a business. If the road ahead looks more risky than usual go for £2 of equity to every £1 of debt. Table 5-1 illustrates some of the differences between risk-averse lenders and risk-taking investors.

Table 5-1	Comparing Benefits of Lenders and Investors	
Category	*Lenders*	*Investors*
Interest	Paid on outstanding loan	None, though dividends sometimes paid if profits warrant it
Capital	Repaid at end of term or sooner if lender has concerns	Returned with substantial growth through new shareholders
Security	Either from assets or personal guarantees	From belief in founders and their business vision

If your business sector is generally viewed as very risky, and perhaps the most reliable measure of that risk is the proportion of firms that go bust, then financing the business almost exclusively with borrowings is tanta-mount to gambling.

Debt has to be serviced whatever your business performance, so it follows that, in any risky, volatile marketplace, you stand a good chance of being caught out one day.

If your business risks are low, the chances are that profits are relatively low too. High profits and low risks always attract a flood of competitors, reducing your profits to levels that ultimately reflect the riskiness of your business sector. As venture capitalists and shareholders generally are looking for much better returns than they could get by lending the money, it follows they will be disappointed in their investment on low-risk, low-return business. So if they are wise they will not get involved in the first place, or if they do they will not put any more money in later.

Examining your own finances

Obviously the first place to start looking for money to finance your business is in your own pockets. Whilst you may not have much in ready cash you may have assets that can be turned into cash or used to support borrowing.

Start by totalling your assets and liabilities. The chances are that your most valuable assets are your house, your car, and any life assurance or pension policies you may have. Your liabilities are the debts you owe. The difference between your assets and liabilities, assuming you have more of the former than the latter, is your 'net worth'. That in effect is the maximum security you can offer anyone outside the business that you want to raise money from.

Now the big questions are: what is your appetite for risk and how certain are you your business will be successful? The more of your own money you can put into your business at the outset, the more you will be truly running your own business in your own way. The more outside money you have to raise, the more power and perhaps value you have to share with others.

Now you have a simple piece of arithmetic to do. How much money do you need to finance your business start-up, as shown in your worst-case scenario cash flow forecast? How much of your own money are you willing and able to put into your business? The difference is the sum you are looking to outside financiers to back you with.

If that sum is more than your net worth, then you will be looking for investors. If it is less then bankers may be the right people to approach.

If you do have free cash or assets that you could but won't put into your business, then you should ask yourself if the proposition is worth pursuing. You can be absolutely certain that any outsider you approach for money will ask you to put up or shut up.

Another factor to consider in reviewing your own finances is your ongoing expenses. You have to live whilst getting your business up and running. So food, heat, and a roof over your head are essential expenses. But perhaps a two-week long-haul summer holiday, the second car, and membership of a health club are not essentials. Great whilst you were a hired hand and had a pay cheque each month, but an expendable luxury once you are working for yourself.

Determining the Best Source of Finance

Choosing which external source of finance to use is to some extent a matter of personal preference. One of your tasks in managing your business's financial affairs is to keep good lines of communication open with as many sources as possible.

The other key task is to consider which is the most appropriate source for your particular requirement at any one time. The main issues you need to consider are explored in the following sections.

Considering the costs

Clearly if a large proportion of the funds you need to start your business are going to be consumed in actually raising the money itself, then your set-up costs are going to be very high. Raising capital, especially if the amounts are relatively small (under £500,000) is generally quite expensive. You have to pay your lawyers and accountants, and those of your investor or lender, to prepare the agreements and to conduct the due diligence examination (the business appraisal). It is not unusual to spend between 10 and 15 per cent of the first £500,000 you raise on set-up costs.

An overdraft or factoring agreement is relatively cheap to set up, usually a couple of per cent or so. However, long-term loans, leasing, and hire-purchase agreements could involve some legal costs.

Sharing ownership and control

The source of your money helps determine how much ownership and control you have to give up in return. Venture capitalists generally want a large share of stock and often a large say in how the business is run. At the other end of the spectrum are providers of long-term loans who generally leave you alone so long as you service the interest and repay the capital as agreed. You have to strike the balance that works best for you and your business.

If you do not want to share the ownership of your business with outsiders then clearly raising equity capital is not a good idea. Even if you recognise that owning 100 per cent of a small venture is not as attractive as owning 40 per cent of a business ten times as large it may not be the right moment to sell any of your shares. Particularly if, in common with many business founders, long-term capital gain is one of your principal goals. If you can hold onto your shares until profits are reasonably high you will realise more gain for every share sold than if you sell out in the early years or whilst profits are low.

Parting with shares inevitably involves some loss of control. Letting 5 per cent go may just be a mild irritation from time to time. However once 25 per cent has gone, outsiders could have a fair amount of say in how things are run. At that point, even relatively small groups of shareholders could find it easy to call an Extraordinary General Meeting and put it to a vote to remove you from the board. Nevertheless, whilst you have over 51 per cent you are in control, if only just. Once past the 51 per cent things could get a little dangerous. Theoretically you could be out voted at any stage.

Some capital providers take a hands-on approach and will have a view on how you should run the business.

Beating the clock

Overdrafts can be arranged in days, raising venture capital can take months. Very different amounts of scarce management time are needed, dependent on the financing route taken. So if speed matters, your funding options may be limited.

Venture capital providers (also called Venture Capitalists or VCs) have been known to string out negotiations long enough to see if the bullish forecasts made in the business plan come to pass. After all, venture capital is there to help businesses to grow faster than they might otherwise do not just to keep them afloat. Don't expect a decision from a venture capital firm in under three months whatever their brochure says. Four to six months is a more realistic timescale and nine months is not too unusual.

Business angels can usually make investment decisions much more quickly than VCs; after all it's their money they are risking. Weeks rather than months, is the timescale here.

Banks finance is usually a fairly speedy process. Even large loans of £100,000 and upwards can be arranged in a few weeks. But the speed depends more on how much collateral you have to give the bank manager comfort that her money is safe.

Staying flexible

As your plans change, the amount of money you actually need may alter during negotiations. Some sources of funds such as leasing, hire-purchase agreements, and long-term loans dictate the amount that has to be agreed at the outset. If you're selling shares in the company, you have some fluidity during negotiations, and if you're arranging overdrafts it is possible to draw down only what you need at any one time, with the upper limit negotiated usually each year.

Once you have investigated and used a source of funds you may want to be able to use that source again as your plans unfold. Loans and hire purchase/leasing agreements are for a specific sum and it can be difficult and expensive going back to the same source for more. Many venture capitalists, for example, already have a full weighting of investments in your business sector and so may not be anxious to invest more, however successful your firm. So that might mean starting all over again with another venture capital firm.

It may pay to make sure that at least some of your financing comes from a source such as factoring, which gives you total flexibility to change the amount of money drawn down to mirror the amount needed at any one time – both upwards and downwards.

Adding value to the business

With some sources of finance you can get useful expertise as well as money. For example, with factoring you could get expertise in managing your home and overseas credit, which could result in better credit control, fewer bad debts, and less capital tied up in debtors. You could even close or reduce your credit control department. With new share capital you may get a director with relevant experience in the industry. While the director's principal task is to ensure the capital provides interest, you also get the benefit of her knowledge.

Gaining security and certainty

For most sources of money, if you comply with the agreed-upon terms, the future is reasonably predictable – in so far as that money is concerned. The exception to this rule is an overdraft. An overdraft is technically, and often actually, repayable on demand. Overdrafts are sometimes called in at the moment you need them most.

Limiting personal liability

As a general rule most providers of long-term loans and overdrafts look to you and other owners to provide additional security if the business assets are in any way inadequate. You may be asked to provide a personal guarantee – an asset such as your house. Only when you raise new share capital, by selling more stock in your company, do you escape increasing your personal liability. Even with the new share capital you may be asked to provide warranties to assure new investors that everything in the company's past history has been declared.

Going for Debt

You can explore borrowing from a number of possible sources in your search for outside finance. It is worth giving them all the once over, but it has to be said that most people start and stop at a bank. The other major first source of money is family and friends, but many business starters feel nervous about putting family money at risk and in any event would rather deal with professional financiers. *Credit Unions* and *mezzanine finance* are relatively unusual sources of finance for a start-up, but finding any money to start a business is a tough task, so no source should be completely overlooked. (These terms are explained later in this chapter.)

Borrowing from banks

Banks are the principal, and frequently the only, source of finance for nine out of every ten new and small businesses.

Banks are usually a good starting point for almost any type of debt financing. They are also able to provide many other cash flow and asset backed financing products, although they are often not the only or the most appropriate provider. As well as the main clearing banks, a number of the former building societies and smaller regional banks are competing hard for small firm lending.

Abbey National, now part of the Spanish banking giant Santander, set out to recruit around 600 staff across the UK as part of a push to snatch market share from its rivals in the business banking market and challenge the 'big four' clearing banks in the business banking and finance markets. The move came hot on the heels of an aggressive push by rival HBOS, the merged Halifax and Bank of Scotland, into the small business banking market. Banks often offer inducements to small businesses to bank with them during such expansion drives, including lower interest rates for a set period or assistance with preparing business plans. So shop around for the best-buy bank just as you do for any other product or service. Check out Money Facts (www.money facts.co.uk/banking/bestbuys), Money Extra (www.moneyextra.com/banking), or Which Bank Account 4u (www.which-bank-account-4u.co.uk) to see who is offering the best deals.

All the major clearing banks offer telephone banking and Internet services to their small business customers or are in the process of doing so. Branch location seems less likely to be a significant factor to bank customers in the future, so you no longer have to confine your search for a bank to those with a branch nearby.

Bankers, and indeed any other sources of debt capital, are looking for property, land, insurance policies, or any other investments you may have to back their loan and the near certainty of getting their money back. They also charge an interest rate that reflects current market conditions and their view of the risk level of the proposal.

If you import raw materials, the bank can provide you with Letters of Credit, which guarantees your suppliers payment from the bank when they present proof of satisfactory delivery. If you have a number of overseas suppliers who prefer settlement in their own currency for which you will need foreign currency, cheque facilities or buying forward, banks can make the necessary arrangements.

Running an overdraft

The principal form of short-term bank funding is an *overdraft*. An overdraft is permission for you to use some of the bank's money when you don't have enough of your own. The permission is usually agreed annually, but can be withdrawn at anytime. A little over a quarter of all bank finance for small firms is in the form of an overdraft. The overdraft was originally designed to cover the time between having to pay for raw materials to manufacture finished goods and selling those goods. The size of an overdraft will usually be limited to a modest proportion of the amount of money owed to you by your customers and the value of your finished goods stock. The bank will see those items as assets, which in the last resort can be used to get their money back.

Seeing the five Cs

Bankers like to speak of the five Cs of credit analysis, factors they look at when they evaluate a loan request. When applying to a bank for a loan, be prepared to address the following points:

✔ **Character:** Bankers lend money to borrowers who appear honest and who have a good credit history. Before you apply for a loan, it makes sense to obtain a copy of your credit report and clean up any problems.

✔ **Capacity:** This is a prediction of the borrower's ability to repay the loan. For a new business, bankers look at the business plan. For an existing business, bankers consider financial statements and industry trends.

✔ **Collateral:** Bankers generally want a borrower to pledge an asset that can be sold to pay off the loan if the borrower lacks funds.

✔ **Capital:** Bankers scrutinise a borrower's net worth, the amount by which assets exceed debts.

✔ **Conditions:** Whether bankers give a loan can be influenced by the current economic climate as well as by the amount requested.

Banks also use CAMPARI, which stand for: Character, Ability, Means, Amount, Repayment, Interest and Insurance. You can find out more on the banking liaison group Web site: www.bankexperts.co.uk/.

Keeping the money men happy

Most owner-managers don't give much thought to how to deal with their bank, factoring company, or venture capitalist. They just jump right into their business and don't think about how they should treat these people, what their bankers can do for them, and what their bankers in turn are looking for in a client. With a little thought and effort, you can ensure that you get the most from your banking relationships.

Your banker, or any other source of finance, has the ability to radically influence the success of your business. It is very important that you develop long-term, personal relationships with them – if you do that, when you hit the inevitable bumps in the road they'll be there to help you.

Keep in mind when you meet your banker for the first time that you want to develop a long-term

relationship with this person. The meeting should be a two-way interview. You should ask yourself: 'Is this person genuinely interested in me? Is she trying to understand my business? Does she understand my objectives?' If the answer to any of these is no, then find another banker.

While you often hire your lawyer and accountant by the hour or job, your banker is another matter – she makes money off the fees that your business generates. Your banker is usually very happy to help you, and can therefore be a great source of free consulting, though you do need to be a little more careful today as bankers are beginning to get wise to the idea of charging out services.

Starting out in a cleaning business, for example, you need sufficient funds initially to buy the mop and bucket. Three months into the contract they will have been paid for and so there is no point in getting a five-year bank loan to cover this, as within a year you will have cash in the bank.

However if your overdraft does not get out of the red at any stage during the year then you need to re-examine your financing. All too often companies utilise an overdraft to acquire long-term assets, and that overdraft never seems to disappear, eventually constraining the business.

The attraction of overdrafts is that they are very easy to arrange and take little time to set up. That is also their inherent weakness. The keywords in the arrangement document are 'repayable on demand', which leaves the bank free to make and change the rules as they see fit. (This term is under review and some banks may remove this term from the arrangement.) With other forms of borrowing, as long as you stick to the terms and conditions, the loan is yours for the duration. Not so with overdrafts.

Taking on a term loan

If you are starting up a manufacturing business, you will be buying machinery to last probably five years, designing your logo and buying stationery, paying the deposit on leasehold premises, buying a vehicle, and investing funds in winning a long-term contract. As the profits on this are expected to flow over a number of years, then they need to be financed over a similarly long period of time, either through a bank loan or inviting someone to invest in shares in the company – in other words a long-term commitment.

Term loans, as these long-term borrowings are generally known, are funds provided by a bank for a number of years. The interest can be either variable – changing with general interest rates – or it can be fixed for a number of years ahead. In some cases it may be possible to move between having a fixed interest rate and a variable one at certain intervals. It may even be possible to have a moratorium on interest payments for a short period, to give the business some breathing space. Provided the conditions of the loan are met in such matters as repayment, interest and security cover, the money is available for the period of the loan. Unlike having an overdraft, the bank cannot pull the rug from under you if their circumstances (or the local manager) change.

Going with a loan guarantee

These are operated by banks at the instigation of governments in the UK, and in Australia, the US, and elsewhere. These schemes guarantee loans from banks and other financial institutions for small businesses with viable business proposals, which have tried and failed to obtain a conventional loan because of a lack of security.

These loans are for firms with an annual turnover up to £1.5 million and guarantee 70 per cent (or 85 per cent if a business has been trading for more than two years) of the loan. Loans can be from £5,000 to £100,000 (£250,000 if a business has been trading for more than two years) and for periods of between two and ten years. Borrowers pay interest at 1.5 per cent per year over the bank's normal lending rate for the outstanding amount of the loan, reducing to 0.5 per cent if they take the loan out at a fixed rate of interest.

Cashflow Acceleration, an independent finance broker and a member of the Federation of Small Business, provides a free independent quotation search service for customers looking for commercial finance. At www.cashflow-acceleration.co.uk/small-firms-loan-guarantee-scheme.htm you can see if a bank may be prepared to lend under the scheme to your business.

Financing cash flow

When your business is trading two other sources of finance open up that can smooth out cash-flow troughs when dealing with business customers. Factoring and invoice discounting are both methods of funding sales once you have submitted an invoice.

Factors provide three related services: Immediate finance of up to 80 per cent of invoiced sales, with the balance (minus administration and finance charges) payable after a set period or when the invoice is paid; managing the sales ledger, including sending out invoices and ensuring they are paid; advising on credit risk and insuring clients against bad debts. This type of finance is provided against the security of trade debts (the amount of money customers owe you). Normally when you raise an invoice you send a copy to the factor, who then funds up to 85 per cent against the invoice in advance of the customer paying. The remainder becomes payable either on a maturity date or when the customer pays. As the invoice is assigned to the factor, payment by the customer is direct to the factor. *Invoice discounting* operates in a similar way, except the seller retains control of its debtors and is responsible for collecting the money.

These forms of finance are directly related to sales levels and can be particularly helpful during growth spurts.

The Factors and Discounters Association (`www.thefda.org.uk/public/membersList.asp`) provides a list of over 40 members on its Web site, which has a search facility to help you define which organisations are best placed to meet your individual business requirements.

Getting physical

You can usually finance assets such as vehicles, computers, office equipment, and the like either by leasing them or buying them on hire purchase, leaving your other funds free to cover less tangible expenses such as advertising or living expenses. You can use a lease to take the risk out of purchasing an asset that becomes obsolete or for taking account of repairs and maintenance costs. In return for this 'certainty' you pay a fee that is added to the monthly or quarterly charge. However, knowing the exact cost of purchasing and using an asset can be attractive and worth paying for. Hire purchase differs from leasing in that you have the option eventually to become the owner of the asset after a series of payments. Important tax implications apply to using these types of finance and you should discuss them with your accountant (I cover finding an accountant in Chapter 12).

The Finance and Leasing Association Web site (`www.fla.org.uk`) gives more information on the different products on offer to finance assets and has a directory of members, which you can only access when you know the name of the proposed provider. While that is helpful if you want to establish if a company is a bona fide provider of finance facilities, if you want to find a lender go to the Startups.co.uk Web site at `www.startups.co.uk/Find_a_leasing_company.YWg1vhBoX8KDRw.html`).

You can also use the calculator at www.leasing.co.uk/leasecalculator/index.html to get some idea of the monthly repayments for different types of assets (e.g. software, furniture, cars) over different time periods.

Uniting with a credit union

If you don't like the terms on offer from the *high street banks,* as the major banks are often known, you may consider forming your own bank. It's not as crazy an idea as it sounds. Credit unions formed by groups of small business people, both in business and aspiring to start up, have been around for decades in the US, UK, and elsewhere. They are an attractive option for people on low incomes, providing a cheap and convenient alternative to banks. Some self-employed people such as taxi drivers have also formed credit unions. They can then apply for loans to meet unexpected capital expenditure either for repairs, refurbishments, or technical upgrading.

Established credit unions will usually require you to be in a particular trade, have paid money in for a number of months or perhaps years and have a maximum loan amount limited to the types of assets people in their trade are most likely to need.

Certainly, few could argue about the attractiveness of an annual interest rate 30 per cent below that of the high-street lenders, which is what credit unions aim for. Members have to save regularly to qualify for a loan, though there is no minimum deposit and, after ten weeks, members with a good track record can borrow up to five times their savings, though they must continue to save while repaying the loan. There is no set interest rate, but dividends are distributed to members from any surplus, usually about 5 per cent a year. This too compares favourably with bank interest on deposit accounts. Credit Union usage in the UK has more than doubled in the past five years and 404,000 people have between them over £350 million on loan. The Association of British Credit Unions (www.abcul.org) offers information and a directory of providers.

Borrowing from family and friends

Those close to you are often willing to lend you money or invest in your business. This helps you avoid the problem of pleading your case to outsiders and enduring extra paperwork and bureaucratic delays. Help from friends, relatives, and business associates can be especially valuable if you've been through bankruptcy or had other credit problems that make borrowing from a commercial lender difficult or impossible.

Involving friends and family in your business brings a range of extra potential benefits, costs, and risks that are not a feature of most other types of finance. You need to decide if these are acceptable.

Some advantages of borrowing money from people you know well are that you may be charged a lower interest rate, may be able to delay paying back money until you're more established, and may be given more flexibility if you get into a jam. But once the loan terms are agreed to, you have the same legal obligations as you would with a bank or any other source of finance.

Borrowing money from relatives and friends can have a major disadvantage. If your business does poorly and those close to you end up losing money, you may well damage your personal relationships. So in dealing with friends, relatives, and business associates be extra careful not only to establish clearly the terms of the deal and put them in writing but also to make an extra effort to explain the risks. In short, it's your job to make sure your helpful friend or relative won't suffer true hardship if you're unable to meet your financial commitments.

Many types of business have loyal and devoted followers, people who care as much about the business as the owners do. A health food restaurant, a specialist bookstore, or an art gallery, for example, may attract people who are enthusiastic about lending money to, or investing in, the business because it fits in with their lifestyle or philosophy. Their decision to participate is driven to some extent by their feelings and is not strictly a business proposition. The rules for borrowing from friends and relatives apply here as well. Put repayment terms in writing, and don't accept money from people who can't afford to risk it.

When raising money from family and friends, follow these guidelines.

1. Do agree proper terms for the loan or investment.

2. Do put the agreement in writing and if it involves a limited partnership, share transaction, or guarantee have a legal agreement drawn up.

3. Do make an extra effort to explain the risks of the business and the possible downside implications to their money.

4. Do make sure when raising money from parents that other siblings are compensated in some way, perhaps via a will.

5. Do make sure you want to run a family business before raising money from them. It will not be the same as running your own business.

6. Don't borrow from people on fixed incomes.

7. Don't borrow from people who can't afford to lose their investment.

8. Don't make the possible rewards sound more attractive than you would say to a bank.

9. Don't offer jobs in your business to anyone providing money unless she is the best person for the job.

10. Don't change the normal pattern of social contact with family and friends after they have put up the money.

Managing mezzanine money

Mezzanine finance (also known as subordinated debt) is a form of debt where the lender takes on more risk than a bank would normally be up for. Mezzanine finance providers accept the fact that they will only get their money back after bank overdraft and loans and the like have been paid back. But in return they expect a higher rate of interest and they may ask for an option to convert some of that debt into shares in the company at a certain point. By doing that they can get a slice of the upside if your business is a success.

The benefit of mezzanine finance is that it often bridges the gap between the funds provided by a bank and the high-risk investment by you, a venture capitalist, and business angels.

Mezzanine finance can now also be considered a stand-alone funding solution, often as an alternative to more expensive equity finance. Mezzanine is now commonly used to provide acquisition finance, development capital, and replacement capital, as well as finance for the more traditional management buy-out, buy-in scenarios.

Sources of mezzanine finance include many of the clearing banks and insurance companies, as well as specialist finance boutiques such as Intermediate Capital Group (www.icgplc.com) and Mezzanine Finance UK (www.mezzanine finance.co.uk), the latter of whom specialises in the property investing and developing sectors.

The amount and cost of funds under a mezzanine arrangement will depend on many factors including industry sector, historic performance, credit ratings, seasonality, and predictability of revenues and forecasts for future cash flow and profitability, as well as the strength of management, the nature of a company's financial backers and the structure of the overall financing package.

It is usual for mezzanine finance to be provided on an interest-only basis until some or all of general bank debt has been repaid, typically after four to five years, with typical loan terms ranging up to ten years. Loans are usually secured with a second charge on a company's assets such as property, plant, and equipment.

Sharing Out the Spoils

If your business is particularly risky, requires a lot of up-front finance, or involves new technology, then you usually have to consider selling a portion of your business's shares to outside investors.

However, if your business plan does not show profit returns in excess of 30 per cent compound (see Book IV Chapter 1 for more on this) and you are not prepared to part with upwards of 15 per cent of your business, then equity finance is probably not for you.

A number of different types of investor could be prepared to put up the funds if the returns are mouth-watering enough. We talk about each type in the following sections.

Going for venture capital

Venture capital is a means of financing the start-up, development, expansion, or the purchase of a company. The venture capitalist acquires a share of the company in return for providing the requisite funding. Venture capital firms often work in conjunction with other providers of finance in putting together a total funding package for a business.

Venture capital providers (*VCs*) invest other people's money, often from pension funds. They are likely to be interested in investing a large sum of money for a large stake in the company.

Venture capital is a medium- to long-term investment, of not just money, but of time and effort. The venture capital firm's aim is to enable growth companies to develop into the major businesses of tomorrow. Before investing, a venture capital provider goes through *due diligence*, a process that involves a thorough examination of both the business and its owners. Accountants and lawyers subject you and your business plan to detailed scrutiny. You and your directors are required to warrant that you have provided *all* relevant information, under pain of financial penalties.

In general VCs expect their investment to pay off within seven years. But they are hardened realists. Two in every ten investments they make are total write-offs, and six perform averagely well at best. So the one star in every ten investments they make has to cover a lot of duds. VCs have a target rate of return of 30 per cent plus, to cover this poor success rate.

Raising venture capital is not a cheap option. The arrangement costs will almost always run to six figures. The cost of the due diligence process is borne by the firm raising the money, but will be paid out of the money raised, if that's any consolation. Raising venture capital is not quick either. Six months is not unusual and over a year has been known. Every VC has a deal done in six weeks in their portfolio, but that truly is the exception.

Venture capital providers want to exit from their investment at some stage. Their preferred route is via a public offering, taking your company onto the stock market, but a trade sale to another, usually larger business in a related line of work, is more usual.

New venture capital funds are coming on stream all the time and they too are looking for a gap in the market.

The British Venture Capital Association (www.bvca.co.uk) and the European Venture Capital Association (www.evca.com) both have online directories giving details of hundreds of venture capital providers. VFinance (www.v finance.com), a global financial services company specialising in high-growth opportunities, has a directory of 1,400 venture capital firms and over 23,000 business angels. Its Web site also contains a useful business plan template. (See Chapter 6 for more on business planning.)

Benefiting by business angels

One source of equity or risk capital is a private individual, with her own funds, and perhaps some knowledge of your type of business, who is willing to invest in your company in return for a share in the business.

Such investors have been christened *business angels,* a term first coined to describe private wealthy individuals who backed theatrical productions, usually a play on Broadway or in London's West End.

By their very nature such investments are highly speculative in nature. The angel typically has a personal interest in the venture and may want to play some role in the company – often an angel is determined upon some involvement beyond merely signing a cheque.

Business angels are informal suppliers of risk capital to new and growing businesses, often taking a hand at the stage when no one else will take the chance; a sort of investor of last resort. But whilst they often lose their shirts, they sometimes make serious money. One angel who backed Sage with £10,000 in their first round of £250,000 financing, saw his stake rise to £40 million, while Ian McGlinn, the former garage owner who advanced Anita

---

A venture capital success story

Karen Darby left school at 16 with just one GCSE. While working in a call centre in 2002 she hit on the idea of helping people find the cheapest gas, electricity, and telephone companies and providing a user-friendly way to switch suppliers for free. She pitched her business proposition to Bridges Community Ventures, a venture capital firm, and raised £300,000. Three years down the road her company, SimplySwitch, was sold to Daily Mail and General Trust, leaving Karen £6 million richer.

Roddick the £4,000 she needed to open a second shop in return for about 25 per cent of the company's shares, eventually wound up with a couple of hundred million pounds from his stake in the Body Shop.

These angels often have their own agenda and frequently operate through managed networks. Angel networks operate throughout the world, in some cases on the Internet. In the UK and the US there are hundreds of networks with tens of thousands of business angels prepared to put up several billion pounds each year into new or small businesses. One estimate is that the UK has approximately 18,000 business angels and that they annually invest in the region of £500 million.

Two organisations that can put you in contact with a business angel are:

- ✔ The British Business Angels Association (BBAA; Web site www.bbaa. org.uk).

- ✔ Venture Capital Report's directory (www.vcrdirectory.co.uk).

Alternatively you could apply to appear on the BBC's business reality show *Dragon's Den* (www.bbc.co.uk/dragonsden/apply.shtml) and put your proposition face to face to five angels and five million television viewers.

Research has unravelled these sketchy facts about business angels as a breed. Knowing them may help you find the right one for your business.

- ✔ Business angels are generally self-made, high net-worth individuals, with entrepreneurial backgrounds. Most are in the 45–65 year age group; 19 per cent are millionaires; and only 1 per cent are women.

- ✔ Fifty per cent of angels conduct minimal or no research on the business in question, meet their entrepreneur an average of 5.4 times before investing (compared with venture capitalists who meet on average 9.5 times), and 54 per cent neglected to take up independent personal references compared to only 6 per cent of venture capitalists. Angels fundamentally back people rather than propositions and venture capitalists do the reverse.

- ✔ Typically, business angels invest 5–15 per cent of their investment portfolio in start-up business ventures and their motivation is, first and foremost, financial gain through capital appreciation, with the fun and enjoyment of being involved with an entrepreneurial business an important secondary motive. A minority are motivated in part by altruistic considerations, such as helping the next generation of entrepreneurs to get started, and supporting their country or state.

- ✔ Business angels invest in only a very small proportion of investments that they see: typically at least seven out of eight opportunities are rejected. More than 90 per cent of investment opportunities are rejected at the initial screening stage.

✔ Around 30 per cent of investments by business angels are in technology-based businesses. Most will tell you that they vigorously avoid investing in industries they know nothing about.

✔ The majority of business angels invest in businesses located in close proximity to where they live – two-thirds of investments are made in businesses located within 100 miles of their home or office. They are, however, prepared to look further afield if they have specific sector-related investment preferences or if they are technology investors.

✔ Ninety-two per cent of angels had worked in a small firm compared, for example, with only 52 per cent of venture capitalists who had similar experience.

✔ On average, business angels sell their shareholding in the most success-ful investments after four years (and 75 per cent after seven years). Conversely, half of the investments in which business angels lost money had failed within two years of the investment being made.

✔ Business angels are up to five times more likely to invest in start-ups and early stage investments than venture capital providers in general.

Looking to corporate venturing

Alongside the venture capital firms are 200 or so other businesses who have a hand in the risk capital business, without it necessarily being their main line of business. For the most part these are firms with an interest in the Internet or high technology that want an inside track to new developments. Their own research and development operations have slowed down and become less and less entrepreneurial as they have become bigger. So they need to look outside for new inspiration.

Even successful firms invest hundreds of millions of dollars each year in scores of other small businesses. Sometimes, if the company looks a particularly good fit, they buy the whole business.

Apple, for example, whilst keeping its management team focused on the core business, has a $12 million stake in Akamai Technologies, the firm whose software tries to keep the Web running smoothly even under unusual traffic demands.

It's not only high-tech firms that go in for corporate venturing. Any firm whose arteries are hardening a bit is on the look out for new blood. McDonald's, for example, hardly a business in the forefront of the technological revolution, has stakes in over a dozen ventures including a 35 per cent stake in Prêt-à-Manger. Table 5-2 lists the top corporate venturers.

Table 5-2	The World's Top Corporate Venturers
Company	*$ millions*
Electronic Data Systems	1,500
Accenture Consulting	1,000
PriceWaterhouseCoopers	500
Time Warner Inc	500
Intel Corporation	450
Cisco Systems	450
Microsoft	450
Softbank	350
News Corporation	300
Comcast Corporation	250
Unilever	200
Sun Microsystems	200
Novell Inc	170

Entering an Incubator

Incubators – also known as accelerators, science parks, innovation centres, technology parks, and a whole variety of other names coined over the years – are places where new businesses can set up in a benign environment, with support services and advice close at hand. The many names try to describe the tasks that incubators perform.

Tempting though it may be to believe that business incubators are an Internet phenomenon, the first serious attempt at incubation is credited to a near derelict building near New York City in 1959. The name came into common usage more by way of a joke, because one of the businesses involved was actually incubating real chicken eggs. Several waves of incubators followed this inauspicious start and by the 1980s several hundred such facilities were scattered around the US, Canada, Europe, and Australia. Later incubator progressions took in the developing economies and the Internet variation, which came into being in the mid-1990s, swept across America, Europe, India, China, Malaysia, Singapore, the Philippines, and elsewhere, bringing the total by 2007 to some 4,400 facilities worldwide.

Finding the right type of incubator

Varieties of incubators now co-exist in the market, with radically different aims and objectives. Some, such as those founded by entrepreneurs and venture capital firms – the 'for profit' variety – only want to get rich by helping entrepreneurs to get rich. That goal at least has the merit of transparency. Some incubators have revenue models that can make the incubator rich without necessarily benefiting anyone else that much. Governments and local governments are more concerned with job creation than wealth, and universities, another major player, want jobs for the students and funding for faculty research rather than riches themselves. Big corporate firms run private incubators to encourage firms who may buy their products or services, or create career opportunities for their more entrepreneurial and potentially less fickle employees.

These incubators are havens for entrepreneurs with innovative or technology-based business ideas that need more help than most to bring to fruition. Such ventures usually have more potential than other business start-ups, but they are also more risky. No one knows how many entrepreneurs graduate from these incubators each year, but a reasonable supposition is that each of the estimated 4,000 incubators has two or three graduates each year. So 10,000 or so 'eggs' are hatched in a safe environment each year – not a big number in terms of business start-ups. Across Europe and the US somewhere between 3 and 4 million new businesses get going in most years. But for at least some of the entrepreneurs who get into an incubator, their chances of success are better than if they go it alone.

Getting into an incubator

You almost invariably face an application process to get into any business incubator. All that does vary is the process itself. Some incubators positively invite and encourage the informal approach, some are highly structured, some have their own models and techniques that they believe can sort the wheat from the chaff. All the application processes take time and if they didn't you would have cause for concern. After all, if an incubator takes in anyone without any serious consideration of what they can do to help their businesses, that particular incubation process is unlikely to be of much value. Most application processes require some sort of business plan. This may be little more than an executive summary created online with your application. Or it may be a more comprehensive written document setting out your latest thinking on what is so special about you and your big idea. Then comes the interview and after that the decision.

Most incubators have details of their application process on their Web sites, as well as case examples of successful clients. Some have business plan application templates to help in the process. You can expect to take anything from a couple of weeks to a couple of months to get through the process.

How much does incubation cost? If you are just paying rent and for services as you use them then the cost of being in an incubator is transparent. Such not-for-profit incubators are usually aimed at non-business-educated people who have good ideas to create traditional small businesses, usually with little technology involved. These incubators are frequently government funded, often in underdeveloped cities, and provide mentoring, business development, and office space. The typical equity stake required ranges from none to nominal (some require CEOs to give back to the community).

But if providing an incubator with an equity stake in your business is involved, as it surely is in any for-profit incubator, then the cost can run the scale from a few per cent of the business to an outrageously expensive 30 to 50 per cent. The amount you pay doesn't always relate to the value you receive. It depends on your business needs and the scale of the opportunity you want to exploit.

Contact either UK Business Incubation (www.ukbi.co.uk) or United Kingdom Science Park Association (UKSPA; www.ukspa.org.uk) to find out all you need to know about incubators or innovation centres that may help you achieve your ambitious goals.

Finding Free Money

Sometimes, if you're very lucky or very smart – or both – you can get at least some of the money you need for free. The following sections tell you how to cash in on government grants and how winning a contest can earn you lots of lovely loot.

Getting help from the government

Unlike debt, which has to be repaid, or equity, which has to earn a return for the investors, grants and awards from the government or the European Union are often not refundable. So, although they are frequently hard to get, they can be particularly valuable.

Almost every country has incentives to encourage entrepreneurs to invest in particular locations or industries. The US, for example, has an allowance of Green Cards (work and residence permits) for up to several hundred immigrants each year prepared to put up sufficient funds to start-up in a substantial business in the country.

In the UK, if you are involved in the development of a new technology then you may be eligible for a grant for Research and Development that is now available. Under the new grant scheme, 60 per cent of eligible project costs up to a maximum grant of £75,000 can be claimed on research projects (previously called 'feasibility studies'); 35 per cent of costs up to £200,000 on development projects; 35 per cent of costs up to £500,000 on exceptional development projects; and 50 per cent of costs up to a maximum grant of £20,000 on micro projects. Business Links can give full details of the new grants.

Support for business comes in a very wide variety of forms. The most obvious is the direct (cash) grant but other forms of assistance are also numerous. The main types of grant also include *soft loans* – money lent on terms more advantageous than would usually be available from a bank – additional share capital, free or subsidised consultancy, which could help you with market research, staff development or identifying business opportunities, or with access to valuable resources such as research facilities.

Though several grant schemes operate across the whole of the UK and are available to all businesses that satisfy the outline criteria, there are a myriad of schemes that are administered locally. Thus the location of your business can be absolutely crucial, and funding may be strongly dependent on the area into which you intend to grow or develop. Additionally, there may well be additional grants available to a business investing in or into an area of social deprivation, particularly if it involves sustainable job creation.

The assistance provided for enterprise is limited so you will be competing for grants against other applicants. You can enhance your chances of success by following these seven rules:

1. **Keep yourself informed about which grants are available.**

   Grants are constantly being introduced (and withdrawn), but there is no system that lets you know automatically. You have to keep yourself informed.

   Business Link (www.businesslink.gov.uk), the Department Business, Enterprise and Regulatory Reform (www.dti.gov.uk), Funders online (www.fundersonline.org/grantseekers), and Grants On-line (www.grantsonline.org.uk) are all Web sites that can help you find out about grants.

2. **Do not start the project for which you want a grant before you make the application.**

   The awarding body will almost certainly take the view that if you can start the project without a grant you must have sufficient funds to complete it without assistance. Much better to show that your project is dependent on the grant being made.

3. **Talk to the awarding body before you apply.**

   Make contact with an individual responsible for administering the scheme. You will be given advice on whether it is worthwhile your applying before you start spending time and effort on making the application;

you may get some help and advice on completing the application form; you may get an insight into how you should shape your application.

4. **Make sure your application is in respect of a project.**

Usually, grants are given for specific projects, not for the normal organic growth of a business. If, for example, you need new equipment to launch a product, make sure your application emphasises the project, not the equipment. State the advantages of the project's success (for example, it will safeguard or create jobs) and explain that the purchase of the equipment is a prerequisite for that success.

5. **Get your application in early.**

The chances of a successful application are always highest just after a scheme is launched. That is when there is the most money in the pot, and it's also the time when those administering the scheme are keenest to get applications in and grants awarded. Competition is likely to be less fierce.

6. **Make your application match the awarding body's objectives.**

The benefits of your project should fit in with the objectives of the awarding body and the grant scheme itself. So if the grant is intended to help the country in the form of potential exports, for example, make sure your application details your exports.

Most grant applications require the submission of a business plan, so make sure you have an up to date one.

7. **Make sure you have matching funds available.**

It is unusual for a grant to finance 100 per cent of the costs of any project. Typically nowadays a grant will contribute 15–50 per cent of the total finance required. Those making the decision about the grant are spending public money. They have a duty to ensure it is spent wisely and they will need to be absolutely convinced that you have, or can raise from other sources, the balance required.

Winning money

If you enjoy publicity and like a challenge then you could look out for a business competition to enter. Like government grants, business competitions are ubiquitous and, like national lotteries, they are something of a hit or miss affair. But one thing is certain. If you don't enter you can't win.

There are more than 100 annual awards in the UK alone, aimed at new or small businesses. For the most part, these are sponsored by banks, the major accountancy bodies, chambers of commerce, local or national newspapers, business magazines, and the trade press. Government departments may also have their own competitions as a means of promoting their initiatives for exporting, innovation, job creation, and so forth.

The nature and the amount of the awards change from year to year, as do the sponsors. But looking out in the national and local press, particularly the small business sections of *The Times*, *Daily Telegraph*, *Daily Mail*, and *The Guardian*, should put you in touch with a competition organiser quickly, as will an Internet search. Money awards constitute 40 per cent of the main competition prizes. For the most part, these cash sums are less than £5,000. However, a few do exceed £10,000 and one UK award is for £50,000.

Business Match (www.businessmatch.org.uk/576.asp), the Design Council (www.designcouncil.org.uk/en/Directory-Listings/Events-and-Competitions), the National Business Awards (www.thenationalbusiness awards.com), and the Growing Business Awards (www.growingbusiness awards.co.uk) are all Web sites that can help you find out about competitions.

Trusting the Prince's Trust

The Prince's Trust (www.princes-trust.org.uk) helps 14–30-year-olds develop confidence, learn new skills, and get into work. It offers opportunities when no one else will. So if you've got an idea for a business but no one will give you the money to get it off the ground, the Prince's Trust may be able to provide you with finance and advice. The Prince's Trust can offer:

- A low-interest loan of up to £5,000

- Test marketing grants of up to £250

- Grants of up to £1,500 in special circumstances

- Advice from a volunteer 'business mentor' during your first three years of trading

- Extra support, including access to a wide range of products and services, such as a free legal helpline sponsored by Barclays and free legal patent, copyright, and trademark guidance.

Each year the Prince's Trust helps about 13,000 young people to set up in business. Over 71 per cent of all start-up applications to the Trust have been converted into new ventures – creating almost 18,000 businesses in just five years. One in ten of those businesses has a turnover in excess of £1 million.

Chapter 6

Operating Effectively

. . . .

In This Chapter

▶ Opting to make it yourself or buy from outside

▶ Choosing and using suppliers

▶ Looking at operating risks

▶ Delving into directors

▶ Deciding on key business advisers

. . . .

*A*lthough you have decided to go into business, it doesn't necessarily mean that you have to make your own product, or carry out every aspect of a business yourself. It might be the best use of your time to out-source the most time-consuming and least valuable aspect of your business. For example, we bet you can't get a package from Milton Keynes to Penzance in under 24 hours and see change of a twenty pound note! But a delivery service could.

Whether you buy in most of what you sell, or just some components and assemble then yourself, you will have to chose between the dozens if not hundreds of suppliers in the market. Price alone is rarely a good enough guide to which supplier to chose. If they can't deliver on time, price is irrelevant.

You will have to face risks in your business, not all of which you will either want to or be able to shoulder yourself. For these you will have to make choices about insurance types and levels. Even as a director some of those company risks will fall on you and the consequences of getting it wrong can be serious, even catastrophic.

Fortunately you don't have to face all these decisions alone. There are plenty of advisers out there to help. This chapter looks at these risks and decisions and helps you to choose someone to help you through the minefield.

Taking the Make-or-Buy Decision

If your business involves making or constructing products then you should address the issue of whether to make the product yourself, or buy it either ready to sell, or as components for assembly.

Making it yourself, pros and cons

If you decide to make the whole of your product, or at least a major part of it, yourself, you will need to decide exactly what plant and equipment you need and how many pieces you can produce at what rate. Then you need to consider such factors as: what engineering support, if any, will you need? How will you monitor and control quality?

To estimate how much space you will need, make a rough sketch of the layout of your manufacturing unit, showing the overall size of facility needed, the positioning of equipment, and the path of materials and finished goods.

The great advantage of manufacturing your product yourself is that you have control over every aspect of the business and its products. You can, in theory at least, step up production to meet extra demand, make minor modifications to a product to meet a customer's particular needs and have the resources in-house to develop prototypes of new products to respond to changing market conditions.

Different strokes for different folks

The following stories illustrate a variety of in-house and outsourcing solutions:

✔ Jenny Row designed her knitwear herself, but had it made up by outworkers. In this way she could expand or contract output quickly, paying only the extra cost of materials and production for more orders. It also left her free to design new toys to add to her existing range.

✔ Tim Brown sold computer systems tailor-made to carry out solicitors' conveyancing work. He commissioned software writers to prepare the programs, bought in computers from the manufacturer, and selected a range of printers to suit individual customers' requirements. His end product was a total system, which he bought in kit parts from his various sub-contractors. Apart from a handful of giants no one company could produce all these elements in-house.

✔ Graham Davy designed and manufactured his own range of furniture. He rented a small workshop and bought in cutting, turning, and polishing tools, and a finish spraying room. He bought in wood and worked on it himself, producing batches of three or four of each design. The equipment needed for design and prototype work was also sufficient for small batch production.

However, some possible disadvantages of making products yourself in a start-up business are:

- ✔ The large outlay of money needed from day one.

- ✔ The deflection of management time, mostly your own, to looking inwards at processes rather than outwards at the marketplace.

- ✔ Established manufacturers may be better and cheaper than you are at various elements of the production process – after all they've been at it longer than you and have the benefit of being further up the learning curve and further down the cost curve than any start-up could realistically expect to be.

Outsourcing, pros and cons

Outsourcing, contracting out the production of your product, has become a buzz-word in our economy. There are thousand s of articles and hundreds of books written on it and you can attend countless seminars on the subject. An Internet search on 'outsourcing' will bring up more links that you could ever hope to handle.

One way to set the boundaries for outsourcing is to decide what you are good at then outsource everything else. In other words focus your company on your core competency, and stick to the knitting. That logic is sound in theory, and to a certain degree in practice, but like everything else you can take it too far. The key is to understand your business and its goals and decide how outsourcing can help you attain them.

There are some things that are central to your business that you should probably not outsource at the outset. You need to keep an eye (your eye!) on them until you have them fully under control. These include cash flow management and most aspects of customer relations. Later on you may consider, for example, outsourcing collecting cash from customers to an invoice discounter or factoring service (which we talk about in Book I Chapter 5), who may have better processes in place to handle larger volumes of invoices than you could afford.

Some tasks make sense to outsource initially and bring in-house later. If you plan to offer a product service that you're not expert at, it makes sense to contract out the core function, at least until you gain confidence and expertise. For example, if you plan to start an upmarket soup kitchen but aren't very experienced at making soup, you could turn to an established soup chef to cook for you. The outside expert will charge you a premium, but for that you get significant value: the contractor understands your requirements, produces the product and delivers to your site with little risk to you. If the quality is

Making the most of simple improvements

James Killick runs a company that grew from £2 million turnover per annum to over £4.5 million within 18 months. In order to achieve his meteoric growth, Killick took a detailed look at everything the firm did with a view to increasing the profitability of every hour worked. Each process was examined and made the subject of a brainstorming session. For example, one part of the manufacturing process of their products required several hundred plastic parts to be tipped onto a table. Invariably, 50 or so fell off the table and were either damaged or took valuable seconds to recover. By putting a 3 inch high rim

around the table, at a cost of £5, the company saved two hours' production time per week.

Several hundred simple ideas like this reduced the total production time for one key product by nearly 40 per cent. The overall effect was quite staggering. James subcontracted his low value-added production processes to a subcontractor who could actually make them cheaper than he could. The subcontractor took on the commitment to buy raw material and hold stocks, and James used the factory space saved for better things.

wrong, send it back. If you need more product, order it. You don't have to wait for your new equipment to arrive before you can step up production. You may find hidden benefits.

Reasons to outsource

Whether you want access to world-class expertise, increased staffing flexibility, a more predictable cost structure, or the ability to focus on your core business, outsourcing offers many strategic advantages.

- ✔ **Meeting unexpected deadlines:** It is often difficult and costly to ramp up your staffing to respond quickly to new technologies, or business needs. Sometimes, it's simply impossible – especially when you're trying to balance your resources to cover numerous other conflicting priorities at the same time. Buying in resources allows you to meet deadlines.

- ✔ **Access to expertise:** The rapid obsolescence of technology and skills is an accepted fact of life, in almost every sphere of business. It can be almost impossible for a small firm, especially in the start-up phase, to attract and retain a team with the latest expertise. It is easier for larger established firms to attract and retain a team with the latest expertise and for you to hire that expertise as needed.

- ✔ **Greater scalability:** It just isn't cost-effective to have production resources on hand from the outset to meet possible future demand. By outsourcing to one or more suppliers you can have, in effect, any level of output you want, all at a variable cost, rather than a fixed cost. (See Book I Chapter 3 for more on fixed costs.)

✔ **More predictable costs:** While outside suppliers and manufacturers can sometimes provide products and services at a lower cost than doing it yourself, the main financial reason for choosing an outsourcing solution is to make costs more predictable and establish a smoother cash flow.

✔ **Free-up your time:** Turning over non-core functions and self-contained projects that require specific, cutting-edge expertise lets you and your team focus on strategic development and core business functions to ensure that you are contributing real value to your enterprise.

✔ **Economies of scale:** An outsource supplier has multiple clients with similar needs, and can often leverage this to your advantage when negotiating price and service agreements with equipment, software and raw material providers, and so forth. The outsourcer's range of experience often allows for a more efficient use of equipment for added cost savings.

Reasons to hesitate before outsourcing

While there are many benefits to outsourcing, there are inherent risks involved as well. Many of these risks can be reduced via a well-structured contract with clearly defined responsibilities and expectations, but sometimes a function is simply not a good candidate for outsourcing. The following are some considerations to examine before going for outsourcing:

✔ **Rapidly changing requirements:** If you anticipate frequent changes to your products, processes, and volumes , cost and communication issues may make handling the process yourself more efficient, especially if you need to respond quickly to user needs or want to maintain direct control over the problem resolution.

✔ **In-house expertise:** If best-in-class knowledge is required to stay in business, as in for example the bio-technology markets, then it may be essential for you to acquire and retain key operations staff from the outset. Expensive though it will be, this is a market-entry cost. On the positive side these costs also act as a barrier, keeping other new small firms off your patch.

✔ **Confidentiality of data:** This is a fundamental concern for any business, and is an obvious and essential part of your relationship with an outsourcing partner. Basic contractual provisions, including copyright and non-disclosure agreements, should be established to protect corporate secrets, confidential information, and intellectual property. If the activity to be outsourced is such that the confidentiality of your critical data cannot be ensured, the task is probably not a good candidate for outsourcing.

Making the decision

Whether to make it yourself or to buy in from outside is rarely a cut and dried decision that you can make using a spreadsheet. You always have questions. Can I trust them to keep our trade secrets? Will they be as reliable as they claim? Will they put their prices up once they have us in the bag? There are no easy answers to any of these questions, you just have to weigh up the pros and cons yourself.

Setting quality standards

Quality may well be, like beauty, in the eye of the beholder, but you would be wise to set clear standards that you expect every aspect of your end product, or for that matter service, to conform to. This is true whether you make in-house or outsource.

There are a number of well-regarded quality standards that may help you monitor and control your quality. The BS EN ISO 9000 series are perhaps the best-known standards. They can ensure that your operating procedure delivers a consistent and acceptable standard of products or services. If you are supplying to large firms they may insist on your meeting one of these quality standards, or on auditing your premises to satisfy themselves. The British Standards Institute (www.bsi.global.com) can provide details of these standards.

A number of commercial organisations provide user-friendly guidelines and systems to help you reach the necessary standard. Searching the Web using keywords such as 'Quality Standards' or 'Measurement' will bring you some useful sites.

Choosing a Supplier

Selecting the wrong supplier for your business can be a stressful and expensive experience. This section offers some pointers on how to find a supplier and make sure your supplier can meet your business needs. (Book I Chapter 3 talks about similar issues, so you may want to consult that chapter too.)

Look for value in the service a supplier offers rather than just the price you pay. The key questions you should ask about any prospective supplier to your business are:

✔ Do they offer a guaranteed level of service?

✔ Do they have a strong business track record and evidence of financial stability? Check out their accounts at Companies House (www.companies house.gov.uk).

✔ Do they have clients in your business sector and local area?

✔ Can they provide you with client references and impartial evidence of their quality? You should check out references to make sure they are reliable and can meet deadlines.

✔ Can they meet rushed deliveries in case of emergency?

✔ What level of after-sales support do they provide?

✔ Do they provide you with value for money when compared to competitor services?

✔ Do you think you will enjoy working with them? If so the relationship will be more productive.

Thomas's Register (www.thomasnet.com), Kelly's (www.kelly.co.uk), and Kompass (www.kompass.com) between them have details on over 1.6 million UK companies and hundreds of thousands of US and Canadian manufacturers, covering 23 million key products and 744,000 trade and brand names. If someone makes it, you will find their details in one of these directories.

Some free search facilities are available online. Your local business library will also have hard copies and may even have Internet access to all the key data you could ever need on suppliers.

Evaluating trading terms

Buying is the mirror image of selling. Remember that as you negotiate with suppliers, who are essentially selling their services. Even if they have no deliberate intention to mislead, you may be left thinking that a supplier will be doing things that they are not committed to in any way. The moral of that story is to get it in writing.

The starting point in establishing trading terms is to make sure the supplier can actually do what you want and what they claim to be able to do. This involves checking them out and taking up references.

The next crunch point is price. As a small business you may feel you are fairly short on buying power. Whilst there is some truth in that, there is always room for negotiation. All suppliers want more customers and there is always a time when they want them badly enough to shift on price.

 If you do your research by contacting several suppliers so you have a good idea of the price parameters before you talk seriously to any supplier set yourself a target discount price, and start negotiating 10 per cent or so below that. In any negotiation you may well have to give ground, so if you start at your target price, you will end up paying more.

The supplier's opening claim is likely to be that they never negotiate on price. Don't be deterred. There are lots of ways to get your costs down without changing the headline price. Some examples are:

✔ Allowing a certain percentage of free product, along the line of the free bottle of wine with every half case, can nudge the price down by 15 per cent.

✔ Agreeing to hold stock in their warehouse that will save you renting your own warehouse.

✔ Extending an extra 30 days' credit eases your cash flow and may be the difference between growing your young business and standing still.

You need to examine all the contract terms, such as delivery, payment terms, risk, and ownership (the point at which title to the goods passes from the maker to you), warranties and guarantees, termination, arbitration rules if you fall out, and the governing law in the case of dealings with overseas suppliers.

Building a relationship

To ensure that problems you have with your suppliers are handled effectively, you need to build relationships with them. That means talking to them and keeping them informed of your plans and intentions. If you're planning a sales drive, new price list, or some other similar activity, let the suppliers know so they can anticipate the possible impact on them. Keeping them informed does not commit you to buying extra product, or indeed any product beyond that contracted for, but it does make your suppliers feel part of the value chain between you and your customers. By involving them you are indirectly encouraging them to commit to helping you meet your goals.

Many business people pay too much for the goods or services they purchase, which shows up as lower gross margin and poorer performance than the competition. Many of these people don't raise the issue with their supplier but instead start looking elsewhere for an alternative source. Don't make their mistake. More often than not, your supplier would rather discuss the terms of your arrangement than lose your business. In many cases, you both end up with a better deal than before.

Three other tips for building good long-term relationships:

✔ Pay your bills on time.

✔ Ask for favours only when you really need them.

✔ Treat your supplier's representatives and agents with courtesy and respect; they are the front line and will convey their experiences of dealing with you to their bosses.

The Chartered Institute of Purchasing and Supply (`www.cips.org`) administers education and qualifications in the field of purchasing and supply chain management.

Buying online

Buying online has a range of important benefits for a small firm. Big companies have buying departments whose job is to find the best suppliers in the world with the most competitive prices and trading terms. A small firm can achieve much the same at a fraction of the cost. By buying online, a small firm can lower costs, save scarce management time, get supplies just in time hence speeding up cash flow and reducing stock space, along with a range of other benefits.

The range of goods and services that can be bought online is vast and getting larger. As well as office supplies you can buy computer equipment, software, motor vehicles, machine tools, vending equipment, insurance, hotel accommodation, airline tickets, business education, building materials, tractors, work clothing, and cleaning equipment online, to name but a few.

You can use several methods to buy business supplies online. We explain the most useful methods in the following sections.

Joining an e-buying group

Various names are given to online buying groups, including trading hubs, e-marketplaces, online communities, aggregators, and cost reducers.

Buying in this way allows you to collect information from potential vendors quickly and easily. These online markets gather multiple suppliers in one place so you can comparison shop without leaving your office or picking up the phone. For example, if you need to buy toner cartridges for your office laser printer, you can go to an online marketplace and search the catalogues of multiple office supplies vendors, buying from the one that offers the best deal. You can also do this for bigger ticket items such as office furniture or photocopiers. No more calling a handful of potential suppliers, sitting through sales presentations, and negotiating prices. You save time for more valuable business activities and get a better rate through comparison shopping.

Going in for auctions

Online auctions are another way to buy supplies online. Their advantage is that you pay only as much as you're willing to pay. The disadvantage is you may have to wait for the right deal to come up.

Auctions are a great way to significantly reduce the funds you need to purchase items on your business *wish list* – items you want now or will need eventually but that aren't a current necessity.

Bartering online

You can avoid using hard cash by taking advantage of online barter exchanges. These e-exchanges let you trade your company's products and services for those of other businesses. You can swap ad space for accounting services, consulting for computers. For start-ups or cash-strapped companies, barter can be an effective way to get products or services you might otherwise be unable to afford. Organisations that can help you get started with bartering include Bartercard (www.bartercard.co.uk, tel. 01276 415739) and Barter Marketing (www.bartermarketing.com, tel. 0870 787 8100).

Minimising Risk and Assessing Liability

As the saying goes, no pain, no gain. Some of the pain is routine and can be allowed for in the normal course of events. Employees come and go, suppliers have to be paid, premises have to be moved in and out of. But some events are less easy to predict and can have serious if not disastrous consequences for your business. What happens if the warehouse burns down or your pizzas send a few customers to hospital?

You can't be expected to know such things will happen ahead of time, but you can be reasonably sure that *something* will happen *sometime.* The laws of probability point to it and the law of averages give you a basis for estimating your chances (see the nearby sidebar for a technical explanation). You have to be prepared to deal with the unexpected, which is what this section helps you do.

Insurance forms a guarantee against loss. You must weigh up to what extent your business assets are exposed to risk and what effect such events could have on the business if they occurred.

One very simple way to assess risk is to get an insurance quote to cover the risk. Insuring against an earthquake in London will be very cheap, but the same cover in Istanbul will be a significant sum.

Insurance is an overhead, producing no benefit until a calamity occurs. It is therefore a commercial decision as to how much to carry, and whilst it is a temptation to minimise cover, you should resist it. You must carry some cover, either by employment law, or as an obligation imposed by a mortgager.

Establish your insurance needs by discussing your business plans with an insurance broker. Make sure you know exactly what insurance you are buying; and, as insurance is a competitive business, get at least three quotations before making up your mind.

The Association of British Insurers (ABI) (www.abi.org.uk) and the British Insurance Association (BIBA) (www.biba.org.uk) can put you in touch with a qualified insurance expert.

Protecting your employees

You must carry at least £2 million of liability insurance to meet your legal liabilities for death or bodily injury incurred by an employee during the course of business. In practice, this cover is usually unlimited, with the premiums directly related to your wage bill.

Employer's liability covers only those accidents in which the employer is held to be legally responsible. You may want to extend this cover to any accident to an employee whilst on your business, whosoever is at fault. You may also have to cover your own financial security, particularly if the business depends on your being fit.

Covering yourself when an employee sues

The advent of the no-win, no-fee legal support is encouraging more individuals to feel confident enough to take on companies both big and small, and often in circumstances where their chances of success are not immediately obvious.

The growing burden of employment legislation facing small firms is forcing more and more businesses to take out legal expense insurance as the risk for being prosecuted for breaking the law rises.

But it is not only the risk that is rising. The consequences are spiralling upwards too. The ceiling for unfair dismissal awards has risen from £12,000 to £50,000 as one example of the burden of new employment laws. In 2001 there was a 40 per cent rise in payouts for discrimination claims, for example, and employment tribunals awarded £3.53million for sex, race, and disability claims.

The remedy for the small firm without its own human resources department to keep it operating clearly within legal boundaries and a legal department to fend of any legal threats, is to take out legal expense insurance.

Firms that sign up for this type of insurance can not only expect any fines and awards to be paid, but their costs associated with defending themselves against allegations will also be met. In many cases, whether the employer wins or loses, they will pay their own legal costs, which makes insurance cover especially attractive. For the small employer, who often takes on the task of handling disputes with employees himself, this is a great benefit, saving not only time but lifting the concerns and anxieties that inevitably accompany litigation.

Protecting assets

Obviously, you need to insure your business premises, plant, and equipment. However, you can choose a couple of ways to do that.

- ✔ **Reinstatement** provides for full replacement cost
- ✔ **Indemnity** meets only the current market value of your asset, which means taking depreciation off first

You have to consider related costs and coverage, as well. For example, who pays for removing debris? Who pays the architect to design the structure if you have to rebuild? Who reimburses employees for any damaged or destroyed personal effects? And potentially the most expensive of all, who covers the cost of making sure that a replacement building meets current, possibly more stringent and more expensive, standards?

These factors are covered in the small print of your insurance policy, so if they matter to you check them out.

Also from raw materials through to finished goods, stock is as exposed as your buildings and plant in the event of hazards such as fire and theft. Theft from commercial property runs to hundreds of millions of pounds per annum.

Once in business you can expect threats from within and without. A *fidelity guarantee*, the name given to this particular type of insurance, can be taken to protect you from fraud or dishonesty on the part of key employees. Normal theft cover can be taken to protect your business premises and its contents.

Covering loss of profits

Meeting the replacement costs of buildings, plant, equipment, and stock does not compensate you for the loss of business and profit arising out of a fire or other disaster. Your overheads, employees' wages, and so on may have to continue during the period of interruption. You may incur expenses such as getting subcontracted work done. Insurance for *consequential loss,* as this type of insurance is known, is intended to restore your business's finances to the position they were in before the interruption occurred.

Goods in transit

Until your goods reach your customer and he accepts them, they are still at your risk. You may need to protect yourself from loss or damage in transit.

One newly established business, planning to expand its activities economically, sought and found a specialist supplier of second-hand reconditioned woodworking machinery – lathes, turners, band saws and so on. After inspecting the machinery in Yorkshire the company arranged for it to be transported by the vendor under his own goods in transit insurance cover to its factory in the West Country. While a particularly heavy piece was being unloaded, it fell from the transporter on to the ground immediately outside the factory, and was damaged beyond repair. The buying company's own insurance only covered machinery inside its workshop, the vendor's only while the goods were on the transporter. The gap in between was an insurance 'no man's land', where neither party had cover.

Protecting yourself

Anyone who puts a substantial amount of money into your business – the bank or a venture capitalist, for example – may require you to have *key man insurance.* This type of insurance provides a substantial cash cushion in the event of your death or incapacity – you being the key man (even if you're a woman) on whom the business's success depends.

Key man insurance is particularly important in small and new firms where one person is disproportionately vital in the early stages. Partners may also consider this a prudent protection.

Warranting goods and services

As well as your own specifications confirming how your products or service will perform, you may have legal obligations put on you under the *Consumer Protection Act,* which sets out safety rules and prohibits the sale of unsafe goods and the *Sale of Goods Acts* that govern your contractual relationship with your customer. In addition the common law rules of negligence also apply to business dealings.

If you're a principal in a partnership with unlimited liability, it would be quite possible to be personally bankrupted in a lawsuit concerning product liability. Even if the business was carried out through a limited company, although the directors may escape personal bankruptcy, the company would not. If you believe the risks associated with your product are real, then you need to consider taking out product liability insurance.

If your business involves foodstuffs, you must also pay close attention to the stringent hygiene regulations that now encompass all food manufacture, preparation, and handling. The defence of 'due diligence' will only hold water if thorough examination and identification of all the hazard points has taken place. Trading Standards (`www.tradingstandards.gov.uk`) and Environmental Health Officers based in your local government office are there to help and advise in a free consultative capacity.

Obligations are placed on producers or importers of certain types of goods under both the Consumer Protection Act 1987 and the Sale of Goods Act 1979. Importers can be sued for defects, they cannot disclaim liability simply because they have not been involved in manufacture.

Other liabilities you should consider taking insurance cover are:

- ✔ Public Liability: Legal liability to pay damages consequent upon bodily injury, illness, or disease contracted by any other person, other than employees, or loss of or damage to their property caused by the insured.

- ✔ Professional Indemnity: Professional indemnity provides protection against any action by clients who believe they received bad or negligent services, and incurred a loss as a result. Most professional bodies have professional indemnity cover – in some cases it is compulsory. Anyone who supplies advice or services such as consultancy should consider professional indemnity insurance.

The main points of liability law in the UK are:

- ✔ Do not make claims like 'So simple a child could understand.' You are laying yourself wide open to rebuttal.

- ✔ Instructions should be crystal clear both on the packet and on the article if possible.

- ✔ Textiles must carry fibre content, labelling, and washing instructions.

- ✔ Because the Acts cover the European Union, if you are exporting to another country in the Union you must double-check translations. It is now possible, for example, for a German person to sue you as manufacturer in a German court for goods exported to Germany that have a product defect.

- ✔ You must keep records for ten years and be ready to institute a product recall operation if necessary.

Dissecting Directors

If you decide to trade as a *limited liability company* (see Book I Chapter 2) then you will in all probability have to become a director of the business. You may be the only director, or you may be one of several, but as well as the status you have responsibilities too.

Some of a director's duties, responsibilities, and potential liabilities are:

- ✔ To act in good faith in the interests of the company; this includes carrying out duties diligently and honestly.

- ✔ Not to carry on the business of the company with intent to defraud creditors or for any fraudulent purpose.

- ✔ Not knowingly to allow the company to trade while insolvent ('wrongful trading'); directors who do so may have to pay for the debts incurred by the company while insolvent.

- ✔ Not to deceive shareholders.

- ✔ To have a regard for the interests of employees in general.

- ✔ To comply with the requirements of the Companies Acts, such as providing what is needed in accounting records or filing accounts.

In the UK alone over 1,500 directors are disqualified each year from being directors, so can no longer legally manage and control their own business. The reasons for their disqualification range from fraud to the more innocuous wrongful trading, which means carrying on doing business whilst the business is insolvent. This latter area is more difficult to recognise by a director before the event, but you need to be aware of the danger signs if you get into financial difficulties and discuss potential remedies with your accountant sooner rather than later.

In practice, a director's general responsibilities are much the same as those for a sole trader or partner (outlined in Book I Chapter 2). By forming a company you can separate your own assets from the business assets (in theory at any rate, unless personal guarantees have been extracted). However, a director also has to cope with more technical and detailed requirements; for example, sending in your accounts to Companies House. More onerous than just signing them, a director is expected and required in law to understand the significance of the balance sheet and profit and loss account and the key performance ratios.

Directors' risks can be insured using Directors Insurance, covering negligent performance of duties and breach of the Companies Acts – particularly the Insolvency Act, which can hold directors personally liable to a company's creditors. The cost of the insurance is borne by the company as the directors are acting on its behalf.

The most dangerous areas of a director's responsibilities are ones that could get you disqualified. In summary the areas to avoid at all costs are:

- ✔ Trading whilst insolvent, which occurs when your liabilities exceed your assets. At this point the shareholders' equity in the business has effectively ceased to exist, which puts directors personally at risk. Directors owe a duty of care to creditors – not shareholders. If you find yourself even approaching this area you need the prompt advice of an insolvency practitioner. Directors who act properly will not be penalised, and will live to fight another day.

- ✔ Wrongful trading can apply if, after a company goes into insolvent liquidation, the liquidator believes that the directors ought to have concluded earlier that the company had no realistic chance of survival. In these circumstances the courts can make directors personally liable for the company's debts.

- ✔ Fraudulent trading is rather more serious than wrongful trading. Here the proposition is that the director(s) were knowingly party to fraud on their creditors. The full shelter of Limited Liability can be removed in these circumstances.

Former directors of insolvent companies can be banned from holding office as a company director for periods of up to 15 years. Fraud, fraudulent trading, wrongful trading, or a failure to comply with company law may result in disqualification.

A register of disqualified directors is available for free access on the Companies House Web site. (www.companieshouse.gov.uk).

Finding and Choosing Business Advisers

You need lots of help to get started in business and even more when you are successful. Here are some tips on dealing with some of the key people you are almost bound to need at some stage. There are dozens of others including: tax consultants, advertising and public relations consultants, technology and IT advisers, and the like. The rules and tips in the following sections should steer you through dealing with most situations involving choosing and using outside advisers. (For information on professional auditors and advisers, see Book IV Chapter 6.)

Tallying up an accountant

Keeping your financial affairs in good order is the key to staying legal and winning any disputes. A good accountant inside or outside the firm can keep you on track. A bad accountant is in the ideal position to defraud you at worst, or derail you through negligence or incompetence. What attributes should you look for and how can you find the right accountant for your business? The key steps to choosing a good accountant are:

- ✔ Check they are members of one of the recognised accounting bodies such as the Chartered Institute of Management Accountants (www.cima global.com) or the Institute of Chartered Accountants in England and Wales (www.icaew.co.uk).

- ✔ Have a clear idea of what services you require. You need to consider how complete your bookkeeping records are likely to be, whether you need the VAT return done, budgets and cash flow forecasts prepared and updated, as well as whether you require an annual audit.

- ✔ Clarify the charges scale at the outset. It may well make more sense to spend a bit more on bookkeeping, both staff and systems, rather than leaving it all to a much higher-charging qualified accountant.

- ✔ Use personal recommendations from respected fellow businesspeople. There is nothing like hearing from a fellow consumer of a product or service. Pay rather less attention to the recommendation of bankers, government agencies, family and friends, without totally ignoring their advice.

- ✔ Take references from the accountant's clients as well as from the person who recommended them. It could just be a lucky event that they get on. They may even be related!

- ✔ Find out what back-up they have for both systems and people. The tax authorities will not be very sympathetic whatever the reason for lateness. It would be doubly annoying to be fined for someone else's tardiness.

- ✔ See at least three accountants before making your choice, making sure they deal with companies your size and a bit bigger. Not so much bigger as to have no relevant advice and help to offer, but big enough for you to have some room for growth without having to change accountants too quickly.

- ✔ Find out which other companies the accountant acts for. You don't want them to be so busy they can't service your needs properly, or to be working for potential competitors.

- ✔ Make the appointment for a trial period only, and set a specific task to see how they get on.

- ✔ Give them the latest accounts of your business and ask them for their comments based on their analysis of the figures. You will quickly see if they have grasped the basics of your financial position.

Investing in a bank

You may wonder why choosing a bank is listed in this section covering choosing business advisers. Well the answer, crazy as it may seem, is that your banker is almost invariably the first person you turn to when the chips are down. It's not so surprising when you think about it. After all most big business problems turn on money and bankers are the people who turn the money on.

Get the wrong bank and you could lose more than your overdraft. You may lose the chance to acquire a free, or at least nearly free, business adviser.

These are the top ten questions to ask before taking on a bank manager:

- ✔ How quickly can you make decisions about lending? Anything longer than ten days is too long.

- ✔ What rate of interest will you charge? Two or three per cent above the Bank of England base rate is fairly normal. Above four per cent is on the high side.

- ✔ What factors do you take into consideration in arriving at that rate? If the bank proposes a high rate of interest, say four per cent above Bank of England base rate or higher, then you need to know why. It may be that all the bank is asking for is some further security for their loan, which you might think worth giving in return for a lower interest rate.

- ✔ What other charges will there be? For example will you be charged for every transaction in and out of the account and if so how much?

- ✔ Do you visit your clients and get to know their business? If the bank doesn't visit it's hard to see how they will ever get to really understand your business.

- ✔ Under what circumstances would you want personal guarantees? When the bank is feeling exposed to greater risk than it wants to take it will ask you to shoulder some of that risk personally. Under the terms of a bank's loan to your business it may state that its lending should not exceed a certain sum. You need to be clear what that sum is.

- ✔ What help and advisory services do you have that could be useful to me? Banks often provide advice on export trade, currency dealing, insurance, and a range of other related services.

- ✔ What is unique about your banking services that would make me want to use your rather than any other bank? This factor rather depends on what you consider to be valuable. A bank that delivers all its service on the Internet may be attractive to one person and anathema and turnoff to another.

✔ How long will it be before my present manager moves on? If managers are routinely moved every few years then it's hard to see any value in forming personal relationships.

✔ Are there any situations when you would ask for repayment of a loan to be made early? A bank may insist that if you break any major condition of the loan, such as the overdraft limit or repayment schedule, the whole loan is repayable. You need to find out if this is so, and what sum will cause this to happen.

Choosing a lawyer

Lawyers or solicitors are people you hope never to have to use and when you do need one you need them yesterday. Even if you don't appoint a company lawyer, you may well need one for basic stuff if you are forming a company or setting up a partnership agreement. Follow the same rules as you would for choosing an accountant (refer to the previous 'Tallying up an accountant' section).

The fact is that in business, you know that one day you will need a lawyer. The complexity of commercial life means that, sooner or later, you will find yourself either initiating or defending legal action. It may be a contract dispute with a customer or supplier, or perhaps the lease on your premises turns out to give you far fewer rights than you hoped. A former employee might claim you fired them without reason. Or the Health and Safety Inspector finds some aspect of your machinery or working practices less than satisfactory.

When things do go wrong, the time and money required to put them right can be an unexpected and unwelcome drain on your cash. By doing things right from the start, you can avoid at least some of the most common disputes and cope more easily with catastrophes.

In addition to ensuring that contracts are correctly drawn up, that leases are free from nasty surprises, and that the right health and safety procedures are followed, a solicitor can also advise on choosing the best structure for your company, on protecting your intellectual property, and on how to go about raising money.

It makes sense to either see your solicitor before your problems arise, and find out what they can do for you or, at the very least, make yourself conversant with the relevant laws. Taking timely action on legal issues may help you gain an advantage over competitors and will almost certainly save you money in the long run.

If you are going to see a lawyer, it is always best to be well prepared. Have all the facts to hand and know what you want help with.

Finding a Lawyer For Your Business

Lawyers For Your Business represents some 1,200 firms of solicitors in England and Wales, which have come together to help ensure that all businesses, and especially the smaller owner-managed ones, get access to sound legal advice whenever they need it. LFYB is administered by the Law Society (www.lawsociety.org.uk), and backed by Business in the Community, the Federation of Small Business, and the Forum of Private Business.

To remove the risk of incurring unexpectedly high legal costs, all Lawyers For Your Business members offer a free consultation, lasting at least half-an-hour, to diagnose your legal problem and any need for action, with full information, in advance, on the likely costs of proceeding.

The Law Society will send you a list of Lawyers For Your Business members in your area, and a voucher for a free consultation.

Simply choose one of the firms in the list and arrange an appointment, mentioning Lawyers For Your Business and the voucher.

Considering management consultants

If you are facing a new major problem you have no expertise in, particularly a problem you don't expect to experience again, then hiring a consultant is an option worth considering. For example if you are moving premises, changing your computer or accounting system, starting to do business overseas, or designing an employee share ownership scheme, it may well make sense to get the help of someone who has covered that area several times before and who is an expert in the field.

The time taken for a consultant to carry out most tasks a small business might require is likely to be between a fortnight and three months. Anything much longer will be too expensive for most small firms and anything much shorter is unlikely to have much of an impact on the business. That's not to say they will be working continuously on your project for that time. After an initial meeting a consultant may do much of the work off site and in chunks of time. Costs vary dependant on both the skill of the consultant and the topic covered. A tax consultant, for example can cost upwards of £450 an hour, whilst a training consultant might cost the same sum for a day.

Take on a consultant using much the same procedures as you would a key employee. Take time to brief them thoroughly. Don't expect to just dump the problem on their doorstep and walk away. Set the consultant a small measurable part of the task first and see how they perform. Never give them a long-term contract or an open book commitment.

Remember you can't delegate decision-making you can only delegate the analysis of problems and the presentation of options. In the end you have to choose which way to go. Don't let consultants implement decisions on their own. The line responsibility between yourself and your staff needs to be preserved. If they see someone else giving orders it will undermine the chain of command. If the consultant's solution is so complex it needs their expertise to implement, you have the wrong solution.

The Institute of Business Consulting (www.ibconsulting.org.uk) offers a free consultancy-finding service on its Web site. You will also find that your local Business Link will have a national register of approved (and insured) specialist consultants for most business needs.

Chapter 7

Improving Performance

. . . .

In This Chapter

▶ Seeing why retaining customers matters

▶ Measuring customer satisfaction

▶ Discovering ways to cut costs and work smarter

▶ Evaluating market growth strategies

▶ Looking at new product opportunities

. . . .

*A*n unpleasant truism in business, and in much else, is that once resources are allocated they become misallocated over time. Another way of looking at this problem is to say that just because something 'ain't broke' it doesn't mean it can't be made to perform better still. To get your business to grow and keep growing needs a continuous effort to improve every aspect of your business.

In this chapter, we tell you how to keep your business going strong by keeping your customers happy, improving your efficiency and effectiveness, and increasing and expanding your business.

Checking Your Internal Systems

In order to improve performance you have to have systems in operation that help you measure performance in the first place. The two sub-sections following give you tips for evaluating how you spend your time and how to keep on top of your markets.

Keeping track of your routine

A good test of whether you are allocating enough time to the task of improving performance is to keep a track of how you spend your time, say, over a month. As well as recording the work you do and the time you spend on each major task, put the letter R, for routine, S for strategic, or I for improving performance next to the task.

A routine task is something like meeting a customer or the bank manager, delivering a product or service, or taking on a new employee. Strategic tasks would include considering a major shift of activities, say from making a product to just marketing it, forming a joint venture, or buying out a competitor. Improvement activities include all the elements we talk about in this chapter – activities focused on getting more mileage, lower costs, or higher yields out of the existing business.

Most owner managers spend 95 per cent of their day on routine tasks and only tackle improvement and strategic issues when they hit the buffers. For example most entrepreneurs don't worry too much about cash until it runs out. Then they pick up the phone and press customers into paying up. What they should have done, however, is introduce new procedures for collecting cash *before* the crunch.

If you are not spending at least 30 per cent of your time on improving your business and strategic issues, then you're probably heading for the buffers.

Analysing market position

A *SWOT analysis* is a way of consolidating everything you know about your competitive market position. SWOT stands for Strengths, Weaknesses, Opportunities, and Threats. Many businesses use SWOT analysis regularly, and very few people try it once and never again. For my money, SWOT is the way to go.

A SWOT analysis can't be carried out on the business as a whole. You have to analyse each important market segment separately. Because customer needs in each segment are different, it follows that you have to do different things in each segment to satisfy those needs. You may be up against different competitors in each segment so your strengths and weaknesses will be particular to that competitive environment. For example, look at travel methods: for families, cars, coaches, and to a lesser extent, trains, compete with each other; for business it's people, cars, planes, and first-class rail travel that are the biggest competitors.

Discovering strengths and weaknesses

A strength or weakness is an element that matters to the customers concerned. In fact it has to be such an important factor in the customers' minds that they would not buy without it. These are known as Critical Success Factors and it is your performance against these that confirm your strengths and weaknesses.

Find out the five or so things you have to get right to succeed in your market. For retail booksellers, location, range of books, hours of operation, knowledgeable staff, and ambiance may be the top five elements. Rank how well you think your competitors perform in these critical areas, or better still ask their existing, soon to be your, customers. If they score badly, you may have a strength.

Keeping an eye on opportunities and threats

It is important to recognise that an idea, invention or innovation is not necessarily an opportunity to grow your business. An opportunity has to be attractive, durable and timely. It is centred on a product or service that creates or adds value for its buyer or end user.

Working out what is attractive to you is fairly straightforward. Estimating the likely life of an opportunity or whether the time is right for its launch is not so easy. In a way that is the essence of an entrepreneur's skill. With opportunities you are looking for those that will bring the maximum benefit to the business whilst at the same time having a high probability of success. The benefits you are looking for may vary over time. In the early years cash flow may feature high on the list. Later fast growth and high margins may be more important.

Threats can come from all directions. Changes in the political or economic climate, new legislation or hackers and computer viruses can all have an impact on your business. For example, one business founder found to his dismay that his new Web site linked into dozens of pornography sites – the work of professional hackers. This set his operation back two months.

Changes in the demographic profile of populations (more older people and fewer of working age) or changing fashions, hit all businesses, old and new economy alike.

There are always too many potential threats for you to consider so you need to focus on those with the greatest possible impact that seem most likely to occur.

Doing the actual analysis

The actual SWOT process is asking various groups to share their thoughts on your company's greatest strength, its most glaring weakness, the area of greatest opportunity, and the direction of greatest threat.

To carry out a SWOT analysis, you need to consider each element separately for each major market segment.

Use the following steps to find out your SWOT quotient in each SWOT area:

1. Determine your own view.

   Decide what you think your business's best feature is, what the greatest weakness is, where your opportunities to gain more customers lie, and what the biggest threat facing your business is.

2. Find out what other entrepreneurs and your management team think about these issues.

3. Ask your newest front-line staff the same questions.

4. Form a customer focus group to consider the same questions.

5. Analyse how far apart the views of each group are.

   If you are close to your customers and to your market, there should be little difference among the various groups. If there is a large difference, figure out what you can do to make sure the gap is narrowed and stays that way.

The question 'so what?' is a good one to apply to all aspects of your SWOT analysis. That will help you concentrate only on the important issues. Once completed the SWOT will provide the ingredients and framework for developing your marketing strategy.

Retaining Customers

Businesses spend an awful lot of time and money winning customers and nothing like enough time and money on keeping them. This behaviour is as pointless as pouring water, or perhaps molten gold might be a better material to keep in mind, into a bucket with a big hole in the bottom. Most if not all of the flow is required to keep the bucket partially full. However fast the flow in, the flow out is just as fast.

Virtually all managers agree that customer care is important. A recent survey of major UK companies showed that 75 per cent had recently instituted customer care quality schemes. Sadly another survey, conducted by Bain and Company, the American consultants, also revealed that less than a third of those companies saw any payback for their efforts in terms of improved market share or profitability.

Bain suggests that the reason companies are disappointed with their attempts to improve customer care is that they don't have anything tangible to measure. To help overcome that problem Bain suggests that managers focus on the Customer Retention Ratio, a Bain invention. For example, if you have 100 customers in January and 110 in December, but only 85 of the original customers are still with you, then your retention rate is 85 per cent. Bain's study demonstrated that a 5 per cent improvement in retention had a fairly dramatic effect on clients. For a credit card client it boosted profits by 125 per cent; for an insurance broker there was a 5 per cent increase in profits; and for a software

house a 35 per cent improvement in profits. Bain claims that the longer customers stay with you the more profitable they become. The next section
explains why.

Realising why retaining customers matters

Studies and common sense indicate several principal reasons why retaining
customers is so vitally important:

✔ It costs more to acquire new customers than to retain the ones you have.
What with market research, prospecting, selling time, and so on, it costs
between three and seven times as much to acquire a new customer as to
retain an old one.

This is nothing more than the old military maxim applied by Montgomery,
that attacking forces need several times the strength of the defenders to
guarantee success.

✔ The longer you retain a customer, the more years you have to allocate
the costs of acquiring that customer. By spreading the costs of acquiring
new customers over ten years, instead of one or two, the annual profit
per customer will be higher. Suppose it costs you £500 to get a new customer, and that customer makes you £1,000 profit each year you keep
her. If you keep the customer one year, your annual profit is £500 (£1,000
minus £500). However, if you keep the customer ten years, your annual
profit is £950 (£1,000 minus £500/10). Customers who stay tend, over
time, to spend more.

✔ Regular customers cost less to serve than new customers. Insurance
and underwriting costs as a percentage of sales fall by 40 per cent for
renewal policies. You don't incur up-front costs again.

✔ Long-term customers are often willing to pay a premium for service. Long-
term customers also are less prone to check your competitors because
they know and like you.

Avoiding the consequences of losing customers is a powerful motivator for
keeping in your customers' good graces. Some of those consequences are:

✔ Dissatisfied customers tell between eight and 15 others about their
experience. Just avoiding this negative publicity has a value.

✔ Your former customers are fertile ground for your competitors. If you
keep your customers, your competitors have to offer inducements to
dislodge your customers and this is expensive and time-consuming for
them.

Working to retain customers

Use these five rules to make sure you retain customers and so improve your profit growth:

✔ Make customer care and retention a specific goal, and reward people for keeping customers, not just for getting them.

✔ Find out why you lose customers. Don't just let them go – have either a follow-up questionnaire or get someone other than the salesperson concerned to visit former customers to find out why they changed supplier. You'd be surprised how pleased people are to tell you why they didn't stay with you, if you explain that it may help you serve them better the next time.

✔ Research your competitors' service levels as well as their products. If it's practical, buy from them on a regular basis. If you can't buy from competitors, keep close to people that do.

✔ If one part of your organisation is good at caring for customers, get them to teach everyone else what they do.

✔ Recognise that the best people to provide customer care are those staff who work directly with customers. But this means you have to train them and give them the authority to make decisions on the spot. Aloof or indifferent employees don't convince customers that you really want to keep their business.

Retaining customers is not the passive activity it sounds. The next sections offer concrete ways to keep your customers happy.

Monitoring complaints

One terrifying statistic is that 98 per cent of complaints never happen. People just don't get round to making the complaint, or worse still, they can find no one to complain to. You would have to be a hermit never to have experienced something to complain about, but just try finding someone to complain to at 8 p.m. on a Sunday at Paddington Station and you will get a fair impression of how the Gobi Desert feels.

You can never be confident that just because you're not hearing complaints your customers and clients aren't dissatisfied and about to defect. It also doesn't mean that they won't run around bad mouthing you and your business. It's as well to remember that on average people share their complaint with a score of others, who in turn are equally eager to share the tidings with others. The viral effect of e-mail has the potential to make any particularly juicy story run around the world in days if not hours.

Set up a system that will ensure your customers have ample opportunity to let you know what they think about your product or service. This could involve a short questionnaire, a follow up phone call or an area on your Web site devoted to customer feedback. As a bonus you will probably get some great ideas on how to improve your business.

Ninety-eight per cent of customers who have a complaint will buy from you again if you handle their complaint effectively and promptly. Not only will they buy from you again, but also they will spread the gospel about how clever they were in getting you to respond to their complaint. Nothing makes people happier than having something to complain about that ends up costing them next to nothing.

Setting customer service standards

Customer service is all those activities that support a customer's purchase, from the time she becomes aware that you could supply her with a particular product or service, to the point at which she owns that product or service and is able to enjoy all the benefits she was led to believe were on offer.

The largest part of the value of many products and services lies in how customer service is delivered. It is also the area most likely to influence whether customers come back again or recommend you to others. Customer service works best when:

- ✔ Customers are encouraged to tell you about any problems.
- ✔ Customers know their rights and responsibilities from the beginning.
- ✔ Customers know the circumstances under which they are entitled to get their money back and how to take advantage of other rights.
- ✔ Customers feel in control. It's far better to provide a full refund if the customer is dissatisfied than to demand that the customer come up with a good reason for the refund. A refund, or any other recourse you offer, should be prompt.

Repeat business is another key profit-maker. Repeat business comes from ensuring customers are genuinely completely satisfied with – and preferably pleasantly surprised by – the quality of your product. Repeat sales save unnecessary expenditure on advertising and promotion to attract new customers.

It is certain that as standards of living rise, the more that quality, convenience, and service will become important relative to price. An investment in a strategy of quality customer service now is an investment in greater future profitability.

Giving customers opportunities to complain

One entrepreneur who is more than aware of the problems (and incidentally opportunities) presented by complaints is Julian Richer, founder of the retail hi-fi chain, Richer Sounds. His maxim is that his staff should maximise customers' opportunities to complain. The operative word in that sentence is *opportunities*, which should not be confused with *reasons*. In order to put this policy into effect Richer has a range of techniques in place. The whole customer satisfaction monitoring process starts from the moment customers enter one of his retail outlets. A bell near the door invites those in the shop to ring it if they have had particularly good service or help whilst in the shop. That help could be simply getting some great advice, or may be finding a product they want to buy at a very competitive price.

Customers find that when they get their hi-fi equipment home there is a short questionnaire on a postcard asking them for their immediate post-purchase feelings. Does the product work as specified, is it damaged in any way, were they delighted with the service they have had? The postcard is addressed to 'Julian Richer, Founder' and not, as is the case with so many other big businesses, to 'Customer Services, Department 126754, PO Box, blah blah blah'.

Richer does surveys on customer satisfaction and encourages his staff to come up with their own ideas for monitoring customer reactions. In fact he insists that they hit minimum targets for getting customer feedback. Silence on the customer satisfaction front is not an option for management in his business.

You need to have a model to follow for effective customer service and you should consider using mystery shopping as a way to keep tabs on your customer service standards – both issues are covered in the next sections.

Customer service is often the difference between keeping customers for life and losing customers in droves. You and your staff have to deliver outstanding customer service at all times.

In order to do this everyone has to know what the important elements of good customer service are and everyone needs to incorporate those elements into her everyday customer interactions.

The key elements of your customer service plan should include:

✔ **Initial contact:** The customers' first contact with staff creates a lasting impression and can win and sustain them. All your staff need to be aware of how to handle enquiries quickly and competently. They should know how to leave potential customers feeling confident that their requirements will be met.

✔ **Information flow:** Keeping customers informed of where their orders are in the process influences their feelings about the way you do business. Your action plan needs to specify each step of your process: quotation;

order confirmation; delivery notification; installation instructions. A regular flow of information throughout this period makes your customers feel that they matter to you.

- ✔ **Delivery:** Delivering the goods or service is a key part of customer service. Your product needs to be available in a timely manner, delivery lead times must be reasonable, and the delivery itself must be in a way that meets the customer's requirements.

- ✔ **After-sales support:** Good coverage in areas such as maintenance, repairs, help-lines, upgrade notification, instruction manuals, returns policy, and fault tracing help customers feel that you care about their total experience with your products and business.

- ✔ **Problem solving:** Often the acid test of customer service; your staff need to be able to recognise when a customer has a real crisis and what your procedure is for helping her.

High customer service standards enable many firms to charge a premium for their products. Yet in many ways, good customer service can be a nil-cost item. After all it takes as much effort to answer the phone politely as it does with a surly and off-putting tone. So improved customer service is one route to increased profitability.

Carrying out mystery shopping

No, mystery shopping is not the feeling of surprise that comes over you when you unpack the result of your weekly family shop at the supermarket. Mystery shopping is the process that investigates your staff's service, friendliness, speed, and product knowledge to ensure that your customers are being well cared for.

Mystery shopping is the evaluation, measurement, and reporting of customer service standards by use of agents acting as if they were customers. It is arguably the fastest and most effective method of obtaining hard objective management data about customer service levels. Your employees have to be on their toes for every customer, since any of them could be a mystery shopper.

Companies such as the aptly named Mystery Shoppers (www.mystery shoppers.co.uk) or http:// gfk NOP (www.gfknop.com) employ thousands of people around the country who routinely visit thousands of locations, make tens of thousands of phone calls, and ask for millions of quotations or pieces of advice, none of which will result in an order for the business concerned.

Key aspects that mystery shopping can measure:

- ✔ Are the staff knowledgeable, helpful and polite?

- ✔ Are the staff competent at selling your products and services?

- Do the staff try to sell products or services that are related to the one(s) they are enquiring about?
- How are customers treated when they are complaining or returning products?
- Do the staff comply with all the regulations governing your industry?
- How competitive are your prices and other terms?
- Is your product being properly displayed with the right literature and any other point-of-sale materials?
- Are the premises in a clean workmanlike condition?
- How do your staff perform on the telephone?
- How effective is your Web site?

Rewarding loyalty

The reasons that loyalty improves profitability are: retaining customers costs less than finding and capturing new ones; loyal customers tend to place larger orders; and loyal customers don't always place price first, whilst new ones do. So what works and what doesn't when it comes to keeping customers loyal?

One of the ideas that hasn't lived up to its promise is customer loyalty cards. When they were launched, retailers made big claims of how they would be gathering tons of invaluable data about customers. But mostly they have been left with huge virtual warehouses of information that hasn't been used.

Analysing the buying habits of millions of shoppers as their cards are swiped at the till can be prohibitively expensive and few companies have used much of the data gathered to make their customers feel special and hence want to stay loyal.

Asked to give reasons for their loyalty, the top five elements consumers list are:

- Convenience
- Price
- Range
- Customer service
- Quality

What this means is that you have to get your basic marketing strategy right and understand what your customer wants and how much she is prepared to pay. If that is wrong no loyalty scheme will keep her on board. Customer service and quality are about getting it right first time, every time. So always under promise and over deliver.

Care and help-lines, where customers are encouraged to call for advice, information or help with problems, will keep customers loyal and make them more likely to buy from you in the future. If the line is a free phone service it will be even more effective.

Keeping in touch with customers can also bind them more securely. Questionnaires, newsletters, magazines, letters about incentive, customer service calls, invitations to sales events, and 'member get member' schemes are all ways of achieving this result.

Improving Productivity

Improving productivity is a constant requirement for a growth-minded business, not simply an activity during periods of economic recession (when it is still, nonetheless, important – much better than adopting the 'turtle position', pulling in your head and your hands and getting off the road!). Productivity needs to be improved by acting on both your costs and your margins.

Increasing margins can be achieved by changing the mix of products and services you sell to focus on those yielding the best return, or by raising your selling price. Cutting cost has the merit of showing quick and certain returns.

Cutting costs

Costs need to be constantly controlled and balanced against the need for good quality and good service. In particular you need to separate and act on your variable and your fixed costs (see Book I Chapter 3 for more on fixed and variable costs).

Variable cost cutting is always in evidence in recession; witness the automotive and banking staff cuts in the early 1990s and in 2002–3. Cutting variable costs include such things as wages and materials that are directly related to the volume of sales.

Cutting fixed cost such as cars, computers and equipment that do not change directly with the volume of sales should not include scrapping investments in technology that could bring economies and extra nimbleness in the future (like flexible-manufacturing facilities, where, for example, Peugeot has invested in product lines that can turn out two models at once). Many firms, following Japanese practice, increase their use of subcontractors to help offset increased risk.

Equally, alliances between firms, aiming to reduce fixed cost investments, can be advantageous. In the soft drinks industry, Perrier provide distribution for Pepsi in France, while Bulmers reciprocated for Perrier in England, avoiding the need for extra investment in warehousing and transport.

Focusing attention on the 20 per cent of items that make up 80 per cent of your costs will probably yield your biggest savings. The 80/20 rule is helpful in getting costs back into line, but what if the line was completely wrong in the first place?

Budgeting from zero

When you sit down with your team and discuss budgets, the arguments always revolve around how much more each section will need next year. The starting point is usually this year's costs, which are taken as the only facts upon which to build. So, for example, if you spent £25,000 on advertising last year and achieved sales of £1 million, your advertising expense was 2.5 per cent of sales. If the sales budget for next year is £1.5 million, then it seems logical to spend £37,500 next year on advertising. That, however, presupposes last year's sum was wisely and effectively spent in the first place, which it almost certainly was not.

Zero-based budgeting turns the cost argument on its head. It assumes that each year every cost centre starts from zero spending and, based on the goals of the business and the resources available, arguments are presented for every pound spent, *not just for the increase.*

Increasing margins

To achieve increased *profit margins*, which is the difference between the costs associated with the product or service you sell and the price you get in the market, you need first to review your sales. This requires accurate costs and gross margins for each of your products or services (see Book III Chapter 1). Armed with that information you can select particular product groups or market segments that are less price sensitive and potentially more profitable.

No one rushes out to buy expensive overpriced products when cheaper ones that are just as good are readily available. The chances are that your most profitable products are also the ones that your customers value the most. You should start your efforts to increase margins by concentrating on trying to sell the products and services that make you the most money

Pricing is the biggest decision your business has to make, one it needs to keep constantly under review. Your decision on pricing is the one that has the biggest impact on company profitability. Try the consultants' favourite exercise of computing and comparing the impact on profits of a 5 per cent:

  ✔ Cut in your overheads

  ✔ Increase in volume sales

  ✔ Cut in materials purchased

  ✔ Price increase

All these actions are usually considered to be within an owner-manager's normal reach. Almost invariably, the 5 per cent price increase scores the highest, as it passes straight to the net profit, bottom line. Even if volume falls, because of the effect price has on growth margin, it is usually more profitable to sell fewer items at a higher price. For example, at a constant gross margin of 30 per cent with a 5 per cent price increase, profits would be unchanged even if sales declined 14 per cent. Yet if prices were cut 5 per cent, an extra 21 per cent increase in sales would be needed to make the same amount of profit.

Frequently, resistance to increasing prices, even in the face of inflationary cost rises, can come from your own team members, eager to apportion blame for performance lapses. In these instances it is important to make detailed price comparisons with competitors.

Working smarter

Making more money doesn't always have to mean working longer hours. You could just work smarter and who knows you may even end up working fewer hours than you do now and still make more money.

One way to get everyone's grey matter working overtime is to create smart circles, comprising of people working in different areas of your business who are challenged to come up with ideas to make the business better (and smart rewards, which include extra resources, holidays and recognition for their achievements, rather than cash). You could formalise the process of encouraging employees to rethink the way they work and reward them in such a way as to make their working environment better still.

Rewarding results

If you can get the people who work for you to increase their output, you can improve productivity. The maxim 'What get measured gets done and what gets rewarded gets done again' is the guiding principle behind rewards, and setting objectives is the starting point in the process.

The objectives you want people to achieve in order to be rewarded beyond their basic pay need to be challenging but achievable too, which is something of a contradiction in terms. Problems start to arise as soon as professional managers and supervisors come on board with experience of working in big companies. They, and probably you yourself, tend to take objectives and the ensuing budgets very seriously. They have to be hit, so it makes sense to pitch on the conservative side.

But in a small business growth and improvement percentages have the potential to be much greater than in larger firms. A big business with a third of its market can only grow very quickly by acquisition or if the market itself is growing very fast. A small firm, on the other hand, can grow by very large amounts very quickly. Moving from 0.01 per cent of a market to 0.02 per cent is hardly likely to upset many other players, but it represents a doubling in size for the small firm. However exceptional performance, even in a small firm, will only be attainable with breakthrough thinking and performance. The question may not be how can we grow the business by 20 per cent a year, but how can we grow it by 20 per cent a month.

Nevertheless, if goals are set too aggressively people may leave. Even, perhaps especially, great performers will balk if the hurdle is put too high.

A way to get the best of both worlds is to have a performance band rather than just one number. The reward for achieving a really great result should be massive, but if this high goal is missed slightly, the employee is rewarded as if the goal had been set at the level reached. The reward is proportionately smaller, so your rewards budget still balances. This technique can get an 'inspiration dividend'. Teams can be persuaded to set higher goals than they might otherwise have set, and even when they miss them, the year-on-year improvements can be stunning.

Increasing Sales

The most obvious way to grow a business is to get more sales. This is often easier said than done, but there are some tried and proven techniques that usually deliver the goods. A helpful framework to keep in mind is the one developed by the business guru, Igor Ansoff, and named after him as Ansoff's Growth Matrix.

Ansoff's model has four major elements:

- ✔ Business development, which is about getting more customers like the ones you already have and getting them to buy more from you.

- ✔ Market development, which involves entering new markets in your home country or overseas.

- ✔ Product or service development, which involves launching new products or extensions to existing products or services. A courier service adding an overnight delivery service to its existing 48-hour service is an example of this activity.

✔ Diversification, which means, in a nutshell, launching off into the unknown.

Getting customers to buy more

This is a no-brainer starting point for achieving profitable growth. Winning a new customer can be an expensive and time-consuming activity, so once you have her the more you can get her to spend with you rather than a competitor, the better your bottom line will be.

You can avoid this experience if you use this framework to categorise your customers:

✔ **Courtship:** This is the stage before a customer has bought anything from you. At this stage the customer is suspicious and your objective is to get your first order. Any order will do just to get the relationship under way.

✔ **Engagement:** Having got your first order in the bag, your customer may still be moderately suspicious of you and is still not sure if your intentions are wholly honourable. Your goal is to get your first repeat order and cement the relationship. Getting to this stage means that your first order must go well and your customer must be at least satisfied, or delighted if you want to get to the honeymoon stage in your relationship. To make that happen you need to stand out from the crowd and go the extra mile to make that customer feel special by meeting her particular needs.

✔ **Honeymoon:** With several repeat orders successfully fulfilled, your customer now trusts you and is susceptible to new ideas. Here you should be looking to increase sales volume. It is almost certain that as a new supplier your customer has not put all her eggs in your basket. Now your task is to get as many eggs as you can and build up to being the preferred and perhaps only supplier.

Rewarding excellent results

Nick White's Ecotravel company sends people to off-the-beaten-track exotic locations and to conservation areas where money goes into research projects. Ecotourists who book with Ecotravel pay to see animals in conservation areas and a proportion of the money they spend on the holiday goes directly to conservation projects.

White expanded slowly until two years ago when he introduced a 'rewarding excellence' initiative and sales shot up by 40 per cent in just six months. The basis of the reward is an accelerating bonus. If the company hits its sales targets staff share in a 5 per cent bonus. If it exceeds targets the bonus rates rise too. For every 20 per cent of achievement above target the bonus rate goes up 1 per cent. Targets are reset each year using a similar formula but starting from a new and higher base level.

✔ **Wedlock:** When you first started talking to your customer you were the new kid on the block, to her at least. Your ideas and products or services were refreshingly new and her existing suppliers had had ample opportunity to disappoint her and let her down. Now you have become, or are fast becoming, that old boring supplier. You need to think of ways to keep your relationship exciting and fresh.

✔ **Deadlock:** Your customer has become disenchanted and is considering divorce. The time has come to bring on new products and services to whet her appetite and make her see you as the exciting vigorous supplier you appeared when your relationship started.

Encouraging referrals

Referrals are the most valuable marketing asset any business can have. Whether you are selling direct to an end consumer or user, or operate in the business-to-business arena your goal is the same – to get those using your product or service to talk in glowing terms about their experience with your business.

Passive word of mouth is rarely as effective as encouraging satisfied customers to pass on the glad tidings. Happy customers tell an average of seven other people if they have had a positive experience with you. Unhappy customers tell 11 to 20 other people.

You can make word-of-mouth advertising work, however. It just requires discipline and a programmed effort to ask your customers for referrals. Make it easy for them – give them brochures, flyers, samples, or whatever it takes to make your case. Then follow up.

Angus Thirlwell and Peter Harris, founders of Hotel Chocolat (www.hotel chocolat.co.uk), have a neat method of getting customers to promote their luxury home-delivered chocolate business. They started a number of Tasting Clubs that have attracted well over 100,000 regular members, who enjoy a brand new selection of exciting, artisan chocolates every month. The idea is that a member receives a selection of chocolates together with a scoring card, then invites their friends to taste and rate the selection. In the process, new members are recruited to the club.

Premier Business Audio (www.premierbusinessaudio.co.uk > referrals), formerly known as On Hold Services, takes a more direct approach. They offer £30 worth of PBA Leisure vouchers, redeemable at Marks & Spencer, Laithwaites, and a host of other firms, for every successful referral. Another business, Big Advertising Ltd, issues Referral Reward Credits onto clients' accounts to the tune of 10 per cent of the first payment made by any new customer directly referred to them (www.bigadvertising.co.uk/referral reward/referral-reward-system.asp).

Discounts for introductions come out of your advertising budget. So you need to work out how much an introduction to a prospect is worth before you can decide on the discount. The rules to follow are:

- ✔ Be specific in the type of introductions you want. In particular make the sales volume and product specifications clear. There is no point in giving a discount for products on which your margins are already tight.

- ✔ Have a sliding scale of discount. The more introductions you get the more you give.

- ✔ Make it easy for people to give you introductions. Send them fax back forms or have a place on your Web site for them to tap in minimum details. A name and company should be enough for you to find the other details you need.

- ✔ Follow up and let people know that their introduction paid off. People are usually interested in more than just the discount when they give introductions.

- ✔ Have a specific programme such as member-gets-member and run it as a campaign for a set period of time. Then change the programme and the discounts. That keeps people interested.

- ✔ Give the discount promptly, but not until the new introduction has bought and paid their bill.

- ✔ Give extra discount for introductions to loyal customers. Perhaps when the new customer has placed her third or fourth order you can give the extra discount.

- ✔ Research the market and find out what introductory schemes are on offer in your sector.

- ✔ Set up a database to monitor the effectiveness of your introductory discount scheme.

Entering new markets at home

Generally the most rewarding market growth for small businesses comes in the first few months and years when the whole of what is known as the home market is up for grabs. New markets can take a number of shapes. The two most common of these are:

- ✔ Geographic. Once you are confident that you have extracted as much business as you can get from your immediate business area, be that a town, city, or region, move onto another one. You need to make sure that the new geographic area is broadly similar to the one you have been successful in already. For example Bristol and Bath, are broadly similar to Bradford and Sheffield, as cities, but if your business has tourists as customers, the last two cities will be less appealing as a new market than the first two.

> ✔ Demographic. This covers factors particular to customer groups. If you make clothes for women in Bristol, you could consider making clothes for children, men or teenagers, sticking to the Bristol area.

You can get help and advice from Business Link (www.businesslink.gov.uk) who can provide practical support in this area and in most other areas of marketing your business.

Selling overseas

Financial web site Motley Fool's entry into the German market involved a modest change in a well-proven product, as for its entry to the British, French, and Italian markets between 1998 and 2001. But expanding overseas is not quite as easy as it looks.

Marks and Spencer made a mess of its foray into America and retired in some ignominy from the French market, closing 38 stores virtually overnight and exciting the wrath of the French trade unions on the way. The Body Shop, a world business if ever there was one, found it hard going in the French market, where people take beauty, as they do wine, rather more seriously than most.

Don't let these stories of failure discourage you. After all, millions of businesses export successfully and you can always get some help in getting started. UK Trade and Investment (www.uktradeinvest.gov.uk), the government's export advisory organisation, can put a package of help together for you. One of the most useful services on offer for businesses new to international trade is its Tradeshow Access Programme (TAP). Using this service small businesses can receive up to three grants of £1,800 (for separate exhibitions) to help acquire knowledge and experience of exhibiting effectively overseas, as part of a longer-term export strategy. Among the 530 exhibitions you can participate in are those in China, Hong Kong, Taiwan, India, Brazil, Gulf Co-operation

EXAMPLE

Painting the landscape with art shops

Megan started her first reproduction modern art shop in St Ives, Cornwall in 2000. That went well, so using the same basic criteria for layout and location, she opened her second shop in Padstow a year later and a third in Falmouth in the following year.

Megan reckoned that tourists, who make up 80 per cent of her market, spend most of their time within a dozen miles of their holiday cottage, caravan, or hotel. So by opening more outlets at least 12 miles apart she is not in danger of cannibalising her sales from an existing shop.

Council States, Indonesia, Japan, Malaysia, Mexico, Russia, Singapore, South Africa, South Korea, Thailand, Turkey, and Vietnam. You're eligible for support if you are new to these markets. Go to www.uktradeinvest.gov.uk, then select Exporting from the UK, Our Services, and finally Market Entry.

Adding new products or services

At one end of a spectrum are truly new and innovative products; at the other are relatively modest product or service line extensions. For example, Amazon's Music and Video/DVD business could be seen as product line extensions of their book trade. Their Tools and Hardware operation looks more like a new product. New to them, of course, not to the thousands of other businesses in that sector.

Most new products are unsuccessful. A new product has to be two or three times better in some respect – price, performance, convenience, availability – to dislodge a well-entrenched rival.

They don't necessarily have to be your new products and services, of course. Alliances, affiliations, joint ventures, and the like abound and may help you to be even more successful.

The sources of successful new products include:

- ✔ Listening to customers, who can tell you their needs and dissatisfactions with current products and services.

- ✔ Your sales team, who are also close to the market and so can form a view as to what might sell well.

- ✔ Competitors who are first to market usually make lots of mistakes on the way. Following in their wake you can avoid the worst of their errors and succeed where they have not.

- ✔ Exhibitions and trade fairs are where other firms, not necessarily competitors, but those on the margins of your sector meet and exchange ideas. Products and services that work well in one environment may be adapted for use in your market with little cost.

- ✔ Markets that are known to be in advance of your own. Many new ideas start their lives in the US and only arrive in Europe 18 months to five years later. Following trends there will give you useful pointers for successful new products in your own market.

- ✔ Research and development departments often throw up innovative ideas for which there are no obvious market need. You may know of profitable ways to exploit those technologies.

Diversifying as a last resort

Diversification involves moving away from the products, service and markets that you currently operate in, to completely new areas of business. This is the riskiest strategy of all – selling things you know little about to people you know even less about. Sure, you can do market research and buy in industry expertise, but there is still a risk. Companies that succeed in diversifying do so slowly, sometimes by acquisition, and above all by listening to customers and front-line staff.

Unless you can quantify the value added in an acquisition or diversification, for example in better buying with quantity discounts or by being able to spread your costs over a bigger sales volume, don't bother. However, if you can get acquisitions right, the growth through diversification can be phenomenal.

Book II
Accounting Basics

'This is <u>real</u> hell – The books
down here <u>never</u> balance!'

In this book . . .

*I*n this Book, we explain the basics of how bookkeeping works and help you to get started with the task of setting up your books. We show you how to monitor your day-to-day business operations by recording sales and purchases as well as any discounts and returns.

We expose you to terms with a unique meaning in the world of bookkeeping, such as ledger, journal, debit, and credit, and show you how to set up the roadmap for your books – the Chart of Accounts. We introduce you to the basics of correctly entering and recording financial transactions and tell you how to put good internal controls in place – a must-have for any bookkeeping system. In addition, you want to be sure that cash coming in and going out of the business is properly handled, and so we provide recommendations of how to separate various money-related duties.

Finally, we introduce you to your options when it comes to computerised accounting systems and share the benefits of using these types of systems to keep your business's books.

Here are the contents of Book II at a glance:

Chapter 1

Getting Down to Bookkeeping Basics

. . . .

In This Chapter

▶ Keeping business records

▶ Getting to know the lingo

▶ Navigating the accounting cycle

▶ Understanding accrual accounting

▶ Making sense of double-entry bookkeeping

▶ Clarifying debits and credits

. . . .

*A*ll businesses need to keep track of their financial transactions, which is why bookkeeping and bookkeepers are so important. Without accurate records, how can you tell whether your business is making a profit or taking a loss?

In this chapter, we cover the key aspects of bookkeeping: We introduce you to the language of bookkeeping, familiarise you with how bookkeepers manage the accounting cycle, and show you how to understand the more complex type of bookkeeping – double-entry bookkeeping.

The Record Keeping of the Business World

Bookkeeping, the methodical way in which businesses track their financial transactions, is rooted in accounting. *Accounting* is the total structure of records and procedures used to record, classify, and report information about a business's financial transactions. Bookkeeping involves the recording of that financial information into the accounting system while maintaining adherence to solid accounting principles.

The bookkeeper's job is to work day in and day out to ensure that transactions are accurately recorded. Bookkeepers need to be very detail-oriented and love working with numbers, because numbers and the accounts the numbers go into are what these people deal with all day long.

Bookkeepers aren't required to belong to any recognised professional body, such as the Institute of Chartered Accountants of England and Wales. You can recognise a chartered accountant by the letters ACA after the name, which indicates that she is an Associate of the Institute of Chartered Accountants. If she's been qualified much longer, she may use the letters FCA, which indicate that the accountant is a Fellow of the Institute of Chartered Accountants.

Of course, both Scotland and Ireland have their own chartered accountant bodies with their own designations. Other accounting qualifications exist, offered by the Institute of Chartered Management Accountants (ACMA and FCMA), the Institute of Chartered Certified Accountants (ACCA and FCMA), and the Chartered Institute of Public Finance Accountants (CIPFA).

The Association of Accounting Technicians offers a bookkeeping certificate (ABC) programme, which provides a good grounding in this subject. In reality, most bookkeepers tend to be qualified by experience.

If you're after an accountant to help your business, use the appropriate chartered accountants or a chartered certified accountant as they have the most relevant experience.

On starting up their businesses, many small businesspeople serve as their own bookkeepers until the business is large enough to hire a dedicated person to keep the books. Few small businesses have accountants on the payroll to check the books and prepare official financial reports; instead, they have bookkeepers (either on the payroll or hired on a self-employed basis) who serve as the outside accountants' eyes and ears. Most businesses do seek out an accountant, usually a chartered accountant (either ACA or FCA), but this is usually to submit annual accounts to the Inland Revenue, which is now part of HM Revenue & Customs.

In many small businesses today, a bookkeeper enters the business transactions on a daily basis while working inside the business. At the end of each month or quarter, the bookkeeper sends summary reports to the accountant who then checks the transactions for accuracy and prepares financial statements such as the profit and loss (see Book III Chapter 1), and balance sheet (see Book III Chapter 2) statements.

In most cases, the accounting system is initially set up with the help of an accountant. The aim is to ensure that the system uses solid accounting principles and that the analysis it provides is in line with that required by the business, the accountant, and HM Revenue & Customs. That accountant periodically reviews the system's use to make sure that transactions are being handled properly.

Accurate financial reports are the only way to ensure that you know how your business is doing. These reports are developed using the information you, as the bookkeeper, enter into your accounting system. If that information isn't accurate, your financial reports are meaningless: As the old adage goes, 'Garbage in, garbage out'.

Wading through Basic Bookkeeping Lingo

Book II

Accounting Basics

Before you can take on bookkeeping and start keeping the books, you first need to get a handle on the key accounting terms. This section describes the main terms that all bookkeepers use on a daily basis.

Note: This list isn't exhaustive, and doesn't contain all the unique terms you have to know as a bookkeeper. For full coverage of bookkeeping terminology, turn to the Glossary at the back of the book.

Accounts for the balance sheet

Here are a few terms you need to know:

- **Balance sheet:** The financial statement that presents a snapshot of the business's financial position (assets, liabilities, and capital) as of a particular date in time. The balance sheet is so-called because the things owned by the business (assets) must equal the claims against those assets (liabilities and capital).

   On an ideal balance sheet, the total assets need to equal the total liabilities plus the total capital. If your numbers fit this formula, the business's books are in balance. (We discuss the balance sheet in greater detail in Book III Chapter 2.)

- **Assets:** All the items a business owns in order to run successfully, such as cash, stock, buildings, land, tools, equipment, vehicles, and furniture.

- **Liabilities:** All the debts the business owes, such as mortgages, loans, and unpaid bills.

- **Capital:** All the money the business owners invest in the business. When one person (sole trader) or a group of people (partnership) own a small business, the owner's capital is shown in a Capital account. In an incorporated business (limited company), the owner's capital is shown as shares.

Another key Capital account is *Retained Earnings,* which shows all business profits that have been reinvested in the business rather than paid out to the owners by way of dividends. Unincorporated businesses show money paid out to the owners in a Drawings account (or individual drawings accounts in the case of a partnership), whereas incorporated businesses distribute money to the owners by paying *dividends* (a portion of the business's profits paid out to the ordinary shareholders, typically for the year).

Accounts for the profit and loss statement

Following are a few terms related to the profit and loss statement that you need to know:

- ✓ **Profit and loss statement:** The financial statement that presents a summary of the business's financial activity over a certain period of time, such as a month, quarter, or year. The statement starts with Sales made, subtracts out the Costs of Goods Sold and the Expenses, and ends with the bottom line – Net Profit or Loss. (We show you how to develop a profit and loss statement in Book III Chapter 1.)

- ✓ **Income:** All sales made in the process of selling the business's goods and services. Some businesses also generate income through other means, such as selling assets the business no longer needs or earning interest from investments. (We discuss how to track income in Book II Chapter 6.)

- ✓ **Cost of Goods Sold:** All costs incurred in purchasing or making the products or services a business plans to sell to its customers. (We talk about purchasing goods for sale to customers in Book II Chapter 6.)

- ✓ **Expenses:** All costs incurred to operate the business that aren't directly related to the sale of individual goods or services. (We review common types of expenses in Book II Chapter 2.)

Other common terms

Some other common terms include the following:

- ✓ **Accounting period:** The time for which financial information is being prepared. Most businesses monitor their financial results on a monthly basis, so each accounting period equals one month. Some businesses choose to do financial reports on a quarterly basis, so the accounting period is three months. Other businesses only look at their results on a yearly basis, so their accounting period is 12 months. Businesses that track their financial activities monthly usually also create quarterly and *annual reports* (a year-end summary of the business's activities and financial results) based on the information they gather.

✔ **Accounting year-end:** In most cases a business accounting year is 12 months long and ends 12 months on from when the business started or at some traditional point in the trading cycle for that business. Many businesses have year-ends of 31st March (to tie in with the tax year) and 31st December (to tie in with the calendar year). You're allowed to change your business year-end to suit your business.

For example if you started your business on July 1, your year-end will be 31 June (12 months later). If, however, it is traditional for your industry to have 31 December as the year-end, it is quite in order to change to this date. For example, most retailers have 31 December as their year-end. You of course have to let HM Revenue & Customs know and get their formal acceptance.

✔ **Debtors (also known as Accounts Receivable):** The account used to track all customer sales made on credit. *Credit* refers not to credit card sales but to sales in which the business gives a customer credit directly, and which the business needs to collect from the customer at a later date. (We discuss how to monitor Accounts Receivable in Book II Chapter 6.)

✔ **Creditors (also known as Accounts Payable):** The account used to track all outstanding bills from suppliers, contractors, consultants, and any other businesses or individuals from whom the business buys goods or services. (We talk about managing Accounts Payable in Book II Chapter 6.)

✔ **Depreciation:** An accounting method used to account for the aging and use of assets. For example, if you own a car, you know that the value of the car decreases each year (unless you own one of those classic cars that goes up in value). Every major asset a business owns ages and eventually needs replacement, including buildings, factories, equipment, and other key assets. (We discuss how to work out depreciation in Book IV Chapter 5.)

✔ **Nominal (or General) Ledger:** Where all the business's accounts are summarised. The Nominal Ledger is the master summary of the bookkeeping system. (We discuss posting to the Nominal Ledger in Book II Chapter 3.)

✔ **Interest:** The money a business needs to pay when it borrows money from anybody. For example, when you buy a car using a car loan, you must pay not only the amount you borrowed (capital or principal) but also additional money, or interest, based on a percentage of the amount you borrowed.

✔ **Stock (or Inventory):** The account that tracks all products sold to customers. (We review stock valuation and control in Book II Chapter 6.)

✔ **Journals:** Where bookkeepers keep records (in chronological order) of daily business transactions. Each of the most active accounts, including cash, Accounts Payable, and Accounts Receivable, has its own journal. (We discuss entering information into journals in Book II Chapter 3.)

Book II

Accounting Basics

✔ **Payroll:** The way a business pays its employees. Managing payroll is a key function of the bookkeeper and involves reporting many aspects of payroll to HM Revenue & Customs, including Pay As You Earn (PAYE) taxes to be paid on behalf of the employee and employer, and National Insurance Contributions (NICs). In addition, a range of other payments such as Statutory Sick Pay (SSP) and maternity/paternity pay may be part of the payroll function. (We discuss employee payroll in Book V Chapter 2 and the government side of payroll reporting in Book V Chapter 3.)

✔ **Trial balance:** How you test to ensure that the books are in balance before pulling together information for the financial reports and closing the books for the accounting period.

Pedalling through the Accounting Cycle

As a bookkeeper, you complete your work by completing the tasks of the accounting cycle, so-called because the workflow is circular: Entering transactions, manipulating the transactions through the accounting cycle, closing the books at the end of the accounting period, and then starting the entire cycle again for the next accounting period.

The accounting cycle has eight basic steps, shown in Figure 1-1.

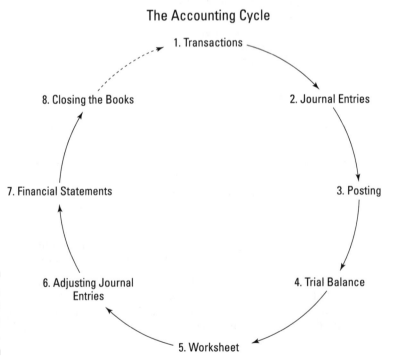

Figure 1-1:
The accounting cycle.

1. **Transactions:** Financial transactions start the process. Transactions can include the sale or return of a product, the purchase of supplies for business activities, or any other financial activity that involves the exchange of the business's assets, the establishment or payoff of a debt, or the deposit from or payout of money to the business's owners. All sales and expenses are transactions that must be recorded. We cover transactions in greater detail throughout the book as we discuss how to record the basics of business activities – recording sales, purchases, asset acquisition, or asset disposal, taking on new debt, or paying off debt.

2. **Journal entries:** The transaction is listed in the appropriate journal, maintaining the journal's chronological order of transactions. (The journal is also known as the 'book of original entry' and is the first place a transaction is listed.) We talk more about journal entries in Book II Chapter 3.

Book II

Accounting Basics

3. **Posting:** The transactions are posted to the relevant account. These accounts are part of the Nominal Ledger, where you can find a summary of all the business's accounts. We discuss posting in Book II Chapter3.

4. **Trial balance:** At the end of the accounting period (which may be a month, quarter, or year depending on your business's practices), you prepare a trial balance.

5. **Worksheet:** Unfortunately, often your first trial balance shows that the books aren't in balance. In this case, you look for errors and make corrections called *adjustments,* which are tracked on a worksheet. Adjustments are also made to account for the depreciation of assets, and to adjust for one-time payments (such as insurance) that need to be allocated on a monthly basis to match monthly expenses with monthly revenues more accurately. After you make and record adjustments, you take another trial balance to be sure that the accounts are in balance.

6. **Adjusting journal entries:** You post any necessary corrections to the relevant accounts after your trial balance shows that the accounts balance (after the necessary adjustments are made to the accounts). You don't need to make adjusting entries until the trial balance process is completed and all needed corrections and adjustments have been identified.

7. **Financial statements:** You prepare the balance sheet and profit and loss statement using the corrected account balances.

8. **Closing the books:** You close the books for the Revenue and Expense accounts and begin the entire cycle again.

At the end of the accounting year (year-end) all the accounting ledgers are closed off. This situation means that Revenue and Expense accounts must start with a zero balance at the beginning of each new accounting year. In contrast, you carry over Asset, Liability, and Capital account balances from year to year, because the business doesn't start each cycle by getting rid of old assets and buying new assets, paying off and then taking on new debt, or paying out all claims to owners and then collecting the money again.

Managing the Bookkeeping and Accounting System

In our experience, far too many business owners either ignore their bookkeeping and accounting systems or take them for granted – unless something obvious goes wrong. The owners assume that if the books are in balance, then everything is OK. The section 'Recording transactions using debits and credits', later in this chapter, covers just exactly what 'the books being in balance' means – it does *not* necessarily mean that everything is OK.

To determine whether your bookkeeping system is up to scratch, check out the following sections, which, taken as a whole, provide a checklist of the most important elements of a good system.

Categorise your financial information

Suppose that you're the accountant for a company and you're faced with the daunting task of preparing the annual income tax return for the business. This demands that you report the following kinds of expenses (and this list contains just the minimum!):

- Advertising
- Bad debts
- Charitable contributions
- Compensation of directors
- Cost of goods sold
- Depreciation
- Employee benefits
- Interest
- Pensions and profit-sharing plans
- Rents
- Repairs and maintenance
- Salaries and wages
- Taxes and licenses

You must provide additional information for some of these expenses. For example, the cost of goods sold expense is determined in a schedule that also requires stock cost at the beginning of the year, purchases during the year, cost of labour during the year (for manufacturers), other costs, and stock cost at year-end.

Where do you start? Well, if it's March 1 and the tax return deadline is March 15, you start by panicking – unless you were smart enough to think ahead about the kinds of information your business would need to report. In fact, when your accountant first designs your business's accounting system, he or she should dissect any financial statements and the tax returns, breaking down all the information into categories such as those we just listed.

For each category, you need an *account,* a record of the activities in that category. An account is basically a focused history of a particular dimension of a business. In bookkeeping this means a basic category of information in which the financial effects of transactions are recorded and which serves as the source of information for preparing financial statements and tax returns.

Book II

Accounting Basics

The term *general ledger* refers to the complete set of accounts established and maintained by a business. The *chart of accounts* is a term used to describe a formal index of these accounts – the complete listing and classification of the accounts used by the business to record its transactions. *General ledger* usually refers to the actual accounts and often to the balances in these accounts at some particular time.

The chart of accounts, even for a relatively small business, normally contains 100 or more accounts. Larger business organisations need thousands of accounts. The larger the number, the more likely that the accounts are given number codes according to some scheme – all assets may be in the 100–300 range, all liabilities in the 400–500 range, and so on. (See Book II Chapter 3 for more on the chart of accounts.)

As a business owner, you should make sure that the person in charge of accounting (or perhaps an outside chartered accountant) reviews the chart of accounts periodically to determine whether the accounts are up-to-date and adequate for the business's needs. Over time, income tax rules change, the company may go into new lines of business, the company could decide to offer additional employee benefits and so on. Most businesses are in constant flux, and the chart of accounts has to keep up with these changes.

Standardise source document forms and procedures

Businesses move on paperwork. Whether placing an order to buy products, selling a product to a customer, or determining the earnings of an employee for the month – virtually every business transaction needs paperwork, known as *source documents.* Source documents serve as evidence of the terms and conditions agreed upon by the business and the other person or organisation that it's dealing with. Both parties receive some kind of source document. For example, for a sale at a cash register, the customer gets a sales receipt, and the business keeps a running record of all transactions in the register.

Clearly, an accounting system needs to standardise the forms and procedures for processing and recording all normal, repetitive transactions and should control the generation and handling of these source documents.

From the bookkeeping point of view, these business forms and documents are very important because they provide the input information needed for recording transactions in the business's accounts. Sloppy paperwork leads to sloppy accounting records, and sloppy accounting records just won't do when the time comes to prepare tax returns and financial statements.

Check out a business office-supply store to see the kinds of forms that you can buy right off the shelf. You can find many – maybe all – of the basic forms and documents that you need for recording business transactions, although most firms have to design at least some of their own forms. Also, personal computer accounting software packages (see Appendix B for more detail) provide templates for common business forms.

Employ competent, trained personnel

What good is meticulously collecting source documents if the information on those documents isn't entered into your system correctly? You shouldn't try to save a few pounds by hiring the lowest-paid people you can find. Book-keepers and accountants, like all other employees in a business, should have the skills and knowledge needed to perform their functions. No-brainer, right? Well, determining what that level is *can* be difficult. Here are some guidelines for choosing the right people to enter and manipulate your business's data and for making sure that those people *remain* the right people:

- **University degree:** Many accountants in business organisations have a degree in accounting. However, as you move down the accounting department you find that more and more employees do not have a degree and perhaps even haven't taken any courses in accounting.

- **ACA, ACCA, or CIMA:** The main professional accounting credentials are: ACA sponsored by the Institute of Chartered Accountants; ACCA sponsored by the Association of Chartered Certified Accountants; and CIMA sponsored by the Chartered Institute of Management Accountants. All of these qualifications are evidence that the person has passed tough exams and has a good understanding of business accounting and income tax. The Association of Chartered Certified Accountants (go to www. accaglobal.com and click on 'Public Interest' and 'Find an Accountant') and The Institute of Chartered Accountants (www.icaewfirms.co.uk) have online directories of qualified accountants searchable by name, useful if you have a personal recommendation from a colleague you respect; location if you just want someone nearby; the business sector you are in, which can be handy if you need to tap into specialist skills; or any specific accountancy skills or knowledge you are looking for.

✔ **Accounting Technicians**: Assist chartered accountants in their work, or can themselves after further study join a chartered institute. The association's Web site (go to `www.aat.org.uk` and click on 'employers' and 'recruitment') provides tips on how to find accountant and guidance on pay structures.

✔ **Bookkeepers:** These are lowest cost players in this game doing the basic entry work covering anything from simply recording the transactions in your books, through to producing accounts, preparing the VAT return or doing the Payroll. The International Association of Book-keepers (IAB), (`www.iab.org.uk`) and the Institute of Certified Bookkeepers (`www.book-keepers.org`), offer free matching services to help small businesses find a bookkeeper to suit their particular needs.

✔ **Continuing education:** Many short-term courses, e-learning, and home-study programmes are available at very reasonable costs for keeping up on the latest accounting developments. Accountancy bodies that give practising certificates which allow accountants to work with businesses in public practice will expect them to take continuing education in approved courses in order to keep their practising certificates.

✔ **Integrity:** What's possibly the most important quality to look for is also the hardest to judge. Bookkeepers and accountants need to be honest people because of the amount of control they have over your business's financial records.

Book II

Accounting Basics

Protect the family jewels: internal controls

Every accounting system should establish and vigorously enforce *internal controls* – basically, additional forms and procedures over and above what's strictly needed to move operations along. These additional controls serve to deter and detect errors (honest mistakes) and all forms of dishonesty by employees, customers, and suppliers. Internal controls are like a public weighbridge that makes sure that a heavy goods vehicle's load doesn't exceed the limits and that the vehicle has a valid licence. You're just checking that your staff is playing by the rules.

For example, to prevent or minimise shoplifting, most retailers now have video surveillance, tags that set off the alarms if the customer leaves the store with the tag still on the product, and so on. Likewise, a business has to implement certain procedures and forms to prevent, as much as possible, any theft, embezzlement, scams and fraud (and simple mistakes) by its own employees.

In our experience, smaller businesses tend to think that they're immune to embezzlement and fraud by their loyal and trusted employees. Yet a recent study found that small businesses are hit the hardest by fraud and usually can least afford the consequences. Your business, too, should put checks and balances into place to discourage dishonest practices and to uncover any fraud and theft as soon as possible. For example, virtually every retailer that deals with the general public installs protections against shoplifting. Likewise, every business should guard against 'internal shoplifting' or fraud by its employees.

Keep the scale in balance: Double-entry accounting

A business needs to be sure that *both* sides of the economic exchange are recorded for all its transactions. Economic exchanges involve a give and take, or something given for something received. Businesses (and other entities as well) use the *double-entry accounting method* to make sure that both sides of their transactions are recorded and to keep their books in balance. This method, which has been used for hundreds of years, involves recording certain changes as debits and the counterbalancing changes as credits. See 'Seeing Double with Double-Entry Bookkeeping,' later in this chapter, for more details.

Check your figures

Like a pilot before take-off, an accountant should have a clear checklist to follow at the end of each period and especially at the end of the accounting year. Two main things have to be done at the end of the period:

- **Normal, routine *adjusting entries* for certain expenses:** For example, depreciation isn't a transaction as such and therefore hasn't been recorded as an expense in the flow of transactions recorded in the day-to-day bookkeeping process. (Book III Chapter 1 explains depreciation expense.) Similarly, certain other expenses and some revenues may not have been associated with a specific transaction and will not have been recorded. These kinds of adjustments are necessary for providing complete and accurate reports.

- *Careful sweep of all matters* **to check for other developments that may affect the accuracy of the accounts:** For example, the company may have discontinued a product line. The remaining stock of these products may have to be removed from the asset account, with a loss recorded in the period. Or the company may have settled a long-standing lawsuit, and the amount of damages needs to be recorded. Layoffs and severance packages are another example of what the chief accountant needs to look for before preparing reports.

Lest you still think of accounting as dry and dull, let us tell you that end-of-period accounting procedures can stir up controversy of the heated-debate variety. These procedures require that the accountant make decisions and judgments that upper management may not agree with. For example, the accountant may suggest recording major losses that would put a big dent in the profit for the year or cause the business to report a loss. The outside auditor (assuming that the business has an audit of its financial statements) often gets in the middle of the argument. These kinds of debates are precisely why you business owners need to know some accounting: to hold up your end of the argument and participate in the great sport of yelling and name-calling – strictly on a professional basis, of course.

Book II

Accounting
Basics

Keep good records

The happy trails that accountants like to walk are called *audit trails.* Good bookkeeping systems leave good audit trails. An audit trail is a clear-cut path of the sequence of events leading up to an entry in the accounts; an accountant starts with the source documents and follows through the bookkeeping steps in recording transactions to reconstruct this path. Even if a business doesn't have an outside accountant do an annual audit, the firm's management accountant has frequent occasion to go back to the source documents and either verify certain information in the accounts or reconstruct the information in a different manner. For example, suppose that a salesperson is claiming some suspicious-looking travel expenses; the accountant would probably want to go through all this person's travel and entertainment reimbursements for the past year.

If HM Revenue and Customs comes in for a field audit of your business, you'd better have good audit trails to substantiate all your expense deductions and sales revenue for the year. There are rules about saving source documents for a reasonable period of time, usually at least five years, and having a well-defined process for making bookkeeping entries and keeping accounts. Think twice before throwing away source documents. Also, ask your accountant to demonstrate, and lay out for your inspection, the audit trails for key transactions – such as cash collections, sales, cash disbursements, stock purchases, and so on. Even in computer-based accounting systems, the importance of audit trails is recognised. Well-designed computer programs provide the ability to backtrack through the sequence of steps in the recording of specific transactions. HM Revenue and Customs (go to www.hmrc.gov.uk and click on 'Businesses and corporations') Web site has everything concerning the rules on what books to keep and how long for. For any topic not listed use the Search pane at the top of the Home page.

Look out for unusual events

Business owners should encourage their accountants to be alert to anything out of the ordinary that may require attention. Suppose that the debtor balance for a particular customer is rapidly increasing – that is, the customer is buying more and more from your company on credit but isn't paying for these purchases quickly. Maybe the customer has switched more of his or her company's purchases to your business and is buying more from you only because he or she is buying less from other businesses. But maybe the customer is planning to stuff your business and take off without paying his or her debts. Or maybe the customer is secretly planning to go into bankruptcy soon and is stockpiling products before the company's credit rating heads south. To some extent, accountants have to act as the eyes and ears of the business. Of course, that's one of your main functions as business owner, but your accountant can play an important role as well.

Design truly useful accounting reports

We have to be careful in this section; we have strong opinions on this matter. We have seen too many hit-and-miss accounting reports to owners – difficult to decipher and not very useful or relevant to the owner's decision-making needs and control functions.

Part of the problem lies with owners themselves. As a business owner, have you told your accounting staff what you need to know, when you need it, and how to present it in the most efficient manner?

On the other hand, accountants bear a good share of the blame for the poor reports. Accountants should proactively study the owner's decision-making responsibilities and provide the information that is most useful, presented in the most easily digestible manner.

 So what's the answer for an owner who receives poorly formatted reports? Demand a report format that suits your needs! See Book IV Chapter 1 for a useful profit analysis model (and make sure that your accountant reads that chapter as well).

Understanding Accounting Methods

Many not-for-profit organisations, such as sports clubs, have very simple accounting needs. These organisations aren't responsible to shareholders to account for their financial performance, though they are responsible to their members for the safe custody of their subscriptions and other funds. Consequently, the accounting focus isn't on measuring profit but more on accounting for receipts and payments. For these cases, a simple cash-based accounting system may well suffice, which allows for only cash transactions – no provisions are made for giving or receiving credit.

However, complications may arise when members don't pay their subscriptions during the current accounting year and the organisation needs to reflect this situation in its accounts. In this case, the accrual accounting method is best.

A few businesses operate on a cash basis, and their owners can put forward a good case for using this method. However most accountants and HM Customs & Revenue don't accept this method as it doesn't give a very accurate measure of profit (or loss) for accounting periods.

Book II

Accounting Basics

In the next sections, we briefly explain how cash-based accounting works before dismissing it in favour of the more accepted and acceptable accrual method.

Realising the limitations of cash-based accounting

With *cash-based accounting,* you record all transactions in the books when cash actually changes hands, which means when the business receives cash payment from customers or pays out cash for purchases or other services. Cash receipt or payment can be in the form of cash, cheque, credit card, electronic transfer, or other means used to pay for an item.

Cash-based accounting can't be used when a business sells products on credit and collects the money from the customer at a later date. No provision exists in the cash-based accounting method to record and track money due from customers at some point in the future.

This situation also applies for purchases. With the cash-based accounting method, the business only records the purchase of supplies or goods that are to be sold later when it actually pays cash. When the business buys goods on credit to be paid later, it doesn't record the transaction until the cash is actually paid out.

Depending on the size of your business, you may want to start out with cash-based accounting. Many small businesses run by a sole proprietor or a small group of partners use the easier cash-based accounting system. When your business model is simple – you carry no stock, start and finish each job within a single accounting period, and pay and get paid within this period – the cash accounting method can work for you. But as your business grows, you may find it necessary to switch to accrual accounting in order to track revenues and expenses more accurately, and to satisfy the requirements of the external accountant and HM Revenue & Customs. The same basic argument also applies to not-for-profit organisations.

Cash-based accounting does a good job of tracking cash flow, but the system does a poor job of matching revenues earned with money laid out for expenses. This deficiency is a problem particularly when, as often happens, a business buys products in one month and sells those products in the next month. For example, you buy products in June paying £1,000 cash, with the intent to sell them that same month. You don't sell the products until July, which is when you receive cash for the sales. When you close the books at the end of June, you have to show the £1,000 expense with no revenue to offset it, meaning you have a loss that month. When you sell the products for £1,500 in July, you have a £1,500 profit. So, your monthly report for June shows a £1,000 loss, and your monthly report for July shows a £1,500 profit, when in reality you had revenues of £500 over the two months. Using cash-based accounting you can never be sure that you have an accurate measure of profit or loss – but as cash-based accounting is for not-for-profit organisations, this is not surprising.

Because accrual accounting is the only accounting method acceptable to accountants and HM Revenue & Customs, we concentrate on this method throughout the book. If you choose to use cash-based accounting because you have a cash only business and a simple trading model, don't panic: Most of the bookkeeping information here is still useful, but you don't need to maintain some of the accounts, such as Accounts Receivable and Accounts Payable, because you aren't recording transactions until cash actually changes hands. When you're using a cash-based accounting system and you start to sell things on credit, though, you better have a way to track what people owe you.

Our advice is to use the accrual accounting method right from the beginning. When your business grows and your business model changes, you need the more sophisticated and legally required accrual accounting.

Recording right away with accrual accounting

With *accrual accounting,* you record all transactions in the books when they occur, even when no cash changes hands. For example, when you sell on credit, you record the transaction immediately and enter it into a Debtors account until you receive payment. When you buy goods on credit, you immediately enter the transaction into a Creditors account until you pay out cash.

Like cash-based accounting, accrual accounting has drawbacks, doing a good job of matching revenues and expenses, but a poor job of tracking cash. Because you record income when the transaction occurs and not when you collect the cash, your profit and loss statement can look great even when you don't have cash in the bank. For example, suppose you're running a contracting business and completing jobs on a daily basis. You can record the revenue upon completion of the job even when you haven't yet collected the cash. When your customers are slow to pay, you may end up with lots of income but little cash. Remember – *never* confuse profit and cash. In the short term cash flow is often more important than profit, but in the long term profit becomes more important. But don't worry just yet; in Book II Chapter 6, we tell you how to manage Accounts Receivable so that you don't run out of cash because of slow-paying customers.

Many businesses that use the accrual accounting method monitor cash flow on a weekly basis to be sure they have enough cash on hand to operate the business. If your business is seasonal, such as a landscaping business with little to do during the winter months, you can establish short-term lines of credit through your bank to maintain cash flow through the lean times.

Seeing Double with Double-Entry Bookkeeping

All businesses use *double-entry bookkeeping* to keep their books, whether they use the cash-based accounting method or the accrual accounting method. Double-entry bookkeeping – so-called because you enter all transactions twice – helps minimise errors and increase the chance that your books balance.

When it comes to double-entry bookkeeping, the key formula for the balance sheet (Assets = Liabilities + Capital) plays a major role.

In the bookkeeping world, you use a combination of debits and credits to adjust the balance of accounts. You may think of a debit as a subtraction, because debits usually mean a decrease in your bank balance. On the other hand, you probably like finding unexpected credits in your bank or credit card, because they mean more money has been added to the account in your favour. Now forget everything you know about debits or credits. In the world of bookkeeping, their meanings aren't so simple.

The only definite thing when it comes to debits and credits in the bookkeeping world is that a debit is on the left side of a transaction and a credit is on the right side of a transaction. Everything beyond that can get very muddled. We show you the basics of debits and credits in this chapter, but don't worry if you find these concepts difficult to grasp at first.

Before we get into all the technical mumbo jumbo of double-entry bookkeeping, here's an example of the practice in action. Suppose you purchase a new desk for your office that costs £1,500. This transaction actually has two parts: You spend an asset – cash – to buy another asset – furniture. So, you must adjust two accounts in your business's books: the Cash account and the Furniture account. The transaction in a bookkeeping entry is as follows (we talk more about how to do initial bookkeeping entries in Book II Chapter 3):

Account	Debit	Credit
Furniture	£1,500	
Cash		£1,500

To purchase a new desk for the office.

In this transaction, you record the accounts impacted by the transaction. The debit increases the value of the Furniture account, and the credit decreases the value of the Cash account. For this transaction, both accounts impacted are Asset accounts so, looking at how the balance sheet is affected, you can see that the only changes are to the asset side of the balance sheet equation:

Assets = Liabilities + Capital

Furniture increase = No change to this side of the equation

Cash decrease

In this case, the books stay in balance because the exact pounds sterling amount that increases the value of your Furniture account decreases the value of your Cash account. At the bottom of any journal entry, include a brief explanation that explains the purpose for the entry. In the first example, we indicate this entry was 'To purchase a new desk for the office'.

To show you how you record a transaction that impacts both sides of the balance sheet equation, here's an example on recording the purchase of stock. Suppose that you purchase £5,000 worth of widgets on credit. (Have you always wondered what widgets were? Can't help you. They're just commonly used in accounting examples to represent something purchased where what is purchased is of no real significance.) These new widgets add value to your Stock Asset account and also add value to your Accounts Payable account. (Remember, the Accounts Payable account is a Liability account where you track bills that need to be paid at some point in the future.) The bookkeeping transaction for your widget purchase looks as follows:

Account	Debit	Credit
Stock	£5,000	
Accounts Payable		£5,000

To purchase widgets for sale to customers.

This transaction affects the balance sheet equation as follows:

Assets = Liabilities + Capital

Stock increases = Accounts Payable increases + No change

In this case, the books stay in balance because both sides of the equation increase by £5,000.

You can see from the two example transactions how double-entry bookkeeping helps to keep your books in balance – as long as you make sure that each entry into the books is balanced. Balancing your entries may look simple here, but sometimes bookkeeping entries can get very complex when the transaction impacts more than two accounts.

Don't worry, you don't have to understand double-entry bookkeeping totally now. We show you how to enter transactions throughout the book depending upon the type of transaction being recorded. We're just giving you a quick overview to introduce the subject right now.

Book II

Accounting Basics

Differentiating Debits and Credits

Because bookkeeping's debits and credits are different from the ones you're used to encountering, you're probably wondering how you're supposed to know whether a debit or credit increases or decreases an account.

Believe it or not, identifying the difference becomes second nature as you start making regular entries in your bookkeeping system. But to make things easier for you, Table 1-1 is a chart that bookkeepers and accountants commonly use. Yep, everyone needs help sometimes.

Double-entry bookkeeping goes way back

No one's really sure who invented double-entry bookkeeping. The first person to put the practice on paper was Benedetto Cotrugli in 1458, but mathematician and Franciscan monk Luca Pacioli is most often credited with developing double-entry bookkeeping. Although Pacioli is called the Father of Accounting, accounting actually occupies only one of five sections of his book, *Everything About Arithmetic, Geometry and Proportions,* which was published in 1494.

Pacioli didn't actually *invent* double-entry bookkeeping; he just described the method used by merchants in Venice during the Italian Renaissance period. He's most famous for his warning to bookkeepers: 'A person should not go to sleep at night until the debits equal the credits!'

Table 1-1	How Credits and Debits Impact Your Accounts	
Account Type	*Debits*	*Credits*
Assets	Increase	Decrease
Liabilities	Decrease	Increase
Income	Decrease	Increase
Expenses	Increase	Decrease

Copy Table 1-1 and post it at your desk when you start keeping your own books (a bit like the chief accountant in the nearby 'Sharing a secret' sidebar). We guarantee that the table helps to keep your debits and credits straight.

Balanced books don't necessarily mean correct balances. If debits equal credits, the entry for the transaction is correct as far as recording equal amounts on both sides of the transaction. However, even if the debits equal the credits, other errors are possible. The bookkeeper may have recorded the debits and credits in a wrong account, or may have entered wrong amounts, or may have missed recording an entry altogether. Having balanced books simply means that the total of accounts with debit balances equals the total of accounts with credit balances. The important thing is whether the books (the accounts) have *correct* balances, which depends on whether all transactions and other developments have been recorded and accounted for correctly.

Sharing a secret

Don't feel embarrassed if you forget which side the debits go on and which side the credits go on. One often-told story is of a young clerk in an accounts office plucking up courage to ask the chief accountant, who was retiring that day, why for 30 years he had at the start of each day opened up his drawer and read the contents of a piece of paper before starting work. The chief accountant at first was reluctant to spill the beans, but ultimately decided he had to pass on his secret – and who better than to an up-and-coming clerk. Swearing the young clerk to secrecy, he took out the piece of paper and showed it to him. The paper read: 'Debit on the left and Credit on the right.'

Chapter 2

Outlining Your Financial Roadmap with a Chart of Accounts

In This Chapter

▶ Introducing the Chart of Accounts

▶ Looking at balance sheet accounts

▶ Going over the profit and loss

▶ Creating your own Chart of Accounts

*C*an you imagine what a mess your cheque book would be if you didn't record each cheque you write? Like us, you've probably forgotten to record a cheque or two on occasion, but you certainly found out quickly enough when an important payment bounced as a result. Yikes!

Keeping the books of a business can be a lot more difficult than maintaining a personal cheque book. Each business transaction must be carefully recorded to make sure that it goes into the right account. This careful bookkeeping gives you an effective tool for figuring out how well the business is doing financially.

As a bookkeeper, you need a roadmap to help you determine where to record all those transactions. This roadmap is called the Chart of Accounts. In this chapter, we tell you how to set up the Chart of Accounts, which includes many different accounts. We also review the types of transactions you enter into each type of account in order to track the key parts of any business – assets, liabilities, capital, income, and expenses.

Getting to Know the Chart of Accounts

The *Chart of Accounts* is the roadmap that a business creates to organise its financial transactions. After all, you can't record a transaction until you know where to put it! Essentially, this chart is a list of all the accounts a business has, organised in a specific order; each account has a description that includes the type of account and the types of transactions to be entered into that account. Every business creates its own Chart of Accounts based on how the business is operated, so you're unlikely to find two businesses with the exact same Charts of Accounts.

However, some basic organisational and structural characteristics are common to all Charts of Accounts. The organisation and structure are designed around two key financial reports: the *balance sheet,* which shows what your business owns and what it owes, and the *profit and loss statement,* which shows how much money your business took in from sales and how much money it spent to generate those sales. (You can find out more about profit and loss statements in Book III Chapter 1 and balance sheets statements in Book III Chapter 2.)

The Chart of Accounts starts with the balance sheet accounts, which include the following:

- ✔ **Fixed Assets:** Includes all accounts that show things the business owns that have a lifespan of more than 12 months, such as buildings, furniture, plant and equipment, motor vehicles, and office equipment.

- ✔ **Current Assets:** Includes all accounts that show things the business owns and expects to use in the next 12 months, such as cash, Accounts Receivable (money collected from customers), prepayments, and stock.

- ✔ **Current Liabilities:** Includes all accounts that show debts the business must repay over the next 12 months, such as Accounts Payable (bills from suppliers, contractors, and consultants), hire purchase and other loans, VAT and income/corporation tax, accruals, and credit cards payable.

- ✔ **Long-Term Liabilities:** Includes all accounts that show debts the business must pay over a period of time longer than the next 12 months, such as mortgages repayable and longer-term loans that are repayable.

- ✔ **Capital:** Includes all accounts that show the owners of the business and their claims against the business's assets, including any money invested in the business, any money taken out of the business, and any earnings that have been reinvested in the business.

The rest of the chart is filled with profit and loss statement accounts, which include the following:

- ✔ **Income:** Includes all accounts that track sales of goods and services as well as revenue generated for the business by other means.

- ✔ **Cost of Goods Sold:** Includes all accounts that track the direct costs involved in selling the business's goods or services.

- ✔ **Expenses:** Includes all accounts that track expenses related to running the businesses that aren't directly tied to the sale of individual products or services.

When developing the Chart of Accounts, start by listing all the Asset accounts, the Liability accounts, the Capital accounts, the Revenue accounts, and finally, the Expense accounts. All these accounts feed into two statements: the balance sheet and the profit and loss statement.

In this chapter, we review the key account types found in most businesses, but this list isn't cast in stone. You need to develop an account list that makes the most sense for how you're operating your business and the financial information you want to track. As we explore the various accounts that make up the Chart of Accounts, we point out how the structure may differ for different types of businesses.

The Chart of Accounts is a money management tool that helps you follow your business transactions, so set it up in a way that provides you with the financial information you need to make smart business decisions. You're probably going to tweak the accounts in your chart annually and, if necessary, you may add accounts during the year if you find something for which you want more detailed tracking. You can add accounts during the year, but don't delete accounts until the end of a 12-month reporting period.

Book II

Accounting Basics

Starting with the Balance Sheet Accounts

The first part of the Chart of Accounts is made up of balance sheet accounts, which break down into the following three categories:

- ✔ **Asset:** These accounts are used to show what the business owns. Assets include cash on hand, furniture, buildings, vehicles, and so on.

- ✔ **Liability:** These accounts show what the business owes, or more specifically claims that lenders have against the business's assets. For example, mortgages on buildings and lines of credit are two common types of liabilities. Also, a mortgage (a legal charge) is a good example of a claim that the lender (bank or building society) has over a business asset (in this case the premises being bought through the mortgage).

- ✔ **Capital:** These accounts show what the owners put into the business and the claims the owners have against the business's assets. For example, shareholders are business owners that have claims against the business's assets.

The balance sheet accounts, and the financial report they make up, are so-called because they have to *balance* out. The value of the assets must be equal to the claims made against those assets. (Remember, these claims are liabilities made by lenders and capital made by owners.)

We discuss the balance sheet in greater detail in Book III Chapter 2, including how to prepare and use it. This section, however, examines the basic components of the balance sheet, as reflected in the Chart of Accounts.

Tackling assets

The accounts that track what the business owns – its assets – are always the first category on the chart. The two types of Asset accounts are fixed assets and current assets.

Fixed assets

Fixed assets are assets that you anticipate your business is going to use for more than 12 months. This section lists some of the most common fixed assets, starting with the key accounts related to buildings and business premises that the business owns:

- ✔ **Land and Buildings:** This account shows the value of the land and buildings the business owns. The initial value is based on the cost at the time of purchase, but this asset can be (and often is) revalued as property prices increase over time. Because of the virtually indestructible nature of this asset it doesn't depreciate at a fast rate. *Depreciation* is an accounting method that shows an asset is being used up. We talk more about depreciation in Book IV Chapter 5.

- ✔ **Accumulated Depreciation – Land and Buildings:** This account shows the cumulative amount this asset has depreciated over its useful lifespan.

- ✔ **Leasehold Improvements:** This account shows the value of improvements to buildings or other facilities that a business leases rather than purchases. Frequently when a business leases a property, it must pay for any improvements necessary in order to use that property as the business requires. For example, when a business leases a shop, the space leased is likely to be an empty shell or filled with shelving and other items that don't match the particular needs of the business. As with land and buildings, leasehold improvements depreciate as the value of the asset ages – usually over the remaining life of the lease.

- ✔ **Accumulated Depreciation – Leasehold Improvements:** This account tracks the cumulative amount depreciated for leasehold improvements.

The following are the types of accounts for smaller long-term assets, such as vehicles and furniture:

- ✔ **Vehicles:** This account shows any cars, lorries, or other vehicles owned by the business. The initial value of any vehicle is listed in this account based on the total cost paid to put the vehicle into service. Sometimes this value is more than the purchase price if additions were needed to make the vehicle usable for the particular type of business. For example, when a business provides transportation for the handicapped and must add additional equipment to a vehicle in order to serve the needs of its customers, that additional equipment is added to the value of the vehicle. Vehicles also depreciate through their useful lifespan.

✔ **Accumulated Depreciation – Vehicles:** This account shows the depreciation of all vehicles owned by the business.

✔ **Furniture and Fixtures:** This account shows any furniture or fixtures purchased for use in the business. The account includes the value of all chairs, desks, store fixtures, and shelving needed to operate the business. The value of the furniture and fixtures in this account is based on the cost of purchasing these items. These items are depreciated during their useful lifespan.

✔ **Accumulated Depreciation – Furniture and Fixtures:** This account shows the accumulated depreciation of all furniture and fixtures.

✔ **Plant and Equipment:** This account shows equipment that was purchased for use for more than 12 months, such as process related machinery, computers, copiers, tools, and cash registers. The value of the equipment is based on the cost to purchase these items. Equipment is also depreciated to show that over time it gets used up and must be replaced.

✔ **Accumulated Depreciation – Plant and Equipment:** This account tracks the accumulated depreciation of all the equipment.

The following accounts show the fixed assets that you can't touch (accountants refer to these as *intangible assets*), but that still represent things of value owned by the business, such as start-up costs, patents, and copyrights. The accounts that track them include:

✔ **Start-up Costs:** This account shows the initial start-up expenses to get the business off the ground. Many such expenses can't be set off against business profits in the first year. For example, special licences and legal fees must be written off over a number of years using a method similar to depreciation, called *amortisation,* which is also tracked.

✔ **Amortisation – Start-up Costs:** This account shows the accumulated amortisation of these costs during the period in which they're being written-off.

✔ **Patents:** This account shows the costs associated with *patents,* grants made by governments that guarantee to the inventor of a product or service the exclusive right to make, use, and sell that product or service over a set period of time. Like start-up costs, patent costs are amortised. The value of this asset is based on the expenses the business incurs to get the right to patent its product.

✔ **Amortisation – Patents:** This account shows the accumulated amortisation of a business's patents.

Book II

Accounting Basics

- ✔ **Copyrights:** This account shows the costs incurred to establish copyrights, the legal rights given to an author, playwright, publisher, or any other distributor of a publication or production for a unique work of literature, music, drama, or art. This legal right expires after a set number of years, so its value is amortised as the copyright gets used up.

- ✔ **Goodwill:** This account is needed only if a business buys another business for more than the actual value of its tangible assets. Goodwill reflects the intangible value of this purchase for things like business reputation, store locations, customer base, and other items that increase the value of the business bought. The value of goodwill is not everlasting, and so like other intangible assets, must be amortised.

- ✔ **Research and Development:** This account shows the investment the business has made in future products and services, which may not see the light of day for several years. These costs are written off (amortised) over the life of the products and services as and when they reach the marketplace.

If you hold a lot of assets that aren't of great value, you can also set up an 'Other Assets' account to show those assets that don't have significant business value. Any asset you show in the Other Assets account that you later want to show individually can be shifted to its own account.

Current assets

Current assets are the key assets that your business uses up within a 12-month period and are likely not to be there the next year. The accounts that reflect current assets on the Chart of Accounts are:

- ✔ **Current account:** This account is the business's primary bank account used for operating activities, such as depositing receipts and paying expenses. Some businesses have more than one account in this category; for example, a business with many divisions may have an account for each division.

- ✔ **Deposit account:** This account is used for surplus cash. Any cash not earmarked for an immediate plan is deposited in an interest-earning savings account. In this way, the cash earns interest while the business decides what to do with it.

- ✔ **Cash on Hand:** This account is used to record any cash kept at retail stores or in the office. In retail stores, cash must be kept in registers in order to provide change to customers. In the office, petty cash is often kept for immediate cash needs that pop up from time to time. This account helps you keep track of the cash held outside the various bank and deposit accounts.

- ✔ **Debtors (also referred to as Accounts Receivable):** This account shows the customers who still owe you money, when you offer your products or services to customers on credit (by which we mean *your* own credit system).

Debtors isn't used to show purchases made on other types of credit cards, because your business gets paid directly by banks, not customers, when credit cards are used. Check out Book II Chapter 6 to read more about this scenario and the corresponding type of account.

✔ **Stock:** This account shows the value of the products you have on hand to sell to your customers. The value of the assets in this account varies depending upon the way you decide to track the flow of stock into and out of the business. We discuss stock valuation and recording in greater detail in Book II Chapter 6.

✔ **Prepayments:** This account shows goods or services you pay for in advance: The payment is credited as it gets used up each month. For example, say you prepay your property insurance on a building you own one year in advance — each month you reduce the amount that you prepaid by one-twelfth as the prepayment is used up.

Book II

Accounting Basics

Depending upon the type of business you're setting up, you may have other current Asset accounts to account for. For example, say you're starting a service business in consulting: You're likely to have a Consulting account for tracking cash collected for those services. If you run a business in which you barter assets (such as trading your services for paper goods from a paper goods company), you may add a Barter account for business-to-business barter.

Laying out your liabilities

After you deal with assets, the next stop on the bookkeeping journey is the accounts that show what your business owes to others. These others can include suppliers from which you buy products or supplies, financial institutions from which you borrow money, and anyone else who lends money to your business. Like assets, liabilities are lumped into current liabilities and long-term liabilities.

Current liabilities

Current liabilities are debts due in the next 12 months. Some of the most common types of current liabilities accounts that appear on the Chart of Accounts are as follows:

✔ **Creditors (also referred to as Accounts Payable):** This account shows money the business owes to suppliers, contractors, and consultants that must be paid in less than 12 months. Most of these liabilities must be paid in 30 to 90 days from initial invoicing.

✔ **Value Added Tax (VAT):** This account shows your VAT liability. You may not think of VAT as a liability, but because the business collects the tax from the customer and doesn't pay it immediately to HM Customs &

Revenue, the taxes collected become a liability. Of course you're entitled to offset the VAT that the business has been charged on its purchases before making a net payment. A business usually collects VAT throughout the month and then pays the net amount due on a quarterly basis. We discuss paying VAT in greater detail in Book VI Chapter 4.

✔ **Accrued Payroll Taxes:** This account shows payroll taxes, such as PAYE and National Insurance, collected from employees and the business itself, which have to be paid over to HM Customs & Revenue. Businesses don't have to pay these taxes over immediately and may pay payroll taxes on a monthly basis. We discuss how to handle payroll taxes in Book V Chapter 2.

✔ **Credit Cards Payable:** This account shows all credit card accounts to which the business is liable. Most businesses use credit cards as short-term debt and pay them off completely at the end of each month, but some smaller businesses carry credit card balances over a longer period of time. Concerning your Chart of Accounts, you can set up one Credit Card Payable account, but you may want to set up a separate account for each card your business holds to improve your ability to track credit card usage.

The way you set up your current liabilities – and how many individual accounts you establish – depends upon the level of detail in which you want to track each type of liability.

Long-term liabilities

Long-term liabilities are debts due in more than 12 months. The number of long-term Liability accounts you maintain on your Chart of Accounts depends on your debt structure. For example, if you have several different loans then set up an account for each one. The most common type of long-term Liability accounts is Loans Payable. This account tracks any long-term loans, such as a mortgage on your business building. Most businesses have separate Loans Payable accounts for each of their long-term loans. For example, you can have 'Loans Payable – Mortgage Bank' for your building and 'Loans Payable – Car Bank' for your vehicle loan.

In addition to any separate long-term debt that you may want to track in its own account, you may also want to set up an account called *Other Liabilities*. You can use this account to track types of debt that are so insignificant to the business that you don't think they need their own accounts.

Controlling the capital

Every business is owned by somebody. *Capital accounts* track owners' contributions to the business as well as their share of ownership. For a limited company, ownership is tracked by the sale of individual shares because each stockholder owns a portion of the business. In smaller businesses owned by one person or a group of people, capital is tracked using Capital and Drawing accounts. Here are the basic Capital accounts that appear in the Chart of Accounts:

- ✔ **Ordinary Share Capital:** This account reflects the value of outstanding ordinary shares sold to investors. A business calculates this value by multiplying the number of shares issued by the value of each share of stock. Only limited companies need to establish this account.

- ✔ **Retained Earnings:** This account tracks the profits or losses accumulated since a business opened. At the end of each year, the profit or loss calculated on the profit and loss statement is used to adjust the value of this account. For example, if a business made a £100,000 profit after tax in the past year, the Retained Earnings account is increased by that amount; if the business lost £100,000, that amount is subtracted from this account. Any dividends paid to shareholders reduce the profit figure transferred to Retained Earnings each year.

- ✔ **Capital:** This account is only necessary for small, unincorporated businesses, such as sole traders or partnerships. The Capital account reflects the amount of initial money the business owner contributed to the business as well as any additional contributions made after initial start-up. The value of this account is based on cash contributions and other assets contributed by the business owner, such as equipment, vehicles, or buildings. When a small company has several different partners, each partner gets his own Capital account to track his contributions.

- ✔ **Drawing:** This account is only necessary for businesses that aren't incorporated. The Drawing account tracks any money that a business owner takes out of the business. If the business has several partners, each partner gets his own Drawing account to track what he takes out of the business.

Keeping an Eye on the Profit and Loss Statement

The profit and loss statement is made up of two types of accounts:

- ✔ **Revenue:** These accounts track all income coming into the business, including sales, interest earned on savings, and any other methods used to generate income.

- ✔ **Expenses:** These accounts track all costs that a business incurs in order to keep itself afloat.

The bottom line of the profit and loss statement shows whether your business made a profit or a loss for a specified period of time. We discuss how to prepare and use a profit and loss statement in greater detail in Book III Chapter 1.

This section examines the various accounts that make up the profit and loss statement portion of the Chart of Accounts.

Recording the profit you make

Accounts that show revenue coming into the business are first up in the profit and loss statement portion of the Chart of Accounts. If you choose to offer discounts or accept returns, that activity also falls within the revenue grouping. The most common income accounts are:

- **Sales of Goods or Services:** This account, which appears at the top of every profit and loss statement, shows all the money that the business earns selling its products, services, or both.

- **Sales Discounts:** This account shows any reductions to the full price of merchandise (necessary because most businesses offer discounts to encourage sales).

- **Sales Returns:** This account shows transactions related to returns, when a customer returns a product.

When you examine a profit and loss statement from a business other than the one you own or are working for, you usually see the following accounts summarised as one line item called *Revenue* or *Net Revenue.* Because not all income is generated by sales of products or services, other income accounts that may appear on a Chart of Accounts include the following:

- **Other Income:** This account shows income a business generates from a source other than its primary business activity. For example, a business that encourages recycling, and earns income from the items recycled, records that income in this account.

- **Interest Income:** This account shows any income earned by collecting interest on a business's savings accounts. If the business lends money to employees or to another business and earns interest on that money, that interest is recorded in this account as well.

Recording the cost of goods sold

Of course, before you can sell a product, you must spend money to buy or make that product. The type of account used to track the money spent is called a Cost of Goods Sold account. The most common Cost of Goods Sold accounts are:

✔ **Purchases:** This account shows the purchases of all items you plan to sell.

✔ **Purchase Discount:** This account shows the discounts you may receive from suppliers when you pay for your purchase quickly. For example, a business may give you a 2 per cent discount on your purchase when you pay the bill in 10 days rather than wait until the end of the 30-day payment period.

✔ **Purchase Returns:** This account shows the value of any returns when you're unhappy with a product you bought.

✔ **Freight Charges:** This account shows any charges related to shipping items you purchase for later sale. You may or may not want to keep this detail.

✔ **Other Sales Costs:** This account is a catchall account for anything that doesn't fit into one of the other Cost of Goods Sold accounts.

Acknowledging the other costs

Expense accounts take the cake for the longest list of individual accounts. Anything you spend on the business that can't be tied directly to the sale of an individual product falls under the Expense account category. For example, advertising a sale isn't directly tied to the sale of any one product, so the costs associated with advertising fall under the Expense account category.

The Chart of Accounts mirrors your business operations, so you decide how much detail you want to keep in your Expense accounts. Most businesses have expenses that are unique to their operations, so your list is likely to be longer than the one we present here. However, you also may find that you don't need some of these accounts. Small businesses typically have expense headings that mirror those required by HM Revenue & Customs on their self assessment returns.

On your Chart of Accounts, the Expense accounts don't have to appear in any specific order, so we list them alphabetically. The most common Expense accounts are:

✔ **Advertising:** This account shows all expenses involved in promoting a business or its products. Expenditure on newspaper, television, magazine, and radio advertising is recorded here as well as any costs incurred to print flyers and mailings to customers. Also, when a business participates in community events such as cancer walks or craft fairs, associated costs are shown in this account.

✔ **Amortisation:** This account is very similar to the depreciation account (later in this list) and shows the ongoing monthly charge for the current financial year for all your intangible assets.

✔ **Bank Service Charges:** This account shows any charges made by a bank to service a business's bank accounts.

✔ **Depreciation:** This account shows the ongoing monthly depreciation charge for the current financial year for all your fixed assets – buildings, cars, vans, furniture, and so on. Of course, when the individual depreciation values are large for each fixed asset category, you may open up individual depreciation accounts.

✔ **Dues and Subscriptions:** This account shows expenses related to business club membership or subscriptions to magazines for the business.

✔ **Equipment Rental:** This account records expenses related to renting equipment for a short-term project. For example, a business that needs to rent a van to pick up some new fixtures for its shop records that van rental in this account.

✔ **Insurance:** This account shows insurance costs. Many businesses break this account down into several accounts, such as 'Insurance – Employees Group', which records any expenses paid for employee insurance, or 'Insurance – Officer's Life', which records the cost of buying insurance to protect the life of a key owner or officer of the business. Businesses often insure their key owners and senior managers because an unexpected death, especially for a small business, may mean facing many unexpected expenses in order to keep the business's doors open. In such a case, the insurance proceeds can be used to cover those expenses.

✔ **Legal and Accounting:** This account shows the cost of legal or accounting advice.

✔ **Miscellaneous Expenses:** This account is a catchall account for expenses that don't fit into one of a business's established accounts. If certain miscellaneous expenses occur frequently, a business may choose to add an account to the Chart of Accounts and move related expenses into that new account by subtracting all related transactions from the Miscellaneous Expenses account and adding them to the new account. With this shuffle, you need to carefully balance out the adjusting transaction to avoid any errors or double counting.

✔ **Office Expenses:** This account shows any items purchased in order to run an office. For example, office supplies such as paper and pens or business cards fit in this account. As with miscellaneous expenses, a business may choose to track some office expense items in their own accounts. For example, when you find your office is using a lot of copy paper and you want to track that separately, set up a Copy Paper Expense account. Just be sure that you really need the detail because a large number of accounts can get unwieldy and hard to manage.

✔ **Payroll Taxes:** This account records any taxes paid related to employee payroll, such as Pay As You Earn (PAYE), Statutory Sick Pay (SSP), and maternity/paternity pay.

✔ **Postage:** This account shows any expenditure on stamps, express package shipping, and other shipping. If your business does a large amount of shipping through suppliers such as UPS or Federal Express, you may want to track that spending in separate accounts for each vendor. This option is particularly helpful for small businesses that sell over the Internet or through mail order sales.

✔ **Profit (or Loss) on Disposal of Fixed Assets:** This account records any profit when a business sells a fixed asset, such as a car or furniture. Make sure that you only record revenue remaining after subtracting the accumulated depreciation from the original cost of the asset.

✔ **Rent:** This account records rental costs for a business's office or retail space.

✔ **Salaries and Wages:** This account shows any money paid to employees as salary or wages.

✔ **Supplies:** This account shows any business supplies that don't fit into the category of office supplies. For example, supplies needed for the operation of retail stores are recorded using this account.

✔ **Travel and Entertainment:** This account records any expenditure on travel or entertainment for business purposes. Some businesses separate these expenses into several accounts, such as 'Travel and Entertainment – Meals'; 'Travel and Entertainment – Travel'; and 'Travel and Entertainment – Entertainment', to keep a close watch.

✔ **Telephone:** This account shows all business expenses related to the telephone and telephone calls.

✔ **Utilities:** This account shows utility costs, such as electricity, gas, and water.

✔ **Vehicles:** This account shows expenses related to the operation of business vehicles.

Book II

Accounting
Basics

Setting Up Your Chart of Accounts

You can use all the lists of accounts provided in this chapter to set up your business's own Chart of Accounts. No secret method exists for creating your own chart – just make a list of the accounts that apply to your business.

When first setting up your Chart of Accounts, don't panic if you can't think of every type of account you may need for your business. You can easily add to the Chart of Accounts at any time. Just add the account to the list and distribute the revised list to any employees who use the Chart of Accounts for recording transactions into the bookkeeping system. (Employees who code invoices or other transactions, and indicate the account to which those transactions are to be recorded, need a copy of your Chart of Accounts as well, even if they aren't involved in actual bookkeeping.)

The Chart of Accounts usually includes at least three columns:

- ✔ **Account:** Lists the account names
- ✔ **Type:** Lists the type of account – Asset, Liability, Capital, Income, Cost of Goods Sold, or Expense
- ✔ **Description:** Contains a description of the type of transaction that is to be recorded in the account

Many businesses also assign numbers to the accounts, to be used for coding charges. If your company is using a computerised system, the computer automatically assigns the account number. Otherwise, you need to plan out your own numbering system. The common number system is:

- ✔ Asset accounts: 1,000 to 1,999
- ✔ Liability accounts: 2,000 to 2,999
- ✔ Capital accounts: 3,000 to 3,999
- ✔ Sales and Cost of Goods Sold accounts: 4,000 to 4,999
- ✔ Expense accounts: 5,000 to 6,999

This numbering system matches the one used by some computerised accounting systems, so you can easily make the transition if you decide to automate your books using a computerised accounting system in the future.

One major advantage of a computerised accounting system is the number of different Charts of Accounts that have been developed based on the type of business you plan to run. When you get your computerised system, whichever accounting software you decide to use, you can review the list of chart options included with that software for the type of business you run, delete any accounts you don't want, and add any new accounts that fit your business plan.

If you're setting up your Chart of Accounts manually, be sure to leave a lot of room between accounts to add new accounts. For example, number your Current Account account 1,000 and your Accounts Receivable account 1,100. That leaves you plenty of room to add other accounts to record cash.

Figure 2-1 is a sample Chart of Accounts developed using Sage 50 Accounts, the accounts package we use throughout this book. In the sample chart, you can see the standard accounts that Sage has already set up for you.

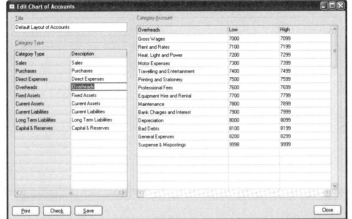

Figure 2-1:
The top
portion of
a sample
Chart of
Accounts.

Book II

**Accounting
Basics**

Chapter 3

Keeping a Paper Trail

. . . .

In This Chapter

▶ Understanding the Nominal Ledger

▶ Developing and adjusting ledger entries

▶ Creating ledgers in computerised accounting software

▶ Using journals to keep track of transactions

▶ Simplifying the journals process with computers

. . . .

*I*n this chapter we introduce you to the basics of entering financial transactions, posting transactions to your Nominal Ledger (the pinnacle of your bookkeeping system), and recording all the transaction details in your journals.

Good internal controls are a must-have for any bookkeeping system, and so we tell you how to put them in place to be sure that all your financial transactions are not just entered into the books, but entered correctly.

Looking at Ledgers

As a bookkeeper, you may dream of having a single source that you can turn to when you need to review all entries that impact your business's accounts. (Okay, so maybe you're not exactly dreaming that, but just work with me here!) The Nominal Ledger is your dream come true, because here you find a summary of transactions and a record of the accounts that those transactions impact.

The Nominal Ledger serves as the figurative eyes and ears of bookkeepers and accountants who want to know what financial transactions have taken place historically in a business. By reading the Nominal Ledger – not exactly interesting reading unless you love numbers – you can see, account by account, every transaction that has taken place in the business. (And to uncover more details about those transactions, you can turn to your business's journals, where transactions are kept on a daily basis. See later in this chapter for the low-down on journals.)

The Nominal Ledger is the master summary of your business. You can find all the transactions that ever occurred in the history of the business in the Nominal Ledger account. In just one place you can find transactions that impact Cash, Stock, Accounts Receivable, Accounts Payable, and any other account included in your business's Chart of Accounts. (See Book II Chapter 2 for more information about setting up the Chart of Accounts and the kind of transactions you can find in each account.)

Developing Entries for the Ledger

Because your business's transactions are first entered into journals you develop many of the entries for the Nominal Ledger based on information pulled from the appropriate journal. For example, cash receipts and the accounts that those receipts impact are listed in the Cash Receipts Book. Cash payments and the accounts those payments impact are listed in the Cash Payments Book. The same is true for transactions found in the Sales journal, Purchases journal, Nominal journal, and any other special journals you may be using in your business.

At the end of each month, you summarise each journal by adding up the columns and then use that summary to develop an entry for the Nominal Ledger. Believe me, this process takes a lot less time than entering every transaction in the Nominal Ledger.

We introduce you to the process of entering transactions and summarising journals later in this chapter. Near the end of the chapter, we even summarise one journal and develop this entry for the Nominal Ledger:

Account	Debit	Credit
Cash	£2,900	
Accounts Receivable		£500
Sales		£900
Capital		£1,500

Note that the Debits and Credits are in balance – £2,900 each. Remember the cardinal rule of double-entry bookkeeping: All entries to the Nominal Ledger must be balanced entries. For more detail about double-entry bookkeeping, read Book II Chapter 1.

In this entry, the Cash account is increased by £2,900 to show that cash was received. The Accounts Receivable account is decreased by £500 to show customers paid their bills, and the money is no longer due. The Sales account is increased by £900, because additional revenue was collected. The Capital account is increased by £1,500 because the owner put more cash into the business.

You need a selection of accountancy pads to write up your journals. We get our pads from high street stationers, and so you shouldn't have a problem doing the same. A good all-purpose pad is the A4 six-column cash pad. Vestry produces a range of pads to suit all purposes, but any similar brand is fine too.

Figures 3-1 to 3-4 summarise the remaining journal pages prepared later in this chapter. Reviewing those summaries, we developed the following entries for the Nominal Ledger:

Figure 3-1 – Summarised Cash Payments Book

Figure 3-2 – Summarised Sales Journal

Figure 3-3 – Summarised Purchases Journal

Figure 3-4 – Summarised Nominal Journal

Figure 3-1 shows a summary of the Cash Payments Book for a business. The following Nominal Ledger entry is based on the transactions that appear in Figure 3-1:

Account	*Debit*	*Credit*
Rent	£800	
Accounts Payable	£750	
Salaries	£350	
Credit Card Payable	£150	
Cash		£2,050

This Nominal Ledger summary balances out at £2,050 each for the debits and credits. The Cash account is decreased to show the cash outlay, the Rent and Salaries Expense accounts are increased to show the additional expenses, and the Accounts Payable and Credit Card Payable accounts are decreased to show that bills were paid and are no longer due.

In a small business, you use the Cash Book to record both payments and receipts made by cheque or cash. In Figure 3-1, a column records the cheque number, which is useful if any queries crop up later.

Figure 3-1:
A Cash Payments Book keeps track of all cash transactions involving cash sent out of the business. This figure shows how to summarise those transactions so that they can be posted to the Nominal Ledger.

Rachel & Zoe's Sewing Shop
Cash Book (Payments)
June 2008

Date	Account Debited	Folio	Cheque No.	Nominal Debit	Account Payable Debit	Salaries Debit		Cash Credit
1/6	Rent		1065	800 —				800 —
3/6	Accts Pay - Henry's		1066		500 —			500 —
3/6	Accts Pay - Helen's		1067		250 —			250 —
4/6	Salaries		1068			350 —		350 —
10/3	Credit Card - Barclays		1069	150 —				150 —
				950 —	750 —	350 —		2,050 —

Figure 3-2:
A Sales journal keeps track of all credit sales transactions. This figure shows how to summarise those transactions so they can be posted to the Nominal Ledger.

Rachel & Zoe's Sewing Shop
Sales journal
June 2008

Date	Customer Acct. Debited		Invoice No.	Accounts Receivable Debit	Sales Credit				
1/6	S. Smith		243	200 —	200 —				
1/6	Charlie's Garage		244	300 —	300 —				
3/6	P. Perry		245	100 —	100 —				
5/6	J. Jones		246	200 —	200 —				
				800 —	800 —				

Figure 3-2 shows the Sales journal for a sample business. The following Nominal Ledger entry is based on the transactions that appear in Figure 3-2:

Account	*Debit*	*Credit*
Accounts Receivable	£800	
Sales		£800

Note that this entry is balanced. The Accounts Receivable account is increased to show that customers owe the business money because they bought items on credit. The Sales account is increased to show that even though no cash changed hands, the business in Figure 3-2 took in revenue. Cash is going to be collected when the customers pay their bills.

Figure 3-3 shows the business's Purchases journal for one month. The following Nominal Ledger entry is based on the transactions that appear in Figure 3-3:

Account	*Debit*	*Credit*
Purchases	£925	
Accounts Payable		£925

Like the entry for the Sales account, this entry is balanced. The Accounts Payable account is increased to show that money is due to suppliers, and the Purchases Expense account is also increased to show that more supplies were purchased.

Figure 3-4 shows the Nominal journal for a sample business. The following Nominal Ledger entry is based on the transactions that appear in Figure 3-4:

Account	*Debit*	*Credit*
Sales Returns	£60	
Accounts Payable	£200	
Vehicles	£10,000	
Accounts Receivable		£60
Purchase Returns		£200
Capital		£10,000

Checking for balance – Debits and Credits both total to £10,260.

In this entry, the Sales Returns and Purchase Returns accounts are increased to show additional returns. The Accounts Payable and Accounts Receivable accounts are both decreased to show that money is no longer owed. The Vehicles account is increased to show new business assets, and the Capital account, which is where the owner's deposits into the business are recorded, is increased accordingly.

Figure 3-3:
A Purchases journal keeps track of all purchases of goods to be sold. This figure shows how to summarise those transactions so they can be posted to the Nominal Ledger.

		Rachel & Zoe's Sewing Shop						
		Purchases journal						
		June 2008						
Date	Supplier Credited	Invoice No.	Purchases Debit	Accounts Payable Credit				
1/6	Supplier from Henry's	1575	750 —	750 —				
5/6	Barry's – packaging	1285	100 —	100 —				
8/6	Helen's – paper	1745	75 —	75 —				
			925 —	925 —				

Figure 3-4:
A General journal keeps track of all miscellaneous transactions not tracked in a specific journal, such as a Sales journal or a Purchases journal. This figure shows how to summarise those transactions so they can be posted to the Nominal Ledger.

		Rachel & Zoe's Sewing Shop				
		General journal				
		June 2008				
Date	Account	Nominal Debit	Nominal Credit	Accounts Payable Debit	Accounts Receivable Credit	
3/6	Sales Return	60 —				
	S. Smith				60 —	
	Credit Memo 124					
5/6	Henry's Bakery			200 —		
	Purchase Return		200 —			
	Debit Memo 346					
8/6	Vehicles	10,000 —				
	Rachel's Capital		10,000 —			
				200 —	60 —	

Posting Entries to the Ledger

After you summarise your journals and develop all the entries you need for the Nominal Ledger (see the previous section), you post your entries into the Nominal Ledger accounts whenever you sit down to do the bookkeeping.

When posting to the Nominal Ledger, include transaction pound amounts as well as references to where material was originally entered into the books so you can track a transaction back if a question arises later. For example, you may wonder what a number means, your boss or the owner may wonder why certain money was spent, or an auditor (an outside accountant who checks your work for accuracy) may raise a question.

Whatever the reason for questioning an entry in the Nominal Ledger, you definitely want to be able to find the point of original entry for every transaction in every account. Use the reference information that guides you to where the original detail about the transaction is located in the journals to answer any question that arises.

For this particular business, three of the accounts – Cash, Accounts Receivable, and Accounts Payable – are carried over month to month, so each has an opening balance. Just to keep things simple, in this example we start each account with a £2,000 balance. One of the accounts, Sales, is closed at the end of each accounting period, and so starts with a zero balance.

Most businesses close their books at the end of each month and produce financial reports. Others close them at the end of a quarter or end of a year. For the purposes of this example, we assume that this business closes its books monthly. And in the figures that follow, we only give examples for the first five days of the month to keep things simple.

As you review the figures for the various accounts in this example, notice that the balance of some accounts increase when a debit is recorded and decrease when a credit is recorded. Other accounts increase when a credit is recorded and decrease when a debit is recorded. This feature is the mystery of debits, credits, and double-entry accounting. For more, flip to Book II Chapter 1.

The Cash account (see Figure 3-5) increases with debits and decreases with credits. Ideally, the Cash account always ends with a debit balance, which means money is still in the account. A credit balance in the cash account indicates that the business is overdrawn, and you know what that means – cheques are returned for non payment.

The Debtors account (see Figure 3-6) increases with debits and decreases with credits. Ideally, this account also has a debit balance that indicates the amount still due from customer purchases. If no money is due from customers, the

Book II

Accounting Basics

account balance is zero. A zero balance isn't necessarily a bad thing if all customers have paid their bills. However, a zero balance may be a sign that your sales have slumped, which can be bad news.

	Rachel & Zoe's Sewing Shop						
	Cash account						
	June 2008						
Date	Description	Ref. No.	Debit	Credit			Balance
1/6	Opening Balance						2,000 —
30/6	From Cash Receipts Journal	Jnl Page 1	2,900 —				
30/6	From Cash Payments Journal	Jnl Page 2		2,050 —			
	Closing Balance						2,850 —

Figure 3-5: Cash account in the Nominal Ledger.

	Rachel & Zoe's Sewing Shop						
	Debtors account						
	June 2008						
Date	Description	Ref. No.	Debit	Credit			Balance
1/6	Opening Balance						2,000 —
30/6	From Cash Receipts Jnl	Jnl Page 1		500 —			
30/6	From Sales Jnl	Jnl Page 3	800 —				
3/6	Credit Memo 124 Gen. Jnl	Jnl Page 5		60 —			
	Closing Balance						2,240 —

Figure 3-6: Debtors account in the Nominal Ledger.

The Creditors account (see Figure 3-7) increases with credits and decreases with debits. Ideally, this account has a credit balance because money is still due to vendors, contractors, and others. A zero balance here means no outstanding bills.

	Rachel & Zoe's Sewing Shop										
	Creditors account										
	June 2008										
Date	Description		Ref. No.	Debit	Credit					Balance	
1/6	Opening Balance									2,000	—
30/6	From Cash Book		Jnl Page 2	750 —							
30/6	From Purchase Jnl.		Jnl Page 4		925 —						
5/6	Debit Memo 346		Jnl Page 5	200 —							
	Closing Balance									1,975	—

Figure 3-7:
Creditors
account in
the Nominal
Ledger.

These three accounts – Cash, Accounts Receivable, and Accounts Payable – are part of the balance sheet, which we explain fully in Book III Chapter 2. Asset accounts on the balance sheet usually carry debit balances because they reflect assets (in this case, cash) that the business owns. Cash and Accounts Receivable are Asset accounts. Liability and Capital accounts usually carry credit balances because Liability accounts show claims made by creditors (in other words, money the business owes to financial institutions, vendors, or others), and Capital accounts show claims made by owners (in other words, how much money the owners have put into the business). Accounts Payable is a Liability account.

Here's how these accounts impact the balance of the business:

Assets	=	Liabilities	+	Capital
Cash		Accounts Payable		Accounts Receivable
(Usually debit balance)		(Usually credit balance)		(Usually debit balance)

Here's how these accounts affect the balances of the business:

The Sales account (see Figure 3-8) isn't a balance sheet account. Instead, the Sales account is used to develop the profit and loss statement, which shows whether or not a business made profit in the period being examined. (For the low-down on profit and loss statements, see Book III Chapter 1.) Credits and debits are pretty straightforward in the Sales account: Credits increase the account, and debits decrease it. Fortunately, the Sales account usually carries a credit balance, which means the business had income.

What's that, you say? The Sales account should carry a credit balance? That may sound strange, but the key is the relationship between the Sales account and the balance sheet. The Sales account is one of the accounts that feed the bottom line of the profit and loss statement, which shows whether your business made a profit or suffered a loss. A profit means that you earned more through sales than you paid out in costs or expenses. Expense and cost accounts usually carry a debit balance.

The profit and loss statement's bottom line figure shows whether or not the business made a profit. When the business makes a profit, the Sales account credits exceed expense and cost account debits. The profit is in the form of a credit, which gets added to the Capital account called Retained Earnings, which tracks how much of your business's profits are reinvested to grow the business. When the business loses money and the bottom line of the profit and loss statement shows that cost and expenses exceeded sales, the number is a debit. That debit is subtracted from the balance in Retained Earnings, to show the reduction to profits reinvested in the business.

When your business earns a profit at the end of the accounting period, the Retained Earnings account increases thanks to a credit from the Sales account. When you lose money, your Retained Earnings account decreases.

Because the Retained Earnings account is a Capital account and Capital accounts usually carry credit balances, Retained Earnings usually carries a credit balance as well.

After you post all the Ledger entries, you need to record details about where you posted the transactions on the journal pages. We show you how to carry out that process later in this chapter.

	Rachel & Zoe's Sewing Shop							
	Sales account							
	June 2008							
Date	Description	Ref. No.	Debit	Credit			Balance
1/6	Opening Balance						— —
30/6	From Cash Receipts Jnl.	Jnl Page 1		900 —			
30/6	From Sales Jnl.	Jnl Page 3		800 —			
	Closing Balance						1,700 —

Figure 3-8: Sales account in the Nominal Ledger.

Adjusting for Ledger Errors

Your entries in the Nominal Ledger aren't cast in stone. If necessary, you can always change or correct an entry with an *adjusting entry.* Four of the most common reasons for Nominal Ledger adjustments are:

✔ **Depreciation:** A business shows the aging of its assets through depreciation. Each year, a portion of the original cost of an asset is written off as an expense, and that change is noted as an adjusting entry. Determining how much is to be written off is a complicated process that we explain in greater detail in Book IV Chapter 5.

✔ **Prepaid expenses:** Expenses that are paid up front, such as a year's worth of insurance, are allocated by the month using an adjusting entry. This type of adjusting entry is usually done as part of the closing process at the end of an accounting period.

✔ **Adding an account:** Accounts can be added by way of adjusting entries at any time during the year. If the new account is being created to track transactions separately that once appeared in another account, you must move all transactions already in the books to the new account. You do this transfer with an adjusting entry to reflect the change.

✔ **Deleting an account:** Only delete an account at the end of an accounting period.

Book II

Accounting
Basics

Using Computerised Transactions

If you keep your books using a computerised accounting system, your accounting software does the posting to the Nominal Ledger behind the scenes. You can view your transactions right on the screen. We now show you how to do this using two simple steps in Sage 50 Accounts, without you having to make a Nominal Ledger entry. Other computerised accounting programs allow you to view transactions right on the screen too. Sage 50 Accounts is the most popular of the computerised accounting systems, which is why we use it to produce examples throughout the book.

1. **Click on the symbol for Nominal Ledger Record.**

    The enquiry screen appears.

2. **Select Nominal Code (NC) 1100 to view a summary of Accounts Payable account.**

    This shows how much in total you owe (see Figure 3-9).

3. Click on the Activity tab for more detail.

Figure 3-10 shows the sales transactions entered for July.

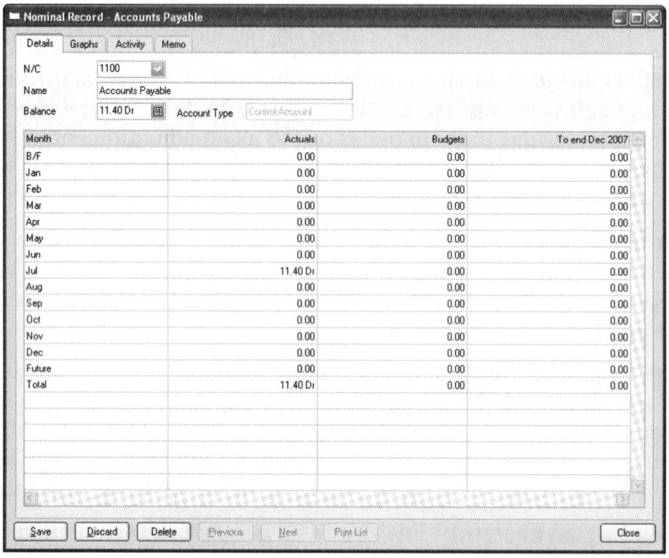

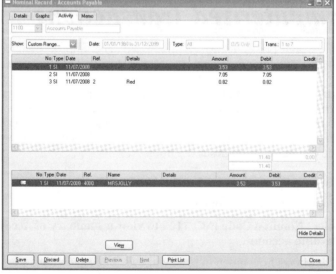

Figure 3-9:
A Chart of
Accounts
appearing
in Sage 50
Accounts.

Figure 3-10:
Look
inside the
Accounts
Payable
account in
Sage 50
Accounts.

If you need to make an adjustment to a payment that appears in your computerised system, highlight the transaction, click Edit Transaction in the line below the account name, and make the necessary changes.

As you navigate the Nominal Ledger created by your computerised bookkeeping system, you can see how easily someone can make changes that alter your financial transactions and possibly cause serious harm to your business. For example, someone may reduce or alter your bills to customers or change the amount due to a supplier. Be sure that you can trust whoever has access to your computerised system and that you set up secure password access. Also, establish a series of checks and balances for managing your business's cash and accounts. Book II Chapter 5 covers safety and security measures in greater detail.

Keeping Journals

When doing your books, you have to start somewhere. You can take a shortcut and just list every transaction in the affected accounts, but after recording hundreds – maybe thousands – of transactions in one month, imagine the nightmare if your books don't balance and you need to find the error. Talk about looking for a needle in a haystack – a haystack of numbers!

Because in a double-entry bookkeeping system you enter every transaction in two places – as a debit in one account and a credit in another account – you need to have a place where you can easily match those debits and credits. (For more on the double-entry system, flip to Book II Chapter 1.)

Long ago, bookkeepers developed a system of *journals* to give businesses a starting point for each transaction. In this chapter, we introduce you to the process of journalising your transactions; we tell you how to set up and use journals, how to post the transactions to the accounts impacted, and how to use a computerised bookkeeping program to simplify this entire process.

Establishing a Transaction's Point of Entry

In most businesses that don't use computerised bookkeeping programs, a transaction's original point of entry into the bookkeeping system is through a system of journals.

Each transaction goes in the appropriate journal in chronological order. The entry includes information about the date of the transaction, the accounts to which the transaction was posted, and the source material used for developing the transaction.

If, at some point in the future, you need to follow how a credit or debit ended up in a particular account, you can find the necessary detail in the journal where you first posted the transaction. (Before being posted to various accounts in the bookkeeping system, each transaction gets a reference number to help you backtrack to the original entry point.) For example, suppose a customer calls you and wants to know why her account has a £500 charge. To find the answer, you go to the posting in the customer's account, follow the charge back to its original point of entry in the Sales journal, use that information to locate the source for the charge, make a copy of the source (most likely a sales invoice or receipt), and post the evidence to the customer.

If you filed everything properly, you can easily find the original source material and settle any issue that arises regarding any transaction. For more on what papers you need to keep and how to file them, see Book II Chapter 5.

Although you can keep a single general journal for all your transactions, one big journal can be very hard to manage because you're likely to have thousands of entries in that journal by the end of the year. Instead, most businesses employ a system of journals that includes a Cash Book (or Books), which are really journals but are traditionally called books, for both incoming cash outgoing cash. In the one-book system, cash receipts are entered on one page (usually the left-hand page) and cash payments are entered on the opposite page (the right-hand page). This system works well if you have roughly equal numbers of cash receipts and payments. However, if your business makes more payments than it has receipts (which is usual), you may want to have a Cash Payments Book and a separate Cash Receipts Book.

Not all transactions involve cash, however, so the two most common non-cash journals are the Sales journal and the Purchases journal. We show you how to set up and use each of these journals in the following sections.

Watching Cash Change Hands

Businesses deal with cash transactions every day, and as a business owner, you definitely want to know where every penny is going. The best way to get a quick daily summary of cash transactions is by reviewing the entries in your Cash Book. In this section, we assume that you're keeping a separate Cash Payments Book and a Cash Receipts Book because you have a very busy business.

Keeping track of incoming cash

The Cash Receipts Book is the first place you record cash received by your business. The majority of cash received each day comes from daily sales; other possible sources of cash include deposits of capital from the business's owner, customer invoice payments, new loan proceeds, and interest from savings accounts.

Each entry in the Cash Receipts Book must not only indicate how the cash was received but also designate the account into which the cash is to be recorded.

Every Cash Receipts Book has at least two columns in common:

- ✔ **Date:** The date of the transaction, whether a sale, a receipt, a credit transaction, or whatever.

- ✔ **Folio:** This column shows where the transaction is to be posted at the end of the month. This information is filled in at the end of the month when you do the posting to the Nominal Ledger accounts. If the entry to be posted to the accounts is summarised and totalled at the bottom of the page, you can just put a tick mark next to the entry in the Folio column. For transactions listed in the General Credit or General Debit columns, indicate an account number for the account in which the transaction is posted.

Book II

Accounting Basics

Remember, in double-entry bookkeeping, every transaction is entered twice – once as a debit and once as a credit. For example, cash taken in for sales is credited to the Sales account and debited to the Cash account. In this case, both accounts increase in value. (For more about debits and credits, flip to Book II Chapter 1.)

In the Cash Receipts Book, the Cash account is always the debit because you initially deposit your money there. The credits vary depending upon the source of the funds. Figure 3-11 shows you what a series of transactions look like when they're entered into a Cash Receipts Book.

Most of your incoming cash (received by the cashier) is recorded each day, and is called *cash register sales* or simply *sales* in the journal. When you record cheques received from customers, you list the customer's cheque number and name as well as the amount. In Figure 3-11, the only other cash received is a cash deposit from H.G. to cover a cash shortfall.

					Accounts					
Date	Account Credited	Folio	General Credit	Receivable Credit	Sales Credit				Cash Debit
1/6	Sales				300 —				300 —
2/6	Sales				250 —				250 —
3/6	Cheque 121 - S. Smith			200 —					200 —
3/6	Sales				150 —				150 —
4/6	H.G. Capital		1,500 —						1,500 —
5/6	Cheque 325 - J. Jones			100 —					100 —
5/6	Cheque 567 - P. Perry			200 —					200 —
5/6	Sales				200 —				200 —

Rachel & Zoe's Sewing Shop
Cash Book (Receipts)
June 2008

Figure 3-11: The Cash Receipts Book is the first point of entry for incoming cash.

The Cash Receipts Book in Figure 3-11 has seven columns of information, including the Date and Folio columns explained earlier in this section:

- **Account Credited:** The name of the account credited.

- **General Credit:** For transactions that don't have their own columns; these transactions are entered individually into the accounts impacted.

   For example, according to Figure 3-11, H.G. deposited £1,500 of her own money into the Capital account on 4 March in order to pay invoices. The credit shown is to be posted to the Capital account at the end of the month, because the Capital account tracks all information about assets H.G. pays into the business.

- **Accounts Receivable Credit:** Any transactions that are posted to the Accounts Receivable account (which tracks information about customers who buy products on credit).

- **Sales Credit:** Credits for the Sales account.

- **Cash Debit:** Anything that is going to be added to the Cash account.

You can set up your Cash Receipts Book with more columns when you have accounts with frequent cash receipts. The big advantage to having individual columns for active accounts is that, when you total the columns at the end of the month, the total for the active accounts is the only thing you have to add to the Nominal Ledger accounts, which is a lot less work than entering every Sales transaction individually in the Nominal Ledger account. This approach saves a lot of time posting to accounts that involve multiple transactions every month. Individual transactions listed in the General Credits column each need to be entered into the affected accounts separately, which takes a lot more time that just entering a column total.

The top right-hand corner of the Cash Receipts Book provides space for the person who prepared the journal, and for someone who approves the entries, to sign and date. If your business deals with cash, incorporate a system of checks and balances to ensure that cash is properly handled and recorded. For more safety measures, see Book II Chapter 5.

Following outgoing cash

Cash going out of the business to pay invoices, salaries, rents, and other necessities has its own journal, the Cash Payments Book. This journal is the point of original entry for all business cash paid out to others.

No businessperson likes to see money go out the door, but imagine what creditors, suppliers, and others think if they don't get the money they're due. Put yourself in their shoes: Would you be able to buy needed supplies if other businesses didn't pay what they owed you? Not a chance.

You need to monitor your outgoing cash just as carefully as you monitor incoming cash (see the preceding section). Each entry in the Cash Payments Book must not only indicate how much cash was paid out but also designate which account is to be decreased in value because of the cash disbursal. For example, cash disbursed to pay invoices is credited to the Cash account (which goes down in value) and is debited to the account from which the invoice or loan is paid, such as Accounts Payable. The debit decreases the amount still owed in the Accounts Payable account.

In the Cash Payments Book, the Cash account is always the credit, and the debits vary depending upon the outstanding debts to be paid. Figure 3-12 shows you what a series of transactions look like when they're entered in a Cash Payments Book.

The Cash Payments Book in Figure 3-12 has eight columns of information. (For an explanation of the Date and Folio columns, see the preceding section 'Keeping track of incoming cash'.)

- ✔ **Account Debited:** The name of the account debited as well as any detail about the reason for the debit.
- ✔ **Cheque No.:** The number of the cheque used to pay the debt.

Rachel & Zoe's Sewing Shop									
Cash Book (Payments)									
June 2008									
Date	Account Debited	Folio	Cheque No.	Nominal Debit	Account Payable Debit	Salaries Debit			Cash Credit
1/6	Rent		1065	800 —					800 —
3/6	Accts Pay – Henry's		1066		500 —				500 —
3/6	Accts Pay – Helen's		1067		250 —				250 —
4/6	Salaries		1068			350 —			350 —
10/3	Credit Card – Barclays		1069	150 —					150 —
				950 —	750 —	350 —			2,050 —

Figure 3-12: The Cash Payments Book is the first point of entry for outgoing cash.

▸ **General Debit:** Any transactions that don't have their own columns; these transactions are entered individually into the accounts they impact.

For example, according to Figure 3-12, rent was paid on 1 June and is to be indicated by a debit in the Rent Expense.

▸ **Accounts Payable Debit:** Any transactions that are posted to the Accounts Payable account (which tracks invoices due).

▸ **Salaries Debit:** Debits to the Salaries Expense account, which increase the amount of salaries expenses paid in a particular month.

▸ **Cash Credit:** Anything deducted from the Cash account.

You can set up your Cash Payments Book with more columns if you have accounts with frequent cash disbursals. For example, in Figure 3-12, the book-keeper for this fictional business added one column each for Accounts Payable and Salaries because cash for both accounts is disbursed on multiple occasions during the month. Rather than having to list each disbursement in the Accounts Payable and Salaries accounts, she can just total each journal column at the end of the month and add totals to the appropriate accounts. This approach saves a lot of time when you're working with your most active accounts.

Managing Sales Like a Pro

Not all sales involve the collection of cash; many businesses allow customers to buy products on credit using a credit account facility.

Credit comes into play when a customer is allowed to take a business's products without paying immediately because her account is invoiced monthly. This can be done by using a credit card issued by the shop (in the case of a retail business) or some other method the business uses to record customer credit purchases, such as having the customer sign a sales receipt indicating that the amount is to be charged to the customer's account.

Sales made on credit don't involve cash until the customer pays her invoice. (In contrast, with credit card sales, the store gets a cash payment from the card-issuing bank before the customer even pays the credit card invoice.) If your business sells on credit, the total value of the products bought on any particular day becomes an item for the Accounts Receivable account, which records all money due from customers. We talk more about managing Accounts Receivable in Book II Chapter 6.

Before allowing customers to buy on credit, make sure that you require them to apply for credit in advance so that you can check their credit references.

When something's sold on credit, usually the cashier or accounts department drafts an invoice for the customer to sign when picking up the product. The invoice lists the items purchased and the total amount due. After getting the customer's signature, the invoice is recorded in both the Accounts Payable account and the customer's individual account.

Transactions for sales made on credit first enter your books in the Sales journal. Each entry in the Sales journal must indicate the customer's name, the invoice number, and the amount charged.

In the Sales journal, the Accounts Receivable account is debited, which increases in value. The bookkeeper must also remember to make an entry to the customer's account records because the customer has not yet paid for the item. The transaction also increases the value of the Sales account, which is credited.

Figure 3-13 shows a few days' worth of transactions related to credit sales.

The columns in the Sales journal in Figure 3-13 include the following:

- **Customer Account Debited:** The name of the customer whose account is debited
- **Invoice Number:** The invoice number for the purchase
- **Accounts Receivable Debit:** Increases to the Accounts Receivable account
- **Sales Credit:** Increases to the Sales account

(For an explanation of the Date and Folio columns, see the preceding 'Keeping track of incoming cash' section.)

Book II

Accounting Basics

Rachel & Zoe's Sewing Shop Sales journal June 2008												
Date	Customer Acct. Debited		Invoice No.	Accounts Receivable Debit		Sales Credit						
1/6	S. Smith		243	200	—	200	—					
1/6	Charlie's Garage		244	300	—	300	—					
3/6	P. Perry		245	100	—	100	—					
5/6	J. Jones		246	200	—	200	—					
				800	—	800	—					

Figure 3-13: The Sales journal is first point of entry for sales made on credit.

At the end of the month, the bookkeeper can just total the Accounts Receivable and Sales columns shown in Figure 3-13 and post the totals to those Nominal Ledger accounts. She doesn't need to post all the detail because she can always refer back to the Sales journal. However, each invoice noted in the Sales journal must be carefully recorded in each customer's account. Otherwise, the bookkeeper doesn't know who and how much to invoice.

Keeping Track of Purchases

Purchases of products to be sold to customers at a later date are a key type of non-cash transaction. All businesses must have something to sell, whether they manufacture it themselves or buy a finished product from some other business. Businesses usually make these purchases on credit from the business that makes the product. In this case, the business becomes the customer of another business.

Transactions for purchases bought on credit first enter your books in the Purchases journal. Each entry in the Purchases journal must indicate the supplier from whom the purchase was made, the supplier's invoice number, and the amount charged.

In the Purchases journal, the Accounts Payable account is credited, and the Purchases account is debited, meaning both accounts increase in value. The Accounts Payable account increases because the business now owes more money to creditors, and the Purchases account increases because the amount spent on goods to be sold goes up.

Figure 3-14 shows some store purchase transactions as they appear in the business's Purchases journal.

Including the standard Date and Folio columns, which are explained in the previous 'Keeping track of incoming cash' section, the Purchases journal in Figure 3-14 has six columns of information:

- ✔ **Supplier Account Credited:** The name of the supplier from whom the purchases were made

- ✔ **Invoice Number:** The invoice number for the purchase that the vendor assigned

- ✔ **Purchases Debit:** Additions to the Purchases account

- ✔ **Accounts Payable Credit:** Increases to the Accounts Payable account

Book II

Accounting Basics

At the end of the month, the bookkeeper can just total the Purchases and Accounts Payable columns and post the totals to the corresponding Nominal Ledger accounts. She can refer back to the Purchases journal for details if necessary. However, each invoice needs to be carefully recorded in each supplier's accounts so that a running total of outstanding invoices exists for each supplier. Otherwise, the bookkeeper doesn't know who, and how much, is owed.

Figure 3-14: The Purchases journal is first point of entry for purchases bought on credit.

					Accounts	
Date	Supplier Credited	Folio	Invoice No.	Purchases Debit	Payable Credit	
1/6	Supplies from Henry's		1575	750 —	750 —	
5/6	Barry's – packaging		1285	100 —	100 —	
8/6	Helen's – paper		1745	75 —	75 —	
				925 —	925 —	

Rachel & Zoe's Sewing Shop
Purchases journal
June 2008

Dealing with Transactions that Don't Fit

Not all your transactions fit in one of the four main journals (Cash Receipts, Cash Payments, Sales, and Purchases). If you need to establish other special journals as the original points of entry for transactions, go ahead. The sky's the limit!

If you keep your books the old-fashioned way – on paper – be aware that paper is vulnerable to being mistakenly lost or destroyed. In this case, you may want to keep the number of journals you maintain to a minimum.

For transactions that don't fit in the 'big four' journals but don't necessarily warrant the creation of their own journals, consider keeping a General Journal for miscellaneous transactions. Using columnar paper similar to that used for the other four journals, create Date and Folio columns (see the previous section, 'Keeping track of incoming cash') as well as the following columns:

- **Account:** The account that the transaction impacts. More detail is needed here because the General Journal impacts so many different accounts with so many different types of transactions. For example, you find only sales transactions in the Sales journal and Purchase transactions in the Purchase journal, but you can find any type of transaction in the General journal affecting many less active accounts. (Place this column after the Date column and before the Folio column.)
- **General Debit:** Contains most debits.
- **General Credit:** Contains most credits.

If you have certain very active accounts, start a column for those accounts as well. In Figure 3-14, we added a column for Accounts Payable and in Figure 3-15 we added columns for Accounts Payable and Accounts Receivable. The big advantage of having a separate column for an account is that you're able to total that column at the end of the month and just put the total in the Nominal Ledger. You don't have to enter each transaction separately.

Many businesses also add columns for Accounts Payable and Accounts Receivable because non-cash transactions commonly impact those accounts.

All the transactions in the General journal are non-cash transactions. Cash transactions go into one of the two cash journals: Cash Receipts (see the section 'Keeping track of incoming cash') and Cash Payments (see the section 'Following outgoing cash').

In a General journal, you enter transactions on multiple lines because each transaction impacts two accounts (and sometimes more than two). For example, in the General journal shown in Figure 3-15, the first transaction listed is the return of product by S. Smith. This return of products sold must be posted to the customer's account as a credit as well as to the Accounts Receivable account. Also, the Sales Return account, where the business tracks all products returned by the customer, has to be debited. Here are some sample transactions from Figure 3-15:

- ✔ 5 June – Return a portion of purchase from Henry's Supplies, £200, Debit memo 346. When a business returns a product purchased, track it in the Purchase Return account, which is credited. A debit must also be made to the Accounts Payable account, as well as to the supplier's account, because less money is now owed. Cash doesn't change hands with this transaction.

- ✔ 8 June – Rachel transfers a car to the business, £10,000. This transaction is posted to the Vehicle Asset account and the Capital account in Owner's Capital. Rather than deposit cash into the business, Rachel made her personal vehicle a business asset.

					Accounts Payable	Accounts Receivable		
Date	Account	Folio	Nominal Debit	Nominal Credit	Debit	Credit		
3/6	Sales Return		60 —					
	S. Smith					60 —		
	Credit Memo 124							
5/6	Henry's Bakery				200 —			
	Purchase Return			200 —				
	Debit Memo 346							
8/6	Vehicles		10,000 —					
	Rachel's Capital			10,000 —				
					200 —	60 —		

Rachel & Zoe's Sewing Shop
General journal
June 2008

Figure 3-15: The General journal is the point of entry for miscellaneous transactions.

In addition to the other columns, the General journal in Figure 3-15 has the following two columns:

✔ **Accounts Payable Debit:** Decreases to the Accounts Payable account

The bookkeeper working with this journal anticipated that many of the business's transactions were going to impact Accounts Payable. She created this column so that she can subtotal it and make just one entry to the Accounts Payable account in the Nominal Ledger.

✔ **Accounts Receivable Credit:** Decreases to the Accounts Receivable account

At the end of the month, the bookkeeper can just total this journal's Accounts Payable and Accounts Receivable columns and post those totals to the corresponding Nominal Ledger accounts. All transaction details remain in the General journal. However, because the miscellaneous transactions impact Nominal Ledger accounts, the transactions need to be posted to each affected account separately (see the section 'Posting Journal Information to Accounts').

Posting Journal Information to Accounts

When you close your books at the end of the month, you summarise all the journals by totalling the columns and posting the information to update all the accounts involved.

Posting journal pages is a four-step process:

1. **Number each journal page at the top if not already numbered.**

2. **Total any column not titled General Debit or General Credit.**

    Any transactions recorded in the General Debit or General Credit columns need to be recorded individually in the Nominal Ledger.

3. **Post the entries to the Nominal Ledger account.**

    Each transaction in the General Credit or General Debit column must be posted separately. You just need to post totals to the Nominal Ledger for the other columns in which transactions for more active accounts were entered in the General journal. List the date and journal page number as well as the amount of the debit or credit, so you can quickly find the entry for the original transaction if you need more details.

    The Nominal Ledger account shows only debit or credit (whichever is appropriate to the transaction). Only the journals have both sides of a transaction. (We show you how to work with Nominal Ledger accounts earlier in this chapter.)

4. **Record information about where the entry is posted in the Folio column.**

   If the entry to be posted to the accounts is summarised and totalled at the bottom of the page, you can just put a tick mark next to the entry in the Folio column. For transactions listed in the General Credit or General Debit columns, indicate an account number for the account into which the transaction is posted. This process helps you confirm that you've posted all entries in the Nominal Ledger.

Posting to the Nominal Ledger is done at the end of an accounting period as part of the process of closing the accounts.

Figure 3-16 shows a summarised journal page, specifically the Cash Receipts Book. You can see that entries listed in the Sales Credit and Cash Debit columns on the Cash Receipts Book are just ticked. Only one entry was placed in the General Credit column, and that entry has an account number in the Folio column. Although we don't list here all the transactions for the month, which would of course be a much longer list, we do show how you summarise the journal at the end of the month.

Book II

Accounting Basics

				Accounts					
	Rachel & Zoe's Sewing Shop								
	Cash Book (Receipts)								
	June 2008								
Date	Account Credited	Folio	General Credit	Receivable Credit	Sales Credit				Cash Debit
1/6	Sales	✓			300 —				300 —
2/6	Sales	✓			250 —				250 —
3/6	Cheque 121 - S. Smith	✓		200 —					200 —
3/6	Sales	✓			150 —				150 —
4/6	H.G. Capital	3300	1,500 —						1,500 —
5/6	Cheque 325 - J. Jones	✓		100 —					100 —
5/6	Cheque 567 - P. Perry	✓		200 —					200 —
5/6	Sales	✓			200 —				200 —
			1,500 —	500 —	900 —				2,900 —
			✓	(1100)	(4000)				(1000)

Nominal Codes

Figure 3-16: Summary of Cash Receipts Book entries after the first five days.

As shown in Figure 3-16, after summarising the Cash Receipts Book, you only need to post entries into four Nominal Ledger accounts (General Credit, Accounts Receivable Credit, Sales Credit, and Cash Debit) and three customer accounts (S. Smith, J. Jones, and P. Perry). For the Nominal Ledger transactions, we show the Nominal Ledger account numbers (or codes) that each posting goes to – 3300, 1100, 4000, and 1000. You use codes like this if you choose to computerise your accounts. Even better, the entries balance: £2,900 in debits and £2,900 in credits! (The customer accounts total £500, which is good news because it matches the amount credited to Accounts Receivable. The Accounts Receivable account is decreased by £500 because payments were received, as is the amount due from the individual customer accounts.)

Simplifying Your Journaling with Computerised Accounting

The process of posting first to the journals and then to the Nominal Ledger and individual customer or vendor accounts can be very time-consuming. Luckily, most businesses today use computerised accounting software, so the same information doesn't need to be entered so many times. The computer does the work for you.

If you're working with a computerised accounting software package (see Book II Chapter 4), you only have to enter a transaction once. All the detail that normally needs to be entered into one of the journal pages, one of the Nominal Ledger accounts, and customer, supplier, and other accounts is posted automatically. Voilà!

The method you use to enter your transaction initially varies depending on the type of transaction. To show you what's involved in making entries into a computerised accounting system, the following figures show one entry each from the Cash Receipts Book (see Figure 3-17 for a customer payment), the Cash Payments Book (see Figure 3-18 for a list of invoices to be paid), and the Sales journal (see Figure 3-19 for an invoice). (The screenshots are all from Sage 50 Accounts, a popular computerised bookkeeping system.)

As shown in Figure 3-17, to enter the payment by Mrs Jolly, all you need to do is choose the Receive Payments option and enter MrsJolly in the A/C box. All outstanding invoices appear. You can then decide to accept payment for individual invoices or let the Wizard work out which invoices are being paid from the amount being paid by the customer. When you are done, click on Save and Close.

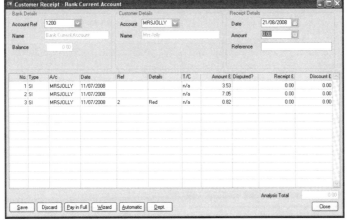

Figure 3-17: Payment by customer Mrs Jolly.

Book II

Accounting Basics

When you use a software package to track your cash receipts, the following accounts are automatically updated:

✔ The Cash account is debited the appropriate amount.

✔ The Accounts Receivable account is credited the appropriate amount.

✔ The corresponding customer account is credited the appropriate amount.

You can see how much simpler this computerised system is than adding the transaction to the Cash Receipts Book, closing the journal at the end of the month, adding the transactions to the accounts impacted by the cash receipts, and then (finally!) closing the books.

Cash disbursements are even easier than cash receipts when you have a computerised system on your side. For example, when paying invoices (see Figure 3-18), all you need to do is go to the invoice-paying screen for Sage 50 Accounts. In this example, all the June invoices are listed, so all you need to do is select the invoices you want to pay, and the system automatically sets the payments in motion.

The invoice-paying perks of this system include:

✔ Cheques can be automatically printed by the software package.

✔ Each of the supplier accounts are updated to show that payment is made.

✔ The Accounts Payable account is debited the appropriate amount for your transaction, which decreases the amount due to suppliers.

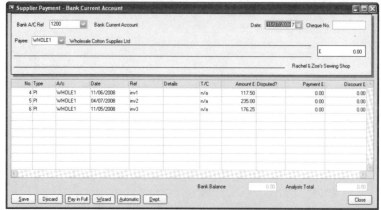

Figure 3-18:
Paying
invoices.

✔ The Cash account is credited the appropriate amount for your transaction, which decreases the amount of cash available (because the cash is designated for use to pay corresponding invoices).

When you make the necessary entries into your computerised accounting system for the information normally to be found in a Sales journal (for example, when a customer pays for your product on credit), you can automatically create an invoice for the purchase. Figure 3-19 shows what that invoice looks like when generated by a computerised accounting system. Adding the customer name in the box marked 'Customer' automatically fills in all the necessary customer information. The date appears automatically, and the system assigns a customer invoice number. You add the quantity and select the type of product bought in the 'Item Code' section, and the rest of the invoice is calculated automatically. When the invoice is final, you print out and send it off to the customer.

Figure 3-19 shows Value Added Tax, which the system automatically calculates. We cover Value Added Tax in Book VI Chapter 4.

Filling out the invoice in the accounting system also updates the affected accounts:

✔ The Accounts Receivable account is debited the appropriate amount, which increases the amount due from customers by that amount.

✔ The Sales account is credited the appropriate amount, which increases the revenue received by that amount.

✔ The invoice is added to the customer's outstanding invoices so that when the customer makes a payment, the outstanding invoice appears on the payment screen.

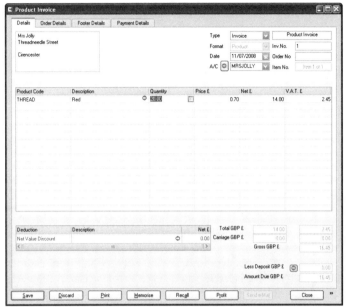

Figure 3-19:
Customer
invoice for
Mrs Jolly.

Book II

Accounting Basics

Chapter 4

Surveying Computer Options

In This Chapter

▶ Finding the right accounting software for your business

▶ Getting your computerised books up and running

S ome small business owners who've been around a while still do things the old-fashioned way – keeping their books in paper journals and ledgers. However, in this age of technology and instant information, the majority of today's businesses computerise their books.

Not only is computerised bookkeeping easier, but it also minimises the chance of errors, because most of the work done to a computerised system's ledgers and journals (see Book II Chapter 3) involves inputting data on forms that can be understood even by someone without training in accounting or bookkeeping. The person entering the information doesn't need to know whether something is a debit or credit (see Book II Chapter 1 for an explanation of the difference) because the computerised system takes care of everything.

In this chapter, we explore three popular accounting software packages for small businesses, discuss the basics of setting up your own computerised books, talk about how you can customise a program for your business, and give you some pointers on converting your manual bookkeeping system into a computerised one.

Most businesses start with a manual accounting system and progress to computerisation as the business grows. The real benefit of computerised accounting systems is that they enable you to do your bookkeeping much faster as your business grows. Also, most reports you may want are available at the click of a menu button. However, we must mention the fact that in a significant number of business situations no accounting software package does exactly what you did before in the same way. Every accounting package is a compromise because it offers the features that someone else decided are important for the majority of businesses. The decision you may have to make is whether to modify your business processes to fall into line with the new accounting software or have some bespoke modification to the accounting software package you decide to buy. The simplest and cheapest solution is to fall into line with your chosen accounting software.

Surveying Your Software Options

More than 50 different types of accounting software programs are on the market, and all are designed to computerise your bookkeeping. The more sophisticated ones target specific industry needs, such as food services or utilities, and can cost thousands of pounds.

Use an Internet search engine to find a list of accounting software in the UK.

As a further resource, ask your auditors or external accountants for their advice. Don't be surprised if they recommend Sage 50 Accounts, the number one accounting software package for small (and bigger) businesses in the UK. Most accountants are resellers of these accounting packages.

Luckily, as a small businessperson, you probably don't need all the bells and whistles that the top-of-the-line programs offer. Instead, the three software programs that we review in this chapter can meet the needs of most small businesspeople. You can buy one of the three systems we recommend from as little as £39.95. Such a program may not be fancy, but basic computerised accounting software can do a good job of helping you keep your books. And you can always upgrade to a more expensive program, if needed, as your business grows. The third accounting solution, Sage 50 Accounts, is a full-featured software package costing around £525. This amount may seem like a big investment, but Sage 50 Accounts accounting system can grow with your business.

The three programs we describe that meet any small business's basic bookkeeping needs are QuickBooks, Mind Your Own Business (MYOB), and Sage 50 Accounts. The most affordable of the three is QuickBooks Simple Start, which we've seen priced as low as £39.95 at various Internet sites. MYOB and Sage also offer simple systems, but if you can afford the cost, we recommend that you step up at least one notch to Sage 50 Accounts or QuickBooks Pro.

Accounting software packages are updated almost every year, because tax laws and laws involving many other aspects of operating a business change so often. In addition, computer software companies are always improving their products to make computerised accounting programs more user-friendly, so ensure that you always buy the most current version of an accounting software package.

QuickBooks

QuickBooks (www.intuit.co.uk) offers an easy user interface (for the novice) and extensive bookkeeping and accounting features (for the experienced bookkeeper or accountant). In 2005, QuickBooks became even better for the novice with the addition of its learning centre, which walks you through every type of key transaction with an interactive program that not only shows you how to do the function but also explains the basics of bookkeeping. You don't have to use the tutorial, but the option pops up when you do a task for the first time, so the choice is always yours. You can also go back to the learning centre to review at any time.

QuickBooks Simple Start, priced around £40 (we found it downloadable from the Internet for £39.95), can meet most of your bookkeeping and accounting needs. If you want to integrate your bookkeeping with a point-of-sale software package, which integrates cash register sales, you need to get QuickBooks Pro 2008, which sells for around £299.95 for a single use and £899 for up to five users (though we found them available on the internet for as little as £250 and £750, respectively). You also need to upgrade if you want to do stock management, generate purchase orders from estimates or sales orders, do job costing and estimates, automatically create a budget, or integrate your data for use with Microsoft Word and Excel programs.

QuickBooks is versatile software if you plan to use it alongside other software packages. QuickBooks can share data with over 325 popular business software applications. Sales, customer, and financial data can be shared easily too, so you don't have to enter that information twice. To find out if QuickBooks can share data with the business software applications you're currently using or plan to use, call Intuit on 0845 606 2161 (sales).

MYOB

MYOB BusinessBasics (www.myob.com) is a cost-effective choice for book-keeping software when you're just starting up and don't have sophisticated bookkeeping or accounting needs. For example, you can process credit card transactions and electronic features from inside the other two accounting software programs we discuss in this chapter, but with MYOB Business Basics you need to upgrade to MYOB Accounting and then add the MYOB RetailBasics module. This program caters to the bookkeeping novice and claims to be ideal if you have little or no accounting knowledge, have just started in business, and run a small or home-based business. Even this basic accounting software package has some nice features, such as the ability to import online bank statement information directly into BusinessBasics. You can choose from 83 starter charts of account, and the sales ledger offers the option to customise your sales invoices.

We particularly like the fact that the hardware requirements aren't too strenuous. You can run MYOB on a fairly low power PC and also, unlike most accounting software, you can run it on Apple Macs.

MYOB offers a full range of accounting solutions ranging from MYOB Business Basics at £79 plus VAT (though we found it available on the Internet for £70) to MYOB Accounting Plus at around £300. In addition, MYOB also offers a range of support software packages.

Sage

We'd be almost negligent if we didn't mention Sage accounting products (www.sage.co.uk). Sage offers a wide range of accounting software for businesses of every size. Sage probably has the biggest user base in the UK among small and medium-sized businesses using accounting software. They offer something for businesses of every size and level of sophistication. Also, Sage products are easy and quick to obtain because virtually every high street software retailer stocks them.

Sage even has software packages designed for businesses that have yet to get started. Sage Start-Up offers business planning tools and online advice to help you run your business. Sage Instant is their budget accounting software package range and offers basic accounting but you can add on payroll, ACT! contact manager, and Forecasting at additional cost.

Sage Instant Accounts covers most of the basic accounting features a small business needs. This software allows you to organise and record your sales and purchases, customer and supplier contacts, invoicing, and VAT. The Accounts Analyser gives you an instant snapshot of your financial situation, so you can see where your money comes from and where it goes. The bank reconciliation process allows you to match money recorded in Instant Accounts with your bank statements. This software package even lets you create and customise quotations and then automate the invoicing process. The program also creates your VAT return.

Sage Instant Accounts starts at £115 plus VAT (though we found it available on the Internet for as little as £65) rising to £200 if you buy the Payroll and ACT! contact manager facility.

One of the real beauties of Sage software is the attractive and familiar screens. For many years, when its competitors were hiding behind off-putting, text-based, non-windows screens, Sage offered a welcoming approach. We know of many bookkeepers and accountants who still have fond memories of using Sage, long after they've moved to businesses that use other accounting software packages. By and large Sage users are happy users.

Most reasonable-sized businesses are really going to start with the Sage 50 Accounts range, which starts at around £525 and rises to £906 for the top of the range Sage 50 Accounts Starter Package. As the name implies, the Starter Package comes with Sage Training vouchers, 1,000 standard invoices and a year of Sage Cover support.

Sage 50 Accounts comes in three versions – Accounts, Accounts Plus, and Accounts Professional. All versions have an impressive feature list and if you aren't an importer/exporter with a need to run multi-currencies, Accounts or Accounts Plus meet most of your needs. Of course, all these software packages cover all your basic accounting needs. Accounts Plus, however, adds some nice touches like project costing, individual customer pricing and custom price lists, multiple delivery addresses, cheque printing, and improved stock allocation and bill of materials. The top of the range package also offers: intrastat support, Foreign Trader, cash sales, sales order processing, and purchase order processing.

In addition to these accounting software packages, Sage also offers payroll and HR software solutions, reporting and analysis software, and customer contact software. However, the real strength of Sage is that you're buying into a family of products and services that can grow with your business. Sage run their own training courses, which are available regionally, and numerous books are available to show you how to use their various packages. Sage offer a full range of stationery that you can use with their software to improve the image of your business.

Book II

Accounting Basics

For all these reasons, we use Sage 50 Accounts to demonstrate various book-keeping functions throughout this book.

Setting Up Your Computerised Books

After you pick your software, the hard work is done because setting up the package probably takes you less time than researching your options and picking your software. All three packages we discuss in this chapter (see the earlier section 'Surveying Your Software Options') have good start-up tutorials to help you set up the books. QuickBooks even has an interactive interview that asks questions about all aspects of how you want to run your business, and then sets up what you need based on your answers.

Add-ons and fees

All the accounting programs recommended in this section offer add-ons and features you're likely to need, such as:

✔ **Tax updates:** If you have employees and want up-to-date tax information and forms to do your payroll using your accounting software, you need to buy an update each year.

✔ **Online credit card processing and electronic bill paying:** For additional fees, you can buy the capabilities to perform these tasks.

✔ **Point-of-sale software:** This add-on helps you integrate your sales at the cash register with your accounting software.

Before signing on for one of the add-ons, make sure that you understand what the fees are going to be. Usually, you're advised of the additional costs whenever you try to do anything that incurs extra fees.

All the featured accounting software packages produce a number of sample Charts of Accounts (see Book II Chapter 2) that automatically appear after you choose the type of business you plan to run and within which industry your business falls. Start with one of the sample charts that the software offers, as shown in Figure 4-1, and then tweak the chart to your business's needs.

Figure 4-1: As part of the initial interview in Sage 50 Accounts, the system generates a Chart of Accounts based on your type of business.

Configuration Editor						
Departments	Fixed Assets	Custom Fields	Dispute Reasons	Credit Control		Project Costing
General	Chart of Accounts	Terms	Tax Codes	Account Status		Products

The configuration editor helps you to match your accounting system to your type of business.

Click on the tabs at the top of this dialog to configure different areas of your Sage Accounts program.

If you want to apply your settings to the company that you currently have open in Sage Accounts, just press "Apply".

If you wish to save your settings to a configuration file, press "Save" or "Save As...". If you create a configuration file you can use it as a template when you set up a new company in your Sage Accounts program.

If you already have a configuration file available, you can load it into the configuration editor to review or modify it by pressing the "Browse" button below.

Note: you will not be able to apply a loaded configuration to your current company data.

Template Name	General Business
Description	General Business - Standard Accounts
Filename	C:\PROGRAM FILES\SAGE\LINE50 V12 WORK\BOOKS\CONFIGS\GBFS\General.XML

Save | Save As | Apply
Press 'Apply' to use this configuration on your accounts data
Press 'Save' or 'Save As' to create a configuration file to use on other accounts data sets. | Close

When your Chart of Accounts appears, all three programs ask you to enter a company name, address, and tax identification numbers to get started. You then select an accounting period (see Figure 4-2). If the calendar year is your accounting period, you don't have to change anything. But if you operate your business based on another 12-month period, you must enter that information. Most accounting packages assume you run on a 12-month financial year.

If you don't change your accounting period to match how you plan to develop your financial statements, you have to delete the business from the system and start over.

Financial year

Many retail businesses don't close their books at the end of December, because the holiday season is not a good time to be closing out for the year. With gift cards and other new ways to give gifts, purchases after the holiday season can be very active. For this reason, many retail businesses operate on a financial year of 1 February to 31 January, so that they can close the books well after the holiday season ends.

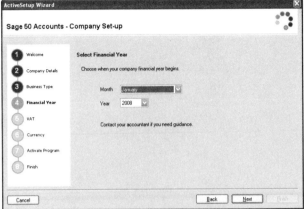

Figure 4-2: Sage 50 Accounts asks you to put in the month that you start your business and the year.

Book II

Accounting Basics

After you set up your business, you can customise the software so that it matches your business's needs.

Customising software to match your operations

With the basics set up (see the preceding section), you can customise the software to fit your business's operations. For example, you're able to pick the type of invoices and other business forms you want to use.

You're also now ready to input information about your bank accounts and other key financial data (see Figure 4-3). Use your main business bank account as the first account listed in your software program.

After entering your bank and other financial information, enter data unique to your business. If you want to use the program's budgeting features, enter your budget information before entering other data. Then add your supplier and customer accounts so that when you start entering transactions, the information is already in the system. If you don't have any outstanding bills or customer payments due, you can wait and enter supplier and customer information as the need arises.

If you have payments to be made or money to be collected from customers, make sure that you input that information so your system is ready when the time comes to pay the bills or input a customer payment. Also, you don't want to forget to pay a bill or collect from a customer!

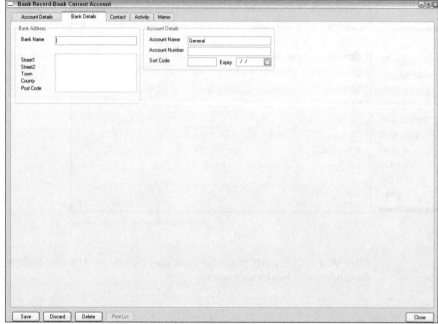

Figure 4-3:
Sage 50
Accounts
collects
information
about your
bank
accounts
via the
Bank
Record
screen,
which is
accessed
from the
Bank tab.

You may be able to import data about your customers, suppliers, and employees from software packages you're currently using to track that information, such as Microsoft Excel or Access. The software program you choose comes with full instructions for importing data.

Don't panic about entering everything into your computerised system right away. All the programs make adding customers, suppliers, and employees very easy at any time.

You also need to enter information about whether you're VAT registered and if so the appropriate VAT rates. Also, you can pick a format for your invoices, set up payroll data, and make arrangements for how you want to pay bills.

Converting your manual bookkeeping to a computerised system

When you're converting a manual bookkeeping system to a computerised system, your conversion takes a bit more time than just starting fresh, because you need to be sure that your new system starts with information that matches your current books. The process for entering your initial data varies depending on the software you've chosen, so we don't go into detail about that process here. To ensure that you properly convert your bookkeeping system, use the information that comes with your software; read through the manual, review the startup suggestions made as you set up the system, and pick the methods that best match your style of operating.

The best time to convert is at the end of an accounting period. That way, you don't have to do a lot of extra work adding transactions that have already occurred during a period. For example, if you decide to computerise your accounting system on 15 March, you have to add all the transactions that occurred between 1 March and 15 March into your new system. Even if you buy the software on 15 March, waiting until 1 April to get started is easier. Although you can convert to a computerised accounting system at the end of a month, the best time is at the end of a calendar or financial year. Otherwise, you have to input data for all the months of the year that have passed.

Whenever you decide to start your computerised bookkeeping, use the data from your trial balance that you used to close the books at the end of the most recent accounting period. In the computerised system, enter the balances for each of the accounts in your trial balance. Asset, Liability, and Capital accounts need to have carry-over balances, but Income and Expense accounts have zero balances.

Of course, when you're starting a new business, you don't have a previous trial balance. In this case, just enter any balances you may have in your cash accounts, any assets your business may own as it starts up, and any liabilities that your business may already owe relating to startup expenses. Also add any contributions from owners that were made to get the business started in the Capital accounts.

After you enter all the appropriate data, run a series of financial reports, such as a profit and loss statement and balance sheet, to be sure that the data is entered and formatted the way as you prefer. Changing the formatting is a lot easier when the system isn't chock-full of data.

You need to be sure that you've entered the right numbers, so verify that the new accounting system's financial reports match what you created manually. If the numbers are different, now's the time to find out why. Otherwise the reports you do at the end of the accounting period are going to be wrong. If the numbers don't match, don't assume that the error is in the data entered. You may find that the error is in the reports you developed manually. Of course, check your entries first, but if the profit and loss statement and balance sheet still don't look right, double-check your trial balances as well.

Chapter 5

Controlling Your Books, Your Records, and Your Money

. . . .

In This Chapter

▶ Protecting your business's cash

▶ Maintaining proper paperwork

▶ Divvying up responsibilities

▶ Insuring your cash handlers

. . . .

*E*very business takes in cash in some form or another: Notes and coins, cheques, and credit card and electronic payments are all eventually deposited as cash into the business's accounts. Before you take in that first penny, your initial concern must be controlling that cash and making sure that none of it walks out the door improperly.

Finding the right level of cash control, while at the same time allowing your employees the flexibility to sell your products or services and provide ongoing customer service, can be a monumental task. If you don't have enough controls, you risk theft or embezzlement. Yet if you have too many controls, employees may miss sales or anger customers.

In this chapter, we explain the basic protections you need to put in place to be sure that all cash coming into or going out of your business is clearly documented and controlled. We also review the type of paperwork you need to document the use of cash and other business assets. Finally, we tell you how to organise your staff to control the flow of your assets properly and insure yourself against possible misappropriation of those assets.

Putting Controls on Your Business's Cash

Think about how careful you are with your personal cash. You find various ways to protect the cash you carry around, you dole it out carefully to your family members, and you may even hide cash in a safe place in the house just in case you need it for unexpected purposes.

You're very protective of your cash when you're the only one who handles it, but consider the vulnerability of your business cash. After all, you aren't the only one handling that cash. You have some employees encountering incoming cash at cash registers, others opening the mail and finding cheques for orders to purchase products or pay bills, as well as cheques from other sources. And don't forget that employees may need petty cash to pay for mail sent COD (Cash on Delivery), or to pay for other unexpected, low-cost needs.

If you watch over every transaction in which cash enters your business, you have no time to do the things you need to do to grow your business. When the business is small, you can sign all cheques and maintain control of cash going out, but as soon as the business grows, you just may not have the time.

The good news is that just putting in place the proper controls for your cash can help protect it. Cash flows through your business in four key ways:

- ✔ Deposits and payments into and out of your current accounts
- ✔ Deposits and payments into and out of your savings accounts
- ✔ Petty cash funds in critical locations where quick access to cash may be needed
- ✔ Transactions made in your cash registers

The following sections cover some key controls for each of these cash flow points.

Current accounts

Almost every penny that comes into your business flows through your business's current account (at least that *should* happen). Whether the cash is collected at your cash registers, payments received in the mail, cash used to fill the cash registers or petty cash accounts, payments sent out to pay business obligations, or any other cash need, this cash enters and exits your current account. Thus, your current account is your main tool for protecting your cash flow.

Choosing the right bank

Finding the right bank to help you set up your current account and the controls that limit access to that account is crucial. When evaluating your banking options, ask yourself the following questions:

- ✔ Does this bank have a branch conveniently located for my business?
- ✔ Does this bank operate at times when I need it most?
- ✔ Does this bank offer secure ways to deposit cash even when the bank is closed?

Most banks have secure drop boxes for cash so you can deposit receipts as quickly as possible at the end of the business day rather than secure the cash overnight yourself.

Visit local bank branches yourself, and check out the type of business services each bank offers. Pay particular attention to:

- ✔ The type of personal attention you receive
- ✔ How questions are handled
- ✔ What type of charges may be tacked on for personalised attention

Some banks require business account holders to call a centralised line for assistance rather than depend on local branches. Most banks charge if you use a cashier rather than an ATM (automatic teller machine). Other banks charge for every transaction, whether a deposit, withdrawal, or cheque. Many banks have charges that differ for business accounts. If you plan to accept credit cards, compare the services offered for that as well.

The general rule is that banks charge businesses for everything they do. However, they charge less for tasks that can be automated and thus involve less manual effort. So, you save money when you use electronic payment and receipt processes. In other words, pay your suppliers electronically and get your customers to pay you the same way, and you reduce your banking costs.

Deciding on types of cheques

After you choose your bank, you need to consider what type of cheques you want to use in your business. For example, you need different cheques depending upon whether you handwrite each cheque or print cheques from your computerised accounting system.

Writing cheques manually

If you plan to write your cheques, you're most likely to use a business cheque book, which in its simplest form is exactly the same as a personal cheque book, with a counterfoil (or cheque stub) on the left and a cheque on the right. This arrangement provides the best control for manual cheques because each cheque and counterfoil is numbered. When you write a cheque, you fill out the counterfoil with details such as the date, the cheque's recipient, and the purpose of the cheque. The counterfoil also has a space to keep a running total of your balance in the account.

Printing computer-generated cheques

If you plan to print cheques from your computerised accounting system, you need to order cheques that match that system's programming. Each computer software program has a unique template for printing cheques. Figure 5-1 shows a common layout for business cheques that a computerised accounting system prints out. The key information is exactly what you expect to see on any cheque – payee details, date, and amount in both words and numbers.

Figure 5-1:
Businesses
that choose
to print their
cheques
using their
comput-
erised
accounting
systems
usually
order them
with their
business
name
already
printed on
the cheque.
This
particular
cheque is
compatible
with
Sage 50
Accounts.

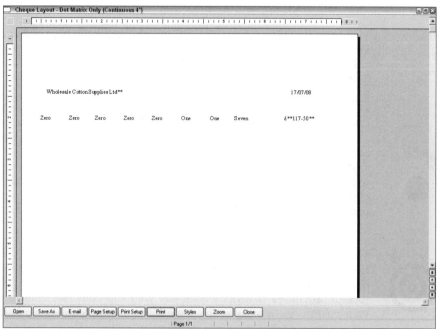

You can also set up your computer accounting system to print out the precise details you'd expect to find on a manual cheque – the current date, name
of the recipient, and the value of the cheque. Unlike a manually prepared
cheque, you don't have a counterfoil to fill in, which is not a problem because
your computerised accounting system records this information for you: It
keeps an internal record of all cheques issued. If you need to check that you
issued a cheque correctly, you can always run a report or make an on-screen
enquiry on your computerised accounting system.

Initially, when the business is small, you can sign each cheque and keep control of the outflow of money. But as the business grows, you may find that you
need to delegate cheque-signing responsibilities to someone else, especially if
you travel frequently. Many small business owners set up cheque-signing procedures that allow one or two of their staff to sign cheques up to a designated
amount, such as £5,000. Any cheques above that designated amount require
the owner's signature, or the signature of an employee and a second designated person, such as an officer of the business.

Making deposits in the current account

Of course, you aren't just withdrawing from your business's current account (that would be a big problem). You also need to deposit money into that account, and you want to be sure that your paying in slips contain all the necessary detail as well as documentation to back up the deposit information. Most banks provide printed paying in slips with all the necessary detail to be sure that the money is deposited into the appropriate account, together with who wrote each cheque, the value, and the date received.

A good practice is to record cheques immediately as part of a daily morning routine. Enter the details onto the paying in slip and update your computerised or manual accounting system at the same time. Make sure that you pay in any money received before 3:30 p.m. on the same day, to ensure that your bank account gets credit that day rather than the next. (We talk more about controls for incoming cash in the 'Dividing staff responsibilities' section, later in this chapter.) If you get both personal and business cheques sent to the same address, instruct the person opening the mail about how to differentiate the types of cheques and how each type of cheque needs to be handled to best protect your incoming cash, whether for business or personal purposes.

Book II

Accounting Basics

You may think that making bank deposits is as easy as 1-2-3, but when it comes to business deposits and multiple cheques, things get a bit more complicated. To make deposits to your business's current account properly, follow these steps:

1. **Record on the paying in slip the full details of all cheques being deposited as well as the total cash being deposited. Also make a note of how many cheques you're paying into the bank on that paying in slip.**

2. **Record the details regarding the source of the deposited cash before you make the deposit; file everything in your daily bank folder.**

   (We talk more about filing in the section 'Keeping the Right Paperwork', later in this chapter.)

3. **Make sure that the cashier at the bank stamps the paying in slip as confirmation that the bank has received all the cheques and cash.**

   If you're paying in cheques via the ATM then treat it exactly as if you were paying in via the cashier. Still prepare your own paying slip and make sure that you pick up the receipt that the ATM gives you. This does not ensure that things will not go wrong but it will ensure you have a paper trail if they do.

Savings accounts

Some businesses find that they have more cash than they need to meet their immediate plans. Rather than keep that extra cash in a non-interest bearing account, many businesses open a savings account to store the extra cash.

If you're a small business owner with few employees, you probably control the flow of money into and out of your savings account yourself. As you grow and find that you need to delegate the responsibility for the business's savings, ensure that you think carefully about who gets access and how you can document the flow of funds into and out of the savings account. Treat a savings account like a current account and use paying in slips to record deposits and cheque book stubs to record payments.

Petty cash accounts

Every business needs cash on almost a weekly basis. Businesses need to keep some cash on hand, called *petty cash,* for unexpected expenses such as money to pay for letters and packages delivered COD, money to buy a few emergency stamps to get the mail out, or money for some office supplies needed before the next delivery.

You certainly don't want to have a lot of cash sitting around in the office, but try to keep £50 to £100 in a petty cash box. If you subsequently find that you're faced with more or less cash expenses than you expected, you can always adjust the amount kept in petty cash accordingly.

No matter how much you keep in petty cash, make sure that you set up a good control system that requires anyone who uses the cash to write a petty cash voucher specifying how much was used and why. Also ask that a cash receipt, for example from the shop or post office, is attached to the voucher in order to justify the cash withdrawal whenever possible. In most cases, a member of staff buys something for the business and then gets reimbursed for that expense. If the expense is small enough, you can reimburse through the petty cash fund. If the expense is more than a few pounds, ask the person to fill out an expense account form and get reimbursed by cheque. Petty cash is usually used for minor expenses of £10 or less.

The best way to control petty cash is to pick one person in the office to manage the use of all petty cash. Before giving that person more cash, she should be able to prove the absence of cash used and why it was used.

Poor control of the petty cash box can lead to small but significant losses of cash. Quite often you can find it difficult or impossible to identify or prove who took the cash. The best solution is to make it slightly more difficult for employees to obtain petty cash, than having a free-for-all system. A locked box in a cupboard works very well.

For the ultimate control of cash, use the imprest system in which a fixed amount is drawn from the bank and paid into petty cash (the float). After that, cash is issued only against a petty cash voucher. This system means that, at any point, cash, or cash plus vouchers, should be equal to the total of the petty cash float. At the end of the week (or month) the vouchers are removed and the cash made up to the original amount.

Cash registers

Have you ever gone into a business and tried to pay with a large note only to find out that the cashier has no change? This frustrating experience happens in many businesses, especially those that don't carefully monitor the money in their cash registers. Most businesses empty cash registers each night and put any cash not being deposited in the bank that night into a safe. However, many businesses instruct their cashiers to deposit their cash in a business safe periodically throughout the day and get a paper voucher to show the cash deposited. These daytime deposits minimise the cash held in case the store is the victim of a robbery.

All these types of controls are necessary parts of modern business operations, but they can have consequences that make customers angry. Most customers just walk out the door and don't come back when they can't buy what they want using the notes they have on hand.

At the beginning of the day, cashiers usually start out with a set amount of cash in the register. As they collect money and give out change, the register records the transactions. At the end of the day, the cashier must count out the amount of change left in the register, run a copy of all transactions that passed through that register, and total the cash collected. Then the cashier must prove that the amount of cash remaining in that register totals the amount of cash the register started with plus the amount of cash collected during the day. After the cashier balances the register, the person in charge of cash deposits (usually the shop manager or someone on the accounting or bookkeeping staff) takes all the cash out, except the amount needed for the next day, and deposits it in the bank. (We talk more about separation of staff duties in the section 'Dividing staff responsibilities', later in this chapter.)

In addition to having the proper amount of cash in the register necessary to give customers the change they need, you also must make sure that your cashiers are giving the right amount of change and actually recording all sales on their cash registers. Keeping an eye on cashier activities is good business practice in any case, but you can also protect against cash theft by your employees in this way. Three ways exist in which cashiers can pocket some extra cash:

- ✔ **They don't record the sale in the cash register and instead pocket the cash.** The best deterrent to this type of theft is supervision. You can decrease the likelihood of theft through unrecorded sales by printing up sales tickets that the cashier must use to enter a sale in the cash register and open the cash drawer. If cash register transactions don't match sales receipts, the cashier must show a voided transaction for the missing ticket, or explain why the cash drawer was opened without a ticket.

- ✔ **They don't provide a sales receipt and instead pocket the cash.** In this scenario the cashier neglects to give a sales receipt to one customer in the queue. The cashier gives the next customer the unused sales receipt but doesn't actually record the second transaction in the cash register. Instead, she just pockets the cash. In the business's books, the second sale never took place. The customer whose sale wasn't recorded has a valid receipt though it may not match exactly what was bought. Therefore, the customer is unlikely to notice any problem unless something needs to be returned later. Your best defence against this type of deception is to post a sign reminding all customers that they must get a receipt for all purchases and that the receipt is required to get a refund or exchange. Providing numbered sales receipts that include a duplicate copy can also help prevent this problem; cashiers need to produce the duplicates at the end of the day when proving the amount of cash flow that passed through their registers.

In addition to protection from theft by cashiers, the printed sales receipt system can be used to monitor shoplifters and prevent them from getting money for merchandise they never bought. For example, suppose a shoplifter takes a blouse out of a store, as well as some blank sales receipts. The next day the shoplifter comes back with the blouse and one of the stolen sales receipts filled out as though the blouse had actually been purchased the day before. You can spot the fraud because that sales receipt is part of a numbered batch of sales receipts that you've already identified as missing or stolen. You can quickly identify that the customer never paid for the merchandise and call the police.

✔ **They record a false credit voucher and keep the cash for themselves.** In this case the cashier writes up a credit voucher for a nonexistent customer and then pockets the cash refund. Most shops use a numbered credit voucher system to control this problem, so each credit can be carefully monitored with some detail that proves its connection to a previous customer purchase, such as a sales receipt. Customers are often asked to provide an address and telephone number before receiving a refund. Although this may not put off the determined fraudster, the opportunist thief is likely to be deterred. Also, shops usually require that a manager review the reason for the credit voucher, whether a return or exchange, and approve the transaction before cash or credit is given. When the bookkeeper records the sales return in the books, the number for the credit voucher is recorded with the transaction so that the detail about that credit voucher is easy to find if a question is raised later about the transaction.

Even if cashiers don't deliberately pocket cash, they can inadvertently give the wrong change. If you run a retail outlet, training and supervising your cashiers is a critical task that you must handle yourself or hand over to a trusted employee.

Keeping the Right Paperwork

When handling cash, you can see that a lot of paper changes hands, whether from the cash register, deposits into your current accounts, or petty cash withdrawals. Therefore, careful documentation is paramount to control the movement of cash into and out of your business properly. And don't forget about organisation; you need to be able to find that documentation if questions about cash flow arise later.

Monitoring cash flow isn't the only reason why you need to keep loads of paperwork. In order to do your taxes and write off business expenses, you need receipts for those expenses. You also need details about the money you pay to employees, and tax and National Insurance contributions collected for your employees, in order to file the proper reports with HM Revenue & Customs. (We discuss taxes in Book VI, and dealing with HM Revenue & Customs in relation to employee matters in Book V Chapter 2.) Setting up a good filing system and knowing what to keep and for how long is very important for any small businessperson.

Creating a filing system

To get started setting up your filing system, you need the following supplies:

- ✔ **Filing cabinets:** Pretty self-explanatory – you can't have a filing system with nothing to keep the files in.

- ✔ **File folders:** Set up separate files for each of your suppliers, employees, and customers who buy on credit, as well as files for backup information on each of your transactions. Many bookkeepers file transaction information using the date the transaction was added to their journal. If the transaction relates to a customer, supplier, or employee, they add a duplicate copy of the transaction to the individual files as well.

  Even if you have a computerised accounting system, you need to file paperwork related to the transactions you enter into your computer system. You still need to maintain employee, supplier, and customer files in hard copy just in case something goes wrong – for example, if your computer system crashes, you need the originals to restore the data. Back up your computerised accounting system's data regularly to minimise the effects of such a crisis. Daily backups are best; one week is the longest you should ever go without a backup.

- ✔ **Ring binders:** These binders are great for things like your Chart of Accounts (see Book II Chapter 2), your Nominal Ledger (see Book II Chapter 3) and your system of journals (see Book II Chapter 3) because you add to these documents regularly and the binders make adding additional pages easy. Make sure that you number the pages as you add them to the binder, so you can quickly spot a missing page. How many binders you need depends on how many financial transactions you have each accounting period. You can keep everything in one binder, or you may want to set up a binder for the Chart of Accounts and Nominal Ledger and then a separate binder for each of your active journals. The decision is based on what makes your job easier.

✔ **Expandable files:** These files are the best way to keep track of current supplier activity and any bills that may be due. Make sure that you have

- **An alphabetical file:** Use this file to track all your outstanding purchase orders by supplier. After you fill the order, you can file all details about that order in the supplier's individual file in case questions about the order arise later.

- **A 12-month file:** Use this file to keep track of bills that you need to pay. Simply place the bill in the slot for the month payment is due. Many businesses also use a 30-day expandable file. At the beginning of the month, the bills are placed in the 30-day expandable file based on the dates that they need to be paid. This approach provides a quick and organised visual reminder for bills that are due.

If you're using a computerised accounting system, you don't need the expandable files because your accounting system can remind you when bills are due (as long as you add the information to the system when the bill arrives).

✔ **Blank computer disks or other storage media:** Use these to backup your computerised system on a weekly or, better yet, daily basis. Keep the backup discs in a fire safe or somewhere unaffected if a fire destroys the business. (A fire safe is the best way to keep critical financial data safe, and is therefore a must for any business.)

Working out what to keep and for how long

As you can probably imagine, the pile of paperwork you need to hold on to can get very large very quickly. As they see their files getting thicker and thicker, most businesspeople wonder what they can toss, what they really need to keep, and how long they need to keep it.

Generally, keep most transaction-related paperwork for as long as HM Revenue & Customs can come and audit your books. For most types of audits, that means six years. But if you fail to file your tax return or file it fraudulently (and we hope this doesn't apply to you), HM Revenue & Customs may question you at any time, because no time limitations exist in these cases.

HM Revenue & Customs isn't the only reason to keep records around for longer than one year. You may need proof-of-purchase information for your insurance company if an asset is lost, stolen, or destroyed by fire or other accident. Also, you need to hang on to information regarding any business loan until paid off, just in case the bank questions how much you paid. After the loan's paid off, ensure that you keep proof of payment indefinitely in case a question about the loan ever arises. Information about property and other asset holdings needs to be kept around for as long as you hold the asset and for at least six years after the asset is sold. You're legally required to keep information about employees for at least three years after the employee leaves.

Keep the current year's files easily accessible in a designated filing area and keep the most recent past year's files in accessible filing cabinets if you have room. Box up records when they hit the two-year-old mark, and put them in storage. Make sure that you date your boxed records with information about what they are, when they were put into storage, and when you can destroy them. Many people forget that last detail, and boxes pile up until total desperation sets in and no more room is left. Then someone must take the time to sort through the boxes and figure out what needs to be kept and what can be destroyed – not a fun job.

It is a legal requirement to keep information about all transactions for six years. After that, make a list of things you want to hold on to longer for other reasons, such as asset holdings and loan information. Check with your lawyer and accountant to get their recommendations on what to keep and for how long.

Book II

Accounting Basics

Protecting Your Business Against Internal Fraud

Many businesspeople start their operations by carefully hiring people they can trust, thinking: 'We're a family – they'd never steal from me.'

Often a business owner finds out too late that even the most loyal employee may steal from the business if the opportunity arises and the temptation becomes too great – or if the employee gets caught up in a serious personal financial dilemma and needs fast cash. In this section, we talk about the steps you can take to prevent people stealing from your business.

Facing the reality of financial fraud

The four basic types of financial fraud are:

- ✔ **Embezzlement,** which is the illegal use of funds by a person who controls those funds. For example, a bookkeeper may use business money for her own personal needs. Many times, embezzlement stories don't appear in the newspapers because businesspeople are so embarrassed that they choose to keep the affair quiet. They usually settle privately with the embezzler rather than face public scrutiny.

- ✔ **Internal theft,** which is the stealing of business assets by employees, such as taking office supplies or products the business sells without paying for them. Internal theft is often the culprit behind stock shrinkage.

✔ **Payoffs and kickbacks,** which are situations in which employees accept cash or other benefits in exchange for access to the business, often creating a scenario where the business that the employee works for pays more for the goods or products than necessary. That extra money finds its way into the pocket of the employee who helped facilitate the access. For example, say Business A wants to sell its products to Business B. An employee in Business B helps Business A get in the door. Business A prices its product a bit higher and gives the employee of Business B the extra profit in the form of a kickback for helping it out. A payoff is paid before the sale is made, essentially saying 'please'. A kickback is paid after the sale is made, essentially saying 'thank you'. In reality, payoffs and kickbacks are a form of bribery, but few businesses report or litigate this problem (although employees are fired when deals are uncovered).

✔ **Skimming,** which occurs when employees take money from receipts and don't record the revenue on the books.

Although any of these financial crimes can happen in a small business, the one that hits small businesses the hardest is embezzlement. This crime happens most frequently when one person has access or control over most of the business's financial activities. For example, a single bookkeeper may write cheques, make deposits, and balance the monthly bank statement – talk about having your fingers in a very big till.

Caught with fingers in the till

Alice is a bookkeeper who's been with Business A for a long time. She was promoted to office manager after being with the business for 20 years. She's like a family member to the business owner, who trusts her implicitly. Because he's so busy with other aspects of running the business, he gives her control of the daily grind of cash flow. The beloved office manager handles or supervises all incoming and outgoing cash, reconciles the bank statements, handles payroll, signs all the cheques, and files the business's tax returns.

All that control gives her the opportunity, credibility, and access to embezzle a lot of money. At first, the trust is well founded, and Alice handles her new responsibilities very well. But after about three years in the role as office manager,

she develops a gambling habit and the debts mount up.

Alice decides to pay herself more money. She adds her husband to the payroll and documents the cheques for him as consulting expenses. She draws large cash cheques to buy non-existent office supplies and equipment, and then, worst of all, she files the business's tax returns and pockets the money that should go to paying the tax due. The business owner doesn't find out about the problem until HM Revenue & Customs comes calling, and by then, the office manager has retired and moved away.

This story may sound far-fetched, but you can read about similar embezzlement schemes in the national newspapers.

The high cost of employee versus customer theft

According to the British Retail Consortium internal theft by employees is the largest single component of white-collar crime. You don't hear much about it, though, because many businesses choose to keep quiet. The reality is that employee theft and embezzlement in UK are estimated to cost employers over £500 million per year. Over 50 per cent of all losses are the result of employee theft. Four key situations in the workplace provide opportunities for theft and embezzlement: poor internal controls, too much control given to certain individuals, lax management, and failure to prescreen employees adequately.

Dividing staff responsibilities

Your primary protection against financial crime is properly separating staff responsibilities when the flow of business cash is involved. Basically, never have one person handling more than one of the following tasks:

- **Bookkeeping:** Involves reviewing and entering all transactions into the business's books. The bookkeeper makes sure that transactions are accurate, valid, appropriate, and have the proper authorisation. For example, if a transaction requires paying a supplier, the bookkeeper makes sure that the charges are accurate and someone with proper authority has approved the payment. The bookkeeper can review documentation of cash receipts and the overnight deposits taken to the bank, but shouldn't actually make the deposit. Also, if the bookkeeper is responsible for handling payments from external parties, such as customers or suppliers, she shouldn't enter those transactions in the books.

- **Authorisation:** Involves being the manager or managers delegated to authorise expenditures for their departments. You may decide that transactions over a certain amount must have two or more authorisations before cheques can be sent to pay a bill. Spell out authorisation levels clearly and make sure that everyone follows them, even the owner or managing director of the business. (Remember, as owner, you set the tone for how the rest of the office operates; when you take shortcuts, you set a bad example and undermine the system you put in place.)

- **Money-handling:** Involves direct contact with incoming cash or revenue, whether cheque, credit card, or credit transactions, as well as outgoing cash flow. The person who handles money directly, such as a cashier, shouldn't also prepare and make bank deposits. Likewise, the person writing cheques to pay business bills shouldn't be authorised to sign those cheques; to be safe, have one person prepare the cheques based on authorised documentation, and a second person sign those cheques, after reviewing the authorised documentation.

When setting up your cash-handling systems, try to think like an embezzler to figure out how someone can take advantage of a system.

✔ **Financial report preparation and analysis:** Involves the actual preparation of the financial reports and any analysis of those reports. Someone who's not involved in the day-to-day entering of transactions in the books needs to prepare the financial reports. For most small businesses, the bookkeeper turns over the raw reports from the computerised accounting system to an outside accountant who reviews the materials and prepares the financial reports. In addition, the accountant does a financial analysis of the business activity results for the previous accounting period.

We realise that you may be just starting up a small business and therefore not have enough staff to separate all these duties. Until you do have that capability, make sure that you stay heavily involved in the inflow and outflow of cash in your business. The following tips tell you how:

✔ **Periodically (once a month) open your business's bank statements, and keep a close watch on the transactions.** Someone else can be given the responsibility of reconciling the statement, but you still need to keep an eye on the transactions listed.

✔ **Periodically look at your business cheque book counterfoils to ensure that no cheques are missing.** A bookkeeper who knows that you periodically check the books is less likely to find an opportunity for theft or embezzlement. If you find that a cheque or page of cheques is missing, act quickly to find out if the cheques were used legitimately. If you can't find the answer, call your bank and put a stop on the missing cheque numbers.

✔ **Periodically observe your cashiers and managers handling cash to make sure that they're following the rules you've established.** This practice is known as *management by walking around* – the more often you're out there, the less likely you are to be a victim of employee theft and fraud.

Balancing control costs

As a small businessperson, you're always trying to balance the cost of protecting your cash and assets with the cost of adequately separating those duties. Putting in place too many controls, which end up costing you money, can be a big mistake. For example, you may create stock controls that require salespeople to contact one particular person who has the key to your product warehouse. This kind of control may prevent employee theft, but can also result in lost sales, because salespeople can't find the key-holder while dealing with an interested customer. In the end, the customer gets mad, and you lose the sale.

When you put controls in place, talk to your staff both before and after instituting the controls to see how they're working and to check for any unforeseen problems. Be willing and able to adjust your controls to balance the business needs of selling your products, managing the cash flow, and keeping your eye on making a profit. Talk to other businesspeople to see what they do and pick up tips from established best practice. Your external accountant can be a good source of valuable information.

Generally, as you make rules for your internal controls, make sure that the cost of protecting an asset is no more than the asset you're trying to protect. For example, don't go overboard to protect office supplies by forcing your staff to wait around for hours to access needed supplies while you and a manager are at a meeting away from the office.

Ask yourself these four questions as you design your internal controls:

- ✔ What exactly do I want to prevent or detect – errors, sloppiness, theft, fraud, or embezzlement?
- ✔ Do I face the problem frequently?
- ✔ What do I estimate the loss to be?
- ✔ What is the cost to me of implementing the change in procedures to prevent or detect the problem?

You can't answer all these questions yourself, so consult with your managers and the staff the changes are likely to impact. Get their answers to these questions, and listen to their feedback.

When you finish putting together the new internal control rule, ensure that you document why you decided to implement the rule and the information you collected in developing it. After the rule's been in place for a while, test your assumptions. Make sure that you are in fact detecting the errors, theft, fraud, or embezzlement that you hoped and expected to detect. Check the costs of keeping the rule in place by looking at cash outlay, employee time and morale, and the impact on customer service. If you find any problems with your internal controls, take the time to fix them and change the rule, again documenting the process. Detailed documentation ensures that, if two or three years down the road someone questions why she is doing something, you have the answers and are able to determine whether the problem is still valid, as well as whether the rule is still necessary or needs to be changed.

Book II

Accounting
Basics

Insuring Your Cash through Employee Bonding

If you have employees who handle a lot of cash, insuring your business against theft is an absolute must. This insurance, known as *employee bonding,* is often offered as an extension to an existing business insurance policy, and helps to protect you against theft and reduce your risk of loss.

If you carry a bond on your cash handlers, you're covered for losses sustained by any employee who's bonded. You also have coverage when an employee's act causes losses to a client of your business. For example, when you're a financial consultant and your bookkeeper embezzles a client's cash, you're protected for the loss.

A *fidelity bond* is a type of insurance that you can buy through the company that handles your business insurance policies. It is a stand alone policy, unlike employee bonding. The cost varies greatly depending on the type of business you operate and the amount of cash or other assets that are handled by the employees you want to bond. If an employee steals from you or one of your customers, the insurance covers the loss.

Employers also bond employees who may be in a position to steal something other than cash. For example, a cleaning service may bond its workers in case a worker steals something from a customer. If a customer reports something missing, the insurance company that bonded the employee covers the loss. Without a bond, an employer must pay back the customer for any loss.

Chapter 6

Tracking Your Purchases and Counting Your Sales

Do you want to know every single financial transaction that happens in your business each and every day? You should. Recording every transaction is the only way you can put all the pieces together and see how well your business is doing financially.

This chapter shows you how to monitor your day-to-day business operations by recording sales and purchases as well as any discounts and returns.

Buying and Tracking Purchases

In order to make money, your business must have something to sell. Whether you sell products or offer services, you have to deal with costs directly related to the goods or services being sold. Those costs primarily come from the purchase or manufacturing of the products you plan to sell or the items you need in order to provide the services.

All businesses must keep careful watch over the cost of the products to be sold or services to be offered. Ultimately, your business's profits depend on how well you manage those costs because, in most cases, costs increase over time rather than decrease. How often do you find a reduction in the price of needed items? Doesn't happen often. When costs increase but the price to the customer remains unchanged, the profit you make on each sale is less.

In addition to the costs to produce products or services, every business has additional expenses associated with purchasing supplies needed to run the business. The bookkeeper has primary responsibility for monitoring all these costs and expenses as invoices are paid and alerting business owners or managers when suppliers increase prices. In the following sections, we cover how to track purchases and their costs, manage stock, buy and manage supplies, and pay the bills for the items your business buys. We also review the basic responsibilities of a business's bookkeeping and accounting staff for tracking sales, making adjustments to those sales, monitoring customer accounts, and alerting management to slow-paying customers.

Keeping Track of Stock

Products to be sold are called *stock*. As a bookkeeper, you use two accounts to track stock:

- ✔ **Purchases:** Where you record the actual purchase of goods to be sold. This account is used to calculate the *Cost of Goods Sold,* which is an item on the profit and loss statement (see Book III Chapter 1 for more on this statement).

- ✔ **Stock:** Where you track the value of stock on hand. This value is shown on the balance sheet as an asset in a line item called *Stock* (Book III Chapter 2 addresses the balance sheet).

Businesses track physical stock on hand using one of two methods:

- ✔ **Periodic stock count:** Conducting a physical count of the stock in the stores and in the warehouse. This count can be done daily, monthly, yearly, or for any other period that best matches your business needs. (Many businesses close for all or part of a day to count stock.)

- ✔ **Perpetual stock count:** Adjusting stock counts as each sale is made. In order to use this method, you must manage your stock using a computerised accounting system tied into your point of sale (usually cash registers).

Even if you use a perpetual stock method, periodically do a physical count of stock to ensure that the numbers match what's in your computer system. Because theft, damage, and loss of stock aren't automatically entered in your computer system, the losses don't show up until you do a physical count of the stock you have on hand in your business.

When preparing your profit and loss statement at the end of an accounting period (whether that period is for a month, a quarter, or a year), you need to calculate the Cost of Goods Sold in order to calculate the profit made.

In order to calculate the Cost of Goods Sold, you must first find out how many items of stock were sold. You start with the amount of stock on hand at the beginning of the month (called *Opening Stock*), as recorded in the Stock account, and add the amount of purchases, as recorded in the Purchases account, to find the Goods Available for Sale. Then you subtract the stock on hand at the end of the month *(Closing Stock)*, which is determined by counting remaining stock.

Here's how you calculate the number of goods sold:

> Opening Stock + Purchases = Goods Available for Sale – Closing Stock = Items Sold

After you determine the number of goods sold, compare that number to the actual number of items the business sold during that accounting period, which is based on sales figures collected through the month. When the numbers don't match, you have a problem. The mistake may be in the stock count, or items may be unaccounted for because they've been misplaced or damaged and discarded. In the worst-case scenario, you may have a problem with customer or employee theft. These differences are usually tracked within the accounting system in a line item called *Stock Shortages.*

Entering initial cost

When your business first receives stock, you enter the initial cost of that stock into the bookkeeping system based on the shipment's invoice. In some cases, invoices are sent separately, and only a delivery note is included in the order. When that situation applies, you still record the receipt of the goods, because the business incurs the cost from the day the goods are received and you must be sure that the money is available to pay for the goods when the invoice arrives and the bill comes due. (You track outstanding bills in the Accounts Payable account.) Where you only have a delivery note, use the price agreed on your purchase order (if you use purchase orders) or the price from your last invoice from that supplier.

Entering the receipt of stock is a relatively easy entry in the bookkeeping system. For example, if your business buys £1,000 of stock to be sold, you make the following record in the books:

	Debit	*Credit*
Purchases	£1,000	
Accounts Payable		£1,000

The Purchases account increases by £1,000 to reflect the additional costs, and the Accounts Payable account increases by the same amount to reflect the amount of the bill that needs to be paid in the future.

When stock enters your business, in addition to recording the actual costs, you need more detail about what was bought, how much of each item was bought, and what each item cost. You also need to track

- How much stock you have on hand
- The value of the stock you have on hand
- When you need to order more stock

Tracking these details for each type of product bought can be a nightmare, especially if you're trying to keep the books for a retail shop, because you need to set up a special Stock journal with pages detailing purchase and sale information for every item you carry. (See Book II Chapter 3 for the low-down on journals.)

However, computerised accounting simplifies this process of tracking stock. Details about stock can be entered initially into your computer accounting system in several ways:

- If you pay by cheque or credit card when you receive the stock, you can enter the details about each item on the cheque counter foil or credit card slip.
- If you use purchase orders, you can enter the detail about each item on the purchase order, record receipt of the items when they arrive, and update the information when you receive the bill.
- If you don't use purchase orders, you can enter the detail about the items when you receive them and update the information when you receive the bill.

To give you an idea of how this information is collected in a computerised accounting software program, Figure 6-1 shows you how to enter the details in Sage 50 Accounts. This particular form is for the receipt of stock without a purchase order and can be used when you receive a supplier invoice.

Figure 6-2 shows a stock item in the computerised accounting system. Note that you must give the item a product code and a description. The product code is a short unique name or code to identify the stock item internally. The longer description is a more user-friendly name that can appear on customer invoices (sales transactions). You can input a cost and sales price if you want, or you can leave them at zero and enter the cost and sales prices with each transaction.

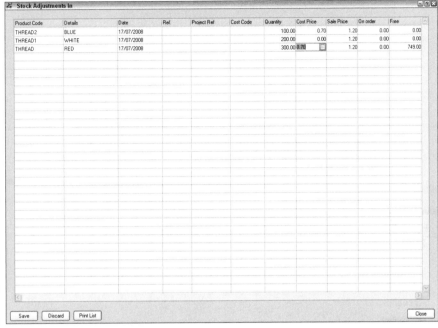

© 2008 Sage (UK) Limited. All rights reserved.

Figure 6-1:
Recording of the receipt of stock using Sage 50 Accounts.

If you have a set contract purchase price or sales price on a stock item, you can enter the price on this form to save time – you don't then have to enter the price each time you record a transaction. But, if the price changes frequently, leave the space blank so you don't forget to enter the updated price when you enter a transaction.

Notice in Figure 6-2 that you can also use this form to give you information about stock on hand and when stock needs to be reordered. To make sure that your shelves are never empty, enter a number for each item that indicates at what point you want to reorder stock. You can indicate the 'Reorder Level' in the section called 'Status'. (A nice feature of Sage 50 Accounts is that you can run a report to see which stock items have fallen below their reorder level and use that to place your next order.)

If you use the Purchase Order Processing order routine and save the form that records the receipt of stock in Sage 50 Accounts, the software automatically

- Adjusts the quantity of stock you have in stock

- Increases the Asset account called Stock

- Lowers the quantity of items on order (if you initially entered the information as a purchase order)

- Averages the cost of stock on hand

- Increases the Accounts Payable account

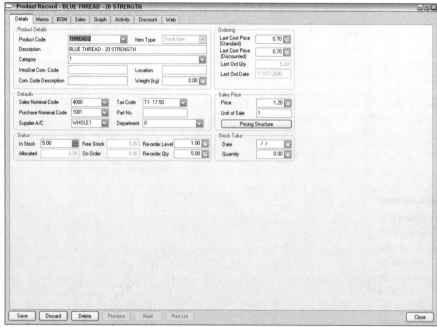

Figure 6-2:
Setting up
a stock
item using
Sage 50
Accounts.

Managing stock and its value

After you record the receipt of stock, you have the responsibility of managing the stock you have on hand. You must also know the value of that stock. You may think that as long as you know what you paid for the items, the value isn't difficult to calculate. Well, accountants can't let things be that simple, and so five different ways exist to value stock:

✓ **LIFO (Last In, First Out):** You assume that the last items put on the shelves (the newest items) are the first items to be sold. Retail shops that sell non-perishable items, such as tools, are likely to use this type of system. For example, when a hardware store gets new hammers, workers probably don't unload the hammers on the shelves and put the newest items in the back. Instead, the new hammers are just put in the front, so they're likely to be sold first.

✓ **FIFO (First In, First Out):** You assume that the first items put on the shelves (the oldest items) are sold first. Shops that sell perishable goods, such as food shops, use this stock valuation method most often. For example, when new milk arrives at a shop, the person stocking the shelves unloads the older milk, puts the new milk at the back of the shelf, and then puts the older milk in front. Each carton of milk (or other perishable item) has a date indicating the last day it can be sold, so food shops always try to sell the oldest stuff first, while those items are still sellable. (They try, but how many times have you reached to the back of a food shelf to find items with the longest shelf life?)

✔ **Averaging:** You average the cost of goods received, to avoid worrying about which items are sold first or last. This method of stock is used most often in any retail or services environment where prices are constantly fluctuating and the business owner finds that an average cost works best for managing his Cost of Goods Sold.

✔ **Specific Identification:** You maintain cost figures for each stock item individually. Retail outlets that sell big-ticket items, such as cars, which often have a different set of extras on each item, use this type of stock valuation method.

✔ **LCM (Lower of Cost or Market):** You set stock values based on whichever is lower: the amount you paid originally for the stock item (the cost), or the current market value of the item. Businesses that deal in precious metals, commodities, or publicly traded securities often use this method because the prices of their products can fluctuate wildly, sometimes even in the same day.

Book II

Accounting Basics

After you choose a stock valuation method, you need to use the same method each year on your financial reports and when you file your accounts. If you decide you want to change the method, you need to explain the reasons for the change to both HM Revenue & Customs and to your financial backers. If you run an incorporated business in which shares have been sold, you need to explain the change to your shareholders. You also have to go back and show how the change in stock method impacts your prior financial reporting, and adjust your profit margins in previous years to reflect the new stock valuation method's impact on your long-term profit history.

Figuring out the best method for you

We're sure that you're wondering why the stock valuation method you use matters so much. The key to the choice is the impact on your bottom line as well as the tax your business pays.

Because FIFO assumes the oldest (and most likely the lowest priced) items are sold first, this method results in a lower Cost of Goods Sold number. Because Cost of Goods Sold is subtracted from sales to determine profit, a lower Cost of Goods Sold number produces a higher profit. (For more on Cost of Goods Sold, see 'Keeping Track of Stock', earlier in this chapter.)

The opposite is true for LIFO, which uses cost figures based on the last price paid for the stock (and most likely the highest price). Using the LIFO method, the Cost of Goods Sold number is higher, which means a larger sum is subtracted from sales to determine profit. Thus, the profit margin is lower. The good news, however, is that the tax bill is also low.

The Averaging method gives a business the best picture of what's happening with stock costs and trends. Rather than constantly dealing with the ups and downs of stock costs, this method smoothes out the numbers used to calculate a business's profits. Cost of Goods Sold, taxes, and profit margins for this method fall between those of LIFO and FIFO. Definitely choose this method when you're operating a business in which stock prices are constantly going up and down.

The Averaging method always falls between LIFO and FIFO as regards the cost of goods sold, taxes, and profit margin.

Sage 50 Accounts uses the LIFO method to calculate Cost of Goods Sold and Stock line items on its financial reports, so if you choose this method, you can use Sage 50 Accounts and the financial reports it generates. However, if you choose to use one of the other four stock methods, you can't use the Sage 50 Accounts financial report numbers. Instead, you have to print out a report of purchases and calculate the accurate numbers to use on your financial reports for the Cost of Goods Sold and Stock accounts.

Check with your accountant to see which stock method he thinks is best for you given the type of business you're operating and which one will be most acceptable to HM Revenue & Customs.

Comparing the methods

To show you how much of an impact stock valuation can have on profit margin, in this section we compare three of the most common methods: FIFO, LIFO, and Averaging. In this example, we assume Business A bought the stock in question at different prices on three different occasions. Opening Stock is valued at £500 (50 items at £10 each).

Here's the calculation to determine the number of items sold (from the earlier 'Keeping Track of Stock' section):

Opening Stock + Purchases = Goods Available for Sale – Closing Stock = Items Sold

50 + 500 = 550 – 75 = 475

Here's what the business paid to purchase the stock:

Date	Quantity	Unit Price
1 April	150	£10
15 April	150	£25
30 April	200	£30

Here's an example of how you calculate the Cost of Goods Sold using the Averaging method:

Category	Quantity (Unit Price)	Total Cost
Opening Stock	50 (£10)	£500
Purchases	150 (£10)	£1,500
	150 (£25)	£3,750
	200 (£30)	£6,000
Total Stock	550	£11,750

Now you can do other calculations:

Average Stock Cost	£11,750 ÷ 550 = £21.36
Cost of Goods Sold	475 × £21.36 = £10,146
Closing Stock	75 @ £21.36 = £1,602

The Cost of Goods Sold number appears on the profit and loss statement and is subtracted from Sales. The Closing Stock number shows up as an asset on the balance sheet. This system applies to all three stock valuation methods.

Now, we demonstrate how you calculate the Cost of Goods Sold using the FIFO method. With this method, you assume that the first items received are the first ones sold, and because the first items received here are those in Opening Stock, we start with them:

Date	Quantity (Unit Price)	Total
Opening Stock	50 (£10)	£500
1 April	150 (£10)	£1,500
15 April	150 (£25)	£3,750
30 April	125 (£30)	£3,750
Cost of Goods Sold	475	£9,500
Closing Stock	75 @ £30	£2,250

Note: Only 125 of the 200 units purchased on April 30 are used in the FIFO method. Because this method assumes that the first items into stock are the first items sold (or taken out of stock), the first items used are those on April 1. Then the April 15 items are used, and finally the remaining needed items are taken from those bought on April 30. Because 200 were bought on April 30 and only 125 were needed, 75 of the items bought on April 30 are left in

Closing Stock. The Cost of Goods Sold figure, which is £9,500, is the sum of the total values of the units above which are deemed to have been sold to arrive at this figure (£500 + £1,500 + £3,750 + £3,750).

Next, we calculate the Cost of Goods Sold using the LIFO method. With this method, you assume that the last items received are the first ones sold, and because the last items received were those purchased on April 30, we start with them:

Date	Quantity (Unit Price)	Total
30 April	200 (£30)	£6,000
15 April	150 (£25)	£3,750
1 April	125 (£10)	£1,250
Cost of Goods Sold	475	£11,000
Closing Stock	75 @ £10	£750

Note: Because LIFO assumes the last items to arrive are sold first, the Closing Stock includes the 25 remaining units (150 purchased less 125 used/sold) from the 1 April purchase plus the 50 units in Opening Stock.

Here's how the use of stock under the LIFO method impacts the business profits. We assume the items are sold to the customers for £40 per unit, which means total sales of £19,000 for the month (£40 × 475 units sold). In this example, we just look at the *Gross Profit,* which is the profit from Sales before considering expenses incurred for operating the business. We talk more about the different profit types and what they mean in Book III Chapter 1. The following equation calculates Gross Profit:

Sales – Cost of Goods Sold = Gross Profit

Table 6-1 shows a comparison of Gross Profit for the three methods used in this example scenario.

Table 6-1	Comparison of Gross Profit Based on Stock Valuation Method		
Profit and Loss Statement Line Item	**FIFO**	**LIFO**	**Averaging**
Sales	£19,000	£19,000	£19,000
Cost of Goods Sold	£9,500	£11,000	£10,146
Gross Profit	£9,500	£8,000	£8,854

Looking at the comparisons of gross profit, you can see that stock valuation can have a major impact on your bottom line. LIFO is likely to give you the lowest profit because the last stock items bought are usually the most expensive. FIFO is likely to give you the highest profit because the first items bought are usually the cheapest. And the profit that the Averaging method produces is likely to fall somewhere in between the two.

Buying and Monitoring Supplies

In addition to stock, all businesses must buy the supplies used to operate the business, such as paper, pens, and paper clips. Supplies that aren't bought in direct relationship to the manufacturing or purchasing of goods or services for sale fall into the category of *expenses*.

Just how closely you want to monitor the supplies you use depends on your business needs. The expense categories you establish may be as broad as 'Office supplies' and 'Retail supplies', or you may want to set up accounts for each type of supply used. Each additional account is just one more thing that needs to be managed and monitored in the accounting system, so you need to determine whether keeping a very detailed record of supplies is worth your time.

Your best bet is to track supplies that make a big dent in your budget carefully with an individual account. For example, if you anticipate paper usage is going to be very high, monitor that usage with a separate account called 'Paper expenses'.

Many businesses don't use the bookkeeping system to manage their supplies. Instead, they designate one or two people as office managers or supply managers and keep the number of accounts used for supplies to a minimum. Other businesses decide to monitor supplies by department or division, and so they set up a supply account for each one. This system puts the burden of monitoring supplies in the hands of the department or division managers.

Staying on Top of Your Bills

Eventually, you have to pay for both the stock and the supplies you purchase for your business. In most cases, the bills are posted to the Accounts Payable account when they arrive, and they're paid when due. A large chunk of the cash paid out of your Cash account (see Book II Chapters 3 and 5 for more information on the Cash account and handling cash) is in the form of the cheques sent out to pay bills due in Accounts Payable, so you need to have careful controls over the five key functions of Accounts Payable:

- ✔ Entering the bills to be paid into the accounting system
- ✔ Preparing cheques to pay the bills

✔ Signing cheques to pay the bills

✔ Sending out payment cheques to suppliers

✔ Reconciling the bank account

In your business, the person who enters the bills to be paid into the system is likely to be the same person who also prepares the payment cheques. However, you must ensure that someone else does the other tasks: Never allow the person who prepares the cheques to review the bills to be paid and sign the cheques, unless of course that person's you, the business owner. (We talk more cash control and the importance of separating duties in Book II Chapter 5.)

Properly managing Accounts Payable allows you to avoid late fees or interest and take advantage of discounts offered for paying early, therefore saving your business a lot of money. If you're using a computerised accounting system, the bill due date and any discount information needs to be entered at the time you receive the stock or supplies (see Figure 6-1 for how you record this information).

If you're working with a paper system rather than a computerised accounting system, you need to set up some way to ensure that you don't miss bill due dates. Many businesses use two accordion files: one set up by the month, and the other set up by the day. On receipt, a bill is put into the first accordion file according to the due month. On the first day of that month, the Accounts Payable clerk pulls all the bills due that month and puts them in the daily accordion file based on the date the bill is due. Payment cheques are then posted in time to arrive in the supplier's office by the due date.

In some cases, businesses offer a discount if their bills are paid early. Sage 50 Accounts allows you to set up for each supplier Settlement Due dates and Settlement Discount percentage figures. For example, a supplier set up as 10 days and 2 per cent means that if the bill is paid in 10 days, the purchasing business can take a 2 per cent discount; otherwise, the amount due must be paid in full in 30 days. In addition, many businesses state that interest or late fees are charged if a bill isn't paid in 30 days (although in reality few dare make this charge if they want to retain the business). If the total amount due for a bill is £1,000 and the business pays the bill in 10 days, that business can take a 2 per cent discount, or £20. This may not seem like much, but if your business buys £100,000 of stock and supplies in a month and each supplier offers a similar discount, you can save £1,000. Over the course of a year, discounts on purchases can save your business a significant amount of money and improve your profits.

Counting Your Sales

Every business loves to take in money, and this means that you, the bookkeeper, have lots to do to ensure that sales are properly recorded in the books.

In addition to recording the sales themselves, you must monitor customer accounts, discounts offered to customers, and customer returns and allowances.

If the business sells products on credit, you have to monitor customer accounts carefully in Accounts Receivable, including monitoring whether customers pay on time and alerting the sales team when customers are behind on their bills and future purchases on credit need to be declined. Some customers never pay, and in that case, you must adjust the books to reflect non-payment as a bad debt.

Collecting Your Cash Sales

Most businesses collect some form of cash as payment for the goods or services they sell. Cash receipts include more than just notes and coins; cheques and credit and debit card payments are also considered cash sales for bookkeeping purposes. In fact, with electronic transaction processing (when a customer's credit or debit card is swiped through a machine), a deposit is usually made to the business's bank account the same day (sometimes within seconds of the transaction, depending on the type of system the business sets up with the bank).

The only type of payment that doesn't fall under the umbrella of a cash payment is purchases made on credit. And by credit, we mean credit your business offers to customers directly rather than through a third party, such as a bank credit card or loan. We talk more about this type of sale in the section 'Selling on Credit', later in this chapter.

Discovering the value of sales receipts

Modern businesses generate sales receipts in one of three ways: by the cash register, by the credit or debit card machine, or by hand (written out by the salesperson). Whichever of these three methods you choose to handle your sales transactions, the sales receipt serves two purposes:

- ✔ Gives the customer proof that the item was purchased on a particular day at a particular price in your shop in case he needs to exchange or return the merchandise.

- ✔ Gives the shop a receipt that can be used at a later time to enter the transaction into the business's books. At the end of the day, the receipts are also used to cash up the cash register and ensure that the cashier has taken in the right amount of cash based on the sales made. (In Book II Chapter 5, we talk more about how to use cash receipts as an internal control tool to manage your cash.)

You're familiar with cash receipts, no doubt, but just to show you how much useable information can be generated for the bookkeeper on a sales receipt, Figure 6-3 shows a sample receipt from a bakery.

Sales Receipt
24/4/2008
VAT No.:

Ashcroft Bakery
Clegg Street
Cardiff

Item	Qty.	Price	Total
White Serving Set	1 £40	£40 —	
Cheesecake, Marble	1 £20	£20 —	
Cheesecake, Blueberry	1 £20	£20 —	
			£80 —
		£80 —	
Cash Paid		£90 —	
Change		£10 —	

Figure 6-3: A sales receipt from Ashcroft Bakery.

Receipts contain a wealth of information that can be collected for your business's accounting system. A look at a receipt tells you the amount of cash collected, the type of products sold, the quantity of products sold, and how much Value Added Tax (VAT) was collected. In the example used in Figure 6-3 there is no VAT chargeable as food products are currently exempt from VAT.

Unless your business uses some type of computerised system that integrates the point of sale (usually the cash register) with the business's accounting system, sales information is collected throughout the day by the cash register and printed out in a summary form at the end of the day. At that point, you enter the details of the sales day in the books.

If you don't use a computerised system to monitor stock, you use the data collected by the cash register to simply enter into the books the cash received, total sales, and VAT collected. Although you're likely to have many more sales and much higher numbers at the end of the day, the entry in the Cash Receipts journal for the receipt appears as follows:

	Debit	*Credit*
Bank Account	£80.00	
Sales		£80.00

Cash receipts for 25 April 2008

In this example entry, Bank Account is an Asset account shown on the balance sheet (see Book III Chapter 2 for more about balance sheets), and its value increases with the debit. The Sales account is a revenue account on the profit and loss statement (see Book III Chapter 1 for more about profit and loss statements), and its balance increases with a Credit, showing additional revenue. (We talk more about debits and credits in Book II Chapter 1.) The VAT Collected account is a Liability account that appears on the balance sheet, and its balance increases with this transaction.

Book II

Accounting Basics

Businesses pay VAT to HM Revenue & Customs monthly or quarterly depending on rules set by HM Revenue & Customs. Therefore, your business must hold the money owed in a Liability account so you're certain you can pay the VAT collected from customers when due. We talk more about VAT and payment in Book VI Chapter 4.

Recording cash transactions

If you're using a computerised accounting system, you can enter more detail from the day's receipts and record stock sold as well. Most of the computerised accounting systems include the ability to record the sale of stock. Figure 6-4 shows you the Sage 50 Accounts sales receipts form that you can use to input data from each day's sales.

In addition to the information included in the Cash Receipts journal, note that Sage 50 Accounts also collects information about the items sold in each transaction. Sage 50 Accounts then automatically updates stock information, reducing the amount of stock on hand when necessary. If the sales receipt in Figure 6-4 is for an individual customer, you enter his name and address in the A/C field. At the bottom of the receipt, the Print tab takes you to a further menu where you have the option to print or e-mail the receipt. You can print the receipt and give it to the customer or, for a phone or Internet order, e-mail it to the customer. Using this option, payment can be made by any method such as cheque, electronic payment, or credit or debit card. (For an additional fee, Sage 50 Accounts allows you to process credit card receipts.)

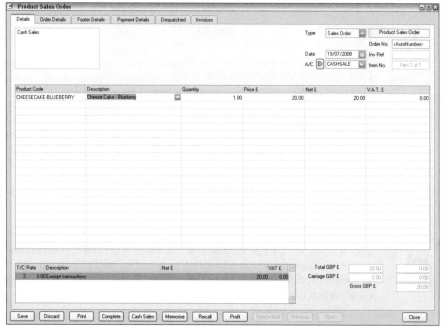

Figure 6-4:
Example of
a sales
receipt in
Sage 50
Accounts.

If your business accepts credit cards, expect sales revenue to be reduced by the fees paid to credit card companies. Usually, you face monthly fees as well as fees per transaction; however, each business sets up individual arrangements with its bank regarding these fees. Sales volume impacts how much you pay in fees, so when researching bank services, ensure that you compare credit card transaction fees to find a good deal.

Selling on Credit

Many businesses decide to sell to customers on credit, meaning credit the business offers and not through a bank or credit card provider. This approach offers more flexibility in the type of terms you can offer your customers, and you don't have to pay bank fees. However, credit involves more work for you, the bookkeeper, and the risk of a customer not paying what he owes.

When you accept a customer's bank-issued credit card for a sale and the customer doesn't pay the bill, you get your money; the bank is responsible for collecting from the customer, taking the loss if he doesn't pay. This doesn't apply when you decide to offer credit to your customers directly. If a customer doesn't pay, your business takes the loss.

Deciding whether to offer credit

The decision to set up your own credit system depends on what your competition is doing. For example, if you run an office supply store and all other office supply stores allow credit to make it easier for their customers to get supplies, you probably need to offer credit to stay competitive.

You need to set up some ground rules when you want to allow your customers to buy on credit. For personal customers you have to decide:

- ✔ How to check a customer's credit history.
- ✔ What the customer's income level needs to be for credit to be approved.
- ✔ How long to give the customer to pay the bill before charging interest or late fees.

If you want to allow your trade or business customers to buy on credit, you need to set ground rules for them as well. The decisions you need to make include:

- ✔ Whether to deal only with established businesses. You may set an outer limit to businesses that have been trading for at least two years.

- ✔ Whether to require *trade references,* which show that the business has been responsible and paid other businesses when they've taken credit. A customer usually provides you with two suppliers that offered him credit. You then contact those suppliers directly to see if the customer has been reliable and on time with his payments.

- ✔ Whether to obtain credit rating information. You may decide to use a third party credit checking agency to provide a credit report on the business applying for credit. This report suggests a maximum credit limit and whether the business pays on time. Of course a fee is charged for this service, but using it may help you avoid making a terrible mistake. A similar service is available for individuals.

The harder you make getting credit and the stricter you make the bill-paying rules, the less chance you have of a taking a loss. However, you may lose customers to a competitor with lighter credit rules. For example, you may require a minimum income level of £50,000 and make customers pay in 30 days to avoid late fees or interest charges. Your sales staff reports that these rules are too rigid because your direct competitor down the street allows credit on a minimum income level of £30,000 and gives customers 60 days to pay before late fees and interest charges. Now you have to decide whether you want to change your credit rules to match those of the competition. If you do lower your credit standards to match your competitor, however, you may end up with more customers who can't pay on time (or at all) because you've qualified customers for credit at lower income levels and given them more time to pay. If you do loosen your qualification criteria and bill-paying requirements, monitor your customer accounts carefully to ensure that they're not falling behind.

The key risk you face is selling products for which you're never paid. For example, if you allow customers 30 days to pay and cut them off from buying goods when their accounts fall more than 30 days behind, the most you can lose is the amount purchased over a two-month period (60 days). But if you give customers more leniency, allowing them 60 days to pay and cutting them off after payment is 30 days late, you're faced with three months (90 days) of purchases for which you may never be paid.

Recording credit sales

When sales are made on credit, you have to enter specific information into the accounting system. In addition to inputting information regarding cash receipts (see 'Collecting on Cash Sales', earlier in this chapter), you update the customer accounts to make sure that each customer is billed and the money is collected. You debit the Accounts Receivable account, an Asset account shown on the balance sheet (see Book III Chapter 2), which shows money due from customers.

Here's how a journal entry of a sale made on credit looks:

	Debit	*Credit*
Accounts Receivable	£80.00	
Sales		£80.00

Cash receipts for 25 April 2008

In addition to making this journal entry, you enter the information into the customer's account so that accurate statements can be sent out at the end of the month. When the customer pays the bill, you update the individual customer's record to show that payment has been received and enter the following into the bookkeeping records:

	Debit	*Credit*
Accounts Receivable	£80.00	
Sales		£80.00

Payment from Mrs Jolly on invoice 5.

If you're using Sage 50 Accounts, you enter purchases on credit using an invoice form like the one in Figure 6-5. Most of the information on the invoice form is similar to the sales receipt form (see 'Collecting on Cash Sales', earlier in this chapter), but the invoice form also has space to enter a different address for shipping (the Delivery Address field) and includes payment terms (the Settlement Terms field).

Sage 50 Accounts uses the information on the invoice form to update the following accounts:

- ✔ Accounts Receivable
- ✔ Stock
- ✔ Customer's account
- ✔ Value Added Tax account

Book II

Accounting Basics

Based on this data, when the time comes to bill the customer at the end of the month, with a little prompting from you (see Figure 6-6), Sage 50 Accounts generates statements for all customers with outstanding invoices. You can easily generate statements for specific customers or all customers on the books. Figure 6-6 shows a statement for Mrs Jolly.

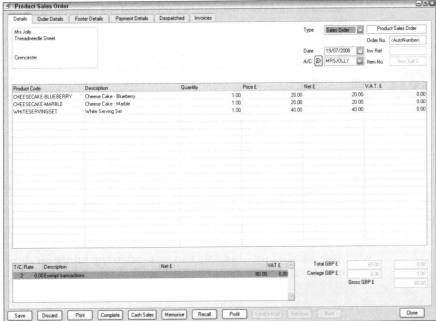

Figure 6-5: Sage 50 Accounts sales invoice for purchases made on credit.

Figure 6-6:
Generating
statements
for cus-
tomers
using
Sage 50
Accounts.

Criteria		✕

Criteria

	From	To
Customer Ref	MRSJOLLY	MRSJOLLY
Transaction Date	01/01/1980	19/07/2008
Exc Later Payments	☐	

Preview a sample report for a
specified number of records or   0 (leave as 0 to see all records)
transactions

Help   OK   Cancel

When you receive payment from a customer, here's what happens:

1. **You enter the customer's name on the customer receipts form (shown in Figure 6-7).**

2. **Sage 50 Accounts automatically lists all outstanding invoices.**

3. **You enter how much the customer is paying in total.**

4. **You select the invoice or invoices paid.**

5. **Sage 50 Accounts updates the Accounts Receivable account, the Cash account, and the customer's individual account to show that payment has been received.**

If your customer is paying a lot of outstanding invoices, Sage 50 Accounts has two very clever options that may save you some time. The first option, Pay in Full, marks every invoice as paid if the customer is settling up in full. The other option, Wizard, matches the payment to the outstanding invoices by starting with the oldest until it matches up the exact amount of the payment.

If your business uses a point of sale program integrated into the computerised accounting system, recording credit transactions is even easier for you. Sales details feed into the system as each sale is made, so you don't have to enter the detail at the end of day. These point of sale programs save a lot of time, but they can get very expensive.

Even if customers don't buy on credit, point of sale programs provide businesses with an incredible amount of information about their customers and what they like to buy. This data can be used in the future for direct marketing and special sales to increase the likelihood of return business.

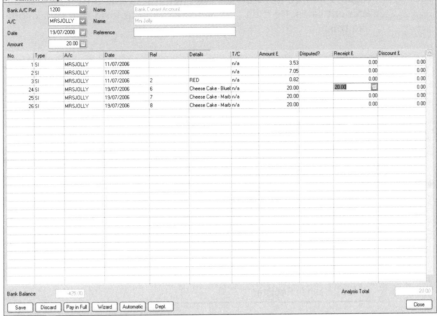

No.	Type	A/c	Date	Ref	Details	T/C	Amount £	Disputed?	Receipt £	Discount £
1	SI	MRSJOLLY	11/07/2006			n/a	3.53		0.00	0.00
2	SI	MRSJOLLY	11/07/2006			n/a	7.05		0.00	0.00
3	SI	MRSJOLLY	11/07/2006	2	RED	n/a	0.82		0.00	0.00
24	SI	MRSJOLLY	19/07/2006	6	Cheese Cake - Blueb	n/a	20.00		20.00	0.00
25	SI	MRSJOLLY	19/07/2006	7	Cheese Cake - Marb	n/a	20.00		0.00	0.00
26	SI	MRSJOLLY	19/07/2006	8	Cheese Cake - Marb	n/a	20.00		0.00	0.00

Figure 6-7:
In Sage 50 Accounts, recording payments from customers who bought on credit starts with the customer receipts form.

Book II

Accounting Basics

Cashing Up the Cash Register

To ensure that cashiers don't pocket a business's cash, at the end of each day, cashiers must *cash up* (show that they have the right amount of cash in the register based on the sales transactions during the day) the amount of cash, cheques, and credit sales they took in during the day.

This process of cashing up a cash register actually starts at the end of the previous day, when cashier John Smith and his manager agree on the amount of cash left in John's register drawer. Cash sitting in cash registers or cash drawers is recorded as part of the Cash on Hand account.

When John comes to work the next morning, he starts out with the amount of cash left in the drawer. At the end of the business day, he or his manager runs a summary of activity on the cash register for the day to produce a report of the total sales taken in by the cashier. John counts the amount of cash in his register as well as totals for the cheques, credit card receipts, and credit account sales. He then completes a cash-out form that looks something like this:

Cash Register: John Smith		25/4/2008
Receipts	*Sales*	*Total*
Opening Cash		£100
Cash Sales		£400
Credit Card Sales	£800	
Credit Account Sales	£200	
Total Sales		£1,400
Sales on Credit		£1,000
Cash Received		£400
Total Cash in Register		£500

A manager reviews John Smith's cash register summary (produced by the actual register) and compares it to the cash-out form. If John's ending cash (the amount of cash remaining in the register) doesn't match the cash-out form, he and the manager try to pinpoint the mistake. If they can't find a mistake, they fill out a cash-overage or cash-shortage form. Some businesses charge the cashier directly for any shortages, whereas others take the position that the cashier's fired after a certain number of shortages of a certain amount (say, three shortages of more than £10).

The manager decides how much cash to leave in the cash drawer or register for the next day and deposits the remainder. He carries out this task for each of his cashiers and then deposits all the cash and cheques from the day in a night deposit box at the bank. He sends a report with details of the deposit to the bookkeeper so that the data appears in the accounting system. The bookkeeper enters the data on the Sales Receipts form (refer to Figure 6-4) if a computerised accounting system is being used, or into the Cash Receipts journal if the books are being kept manually.

Monitoring Sales Discounts

Most business offer discounts at some point in time to generate more sales. Discounts are usually in the form of a sale with 10 per cent, 20 per cent, or even more off purchases.

When you offer discounts to customers, monitor your sales discounts in a separate account so you can keep an eye on how much you discount sales in each month. If you find you're losing more and more money to discounting, look closely at your pricing structure and competition to find out why you're having to lower your prices frequently to make sales. You can monitor discount information very easily by using the data found on a standard sales register receipt. Figure 6-8 shows a bakery receipt that includes sales discount details.

Sales Receipt
25/4/2008
VAT No.:

Ashcroft Bakery
Clegg Street
Cardiff

Item	Qty.	Price	Total
White Serving Set	1	£40 —	£40 —
Cheesecake, Marble	1	£20 —	£20 —
Cheesecake, Blueberry	1	£20 —	£20 —
			£80 —
Sales Discount @ 10%		(8.00) —	
			£72 —
Cash Paid		£80 —	
Change		£8 —	

Figure 6-8:
A sales receipt from Ashcroft Bakery showing sales discount.

From this example, you can see clearly that the business takes in less cash when discounts are offered. When recording the sale in the Cash Receipts journal, you record the discount as a debit. This debit increases the Sales Discount account, which is subtracted from the Sales account to calculate the Net Sales. (We walk you through all these steps and calculations when we discuss preparing the profit and loss statement in Book III Chapter 1.) Here's what the bakery's entry for this particular sale looks like in the Cash Receipts journal:

	Debit	*Credit*
Bank Account	£72.00	
Sales Discounts	£8.00	
Sales		£80.00

Cash receipts for 25 April 2008

If you use a computerised accounting system, add the sales discount as a line item on the sales receipt or invoice, and the system automatically adjusts the sales figures and updates your Sales Discount account.

Recording Sales Returns and Allowances

Most businesses deal with *sales returns* on a regular basis. Customers regularly return purchased items because the item is defective, they change their minds, or for any other reason. Instituting a no-return policy is guaranteed to produce very unhappy customers: Ensure that you allow sales returns to maintain good customer relations.

Accepting sales returns can be a complicated process. Usually, a business posts a set of rules for returns that may include:

- ✔ Returns allowed only within 30 days of purchase.

- ✔ You must have a receipt to return an item.

- ✔ When you return an item without a receipt, you can receive only a credit note.

You can set up whatever rules you want for returns. For internal control purposes, the key to returns is monitoring how your staff handles them. In most cases, ensure that a manager's approval is required on returns. Also, make sure that your staff pays close attention to how the customer originally paid for the item being returned. You certainly don't want to give a customer cash when they took credit – you're just handing over your money! After a return's approved, the cashier returns the amount paid by cash or credit card. Customers who bought the items on credit don't get any money back, because they didn't pay anything but expected to be billed later. Instead, a form is filled out so that the amount of the original purchase can be subtracted from the customer's credit account.

Sales allowances (sales incentive programmes) are becoming more popular with businesses. Sales allowances are most often in the form of a gift card. A sold gift card is actually a liability for the business because the business has received cash, but no merchandise has gone out. For that reason, gift card sales are entered in a Gift Card Liability account. When a customer makes a purchase at a later date using the gift card, the Gift Card Liability account is reduced by the purchase amount. Monitoring the Gift Card Liability account allows businesses to keep track of how much is yet to be sold without receiving additional cash.

You use the information collected by the cashier who handled the return to input the sales return data into the books. For example, a customer returns a

£40 item that was purchased with cash. You record the cash refund in the Cash Receipts Journal like this:

	Debit	Credit
Sales Returns and Allowances	£40.00	
Value Added Tax @ 17.5%	£7.00	
Bank Account		£47.00

To record return of purchase, 30/4/2008.

If the item was bought with a discount, you list the discount as well and adjust the price to show that discount.

In this journal entry:

- ✔ The Sales Returns and Allowances account increases. This account normally carries a debit balance and is subtracted from Sales when preparing the profit and loss statement, thereby reducing revenue received from customers.

- ✔ The debit to the Value Added Tax account reduces the amount in that account because Value Added Tax is no longer due on the purchase.

- ✔ The credit to the Bank Account reduces the amount of cash in that account.

Book II

Accounting Basics

Monitoring Accounts Receivable

Making sure that customers pay their bills is a crucial responsibility of the bookkeeper. Before sending out the monthly bills, prepare an *Aged Debtor Report* that lists all customers who owe money to the business and the age of each debt. If you keep the books manually, you collect the necessary information from each customer account. If you keep the books in a computerised accounting system, you can generate this report automatically. Either way, your Aged Debtor Report looks similar to this example report from a bakery:

Aged Debtor Report – as of 1 May 2008				
Customer	*Current*	*31– 60 Days*	*61–90 Days*	*>90 Days*
S. Smith	£84.32	£46.15		
J. Smith			£65.78	

(continued)

Aged Debtor Report – as of 1 May 2008 *(continued)*				
Customer	*Current*	*31– 60 Days*	*61–90 Days*	*>90 Days*
H. Harris	£89.54			
M. Man				£125.35
Totals	£173.86	£46.15	£65.78	£125.35

The Aged Debtor Report quickly tells you which customers are behind in their bills. In this example, customers are put on stop when their payments are more than 60 days late, so J. Smith and M. Man aren't able to buy on credit until their bills are paid in full.

Give a copy of your Aged Debtor Report to the sales manager so he can alert staff to problem customers. The sale manager can also arrange for the appropriate collections procedures. Each business sets up its own specific collections process, usually starting with a phone call, followed by letters, and possibly legal action, if necessary.

Accepting Your Losses

You may encounter a situation in which a customer never pays your business, even after an aggressive collections process. In this case, you have no choice but to write off the purchase as a *bad debt* and accept the loss.

Most businesses review their Aged Debtor Reports every 6 to 12 months and decide which accounts need to be written off as bad debt. Accounts written off are recorded in a Nominal Ledger account called *Bad Debt*. (See Book II Chapter 3 for more information about the Nominal Ledger.) The Bad Debt account appears as an Expense account on the profit and loss statement. When you write off a customer's account as bad debt, the Bad Debt account increases, and the Accounts Receivable account decreases.

To give you an idea of how you write off an account, assume that one of your customers never pays £105.75 due. Here's what your journal entry looks like for this debt:

	Debit	*Credit*
Bad Debt	£105.75	
Accounts Receivable		£105.75

In a computerised accounting system, you enter the information using a customer payment form and allocate the amount due to the Bad Debt Expense account.

If the bad debt included Value Added Tax (VAT), you have suffered a double loss because you've paid over the VAT to HM Revenue & Customs, even though you never received it. Fortunately, you can reclaim this VAT when you do your next VAT return.

Book II

Accounting Basics

Book III
Reporting Results

'So for all you eager investors, our latest financial report will be read to you by our new accountant, Mr Mesmero.'

In this book . . .

Financial statements are like the tip of an iceberg –
they only show the visible part, underneath which are
a lot of record-keeping, accounting methods, and reporting decisions. The managers of a business, the investors
in a business, and the lenders to a business need a firm
grasp on these accounting communications. They need to
know which handles to grab hold of and how to find both
the good and bad signals in financial statements – and,
ugh, this includes the small-print footnotes that go with
financial statements.

Accountants prepare three primary financial statements.
The *profit and loss account* reports the profit-making activities of the business and how much profit or loss the business made. (Sounds odd, doesn't it, to say a business
made a loss? But to make profit, a business has to take the
risk that it may suffer a loss.) The *balance sheet* reports
the financial situation and position of the business at a
point in time – usually the last day of the profit period.
The *cash flow statement* reports how much cash was actually realised from profit and other sources of cash, and
what the business did with this money. In short, the financial life of a business and its prospects for success or
potential danger of failing is all revealed in its financial
statements, as this part of the book exposes.

Here are the contents of Book III at a glance:

Chapter 1

Profit Mechanics

*I*n this chapter we lift up the bonnet and investigate how the profit engine runs. At first glance, making profit may seem fairly simple – sell stuff and control expenses. Bring in more pounds from sales revenue than the pounds paid out for expenses. The excess of revenue over expenses is profit. What's the big deal?

Well, making a profit and determining its amount isn't nearly as simple as you may think. This chapter starts with a simple case in which the increase in cash is equal to profit – the business collects cash for all of its sales during the period and pays out cash for all of its expenses, and profit equals the cash left over. But alas, the business world is not so simple. So the chapter continues one step at a time to build a realistic profit model. Walking through this example lets you answer one very important question: At the end of the day, where exactly is your profit that you worked so hard to earn?

Swooping Profit into One Basic Equation

For a business that sells products, its profit equation is simply sales revenue – expenses = profit, which almost always is reported in a vertical format like this:

Basic Profit Equation	
Sales Revenue	£100,000
Less Expenses	94,000
Equals Profit	£6,000

Profit, in short, equals what's left over from sales revenue after you deduct all expenses. (You never see the term *net sales revenue* instead of *profit.*) This business earned £6,000 on £100,000 total sales revenue for the period, which is 6%. Expenses used up 94% of sales revenue. Although it may seem rather thin, a 6 percent profit margin on sales is typical for many businesses – although some businesses consistently make a bottom-line profit of 10–20% of sales, and others are satisfied with a 1% or 2% profit margin on sales revenue. Normal profit ratios vary widely from industry to industry.

Businesses that sell services instead of products also use the term *sales revenue* for *gross income* (total income before deducting expenses) from sales of their services – but you also see variations on this term. Businesses that don't sell anything as such – financial institutions that earn investment income, for example – use other terms for their gross income.

Notice the following points about the basic profit equation:

✔ Even though you're deducting expenses from sales revenue, you generally don't use a minus sign or parentheses to indicate that the expense amount is a negative number (although some people do).

✔ Using a double underline under the profit number is common practice but not universal. Some people use bold type. You generally don't see anything as garish as a fat arrow pointing to the profit number or a big smiley encircling the profit number – but again, tastes vary.

✔ Profit isn't always called *profit*. It's often called *net income* or the *bottom line* or – particularly on financial reports intended for people outside the business – *net earnings.* (Can't accountants agree on *anything?*) Throughout this book we use the terms *net income* and *profit* pretty much interchangeably.

✔ *Sales revenue* is the total amount of money or other assets received from sales of the company's products for the entire year. The number used in the profit equation represents all sales – you can't tell how many different sales were made, how many different customers the company sold products to, or how the sales were distributed over the 12 months of the year.

Sales revenue is strictly what belongs to the business and doesn't include money that anyone else can claim (for example, VAT that the business collects from customers and then remits to the government).

Note: A business may have other sources of income in addition to the sales revenue from its products. One common alternative source of income is interest or other return earned on investments the company makes. In the profit report, investment income goes on a separate line and is not included with sales revenue – to make clear that this source of income is secondary to the mainstream sales revenue of the business.

✔ *Expenses* consist of a wide variety of costs of operating the business and making sales, starting with the cost of the goods (products) sold to the customers and including many other costs of operating the business:

- Payroll costs (wages, salaries, and benefits paid to employees)

- Insurance costs

- Property taxes on buildings and land

- Cost of gas and electric utilities

- Telephone and Internet charges

- Depreciation of operating assets that last more than one year (such as buildings, cars and trucks, computers, office furniture, tools and machinery, and shelving)

- Advertising and sales promotion costs

- Office supplies

- Legal and audit costs

- Interest paid on loans

- Income taxes

As is the case with sales revenue, you can't tell from the amount reported as an expense how much was spent on each component making up the total. For example, the total depreciation expense amount doesn't tell you how much was for buildings and how much was for vehicles.

By the way, notice that only one total is shown for all the business's expenses – to keep the profit equation as short as possible. However, when preparing a formal profit report – which is called a *profit and loss account* or *statement* – expenses are broken down into several basic categories. (See 'Lining Up the Profit and Loss Account' later in the chapter.)

Measuring the Financial Effects of Profit-Making Activities

In the basic profit equation example introduced earlier in this chapter, a business earned £6,000 net income for the year. That means it's £6,000 richer now, right? Well, that could happen in a make-believe world, and we start this section with a hypothetical profit example in which the business checking account *does* increase by £6,000 – but this example is extremely oversimplified. In the real world, nothing is that simple.

The financial effects of making profit go far beyond a fatter bank account. To get a clear picture, a balance sheet equation is handy to sort out the various effects. The general format of the balance sheet equation (also called the *accounting equation*) is as follows:

Assets = liabilities + invested capital

See Book III Chapter 2 for more information about developing a balance sheet.

Making a profit increases the assets of a business. Assets also increase when the owners invest money in the business and when the business borrows money. These two types of increases in assets are not profit. Profit is the net increase of assets from sales revenue less expenses, not from borrowing and not from its owners investing capital in the business.

Most businesses do not distribute all of their annual profit to their owners; they could, but they don't. Instead, the increase in assets from making profit is used to expand the resource base of the business. Profit not distributed is called reserves or *retained earnings*. The nature of retained earnings is shown in the following rearrangement of the balance sheet equation:

Assets – liabilities – invested capital = retained earnings

The key idea here is that if you start with total assets and then take away how much of the assets came from liabilities and how much was invested by the owners, the remainder must have come from retained earnings. For example, if a business has £600,000 in assets, of which £500,000 is in liabilities, and £400,000 in invested capital, the remaining £100,000 must be due to retained earnings.

The retained earnings account is *not* – we repeat, *not* – an asset, even though its name may suggest otherwise. It is a *source*-of-assets account, not an asset account. See the 'So why is it called retained earnings?' sidebar for more information about the retained earnings account.

The profit-making activities of a business affect several assets and also some liabilities – not the kind recorded when borrowing money (interest-bearing debt), but the kind recorded for expenses that have not been paid immediately. The accounts used to record unpaid expenses are referred to as *operating liabilities*. Interest is paid on debt (borrowed money), but not on operating liabilities. The term *operating* simply refers to the sales and expense operations of a business that are necessary for making profit.

An example: During a period, a business records the full cost of all wages and benefits that its employees earn. The full cost is the correct amount of expense to record in the period to measure profit for the period. But at the end of the period, some part of this total cost has not been paid. The unpaid balance of the total cost is recorded in an operating liability account.

So why is it called retained earnings?

The retained earnings account, like all balance sheet accounts, reports the net balance in the account after recording both the increases *and the decreases* in the account through the end of the period. The retained earnings account increases when the business makes a profit and then decreases when the business distributes some of the profit to the owners. That is, the total amount of profit paid out to the owners is recorded as a decrease in the retained earnings account. (Exactly how the profit is divided among the owners depends on the ownership structure of the business – see Book IV Chapter 3.)

Preparing the balance sheet equation

Each asset of a business is different from the others, but cash is in a class by itself. Furthermore, the cash flow aspects of profit are receiving a great deal of attention these days – almost to the level of being an equal concern with profit itself. So separating assets into cash and non-cash assets is useful. Moreover, separating liabilities into operating liabilities and borrowed money (generally referred to as *debt*) is useful, and separating owners' equity into invested capital and retained earnings is useful. This six-fold subdivision of the balance sheet equation looks like this:

Cash + non-cash assets = operating liabilities + debt + invested capital + retained earnings

On the one hand, this expansion of the balance sheet equation helps clarify the different types of assets, liabilities, and owners' equity. On the other hand, for exploring the profit-making process debt and invested capital are not needed because revenue and expenses do not involve these two types of accounts. Debt and invested capital are excess baggage for the following journey through the profit-making process of a business. So to simplify the equation assume that the business has no debt and no invested capital (not realistic, but very convenient here). Thus the balance sheet equation that we use in the following sections is as follows:

Cash + Non-cash Assets = Operating Liabilities + Retained Earnings

A simple, all-cash example to start things off: Suppose your business collected all sales revenue for the year immediately in cash and paid all expenses for the year immediately in cash. Your profit for the year was £6,000. Here's how that profit affects the financial condition of your business (to simplify, pound signs are not used):

Cash +	Non-cash Assets	= Operating Liabilities +	Retained Earnings
+6,000			+6,000

The cash asset account increases by £6,000, which is the net difference between sales revenue and expenses – your business bank account balance is £6,000 higher at the end of the year than at the beginning of the year. (If you had distributed some of the profit, the balance of the retained earnings account would be the amount you distributed subtracted from £6,000, and your cash would be lower by the same amount.)

Exploring the Profit-Making Process

We don't mean to scare you off but the profit picture gets more complex than the simple all-cash example just discussed. Many businesses sell their products on credit rather than cash, for example, and usually don't collect all their sales revenue by the end of the year. In other words some of the expenses for the year aren't paid by the end of the year. Each of the following steps adds a layer of reality, one at a time, to make the profit picture more realistic. The following sections start with the all-cash scenario as the point of departure and then make one change at a time to show you how the additional factor affects the balance sheet equation.

Making sales on credit

If your business allows customers to buy its products or services on credit, you need to add an asset account called debtors or *accounts receivable* (also terms we will use interchangeably) which records the total amount owed to the business by its customers who made purchases unofficially and haven't paid up yet. You probably wouldn't have collected all your receivables by the end of the year, especially for credit sales that occurred in the last weeks of the year. However, you still record the sales revenue and the cost-of-goods-sold expense for these sales in the year in which the sales occurred. The initial scenario in which all sales were collected in cash and all expenses were paid in cash is used as the point of reference in the following steps.

Your business had sales revenue of £100,000 and total expenses of £94,000, all of which were paid by year-end, making for a bottom-line profit of £6,000. Now assume that £8,000 of the sales revenue came from credit sales that haven't yet been collected at the end of the year. Here's what the financial effects look like (for convenience, pound signs in the balance sheet equation are not used):

Cash	+ Noncash Assets	= Operating Liabilities	+ Retained Earnings
	+6,000		+6,000

	Accounts receivable		
–8,000			+8,000

Note that the first line in the balance sheet equation (which is underlined) is from the initial all-cash scenario and serves as the point of reference. Everything in the new scenario is the same as in the all-cash scenario except for the changes shown below the line. Also note that the name of the specific non-cash asset – in this case, accounts receivable – is entered in the balance sheet equation column. When a change in a non-cash asset is entered in the balance sheet equation, the corresponding effect on cash is shown in the cash column.

The £8,000 of uncollected sales revenue at year-end has the effect of decreasing the cash you have by £8,000. Accounts receivable represents cash waiting in the wings to be collected in the near future (assuming that all your customers will pay their accounts receivable to you on time). But until the money is actually received, your business is without the £8,000 cash inflow. This situation may appear to be pretty serious. But hang on; there are several more steps to go.

Whether collected entirely in cash or not, the entire £100,000 in sales revenue for the year is recorded and used to calculate profit. So bottom-line profit is £6,000 – the same as in the all-cash scenario. But the cash effects between the two scenarios are quite different. When making sales on credit, you count the sales in calculating your profit, even though the cash is not collected from customers until sometime later. This is one feature of the *accrual basis of accounting,* which is explained in Book III Chapter 3. The accrual basis of accounting records revenue when sales are made and records expenses when these costs are incurred. When sales are made on credit, the accounts receivable asset account is increased; later, when cash is received from the customer, cash is increased and the accounts receivable account is decreased.

Book III

Reporting Results

Depreciation expense

Depreciation expense accounting is the method of spreading out the cost of a fixed asset instead of charging the entire cost to the year of purchase. That way, each year of use bears a share of the total cost. *Fixed assets* are long-lived operating assets – buildings, machinery, office equipment, vehicles, computers and data-processing equipment, shelving and cabinets, and so on.

For example, cars and light trucks may be depreciated over five years. (Businesses apply the five-year rule to other kinds of assets as well.) The basic idea of depreciation is to charge a fraction of the total cost to depreciation expense for each of the five years. (The actual fraction each year depends on which method of depreciation you choose, which is explained in Book IV Chapter 5.)

Suppose your £94,000 total of expenses for the year includes £2,500depreciation for fixed assets. (You bought these assets for £12,500 and are charging one-fifth of the cost each year for five years.) But you didn't actually pay anything for the fixed assets this year – you bought the assets in previous years. Depreciation is a real expense, but not a *cash outlay* expense after the fixed assets are already bought and paid for. (See the 'Appreciating the positive impact of depreciation on cash flow' sidebar if you're confused about this point.)

Here's what the financial effects of depreciation expense look like:

Cash	+ Non-cash Assets	= Operating Liabilities	+ Retained Earnings
+6,000			+6,000
+2,500		Fixed assets –2,500	

Compared with the cash flow effects of accounts receivable, depreciation is good news. Let us put it this way: If all sales revenue had been collected and all expenses except depreciation had been paid during the year, your cash would have increased by £8,500. The company would have realised £6,000 from your profit-making activities plus the £2,500 depreciation recovery during the year. The positive impact of depreciation on cash is just the prelude. Next in line are the favourable cash flow effects of unpaid expenses.

Unpaid expenses

A typical business pays many expenses after the period benefited by the expense. For example, suppose that your business hires a law firm that does a lot of legal work for the company during the year but you don't pay the bill until the following year. Your business may match retirement contributions made by employees but you may not pay your share until the following year. Or your business may have unpaid bills for telephone, gas, electricity, and water that it has used during the year.

Appreciating the positive impact of depreciation on cash flow

Whereas making sales on credit does not generate immediate cash inflow and thus has a temporarily negative impact on your cash flow, depreciation is good news for cash flow. This concept gets a little complex, so stay with us here.

Fundamentally, a business sets its sales prices high enough to recover its expenses plus provide a profit. In a real sense, the business is passing on the cost of its fixed assets to its customers and recovering some of the cost of the fixed assets each year through sales revenue. A good example to illustrate this critical point is a taxicab driver who owns his cab. He sets his fares high enough to pay for his time; to pay for the insurance, license, petrol and oil; and to recover the cost of the cab. Included in each fare is a tiny fraction of the cost of the cab, which over the course of the year adds up to the depreciation expense that he passed on to his passengers and collected in fares. At the end of the year, he has collected a certain amount of money that pays him back for part of the cost of the cab.

In short, fixed assets are gradually *liquidated*, or turned back into cash, each year. Part of sales revenue recovers a fraction of the cost of fixed assets which is why the decrease in the fixed assets account to record depreciation expense has the effect of increasing cash (assuming your sales revenue was collected in cash during the year). What the company does with this cash recovery is another matter. Sooner or later, you need to replace the fixed assets to continue in business. In this chapter, we do not look beyond the cash recovery of part of the original cost invested in the fixed asset.

Accountants use three different types of operating liability accounts to record a business's unpaid expenses:

- **Accounts payable, or creditors:** For items that the business buys on credit and for which it receives an invoice (a bill).

- **Accrued expenses payable:** For unpaid costs that a business generally has to estimate because it doesn't receive an invoice for them. An examples of accrued expenses are unused holiday that your employees carry over to the following year, which you will have to pay for in the coming year.

- **Income tax payable:** For income taxes, or corporation tax, that a business still owes to the Inland Revenue.

Your business has each of the three operating liabilities we just listed. Some of your total expenses for the year are unpaid at year-end – part in the accounts payable account, part in the accrued expenses payable account, and part in the income tax payable account. Here's what the financial effects of your unpaid expenses look like in the balance sheet equation:

Cash	+ **Non-cash Assets** =	**Operating Liabilities** +	**Retained Earnings**
+6,000		+6,000	
+3,000		Accounts payable +3,000	
+3,500		Accrued expenses payable +3,500	
+500		Income tax payable +500	

The total of these three unpaid operating liabilities is £7,000 (£3,000 accounts payable + £3,500 accrued expenses payable + £500 income tax payable). Your balance sheet would report these liabilities because they are claims against the business. You may think that liabilities are bad, but for cash flow, liabilities are good. Your business has not yet paid £7,000 of the expenses for the year, and your cash balance is higher by this amount – you get to hang on to the cash until you pay the liabilities. Of course, you have to pay these liabilities next year, but isn't it nice to have your balance sheet show a big, fat cash increase for this year even though you have to show the liabilities as well?

Prepaid expenses

Prepaid expenses are the opposite of unpaid expenses. For example, a business buys fire insurance and general liability insurance (in case a customer who slips on a wet floor sues the business). You pay insurance premiums ahead of time, before the period in which you're covered, but you charge that expense to the actual period benefited. At the end of the year, the business may be only halfway through the insurance coverage period, so it charges off only half the premium cost as an expense (for a six-month policy, you charge one-sixth of the premium cost to each of the six months covered). So at the time you pay the premium, you charge the entire amount to the prepaid expenses asset account, and for each month of coverage, you transfer the appropriate fraction of the cost to the insurance expense account.

Here's what the financial effects of your prepaid expenses look like in the balance sheet equation:

Cash	+ **Non-cash Assets** =	**Operating Liabilities**	+ **Retained Earnings**
+6,000			+6,000
–1,500		Prepaid expenses +1,500	

The build-up of prepaid expenses has a negative impact on the business's cash. In other words you had to write cheques for the prepaid expenses so your cash balance is smaller. The prepayment of these expenses lays the groundwork for continuing your operations seamlessly into next year. What it comes down to is that certain costs of your profit-making operations must be paid in advance – you don't have a choice. Remember that although your business is £1,500 cash poorer, profit remains the same (£6,000) as it is in all the previous scenarios.

Stock and Cost of Goods Sold expense

Cost of Goods Sold is one of the primary expenses of businesses that sell products. It's just what its name implies: the cost that a business paid for the products it sells to customers. A business makes profit by setting its sales prices high enough to cover the actual costs of products sold, the costs of operating the business, interest on borrowed money, and income taxes (assuming that the business pays income tax), with something left over for profit.

When the business acquires a product, the cost of the product goes into a *stock asset account* (and, of course, the cost is either deducted from the cash account or added to the accounts payable liability account, depending on whether the business paid with cash or bought on credit). When a customer buys that product, the business transfers the cost of the product from the stock asset account to the Cost of Goods Sold expense account because the product is no longer in the business's stock; the product has been delivered to the customer.

Book III

Reporting Results

The first step in determining profit for the period is deducting the Cost of Goods Sold expense from the sales revenue for the goods sold. Most profit and loss accounts report the cost of goods sold as a separate expense (refer to 'Formatting The Profit and Loss Statement,' later in this chapter).

So assume that your business did, in fact, start the year with a sizeable stock of products whose cost is recorded in the stock asset account. As your business sold the products early in the year, the cost of the goods sold was removed from the stock account, and that cost was charged to expense.

Your business sells products so you need to have a stock of products on hand to sell to your customers. This stockpile of goods on the shelves waiting to be sold (or in storage space in the back room) is called *stock*. When you drive by a car dealer and see all the cars waiting to be sold, remember that these products are called stock. The cost of unsold products (goods held in stock) is not charged to expense until the products are actually sold. In this way, the Cost of Goods Sold expense is correctly matched against the sales revenue from the goods sold.

During the year you increased the number of products offered for sale. Therefore, your total purchases of products during the year was £5,500 more than your total cost of goods sold. In other words, you increased the size of your stock by £5,500 cost. The financial effects of your ending stock increase in the balance sheet equation are as follows:

Cash	+ Non-cash Assets	=	Operating Liabilities	+ Retained Earnings
+6,000				+6,000
–5,500	Stock +5,500			

You not only replaced the products sold to customers during the year, but you also bought additional products that cost £5,500. This stock build-up requires cash – notice the £5,500 drain on cash. Your increase in stock may be a smart move but it did use £5,500 in cash.

 An increase in the accounts payable liability account may provide part of the stock increase because businesses that have established good credit histories can buy their stock on credit. However, we didn't want to add another change in the accounts payable account and in most situations, a good part of the stock increase would have to be paid for by the end of the year.

So Where's Your Hard-Earned Profit?

As a business owner, not only should you make profit, but you should also understand and manage the financial effects of profit. In particular, understand that profit does not simply mean an increase in cash. Sales revenue and expenses, the two factors of profit, affect many assets and operating liabilities – making sales on credit impacts accounts receivable, expenses paid in advance impact prepaid assets, unpaid expenses impact operating liabilities and so on. You simply can't have expenses without a smorgasbord of changes in assets and operating liabilities.

 Knowing how much profit your business made isn't enough. You need to take another step and ask, 'Did the profit generate an increase in cash equal to the profit?' and, because it hardly ever does, 'Where is the rest of the profit?'

 So far, we've looked at each step along the reality road separately, as if it were the only change from the simple cash-basis example. Now we assemble all the steps together that we've analysed since starting with the simple all-cash example. In reading the following summary remember that increases in assets hurt your cash balance but that increases in operating liabilities help your cash balance:

Summary of Changes During Year in Non-cash Assets and Operating Liabilities

Changes in Non-cash Assets:		
Accounts receivable	+8,000	
Stock	+5,500	
Prepaid expenses	+1,500	
Fixed assets	−2,500	
Net increase in non-cash assets		£12,500
Changes in Operating Liabilities:		
Creditors (Accounts payable)	+3,000	
Accrued expenses payable	+3,500	
Income tax payable	+500	
Increase of operating liabilities		£7,000
Net decrease in cash balance during year		£5,500

Our purpose right now is simply to explain that £5,500 of your profit for the year is not found in an increase in cash but rather consists of the changes in non-cash assets and operating liabilities. Profit is a mixture, or you could say a smorgasbord, of changes in the assets and operating liabilities that are an integral part of the profit-making process.

If it isn't in cash, where is it? The following schedule summarises the changes in your non-cash assets and operating liabilities caused by the profit-making steps we showed you earlier in this chapter:

Changes in Non-cash Assets		
Accounts receivable	+8,000	
Stock	+5,500	
Prepaid expenses	+1,500	
Fixed assets	−2,500	
Net increase of assets		+£12,500
Changes in Operating Liabilities		
Creditors (Accounts payable)	+3,000	
Accrued expenses payable	+3,500	
Income tax payable	+500	
Less increase of operating liabilities		−£7,000
Non-cash components of profit		+£5,500

Book III

Reporting Results

Note: The amounts shown in this summary are the *changes* – the increases and decreases – in the accounts caused by the sales revenue and expense transactions of your business during the year.

And there you have the story of the £6,000 profit – equal to the £500 increase of cash plus the £12,500 increase of non-cash assets minus the £7,000 increase in operating liabilities. Probably your biggest surprise here is that, even though your business earned £6,000 in profit for the year, your cash balance increased only £500. In managing your profit-making activities (sales revenue and expenses) during the year, you caused cash and three other assets to increase, one asset to decrease, and three operating liabilities to increase. Notice that we've put the onus on you, the owner or manager of the business. The point is that these increases and decreases don't happen automatically – they are the result of management decisions.

By the by, you may not like referring to expenses as profit-making activity but they are! The main point is that expenses should generate sales revenue. Advertising expense creates the incentive in customers to buy products sold by the business. Buying products at £6 cost per unit and selling them for £10 per unit generates £4 profit before other expenses are considered – even though the business has £6 of expense (cost of goods sold). Much of business profit-making is built on the model of incurring, say, £9 in expenses to generate, say, £10 in sales revenue.

Other transactions also change the assets, debt, and owners' equity accounts of a business – such as borrowing money and buying new fixed assets. The balance sheet, in other words, is changed by all the business's transactions. The profit-making transactions (sales and expenses) are the main transactions changing the balance sheet, but many other transactions are recorded in the asset, liability, and owners' equity accounts. Therefore, a separate summary of the profit-making transactions – limited to sales revenue and expenses – that ends with the profit for the period is a standard part of a complete financial report. This separate profit report is called the *profit and loss account.*

Lining Up the Profit and Loss Account

At the end of each period, the accountant prepares a profit report called a *profit and loss account.* You may think that the report would be called the *net profit and loss account* because the bottom-line profit term preferred by accountants is *net income* – but the word *net* is dropped off the title. Other variations of the term are also used, such as *statement of operating results* and *statement of earnings.* Traditionally, the profit and loss account has been called the *profit and loss statement,* or simply the *P&L,* although in external financial reports, businesses and accountants often use the term *income statement.*

Profit and loss accounts summarise the sales and expense transactions of a business during a particular accounting period (which can be a month, quarter, year, or some other period of time that makes sense for a business's needs), with the final profit result on the bottom line. These transactions are *inflows* and *outflows*: Sales revenue is an inflow, and expenses are outflows. Profit, the bottom line, is the *net* inflow. Please note that we didn't say *cash* flow. Making profit involves the inflows and outflows of many assets other than cash, as demonstrated in the steps in the profit-making process examined earlier in the chapter.

The annual profit and loss account included in an external financial report that circulates outside a business has two basic sections (or *layers*):

- ✔ The first section presents the usual, ordinary, continuing sales and expense operations of the business for the year.

- ✔ The second section presents any unusual, extraordinary, and nonrecurring gains and losses that the business recorded in the year (see 'Reporting Unusual Gains and Losses' later in this chapter).

However, a business that didn't experience any extraordinary gains or losses wouldn't include that second section in its profit and loss account – its profit and loss account would consist simply of the first section.

Normal practice is to include two accounting periods on a profit and loss account: the current period plus the year to date. The five key lines that make up a profit and loss account are:

- ✔ **Sales or Revenue:** The total amount of invoiced sales taken in from selling the business's products or services. You calculate this amount by totalling all the sales or revenue accounts. The top line of the profit and loss statement is sales or revenues; either is okay.

- ✔ **Cost of Goods Sold:** How much was spent in order to buy or make the goods or services that were sold during the accounting period under review. The section 'Finding Cost of Goods Sold' below shows you how to calculate Cost of Goods Sold.

- ✔ **Gross Profit:** How much a business made before taking into account operations expenses; calculated by subtracting the Cost of Goods Sold from the Sales or Revenue.

✔ **Operating Expenses:** How much was spent on operating the business; these expenses include administrative fees, salaries, advertising, utilities, and other operations expenses. You add all your expenses accounts on your profit and loss account to get this total.

✔ **Net Profit or Loss:** Whether or not the business made a profit or loss during the accounting period in review; calculated by subtracting total expenses from Gross Profit.

Formatting the Profit and Loss Account

Before you actually create your business's profit and loss account, you have to pick a format in which to organise your financial information. You have two options to choose from: the single-step format or the multi-step format. They contain the same information but present it in slightly different ways.

The *single-step format* groups all data into two categories: revenue and expenses. The *multi-step format* divides the profit and loss account into several sections and offers some key subtotals to make analysing the data easier.

You can calculate the same subtotals from the single-step format in the multi-step format, although it means more work. Therefore, most businesses choose the multi-step format to simplify profit and loss account analysis for those who read their external financial reports.

The following is a simplified example of a basic profit and loss account prepared in the single-step format:

Revenues	
Net Sales	£1,000
Interest Income	£100
Total Revenue	£1,100
Expenses	
Costs of Goods Sold	£500
Depreciation	£50
Advertising	£50
Salaries	£100
Supplies	£100
Interest Expenses	£50
Total Expenses	£850
Net Profit	£250

Using the same numbers, the following is an example of a basic profit and loss account prepared in the multi-step format.

Revenues

Sales	£1,000
Cost of Goods Sold	£500
Gross Profit	£500

Operating Expenses

Depreciation	£50
Advertising	£50
Salaries	£100
Supplies	£100
Interest Expenses	£50
Total Operating Expenses	£350
Operating Profit	£150

Other Income

Interest Income	£100
____Total Profit	£250

Of course in both examples you end up with the same profit but the second profit and loss account provides the reader with a better analysis of what happened in the business.

Preparing the Profit and Loss Account

Before you can prepare your profit and loss account, you have to calculate Net Sales and Cost of Goods Sold.

Finding Net Sales

Net Sales is a total of all your sales minus any discounts. In order to calculate Net Sales, you add up sales, discounts, and any sales fees. For example, suppose that your Total Sales amount to £20,000 and discounts given to customers come to £1,000. Also, your business paid £125 in credit card fees on sales. To find your Net Sales, you subtract the discounts and credit card fees from your Total Sales amount, leaving you with £18,875.

Finding Cost of Goods Sold

Cost of Goods Sold is the total amount your business spent to buy or make the goods or services that you sold. To calculate this amount for a business that buys its finished products from another business in order to sell them to customers, you start with the value of the business's Opening Stock (the amount in the stock account at the beginning of the accounting period), add all purchases of new stock, and then subtract any Closing Stock (stock that's still on the shelves or in the warehouse; it appears on the balance sheet, which is covered in Book III Chapter 2).

The following is a basic Cost of Goods Sold calculation:

Opening Stock + Purchases = Goods Available for Sale

£100 + £1,000 = £1,100

Goods Available for Sale – Closing Stock = Cost of Goods Sold

£1,100 – £200 = £900

To simplify the example for calculating Cost of Goods Sold, these numbers assume the Opening (the value of the stock at the beginning of the accounting period) and Closing Stock (the value of the stock at the end of the accounting period) values are the same. See Book II Chapter 6 for details about calculating stock value. So to calculate Cost of Goods Sold you need just two key lines: the purchases made and the discounts received to lower the purchase cost, as in the following example.

Purchases – Purchases Discounts = Cost of Goods Sold

£8,000 – £1,500 = £6,500

Calculating remaining amounts

After you calculate Net Sales and Cost of Goods Sold (see the preceding sections), you can use your accounting system (see Book II Chapter 1) to prepare your business's profit and loss account. Figure 1-1 shows a sample profit and loss account.

Profit and Loss Statement

May 2008

Month Ended	May
Revenues:	
Net Sales	£ 18,875
Cost of Goods Sold	(£ <u>6,500</u>)
Gross Profit	£ 12,375
Operating Expenses:	
Advertising	£ 1,500
Bank Service Charges	£ 120
Insurance Expenses	£ 100
Interest Expenses	£ 125
Legal & Accounting Fees	£ 300
Office Expenses	£ 250
Payroll Taxes Expenses	£ 350
Postage Expenses	£ 75
Rent Expenses	£ 800
Salaries	£ 3,500
Supplies	£ 300
Telephone Expenses	£ 200
Utilities	£ <u>255</u>
Total Operating Expenses	£ 7,875
Net Profit	£ 4,500

Figure 1-1: A sample profit and loss account.

You and anyone else in-house are likely to want to see the type of detail shown in the example in Figure 1-1, but most business owners prefer not to show all their operating detail to outsiders: They prefer to keep the detail private. Fortunately, if you operate as a sole trader or partnership, only HM Revenue & Customs needs to see your detailed profit and loss figures. If your turnover is less than £15,000 per annum even HM Revenue & Customs only wants to see your profit figure. Also, if you are a small limited company, when you file your accounts at Companies House you can file abbreviated accounts, which means that you can keep your detailed profit and loss figures secret. Speak with your external accountant about whether you qualify as a small company because the exemption levels do change from time to time.

Gauging Your Cost of Goods Sold

Businesses that make their own products rather than buy them for future sale must record stock at three different levels:

- ✔ **Raw materials:** This line item includes purchases of all items used to make your business's products. For example, a fudge shop buys all the ingredients to make the fudge it sells, so the value of any stock on hand that hasn't been used to make fudge yet needs to appear in the raw materials line item.

- ✔ **Work-in-progress stock:** This line item shows the value of any products being made but that aren't yet ready for sale. A fudge shop is unlikely to have anything in this line item because fudge doesn't take more than a few hours to make. However, many manufacturing businesses take weeks or months to produce products and therefore usually have some portion of the stock value in this line item.

  Valuing work in progress can be very complex. As well as the raw material content, you need to add in direct wages and production overheads consumed to produce the products to the stage they're at. In reality most small businesses do not attempt to value work in progress.

- ✔ **Finished-goods stock:** This line item lists the value of stock that's ready for sale. (For a business that doesn't make its own products, finished-goods stock is the same as the stock line item.)

If you keep the books for a business that manufactures its own products, you can use a computerised accounting system to record the various stock accounts described here. However, your basic accounting system software won't cut it – you need a more advanced package in order to record multiple stock types. One such system is Sage 50 Accounts.

Deciphering Gross Profit

Business owners must carefully watch their Gross Profit trends on monthly profit and loss accounts. Gross Profit trends that appear lower from one month to the next can mean one of two things: Sales revenue is down, or Cost of Goods Sold is up.

If revenue is down month-to-month, you may need to find out quickly why, and fix the problem in order to meet your sales goals for the year. Or, by examining sales figures for the same month in previous years, you may determine that the drop is just a normal sales slowdown given the time of year and isn't cause to hit the panic button.

If the downward trend isn't normal, it may be a sign that a competitor's successfully drawing customers away from your business, or it may indicate that customers are dissatisfied with some aspect of the products or services you supply. Whatever the reason, preparing a monthly profit and loss account gives you the ammunition you need to find and fix a problem quickly, thereby minimising any negative hit to your yearly profits.

The other key element of Gross Profit, Cost of Goods Sold, can also be a big factor in a downward profit trend. For example, if the amount you spend to purchase products that you sell goes up, your Gross Profit goes down. As a business owner, you need to do one of five things if the Cost of Goods Sold is reducing your Gross Profit:

✔ Find a new supplier who can provide the goods cheaper.

✔ Increase your prices, as long as you don't lose sales because of the increase.

✔ Find a way to increase your volume of sales so that you can sell more products and meet your annual profit goals.

✔ Find a way to reduce other expenses to offset the additional product costs.

✔ Accept the fact that your annual profit is going to be lower than expected.

The sooner you find out that you have a problem with costs, the faster you can find a solution and minimise any reduction in your annual profit goals.

Book III

Reporting Results

Monitoring Expenses

The Expenses section of your profit and loss account gives you a good summary of how much you spent to keep your business operating that wasn't directly related to the sale of an individual product or service. For example, businesses usually use advertising both to bring customers in and with the hopes of selling many different types of products. That's why you need to list advertising as an Expense rather than a Cost of Goods Sold. After all, rarely can you link an advertisement to the sale of an individual product. The same is true of all the administrative expenses that go into running a business, such as rent, wages and salaries, office costs, and so on.

Business owners watch their expense trends closely to be sure that they don't creep upwards and lower the business's bottom lines. Any cost-cutting you can do on the expense side is guaranteed to increase your bottom-line profit.

Reporting Unusual Gains and Losses

The road to profit is anything but smooth and straight. Every business experiences an occasional *discontinuity* – a serious disruption that comes out of the blue, doesn't happen regularly or often, and can dramatically affect bottom-line profit. In other words, a discontinuity is something that disturbs the basic continuity of business operations – the regular flow of profit-making activities.

Here are some examples of discontinuities:

- Downsizing and restructuring the business
- Abandoning product lines
- Settling lawsuits and other legal actions
- Writing down (also called *writing off*) damaged and impaired assets
- Changing accounting methods
- Correcting errors from previous financial reports

With all these extraordinary losses and gains, how can you distinguish the profit that a business earned from its normal revenue and expense activities from profit caused by other forces entirely? This is one case where accounting rules are actually working *for you*, the non-accountant reader of financial reports.

According to financial reporting standards a business must make these one-time losses and gains very visible in the profit and loss account. So in addition to the normal part of the profit and loss account, which reports normal profit activities, a business with unusual, extraordinary losses or gains must add a second layer to the profit and loss account to report on *these* happenings.

If a business has no unusual gains or losses in the year its profit and loss account ends with one bottom line, usually called *net income* or *profit/loss for the period*. When a profit and loss account includes a second layer, that line becomes *net income from continuing operations before unusual gains and losses*. Below this line, those unusual gains and losses appear for each significant, non-recurring gain or loss.

Say that a business suffered a relatively minor loss from quitting a product line and a very large loss from adopting a new accounting standard. Here's what the second layer of this business's profit and loss account looks like:

Net income from continuing operations	+267,000
Discontinued operations, net of applicable income taxes	–20,000
Earnings before cumulative effect of changes in accounting principles	+247,000
Cumulative effect of changes in accounting principles, net of applicable income taxes	–456,000
Net earnings (loss)	–209,000

The gains and losses reported in the second layer of the external profit and loss account are generally complex and are not always fully explained in the financial report. So where does that leave you?, Your best bet is to seek the counsel of expert financial report readers – financial reports are, for all practical purposes, designed for an audience of stockbrokers, sophisticated readers of *The Financial Times,* and the like, so don't feel bad that you can't understand a report without a degree in accounting-ese.

Even if you have someone else analyse a two-layer profit and loss account for you, you should be aware of controversial issues that extraordinary losses or gains raise. To really get some respect from your stockbroker or accountant, ask these questions about an unusual loss that a business reports:

✔ Were the annual profits reported in prior years overstated?

✔ Why wasn't the loss recorded on a more piecemeal and gradual year-by-year basis instead of as a one-time charge?

✔ Was the loss really a surprising and sudden event that could not have been anticipated?

✔ Will such a loss occur again in the future?

Every company that stays in business for more than a couple of years experiences a discontinuity of one sort or another. But beware of a business that takes advantage of discontinuities in either of the following ways:

✔ **Discontinuities become 'continuities':** This business makes an extraordinary loss or gain a regular feature on its profit and loss account. Every year or so, the business loses a lawsuit, abandons product lines, or restructures itself. It reports 'non-recurring' gains or losses from the same source on a recurring basis every year.

✔ **A discontinuity becomes an opportunity to dump all sorts of write-downs and losses:** When recording an unusual loss (such as settling a lawsuit), the business opts to record other losses at the same time – everything but the kitchen sink (and sometimes that, too) gets written off. This *big-bath theory* says that you may as well take a big bath now in order to avoid taking little showers in the future.

Book III

Reporting Results

Using the Profit and Loss Account to Make Business Decisions

Many business owners find it easier to compare their profit and loss account trends using percentages rather than the actual numbers. Calculating these percentages is easy enough – you simply divide each line item by Net Sales. Figure 1-2 shows a business's percentage breakdown for one month.

Looking at this percentage breakdown, you can see that the business had a gross profit of 65.6 per cent, and its Cost of Goods Sold, at 34.4 per cent, accounted for just over one-third of the revenue. If the prior month's Cost of Goods Sold was only 32 per cent, the business owner needs to find out why the cost of the goods used to make this product seems to have increased. If this trend of increased Cost of Goods Sold continues through the year without some kind of fix, the business makes at least 2.2 per cent less net profit.

You may find it helpful to see how your profit and loss account results compare to industry trends for similar businesses with similar revenues, a process called *benchmarking*. By comparing results, you can find out if your costs and expenses are reasonable for the type of business you operate, and you can identify areas with room to improve your profitability. You also may spot some red flags for line items upon which you spend much more than the national average.

To find industry trends for businesses similar to yours with similar revenues, visit http:// www.fame.bvdep.com. The FAME database contains full financial data on 2.6 million limited companies that file their accounts at Companies House. A word of warning though: Small companies are required to file very little financial information – typically just a balance sheet. This means that if you want to see detailed profit and loss information you have to look at the big businesses with turnover above £22.8 million, more than 250 employees, and a balance sheet greater than £5.6 million.

However, the information available for all the companies on this database is useful and can be interrogated in a number of ways. For example, you can compile industry average statistics, which can be a useful way to see how your business compares with others in the same line of business. You can take this a stage farther and compare your business to other businesses that you already know or have found on this database.

You can also find out how your business looks to the outside world if you use FAME to dig out the financials for your business. A credit rating, details of any court judgements, and other interesting information are all included in the reports.

Profit and Loss Statement

May 2008

Month Ended	May	
Net Sales	£ 18,875	100.0%
Cost of Goods Sold	(£ 6,500)	34.4%
Gross Profit	£ 12,375	65.6%
Operating Expenses:		
Advertising	£ 1,500	7.9%
Bank Service Charges	£ 120	0.6%
Insurance Expenses	£ 100	0.5%
Interest Expenses	£ 125	0.7%
Legal & Accounting Fees	£ 300	1.6%
Office Expenses	£ 250	1.3%
Payroll Taxes Expenses	£ 350	1.9%
Postage Expenses	£ 75	0.4%
Rent Expenses	£ 800	4.2%
Salaries	£ 3,500	18.5%
Supplies	£ 300	1.6%
Telephone Expenses	£ 200	1.1%
Utilities	£ 255	1.4%
Total Operating Expenses	£ 7,875	41.7%
Net Profit	£ 4,500	23.8%

Figure 1-2:
Percentage breakdown of a profit and loss account.

Book III

Reporting Results

FAME is available by subscription, which may make it expensive for the occasional user. You may find that a regional library has FAME available to the public on a free basis or through a per session cost. Most of the UK universities have FAME, and so if you can access one of their library services you can also use this facility. This service may be available through an annual library subscription.

Another source of financial information is your local business link (www.businesslink.gov.uk). Business link acts as a signpost to help small and medium-sized businesses. They can help you access your trade association, and other business support agencies and consultancies that run benchmarking.

Testing Profits

With a completed profit and loss account, you can do a number of quick ratio tests of your business's profitability. You certainly want to know how well your business did compared to other similar businesses. You also want to be able to measure your *return* (the percentage you made) on your business.

Three common tests are Return on Sales, Return on Assets, and Return on Shareholders' Capital. These ratios have much more meaning if you can find industry averages for your particular type of business, so you can compare your results. Check with your local Chamber of Commerce to see whether it has figures for local businesses, or order a report for your industry online from FAME.

Return on Sales

The Return on Sales (ROS) ratio tells you how efficiently your business runs its operations. Using the information on your profit and loss account, you can measure how much profit your business produced per pound of sales and how much extra cash you brought in per sale.

You calculate ROS by dividing net profit before taxes by sales. For example, suppose your business had a net profit of £4,500 and sales of £18,875. The following shows your calculation of ROS.

Net profit before taxes ÷ Sales = Return on Sales

£4,500 ÷ £18,875 = 23.8%

As you can see, your business made 23.8 per cent on each pound of sales. To determine whether that amount calls for celebration, you need to find the ROS ratios for similar businesses. You may be able to get such information from your local Chamber of Commerce, or you can order an industry report online from FAME.

Return on Assets

The Return on Assets (ROA) ratio tests how well you're using your business's assets to generate profits. If your business's ROA is the same or higher than other similar companies, you're doing a good job of managing your assets.

To calculate ROA, you divide net profit by total assets. You find total assets on your balance sheet, which you can read more about in Book III Chapter 2. Suppose that your business's net profit was £4,500 and total assets were £40,050. The following shows your calculation of ROA.

Net profit ÷ Total assets = Return on Assets

£4,500 ÷ £40,050 = 11.2%

Your calculation shows that your business made 11.2 per cent on each pound of assets it held.

ROA can vary significantly depending on the type of industry in which you operate. For example, if your business requires you to maintain lots of expensive equipment, such as a manufacturing firm, your ROA is much lower than a service business that doesn't need as many assets. ROA can range from below 5 per cent, for manufacturing businesses that require a large investment in machinery and factories, to as high as 20 per cent or even higher for service businesses with few assets.

Return on Shareholders' Capital

To measure how successfully your business earned money for the owners or investors, calculate the Return on Shareholders Capital (ROSC) ratio. This ratio often looks better than Return on Assets (see the preceding section) because ROSC doesn't take debt into consideration.

Book III

Reporting Results

You calculate ROSC by dividing net profit by shareholders' or owners' capital. (You find capital amounts on your balance sheet; see Book III Chapter 2.) Suppose your business's net profit was £4,500 and the owners' capital was £9,500. Here is the formula:

Net profit ÷ Shareholders' or owners' capital =
Return on Shareholders' Capital

£4,500 ÷ £9,500 = 47.3%

Most business owners put in a lot of cash upfront to get a business started, so seeing a business whose liabilities and capital are split close to 50 per cent each is fairly common.

Branching Out with Profit and Loss Account Data

The profit and loss account you produce for external use – financial institutions and investors – may be very different from the one you produce for in-house use by your managers. Most business owners prefer to provide the minimum amount of detail necessary to satisfy external users of their financial statements, such as summaries of expenses instead of line-by-line expense details, a Net Sales figure without reporting all the detail about discounts and fees, and a cost of goods number without reporting all the detail about how that was calculated.

Internally, the contents of the profit and loss account are a very different story. With more detail, your managers are better able to make accurate business decisions. Most businesses develop detailed reports based on the data collected to develop the profit and loss account. Items such as discounts, returns, and allowances are commonly pulled out of profit and loss accounts and broken down into more detail.

- **Discounts** are reductions on the selling price as part of a special sale. They may also be in the form of volume discounts provided to customers who buy large amounts of the business's products. For example, a business may offer a 10 per cent discount to customers who buy 20 or more of the same item at one time. In order to put their Net Sales numbers in perspective, business owners and managers must monitor how much they reduce their revenues to attract sales.

- **Returns** are transactions in which the buyer returns items for any reason – not the right size, damaged, defective, and so on. If a business's number of returns increases dramatically, a larger problem may be the cause; therefore business owners need to monitor these numbers carefully in order to identify and resolve any problems with the items they sell.

- **Allowances** cover gifts cards and other accounts that customers pay for upfront without taking any merchandise. Allowances are actually a liability for a business because the customer (or the person who was given the gift card) eventually comes back to get merchandise and doesn't have to pay any cash in return.

Another section of the profit and loss account that you're likely to break down into more detail for internal use is the Cost of Goods Sold. Basically, you take the detail collected to calculate that line item, including Opening Stock, Closing Stock, purchases, and purchase discounts, and present it in a separate report. (We explain how to calculate Cost of Goods Sold in the section 'Finding Cost of Goods Sold', earlier in this chapter.)

No limit exists to the number of internal reports you can generate from the detail that goes into your profit and loss account and other financial statements. For example, many businesses design a report that looks at month-to-month trends in revenue, Cost of Goods Sold, and profit. In fact, you can set up your computerised accounting system (if you use one) to generate this and other custom-designed reports automatically. Using your computerised system, you can produce these reports at any time during the month if you want to see how close you are to meeting your month-end, quarter-end, or year-end goal.

Many businesses also design a report that compares actual spending to the budget. On this report, each of the profit and loss account line items appear with their accompanying planned budget figures and the actual figures. When reviewing this report, you flag any line item that's considerably higher or lower than expected and then research them to find a reason for the difference.

Book III

Reporting Results

Chapter 2

Developing a Balance Sheet

. . . .

. . . .

*P*eriodically, you want to know how well your business is doing. Therefore, at the end of each accounting period, you draw up a balance sheet – a snapshot of your business's condition. This snapshot gives you a picture of where your business stands – its assets, its liabilities, and how much the owners have invested in the business at a particular point in time.

This chapter explains the key ingredients of a balance sheet and tells you how to pull them all together. You also find out how to use some analytical tools called ratios to see how well your business is doing.

Breaking Down the Balance Sheet

Basically, creating a balance sheet is like taking a picture of the financial aspects of your business.

The business name appears at the top of the balance sheet along with the ending date for the accounting period being reported. The rest of the report summarises:

   ✔ **The business's assets,** which include everything the business owns in order to stay in operation.

   ✔ **The business's debts,** which include any outstanding bills and loans that must be paid.

   ✔ **The owners' capital,** which is basically how much the business owners have invested in the business.

Assets, liabilities, and capital probably sound familiar – they're the key elements that show whether or not your books are in balance. If your liabilities plus capital equal assets, your books are in balance. All your bookkeeping efforts are an attempt to keep the books in balance based on this formula, which we talk more about in Book II Chapter 1.

Gathering Balance Sheet Ingredients

To keep this example simple, we assume that the fictitious business has no adjustments for the balance sheet as of 31 May 2008. In the real world, every business needs to adjust something (usually stock levels at the very least) every month.

To prepare the example trial balances in this chapter, we use the key accounts listed in Table 2-1.

Table 2-1	Balance Sheet Accounts
Account Name	*Balance in Account*
Cash	£2,500
Petty Cash	£500
Accounts Receivable	£1,000
Stock	£1,200
Equipment	£5,050
Vehicles	£25,000
Furniture	£5,600
Accounts Payable	£2,200
Loans Payable	£29,150
Capital	£5,000

Dividing and listing your assets

The first part of the balance sheet is the Assets section. The first step in developing this section is dividing your assets into two categories: current assets and long-term assets.

Current assets

Current assets are things your business owns that you can easily convert to cash and expect to use in the next 12 months to pay your bills and your employees. Current assets include cash, Accounts Receivable (money due from customers), marketable securities (including shares, bonds, and other types of securities), and stock. (We cover stock and Accounts Receivable in Book II Chapter 6.)

When you see cash as the first line item on a balance sheet, that account includes what you have on hand in the tills and what you have in the bank, including current accounts, savings accounts, money market accounts, and certificates of deposit. In most cases, you simply list all these accounts as one item, Cash, on the balance sheet.

The current assets for the fictional business are:

Cash	£2,500
Petty Cash	£500
Accounts Receivable	£1,000
Stock	£1,200

You total the Cash and Petty Cash accounts, giving you £3,000, and list that amount on the balance sheet as a line item called Cash.

Long-term assets

Long-term assets are things your business owns that you expect to have for more than 12 months. Long-term assets include land, buildings, equipment, furniture, vehicles, and anything else that you expect to have for longer than a year.

The long-term assets for the fictional business are:

Equipment	£5,050
Vehicles	£25,000
Furniture	£5,600

Most businesses have more items in the long-term assets section of a balance sheet than the few long-term assets we show here for the fictional business. For example:

✔ A manufacturing business that has a lot of tools, dies, or moulds created specifically for its manufacturing processes needs to have a line item called Tools, Dies, and Moulds.

- ✔ A business that owns one or more buildings needs to have a line item labelled Land and Buildings.

- ✔ A business that leases a building with an option to purchase it at some later date considers that *capitalised lease* to be a long-term asset, and lists it on the balance sheet as Capitalised Lease. An example of a capitalised lease is where you pay a premium for a lease and regard that premium as a long-term asset rather than an expense. The premium becomes a capitalised lease and set against profits over the life of the lease.

- ✔ A business may lease its business space and then spend lots of money doing it up. For example, a restaurant may rent a large space and then furnish it according to a desired theme. Money spent on doing up the space becomes a long-term asset called Leasehold Improvements and is listed on the balance sheet in the long-term assets section.

Everything mentioned so far in this section – land, buildings, capitalised leases, leasehold improvements, and so on – is a *tangible asset.* These items are ones that you can actually touch or hold. Another type of long-term asset is the *intangible asset.* Intangible assets aren't physical objects; common examples are patents, copyrights, and trademarks.

- ✔ A **patent** gives a business the right to dominate the markets for the patented product. When a patent expires (usually after 20 years), competitors can enter the marketplace for the product that was patented, and the competition helps to lower the price to consumers. For example, pharmaceutical businesses patent all their new drugs and therefore are protected as the sole providers of those drugs. When your doctor prescribes a brand-name drug, you're getting a patented product. Generic drugs are products whose patents have run out, meaning that any pharmaceutical business can produce and sell its own version of the same product.

- ✔ A **copyright** protects original works, including books, magazines, articles, newspapers, television shows, movies, music, poetry, and plays, from being copied by anyone other than the creator(s). For example, this book is copyrighted, so no one can make a copy of any of its contents without the permission of the publisher, John Wiley & Sons, Ltd.

- ✔ A **trademark** gives a business ownership of distinguishing words, phrases, symbols, or designs. For example, check out this book's cover to see the registered trademark, *For Dummies,* for this brand. Trademarks can last forever, as long as a business continues to use the trademark and file the proper paperwork periodically.

In order to show in financial statements that their values are being used up, all long-term assets are depreciated or amortised. Tangible assets are depreciated; see Book IV Chapter 5 for details on how to depreciate. Intangible assets such as patents and copyrights are amortised (amortisation is very similar to depreciation). Each intangible asset has a lifespan based on the number of years for which the rights are granted. After setting an initial value for the intangible asset, a business then divides that value by the number of years it has protection, and the resulting amount is then written off each year as an Amortisation Expense, which is shown on the profit and loss statement. You can find the total amortisation or depreciation expenses that have been written off during the life of the asset on the balance sheet in a line item called Accumulated Depreciation or Accumulated Amortisation, whichever is appropriate for the type of asset.

Acknowledging your debts

The Liabilities section of the balance sheet comes after the Assets section and shows all the money that your business owes to others, including banks, vendors, contractors, financial institutions, and individuals. Like assets, you divide your liabilities into two categories on the balance sheet:

- ✔ **Current liabilities:** All bills and debts that you plan to pay within the next 12 months. Accounts appearing in this section include Accounts Payable (bills due to suppliers, contractors, and others), Credit Cards Payable, and the current portion of a long-term debt (for example, if you have a mortgage on your premises, the payments due in the next 12 months appear in the Current Liabilities section).

- ✔ **Long-term liabilities:** All debts you owe to lenders that are to be paid over a period longer than 12 months. Mortgages Payable and Loans Payable are common accounts in the long-term liabilities section of the balance sheet.

Most businesses try to minimise their current liabilities because the interest rates on short-term loans, such as credit cards, are usually much higher than those on loans with longer terms. As you manage your business's liabilities, always look for ways to minimise your interest payments by seeking longer-term loans with lower interest rates than you can get on a credit card or short-term loan.

Book III

Reporting Results

The fictional business used for the example balance sheets in this chapter has only one account in each liabilities section:

Current liabilities:

Accounts Payable £2,200

Long-term liabilities:

Loans Payable £29,150

Naming your investments

Every business has investors. Even a small family business requires money upfront to get the business on its feet. Investments are reflected on the balance sheet as *capital*. The line items that appear in a balance sheet's Capital section vary depending upon whether or not the business is incorporated. (Businesses incorporate primarily to minimise their personal legal liabilities; we talk more about incorporation in Book VI Chapter 2.)

If you're preparing the books for a business that isn't incorporated, the Capital section of your balance sheet contains these accounts:

- ✔ **Capital:** All money invested by the owners to start up the business as well as any additional contributions made after the start-up phase. If the business has more than one owner, the balance sheet usually has a Capital account for each owner so that individual stakes in the business can be recorded.

- ✔ **Drawings:** All money taken out of the business by the business's owners. Balance sheets usually have a Drawing account for each owner in order to record individual withdrawal amounts.

- ✔ **Retained Earnings:** All profits left in the business.

For an incorporated business, the Capital section of the balance sheet contains the following accounts:

- ✔ **Shares:** Portions of ownership in the business, purchased as investments by business owners.

- ✔ **Retained Earnings:** All profits that have been reinvested in the business.

Because the fictional business isn't incorporated, the accounts appearing in the Capital Section of its balance sheet are:

Capital £5,000

Retained Earnings £4,500

Sorting out share investments

You're probably most familiar with the sale of shares on the open market through the various stock market exchanges, such as the London Stock Exchange (LSE) and the Alternative Investment Market (AIM). However, not all companies sell their shares through public exchanges; in fact, most companies aren't public companies but rather remain private operations.

Whether public or private, ownership in a business is obtained by buying shares. If the business isn't publicly traded, shares are bought and sold privately. In most small businesses, these exchanges are made among family members, close friends, and occasionally outside investors who have been approached individually as a means to raise additional money to build the business.

The value of each share is set at the time the share is sold. Many businesses set the initial share value at £1 to £10.

Pulling Together the Final Balance Sheet

After you group together all your accounts (see the preceding section 'Gathering Balance Sheet Ingredients'), you're ready to produce a balance sheet. Businesses in the United Kingdom usually choose between two common formats for their balance sheets: the Horizontal format or the Vertical format, with the Vertical format preferred. The actual line items appearing in both formats are the same; the only difference is the way in which you lay out the information on the page.

Book III

Reporting Results

Horizontal format

The Horizontal format is a two-column layout with assets on one side and liabilities and capital on the other side.

Figure 2-1 shows the elements of a sample balance sheet in the Horizontal format.

Balance Sheet
As of 31 May 2008

Fixed Assets			**Capital**		
Equipment	£ 5,050		Opening balance	£ 5,000	
Furniture	£ 5,600		Net Profit for year	£ 14,500	
Vehicles	£ 25,000			£ 19,500	
		£ 35,650	Less Drawings	£ 10,000	
					£ 9,50
			Long-term Liabilities		
			Loans Payable		£ 29,150
Current Assets			**Current Liabilities**		
Stock	£ 1,200		Accounts Payable		£ 2,200
Accounts Receivable	£ 1,000				
Cash	£ 3,000				
		£ 5,200			
		£ 40,850			£ 40,850

Figure 2-1:
A sample balance sheet using the Horizontal format.

Vertical format

The Vertical format is a one-column layout showing assets first, followed by liabilities, and then capital.

Using the Vertical Format, Figure 2-2 shows the balance sheet for a fictional business.

Whether you prepare your balance sheet as per Figure 2-1 or Figure 2-2, remember that Assets = Liabilities + Capital, so both sides of the balance sheet must balance to reflect this.

The Vertical format includes:

- ✔ **Net current assets:** Calculated by subtracting current assets from current liabilities – a quick test to see whether or not a business has the money on hand to pay bills. Net current assets is sometimes referred to as *working capital*.

- ✔ **Total assets less current liabilities:** What's left over for a business's owners after all liabilities have been subtracted from total assets. Total assets less current liabilities is sometimes referred to as *net assets*.

Balance Sheet
As of 31 May 2008

Fixed Assets		
Equipment	£ 5,050	
Furniture	£ 5,600	
Vehicles	£ 25,000	
		£ 35,650
Current Assets		
Stock	£ 1,200	
Accounts Receivable	£ 1,000	
Cash	£ 3,000	
	£ 5,200	
Less: Current Liabilities		
Accounts Payable	£ 2,200	
Net Current Assets		£ 3,000
Total Assets Less Current Liabilities		£ 38,650
Long-term Liabilities		
Loans Payable		£ 29,150
		£ 9,500
Capital		
Opening Balance		£ 5,000
Net Profit for Year		£ 14,500
		£ 19,500
Less Drawings		£ 10,000
		£ 9,500

Figure 2-2:
A sample balance sheet using the Vertical format.

Book III

Reporting Results

Putting Your Balance Sheet to Work

With a complete balance sheet in your hands, you can analyse the numbers through a series of ratio tests to check your cash status and monitor your debt. These tests are the type of tests that financial institutions and potential investors use to determine whether or not to lend money to or invest in your business. Therefore, a good idea is to run these tests yourself before seeking loans or investors. Ultimately, the ratio tests in this section can help you determine whether or not your business is in a strong cash position.

Testing your cash

When you approach a bank or other financial institution for a loan, you can expect the lender to use one of two ratios to test your cash flow: the *current ratio* and the *acid test ratio* (also known as the *quick ratio*).

Current ratio

This ratio compares your current assets to your current liabilities, and provides a quick glimpse of your business's ability to pay its bills in the short term.

The formula for calculating the current ratio is:

Current assets ÷ Current liabilities = Current ratio

The following is an example of a current ratio calculation:

£5,200 ÷ £2,200 = 2.36 (current ratio)

Lenders usually look for current ratios of 1.2 to 2, so any financial institution considers a current ratio of 2.36 a good sign. A current ratio under 1 is considered a danger sign because it indicates the business doesn't have enough cash to pay its current bills. This rule is only a rough guide and some business sectors may require a higher or lower current ratio figure. Get some advice to see what is the norm for your business sector.

A current ratio over 2.0 may indicate that your business isn't investing its assets well and may be able to make better use of its current assets. For example, if your business is holding a lot of cash, you may want to invest that money in some long-term assets, such as additional equipment, that you can use to help grow the business.

Acid test (quick) ratio

The acid test ratio uses only the financial figures in your business's Cash account, Accounts Receivable, and Marketable Securities – otherwise known as *liquid assets*. Although similar to the current ratio in that it examines current assets and liabilities, the acid test ratio is a stricter test of a business's ability to pay bills. The assets part of this calculation doesn't take stock into account because it can't always be converted to cash as quickly as other current assets and because, in a slow market, selling your stock may take a while.

Many lenders prefer the acid test ratio when determining whether or not to give a business a loan because of its strictness.

Calculating the acid test ratio is a two-step process:

1. **Determine your quick assets.**

   Cash + Accounts Receivable + Marketable securities = Quick assets

2. **Calculate your quick ratio.**

   Quick assets ÷ Current liabilities = Quick ratio

The following is an example of an acid test ratio calculation:

£2,000 + £1,000 + £1,000 = £4,000 (quick assets)

£4,000 ÷ £2,200 = 1.8 (acid test ratio)

Lenders consider that a business with an acid test ratio around 1 is in good condition. An acid test ratio less than 1 indicates that the business may have to sell some of its marketable securities or take on additional debt until it can sell more of its stock.

Assessing your debt

Before you even consider whether or not to take on additional debt, always check out your debt condition. One common ratio that you can use to assess your business's debt position is the *gearing ratio*. This ratio compares what your business owes – *external borrowing* – to what your business owners have invested in the business – *internal funds*.

Calculating your debt to capital ratio is a two-step process:

1. **Calculate your total debt.**

   Current liabilities + Long-term liabilities = Total debt

2. **Calculate your gearing ratio.**

   Total debt ÷ Capital = Gearing ratio

The following is an example of a debt to capital ratio calculation:

£2,200 + £29,150 = £31,350 (total debt)

£31,350 ÷ £9,500 = 3.3 (gearing ratio)

Book III

Reporting Results

Lenders like to see a gearing ratio close to 1 because it indicates that the amount of debt is equal to the amount of capital. Most banks probably wouldn't lend any more money to a business with a debt to capital ratio of 3.3 until its debt levels were lowered or the owners put more money into the business. The reason for this lack of confidence may be one of two:

✔ They don't want to have more money invested in the business than the owner.

✔ They are concerned about the business's ability to service the debt.

Generating Balance Sheets Electronically

If you use a computerised accounting system, you can take advantage of its report function to generate your balance sheets automatically. These balance sheets give you quick snapshots of the business's financial position but may require adjustments before you prepare your financial reports for external use.

One key adjustment you're likely to make involves the value of your stock. Most computerised accounting systems use the averaging method to value stock. This method totals all the stock purchased and then calculates an average price for the stock. However, your accountant may recommend a different valuation method that works better for your business. (We discuss the options in Book II Chapter 6.) Therefore, if you use a method other than the default averaging method to value your stock, you need to adjust the stock value that appears on the balance sheet generated from your computerised accounting system.

Chapter 3

Cash Flow and the Cash Flow Statement

This chapter talks about *cash flows* – which in general refers to cash inflows and outflows over a period of time. Suppose you tell us that last year you had total cash inflows of £145,000 and total cash outflows of £140,000. We know that your cash balance increased £5,000. But we don't know where your £145,000 cash inflows came from. Did you earn this much in salary? Did you receive an inheritance from your rich uncle? Likewise, we don't know what you used your £140,000 cash outflow for. Did you make large payments on your credit cards? Did you lose a lot of money at the races? In short, cash flows have to be sorted into different sources and uses to make much sense.

The Three Types of Cash Flow

Accountants categorise the cash flows of a business into three types:

✔ Cash inflows from making sales and cash outflows for expenses; sales and expense transactions are called the *operating activities* of a business (although they could be called profit activities just as well, because their purpose is to make profit).

> ✔ Cash outflows for making investments in new assets (buildings, machinery, tools, and so on), and cash inflows from liquidating old investments (assets no longer needed that are sold off); these transactions are called *investment activities*.
>
> ✔ Cash inflows from borrowing money and from the additional investment of money in the business by its owners, and cash outflows for paying off debt, returning capital that the business no longer needs to owners and making cash distributions of profit to its owners; these transactions are called *financing activities*.

The cash flow statement (or *statement of cash flows*) summarises the cash flows of a business for a period according to this three-way classification. Generally accepted accounting principles (GAAP) require that whenever a business reports its income statement, it must also report its cash flow statement for the same period – a business shouldn't report one without the other. A good reason exists for this dual financial statement requirement.

The income statement is based on the *accrual basis of accounting* that records sales when made, whether or not cash is received at that time, and records expenses when incurred, whether or not the expenses are paid at that time. Because accrual basis accounting is used to record profit, you can't equate bottom-line profit with an increase in cash. Suppose a business's annual income statement reports that it earned £160,000 net income for the year. This does not mean that its cash balance increased £160,000 during the period. You have to look in the cash flow statement to find out how much its cash balance increased (or, possibly, decreased!) from its operating activities (sales revenue and expenses) during the period.

In the chapter, we refer to the net increase (or decrease) in the business's cash balance that results from collecting sales revenue and paying expenses as *cash flow from profit*, as the alternative term for *cash flow from operating activities*. Cash flow from profit seems more user-friendly than cash flow from operating activities, and in fact the term is used widely. In any case, do not confuse cash flow from profit with the other two types of cash flow – from the business's investing activities and financing activities during the period.

Before moving on, here's a short problem for you to solve. Using the three-way classification of cash flows explained earlier, below is a summary of a business's net cash flows for the year just ended, with one amount missing:

(1) From profit (operating activities)	?
(2) From investing activities	– £127,500
(3) From financing activities	+ £16,000
Decrease in cash balance during year	– £1,500

Note that the business's cash balance from all sources and uses decreased £1,500 during the year. The amounts of net cash flows from the company's investing and financing activities are given. So you can determine that the net cash flow from profit was £110,000 for the year. Understanding cash flows from investing activities and financing activities is fairly straightforward. Understanding the net cash flow from profit, in contrast, is more challenging – but business owners should have a good grip on this very important number.

Setting the Stage: Changes in Balance Sheet Accounts

The first step in understanding the amounts reported by a business in its cash flow statement is to focus on the *changes* in the business's assets, liabilities, and owners' equity accounts during the period – the increases or decreases of each account from the start of the period to the end of the period. These changes are found in the comparative two-year balance sheet reported by a business. Figure 3-1 presents the increases and decreases during the year in the assets, liabilities and owners' equity accounts for a business example. Figure 3-1 is not a balance sheet but only a summary of *changes* in account balances. We do not want to burden you with an entire balance sheet, which has much more detail than is needed here.

Take a moment to scan Figure 3-1. Note that the business's cash balance decreased £1,500 during the year. (An increase is not necessarily a good thing, and a decrease is not necessarily a bad thing; it depends on the overall financial situation of the business.) One purpose of reporting the cash flow statement is to summarise the main reasons for the change in cash – according to the three-way classification of cash flows explained earlier. One question on everyone's mind is this: How much cash did the profit for the year generate for the business? The cash flow statement begins by answering this question.

Assets	
Cash	£1,500
Debtors	£80,000
Stock	£97,500
Prepaid Expenses	£14,500
Fixed Assets	£127,500
Accumulated Depreciation*	£120,000
Total	£198,000
Liabilities & Owners' Equity	
Creditors	£8,000
Accrued Expenses Payable	£12,000
Income Tax Payable	£2,000
Overdraft	£20,000
Long-term Loans	£30,000
Owners' Invested Capital	£6,000
Retained Earnings	£120,000
Total	£198,000

* Accumulated Depreciation is a negative asset account which is deducted from Fixed Assets. The negative £120,000 change increases the negative balance of the account.

Figure 3-1: Changes in balance sheet assets and operating liabilities that affect cash flow from profit.

Getting at the Cash Increase from Profit

Although all amounts reported on the cash flow statement are important, the one that usually gets the most attention is *cash flow from operating activities,* or *cash flow from profit* as we prefer to call it. This is the increase in cash generated by a business's profit-making operations during the year, exclusive of its other sources of cash during the year (such as borrowed money, sold-off fixed assets, and additional owners' investments in the business). *Cash flow from profit* indicates a business's ability to turn profit into available cash – cash in the bank that can be used for the needs of business. Cash flow from profit gets just as much attention as net income (the bottom-line profit number in the income statement).

Before presenting the cash flow statement – which is a rather formidable, three-part accounting report – in all its glory, in the following sections we build on the summary of changes in the business's assets, liabilities, and owners' equities shown in Figure 3-1 to explain the components of the £110,000 increase in cash from the business's profit activities during the year. (The £110,000 amount of cash flow from profit was determined earlier in the chapter by solving the unknown factor.)

Computing cash flow from profit

Here's how to compute cash flow from profit based on the changes in the company's balance sheet accounts presented in Figure 3-1:

Computation of Cash Flow from Profit		
	Negative Cash Flow Effects	**Positive Cash Flow Effects**
Net income for the year		$160,000
Debtors increase	$80,000	
Stock increase	$97,500	
Prepaid expenses increase	$14,500	
Depreciation expense		$120,000
Creditors increase		$8,000
Accrued expenses payable increase		$12,000
Income tax payable increase		$2,000
Totals	$192,000	$302,000
Cash flow from profit ($302,000 positive increases minus $192,000 negative increases)		$110,000

Book III

Reporting Results

The business in the example experienced a rather strong growth year. Its accounts receivable and stock increased by relatively large amounts. In fact, all the relevant accounts increased; their ending balances are larger than their beginning balances (which are the amounts carried forward from the end of the preceding year). At this point, we need to provide some additional information. The $120,000 increase in retained earnings is the net difference of two quite different things.

The $160,000 net income earned by the business increased retained earnings by this amount. As you see in Figure 3-1, the account increased only $120,000. Thus there must have been a $40,000 decrease in retained earnings during the year. The business paid $40,000 cash dividends from profit to its owners (the shareholders) during the year, which is recorded as a decrease in retained earnings. The amount of cash dividends is reported in the *financing activities* section of the cash flow statement. The entire amount of net income is reported in the *operating activities* section of the cash flow statement.

Note that net income (profit) for the year – which is the correct amount of profit based on the accrual basis of accounting – is listed in the positive cash flow column. This is only the starting point. Think of this the following way: If the business had collected all its sales revenue for the year in cash, and if it had made cash payments for its expenses exactly equal to the amounts recorded for the expenses, then the net income amount would equal the increase in cash. These two conditions are virtually never true, and they are not true in this example. So the net income figure is just the jumping-off point for determining the amount of cash generated by the business's profit activities during the year.

We'll let you in on a little secret here. The analysis of cash flow from profit asks what amount of profit would have been recorded if the business had been on the cash basis of accounting instead of the accrual basis. This can be confusing and exasperating, because it seems that two different profit measures are provided in a business's financial report – the true economic profit number, which is the bottom line in the income statement (usually called *net income*), and a second profit number called *cash flow from operating activities* in the cash flow statement.

When the cash flow statement was made mandatory many accountants worried about this problem, but the majority opinion was that the amount of cash increase (or decrease) generated from the profit activities of a business is very important to disclose in financial reports. In reading the income statement, you have to wear your accrual basis accounting lenses, and in the cash flow statement you have to put on your cash basis lenses. Who says accountants can't see two sides of something?

The following sections explain the effects on cash flow that each balance sheet account change causes (refer to Figure 3-1).

Getting specific about changes in assets and liabilities

As a business owner, you should keep a close watch on each of your assets and liabilities and understand the cash flow effects of increases (or decreases) caused by these changes. Investors should focus on the business's ability to generate a healthy cash flow from profit, so investors should be equally concerned about these changes.

Debtors increase

Remember that the debtors asset shows how much money customers who bought products on credit still owe the business; this asset is a promise of cash that the business will receive. Basically, debtors is the amount of uncollected sales revenue at the end of the period. Cash does not increase until the business collects money from its customers.

But the amount in debtors *is* included in the total sales revenue of the period – after all, you did make the sales, even if you haven't been paid yet. Obviously, then, you can't look at sales revenue as being equal to the amount of cash that the business received during the period.

To calculate the actual cash flow from sales, you need to subtract from sales revenue the amount of credit sales that you did not collect in cash over the period – but you add in the amount of cash that you collected during the period just ended for credit sales that you made in the *preceding* period. Take a look at the following equation for our business example (the asset and liability changes for which are shown in Figure 3-1).

**£2.5 million sales revenue – £80,000 increase in debtors =
£2.42 million cash collected from customers during the year**

The business started the year with £170,000 in debtors and ended the year with £250,000 in debtors. The beginning balance was collected during the year but at the end of the year the ending balance had not been collected. Thus the net effect is a shortfall in cash inflow of £80,000, which is why it's called a negative cash flow factor. The key point is that you need to keep an eye on the increase or decrease in debtors from the beginning of the period to the end of the period.

Book III

Reporting Results

- ✔ If the amount of credit sales you made during the period is greater than the amount collected from customers during the same period, your debtors *increased* over the period. Therefore you need to *subtract* from sales revenue that difference between start-of-period debtors and end-of-period debtors. In short, an increase in debtors hurts cash flow by the amount of the increase.

- ✔ If the amount you collected from customers during the period is greater than the credit sales you made during the period, your debtors *decreased* over the period. In this case you need to *add* to sales revenue that difference between start-of-period debtors and end-of-period debtors. In short, a decrease in debtors helps cash flow by the amount of the decrease.

In the example we've been using, debtors increased £80,000. Cash collections from sales were £80,000 less than sales revenue. Ouch! The business increased its sales substantially over last period, so you shouldn't be surprised that its debtors increased. The higher sales revenue was good for profit but bad for cash flow from profit.

An occasional hiccup in cash flow is the price of growth – managers and investors need to understand this point. Increasing sales without increasing debtors is a happy situation for cash flow, but in the real world you can't have one increase without the other (except in very unusual circumstances).

Stock increase

Stock is the next asset in Figure 3-1 – and usually the largest short-term, or *current,* asset for businesses that sell products. If the stock account is greater at the end of the period than at the start of the period – because either unit costs increased or the quantity of products increased – what the business actually paid out in cash for stock purchases (or manufacturing products) is more than the business recorded as its cost-of-goods-sold expense in the period. Therefore, you need to deduct the stock increase from net income when determining cash flow from profit.

In the example, stock increased £97,500 from start-of-period to end-of-period. In other words, this business replaced the products that it sold during the period *and* increased its stock by £97,500. The easiest way to understand the effect of this increase on cash flow is to pretend that the business paid for all its stock purchases in cash immediately upon receiving them. The stock on hand at the start of the period had already been paid for *last* period, so that cost does not affect this period's cash flow. Those products were sold during the period and involved no further cash payment by the business. But the business did pay cash *this* period for the products that were in stock at the end of the period.

In other words, if the business had bought just enough new stock (at the same cost that it paid out last period) to replace the stock that it sold during the period, the actual cash outlay for its purchases would equal the cost-of-goods-sold expense reported in its income statement. Ending stock would equal the beginning stock; the two stock costs would cancel each other out and thus would have a zero effect on cash flow. But this hypothetical scenario doesn't fit the example because the company increased its sales substantially over the last period.

To support the higher sales level, the business needed to increase its stock level. So the business bought £97,500 more in products than it sold during the period – and it had to come up with the cash to pay for this stock increase. Basically, the business wrote cheques amounting to £97,500 more than its cost-of-goods-sold expense for the period. This step-up in its stock level was necessary to support the higher sales level, which increased profit – even though cash flow took a hit.

It's that accrual basis accounting thing again: The cost that a business pays *this* period for *next* period's stock is reflected in this period's cash flow but isn't recorded until next period's income statement (when the products are actually sold). So if a business paid more *this* period for *next* period's stock than it paid *last* period for *this* period's stock, you can see how the additional expense would adversely affect cash flow but would not be reflected in the bottom-line net income figure. This cash flow analysis stuff gets a little complicated, we know, but hang in there. The cash flow statement, presented later in the chapter, makes a lot more sense after you go through this background briefing.

Prepaid expenses increase

The next asset, after stock, is prepaid expenses (refer to Figure 3-1). A change in this account works the same way as a change in stock and debtors, although changes in prepaid expenses are usually much smaller than changes in those other two asset accounts.

Again, the beginning balance of prepaid expenses is recorded as an expense this period but the cash was actually paid out last period, not this period. This period, a business pays cash for next period's prepaid expenses – which affects this period's cash flow but doesn't affect net income until next period. So the £14,500 increase in prepaid expenses from start-of-period to end-of-period in this business example has a negative cash flow effect.

As it grows, a business needs to increase its prepaid expenses for such things as fire insurance (premiums have to be paid in advance of the insurance coverage) and its stocks of office and data processing supplies. Increases in debtors, stock, and prepaid expenses are the price a business has to pay for growth. Rarely do you find a business that can increase its sales revenue without increasing these assets.

The simple but troublesome depreciation factor

Depreciation expense recorded in the period is both the simplest cash flow effect to understand and, at the same time, one of the most misunderstood elements in calculating cash flow from profit. (Refer to Book III Chapter 1 and Book IV Chapter 5 for more about depreciation.) To start with, depreciation is not a cash outlay during the period. The amount of depreciation expense recorded in the period is simply a fraction of the original cost of the business's fixed assets that were bought and paid for years ago. (Well, if you want to nit-pick here, some of the fixed assets may have been bought during this period, and their cost is reported in the investing activities section of the cash flow statement.) Because the depreciation expense is not a cash outlay this period, the amount is added back to net income in the calculation of cash flow from profit – so far so good.

When measuring profit on the accrual basis of accounting you count depreciation as an expense. The fixed assets of a business are on an irreversible journey to the junk heap. Fixed assets have a limited, finite life of usefulness to a business (except for land); depreciation is the accounting method that allocates the total cost of fixed assets to each year of their use in helping the business generate sales revenue. Part of the total sales revenue of a business constitutes *recovery of cost invested in its fixed assets*. In a real sense, a business 'sells' some of its fixed assets each period to its customers – it factors the cost of fixed assets into the sales prices that it charges its customers. For example, when you go to a supermarket a very small slice of the price you pay for that box of cereal goes toward the cost of the building, the shelves, the refrigeration equipment, and so on. (No wonder they charge so much for a box of cornflakes!)

Each period, a business recoups part of the cost invested in its fixed assets. In other words, £120,000 of sales revenue (in the example) went toward reimbursing the business for the use of its fixed assets during the year. The problem regarding depreciation in cash flow analysis is that many people simply add back depreciation for the year to bottom-line profit and then stop, as if this is the proper number for cash flow from profit. It ain't so. The changes in other assets as well as the changes in liabilities also affect cash flow from profit. You should factor in *all* the changes that determine cash flow from profit, as explained the following section.

Adding net income and depreciation to determine cash flow from profit is mixing apples and oranges. The business did not realise £160,000 cash increase from its £160,000 net income. The total of the increases of its debtors, stock, and prepaid expenses is £192,000 (refer to Figure 3-1), which wipes out the net income amount and leaves the business with a cash balance hole of £32,000. This cash deficit is offset by the £22,000 increase in liabilities (explained later) leaving a £10,000 net income *deficit* as far as cash flow is concerned. Depreciation recovery increased cash flow £120,000. So the final cash flow from profit equals £110,000. But you'd never know this if you simply added depreciation expense to net income for the period.

The managers did not have to go outside the business for the £110,000 cash increase generated from its profit for the year. Cash flow from profit is an *internal* source of money generated by the business itself, in contrast to *external* money that the business raises from lenders and owners. A business does not have to 'go begging' for external money if its internal cash flow from profit is sufficient to provide for its growth.

Net income + depreciation expense doesn't equal cash flow from profit!

The business in our example earned £160,000 in net income for the year, plus it received £120,000 cash flow because of the depreciation expense built into in its sales revenue for the year. The sum of these is £280,000. Is £280,000 the amount of cash flow from profit for the period? The knee-jerk answer of many investors and managers is 'yes'. But if net income + depreciation truly equals cash flow, then *both* factors in the brackets – both net income and depreciation – must be fully realised in cash. Depreciation is, but the net income amount is not fully realised in cash because the company's debtors, stock, and prepaid expenses increased during the year, and these increases have negative impacts on cash flow.

In passing, we should mention that a business could have a negative cash flow from profit for a year – meaning that despite posting a net income for the period, the changes in the company's assets and liabilities caused its cash balance to decrease. In reverse, a business could report a bottom line *loss* in its income statement yet have a *positive* cash flow from its operating activities: The positive contribution from depreciation expense plus decreases in its debtors and stock could amount to more than the amount of loss. More realistically, a loss often leads to negative cash flow or very little positive cash flow.

Book III

Reporting Results

Operating liabilities increases

The business in the example, like almost all businesses, has three basic liabilities that are inextricably intertwined with its expenses: creditors, accrued expenses payable and income tax payable. When the beginning balance of one of these liability accounts is the same as the ending balance of the same account (not too likely, of course), the business breaks even on cash flow for that account. When the end-of-period balance is higher than the start-of-period balance, the business did not pay out as much money as was actually recorded as an expense on the period's income statement.

In the example we've been using, the business disbursed £72,000 to pay off last period's creditors balance. (This £72,000 was reported as the creditors balance on last period's ending balance sheet.) Its cash flow this period decreased by £72,000 because of these payments. But this period's ending balance sheet shows the amount of creditors that the business will need to pay next period – £80,000. The business actually paid off £72,000 and recorded £80,000 of expenses to the year, so this time, cash flow is *richer* than what's reflected in the business's net income figure by £8,000 – in other words, the increase in creditors has a positive cash flow effect. The increases in accrued expenses payable and income tax payable work the same way.

Therefore, liability increases are favourable to cash flow – in a sense the business borrowed more than it paid off. Such an increase means that the business delayed paying cash for certain things until next year. So you need to add the increases in the three liabilities to net income to determine cash flow from profit, following the same logic as adding back depreciation to net income. The business did not have cash outlays to the extent of increases in these three liabilities.

The analysis of the changes in assets and liabilities of the business that affect cash flow from profit is complete for the business example. The bottom line (oops, we shouldn't use that term when referring to a cash flow amount) is that the company's cash balance increased £110,000 from profit. You could argue that cash should have increased £280,000 – £160,000 net income plus £120,000 depreciation that was recovered during the year – so the business is £170,000 behind in turning its profit into cash flow (£280,000 less the £110,000 cash flow from profit). This £170,000 lag in converting profit into cash flow is caused by the £192,000 increase in assets less the £22,000 increase in liabilities, as shown in Figure 3-1.

Presenting the Cash Flow Statement

The cash flow statement is one of the three primary financial statements that a business must report to the outside world, according to generally accepted accounting principles (GAAP). To be technical, the rule says that whenever a business reports a profit and loss account, it should also report a cash flow statement. The *profit and loss account* summarises sales revenue and expenses and ends with the bottom-line profit for the period. The *balance sheet* summarises a business's financial condition by reporting its assets, liabilities, and owners' equity. (Refer to Book III Chapters 1 and 2 for more about these reports.)

You can probably guess what the *cash flow statement* does by its name alone: This statement tells you where a business got its cash and what the business did with its cash during the period. We prefer the name given in the old days in the US to the predecessor of the cash flow statement, the *Where Got, Where Gone* statement. This nickname goes straight to the purpose of the cash flow statement: asking where the business got its money and what it did with the money.

The history of the cash flow statement

The cash flow statement was not required for external financial reporting until the late 1980s. Until then, the accounting profession had turned a deaf ear to calls from the investment community for cash flow statements in annual financial reports. (Accountants had presented a *funds flow statement* prior to then, but that report proved to be a disaster – the term *funds* included more assets than just cash and represented a net amount after deducting short-term liabilities from short-term, or current, assets.)

In our opinion, the reluctance to require cash flow statements came from fears that the *cash flow from profit* figure would usurp net income – people would lose confidence in the net income line.

Those fears have some justification – considering the attention given to cash flow from profit and what is called 'free cash flow' (discussed later in the chapter). Although the profit and loss account continues to get most of the fanfare (because it shows the magic bottom-line number of net income), cash flow gets a lot of emphasis these days.

To give you a rough idea of what a cash flow statement reports, we repeat some of the questions we asked at the start of the chapter: How much money did you earn last year? Did you get all your income in cash (did some of your wages go straight into a pension plan or did you collect a couple of IOUs)? Where did you get other money (did you take out a loan, win the lottery, or receive a gift from a rich uncle)? What did you do with your money (did you buy a house, support your out-of-control Internet addiction, or lose it playing bingo)?

Book III

Reporting Results

Getting a little too personal for you? That's exactly why the cash flow statement is so important: It bares a business's financial soul to its lenders and owners. Sometimes the cash flow statement reveals questionable judgment calls that the business's managers made. At the very least, the cash flow statement reveals how well a business handles the cash increase from its profit.

As explained at the start of the chapter, the cash flow statement is divided into three sections according to the three-fold classification of cash flows for a business:

- ✔ Cash flow from **operating activities** (which we also call *cash flow from profit* in the chapter): The activities by which a business makes profit and turns the profit into cash flow (includes depreciation and changes in operating assets and liabilities).

✔ Cash flow from **investing activities:** Investing in long-term assets needed for a business's operations; also includes money taken out of these assets from time to time (such as when a business disposes of some of its long-term assets).

✔ Cash flow from **financing activities:** Raising capital from debt and owners' equity, returning capital to these capital sources, and distributing profit to owners.

The cash flow statement reports a business's net cash increase or decrease based on these three groupings of the cash flow statement. Figure 3-2 shows what a cash flow statement typically looks like – in this example, for a *growing* business (which means that its assets, liabilities, and owners' equity increase during the period).

Cash Flow Statement for Year		
Cash Flows from Operating Activities		
Net Income		£160,000
Debtors	£(80,000)	
Stock Increase	£(97,500)	
Prepaid Expenses Increase	£(14,500)	
Depreciation Expense	£120,000	
Creditors Increase	£8,000	
Accrued Expense Increase	£12,000	
Income Tax Payable Increase	£2,000	£(50,000)
Cash Flow from Operating Activities		
Cash Flows from Investing Activities		
Purchases of Property, Plant & Equipment		£(127,500)
Cash Flows from Financing Activities		
Short-term Debt Borrowing Increase	£20,000	
Long-term Debt Borrowing Increase	£30,000	
Share Issue	£6,000	
Dividends Paid Stockholders	£(40,000)	£16,000
Increase (Decrease) In Cash During Year		£(1,500)
Beginning Cash Balance		£201,500
Ending Cash Balance		£200,000

Figure 3-2: Cash flow statement for the business in the example.

Where to put depreciation?

Where the depreciation line goes within the first section (operating activities) of the cash flow statement is a matter of personal preference – no standard location is required. Many businesses report it in the middle or toward the bottom of the changes in assets and liabilities – perhaps to avoid giving people the idea that cash flow from profit simply requires adding back depreciation to net income.

The trick to understanding cash flow from profit is to link the sales revenue and expenses of the business with the changes in the business's assets and liabilities that are directly connected with its profit-making activities. Using this approach earlier in the chapter, we determine that the cash flow from profit is £110,000 for the year for the sample business. This is the number you see in Figure 3-2 for cash flow from operating activities. In our experience, many business managers, lenders, and investors don't fully understand these links, but the savvy ones know to keep a close eye on the relevant balance sheet changes.

What do the figures in the first section of the cash flow statement (refer to Figure 3-2) reveal about this business over the past period? Recall that the business experienced rapid sales growth over the last period. However, the downside of sales growth is that operating assets and liabilities also grow – the business needs more stock at the higher sales level and also has higher debtors.

The business's prepaid expenses and liabilities also increased, although not nearly as much as debtors and stock. The rapid growth of the business yielded higher profit but also caused quite a surge in its operating assets and liabilities – the result being that cash flow from profit is only £110,000 compared with £160,000 in net income – a £50,000 shortfall. Still, the business had £110,000 at its disposal after allowing for the increases in assets and liabilities. What did the business do with this £110,000 of available cash? You have to look to the remainder of the cash flow statement to answer this key question.

A very quick read through the rest of the cash flow statement (refer to Figure 3-2) goes something like this: The company used £127,500 to buy new fixed assets, borrowed £50,000, and distributed £40,000 of the profit to its

Book III

Reporting Results

owners. The bottom line (should we use that term here?) is that cash decreased £1,500 during the year. Shouldn't the business have increased its cash balance, given its fairly rapid growth during the period? That's a good question! Higher levels of sales generally require higher levels of operating cash balances. However, you can see in its balance sheet at the end of the year that the company has £200,000 in cash, which, compared with its £2.5 million annual sales revenue, is probably enough.

A better alternative for reporting cash flow from profit?

We call your attention, again, to the first section of the cash flow statement in Figure 3-2. You start with net income for the period. Next, changes in assets and liabilities are deducted or added to net income to arrive at cash flow from operating activities (the cash flow from profit) for the year. This format is called the *indirect method.* The alternative format for this section of the cash flow statement is called the *direct method* and is presented like this (using the same business example):

Cash inflow from sales	£2.42 million
Less cash outflow for expenses	£2.3 million
Cash flow from operating activities	£110,000

You may remember from the earlier discussion that sales revenue for the year is £2.5 million, but that the company's debtors increased £80,000 during the year, so cash flow from sales is £2.42 million. Likewise, the expenses for the year can be put on a cash flow basis. But we 'cheated' here – we have already determined that cash flow from profit is £110,000 for the year, so we plugged the figure for cash outflow for expenses. We would take more time to explain the direct approach, except for one major reason.

Although the Accounting Standards Board (ASB) expresses a definite preference for the direct method, this august rule-making body does permit the indirect method to be used in external financial reports – and, in fact, the overwhelming majority of businesses use the indirect method. Unless you're an accountant, we don't think you need to know much more about the direct method.

Sailing through the Rest of the Cash Flow Statement

After you get past the first section, the rest of the cash flow statement is a breeze. The last two sections of the statement explain what the business did with its cash and where cash that didn't come from profit came from.

Investing activities

The second section of the cash flow statement reports the investment actions that a business's managers took during the year. Investments are like tea leaves, which serve as indicators regarding what the future may hold for the company. Major new investments are the sure signs of expanding or modernising the production and distribution facilities and capacity of the business. Major disposals of long-term assets and the shedding of a major part of the business could be good news or bad news for the business, depending on many factors. Different investors may interpret this information differently, but all would agree that the information in this section of the cash flow statement is very important.

Certain long-lived operating assets are required for doing business – for example, Federal Express wouldn't be terribly successful if it didn't have aeroplanes and vans for delivering packages and computers for tracking deliveries. When those assets wear out, the business needs to replace them. Also, to remain competitive, a business may need to upgrade its equipment to take advantage of the latest technology or provide for growth. These investments in long-lived, tangible, productive assets, which we call *fixed assets* in this book, are critical to the future of the business and are called *capital expenditures* to stress that capital is being invested for the long haul.

One of the first claims on cash flow from profit is capital expenditure. Notice in Figure 3-2 that the business spent £127,500 for new fixed assets, which are referred to as *property, plant, and equipment* in the cash flow statement (to keep the terminology consistent with account titles used in the balance sheet, because the term *fixed assets* is rather informal).

Cash flow statements generally don't go into much detail regarding exactly what specific types of fixed assets a business purchased – how many additional square feet of space the business acquired, how many new drill presses it bought, and so on. (Some businesses do leave a clearer trail of their investments, though. For example, airlines describe how many new aircraft of each kind were purchased to replace old equipment or expand their fleets.)

Note: Typically, every year a business disposes of some of its fixed assets that have reached the end of their useful lives and will no longer be used. These fixed assets are sent to the junkyard, traded in on new fixed assets, or sold for relatively small amounts of money. The value of a fixed asset at the end of its useful life is called its *salvage value*. The disposal proceeds from selling fixed assets are reported as a source of cash in the investments section of the cash flow statement. Usually, these amounts are fairly small. In contrast, a business may sell off fixed assets because it's downsizing or abandoning a major segment of its business. These cash proceeds can be fairly large.

Financing activities

Note that in the annual cash flow statement (refer to Figure 3-2) of the business example we've been using, the positive cash flow from profit is £110,000 and the negative cash flow from investing activities is £127,500. The result to this point, therefore, is a net cash outflow of £17,500 – which would have decreased the company's cash balance this much if the business did not go to outside sources of capital for additional money during the year. In fact, the business increased its short-term and long-term debt during the year, and its owners invested additional money in the business. The third section of the cash flow statement summarises these financing activities of the business over the period.

The term *financing* generally refers to a business raising capital from debt and equity sources – from borrowing money from banks and other sources willing to loan money to the business and from its owners putting additional money in the business. The term also includes the flip side; that is, making payments on debt and returning capital to owners. The term *financing* also includes cash distributions (if any) from profit by the business to its owners.

Most businesses borrow money for a short term (generally defined as less than one year), as well as for longer terms (generally defined as more than one year). In other words, a typical business has both short-term and long-term debt. (Book III Chapter 2 explains that short-term debt is presented in the current liabilities section of the balance sheet.) The business in our example has both short-term and long-term debt. Although not a hard-and-fast rule most cash flow statements report just the *net* increase or decrease in short-term debt, not the total amount borrowed and the total payments on short-term debt during the period. In contrast, both the total amount borrowed from and the total amount paid on long-term debt during the year are reported in the cash flow statement.

For the business we've been using as an example, no long-term debt was paid down during the year but short-term debt was paid off during the year and replaced with new short-term notes payable. However, only the net increase (£20,000) is reported in the cash flow statement. The business also increased its long-term debt by £30,000 (refer to Figure 3-2).

The financing section of the cash flow statement also reports on the flow of cash between the business and its owners (who are the stockholders of a corporation). Owners can be both a *source* of a business's cash (capital invested by owners) and a *use* of a business's cash (profit distributed to owners). This section of the cash flow statement reports capital raised from its owners, if any, as well as any capital returned to the owners. In the cash flow statement (Figure 3-2), note that the business did issue additional stock shares for £6,000 during the year, and it paid a total of £40,000 cash dividends (distributions) from profit to its owners.

Free Cash Flow: What Does That Mean?

A new term has emerged in the lexicon of accounting and finance – *free cash flow*. This piece of language is not – we repeat, *not* – an officially defined term by any authoritative accounting rule-making body. Furthermore, the term does *not* appear in the cash flow statements reported by businesses. Rather, free cash flow is street language, or slang, even though the term appears often in *The Financial Times* and *The Economist*. Securities brokers and investment analysts use the term freely (pun intended). Like most new words being tossed around for the first time, this one hasn't settled down into one universal meaning although the most common usage of the term pivots on cash flow from profit.

The term *free cash flow* is used to mean any of the following:

✔ Net income plus depreciation (plus any other expense recorded during the period that does not involve the outlay of cash but rather the allocation of the cost of a long-term asset other than property, plant, and equipment – such as the intangible assets of a business).

✔ Cash flow from operating activities (as reported in the cash flow statement).

✔ Cash flow from operating activities minus some or all of the capital expenditures made during the year (such as purchases or construction of new, long-lived operating assets such as property, plant, and equipment).

✔ Cash flow from operating activities plus interest, and depreciation, and income tax expenses, or, in other words, cash flow before these expenses are deducted.

In the strongest possible terms, we advise you to be very clear on which definition of *free cash flow* the speaker or writer is using. Unfortunately, you can't always determine what the term means in any given context. The reporter or investment professional should define the term.

One definition of free cash flow, in our view, is quite useful: cash flow from profit minus capital expenditures for the year. The idea is that a business needs to make capital expenditures in order to stay in business and thrive. And to make capital expenditures, the business needs cash. Only after paying for its capital expenditures does a business have 'free' cash flow that it can use as it likes. In our example, the free cash flow is, in fact, negative – £110,000 cash flow from profit minus £127,500 capital expenditures for new fixed assets equals a *negative* £17,500.

This is a key point. In many cases, cash flow from profit falls short of the money needed for capital expenditures. So the business has to borrow more money, persuade its owners to invest more money in the business, or dip into its cash reserve. Should a business in this situation distribute some of its profit to owners? After all, it has a cash *deficit* after paying for capital expenditures. But many companies like the business in our example do, in fact, make cash distributions from profit to their owners.

Scrutinising the Cash Flow Statement

Analysing a business's cash flow statement inevitably raises certain questions: What would I have done differently if I was running this business? Would I have borrowed more money? Would I have raised more money from the owners? Would I have distributed so much of the profit to the owners? Would I have let my cash balance drop by even such a small amount?

One purpose of the cash flow statement is to show readers what judgment calls and financial decisions the business's managers made during the period. Of course, management decisions are always subject to second-guessing and criticising, and passing judgment based on a financial statement isn't totally fair because it doesn't reveal the pressures the managers faced during the period. Maybe they made the best possible decisions given the circumstances. Maybe not.

The business in our example (refer to Figure 3-2) distributed £40,000 cash from profit to its owners – a 25% *pay-out ratio* (which is the £40,000 distribution divided by £160,000 net income). In analysing whether the pay-out ratio is too high, too low, or just about right, you need to look at the broader context of the business's sources of, and needs for, cash.

First look at cash flow from profit: £110,000, which is not enough to cover the business's £127,500 capital expenditures during the year. The business increased its total debt £50,000. Given these circumstances, maybe the business should have hoarded its cash and not paid so much in cash distributions to its owners.

So does this business have enough cash to operate with? You can't answer that question just by examining the cash flow statement – or any financial statement for that matter. Every business needs a buffer of cash to protect against unexpected developments and to take advantage of unexpected opportunities as we explain in Book IV Chapter 2 on forecasting and budgeting. This particular business has a £2 million cash balance compared with £25 million annual sales revenue for the period just ended which probably is enough. If you were the boss of this business how much working cash balance would you want? Not an easy question to answer! Don't forget that you need to look at all three primary financial statements – the profit and loss account and the balance sheet as well as the cash flow statement – to get the big picture of a business's financial health.

You probably didn't count the number of lines of information in Figure 3-2, the cash flow statement for the business example. Anyway, the financial statement has 17 lines of information. Would you like to hazard a guess regarding the average number of lines in cash flow statements of publicly-owned companies? Typically, their cash flow statements have 30 to 40 lines of information by our reckoning. So it takes quite a while to read the cash flow statement – more time than the average investor probably has to read this financial statement. (Professional stock analysts and investment managers are paid to take the time to read this financial statement meticulously.) Quite frankly, we find that many cash flow statements are not only rather long but also difficult to understand – even for an accountant. We won't get on a soapbox here but we definitely think businesses could do a better job of reporting their cash flow statements by reducing the number of lines in their financial statements and making each line clearer.

Book III

Reporting Results

Book IV
Managing the Finances

'It's nothing to do with the full moon — he always goes through a change when he tries to reorganise our finances.'

In this book . . .

*B*usiness managers and owners depend on financial statements as well as other internal accounting reports to know how much profit they're making, where that profit is at the end of the period, and whether the business is in good financial shape or needs improvement. They also use financial statements to keep a close watch on the lifeblood of the business: cash flows. Managers must know how to read their financial statements. Also, they should take advantage of proven accounting tools and techniques to assist them in making profit, controlling cash flow, and keeping the business in good financial condition.

Managers need a good accounting model for analysing profit; they can use budgeting to plan, make projections, and achieve the financial goals of the business, which is the essence of management control. Business managers and owners must decide which ownership structure to use, taking into account risk to personal wealth and the prospects for tax minimisation. Finally, managers should clearly understand how the costs of the business are determined, and they should get involved in choosing the basic accounting methods for measuring profit and for recording values of their assets and liabilities. This part of the book, in short, explains how accounting helps managers achieve the financial goals of the business.

Here are the contents of Book IV at a glance:

Chapter 1

Managing Profit Performance

*A*s a manager you get paid to make profit happen. That's what separates you from the non-manager employees at your business. Of course, you have to be a motivator, innovator, consensus builder, lobbyist, and maybe sometimes a babysitter too. But the real purpose of your job is to control and improve the profit of your business. No matter how much your staff love you (or do they love those doughnuts you bring in every Monday?), if you don't meet your profit goals, you're facing the unemployment line.

You have to be relentless in your search for better ways to do things. Competition in most industries is fierce, and you can never take profit performance for granted. Changes take place all the time – changes initiated by the business and changes pressured by outside forces. Maybe a new superstore down the street is causing your profit to fall off, and you realise that you'll have a huge sale to draw customers, complete with splashy ads on TV, into the shop.

Slow down, not so fast! First make sure that you can afford to cut prices and spend money on advertising and still turn a profit. Maybe price cuts and splashy ads will keep your cash register singing and the kiddies smiling, but you need to remember that making sales does not guarantee that you make a profit. As all you experienced business managers know, profit is a two-headed beast – profit comes from making sales *and* controlling expenses.

So how do you determine what effect price cuts and advertising costs may have on your bottom line? By turning to your beloved accounting staff, of course, and asking for some *what-if* reports (like 'What if we offer a 15% discount?').

This chapter shows you how to identify the key variables that determine what your profit would be if you changed certain factors (such as prices).

Redesigning the External Profit and Loss Account

To begin, Figure 1-1 presents the profit and loss account of a business. Figure 1-1 shows an *external profit and loss account* – the profit and loss account that's reported to the outside investors and creditors of the business. The expenses in Figure 1-1 are presented as they are usually disclosed in an external statement. (Book III Chapter 1 explains sales revenue, expenses, and the format of the external profit and loss account.)

External Profit and Loss Account For Year	
Sales Revenue	£520,000
Cost of Goods Sold Expense	£312,000
Gross Margin	£208,000
Sales, Administration, and General Expenses	£156,000
Depreciation Expense	£16,500
Earnings Before Interest and Tax	£35,500
Interest Expense	£7,500
Earnings Before Tax	£28,000
Tax Expense	£9,000
Net Income	£19,000

Figure 1-1: Example of a business's external profit and loss account.

The managers of the business should understand this profit and loss account, of course. But, the external profit and loss account is not entirely adequate for management decision-making; this profit report falls short of providing all the information about expenses needed by managers. But, before moving on to the additional information managers need, take a quick look at the external profit and loss account (Figure 1-1) before the train leaves the station.

For more information about the external profit and loss account and all its sundry parts, see Book III Chapter 1. Let us just point out the following here about this particular financial statement:

✔ The business represented by this profit and loss account sells products and therefore has a *cost of goods sold expense.* In contrast, companies that sell services (airlines, cinemas, law firms and so on) don't have a cost of goods sold expense, as all their sales revenue goes toward meeting operating expenses and then providing profit.

✔ The external profit and loss account shown in Figure 1-1 is prepared according to accounting methods and disclosure standards called *generally accepted accounting principles* (GAAP) but keep in mind that these financial reporting standards are designed for reporting information *outside* the business. Once a profit and loss account is released to people outside the business, a business has no control over the circulation of its statement. The accounting profession, in deciding on the information for disclosure in external profit and loss accounts, has attempted to strike a balance. On the one side are the needs of those who have invested capital in the business and have loaned money to the business; clearly they have the right to receive enough information to evaluate their investments in the business and their loans to the business. On the other side is the need of the business to keep certain information confidential and out of the hands of its competitors. What it comes down to is that certain information that outside investors and creditors might find interesting and helpful does not, in fact, have to be disclosed according to GAAP.

✔ The profit and loss account does not report the *financial effects* of the company's profit-making activities – that is, the increases and decreases in its assets and liabilities caused by revenue and expenses. Managers need to control these financial effects, for which purpose they need the complete financial picture provided by the two other primary financial statements (the balance sheet and the cash flow statement) in addition to the profit and loss account. See Book III Chapters 2 and 3 for more about these two other primary financial statements.

Basic Model for Management Profit and Loss Account

Figure 1-2 presents a model for a *management* profit and loss account using the same business as the example whose external profit and loss account is shown in Figure 1-1. Many lines of information are exactly the same – sales revenue and cost of goods sold expense for instance – and thus gross margins are the same. The last five lines in the two statements are the same, starting with operating profit (earnings before interest and corporation tax) down to the bottom line. In other respects, however, there are critical differences between the two profit reports.

Book IV

Managing the Finances

Management Profit and Loss Account For Year

	Totals for Period	Per Unit
Unit Sales Volume =	£5,200	
Sales Revenue	£520,000	£100
Cost of Goods Sold Expense	£312,000	£60
Gross Margin	£208,000	£40
Revenue-driven Operating Expenses	£41,600	£8
Contribution Margin	£166,400	£32
Fixed Operating Expenses	£130,900	
Operating Profit, or Earnings Before Interest and Tax Expenses (EBIT)	£35,500	
Interest Expense	£7,500	
Earnings Before Tax	£28,000	
Tax Expense	£9,000	
Net Income	£19,000	

Figure 1-2: Management profit and loss account model.

First, note that total *unit sales volume* and *per unit amounts* are included in the management profit and loss account (Figure 1-2). The business appears to sell only one product; the 5,200 units total sales volume is from sales of this product. In fact, most businesses sell a mix of many different products. The company's various managers need detailed sales revenue and cost information for each product, or product line, or segment of the business they are responsible for. To keep the illustration easy to follow we have collapsed the business's entire sales into one 'average' product. Instead of grappling with 100 or 1,000 different products we condensed them all into one proxy product. The main purpose of Figure 1-2 is to show a basic template, or model, that can be used for more detailed reports.

Variable versus fixed operating expenses

Another fundamental difference between the external profit report (Figure 1-1) and the internal profit report (Figure 1-2) is that the company's *operating expenses* (sales, administration, and general expenses plus depreciation expense) are separated into two different categories in the management report:

✔ **Variable expenses:** The *revenue-driven expenses* that depend directly on the total sales revenue amount for the period. These expenses move in step with changes in total sales revenue. Commissions paid to salespersons based on a percentage of the amount of sales are a common example of variable operating expenses.

✔ **Fixed expenses:** The operating expenses that are relatively fixed in amount for the period, regardless of whether the company's total unit sales (sales volume) had been substantially more, or substantially less, than the 5,200 units that it actually sold during the year. An example of a fixed operating expense is the annual business rates on the company's property. Also, depreciation is a fixed expense; a certain amount of depreciation expense is recorded to the year regardless of actual sales volume.

The management profit and loss account does not, we repeat *not*, present different profit numbers for the year compared with the profit numbers reported in the company's external profit and loss account. Note that operating profit for the year (or, earnings before interest and tax expenses) is the same as reported outside the business – in Figures 1-1 and 1-2 this number is the same. And in reading down the rest of the two profit and loss accounts note that earnings before tax and bottom-line net income are the same in both the external and internal reports. The external profit and loss account of the business reports a broad, all-inclusive group of 'sales, administration, and general expenses' and a separate expense for depreciation. In contrast, the management profit and loss account reveals information about *how the operating expenses behave relative to the sales of the business*. The actual reporting of expenses in external profit and loss accounts varies from business to business – but you never see profit and loss accounts in which operating expenses are sorted between variable and fixed.

Virtually every business has *variable operating expenses*, which move up and down in tight proportion to changes in unit sales volume or sales revenue. Here are some examples of common variable operating expenses:

✔ Cost of goods sold expense – the cost of the products sold to customers.

✔ Commissions paid to salespeople based on their sales.

✔ Transportation costs of delivering products to customers.

✔ Fees that a business pays to a bank when a customer uses a credit card such as Visa, MasterCard, or American Express. (When a business deposits its copy of the credit card slip, the local bank deducts a certain percentage of the amount deposited as the bank's fee for handling the transaction, and a part of the fee is shared with the credit card issuer.)

Book IV

Managing the Finances

The management profit and loss account (Figure 1-2) can be referred to as the *internal profit report*, since it is for management eyes only and does not circulate outside the business – although it may be the target of industrial intelligence gathering and perhaps even industrial espionage by competitors. Remember that in the external profit and loss account only one lump sum for the category of sales, administrative, and general (SA&G) expenses is reported – a category for which some of the expenses are fixed but some are variable. What you need to do is have your accountant carefully examine these expenses to determine which are fixed and which are variable. (Some expenses may have both fixed and variable components, but we don't go into these technical details.)

Further complicating the matter somewhat is the fact that the accountant needs to divide variable expenses between those that vary with sales *volume* (total number of units sold) and those that vary with sales *revenue* (total pounds of sales revenue). This is an important distinction.

✔ An example of an expense driven by sales volume is the cost of shipping and packaging. This cost depends strictly on the *number* of units sold and generally is the same regardless of how much the item inside the box costs.

✔ An example of an expense driven by sales revenue are sales commissions paid to salespersons, which directly depend on the amounts of sales made to customers. Other examples are franchise fees based on total sales revenue of retailers, business premises rental contracts that include a clause that bases monthly rent on sales revenue, and royalties that are paid for the right to use a well-known name or a trademarked logo in selling the company's products and which are based on total sales revenue.

The business represented in Figure 1-2 has just one variable operating expense – an 8% sales commission, resulting in an expense total of £41,600 (£520,000 sales revenue × 8%). Of course, a real business probably would have many different variable operating expenses, some driven by unit sales volume and some driven by total sales revenue pounds. But the basic idea is the same for all of them and one variable operating expense serves the purpose here. Also, cost of goods sold expense is itself a sales volume driven expense (see Book IV Chapter 5 regarding different accounting methods for measuring this expense). The example shown in Figure 1-2 is a bit oversimplified – the business sells only one product and has only one variable operating expense – but, the main purpose is to present a general template that can be tailored to fit the particular circumstances of a business.

Fixed operating expenses are the many different costs that a business is obliged to pay and cannot decrease over the short run without major surgery on the human resources and physical facilities of the business. You must distinguish fixed expenses from your variable operating expenses.

As an example of fixed expenses, consider a typical self-service car wash business – you know, the kind where you drive in, put some coins in a box, and use the water spray to clean your car. Almost all the operating costs of this business are fixed: Rent on the land, depreciation of the structure and the equipment, and the annual insurance premium cost don't depend on the number of cars passing through the car wash. The only variable expenses are probably the water and the soap.

If you want to decrease fixed expenses significantly, you need to downsize the business (lay off workers, sell off property and so on). When looking at the various ways you have for improving your profit, significantly cutting down on fixed expenses is generally the last-resort option. Refer to 'Improving profit' later in this chapter for the better options.

Better than anyone else, managers know that sales for the year could have been lower or higher. A natural question is, 'What difference in the profit would there have been at the lower or higher level of sales?' If you'd sold 10% fewer total units during the year, what would your net income (bottom-line profit) have been? You might guess that profit would have slipped 10% but that would *not* have been the case. In fact, profit would have slipped by much more than 10%. Are you surprised? Read on for the reasons.

Why wouldn't profit fall the same percentage as sales? The answer is because of the nature of fixed expenses – just because your sales are lower doesn't mean that your expenses are lower. *Fixed expenses* are the costs of doing business that, for all practical purposes, are stuck at a certain amount over the short term. Fixed expenses do not react to changes in the sales level. Here are some examples of fixed expenses:

- Interest on money that the business has borrowed
- Employees' salaries and benefits
- Business rates
- Fire insurance

A business can downsize its assets and therefore reduce its fixed expenses to fit a lower sales level, but that can be a drastic reaction to what may be a temporary downturn. After deducting cost of goods sold, variable operating expenses, and fixed operating expenses, the next line in the management profit and loss account is operating profit, which is also called *earnings before interest and tax* (or *EBIT*). This profit line in the report is a critical juncture that managers need to fully appreciate.

Book IV

Managing the Finances

From operating profit (EBIT) to the bottom line

After deducting all operating expenses from sales revenue, you get to earnings before interest and tax (EBIT), which is £35,500 in the example. *Operating* is an umbrella term that includes cost of goods sold expense and all other expenses of making sales and operating your business – but not interest and tax. Sometimes EBIT is called *operating profit*, or *operating earnings*, to emphasise that profit comes from making sales and controlling operating expenses. This business earned £35,500 operating profit from its £520,000 sales revenue – which seems satisfactory. But is its £35,500 EBIT really good enough? What's the reference for answering this question?

How much net income is needed to make owners happy?

People who invest in a business usually aren't philanthropists who don't want to make any money on the deal. No, these investors want a business to protect their capital investment, earn a good bottom-line profit for them, and enhance the value of their investment over time. They understand that a business may not earn a profit but suffer a loss – that's the risk they take as owners.

As described in Book IV Chapter 3, how much of a business's net income (bottom-line profit) is distributed to the owners depends on the business and the arrangement that it made with the owners. But regardless of how much money the owners actually receive, they still have certain expectations of how well the business will do – that is, what the business's earnings before interest and tax will be. After all, they've staked their money on the business's success.

One test of whether the owners will be satisfied with the net income (after interest and tax) is to compute the *return on equity* (ROE), which is the ratio of net income to total owners' equity (net income ÷ owners' equity). In this chapter's business example, the bottom-line profit is £19,000. Suppose that the total owners' equity in the business is £159,000. Thus, the ROE is 12% (£19,000 ÷ £159,000). Is 12% a good ROE? Well, that depends on how much the owners could earn from an alternative investment. We'd say that a 12% ROE isn't bad. By the way, ROE is also know as ROSI: *return on shareholders' investment.*

Note: ROE does not imply that all the net income was distributed in cash to the owners. Usually, a business needs to retain a good part of its bottom-line net income to provide capital for growing the business. Suppose, in this example, that none of the net income is distributed in cash to its owners. The ROE is still 12%; ROE does not depend on how much, if any, of the net income is distributed to the owners. (Of course, the owners may prefer that a good part of the net income be distributed to them.)

The main benchmark for judging EBIT is whether this amount of profit is adequate to cover the *cost of capital* of the business. A business must secure money to invest in its various assets – and this capital has a cost. A business has to pay interest on its debt capital, and it should earn enough after-tax net income (bottom-line profit) to satisfy its owners who have put their capital in the business. See the sidebar 'How much net income is needed to make owners happy?' in this chapter.

Nobody – not even the most die-hard humanitarian – is in business to make a zero EBIT. You simply can't do this, because profit is an absolutely necessary part of doing business – and recouping the cost of capital is why profit is needed.

Don't treat the word *profit* as something that's whispered in the hallways. Profit builds owners' value and provides the basic stability for a business. Earning a satisfactory EBIT is the cornerstone of business. Without earning an adequate operating profit, a business could not attract capital, and you can't have a business without capital.

Travelling Two Trails to Profit

How is the additional information in the management profit and loss account useful? Well, with this information you can figure out how the business earned its profit for the year. We're not referring to how the company decided which products to sell, and the best ways to market and advertise its products, and how to set sales prices, and how to design an efficient and smooth running organisation, and how to motivate its employees, and all the other things every business has to do to achieve its financial goals. We're talking about an *accounting explanation of profit* that focuses on methods for calculating profit – going from the basic input factors of sales price, sales volume, and costs to arrive at the amount of profit that results from the interaction of the factors. Business managers should be familiar with these accounting calculations. They are responsible for each factor and for profit, of course. With this in mind, therefore: How did the business earn its profit for the year?

First path to profit

We can't read your mind. But, if we had to hazard a guess regarding how you would go about answering the profit question, we'd bet that, after you had the chance to study Figure 1-2, you would do something like the following, which is correct as a matter of fact:

Computing profit before tax

Contribution margin per unit	£32
× Unit sales volume	5,200
Equals: Total contribution margin	£166,400
Less: Total fixed operating expenses	£130,900
Equals: Operating profit (EBIT)	£35,500
Less: Interest Expense	£7500
Equals: Earnings before tax	£28,000

Note that we stop at the earnings before tax line in this calculation. You're aware, of course, that business profit is subject to tax. Book VI Chapter 3 provides a general overview of the taxation of business profit. This chapter focuses on profit above the taxation expense line. Nevertheless, please keep in mind as a broad rule of thumb that taxable income of a regular business corporation is subject to around 30% tax in addition to value added – except small businesses whose taxable income is taxed at a lower rate.

Contribution margin is what's left over after you subtract cost of goods sold expense and other variable expenses from sales revenue. On a *per unit* basis the business sells its product for £100, its variable product cost (cost of goods sold) is £60, and its variable operating cost per unit is £8 – which yields £32 contribution margin per unit. *Total* contribution margin for a period equals contribution margin per unit times the units sold during the period – in the business example, £32 × 5,200 units, which is £166,400 total contribution margin. Total contribution margin is a measure of profit *before fixed expenses are deducted*. To pay for its fixed operating expenses and its interest expense a business needs to earn a sufficient amount of total contribution margin. In the example, the business earned more total contribution margin than its fixed expenses, so it earned a profit for the year.

Here are some other concepts associated with the term *margin*, which you're likely to encounter:

- **Gross margin, also called gross profit:** Gross margin = sales revenue – cost of goods sold expense. Gross margin is profit from sales revenue *before* deducting the other variable expenses of making the sales. So gross margin is one step short of the final contribution margin earned on making sales. Businesses that sell products must report gross margin on their *external* profit and loss accounts. However, GAAP standards do *not* require that you report other variable expenses of making sales on external profit and loss accounts. In their external financial reports, very few businesses divulge other variable expenses of making sales. In other words, managers do not want the outside world and competitors to know their contribution margins. Most businesses carefully guard information about contribution margins because the information is very sensitive.

How variable expenses mow down your sales price

Consider a retail hardware store that sells, say, a Flymo lawnmower to a customer. The purchase cost per unit that the retailer paid to Flymo, the manufacturer, when the retailer bought its shipment of these lawnmowers is the *product cost* in the contribution margin equation. The retailer also provides one free servicing of the lawnmower after the customer has used it a few months (cleaning it and sharpening the blade) and also pays its salesperson a commission on the sale. These two additional expenses, for the service and the commission, are examples of variable expenses in the margin equation.

- **Gross margin ratio:** Gross margin ratio = gross margin ÷ sales revenue. In the business we use as an example in this chapter, the gross margin on sales is 40%. Gross margins of companies vary from industry to industry, from over 50% to under 25% – but very few businesses can make a bottom-line profit with less than a 20% gross margin.

- **Markup:** Generally refers to the amount added to the product cost to determine the sales price. For example, suppose a product that cost £60 is marked up (based on cost) by 66⅔% to determine its sales price of £100 – for a gross margin of £40 on the product. *Note:* The markup based on *cost* is 66⅔% (£40 markup ÷ £60 product cost). But the gross margin ratio is only 40%, which is based on *sales price* (£40 ÷ £100).

Second path to profit

The second method of computing a company's profit starts with a particular sales volume as the point of reference. So, the first step is to compute this specific sales volume of the business (which is not its actual sales volume for the year) by dividing its total annual fixed expenses by its contribution margin per unit. Interest expense is treated as a fixed expense (because for all practical purposes it is more or less fixed in amount over the short-run). For the business in the example the interest expense is £7,500 (see Figure 1-2), which, added to the £130,900 fixed operating expenses, gives total fixed expenses of £138,400. The company's *break-even point*, also called its *break-even sales volume*, is computed as follows:

£138,400 total annual fixed expenses for year ÷ £32 contribution margin per unit = 4,325 units break-even point (or, break-even sales volume) for the year

Book IV

Managing the Finances

In other words, if you multiply £32 contribution margin per unit times 432,500 units you get a total contribution margin of £138,400, which exactly equals the company's total fixed expenses for the year. The business actually sold more than this number of units during the year but, if it had sold only 4,325 units, the company's profit would have been exactly zero. Below this sales level the business suffers a loss, and above this sales level the business makes profit. The break-even sales volume is the crossover point from the loss column to the profit column. Of course, a business's goal is to do better than just reaching its break-even sales volume.

Calculating its break-even point calls attention to the amount of fixed expenses hanging over a business. As explained earlier, a business is committed to its fixed expenses over the short-run and cannot do much to avoid these costs – short of breaking some of its contracts and taking actions to downsize the business that could have disastrous long-run effects. Sometimes the total fixed expenses for the year are referred to as the 'nut' of the business – which may be a hard nut to crack (by exceeding its break-even sales volume).

In the example (see Figure 1-2) the business actually sold 5,200 units during the year, which is 875 units more than its break-even sales volume (5,200 units sold minus its 4,325 break-even sales volume). Therefore, you can determine the company's earnings before tax as follows:

Second Way of Computing Profit	
Contribution margin per unit	£32
× Units sold in excess of breakeven point	875
Equals: Earnings before tax	£28,000

This second way of analysing profit calls attention to the need of the business to achieve and exceed its break-even point to make profit. The business makes no profit until it clears its break-even hurdle, but once over this level of sales it makes profit hand-over-fist because the units sold from here on are not burdened with any fixed costs which have been covered by the first 4,325 of units sold during the year. Be careful in thinking that only the last 875 units sold during the year generate all the profit for the year. The first 4,325 units sold are necessary to get the business into position in order for the next 875 units to make profit.

The key point is that once the business has reached its break-even sales volume (thereby covering its annual fixed expenses) each additional unit sold brings in pre-tax profit equal to the contribution margin per unit. Each additional unit sold brings in 'pure profit' of £32 per unit, which is the company's contribution margin per unit. A business has to get into this upper region of sales volume to make a profit for the year.

Calculating the margin of safety

The *margin of safety* is the excess of its actual sales volume over a company's break-even sales volume. This business sold 5,200 units, which is 875 units above its break-even sales volume – a rather large cushion against any down-turn in sales. Only a major sales collapse would cause the business to fall all the way down to its break-even point, assuming that it can maintain its £32 contribution margin per unit and that its fixed costs don't change. You may wonder what a 'normal' margin of safety is for most businesses. Sorry, we can't give you a definitive answer on this. Due to the nature of the business or industry-wide problems, or due to conditions beyond its control, a business may have to operate with a smaller margin of safety than it would prefer.

Doing What-If Analysis

Managing profit is like driving a car – you need to be glancing in the rear-view mirror constantly as well as looking ahead through the windscreen. You have to know your profit history to see your profit future. Understanding the past is the best preparation for the future.

The model of a *management profit and loss account* shown in Figure 1-2 allows you to compare your actual profit with what it would've looked like if you'd done something differently – for example, raised prices and sold less units. With the profit model, you can test-drive adjustments before putting them into effect. It lets you plan and map out your profit strategy for the *coming* period. Also, you can analyse why profit went up or down from the *last* period, using the model to do hindsight analysis.

The management profit and loss account profit model focuses on the key factors and variables that drive profit. Here's what you should know about these factors:

- ✔ Even a small decrease in the contribution margin per unit can have a drastic impact on profit because fixed expenses don't go down over the short run (and may be hard to reduce even over the long run).

- ✔ Even a small increase in the contribution margin per unit can have a dramatic impact on profit because fixed expenses won't go up over the short run – although they may have to be increased in the long run.

- ✔ Compared with changes in contribution margin per unit, sales volume changes have secondary profit impact; sales volume changes are not trivial, but even relatively small margin changes can have a bigger effect on profit.

Book IV

Managing the Finances

✔ You can, perhaps, reduce fixed expenses to improve profit, but you have to be very careful to cut fat and not muscle; reducing fixed expenses may very well diminish the capacity of your business to make sales and deliver high-quality service to customers.

The following sections expand on these key points.

Lower profit from lower sales

The management profit and loss account shown in Figure 1-2 is designed for managers to use in profit analysis – to expose the critical factors that drive profit. Remember what information has been added that isn't included in the external profit and loss account:

✔ **Unit sales volume** for the year

✔ **Per-unit values**

✔ **Fixed versus variable** operating expenses

✔ **Contribution margin** – total and per unit

Handle this information with care. The contribution margin per unit is confidential, for your eyes only. This information is limited to you and other managers in the business. Clearly, you don't want your competitors to find out your margins. Even within a business, the information may not circulate to all managers – just those who need to know.

The contribution margin per unit is one of the three most important determinants of profit performance, along with sales volume and fixed expenses – as shown in the upcoming sections.

With the information provided in the management profit and loss account you're ready to paint a what-if scenario. We're making you the chief executive officer of the business in this example. What if you had sold 5% fewer units during this period? In this example, that would mean you had sold only 4,940 units rather than 5,200 units, or 260 units less. The following computation shows you how much profit damage this seemingly modest drop in sales volume would've caused.

Impact of 5% Lower Sales Volume on Profit

Contribution margin per unit	£32
× 260 fewer units sold	260
Equals: Decrease in earnings before tax	£8,320

By selling 260 fewer units you missed out on the £8,320 profit that these units would have produced – this is fairly straightforward. What is not so obvious, however, is that this £8,320 decrease in profit would have been a 30% drop in profit: (£8,320 decrease ÷ £28,000 profit = 30% decrease). Lose just 5% of your sales and lose 30% of your profit? How can such a thing happen? The next section expands on how a seemingly small decrease in sales volume can cause a stunning decrease in profit. Read on.

Violent profit swings

First, the bare facts for the business in the example: the company's contribution margin per unit is £32 and, before making any changes, the company sold 5,200 units during the year, which is 875 units in excess of its break-even sales volume. The company earned a total contribution margin of £166,400 (see Figure 1-2), which is its contribution per unit times its total units sold during the year. If the company had sold 5% less during the year (260 fewer units), you'd expect its total contribution margin to decrease 5%, and you'd be absolutely correct – £8,320 decrease ÷ £166,400 = 5% decrease. Compared with its £28,000 profit before tax, however, the £8,320 drop in total contribution margin equals a *30%* fall-off in profit.

The main focus of business managers and investors is on profit, which in this example is profit before tax. Therefore, the 30% drop in profit would get more attention than the 5% drop in total contribution margin. The much larger percentage change in profit caused by a relatively small change in sales volume is the effect of *operating leverage*. Leverage means that there is a multiplier effect – that a relatively small percentage change in one factor can cause a much larger change in another factor. A small push can cause a large movement – this is the idea of leverage.

In the above scenario for the 5%, 260 units decrease in sales volume, note that the 5% is based on the total 5,200 units sales volume of the business. But, if the 260 units decrease in sales volume is divided by the 875 units in excess of the company's break-even point – which are the units that generate profit for the business – the sales volume decrease equals 30%. In other words, the business lost 30% of its profit layer of sales volume and, thus, the company's profit would have dropped 30%. This dramatic drop is caused by the operating leverage effect.

Note: If the company had sold 5% *more* units, with no increase in its fixed expenses, its pre-tax profit would have *increased* by 30%, reflecting the operating leverage effect. The 260 additional units sold at a £32 contribution margin per unit would increase its total contribution margin by £8,320 and this increase would increase profit by 30%. You can see why businesses are always trying to increase sales volume.

Cutting sales price can gut profit

So, what effect would a 5% decrease in the sales price have caused? Around a 30% drop similar to the effect of a 5% decrease in sales volume? Not quite. Check out the following computation for this 5% sales price decrease scenario:

Impact of 5% Lower Sales Price on Profit

Contribution margin per unit decrease	£4.60
× Units sold during year	5200
Equals: Decrease in earnings before tax	£23,920

Hold on! Earnings before tax would drop from £280,000 at the £100 sales price (refer to Figure 1-2) to only £4,080 at the £95 sales price – a plunge of 85%. What could cause such a drastic dive in profit?

The sales price drops £5 per unit – a 5% decrease of the £100 sales price. But, contribution margin per unit does not drop by the entire £5 because the variable operating expense per unit (sales commissions in this example) would also drop 5%, or £0.40 per unit – for a net decrease of £4.60 per unit in the contribution margin per unit. (This is one reason for identifying the expenses that depend on sales revenue – as shown in the management profit and loss account in Figure 1-2.) For this what-if scenario that examines the case of the company selling all units at a 5% lower sales price than it did, the company's contribution margin would have been only £27.40 per unit. Such a serious reduction in its contribution margin per unit would have been intolerable.

At the lower sales price, the company's contribution margin would be £27.40 per unit (£32.00 in the original example minus the £4.60 decrease = £27.40). As a result, the break-even sales volume would be much higher, and the company's 5,200 sales volume for the year would have been only 149 units over its break-even point. So, the lower £27.40 contribution margin per unit would yield only £4,080 profit before tax.

The moral of the story is to protect contribution margin per unit above all else. Every pound of contribution margin per unit that's lost – due to decreased sales prices, increased product cost, or increases in other variable costs – has a tremendously negative impact on profit. Conversely, if you can increase the contribution margin per unit without hurting sales volume, you reap very large profit benefits, as described next.

Improving profit

The preceding sections explore the downside of things – that is, what would've happened to profit if sales volume or sales prices had been lower. The upside – higher profit – is so much more pleasant to discuss and analyse, don't you think?

Profit improvement boils down to the three critical profit-making factors, listed in order from the most effective to the least effective:

- ✔ Increasing the contribution margin per unit

- ✔ Increasing sales volume

- ✔ Reducing fixed expenses

Say you want to improve your bottom-line profit from the £19,000 net income you earned the year just ended to £21,100 next year. How can you pump up your net income by £2,100? (By the way, this is the only place in the chapter we bring the tax factor into the analysis.)

First of all, realise that to increase your net income *after taxes* by £2,100, you need to increase your before-tax profit by much more – to provide for the amount that goes to tax. Your accountant calculates that you would need a £3,120 increase in earnings before tax next year because your tax increase would be about £1,020 on the £3,120 increase in pre-tax earnings. So, you have to find a way to increase earnings, before tax, by £3,120.

You should also take into account the possibility that fixed costs and interest expense may rise next year, but for this example we're assuming that they won't. We're also assuming that the business can't cut any of its fixed operating expenses without hurting its ability to maintain and support its present sales level (and a modest increase in the sales level). Of course, in real life, every business should carefully scrutinise its fixed expenses to see if some of them can be cut.

Okay, so how can you increase your business's before-tax profit by £3,120? You have two choices (well, actually three choices). Take another look at Figure 1-2 and study these options:

- ✔ Increase your contribution margin per unit by £0.60, which would raise the total contribution margin by £3,120, based on a 5,200 units sales volume (£0.60 × 5,200 = £3,120).

Book IV

Managing the Finances

✔ Sell 997.5 additional units at the current contribution margin per unit of £32, which would raise the total contribution margin by £3,120 (97.5 × £32 = £3,120).

✔ Use a combination of these two approaches: Increase both the margin per unit and the sales volume.

The second approach is obvious – you just need to set a sales goal of increasing the number of products sold by 97.5 units. (How you motivate your already overworked sales staff to accomplish that sales volume goal is up to you.) But how do you go about the first approach, increasing the contribution margin per unit by £0.60?

The simplest way to increase contribution margin per unit by £0.60 would be to decrease your product cost per unit by £0.60. Or you could attempt to reduce sales commissions from £8 per £100 of sales to £7.40 per £100 – which may adversely affect the motivation of your sales force, of course. Or you could raise the sales price about £0.65 (remember that 8% comes off the top for the sales commission, so only £0.60 would remain from that £0.65 to improve the unit contribution margin). Or you could combine two or more such changes so that your unit contribution next year would increase £0.60. However you do it, the improvement would increase your earnings before tax the desired amount:

Impact of £0.60 Higher Unit Contribution Margin on Profit	
Contribution margin per unit increase	£0.60
× Units sold during year	5200
Equals: Increase in earnings before tax	£3,120

Cutting prices to increase sales volume

A word of warning: Be sure to *run the numbers* (accountant speak for using a profit model) before deciding to drop sales prices in an effort to gain more sales volume. Suppose, for example, you're convinced that if you decrease sales prices by 5% your sales volume will increase by 10%. Seems like an attractive trade-off, one that would increase both profit performance and market share. But are you sure that those positive changes are the results you'll get?

The impact on profit may surprise you. Get a piece of notepaper and do the computation for this lower sales price and higher sales volume scenario:

Lower Sales Price and Higher Sales Volume Impact on Profit	
New sales price (lower)	£95.00
Less: Product cost per unit (same)	£60.00
Less: Variable operating expenses (lower)	£7.60
Equals: New unit contribution margin (lower)	£27.40
× Sales volume (higher)	5,720
Equals: Total contribution margin	£156,728
Less: Previous total contribution margin	£166,400
Equals: Decrease in total contribution margin	£9,672

Your total contribution margin would not go up; instead, it would go down £9,672! In dropping the sales price by £5, you would give up too much of your contribution margin per unit. The increase in sales volume would not make up for the big dent in unit contribution margin. You may gain more market share but would pay for it with a £9,672 drop in earnings before tax.

To keep profit the same, you would have to increase sales volume more than 10%. By how much? Divide the total contribution margin for the 5,200 units situation by the contribution margin per unit for the new scenario:

£166,400 ÷ £27.40 = 6,073 units

In other words, just to keep your total contribution margin the same at the lower sales price, you would have to increase sales volume to 6,703 units – an increase of 873 units, or a whopping 17%. That would be quite a challenge, to say the least.

Cash flow from improving profit margin vs. improving sales volume

Book VI Chapter 1 discusses increasing profit margin versus increasing sales volume to improve bottom-line profit. Improving your profit margin is the better way to go, compared with increasing sales volume. Both actions increase profit, but the profit margin tactic is much better in terms of cash flow. When sales volume increases, so does stock. On the other hand, when you improve profit margin (by raising the sales price or by lowering product cost), you don't have to increase stock – in fact, reducing product cost may actually cause stock to decrease a little. In short, increasing your profit margin yields a higher cash flow from profit than does increasing your sales volume.

A Final Word or Two

Recently, some friends pooled their capital and opened an up-market off-licence in a rapidly growing area. The business has a lot of promise. We can tell you one thing they should have done before going ahead with this new venture – in addition to location analysis and competition analysis, of course. They should have used the basic profit model (in other words, the management profit and loss account) discussed in this chapter to figure out their break-even sales volume – because we're sure they have rather large fixed expenses. And they should have determined how much more sales revenue over their break-even point that they will need to earn a satisfactory return on their investment in the business.

During their open house for the new shop we noticed the very large number of different beers, wines, and spirits available for sale – to say nothing of the different sizes and types of containers many products come in. Quite literally, the business sells thousands of distinct products. The shop also sells many products like soft drinks, ice, corkscrews, and so on. Therefore, the company does not have a single sales volume factor (meaning the number of units sold) to work with in the basic profit model. So, you have to adapt the profit model to get along without the sales volume factor.

The trick is to determine your *average contribution margin as a percent of sales revenue*. We'd estimate that an off-licence's average gross margin (sales revenue less cost of goods sold) is about 25%. The other variable operating expenses of the shop probably run about 5% of sales. So, the average contribution margin would be 20% of sales (25% gross margin less 5% variable operating expenses). Suppose the total fixed operating expenses of the shop are about £100,000 per month (for rent, salaries, electricity, and so on), which is £1.2 million per year. So, the shop needs £6 million in sales per year just to break even:

> £1.2 million fixed expenses ÷ 20% average contribution margin =
> £6 million annual sales to break even

Selling £6 million of product a year means moving a lot of booze. The business needs to sell another £1 million to provide £200,000 of operating earnings (at the 20% average contribution margin) – to pay interest expense, tax, and leave enough net income for the owners who invested capital in the business and who expect a good return on their investment.

By the way, some disreputable off-licence owners are known (especially to HM Revenue and Customs) to engage in *sales skimming*. This term refers to not recording all sales revenue; instead, some cash collected from customers is put in the pockets of the owners. They don't report the profit in their tax returns or in the profit and loss accounts of the business. Our friends who started the off-licence are honest businessmen, and we're sure they won't engage in sales skimming – but they do have to make sure that none of their store's employees skim off some sales revenue.

When sales skimming is being committed, not all of the actual sales revenue for the year is recorded even though the total cost of all products sold during the year is recorded. Obviously, this distorts the profit and loss account and throws off normal ratios of gross profit and operating profit to sales revenue. If you have the opportunity to buy a business, please be alert to the possibility that some sales skimming may have been done by the present owner. Indeed, we've been involved in situations in which the person selling the business bragged about how much she was skimming off the top.

Chapter 2

Forecasting and Budgeting

· ·

In This Chapter

▶ Constructing your financial forecast

▶ Putting together a pro-forma profit and loss account

▶ Estimating a balance sheet

▶ Projecting your cash flow

▶ Preparing your company's budget

· ·

*H*ow many times have you sat around the table with your family (or maybe just your dog) and talked about the importance of putting the household on a budget? Everybody knows what a budget is, of course: It's a way of figuring out how much you're going to spend on essentials (the things that you need) and incidentals (all the frills). By its very nature, a budget is something that looks ahead, combining a forecast and a set of guidelines for spending money.

As you probably know from experience, it's a lot easier to put together a budget if you have some basic financial information to work with. It's nice to know how much money's going to come in, for example, and when you expect it to arrive. It's also important to keep track of the expenses that absolutely have to be taken care of, such as the mortgage and the car payment. Only then can you begin to get a handle on what you have left over, which is called your *working capital*.

For your company, this kind of basic financial information resides in its financial statements. (For more information on financial statements, refer to Book III.) These financial statements – profit and loss accounts, balance sheets, cash flow – are fairly straightforward, because they're based on how your company performed last year or the year before. Unfortunately, financial information is not quite as easy to put together and use when you have to plan for next year, three years from now, or even five years from now.

Why go to all the trouble of putting financial information together in the first place? The answer is simple: Although the numbers and financials aren't your business plan by themselves, they help you to fulfil your business plan. Without them, you're in real danger of allowing your financial condition – money (or the lack of it) – to take control of, or even replace, your business plan.

In this chapter, we help you construct a financial forecast for your company, including a pro-forma profit and loss account, an estimated balance sheet, and a projected cash-flow statement. Because nothing in the future is certain, we also introduce scenario planning and what-if analysis as ways to consider several financial alternatives. Finally, we talk about how you can use the financial information to create a budget, explaining what goes into a budget and how to go about making one.

Constructing a Financial Forecast

Every philosopher-wannabe has spoken profound words about the future and about whether we should try to predict it. But we can't avoid the future. It's there, it's uncertain, and we're going to spend the rest of our lives in it.

All of us make decisions every day based on our own personal view of what's ahead. Although things often end up surprising us, our assumptions about the future at least give us a basic framework to plan our lives around. Our expectations, no matter how far off the mark they are, encourage us to set objectives, to move forward, and to achieve our goals somewhere down the road.

You can think about the future of your company in much the same way. Assumptions about your own industry and marketplace – that you'll have no new competitors, that a new technology will catch on, or that customers will remain loyal, for example – provide a framework to plan around. Your expectations of what lies ahead influence your business objectives and the long-term goals that you set for the company.

You want to be clear about what your business assumptions are and where they come from, because your assumptions are as important as the numbers themselves when it comes to making a prediction. If you are convinced that no new competitors will enter the market, say why. If you see a period of rapid technological change ahead, explain your reasons. Don't try to hide your business assumptions in a footnote somewhere; place them in a prominent position. That way, you make your financial forecast as honest, adaptable, and useful as it can be. If all your assumptions are out in the open, nobody can possibly miss them.

- Everybody who looks at your forecast knows exactly what's behind it.
- You know exactly where to go when your assumptions need to be changed.

As you may have guessed, coming up with predictions that you really believe in isn't always easy. You may trust some of the numbers (next year's sales figures) more than you do others (the size of a brand-new market). Some of your financial predictions are based on your best estimate. You may arrive at others by using sophisticated number-crunching techniques. When you get the hang of it, though, you begin to see what a broad and powerful planning tool a financial forecast can be. You'll find yourself turning to it to help answer all sorts of important questions, such as the following:

- What cash demands does your company face in the coming year?
- Can your company cover its debt obligations over the next three years?
- Does your company plan to make a profit next year?
- Is your company meeting its overall financial objectives?
- Do investors find your company to be an attractive business proposition?

With so many important questions at stake, a financial forecast is worth all the time and effort that you can spend on it. Because if you're not careful, a forecast can turn out to be way off base. Did you ever hear the old computer programmer's expression 'Rubbish in, rubbish out'? The same is true of financial forecasts. Your financial forecast is only as good as the numbers that go into it. If the numbers are off the mark, it's usually for one of the following reasons:

- Expectations were unrealistic.
- Assumptions weren't objective.
- Predictions weren't checked and rechecked.

The following sections examine the financial statements that make up a financial forecast. After we explain how to put these statements together, we point out which of the numbers are most important and which are the most sensitive to changes in your assumptions and expectations about the future.

Pro-forma profit and loss account

Pro forma refers to something that you describe or estimate in advance. (It can also mean something that is merely a formality and can be ignored – but don't get your hopes up; we're talking about a serious part of a business plan.) When you construct your financial forecast, you should try to include *pro-forma profit and loss accounts* – documents that show where you plan to get your money and how you'll spend it – for at least three years and for as long as five years in the future, depending on the nature of your business. You should subdivide the first two years into quarterly profit projections. After two years, when your profit projections are much less certain, annual projections are fine. (For a look at a profit and loss account, flip to Book III Chapter 1.)

Your company's pro-forma profit and loss accounts predict what sort of profit you expect to make in the future by asking you to project your total business revenue and then to subtract all your anticipated costs. The following should help you get ready:

✔ If you're already in business and have a financial history to work with, get all your past financial statements out right away. You can use them to help you figure out what's likely to happen next.

✔ If you have a new company on your hands and don't have a history to fall back on, you have to find other ways to get the information that you need. Talk to people in similar businesses, sit down with your banker and your accountant, visit a trade association, and read industry magazines and newspapers.

The pro-forma profit and loss account has two parts – projected revenue and anticipated costs.

Projected revenue

Your company's projected revenue is based primarily on your sales forecast – exactly how much of your product or service you plan to sell. You have to think about two things: how much you expect to sell, naturally, and how much you're going to charge. Unfortunately, you can't completely separate the two things, because any change in price usually affects the level of your sales.

Your sales forecast is likely to be the single most important business prediction that you'll ever make. If you get it wrong, the error can lead to mountains of unsold stock or a sea of unhappy, dissatisfied customers – a financial disaster in the making. A souvenir-T-shirt company that *over*estimates how many Cup Final T-shirts customers will buy, for example, is going to be left with an awful lot of worthless merchandise. By the same token, the corner toy shop that *under*estimates how many kids will want the latest Bratz will have to answer to many frustrated parents and unhappy children – and will suffer lost sales.

How do you get the sales forecast right? Start by looking at its formula:

Sales forecast = market size × growth rate × market-share target

- Market size estimates the current number of potential customers.

- Growth rate estimates how fast the market will grow.

- Market-share target estimates the percentage of the market that you plan to capture.

Because your sales forecast has such a tremendous impact on the rest of your financial forecast – not to mention on the company itself – you should try to support the estimates that you make with as much hard data as you can get your hands on. Depending on your situation, you can also rely on the following guides:

Company experience. If you already have experience and a track record in the market, you can use your own sales history to make a sales prediction. But remember that your sales are a combination of the size of the market and your own share of the market. You may still need other sources of data (listed in the following paragraphs) to help you estimate how the market and your share of it are likely to change in the future.

Using data from outside your company also ensures that you're taking full advantage of all the growth opportunities that are available. All too often, companies use last year's sales as a shortcut to estimating next year's sales, without taking the time to look at how their markets are changing. Because a sales forecast can be self-fulfilling, those companies may never know what they missed!

Industry data. Industry data on market size and estimates of future growth come from all quarters, including trade associations, investment companies, and market-research firms. You can also get practical and timely information from industry suppliers and distributors.

Outside trends. In certain markets, sales levels are closely tied to trends in other markets, social trends, or economic trends. Car sales, for example, tend to move with the general economy. So when car dealers track what's happening with the Gross Domestic Product (GDP), they get an estimate of where car sales are headed.

Even if a product is brand-new, you can sometimes find a substitute market to track as a reference. When frozen yogurt first appeared on the scene, for example, frozen-yogurt makers turned to the sales history of ice cream to help support their own sales forecasts.

Speaking of ice cream, don't forget to factor sales cycles into your forecast; in most of the UK, ice cream sales freeze over in January and February. Other markets may have other cycles.

Next, multiply your sales forecast by the average price that you expect to charge. The result is your projected revenue and it looks like this:

Projected revenue = sales forecast × average price

Where does the average price come from? Your average price is based on what you think your customers are willing to pay and what your competitors are charging. Use the information that you pack away on your industry and the marketplace. (Refer to Part II for how to analyse your industry and customers.) The price should also take into account your own costs and your company's overall financial situation.

Now put all the numbers together and see how they work. We'll use a company called Global Gizmos as an example. Sally Smart, widgets product manager, is putting together a three-year revenue projection. Using industry and market data along with the company's own sales history, Sally estimates that the entire market for widgets will grow about 10 per cent a year and that Global Gizmos' market share will increase by roughly 2 per cent a year, with projected price increases of approximately £1 to £2. She puts the numbers together in a table so that she can easily refer to the underlying estimates and the assumptions that support them (see Table 2-1).

Table 2-1   Widget Revenue Projection for Global Gizmos Company

Revenue projection	Year 1	Year 2	Year 3
Projected market size (units)	210,000	231,000	254,100
Projected market share (%)	20	22	24
Sales forecast (units)	42,000	50,820	60,980
Average price	£26	£27	£29
Projected revenue	£1,092,000	£1,372,140	£1,768,420

Anticipated costs

When you complete your revenue projection, you're still not quite finished. You still have to look at anticipated costs – the price tag of doing business over the next several years. To make life a little easier, you can break anticipated costs down into the major categories that appear in a pro-forma profit and loss account: projected cost of goods sold, projected sales, general and administration expenses, projected interest expenses, and projected taxes and depreciation. The following list defines these categories.

Projected cost of goods sold (COGS). COGS, which combines all the direct costs associated with putting together your product or delivering your service, is likely to be your single largest expense. If you have a track record in the industry, you have a useful starting point for estimating your company's future COGS.

Even though the following formula may look ugly, it's actually a simple way to calculate your projected COGS. Based on the assumption that the ratio of your costs to your revenue will stay the same:

Projected COGS = (current COGS ÷ current revenue on sales) × projected revenue

If you haven't been in business long or if you're just starting a company, you won't have access to this kind of information. But you can still estimate your projected COGS by substituting industry averages or by using data that you find on other companies that have similar products or services.

Although this ratio approach has the advantage of being simple, you can get into trouble if you don't confirm the COGS that you come up with. At the very least, you should sum up the estimates of the major costs looming ahead (materials, labour, utilities, facilities, and so on) to make sure that the projected COGS makes sense. This method is tougher, but it gives you a chance to make separate assumptions and projections for each of the underlying costs. You may be pleasantly surprised; you may discover that as your company gets bigger and you're in business longer, your projected revenue goes up faster than your costs do. The effect is called the experience curve and it means that your COGS-to-revenue ratio will actually get smaller in the coming years.

Sales, general, and administration (SG&A). SG&A represents your company's overheads: sales expenses, advertising, travel, accounting, telephones, and all the other costs associated with supporting your business. If your company is brand-new, try to get a feel for what your support costs may be by asking people in similar businesses, cornering your accountant, or checking with a trade association for average support costs in your industry. Also come up with ballpark numbers of your own, including estimates for all the major overhead expenses that you can think of.

If you've been in business for a while, you can estimate a range for your SG&A expenses using two calculations. The first method projects a constant spending level, even if your company's sales are growing. In effect, you assume that your support activities will all get more efficient and will accommodate your additional growth without getting bigger themselves. The other method projects a constant SG&A-to-revenue ratio. In this case, you assume

Book IV

Managing the Finances

that support costs will grow as fast as your revenue and that you won't see any increase in efficiency. An accurate SG&A forecast probably lies somewhere in between. Given what you know about your company's operations, come up with your own estimate, and include the assumptions that you make.

Interest expense. Your interest expense is largely the result of decisions that you make about your company's long-term financing. Those decisions, in turn, are influenced by your ability to pay your interest costs out of profits. Think about what sort of financing you will need and what interest rates you may be able to lock in, then estimate your interest expense as best you can.

Taxes and depreciation. Taxes certainly affect your bottom line, and you want to include your projections and assumptions in your anticipated costs. It's usually pretty simple to estimate their general impact in the future by looking at their impact on your company now. If you're starting a new business, do a bit of research on tax rates.

Depreciation, on the other hand, is an accountant's way of accounting for the value that your asset purchases lose over the time in which you will be using them. As such, it's an expense that doesn't really come out of your pocket every year. You can estimate the numbers, but don't get too carried away. In the future, your depreciation expense will include a portion of those expensive items that you have to buy to keep the business healthy and growing (computers, cars, forklifts, and so on).

When you plug the numbers into your pro-forma profit and loss account and calculate your net profit, be prepared for a shock. You may discover that the profit you were expecting in the first year or two has turned into a projected loss. But don't panic. New business ventures often lose money for some time, until their products catch on and some of the startup costs begin to get paid off. Whatever you do, don't try to turn a projected loss into a profit by fiddling with the numbers. The point isn't to make money on paper; the point is to use the pro-forma profit and loss account as a tool that can tell you what sort of resources and reserves you need to survive until losses turn into predicted profits.

Even if your projection shows a healthy profit, ensure you also complete a Cash Flow Projection (see below) to make sure you can afford to trade at the projected level. Making a profit does not always mean that you will have *cash* on hand to buy raw materials, pay staff and pay taxes.

Estimated balance sheet

Another part of your financial forecast is the *estimated balance sheet,* which, like a regular balance sheet, is a snapshot of what your company looks like at a particular moment – what it owns, what it owes, and what it's worth. Over the years, these snapshots (estimated balance sheets) fill a photo album of sorts, recording how your company changes over time. Your estimated balance sheets describe what you want your company to become and how you plan to get it there. The estimated balance sheets that you put together as part of your financial forecast should start with the present and extend out three to five years in a series of year-end projections. (For much more information on balance sheets, check out Book III Chapter 2.)

While the pro-forma profit and loss accounts in your financial forecast project future revenue, costs, and profits, your estimated balance sheets lay out exactly how your company will grow so that it can meet those projections. First, you want to look at what sorts of things (*assets*) you'll need to support the planned size and scale of your business. Then you have to make some decisions about how you're going to pay for those assets. You have to consider how you'll finance your company – how much debt you plan to take on (*liabilities*) and how much of the company's own money (*equity*) you plan to use.

Assets

Your company's projected assets at the end of each year include everything from the money that you expect to have in the petty-cash drawer to the buildings and machines that you plan to own. Some of these assets will be current assets, meaning that you can easily turn them into cash; others will be fixed assets. Don't be confused by the word *current;* we're still talking about the future.

Current assets. The cash on hand and your investment portfolio, as well as debtors and stocks, add up to your current assets. How much should you plan for? That depends on the list of current liabilities (debts) you expect to have, for one thing, because you'll have to pay short-term debts out of your current assets. What's left over is your working capital. The amount of working capital that you will need depends on your future cash-flow situation.

Your estimates of future debtors (money that customers will owe you) depend on the payment terms that you offer and on the sales that you expect to make on credit.

Projected stocks (the amount of stuff in your warehouse) depend on how fast your company can put together products or services and get them to customers. The longer it takes to build products, the bigger the stock cushion you may need.

Fixed assets. Land, buildings, equipment, machinery, and all the other things that aren't easy to dispose of make up your company's fixed assets. Your estimated balance sheets should account for the expensive items that you expect to purchase or get rid of. Your capital purchases (such as additional buildings, more equipment, and newer machines) can play a major role in company growth, increasing both your revenue and the scale of your business operations.

Keep an eye on how each machine or piece of equipment will help your bottom line. If you plan to buy something big, make a quick calculation of its *payback period* (how long it will take to pay back the initial cost of the equipment out of the extra profit that you'll make). Is the payback period going to be months, years, or decades? As you plan for the future, you also want to keep track of your overall expected *return on assets* (ROA), which is your net profits divided by your total assets. This figure monitors how well you expect all your assets to perform in the future. Compare your estimated ROA with industry averages and even with other types of investments.

Liabilities and owners' equity

Estimated balance sheets have to balance, of course, and your projected assets at the end of each future year have to be offset by all the liabilities that you intend to take on, plus your projected equity in the company. Think about how *leveraged* you intend to be (how much of your total assets you expect to pay for out of money that you borrow). Your use of leverage in the future says a great deal about your company. It shows how confident you are about future profits; it also says, loud and clear, how willing you are to take risks for future gain. For more about how leverage works, check out the sidebar 'Extruding better returns'.

Current liabilities. This category consists of all the money that you expect to owe on a short-term basis. That's why these debts are called *current liabilities,* although we're still talking about the future. Current liabilities include the amounts that you expect to owe other companies as part of your planned business operations, as well as payments that you expect to send to the tax people. You have to plan your future current assets so that they not only cover these estimated liabilities, but also leave you some extra capital to work with.

Extruding better returns

A small, up-and-coming West Country company (we'll call it Klever Kitchens) has made a big name for itself in the kitchen-accessories business. Klever Kitchens produces all sorts of new-fangled gadgets and utensils for the gourmet chef – everything from pasta hooks to melon scoops. Because many of the company's products are made of plastic, the owners face a decision about the purchase of a second plastic-extruding machine. They know that the investment is sound, because the new £20,000 machine will allow the company to grow, and they expect it to generate an additional £4,000 a year in profit, resulting in an estimated payback period of about five years (£20,000 divided by £4,000). The question is whether to pay for the extruder by borrowing the funds or by using some of the company's equity reserves.

The owners understand that using debt is a way to leverage the company. The bank has already agreed to loan Klever Kitchens 75 per cent of the £20,000 investment at a fixed 8 per cent interest rate. But what do the numbers say?

Return on equity (ROE) really measures how much money Klever Kitchens makes on the money that it invests (ROE = (added profit – interest expense) ÷ equity). By taking on debt, the owners expect to earn an additional £2,800 on their investment of £5,000 in the new extruder, for an ROE of 56 per cent. That figure is almost three times the return that they would receive by putting up the funds themselves.

Acting like a financial crowbar, leverage allows Klever Kitchens to use other people's money to generate profits for itself. The risks are also a bit higher, of course, because the owners have to make added interest payments or face losing the extruder and maybe the entire company. In this case, Klever Kitchens should borrow the funds, deciding that the rewards are well worth the risks.

Additional plastic extruder	*No leverage*	*Leverage*
Liability	£0	£15,000
Equity	£20,000	£5,000
Added net profit	£4,000	£4,000
Added interest expense	£0	£1,200
Added profit minus interest expense	£4,000	£2,800
Return on equity (ROE)	20%	56%

Book IV

Managing the Finances

Long-term liabilities. The long-term debt that you plan to take on represents the piece of your company that you intend to finance. Don't be surprised, however, if potential creditors put a strict limit on how much they will loan you, especially if you're just starting out. It's hard to buy a house without a down payment, and it's almost impossible to start a company without one. The down payment is your equity contribution. In general, bankers and other lenders alike want to see enough equity put into your business to make them feel that you're all in the same boat, risk-wise. Equity reassures them that you and other equity investors have a real financial stake in the company, as well as tangible reasons to make it succeed.

How much are lenders willing to loan you, and how much of a down payment do you need to come up with to satisfy them? The answer depends on several things. If you're already in business, the answer depends on how much debt your company already has, how long your company's been around, how you've done up to now, and what the prospects are in your industry. If your company is new, financing depends on your track record in other businesses or on how well you do your homework and put together a convincing business plan.

Before you take on a new loan, find out what kind of debt-to-equity ratios similar companies have. (For help, turn to Book III Chapter 2.) Make sure that yours will fall somewhere in the same range. As an additional test, run some numbers to make sure that you can afford the debt and the interest payments that come along with it.

 Owners' equity. The pieces of your company that you, your friends, relatives, acquaintances, and often total strangers lay claim to are all lumped together as *owners' equity*. Although the details of ownership can become ridiculously complex, the result of the process is fairly straightforward. All owners own part of your company, and everybody sinks or swims, depending on how well the company does.

In general, you can estimate how well the company is likely to do for its owners by projecting the return that you expect to make on the owners' investment (refer to Book III Chapter 1 for the details). Then you can compare that return with what investors in other companies, or even other industries, are earning.

In the initial stages of your company, equity capital is likely to come from the owners themselves, either as cash straight out of the wallet or from the sale of shares to other investors. The equity at this stage is crucial, because if you want to borrow money later, you're going to have to show your bankers that you have enough invested in your business to make your company a sound financial risk. When the company is up and running, of course, you can take some of your profits and (rather than buy the little sports car that you've always wanted) give them back to the company, creating additional equity.

Unfortunately, profit has another side, and the down side is definitely in the red. Although you probably don't want to think about it, your company may lose money some years (especially during the early years). Losses don't generate equity; on the contrary, they eat equity up. So you have to plan to have enough equity available to cover any anticipated losses that you project in your pro-forma profit and loss accounts (refer to the section 'Pro-forma profit and loss account' earlier in this chapter).

Projected cash flow

The flow of cash through a business is much like the flow of oil through an engine; it supports and sustains everything that you do and keeps the various parts of your company functioning smoothly. We all know what happens when a car's oil runs dry: the car belches blue smoke and dies. Running out of cash can be just as catastrophic for your company. If you survive the experience, it may take months or even years for your company to recover.

Cash-flow statements keep track of the cash that comes in and the cash that goes out of your company, as well as where the money ends up. These statements are crucial. Projected cash-flow statements ensure that you never find the cash drawer empty at the end of the month when you have a load of bills left to pay.

Cash-flow statements should project three to five years into the future, and for the first two years, they should include monthly cash-flow estimates. Monthly estimates are particularly important if your company is subject to seasonal cycles or to big swings in sales or expenses. (If you're not sure what a cash-flow statement looks like and how it's different from a profit and loss account, flip to Book II Chapter 2.)

You get a bonus from all this work: The effort that you put into creating cash-flow statements for the company gives you a head start when the time comes to create a budget for your business (see 'Making a Budget' later in this chapter).

✔ Your financial forecast should include a pro-forma profit and loss account, an estimated balance sheet, and a projected cash-flow statement.

✔ The business assumptions behind your forecast are as important as the numbers themselves.

✔ Your company's pro-forma profit and loss account predicts the profit that you expect to make in future years.

✔ Your estimated balance sheet lays out how you expect your company to grow in the future.

✔ Your company's projected cash-flow statement tracks your expected cash position in coming years.

Book IV

Managing the Finances

Exploring Alternatives

Wouldn't it be nice if you could lay out a financial forecast – create your pro-forma profit and loss accounts, estimated balance sheets, and projected cash-flow statements – and then just be done with it? Unfortunately the uncertain future that makes your financial forecast necessary in the first place is unpredictable enough to require constant attention. To keep up, you have to do the following things:

✔ Monitor your financial situation and revise the parts of your forecast that change when circumstances – and your own financial objectives – shift.

✔ Update the entire financial forecast regularly, keeping track of when past predictions were on target or off, and extending your projections another month, quarter, or year.

✔ Consider financial assumptions that are more optimistic and more pessimistic than your own best predictions, paying special attention to the estimates that you're the least certain about.

Why take the time to look at different financial assumptions? For one thing, they show you just how far off your forecast can be if things happen to turn out a bit differently than you expect. Also, the differences that you come up with are an important reminder that your forecasts are only that. You have to be prepared for alternatives.

The DuPont formula

If you really want to get a feel for what's going to happen when you change any of the estimates that make up your company's financial forecast, you have to understand a little bit about how the numbers relate to one other. The DuPont company came up with a formula that turned out to be so useful that other companies have been using a similar one ever since.

The idea behind the *DuPont formula* is simple. The recipe describes all the ingredients that play a role in determining your return on equity (ROE) – a number that captures the overall profitability of your company. ROE is your company's overall net profit divided by the owners' equity. But knowing that your ROE is 13 per cent, for example, is a lot like getting B+ on a test. You think that you did relatively well, but why did you get that particular mark? Why didn't you get an A? You want to know what's behind the mark so that you can do better next time.

By learning what's behind your company's ROE, you have a way to measure the impact of your financial predictions on your profitability. The DuPont chart shown in Figure 2-1 turns the formula into a pyramid, with the ROE at the top. Each level of the pyramid breaks the ratio into more basic financial ingredients.

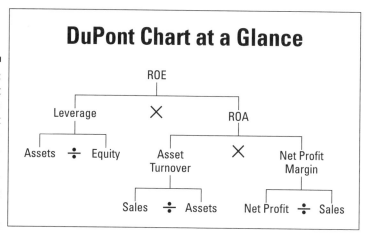

Figure 2-1:
The DuPont chart turns the DuPont formula into a pyramid, with return on equity (ROE) at the top.

First level

ROE = ROA × leverage

You can increase your company's return on equity by increasing the overall return on your company assets or by increasing your leverage (the ratio of your total company assets to equity).

Second level

Leverage = assets ÷ equity

As your debt increases relative to equity, so does your company's leverage.

ROA = asset turnover × net profit margin

You can increase your return on company assets by turning those assets into more sales or by increasing the amount of money that you make on each sale.

Third level

Asset turnover = sales ÷ assets

Asset turnover is the amount of money that you take in on sales relative to your company's assets. The bigger your asset turnover, the more efficient you are at turning assets into sales.

Book IV

Managing the Finances

Net profit margin = net profit ÷ sales

Net profit margin is the profit that you make after subtracting expenses divided by the amount of money you take in on sales. The larger your profit margin, the lower your overall costs relative to the prices that you charge.

What-if analysis

After you see how the DuPont formula is put together, you can start exploring different assumptions and what happens when you change the financial forecast. With the DuPont formula, you can look at how those changes are likely to affect your projected profitability, measured by your return on equity. The DuPont formula makes answering questions like the following much easier:

- ✔ What if you cut prices by 3 per cent?
- ✔ What if you increase sales volume by 10 per cent?
- ✔ What if cost of goods sold goes up by 8 per cent?
- ✔ What if you reduce your leverage by 25 per cent?

If you get your computer and a spreadsheet program involved in the analysis (see your local computer guru for help, if necessary), you can ask ten what-if questions and get the answers before you have time to think of the next ten.

The better you understand where your revenue and profits come from, the better prepared you are to meet financial challenges.

- ✔ Looking at different financial assumptions allows you to cover your bets in an uncertain future.
- ✔ The DuPont formula describes exactly what goes into your return on equity, which is a measure of your overall profitability.
- ✔ Using the DuPont formula, you can ask what-if questions to gauge the effects of changing your financial assumptions.

Making a Budget

The pieces of your financial forecast – the pro-forma profit and loss accounts, estimated balance sheets, and projected cash-flow statements – are meant to create a moving picture of your financial situation tomorrow, next month, next year, and three or even five years out. Your financial picture is likely to be much clearer in the near term, of course, and much cloudier the farther out you try to look. Fortunately, you can use the best of your forecasts to make near-term decisions about where, when, and how much money to spend on your company in the future.

Making a budget for your company is one of the most important steps that you'll take as you prepare your business plan. Your budget, in effect, consists of a series of bets that you're willing to place, based on what you expect to happen in your industry and in the marketplace in general. Your budget spells out exactly where your company's resources will come from and where they're going to go, and helps ensure that you make the right financial decisions.

A budget is more than a collection of numbers, though. Your budget is also a business tool that helps you communicate, organise, monitor, and control what's going on in your business. Your company's budget does the following things:

- ✔ Requires managers to communicate with one another so that they can agree on specific financial objectives, including revenue levels and spending targets.

- ✔ Establishes roles and responsibilities for managers, based on how much money they're in charge of bringing in and how much they're allowed to spend.

- ✔ Creates a standard way of measuring and monitoring management performance by keeping track of how well the revenue targets and spending limits are met.

- ✔ Promotes the efficient and effective use of your financial resources by making sure that all your resources point toward a common set of business goals.

What's in the budget

The rough outlines of your company's budget look a lot like your projected cash-flow statement. In fact, the cash-flow statement is the perfect place to start. Projected cash flow is a forecast of where you think the company's money will come from and where it's going to go in the future. Your budget fills in all the details, turning your financial forecast into a specific plan for taking in money and doling it out.

Book IV

Managing the Finances

The *master budget* that you create is meant to account for everything that your company plans to do over the next year or two. Although you spend your company's money in all sorts of ways, all those ways can be divided into short-term and long-term spending. In the short term, you use money to keep the business up and running every day, covering the costs and expenses of putting together and selling products and services. Over the longer term, you use money to invest in things that will make your company bigger, better, or more profitable.

If your company is small and you have only a few employees, a single master budget should be all that you need to keep your day-to-day finances on track as well as to make decisions in the future. When your company gets a little bigger, however, you may want to think about your company's finances in terms of more than one budget, each of which covers a different aspect of your business. You may want to create the following budgets:

- ✔ **Operating.** This budget deals with all the costs that are directly associated with putting your product or service together, such as materials, supplies, labour, utilities, services, and facilities.

- ✔ **Administrative.** This budget deals with the expenses that are involved in supporting your products and services, sales and advertising, administrative salaries, phone and fax lines, and travel expenses.

- ✔ **Financial.** This budget deals with the overhead expenses involved in managing your assets, including keeping your books, doing your taxes, controlling your product stock, and keeping track of your debtors (the money that customers owe you).

- ✔ **Capital.** This budget deals with funds that are earmarked for the purchase of expensive items, such as new equipment, computers, a company car, and additional office space.

- ✔ **Development.** This budget deals with money that is set aside for developing new products, opening branches in other cities, or marketing to brand-new groups of customers.

When you need several budgets, like those in the preceding list, you use a master budget to pull all the separate budgets together and make sure that they meet your company's larger goals and financial objectives.

Global Gizmos Company put together a budget for the next two years based on a financial forecast and its projected cash flow (see Figure 2-2). The budget goes into considerable detail in dividing the broad financial objectives into actual revenue and expense targets for specific company activities. The cost of goods produced, for example, is broken down into the cost of raw materials and supplies, labour, and utilities and facilities.

Master Budget

Global Gizmos Company

REVENUE AND EXPENSES		
	Next Year	Year After
Budgeted Revenue:		
Gross receipts on sales	£895,000	£970,000
Dividend and interest income	£4,000	£5,000
Total Revenue Available	**£ 899,000**	**£ 975,000**
Budgeted Expenses:		
Cost of goods produced	£600,000	£650,000
Raw materials and supplies	£250,000	£275,000
Labor costs	£300,000	£325,000
Utilities and facilities	£50,000	£50,000
Sales, general, and administration	£165,000	£170,000
Sales and distribution	£90,000	£95,000
Advertising and promotion	£30,000	£30,000
Product service	£15,000	£20,000
Accounting and office support	£30,000	£30,000
Interest expense	£12,500	£12,000
Taxes	£22,000	£24,000
Buildings, equipment, machinery	£40,000	£100,000
Equipment and computers	£35,000	£25,000
Expanded warehouse	£5,000	£75,000
Development projects	£10,000	£15,000
New product development	£8,000	£5,000
New market development	£2,000	£10,000
Long-term debt reduction	£2,500	£2,000
Dividend distribution to owners	£6,000	£7,000
Total Expenses Out	**£858,000**	**£980,000**
NET CHANGE IN CASH POSITION	**£41,000**	**£-5,000**

The numbered markers **1** and **2** appear to the left of the table pointing to the Budgeted Revenue section and the Interest expense/Taxes section respectively.

Figure 2-2:
The master budget looks a lot like the company's projected cash-flow statement.

How budgets are made

Somehow, it's never the right time to sit down and make a budget, there's always something much more important to do. This situation seems to hold true for household and company budgets alike. Why doesn't anybody like to do them? Often, there doesn't seem to be enough financial information around to make a budget that's of any real use. If you complete a financial forecast first, however, your company's budget is much easier to complete.

So when do you get started? If you're just starting your company, there's no time like the present. If you're already up and running, when you create a budget depends on the company's size. For really big companies, the yearly budget process may begin six to nine months in advance. No wonder that the job can feel a bit like never-ending drudgery! Most companies, however, can count on spending some serious time with their budgets three or four months before the next year gets under way.

Established companies can use their track records and financial histories as starting points for next year's budget. But be careful. When you're a veteran, it's all too easy to get a bad case of budgetary laziness, using last year's numbers as a shortcut to next year's numbers. Unfortunately, you can veer off financial course before you know it. A good compass for this situation is something called *zero-based budgeting*. When you insist on zero-based budgeting, you ask everybody – including yourself – to go back and start from the bottom in preparing a budget. Rather than use last year's budget numbers, you make full use of your financial forecast, building up a new set of numbers from scratch. The process takes a little longer but is almost always worthwhile.

The process of making a budget often gets a bad name in the business world. Rather than see budgeting as being a helpful business tool, business owners often rank budgeting among the greatest evils on earth, and managers often talk about it in unprintable ways. So what gives? When the budgeting process falls apart in a company, at least one of the following things probably happened:

- ✔ The budget was handed down from above and used to control the company's managers, taking away their ability to influence the business decisions that they were ultimately responsible for carrying out.

- ✔ The budget was based on short-term thinking, ignoring the company's longer-term plans and strategic goals.

- ✔ The budgeted revenue and expense targets had nothing to do with the company's larger financial objectives or its real financial situation.

To make sure that your own company's budget doesn't suffer these fatal flaws, take a close look at two ways to put together a budget.

Top-down budgeting approach

The top-down approach to making your budget is the simplest way to work through your company's financial plans. The process pretty much begins and ends with the people who are in charge. If your company is small, you may want to invite some outside people to join you – people whom you trust, such as your banker, accountant, or maybe a close business associate. The process goes something like this:

1. **Put the finishing touches on your company's financial forecast, including pro-forma profit and loss accounts, expected balance sheets, and projected cash-flow statements.**

   If certain pieces are missing or incomplete, try to get the information that you need, or make a note that the document you need is unavailable.

2. **Meet with the company's decision-makers (or your trusted group, if you're self-employed) to review the financial forecast.**

   Take time to discuss general expectations about the future. Talk about the business assumptions that go into the forecast and the key predictions and estimates that come out of it.

3. **Meet again to explore possible financial alternatives.**

   Look at different sets of business assumptions and weigh their potential effects on the forecast. Continue to meet until the group either agrees or agrees to disagree about the future.

4. **Come up with revenue and expense targets for each of your company's major business activities or functional areas (whichever is more appropriate to your company).**

5. **Meet one last time after the budget is in place to review the numbers and get it approved.**

   Put together a written summary to go along with the numbers so that everyone in the company knows what the budget is, where it comes from, and what it means.

Although top-down budgeting does a fairly good job when you know all the people in your company by their first names, the approach has some definite disadvantages when your company gets bigger. By including only the managers at the top, you run the risk of leaving out large chunks of the organisation and losing track of your real business situation when it comes time to plug in the numbers.

Book IV

Managing the Finances

Bottom-up budgeting approach

The bottom-up approach to creating your budget really is just an expanded version of the top-down process, taking into account the demands of a bigger company and of more people who have something to say. You still want to begin putting together your budget by getting a group of senior managers together. That group should still spend time coming to a general understanding of, and agreement on, your company's financial forecast, along with the business assumptions and expectations for the future that go with it. But rather than forcing a budget from the top, this approach allows you to build the budget up from the bottom.

Don't ask the group of senior managers to go on and dictate the company's budget. At this point in the budget process, the bottom-up approach means that it's time to get managers and supervisors at all levels of the company involved. The process goes like this:

1. **Meet with senior managers and ask them to review the company's broad financial objectives for each of the major business areas.**

   Try to come up with guidelines that set the tone and direction for budget discussions and negotiations throughout the company.

2. **Ask managers to meet with their managers and supervisors at all levels in the organisation.**

   Meetings can start with a recap of the budget guidelines, but discussions should focus on setting revenue and expense targets. After all, these managers are the ones who actually have to achieve the numbers and stay within the spending limits.

3. **Summarise the results of the budget negotiations.**

   If necessary, get the senior group members together again to discuss revisions in the financial objectives, based on the insights, perceptions, and wisdom of the company's entire management team.

4. **Go through the process again, if you have to, so that everyone at every level of the organisation is on board (or at least understands the reasoning behind the budget and its numbers).**

5. **Approve the budget at the top.**

   Make sure that everybody in the company understands what the budget means, applying the budget not only to financial objectives but also to larger business goals.

   • Your budget spells out exactly where your company's resources will come from and where they will go.

   • Your budget should be based on your projected cash-flow statements.

- Top-down budgeting is done by the top people – owners or senior managers – and works best in small companies.

- Bottom-up budgeting involves all management levels, which can mean more realistic revenue targets and spending limits.

Staying Flexible with Budgets

One thing never to lose sight of is that budgeting is a *means to an end*. It's a tool for doing something better than you could without the tool. Preparing budgeted financial statements is not the ultimate objective; a budget is not an end in itself. The budgeting process should provide definite benefits, and businesses should use their budgeted financial statements to measure progress toward their financial objectives – and not just file them away someplace.

Budgets are not the only tool for management control. Control means accomplishing your financial objectives. Many businesses do not use budgeting and do not prepare budgeted financial statements. But they do lay down goals and objectives for each period and compare actual performance against these targets. Doing at least this much is essential for all businesses.

Keep in mind that budgets are not the only means for controlling expenses. Actually, we shy away from the term *controlling* because we've found that, in the minds of most people, *controlling* expenses means minimising them. The *cost/benefits* idea captures the better view of expenses. Spending more on advertising, for example, may have a good payoff in the additional sales volume it produces. In other words, it's easy to cut advertising to zero if you really want to minimise this expense – but the impact on sales volume may be disastrous.

Business managers should eliminate any *excessive* amount of an expense – the amount that really doesn't yield a benefit or add value to the business. For example, it's possible for a business to spend too much on quality inspection by doing unnecessary or duplicate steps, or by spending too much time testing products that have a long history of good quality. But this doesn't mean that the business should eliminate the expense entirely. Expense control means trimming the cost down to the right size. In this sense, expense control is one of the hardest jobs that business managers do, second only to managing people, in our opinion.

Book IV

Managing the Finances

Chapter 3

Choosing the Right Ownership Structure

In This Chapter

▶ Seeing profit as a small piece of the sales revenue pie

▶ Taking stock of the company as an important ownership structure

▶ Watching out for negative factors affecting share value

▶ Discerning profit allocation and liability issues

▶ Looking out for Number One in a sole proprietorship

*T*he obvious reason for investing in a business as an owner rather than a safer kind of investment is the potential for greater rewards. As one of the partners or shareholders of a business, you're entitled to part of the business's profit – and you're also subject to the risk that the business will go down the tubes, taking your money down with it. This chapter shows you how ownership structure affects your share of the profit – especially how changes beyond your control can make your share less valuable. It also explains how the ownership structure has a dramatic impact on the taxes paid by the business and its owners.

From the Top Line to the Bottom Line

Book III Chapter 1 explains the business profit-making process and the accounting profit report for a period, which is called the *profit and loss account*. The chapter focuses on the financial effects on the various operating assets and operating liabilities of a business of its sales revenue and expense activities. To make sense of a company's *balance sheet* (its statement of financial condition at the end of the profit period), which is explained in Book III Chapter 2, you need to understand how its sales revenue and expenses propel the company's operating assets and operating liabilities. And to round out the financial picture of a business you need to look at its sources and uses of cash flows for the period, which are presented in its *cash flow statement* – see Book III Chapter 3.

Whew! These three business financial statements present a lot of information. But, if you're a manager or owner of a business you should have a good grip on these three *accounting reports* (as they're sometimes called). Accounting often is called the language of business, and learning the basic vocabulary of accounting is extraordinarily helpful, if not downright essential, for business managers and owners.

There is one aspect of the business profit-making process that it is easy to lose sight of when reading a profit and loss account. How does a business get from the top line in its profit and loss account (sales revenue) down to its bottom line (net income)?

In our free enterprise, largely unregulated and non-government-controlled economy, business managers have the responsibility of negotiating the prices paid for labour, subject only to minimum wages legislation, and most of the other services, supplies, and other factors used in the profit-making process. This book isn't the place to delve into the fields of labour economics and political economy. But we would point out that business profit and loss accounts are one key source of information for scholars who do research in these areas. In particular, the financial statements prepared by accountants report how sales revenue is divided among the different parties in a business's profit-making process.

A business collects money from its customers and then redistributes that sales revenue to the many parties clamouring for their fair share. You may think that the second part of this process would be the easy part, but business managers sometimes have a tough time deciding what constitutes a fair share for each claimant. For example, in deciding how much to pay employees in regular wages and fringe benefits, business managers have to ask what value each employee adds to the business, whether to raise sales prices in order to pay higher wages, and so on.

The distribution of total sales revenue among the various claimants on the revenue is a *zero-sum game*. This means that if one party gets a bigger piece of the revenue pie then some other party gets a smaller piece, keeping the size of the pie (total sales revenue) the same. (The alternative is for the business to increase the size of its sales revenue pie – by raising its sales prices or selling more units.) If a business increases compensation to its employees, for instance, without changing the prices paid for all other services and supplies, then the shares of total sales revenue going to the Chancellor in tax and to the owners as after-tax net income decrease. (Note that a business may increase wages expecting that labour productivity gains will offset the wage gains.) Business managers must constantly calculate how changes in the prices they charge customers and changes in the prices they pay for labour, materials, products, utilities, and many other expenses affect bottom-line profit.

Net income, or net profit as it is often referred to, is the bottom-line profit that the business earned this period (or, to be more precise, the period just concluded, which often is called 'this period' to mean the most recent period). This figure is the starting point for determining how much cash – if any – to distribute to the owners. Businesses are not legally required to distribute any of their profit for the period, but if they do distribute some or all of their profit, the amounts distributed to each owner depend on the business's ownership structure, as described in the following section, 'What Owners Expect for Their Money'.

The owners of a business, in a real sense, stand at the end of the line for their piece of the sales revenue pie. How can you tell whether a business is doing well for its owners? What's a good net income figure? One test is to compare bottom-line profit with sales revenue. Dividing profit by sales revenue gives the *profit ratio*, which is expressed as a percentage. Many people don't really know what's a typical profit ratio for a businesses. They think it's high – 20%, 30%, or even 50% of sales revenue. In fact, the large majority of businesses earn profit ratios of less than 10%.

Although profit ratio is a useful test of profit performance, it ignores the amount of capital the owners have tied up in the business. Every business needs owners' capital to invest in the assets needed for making profit. The ratio of profit over owners' equity is called *return on equity*. To calculate a business's return on equity (ROE) you divide net income by total owners' equity (you can find owners' equity listed on the business's balance sheet). Compare the ROE of a business with the ROEs of investment alternatives that have the same kinds of risks and advantages when you're deciding whether to invest in a business. Business managers keep a close watch on their ROE in order to judge their business's profit performance relative to the amount of its owners' capital being used to make that profit.

Usually, managers have an ownership interest in the business – although in large, public companies, managers usually own only a small percentage of the total owners' equity. For a small business, the two or three chief managers may be the only owners. But many small businesses have outside, non-manager investors who put money in the business and share in the profit that the business earns.

Book IV

Managing the Finances

What Owners Expect for Their Money

Every business – regardless of how big it is and whether it's publicly- or privately-owned – has owners; no business can get all the financing it needs just by borrowing. An *owner* is someone who:

- Invested money in the business when it originally raised capital from its owners – or, who bought ownership shares from one of the existing owners of the business.

- ✔ Expects the business to earn profit on the owners' capital and expects to share in that profit by receiving cash distributions from profit and by benefiting from increases in the value of the ownership shares – with no guarantee of either.

- ✔ Directly participates in the management of the business or hires others to manage the business – in smaller businesses an owner may be one of the managers or may sit on the board of directors of the business, but in very large businesses you are just one of thousands of owners who elect a representative board of directors to oversee the managers of the business and to protect the interests of the owners.

- ✔ Receives a proportionate share of the proceeds if the business is sold or if the business sells off its assets.

- ✔ Takes risks and may lose the amount of their shareholding.

When owners invest money in a business the accountant records the amount of money received as an increase in the company's *cash* account (note the account is not called 'money'). And, to keep things in balance, the amount invested in the business is recorded as an increase in an *owners' equity* account. (This is one example of *double entry accounting*, which is explained in Book II Chapter 1.) Owners' equity also increases when a business makes profit. Because of the two different reasons for increases, the owners' equity of a business is divided into two separate accounts:

- ✔ **Share capital (also referred to as Invested capital):** Represents the amounts of money that owners have invested in the business, which could have been many years ago. Owners may invest additional capital from time to time, but generally speaking they cannot be forced to put additional money in a business.

- ✔ **Retained earnings (also referred to as Reserves):** Represents the profit earned by a business over the years that has not been distributed to its owners. If all profit had been distributed every year, retained earnings would have a zero balance. (If a business has never made a profit, its accumulated loss would cause retained earnings to have a negative balance, called a *deficit*.) If none of the annual profits of a business had been distributed to its owners, the balance in retained earnings would be the cumulative profit earned by the business since it opened its doors.

The account title *retained earnings* for the profit that a business earns and does not distribute to its owners is appropriate for any type of business entity. Business companies – one of the most common types of business entities – use this title. The other types of business entities discussed in this chapter may use this title, but they may collapse both sources of owners' equity into just one account for each owner. Companies are legally required to distinguish between the two sources of owners' equity: invested capital versus retained earnings. The other types of business entities may not be.

Whether to retain some or all of annual net income is one of the most important decisions that a business makes; distributions from profit have to be decided at the highest level of a business. A growing business needs additional capital for expanding its assets, and increasing the debt load of the business usually cannot supply all the additional capital. So, the business *ploughs back* some of its profit for the year – it keeps some (perhaps all) of the profit, rather than giving it out to the owners. In the long run this may be the best course of action, a step back before a leap forward.

Banks are one major source of loans to businesses. Of course, banks charge interest on the loans; a business and its bank negotiate an interest rate acceptable to both. Also, many other terms and conditions are negotiated, such as the term (time period) of the loan, whether collateral is required to secure the loan, and so on. The loan contract between a business and its lender may prohibit the business from distributing profit to owners during the period of the loan. Or, the loan agreement may require that the business maintain a minimum cash balance – which could mean that money the business would like to distribute to owners from profit has to stay in its cash account instead.

The chairman or other appropriate officer of the business signs the lending agreement with the bank. In addition, the bank may ask the major investors in the business to sign the agreement *as individuals*, in their personal capacities – and perhaps ask their spouses to sign the agreement as well. You should definitely understand your personal obligations if you are considering signing a lending agreement for a business. You take the risk that you may have to pay some part – or perhaps all – of the loan out of your personal assets.

Now, who are the owners and how do they organise themselves? A business may have just one owner, or two or more owners. A one-owner business may choose to operate as a *sole trader or proprietorship*; a multi-owner business must choose to be a *partnership, a limited partnership*, or a *limited liability company*. The most ordinary type of business is a sole trader – there are 1.5 million of them in the UK. Around a million limited companies are in operation at present, too.

No ownership structure is inherently better than another; which one is right for a particular business is something that the business's managers and owners need to decide (or should consult a tax adviser about, as discussed later in this chapter). The following discussion focuses on how ownership structure affects profit distribution to owners. Later, this chapter explains how the ownership structure determines the tax paid by the business and its owners – which is always an important consideration.

Book IV

Managing the Finances

Companies

The law views a *company* as a real, live person. Like an adult, a company is treated as a distinct and independent individual who has rights and responsibilities. A company's 'birth certificate' is the legal form that is filed with the Department for Business Enterprise and Regulatory Reform if the company is domiciled in the UK. A company must have a legal name, of course, like an individual. Just as a child is separate from her parents, a company is separate from its owners. The company is responsible for its own debts, just like a person is. The bank can't come after you if your neighbour defaults on her loan, and the bank can't come after you if the company you have invested money in goes belly up. If a company doesn't pay its debts, its creditors can seize only the company's assets, not the assets of the company's owners.

This important legal distinction between the obligations of the business entity and its individual owners is known as *limited liability* – that is, the limited liability of the owners. Even if the owners are excessively wealthy they have no legal liability for the unpaid debts of the company (unless they've used the corporate shell to defraud creditors, or are trading in some fraudulent or illegal manner). So, when you invest money in a company as an owner you know that the most you can lose is the same amount you put in. You may lose every pound you put in, but that's the most you can lose. The company's creditors cannot reach through the corporate entity to grab your assets to pay off the liabilities of the business.

Stock shares

A company issues ownership shares to persons who invest money in the business. These ownership shares are documented by *stock certificates,* which state the name of the owner and how many shares are owned. The company has to keep a *register* (list) of how many shares everyone owns, of course. (An owner can be another company, or any other legal entity.) The owners of a company are called its *shareholders* because they own *shares* issued by the company. The shares are fully *negotiable*, which means the owner can sell them at any time to anyone willing to buy them without having to get the approval of the company or the other shareholders to sell the shares. *Publicly-owned companies* are those whose shares are traded in public markets, most notably the London Stock Exchange, the New York Stock Exchange, and NASDAQ (National Association of Securities Dealers Automated Quotation).

One share is one unit of ownership; how much one share is worth with respect to the value of the whole business depends on the total number of shares that the business issues. If a business has issued 40,000 shares and you own 4,000 of them, you own ⅒ of the business. But suppose that the business issues an additional 4,000 shares; you now have 4,000 of 44,000, giving you a ¹⁄₁₁ interest in the business. The more shares a business issues, the smaller the percentage of total owners' equity each share represents. Issuing additional shares may dilute, or decrease the value of each share of stock. A good example is when a publicly-owned company doubles the number of its shares by issuing a two-for-one stock split. Each shareholder gets one new share for each share presently owned, without investing any additional money in the business. As you would expect, the market value of the stock drops in half – which is exactly the purpose of the split because the lower stock price is better for stock market trading (according to conventional wisdom).

If new shares are issued at a price equal to the going value of the shares, the value of the existing shares should not be adversely affected. But if new shares are issued at a discount from the going value, the value of each share after the additional shares are issued may decline. For example, assume you own shares in a business and the shares are selling for £100 per share. Suppose the company issues some shares for £50 per share. Each new share adds only £50 value to the business, which drags down the average value of all shares of the company. We quickly admit here that the valuation of company shares is not nearly so simple – but, our purpose is to emphasise that shareholders should pay attention to the issue of additional shares for less than the going market price of a company's shares. Management stock options are the prime example of issuing shares at below market prices.

Many publicly-owned companies give their managers share options in addition to their salaries and other benefits. A *share option* gives a manager the legal right to buy a certain number of shares at a fixed price starting at some time in the future – assuming conditions of continued employment and other requirements are satisfied. Usually the *exercise price* (also called the *strike price*) of a management share option is set equal to or higher than the present market value of the shares. So, granting the manager the share option does not produce any immediate gain to the manager – and these options can't be exercised for some time anyway. If the market price of the shares rises above the exercise price of the share option sometime in the future the share options become valuable – indeed, many managers have become multi-millionaires from their share options.

Suppose that the market value of a company's shares has risen to, say, £100 and that the exercise price of the share options awarded to several managers a few years ago was set at £50 per share. And, assume that all the other conditions of the share options are satisfied. The managers' share options will certainly be exercised to realise their gains. It would seem, therefore, that the management share options would have a negative impact on the market price of the company's shares – because the total value of the business has to be divided over a larger number of shares and this results in a smaller value per share. On the other hand, it can be argued that the total value of the business is higher than it would have been without the management share options because better qualified managers were attracted to the business or that the managers performed better because of their options. Even with the decrease in the value per share, it is argued, the shareholders are better off than they would have been if no share options had been awarded to the managers. The shares' market value may have been only £90 or £80 without the management share options – so the story goes.

Classes of shares

Before you invest in shares, you should ascertain whether the company has issued just one *class* of share. A class is one group, or type of share all having have identical rights; every share is the same as every other share. A company can issue two or more different classes of shares. For example, a business may offer Class A and Class B shares, where Class A shareholders are given the vote in elections for the board of directors but Class B shareholders do not get a vote. Of course, if you want to vote in the annual election of directors you should buy Class A shares. Laws generally are very liberal regarding the different classes of shares that can be issued by companies. For a whimsical example, one class could get the best seats at the annual meetings of the shareholders. To be serious, differences between classes of shares are very significant and affect the investment value of the shares of each class of share.

Two classes of corporate shares are fundamentally different: *ordinary shares* (called *common shares* in the US) and *preference shares*. Preference shareholders are promised a certain amount of cash dividends each year (note we said 'promised', not 'guaranteed') but the company makes no such promises to its ordinary shareholders. If the business ends up liquidating its assets and after paying off its liabilities returns money to its owners, the preference shareholders have to be paid before any money goes to the ordinary shareholders. The ordinary shareholders are at the top of the risk chain: A business that ends up in deep financial trouble is obligated to pay off its liabilities first, and then its preferred shareholders, and by the time the ordinary shareholders get their turn the business may have no money left to pay them. So, preference shareholders have the promise of annual dividends and stand ahead of ordinary shareholders in the liquidation of the business. What's the attraction of ordinary shares, therefore? The main advantage of ordinary shares is that they have unlimited upside potential. After obligations to its preference shareholders are satisfied, the rest of the profit earned by the company accrues to the benefit of its ordinary shareholders.

The main difference between preference shares and ordinary shares concerns *cash dividends* – what the business pays its owners from its profit. Here are the key points:

- ✔ A business must pay dividends to its preference shareholders because it has a contractual obligation to do so, whereas each year the board of directors must decide how much, if any, cash dividends to distribute to its ordinary shareholders.

- ✔ Preference Shareholders are usually promised a fixed (limited) dividend per year and typically don't have a claim to any profit beyond the stated amount of dividends. (Some companies issue *participating preference shares*, or convertible preference shares which give the preference shareholders a contingent right to more than just their basic amount of dividends, something which gets too technical for this book.)

- ✔ Preference shareholders don't have voting rights – unless they don't receive dividends for one period or more. In other words, preference shareholders usually do not have voting rights in electing the company's board of directors or on other critical issues facing the company. Needless to say, these matters can become complex, and they vary from company to company – no wonder there are so many corporate lawyers! If you need more information we recommend *Investing For Dummies* by Tony Levene.

Here are some other general things to know about ordinary shares:

- ✔ Each share is equal to every other share in its class. This way, ownership rights are standardised, and the main difference between two shareholders is how many shares each owns.

- ✔ The only way a business has to return shareholders' capital (composed of invested capital and retained earnings) is if the majority of shareholders vote to liquidate the business in part or in total. Other than that, the business's managers don't have to worry about losing the shareholders' capital. Of course, shareholders are free to sell their shares at any time, as noted next.

- ✔ A shareholder can sell her shares at any time, without the approval of the other shareholders. However, shareholders of a privately-owned business may have agreed to certain restrictions on this right when they invested in the business. You may also find the stock market takes a dim view if a shareholder who also works in the business suddenly dumps a whole lot of shares, without some compelling reason. You can find details of directors' dealings in their own shares at the Investigate Web site (go to www.investegate.co.uk and click on 'Transaction in Own Shares').

Book IV

Managing the Finances

✔ Shareholders can either put themselves in key management positions or delegate the task of selecting top managers and officers to a *board of directors*, which is a small group of persons selected by the shareholders to set the business's policies and represent shareholders' interests. If you put up more than half the money in a business, you can put yourself on the board and elect yourself president of the business. The shareholders who own 50% plus one share constitute the controlling group that decides who goes on the board of directors.

If you want to sell your shares, how much can you get for them? Shares in privately-owned businesses aren't publicly traded, so how can you determine the value of your shares in such a business? To be frank, you can't really. Until you actually sell your shares for a certain price per share you simply don't know their market value for sure. On the other hand, you can use certain benchmarks, or valuation methods to estimate market value. For example, you could look to the *book value per share*, which is based on values reported on the business's latest balance sheet:

Total shareholders' equity ÷ total number of shares = book value per share

Book values are historical – based on the past transactions of the business – whereas market pricing looks to how the business is likely to do in the future. The past is important, but the future prospects of the business are more important in setting a value on the business. Market value depends on forecast profit performance (future earnings), which in many cases is much more important than book value per share. One way of estimating the value of your shares in a private business company is the *earnings multiple* method, in which you calculate the theoretical value of a share by using a certain multiple of the business's earnings (net income) per share

For example, suppose a privately-owned business company earned £3.20 net income per share last year. You calculate the book value per share at the end of the year, which, let's assume is £20. You may be able to sell your shares at ten times earnings per share, or £32 per share, which is considerably more than the book value per share. If someone paid £32 per share for the shares and the business earned £3.20, again per share, next year, the new shareholder might be satisfied to earn 10% on her £32 investment – calculated by dividing the £3.20 earnings per share by the £32 cost of the share. (Not all of the £3.20 may be paid out as a cash dividend, so part of the 10% earnings on the investment consists of the increase in retained earnings of the business.)

Keep in mind that the £32 market value is only an estimate and just a theoretical price. However, you don't know the market price until you sell the shares. As potential investors in the business, we may be willing to offer you £35 or £40 per share – or we may offer less than the book value per share.

EXAMPLE

Where profit goes in a company

Suppose that your business earned £1.32 million in net income for the year just ended and has issued a total of 400,000 shares of capital stock. Divide net income by the number of shares, and you come up with an earnings per share of £3.30.

The cash flow statement reports that the business paid £400,000 total cash dividends during the year, or £1 per share. (Cash dividends are usually paid half-yearly or sometimes quarterly, so the business most likely paid £0.25 dividends per share each of the four quarters.) The rest of the net income – £920,000 – remains in the retained earnings account. (*Remember:* Net income is first entered as an increase in the retained earnings account, and distributions are taken out of this account.) The retained earnings account thus increased by £2.30 per share (the difference between the net income, or earnings per share, and the dividends per share).

Although shareholders don't have the cash to show for it, their investment is better off by £2.30 per share – which shows up in the balance sheet as an increase in the retained earnings account in owners' equity. They can just hope that the business will use the cash flow provided from profit this year to make more profit in the future, which should lead to higher cash dividends.

If the business is a publicly-owned company whose shares are actively traded, its shareholders look to the change in the *market price* of the stock shares during the year. Did the market value go up or down during the year? You may think that the market value should increase £2.30 per share, because the business earned this much per share that it kept in the business and did not distribute to its shareholders. Your thinking is quite logical: Profit is an increase in the net assets of a business (assets less liabilities). The business is £2.30 per share richer at the end of the year than it was at the start of the year, due to profit earned and retained.

Yet it's entirely possible that the market price of the stock shares actually *decreased* during the year. Market prices are governed by psychological, political, and economic factors that go beyond the information in the financial reports of a business. Financial statements are one – but only one – of the information sources that stock investors use in making their buy-and-sell decisions.

Shareholders and managers

Shareholders (including managers who own shares in the business) are concerned, first and foremost, with the profit performance of their business. The dividends they receive, and the value of their shares, depend on profit. Managers, too, are concerned with profit – their jobs depend on living up to the business's profit goals. But even though shareholders and managers strive toward the common goal of making the business profitable, they have an inherent conflict of interest that revolves around money and power:

✔ The more money that managers make in wages and benefits, the less shareholders see in the bottom-line net income. Shareholders obviously want the best managers for the job, but they don't want to pay any more than they have to. In many companies, top-level managers, for all practical purposes, set their own salaries and compensation packages.

The best solution is often to have outside directors (with no management position in the business) set the compensation of the top-level managers instead.

✔ Who should control the business: the managers, who were hired for their competence and are intimately familiar with the business, or the shareholders, who probably have no experience relevant to running this particular business but who put up the money that the business is running on? In ideal situations, the two sides respect each other's importance to the business and use this tension constructively. Of course, the real world is far from ideal, and you have situations in which managers are controlling the board of directors rather than the other way around. But this book isn't the proper place to get into all that.

In particular, watch out for actions that cause a *dilution effect* on the value of your shares – that is, cause each share to drop in value. Now, the dilution effect may be the result of a good business decision, so even though your share of the business has decreased in the short term, the long-term profit performance of the business (and, therefore, your investment) may benefit. But you need to watch these decisions closely. The following situations cause a dilution effect:

✔ A business issues additional shares at the going market value, but doesn't really need the additional capital – the business is in no better profit-making position than it was before issuing the new shares. For example, a business may issue new shares in order to let a newly hired chief executive officer buy them. The immediate effect may be a dilution in the market value per share. Over the long term, however, the new CEO may turn the business around and lead it to higher levels of profit performance that increase the share's value.

✔ A business issues new shares at a discount below its shares' current value. For example, the business may issue a new batch of shares at a price lower than the current market value to employees who take advantage of an employee share-purchase plan. Selling shares at a discount, by itself, has a dilution effect on the market value of the shares. But in the grand scheme of things the share-purchase plan may motivate its employees to achieve higher productivity levels, which leads to superior profit performance of the business.

Partnerships and Limited Partnerships

Suppose you're starting a new business with one or more other owners, but you do not want it to be a company. You can choose to form a *partnership* or a *limited partnership*, which are the main alternatives to the corporate form of a business. ***Note:*** A partnership is sometimes also called a *firm*. (You don't see this term used to refer to a company nearly as often as you do to a partnership.) The term firm connotes an association of a group of individuals working together in a business or professional practice, as in a *firm of lawyers*.

Compared with the relatively rigid structure of companies, partnership and limited partnership ownership structures allow the division of management authority, profit sharing, and ownership rights among the owners to be very flexible. Here are the key features of these two ownership structures:

- **Partnerships** avoid the double-taxation feature that companies are subject to (see 'Choosing the Right Legal Structure for Tax Purposes', later in this chapter, for details). Partnerships also differ from companies with respect to liability. A partnership's owners fall into two categories:

- **General partners** are subject to *unlimited liability*. If a business can't pay its debts, its creditors can reach into general partners' personal assets. General partners have the authority and responsibility to manage the business. They are roughly equivalent to the managing director and other high-level managers of a business company. The general partners usually divide authority and responsibility among themselves, and often they elect one member of their group as the senior general partner or elect a small executive committee to make major decisions.

- **Limited partners** escape the unlimited liability that the general partners have hanging around their necks. You can reduce the more painful consequences of entering a partnership by having your involvement registered as a limited partnership. A limited partnership is very different from a 'general' partnership. It is a legal animal that, in certain circumstances, combines the best attributes of a partnership and a corporation.

A limited partnership works like this. There must be one or more general partners with the same basic rights and responsibilities (including unlimited liability) as in any general partnership, and one or more limited partners who are usually passive investors. The big difference between a general partner and a limited partner is that the limited partner isn't personally liable for debts of the partnership. The most a limited partner can lose is the amount that she paid or agreed to pay into the partnership as a capital contribution; or received from the partnership after it became insolvent.

To keep this limited liability, a limited partner may not participate in the management of the business, with very few exceptions. A limited partner who does get actively involved in the management of the business risks losing immunity from personal liability and having the same legal exposure as a general partner.

Caution: We would advise you as a member of a partnership, either as a general or limited partner, to get up to speed on the special accounting practices of the business regarding how salaries and other payments for services to owners and partners are accounted for in the entity's financial statements and how they are treated in determining annual taxable income. Don't take anything for granted; investigate first. Call a tax professional if you have questions or need advice in this area.

Going into partnership

Partnerships are effectively collections of sole traders or proprietors. It is a common structure used by people who started out on their own, but want to expand. There are very few restrictions to setting up in business with another person (or persons) in partnership, and several definite advantages. By pooling resources you may have more capital; you will be bringing, hopefully, several sets of skills to the business; and if you are ill the business can still carry on.

The legal regulations governing partnerships in essence assume that competent businesspeople should know what they are doing. The law merely provides a framework of agreement which applies 'in the absence of agreement to the contrary'. It follows from this that many partnerships are entered into without legal formalities and sometimes without the parties themselves being aware that they have entered a partnership! Just giving the impression that you are partners may be enough to create an 'implied partnership'.

In the absence of an agreement to the contrary these rules apply to partnerships:

- ✔ All partners contribute capital equally.
- ✔ All partners share profits and losses equally.
- ✔ No partner shall have interest paid on her capital.
- ✔ No partner shall be paid a salary.
- ✔ All partners have an equal say in the management of the business.

It is unlikely that all these provisions will suit you so you would be well advised to get a partnership agreement drawn up in writing before trading.

Partnerships have three serious financial drawbacks that merit particular attention.

1. If your partner makes a business mistake, perhaps by signing a disastrous contract without your knowledge or consent, every member of the partnership must shoulder the consequences. Under these circumstances your personal assets could be taken to pay the creditors even though the mistake was no fault of your own.

2. If your partner goes bankrupt in her personal capacity, for whatever reason, her creditors can seize their share of the partnership. As a private individual you are not liable for your partner's private debts, but having to buy her out of the partnership at short notice could put you and the business in financial jeopardy.

3. If your partnership breaks up for any reason, those continuing with it will want to recover control of the business; those who remain shareholders will want to buy back shares; the leaver wants a realistic price. The agreement you have on setting up the business should specify the procedures, and how to value the leaver's share, otherwise resolving the situation will be costly. The traditional route to value the leaver's share is to ask an independent accountant. This is rarely cost-effective. The valuation costs money and worst of all it is not definite and consequently there is room for argument. Another way is to establish a formula, an agreed eight times the last audited pre-tax profits, for example. This approach is simple but difficult to get right. A fast-growing business is undervalued by a formula using historic data unless the multiple is high; a high multiple may overvalue 'hope' or goodwill thus unreasonably profiting the leaver. Under a third option, one partner offers to buy out the others at a price she specifies. If they do not accept her offer, the continuing partners must buy the leaver out at that price. In theory, such a price should be acceptable to all.

Even death may not release you from partnership obligations and in some circumstances your estate can remain liable. Unless you take public leave of your partnership by notifying your business contacts, and legally bringing your partnership to an end, you will remain liable indefinitely.

The partnership agreement specifies how to divide profit among the owners. Whereas owners of a company receive a portion of profit that's directly proportional to the number of shares they own and, therefore, how much they invested, a partnership does not have to divide profit according to how much each owner invested. Invested capital is only one of three factors that generally play into profit allocation in partnerships:

✔ **Treasure:** Owners may be rewarded according to how much of the 'treasure' – invested capital – they contributed; they get back a certain percentage (return) on their investment. So if Joe invested twice as much as Jane did, his cut of the profit may be set at twice as much as Jane's.

Book IV

Managing the Finances

✔ **Time:** Owners who invest more time in the business may receive more of the profit. In some businesses, a partner may not contribute much more than capital and her name, whereas other partners work long hours. This way of allocating profit works like a salary.

✔ **Talent:** Regardless of capital or time, some partners bring more to the business than others. Whatever it is that they do for the business, they contribute much more to the business's success than their capital or time suggests.

Note: A partnership needs to maintain a separate capital (or *ownership*) account for each partner. The total profit of the entity is allocated into these capital accounts, as spelled out in the partnership agreement. The agreement also specifies how much money each partner can withdraw from her capital account – for example, partners may be limited to withdrawing no more than 80% of their anticipated share of profit for the coming year, or they may be allowed to withdraw only a certain amount until they've built up their capital accounts.

Sole Proprietorships

A *sole proprietorship* or, as it is frequently known, *sole tradership*, is, basically the business arm of an individual who has decided *not* to carry on her business activity as a separate legal entity (as a partnership, or limited liability company) – it's the default option. An individual may do house repair work for homeowners on a part-time basis, or be a full-time barber who operates on her own. Both are sole proprietorships. Anytime you regularly provide services for a fee, or sell things at a flea market, or engage in any business activity whose primary purpose is to make profit, you are a sole proprietor.

If you carry on business activity to make profit or income, the Inland Revenue requires that you file a separate schedule summarising your profit or loss from trading with your annual individual income tax return. If your business activities are substantial the Inland Revenue may ask for both a profit and loss account and a balance sheet, but for most small businesses a few lines of figures showing income, main cost categories, and the resultant profit will be sufficient.

As the sole owner (proprietor), you have *unlimited liability*, meaning that if your business can't pay all its liabilities, the creditors to whom your business owes money can come after your personal assets. Many part-time entrepreneurs may not know this or may put it out of their minds, but this is a big risk to take.

Spreading the joy of profit to your employees and customers: Business co-operatives

A *co-operative* pays its customers *patronage dividends* based on its profit for the year – each customer receives a year-end refund based on her purchases from the business over the year. Imagine that.

A co-operative is also an enterprise owned and controlled by the people working in it. Once in danger of becoming extinct, the workers' cooperative is enjoying something of a comeback with thousands being set up each year around Europe.

If this is to be your chosen legal form you can pay from £90 a year to register with the Financial

Services Authority (www.fsa.gov.uk). You must have at least seven members at the outset, though they do not all have to be full-time workers at first. Like a limited company, a registered co-operative has limited liability (see 'Limited Liability Companies') for its members; it must notify the FSA of any changes and file annual accounts, but there is no additional charge for this. Not all co-operatives bother to register as it is not mandatory, in which case they are treated in law as a partnership with unlimited liability.

One other piece of advice for sole proprietors: Although you don't have to separate invested capital from retained earnings like companies do, you should still keep these two separate accounts for owners' equity – not only for the purpose of tracking the business but for the benefit of any future buyers of the business as well.

Limited Companies and Public Limited Companies

As the name suggests, in this form of business your liability is limited to the amount you contribute by way of share capital.

Limited companies

A *limited company* has a legal identity of its own, separate from the people who own or run it. This means that, in the event of failure, creditors' claims are restricted to the assets of the company. The shareholders of the business are not liable as individuals for the business debts beyond the paid-up value of their shares. This applies even if the shareholders are working directors, unless of course the company has been trading fraudulently. In practice, the

Book IV

Managing the Finances

ability to limit liability is restricted these days as most lenders, including the banks, often insist on personal guarantees from the directors. Other advantages include the freedom to raise capital by selling shares.

Disadvantages include the legal requirement for the company's accounts to be audited and filed for public inspection.

A limited company can be formed by two shareholders, one of whom must be a director. A company secretary must also be appointed, who can be a shareholder, director, or an outside person such as an accountant or lawyer.

The company can be bought 'off the shelf' from a registration agent, then adapted to suit your own purposes. This will involve changing the name, shareholders, and articles of association and takes a couple of weeks to arrange. Alternatively you can form your own company. But before you can form a company you need to decide which of the two main structures of company to use.

A limited company (Ltd) is the most common type. This is a private company limited by shares. A limited company can be started with, say, an authorised share capital of £1,000. This is then divided into $1,000 \times £1$ shares. You can then issue as few or as many of the shares as you want. As long as the shares you have issued are paid for in full, if the company liquidates, the shareholders have no further liabilities. If the shares have not been paid for, the shareholders are liable for the value, i.e. if they have 100 £1 shares, they only are liable for £100.

Plcs

A *plc company* is a public limited company and may be listed on the Stock Exchange. Before a plc can start to trade it must have at least £50,000 of shares issued and at least 25% of the value must have been paid for. A plc company has a better status due to its larger capital.

Choosing the Right Legal Structure for Tax Purposes

In deciding which type of ownership structure is best for securing capital and managing their business, owners should also consider the tax factor. See Book VI Chapter 2 for more on tax issues relating to the status of your business.

Chapter 4

Cost Conundrums

*M*easuring costs is the second most important thing accountants do, right after measuring profit. But really, can measuring a cost be very complicated? You just take numbers off a purchase invoice and call it a day, right? Not if your business manufactures the products you sell – that's for sure! Businesses must carefully record all their costs correctly so that profit can be determined each period, and so that managers have the information they need to make decisions and to control profit performance.

Previewing What's Coming Down the Road

One main function of accounting for a manufacturing business is measuring *product cost*. Examples are the cost of a new car just rolling off the assembly line or the cost of this book, *Understanding Business Accounting For Dummies*. Most production (manufacturing) processes are fairly complex, so measuring product cost is also fairly complex in most cases. Every step in the production process has to be tracked very carefully from start to finish. One major problem is that many manufacturing costs cannot be directly matched with particular products; these are called *indirect costs*. To arrive at the *full cost* of each separate product manufactured, accountants devise methods for allocating the indirect production costs to specific products. Different accountants use different allocation methods. In other respects, as well, product cost accounting is characterised by a diversity of methods. Generally accepted accounting principles provide very little guidance for measuring product cost. Manufacturing businesses have a lot of leeway in how their product costs are determined; even businesses in the same industry use different product cost accounting methods.

In addition to measuring product costs of manufacturers, accountants in all businesses determine many other costs: the costs of the departments and other organisational units of the business; the cost of pensions for the company's employees; the cost of marketing initiatives and advertising campaigns; and, on occasion the cost of restructuring the business or the cost of a major recall of products sold by the business. A common refrain among accountants is 'different costs for different purposes'. True enough, but at its core cost accounting serves two broad purposes – measuring profit and providing relevant information to managers.

This chapter covers cost concepts and cost measurement methods that are used by both retail and manufacturing businesses, along with additional stuff for manufacturers to worry about. We also discuss how having a good handle on cost issues can help you recognise when a business is monkeying around with product cost to deliberately manipulate its profit figure. Service businesses – which sell a service such as transportation or entertainment – have a break here. They do not encounter the cost-accounting problems of manufacturers, but they have plenty of cost allocation issues to deal with in assessing the profitability of each of their separate sales revenue sources.

What Makes Cost So Important?

Without good cost information, a business operates in the dark. Cost data is needed for different purposes in business, including the following:

- ✓ **Setting sales prices:** The common method for setting sales prices (known as *cost-plus* or *mark-up on cost*) starts with cost and then adds a certain percentage.

- ✓ **Measuring gross margin:** Investors and managers judge business performance by the bottom-line profit figure. This profit figure depends on the *gross margin* figure you get when you subtract your cost of goods sold expense from your sales revenue. Gross margin (also called *gross profit*) is the first profit line in the profit and loss account (see Figure 1-1 of Book IV Chapter 1 and Figure 4-1 in this chapter for examples).

- ✓ **Valuing assets:** The balance sheet reports cost values for many assets, and these values are, of course, included in the overall financial position of your business.

- ✓ **Making optimal choices:** You often must choose one alternative over others in making business decisions. The best alternative depends heavily on cost factors, and you have to be careful to distinguish *relevant* costs from *irrelevant* costs, as described in the section 'Relevant vs. irrelevant costs', later in this chapter.

In most situations, the book value of a fixed asset is an *irrelevant* cost. Say the book value is £35,000 for a machine used in the manufacturing operations of the business. This is the amount of original cost that has not yet been charged to depreciation expense since it was acquired, and it may seem quite relevant. However, in deciding between keeping the old machine or replacing it with a newer, more efficient machine, the *disposable value* of the old machine is the relevant amount, not the undepreciated cost balance of the asset. Suppose the old machine has only a £20,000 salvage value at this time; this is the relevant cost for the alternative of keeping it for use in the future – not the £35,000 that hasn't been depreciated yet. In order to keep using it, the business forgoes the £20,000 it could get by selling the asset, and this £20,000 is the relevant cost in this decision situation. Making decisions involves looking at the future cash flows of each alternative – not looking back at historical-based cost values.

Sharpening Your Sensitivity to Cost

The following sections explain important distinctions between costs that managers should understand in making decisions and exercising control. Also, these cost distinctions help managers better appreciate the cost figures that accountants attach to products that are manufactured or purchased by the business. In a later section we focus on the special accounting methods and problems of computing product costs of *manufacturers*. Retailers purchase products in a condition ready for sale to their customers – although the products have to be removed from shipping containers and a retailer does a little work making the products presentable for sale and putting the products on display.

Manufacturers don't have it so easy; their product costs have to be 'manufactured' in the sense that the accountants have to compile production costs and compute the cost per unit for every product manufactured. We cannot exaggerate the importance of correct product costs (for businesses that sell products, of course). The total cost of goods (products) sold is the first, and usually the largest, expense deducted from sales revenue in measuring profit. The bottom-line profit amount reported in the profit and loss account of a business for the period depends heavily on whether its product costs have been measured properly. Also, keep in mind that product cost is the value for the stock asset reported in the balance sheet of a business.

Book IV

Managing the Finances

Direct vs. indirect costs

✔ **Direct costs:** Can be clearly attributed to one product or product line, or one source of sales revenue, or one organisational unit of the business, or one specific operation in a process. An example of a direct cost in the book publishing industry is the cost of the paper that a book is printed on; this cost can be squarely attached to one particular phase of the book production process.

✔ **Indirect costs:** Are far removed from and cannot be obviously attributed to specific products, organisational units, or activities. A book publisher's phone bill is a cost of doing business but can't be tied down to just one step in the book's editorial and production process. The salary of the purchasing officer who selects the paper for all the books is another example of a cost that is indirect to the production of particular books.

Indirect costs are allocated according to some methods to different products, sources of sales revenue, organisational units, and so on. Most allocation methods are far from perfect, and in the last analysis end up being rather arbitrary. Business managers should always keep an eye on the allocation methods used for indirect costs, and take the cost figures produced by these methods with a grain of salt.

The cost of filling the fuel tank in driving your car from London to Bristol and back is a direct cost of making the trip. The annual road tax that the government charges you is an indirect cost of the trip, although it is a direct cost of having the car available during the year.

Fixed vs. variable costs

✔ **Fixed costs** remain the same over a relatively broad range of sales volume or production output. For example, the cost of renting office space doesn't change regardless of how much a business's sales volume increases or decreases. Fixed costs are like a dead weight on the business. Its total fixed costs is the hurdle that the business must overcome by selling enough units at high enough profit margins per unit in order to avoid a loss and move into the profit zone. (Book IV Chapter 1 explains the break-even point, which is the level of sales needed to cover fixed costs for the period.)

✔ **Variable costs** increase and decrease in proportion to changes in sales or production level. If you increase the number of books that your business produces, the cost of the paper and ink also goes up.

Relevant vs. irrelevant costs

✔ **Relevant costs:** Costs that should be considered when deciding on a future course of action. Relevant costs are *future* costs – costs that you would incur, or bring upon yourself, depending on which course of action you take. For example, say that you want to increase the number of books that your business produces next year in order to increase your sales revenue, but the cost of paper has just shot up. Should you take the cost of paper into consideration? Absolutely: That cost will affect your bottom-line profit and may negate any increases in sales volume that you experience (unless you increase the sales price). The cost of paper is a relevant cost.

✔ **Irrelevant (or sunk) costs:** Costs that should be disregarded when deciding on a future course of action: If brought into the analysis, these costs could cause you to make the wrong decision. An irrelevant cost is a vestige of the past; that money is gone, so get over it. For example, suppose that your supervisor tells you to expect a load of new recruits next week. All your staff members use computers now, but you have loads of typewriters gathering dust in the cupboard. Should you consider the cost paid for those typewriters in your decision to buy computers for all the new staff? Absolutely not: That cost should have been written off and is no match for the cost you'd pay in productivity (and morale) for new employees who are forced to use typewriters.

Generally speaking, fixed costs are irrelevant when deciding on a future course of action, assuming that they're truly fixed and can't be increased or decreased over the short term. Most variable costs are relevant because they depend on which alternative is decided on.

Fixed costs are usually irrelevant in decision-making because these costs will be the same no matter which course of action you decide upon. Looking behind these costs, you usually find that the costs provide *capacity* of one sort or another – so much building space, so many machine-hours available for use, so many hours of labour that will be worked, and so on. Managers have to figure out the best overall way to utilise these capacities.

Separating between actual, budgeted, and standard costs

✔ **Actual costs:** Historical costs, based on actual transactions and operations for the period just ended, or going back to earlier periods. Financial statement accounting is based on a business's actual transactions and operations; the basic approach to determining annual profit is to record the financial effects of actual transactions and allocate historical costs to the periods benefited by the costs.

✔ **Budgeted costs:** Future costs, for transactions and operations expected to take place over the coming period, based on forecasts and established goals. Note that fixed costs are budgeted differently than variable costs – for example, if sales volume is forecast to increase by 10%, variable costs will definitely increase accordingly, but fixed costs may or may not need to be increased to accommodate the volume increase (see 'Fixed vs. variable costs', earlier in this chapter). Book IV Chapter 2 explains the budgeting process and budgeted financial statements.

Book IV

Managing the Finances

✔ **Standard costs:** Costs, primarily in manufacturing, that are carefully engineered based on detailed analysis of operations and forecast costs for each component or step in an operation. Developing standard costs for variable production costs is relatively straightforward because many of these are direct costs, whereas most fixed costs are indirect, and standard costs for fixed costs are necessarily based on more arbitrary methods (see 'Direct vs. indirect costs' earlier in this chapter). *Note:* Some variable costs are indirect and have to be allocated to specific products in order to come up with a full (total) standard cost of the product.

Product vs. period costs

✔ **Product costs:** Costs attached to particular products. The cost is recorded in the stock asset account until the product is sold, at which time the cost goes into the cost of goods sold expense account. (See Book II Chapter 2 and Book III Chapter 1 for more about these accounts; also, see Book IV Chapter 5 for alternative methods for selecting which product costs are first charged to the cost of goods sold expense.) One key point to keep in mind is that product cost is deferred and not recorded to expense until the product is sold.

For example, the cost of a new Ford Focus sitting on a car dealer's showroom floor is a product cost. The dealer keeps the cost in the stock asset account until you buy the car, at which point the dealer charges the cost to the cost of goods sold expense.

✔ **Period costs:** Costs that are *not* attached to particular products. These costs do not spend time in the 'waiting room' of stock. Period costs are recorded as expenses immediately; unlike product costs, period costs don't pass through the stock account first. Advertising costs, for example, are accounted for as period costs and recorded immediately in an expense account. Also, research and development costs are treated as a period cost.

Separating between product costs and period costs is particularly important for manufacturing businesses, as you find out in the following section.

Putting Together the Pieces of Product Cost

Businesses that manufacture products have several additional cost problems to deal with. We use the term *manufacture* in the broadest sense: Car makers assemble cars, beer companies brew beer, oil companies refine oil, ICI makes products through chemical synthesis, and so on. *Retailers*, on the other hand, buy products in a condition ready for resale to the end consumer. For example, Levi Strauss manufactures clothing, and Selfridges is a retailer that buys from Levi Strauss and sells the clothes to the public.

The following sections describe costs that are unique to manufacturers and address the issue of determining the cost of products that are manufactured.

Minding manufacturing costs

Manufacturing costs consist of four basic types:

- ✔ **Raw materials:** What a manufacturer buys from other companies to use in the production of its own products. For example, The Ford Motor Company buys tyres from Goodyear (and other tyre manufacturers) that then become part of Ford's cars.

- ✔ **Direct labour:** The employees who work on the production line.

- ✔ **Variable overhead:** Indirect production costs that increase or decrease as the quantity produced increases or decreases. An example is the cost of electricity that runs the production equipment: You pay for the electricity for the whole plant, not machine by machine, so you can't attach this cost to one particular part of the process. But if you increase or decrease the use of those machines, the electricity cost increases or decreases accordingly.

- ✔ **Fixed overhead:** Indirect production costs that do *not* increase or decrease as the quantity produced increases or decreases. These fixed costs remain the same over a fairly broad range of production output levels (see 'Fixed vs. variable costs' earlier in this chapter). Three significant fixed manufacturing costs are:

  - • Salaries for certain production employees who don't work directly on the production line, such as a department managers, safety inspectors, security guards, accountants, and shipping and receiving workers.

  - • Depreciation of production buildings, equipment, and other manufacturing fixed assets.

  - • Occupancy costs, such as building insurance, property rental and heating and lighting charges.

Book IV

Managing the Finances

Figure 4-1 shows a sample management profit and loss account for a manufacturer, including supplementary information about its manufacturing costs. Notice that the cost of goods sold expense depends directly on the product cost from the manufacturing cost summary that appears below the management profit and loss account. A business may manufacture 100 or 1,000 different products, or even more. To keep the example easy to follow, Figure 4-1 presents a scenario for a one-product manufacturer. The example is realistic yet avoids the clutter of too much detail. The multi-product manufacturer has some additional accounting problems, but these are too technical for a book like this. The fundamental accounting problems and methods of all manufactures are illustrated in the example.

TIP

The information in the manufacturing cost summary schedule below the profit and loss account (see Figure 4-1) is highly confidential and for management eyes only. Competitors would love to know this information. A company may enjoy a significant cost advantage over its competitors and definitely would not want its cost data to get into the hands of its competitors.

Management Profit and Loss Account for Year

Sales Volume		1,100 Units

	Per Unit	Totals
Sales Revenue	£140	£154,000
Cost of Goods Sold Expense	(£76)	(£83,600)
Gross Margin	£64	£70,400
Variable Operating Expenses	(£30)	(£33,000)
Contribution Margin	£34	£37,400
Fixed Operating Expenses	(£19.50)	(£21,450)
Earnings Before Interest and Tax (EBIT)	£14.50	£15,950
Interest Expense		(£2,750)
Earnings Before Tax		£13,200
Corporation Tax Expense		(£4,488)
Net Income		£8,712

Manufacturing Cost Summary for Year

Annual Production Capacity		1,500 Units
Actual Output		1,200 Units

Production Cost Components	Per Unit	Totals
Raw Materials	£21.50	£25,800
Direct Labour	£12.50	£15,000
Variable Overhead	£7	£8,400
Total Variable Manufacturing Costs	£41	£49,200
Fixed Overhead	£35	£42,000
Total Manufacturing Costs	£76	£91,200
To Units Stock Increase		(£7,600)
To Units Sold		£83,600

Figure 4-1:
Example for determining product cost of a manufacturer.

Unlike a retailer, a manufacturer does not *purchase* products but begins by buying the raw materials needed in the production process. Then the manufacturer pays workers to assemble, pack, store, market, and sell the products. All this is generally done in a workshop or factory that has many indirect overhead costs. All these different production costs have to be funnelled into the product cost so that the product cost can be entered in the stock account, and then to cost of goods sold expense when products are sold.

Allocating costs properly: Not easy!

Two vexing issues rear their ugly heads in determining product cost for a manufacturer:

- ✔ **Drawing a defining line between manufacturing costs and non-manufacturing operating costs:** The key difference here is that manufacturing costs are categorised as product costs, whereas non-manufacturing operating costs are categorised as period costs (refer to 'Product vs. period costs' earlier in this chapter). In calculating product cost, you factor in only manufacturing costs and not other costs. Period costs are recorded right away as an expense – either in variable operating expenses or fixed operating expenses for the example shown in Figure 4-1.

  Wages paid to production line workers are a clear-cut example of a manufacturing cost. Salaries paid to salespeople are a marketing cost and are not part of product cost; marketing costs are treated as period costs, which means these costs are recorded immediately to the expenses of the period. Depreciation on production equipment is a manufacturing cost, but depreciation on the warehouse in which products are stored after being manufactured is a period cost. Moving the raw materials and works-in-progress through the production process is a manufacturing cost, but transporting the finished products from the warehouse to customers is a period cost. In short, product cost stops at the end of the production line – but every cost up to that point should be included as a manufacturing cost. The accumulation of direct and variable production costs starts at the beginning of the manufacturing process and stops at the end of the production line. All fixed and indirect manufacturing costs during the year are allocated to the actual production output during the year.

  If you mis-classify some manufacturing costs as operating costs, your product cost calculation will be too low (refer to 'Calculating product cost' later in this chapter).

- ✔ **Whether to allocate indirect costs among different products, or organisational units, or assets:** Indirect *manufacturing* costs must be allocated among the products produced during the period. The full product cost includes both direct and indirect manufacturing costs. Coming up with a completely satisfactory allocation method is difficult and ends up being somewhat arbitrary – but must be done to determine product cost. For non-manufacturing operating costs, the basic test of whether to allocate indirect costs is whether allocation helps managers make better decisions and exercise better control. Maybe, maybe not. In any case, managers should understand how manufacturing indirect costs are allocated to products and how indirect non-manufacturing costs are allocated, keeping in mind that every allocation method is arbitrary and that a different allocation method may be just as convincing.

Calculating product cost

The basic equation for calculating product cost is as follows (using the example of the manufacturer from Figure 4-1):

£91,200 total manufacturing costs ÷ 1,200 units production output = £76 product cost per unit

Looks pretty straightforward, doesn't it? Well, the equation itself may be simple, but the accuracy of the results depends directly on the accuracy of your manufacturing cost numbers. And because manufacturing processes can be fairly complex, with many steps and operations, your accounting systems must be very complex and detailed to keep accurate track of all the manufacturing costs.

As we explain earlier, when introducing the example, this business manufactures just one product. Also, its product cost per unit is determined for the entire year. In actual practice, manufacturers calculate their product costs monthly or quarterly. The computation process is the same, but the frequency of doing the computation varies from business to business.

In this example the business manufactured 1,200 units and sold 1,100 units during the year. As just computed, its product cost per unit is £76. The 1,100 total units sold during the year is multiplied by the £76 product cost to compute the £83,600 cost of goods sold expense, which is deducted against the company's revenue from selling 1,100 units during the year. The company's total manufacturing costs for the year were £91,200, which is £7,600 more than the cost of goods sold expense. This remainder of the total annual manufacturing costs is recorded as an increase in the company's stock asset account, to recognise the 1,000 units increase of units awaiting sale in the future. In Figure 4-1, note that the £76 product cost per unit is applied both to the 1,100 units sold and to the 1,000 units added to stock.

Note: As just mentioned, most manufacturers determine their product costs monthly or quarterly rather than once a year (as in the example). Product costs likely will vary each successive period the costs are determined.

Because the product costs vary from period to period the business must choose which cost of goods sold and stock cost method to use – unless product cost remains absolutely flat and constant period to period, in which case the different methods would yield the same results. Book IV Chapter 5 explains the alternative accounting methods for determining cost of goods sold expense and stock cost value.

Fixed manufacturing costs and production capacity

Product cost consists of two very distinct components: *variable manufacturing costs* and *fixed manufacturing costs*. In Figure 4-1 note that the company's variable manufacturing costs are £41 per unit, and that its fixed manufacturing costs are £35 per unit. Now, what if the business had manufactured just one more unit? Its total variable manufacturing costs would have been £41 higher; these costs are driven by the actual number of units produced, so even one more unit would have caused the variable costs to increase. But, the company's total fixed costs would have been the same if it had produced one more unit, or 10,000 more units for that matter. Variable manufacturing costs are bought on a per unit basis, as it were, whereas fixed manufacturing costs are bought in bulk for the whole period.

Fixed manufacturing costs are needed to provide *production capacity* – the people and physical resources needed to manufacture products – for the period. Once the business has the production plant and people in place for the year, its fixed manufacturing costs cannot be easily scaled down. The business is stuck with these costs over the short run. It has to make the best use it can from its production capacity.

Production capacity is a critical concept for business managers to grasp. You need to plan your production capacity well ahead of time because you need plenty of lead time to assemble the right people, equipment, land, and buildings. When you have the necessary production capacity in place, you want to make sure that you're making optimal use of that capacity. The fixed costs of production capacity remain the same even as production output increases or decreases, so you may as well make optimal use of the capacity provided by those fixed costs.

Book IV

Managing the Finances

The fixed cost component of product cost is called the *burden rate*. In our manufacturing example the burden rate is computed as follows (see Figure 4-1 for data):

£42,000 total fixed manufacturing costs for period ÷ 1,200 units production output for period = £35 burden rate

Note that the burden rate depends on the number divided into total fixed manufacturing costs for the period; that is, the production output for the period. Now, here's a very important twist on our example: Suppose the company had manufactured only 1,100 units during the period – equal exactly to the quantity sold during the year. Its variable manufacturing cost per unit would have been the same, or £41 per unit. But, its burden rate would have been £38.18 per unit (computed by dividing the £42,000 total fixed manufacturing costs by the 1,100 units production output). Each unit sold, therefore, would have cost £3.18 more simply because the company produced fewer units (£38.18 burden rate at the 1,100 output level compared with the £35 burden rate at the 1,200 output level).

In this alternative scenario (in which only 1,100 units are produced), the company's product cost would have been £79.18 (£41 variable costs plus the £38.18 burden rate). The company's cost of goods sold, therefore, would have been £3,500higher for the year (£3.18 higher product cost × 1,100 units sold). This rather significant increase in its cost of goods sold expense is caused by the company producing fewer units, although it did produce all the units that it needed for sales during the year. The same total amount of fixed manufacturing costs would be spread over fewer units of production output.

Shifting the focus back to the example shown in Figure 4-1, the company's cost of goods sold benefited from the fact that it produced 1,000 more units than it sold during the year – these 1,000 units absorbed £3,500 of its total fixed manufacturing costs for the year, and until the units are sold this £3,500 stays in the stock asset account. It's entirely possible that the higher production level was justified – to have more stock on hand for sales growth next year. But, production output can get out of hand – see the following section, 'Excessive production output for puffing up profit'.

Managers (and investors as well) should understand the stock increase effect caused by manufacturing more units than are sold during the year. In the example shown in Figure 4-1, cost of goods sold expense escaped from £3,500 of fixed manufacturing costs because the company produced 1,000 more units than it sold during the year, thus pushing down the burden rate. The company's cost of goods sold expense would have been £3,500 higher if it had produced just the number of units it sold during the year. The lower output level would have increased cost of goods sold expense, and would have caused a £3,500 drop in gross margin and earnings before income tax. Indeed, earnings before income tax would have been 27% lower (£3,500 ÷ £13,200 = 27% decrease).

For the example illustrated in Figure 4-1, the business's production capacity for the year is 1,500 units. However, this business produced only 1,200 units during the year, which is 3,000 units fewer than it could have produced. In other words, it operated at 80% percent of production capacity, which is 20% *idle capacity* (which isn't unusual):

1,200 units output ÷ 1,500 units capacity = 80% utilisation

TECHNICAL STUFF

The actual costs/actual output method and when not to use it

To determine its product cost, the business in the Figure 4-1 example uses the *actual cost/actual output method,* in which you take your actual costs – which may have been higher or lower than the budgeted costs for the year – and divide by the actual output for the year.

The actual costs/actual output method is appropriate in most situations. However, this method is not appropriate and would have to be modified in two extreme situations:

✔ **Manufacturing costs are grossly excessive or wasteful due to inefficient production operations:** For example, suppose that the business represented in Figure 4-1 had to throw away £1,200 of raw materials during the year. The £1,200 is included in the total raw materials cost, but should be removed from the calculation of the raw material cost per unit. Instead, you treat it as a period cost – meaning that you take it

directly into expense. Then the cost of goods sold expense would be based on £75 per unit instead of £76, which lowers this expense by £1,100 (based on the 1,100 units sold). But you still have to record the £1,200 expense for wasted raw materials, so EBIT would be £100 lower.

✔ **Production output is significantly less than normal capacity utilisation:** Suppose that the Figure 4-1 business produced only 750 units during the year but still sold 1,100 units because it was working off a large stock carryover from the year before. Then its production capacity would be 50% instead of 80%. In a sense, the business wasted half of its production capacity, and you can argue that half of its fixed manufacturing costs should be charged directly to expense on the profit and loss account and not included in the calculation of product cost.

Running at 80% of production capacity, this business's burden rate for the year is £35 per unit (£42,000 total fixed manufacturing costs ÷ 1,200 units output). The burden rate would have been higher if the company had produced, say, only 1,100 units during the year. The burden rate, in other words, is sensitive to the number of units produced. This can lead to all kinds of mischief, as explained next.

Book IV

Managing the Finances

Excessive production output for puffing up profit

Whenever production output is higher than sales volume, be on guard. Excessive production can puff up the profit figure. How? Until a product is sold, the product cost goes in the stock asset account rather than the cost of goods sold expense account, meaning that the product cost is counted as a *positive* number (an asset) rather than a *negative* number (an expense). The burden rate is included in product cost, which means that this cost component goes into stock and is held there until the products are sold later. In short, when you overproduce, more of your fixed manufacturing costs for the period are moved to the stock asset account and less are moved into cost of goods sold expense, which is based on the number of units sold.

You need to judge whether a stock increase is justified. Be aware that an unjustified increase may be evidence of profit manipulation or just good old-fashioned management bungling. Either way, the day of reckoning will come when the products are sold and the cost of stock becomes cost of goods sold expense – at which point the cost subtracts from the bottom line.

Recapping the example shown in Figure 4-1: The business manufactured 1,000 more units than it sold during the year. With variable manufacturing costs at £41 per unit, the business took on £4,100 more in manufacturing costs than it would have if it had produced only the 1,100 units needed for its sales volume. In other words, if the business had produced 1,000 fewer units, its variable manufacturing costs would have been £4,100 less. That's the nature of variable costs. In contrast, if the company had manufactured 1,000 fewer units, its *fixed* manufacturing costs would not have been any less – that's the nature of fixed costs.

Of its £42,000 total fixed manufacturing costs for the year, only £38,500 ended up in the cost of goods sold expense for the year (£35 burden rate × 1,100 units sold). The other £3,500 ended up in the stock asset account (£35 burden rate × 1,000 units stock increase). Let us be very clear here: We're not suggesting any hanky-panky. But the business did help its pre-tax profit to the amount of £3,500 by producing 1,000 more units than it sold. If the business had produced only 1,100 units, equal to its sales volume for the year, then all the fixed manufacturing costs would have gone into cost of goods sold expense. As explained above, the expense would have been £3,500 higher, and EBIT would have been that much lower.

Now suppose that the business manufactured 1,500 units during the year and increased its stock by 400 units. This may be a legitimate move if the business is anticipating a big jump in sales next year. But on the other hand, a stock increase of 400 units in a year in which only 1,100 units were sold may be the result of a serious overproduction mistake, and the larger stock may not be needed next year. In any case, Figure 4-2 shows what happens to production costs and – more importantly – what happens to profit at the higher production output level.

Management Profit and Loss Account for Year

Sales Volume — 1,100 Units

	Per Unit	Totals
Sales Revenue	£140	£154,000
Cost of Goods Sold Expense	(£69)	(£75,900)
Gross Margin	£71	£78,100
Variable Operating Expenses	(£30)	(£33,000)
Contribution Margin	£41	£45,100
Fixed Operating Expenses	(£19.50)	(£21,450)
Earnings Before Interest and Tax (EBIT)	£21.50	£23,650
Interest Expense		(£2,750)
Earnings Before Tax		£20,900
Corporation Tax Expense		(£7,106)
Net Income		£13,794

Manufacturing Cost Summary for Year

Annual Production Capacity — 1,500 Units
Actual Output — 1,500 Units

Production Cost Components	Per Unit	Totals
Raw Materials	£21.50	£32,250
Direct Labour	£12.50	£18,750
Variable Overhead	£7	£10,500
Total Variable Manufacturing Costs	£41	£61,500
Fixed Overhead	£28	£42,000
Total Manufacturing Costs	£69	£103,500
To 400 Units Stock Increase		(£27,600)
To 1,100 Units Sold		£75,900

Figure 4-2: Example in which production output greatly exceeds sales volume, thereby boosting profit for the period.

The additional 3,000 units (over and above the 1,200 units manufactured by the business in the original example) cost £41 per unit. (The precise cost may be a little higher than £41per unit because as you start crowding your production capacity, some variable costs may increase a little.) The business would need about £12,300 more for the additional 3,000 units of production output:

£41 variable manufacturing cost per unit × 3,000 additional units produced = £12,300 additional variable manufacturing costs invested in stock

Again, its fixed manufacturing costs would not have increased, given the nature of fixed costs. Fixed costs stay put until capacity is increased. Sales volume, in this scenario, also remains the same.

But check out the business's EBIT in Figure 4-2: £23,650, compared with £15,950 in Figure 4-1 – a £7,700 increase, even though sales volume, sales prices, and operating costs all remain the same. Whoa! What's going on here? The simple answer is that the cost of goods sold expense is £7,700 less than before. But how can cost of goods sold expense be less? The business sells 1,100 units in both scenarios. And, variable manufacturing costs are £41 per unit in both cases.

The burden rate component of product cost in the first case is £35 (see Figure 4-1). In the second case the burden rate is only £28 (see Figure 4-2). Recall that the burden rate is computed by dividing total fixed manufacturing costs for the period by the production output during the period. Dividing by 1,500 units compared with 1,200 units reduces the burden rate from £35 to £28. The £7 lower burden rate multiplied by the 1,100 units sold results in a £7,700 smaller cost of goods sold expense for the period, and a higher pre-tax profit of the same amount.

In the first case the business puts £3,500 of its total annual fixed manufacturing costs into the increase in stock (1,000 units increase × £35 burden rate). In the second case, in which the production output is at capacity, the business puts £11,200 of its total fixed manufacturing costs into the increase in stock (4,000 units increase × £28 burden rate). Thus, £7,700 more of its fixed manufacturing costs go into stock rather than cost of goods sold expense. But don't forget that stock increased 4,000 units, which is quite a large increase compared with the annual sales of 1,100 during the year just ended.

Who was responsible for the decision to go full blast and produce up to production capacity? Do the managers really expect sales to jump up enough next period to justify the much larger stock level? If they prove to be right, they'll look brilliant. But if the output level was a mistake and sales do not go up next year, they'll have you-know-what to pay next year, even though profit looks good this year. An experienced business manager knows to be on guard when stock takes such a big jump.

A View from the Top Regarding Costs

The CEO of a business gets paid to take the big picture point of view. Using the business example in the chapter (refer to Figure 4-1 again), a typical CEO would study the management profit and loss account and say something like the following:

Not a bad year. Total costs were just about 90% of sales revenue. EBIT per unit was a little more than 10% of sales price (£14.50 per unit ÷ £140 sales price). I was able to spread my fixed operating expenses over 1,100 units of sales, for an average of £19.50 per unit. Compared with the £34 contribution margin per unit this yielded £14.50 EBIT per unit. I can live with this.

I'd like to improve our margins, of course, but even if we don't, we should be able to increase sales volume next year. In fact, I notice that we produced 1,000 units more than we sold this year. So, I'll put pressure on the sales manager to give me her plan for increasing sales volume next year.

I realise that cost numbers can be pushed around by my sharp-pencil accountant. He keeps reminding me about cost classification problems between manufacturing and non-manufacturing costs – but, what the heck, it all comes out in the wash sooner or later. I watch the three major cost lines in my profit and loss account – cost of goods sold, variable operating expenses, and fixed operating expenses.

I realise that some costs can be classified in one or another of these groupings. So, I expect my accountant to be consistent period to period, and I have instructed him not to make any changes without my approval. Without consistency of accounting methods, I can't reliably compare my expense numbers from period to period. In my view, it's better to be arbitrary in the same way, period after period, rather than changing cost methods to keep up with the latest cost allocation fads.

Chapter 5

Choosing Accounting Methods

Some people put a great deal of faith in numbers: 2 + 2 = 4, and that's the end of the story. They see a number reported to the last digit on an accounting report, and they get the impression of exactitude. But accounting isn't just a matter of adding up numbers. It's not an exact science.

Accountants *do* have plenty of rules that they must follow. The official rule book of generally accepted accounting principles (GAAP) laid down by the Accounting Standards Board (and its predecessors) is more than 1,200 pages long and growing fast. In addition there are the rules and regulations issued by the various government regulatory agencies that govern financial reporting and accounting methods and those issued by publicly-owned companies such as the London Stock Exchange. Also, the Institute of Chartered Accountants and the other professional accountancy institutes also play a role in setting accounting standards.

Although we're still in the early stages, standards are going *international* – the goal being to establish worldwide accounting standards. With the advent of the European Union and the ever-increasing amount of international trade and investing, business and political leaders in many nations recognise the need to iron out differences in accounting methods and disclosure standards from country to country. You can keep alert about what's going on at the International Accounting Standards Board Web site, www.iasb.org.

Perhaps the most surprising thing – considering that formal rule-making activity has been going on since the 1930s – is that a business still has options for choosing among alternative accounting methods. Different methods lead to inconsistent profit measures from company to company. The often-repeated goal for standardising accounting methods is to make like things look alike and different things look different – but the accounting profession hasn't reached this stage of nirvana yet. In addition, accounting methods change over the years, as the business world changes. GAAP are, to one degree or another, in a state of flux.

Because the choice of accounting methods directly affects the profit figure for the year and the values reported in the ending balance sheet, business managers (and investors) need to know the difference between accounting methods. You don't need to probe into these accounting methods in excruciating, technical detail, but you should at least know whether one method versus another yields higher or lower profit measures and higher or lower asset values in financial statements. This chapter explains accounting choices for measuring cost of goods sold, depreciation, and other expenses. Get involved in making these important accounting decisions – it's your business, after all.

Decision-Making Behind the Scenes in Profit and Loss Accounts

Book III Chapter 1 introduces the conventional format for presenting profit and loss accounts in *external* financial reports. (Also see Figure 1-1 of Book IV Chapter 1 for another example.) Figure 5-1 presents another profit and loss account for a business – with certain modifications that you won't see in actual external profit and loss accounts. For explaining the choices between alternative accounting methods, certain specific expenses are broken down under the company's sales, administrative, and general expenses (SA&G) category in Figure 5-1. Of these particular expenses only depreciation is disclosed in external profit and loss accounts. Don't expect to find in external profit and loss accounts the other expenses shown under the SA&G category in Figure 5-1. Businesses are a very reluctant to divulge such information to the outside world.

Here's a quick overview of the accounting matters and choices relating to each line in the profit and loss account shown in Figure 5-1, from the top line to the bottom line.

Profit and Loss Account for Year		
Sales Revenue		£260,000
Cost of Goods Sold Expense		£143,000
Gross Margin		£117,000
Sales, Administrative, and General Expenses:		
Stock Shrinkage and Write-downs	£3,787	
Bad Debts	£3,850	
Asset Impairment Write-downs	£2,870	
Depreciation	£7,800	
Warranty and Guarantee Expenses	£9,672	
All Other SA&G Expenses	£63,020	
Total		£91,000
Earnings Before Interest and Tax		£26,000
Interest Expense		£4,000
Earnings Before Tax		£22,000
Corporation Tax Expense		£8,800
Net Income		£13,200

Figure 5-1: A profit and loss account including certain expenses that are not reported outside the business.

✔ **Sales revenue:** Timing the recording of sales is something to be aware of. Generally speaking, sales revenue timing is not a serious accounting problem, but businesses should be consistent from one year to the next. For some businesses, however, the timing of recording sales revenue is a major problem – such as software and other high-tech companies, and companies in their early start-up phases. A footnote to the company's financial statements should explain its revenue recognition method if there is anything unusual about it.

Note: If products are returnable and the deal between the seller and buyer does not satisfy normal conditions for a completed sale, then recognition of sales revenue should be postponed until the return privilege no longer exists. For example, some products are sold *on approval*, which means the customer takes the product and tries it out for a few days or longer to see if the customer really wants it. This area has taken on a new significance with the accelerating growth of the Internet as a medium for selling. Distance Selling Regulations brought into effect in the UK in October 2001 gives consumers additional rights to obtaining a full refund without having to give any reason.

Book IV

Managing the Finances

✔ **Cost of goods sold expense:** Whether to use the first-in, first-out (FIFO) method, or the last-in, first-out (LIFO) method, or the average cost method (each of which is explained in the section 'Calculating Cost of Goods Sold and Cost of Stock' later in this chapter), cost of goods sold is a big expense for companies that sell products and naturally the choice of method can have a real impact.

✔ **Gross margin:** Can be dramatically affected by the method used for calculating cost of goods sold expense (and the method of revenue recognition, if this is a problem).

✔ **Stock write-downs:** Whether to count and inspect stock very carefully to determine loss due to theft, damage, and deterioration, and whether to apply the net realisable value (NRV) method strictly or loosely are the two main questions that need to be answered. See 'Identifying Stock Losses: Net Realisable Value' later in this chapter. Stock is a high-risk asset that's subject to theft, damage, and obsolescence.

✔ **Bad debts expense:** When to conclude that the debts owed to you by customers who bought on credit (debtors) are not going to be paid – the question is really when to *write down* these debts (that is, remove the amounts from your asset column). You can wait until after you've made a substantial effort at collecting the debts, or you can make your decision before that time. See 'Collecting or Writing Off Bad Debts' later in this chapter.

✔ **Asset impairment write-downs:** Whether (and when) to *write down* or *write off* an asset – that is, remove it from the asset column. Stock shrinkage, bad debts, and depreciation by their very nature are asset write-downs. Other asset write-downs are required when any asset becomes *impaired*, which means that it has lost some or all of its economic utility to the business and has little or no disposable value. An asset write-down reduces the book (recorded) value of an asset (and at the same time records an expense or loss of the same amount). A *write-off* reduces the asset's book value to zero and removes it from the accounts, and the entire amount becomes an expense or loss.

For example, your delivery truck driver had an accident. The repair of the truck was covered by insurance, so no write-down is necessary. But the products being delivered had to be thrown away and were not insured while in transit. You write off the cost of the stock lost in the accident.

✔ **Depreciation expense:** Whether to use a short-life method and load most of the expense over the first few years, or a longer-life method and spread the expense evenly over the years. Refer to 'Appreciating Depreciation Methods' later in this chapter. Depreciation is a big expense for some businesses, making the choice of method even more important.

✔ **Warranty and guarantee (post-sales) expenses:** Whether to record an expense for products sold with warranties and guarantees in the same period that the goods are sold (along with the cost of goods sold expense, of course) or later, when customers actually return products for repair or replacement. Businesses can usually forecast the percentage of products sold that will be returned for repair or replacement under the guarantees and warranties offered to customers – although a new product with no track record can be a problem in this regard.

✓ **All other SA&G expenses:** Whether to disclose separately one or more of the specific expenses included in this conglomerate total. For example, the SEC requires that *advertising* and *repairs and maintenance* expenses be disclosed in the documents businesses file with the SEC, but you hardly ever see these two expenses reported in external profit and loss accounts. Nor do you find individual top management compensation revealed in external profit and loss accounts, other than that for directors. GAAP does not require such disclosures – much less revealing things like bribes or other legally questionable payments by a business.

✓ **Earnings before interest and tax (EBIT):** This profit measure equals sales revenue less all the expenses above this line; therefore, EBIT depends on the particular choices made for recording sales revenue and expenses. Having a choice of accounting methods means that an amount of wriggle is inherent in recording sales revenue and many expenses. How much wriggle effect do all these accounting choices have on the EBIT profit figure? This is a very difficult question to answer. The business itself may not know. We would guess (and it's no more than a conjecture on our part) that the EBIT for a period reported by most businesses could easily be 10–20% lower or higher if different accounting choices had been made.

✓ **Interest expense:** Usually a cut-and-dried calculation, with no accounting problems. (Well, we can think of some really hairy interest accounting problems, but we won't go into them here.)

✓ **Corporation tax expense:** You can use different accounting methods for some of the expenses reported in your profit and loss account than you use for calculating taxable income. Oh, crikey! The hypothetical amount of taxable income, if the accounting methods used in the profit and loss account were used in the tax return, is calculated; then the corporation tax based on this hypothetical taxable income is figured. This is the corporation tax expense reported in the profit and loss account. This amount is reconciled with the actual amount of corporation tax owed based on the accounting methods used for tax purposes. A reconciliation of the two different tax amounts is provided in a rather technical footnote to the financial statements. See 'Reconciling Corporation Tax' later in this chapter.

Book IV

Managing the Finances

✓ **Net income:** Like EBIT, can vary considerably depending on which accounting methods you use for measuring expenses.

Whereas bad debts, post-sales expenses, and asset write-downs vary in importance from business to business, cost of goods sold and depreciation methods are so important that a business must disclose which methods it uses for these two expenses in the footnotes to its financial statements. The Inland Revenue requires that a company actually record in its cost of goods sold expense and stock asset accounts the amounts determined by the accounting method they use to determine taxable income – a rare requirement in the company tax law

Considering how important the bottom-line profit number is, and that different accounting methods can cause a major difference on this all-important number, you'd think that accountants would have developed clear-cut and definite rules so that only one accounting method would be correct for a given set of facts. No such luck. The final choice boils down to an arbitrary decision, made by top-level accountants in consultation with, and consent of, managers. If you own a business or are a manager in a business, we strongly encourage you to get involved in choosing which accounting methods to use for measuring your profit and for presenting your balance sheet.

Accounting methods vary from business to business more than you'd probably suspect, even though all of them stay within the boundaries of GAAP. The rest of this chapter expands on the methods available for measuring certain expenses. Sales revenue accounting can be a challenge as well, but profit accounting problems lie mostly on the expense side of the ledger.

Calculating Cost of Goods Sold and Cost of Stock

One main accounting problem of companies that sell products is how to measure their *cost of goods sold expense*, which is the sum of the costs of the products sold to customers during the period. You deduct cost of goods sold from sales revenue to determine *gross margin* – the first profit line on the profit and loss account (see Book III Chapter 1 for more about profit and loss accounts, and Figure 1-1 of Book IV Chapter 1 for a typical profit and loss account). Cost of goods sold is therefore a very important figure, because if gross margin is wrong, bottom-line profit (net income) is wrong.

First a business acquires products, either by buying them (retailers) or by producing them (manufacturers). Book IV Chapter 4 explains how manufacturers determine product cost; for retailers product cost is simply the purchase cost. (Well, it's not entirely this simple, but you get the point.) Product cost is entered in the stock asset account and is held there until the products are sold. Then, but not before, product cost is taken out of stock and recorded in the cost of goods sold expense account. You must be absolutely clear on this point. Suppose that you clear £700 from your salary for the week and deposit this amount in your bank account. The money stays in there and is an asset until you spend it. You don't have an expense until you write a cheque.

Likewise, not until the business sells products does it have a cost of goods sold expense. When you write a cheque, you know how much it's for – you have no doubt about the amount of the expense. But when a business withdraws products from its stock and records cost of goods sold expense, the expense amount is in some doubt. The amount of expense depends on which accounting method the business selects.

The essence of this accounting issue is that you have to divide the total cost of your stock between the units sold (cost of goods sold expense, in the profit and loss account) and the unsold units that remain on hand waiting to be sold next period (stock asset, in the balance sheet).

For example, say you own a shop that sells antiques. Every time an item sells, you need to transfer the amount you paid for the item from the stock asset account into the cost of goods sold expense account. At the start of a fiscal period, your cost of goods sold expense is zero, and if you own a medium-sized shop selling medium-quality antiques, your stock asset account may be £20,000. Over the course of the fiscal period, your cost of goods sold expense should increase (hopefully rapidly, as you make many sales).

You probably want your stock asset account to remain fairly static, however. If you paid £200 for a wardrobe that sells during the period, the £200 leaves the stock asset account and finds a new home in the cost of goods sold expense account. However, you probably want to turn around and replace the item you sold, ultimately keeping your stock asset account at around the same level – although more complicated businesses have more complicated strategies for dealing with stock and more perplexing accounting problems.

You have three methods to choose from when you measure cost of goods sold and stock costs: You can follow a first-in, first-out (FIFO) cost sequence, follow a last-in, first-out cost sequence (LIFO), or compromise between the two methods and take the average costs for the period. Other methods are acceptable, but these three are the primary options. *Caution:* Product costs are entered in the stock asset account in the order acquired, but they are not necessarily taken out of the stock asset account in this order. The different methods refer to the order in which product costs are *taken out* of the stock asset account. You may think that only one method is appropriate – that the sequence in should be the sequence out. However, generally accepted accounting principles permit other methods.

Book IV

Managing the Finances

In reality, the choice boils down to FIFO versus LIFO; the average cost method runs a distant third in popularity. If you want our opinion, FIFO is better than LIFO for reasons that we explain in the next two sections. You may not agree, and that's your right. For your business, you make the call.

The FIFO method

With the FIFO method, you charge out product costs to cost of goods sold expense in the chronological order in which you acquired the goods. The procedure is that simple. It's like the first people in line to see a film get in the cinema first. The usher collects the tickets in the order in which they were bought.

We think that FIFO is the best method for both the expense and the asset amounts. We hope that you like this method, but also look at the LIFO method before making up your mind. You should make up your mind, you know. Don't just sit on the sidelines. Take a stand.

Suppose that you acquire four units of a product during a period, one unit at a time, with unit costs as follows (in the order in which you acquire the items): £100, £102, £104, and £106. By the end of the period, you have sold three of those units. Using FIFO, you calculate the cost of goods sold expense as follows:

£100 + £102 + £104 = £306

In short, you use the first three units to calculate cost of goods sold expense. (You can see the benefit of having such a standard method if you sell hundreds or thousands of different products.)

The ending stock asset, then, is £106, which is the cost of the most recent acquisition. The £412 total cost of the four units is divided between the £306 cost of goods sold expense for the three units sold and the £106 cost of the one unit in ending stock. The total cost has been taken care of; nothing fell between the cracks.

FIFO works well for two reasons:

✔ In most businesses, products actually move into and out of stock in a first-in, first-out sequence: The earlier acquired products are delivered to customers before the later acquired products are delivered, so the most recently purchased products are the ones still in ending stock to be delivered in the future. Using FIFO, the stock asset reported on the balance sheet at the end of the period reflects the most recent purchase cost and therefore is close to the current *replacement cost* of the product.

✔ When product costs are steadily increasing, many (but not all) businesses follow a first-in, first-out sales price strategy and hold off on raising sales prices as long as possible. They delay raising sales prices until they have sold all lower-cost products. Only when they start selling from the next batch of products, acquired at a higher cost, do they raise sales prices. We strongly favour using the FIFO cost of goods sold expense method when the business follows this basic sales pricing policy because both the expense and the sales revenue are better matched for determining gross margin.

The LIFO method

Remember the cinema usher we mentioned earlier? Think about that usher going to the *back* of the queue of people waiting to get into the next showing and letting them in from the rear of the queue first. In other words, the later you bought your ticket, the sooner you get into the cinema. This is the LIFO method, which stands for *last-in, first-out*. The people in the front of the queue wouldn't stand for it, of course, but the LIFO method is quite acceptable for determining the cost of goods sold expense for products sold during the period. The main feature of the LIFO method is that it selects the *last* item you purchased first and then works backward until you have the total cost for the total number of units sold during the period. What about the ending stock, the products you haven't sold by the end of the year? Using the LIFO method, you never get back to the cost of the first products acquired (unless you sold out your entire stock); the earliest cost remains in the stock asset account.

Using the same example from the preceding section, assume that the business uses the LIFO method instead of FIFO. The four units, in order of acquisition, had costs of £100, £102, £104, and £106. If you sell three units during the period, LIFO gives you the following cost of goods sold expense:

£106 + £104 + £102 = £312

The ending stock cost of the one unit not sold is £100, which is the oldest cost. The £412 total cost of the four units acquired less the £312 cost of goods sold expense leaves £100 in the stock asset account. Determining which units you actually delivered to customers is irrelevant; when you use the LIFO method, you always count backward from the last unit you acquired.

If you really want to argue in favour of using LIFO – and we have to tell you that we won't back you up on this one – here's what you can say:

- ✔ Assigning the most recent costs of products purchased to the cost of goods sold expense makes sense because you have to replace your products to stay in business, and the most recent costs are closest to the amount you will have to pay to replace your products. Ideally, you should base your sales prices not on original cost but on the cost of replacing the units sold.

- ✔ During times of rising costs, the most recent purchase cost maximises the cost of goods sold expense deduction for determining taxable income, and thus minimises the taxable income. In fact, LIFO was invented for income tax purposes. True, the cost of stock on the ending balance sheet is lower than recent acquisition costs, but the profit and loss account effect is more important than the balance sheet effect.

The more product cost you take out of the stock asset to charge to cost of goods sold expense, the less product cost you have in the ending stock. In maximising cost of goods sold expense, you minimise the stock cost value.

Book IV

Managing the Finances

But here are the reasons why LIFO, in our view, is usually the wrong choice (the following sections of this chapter go into more details about these issues):

✔ Unless you base your sales prices on the most recent purchase costs or you raise sales prices as soon as replacement costs increase – and most businesses don't follow either of these pricing policies – using LIFO depresses your gross margin and, therefore, your bottom-line net income.

✔ The LIFO method can result in an ending stock cost value that's seriously out-of-date, especially if the business sells products that have very long lives.

✔ Unscrupulous managers can use the LIFO method to manipulate their profit figures if business isn't going well. Refer to 'Manipulating LIFO stock levels to give profit a boost' later in the chapter.

Note: In periods of rising product costs, it's true that FIFO results in higher taxable income than LIFO does – something you probably want to avoid, we're sure. Nevertheless, even though LIFO may be preferable in some circumstances, we still say that FIFO is the better choice in the majority of situations, for the reasons discussed earlier, and you may come over to our way of thinking after reading the following sections. By the way, if the products are intermingled such that they cannot be identified with particular purchases, then the business has to use FIFO for its income tax returns.

The greying of LIFO stock cost

If you sell products that have long lives and for which your product costs rise steadily over the years, using the LIFO method has a serious impact on the ending stock cost value reported on the balance sheet and can cause the balance sheet to look misleading. Over time, the cost of replacing products becomes further and further removed from the LIFO-based stock costs. Your 2008 balance sheet may very well report stock based on 1985, 1975, or 1965 product costs. As a matter of fact, the product costs used to value stock can go back even further.

Suppose that a major manufacturing business has been using LIFO for more than 45 years. The products that this business manufactures and sells have very long lives – in fact, the business has been making and selling many of the same products for many years. Believe it or not, the difference between its LIFO and FIFO cost values for its ending stock is about £2 billion because some of the products are based on costs going back to the 1950s, when the company first started using the LIFO method. The FIFO cost value of its ending stock is disclosed in a footnote to its financial statements; this disclosure is how you can tell the difference between a business's LIFO and FIFO cost values. The gross margin (before income tax) over the business's 45 years would have been £2 billion higher if the business had used the FIFO method – and its total taxable income over the 45 years would have been this much higher as well.

Of course, the business's income taxes over the years would have been correspondingly higher as well. That's the trade-off.

Note: A business must disclose the difference between its stock cost value according to LIFO and its stock cost value according to FIFO in a footnote on its financial statements – but, of course, not too many people outside of stock analysts and professional investment managers read footnotes. Business managers get involved in reviewing footnotes in the final steps of getting annual financial reports ready for release. If your business uses FIFO, your ending stock is stated at recent acquisition costs, and you do not have to determine what the LIFO value may have been. Annual financial reports do not disclose the estimated LIFO cost value for a FIFO-based stock.

Many products and raw materials have very short lives; they're regularly replaced by new models (you know, with those 'New and Improved!' labels) because of the latest technology or marketing wisdom. These products aren't around long enough to develop a wide gap between LIFO and FIFO, so the accounting choice between the two methods doesn't make as much difference as with long-lived products.

Manipulating LIFO stock levels to give profit a boost

The LIFO method opens the door to manipulation of profit – not that you would think of doing this, of course. Certainly, most of the businesses that choose LIFO do so to minimise current taxable income and delay paying taxes on it as long as possible – a legitimate (though perhaps misguided in some cases) goal. However, some unscrupulous managers know that they can use the LIFO method to 'create' some profit when business isn't going well.

So if a business that uses LIFO sells more products than it purchased (or manufactured) during the period, it has to reach back into its stock account and pull out older costs to transfer to the cost of goods sold expense. These costs are much lower than current costs, leading to an artificially low cost of goods sold expense, which in turn leads to an artificially high gross margin figure. This dipping into old cost layers of LIFO-based stock is called a *LIFO liquidation gain*.

This unethical manipulation of profit is possible for businesses that have been using LIFO for many years and have stock cost values far lower than the current purchase or manufacturing costs of products. By not replacing all the quantities sold, they let stock fall below normal levels.

Suppose that a retailer sold 10,000 units during the year and normally would have replaced all units sold. Instead, it purchased only 9,000 replacement units. Therefore, the other 1,000 units were taken out of stock, and the accountant had to reach back into the old cost layers of stock to record some of the cost of goods sold expense. To see the impact of LIFO liquidation gain on the gross margin, check out what the gross margin would look like if this business had replaced all 10,000 units versus the gross margin for replacing only 9,000. In this example, the old units in stock carry a LIFO-based cost of only £3, and the current purchase cost is £6.50. Assume that the units have a £100 price tag for the customer.

Gross margin if the business replaced all 10,000 of the units sold

Sales revenue (10,000 units at £10 per unit)	£100,000
Cost of goods sold expense (10,000 units at £6.50 per unit)	65,000
Gross margin	£35,000

Gross margin if the business replaced only 9,000 of the units sold

Sales revenue (10,000 units at £10 per unit)		£100,000
Cost of goods sold expense:		
Units replaced (9,000 units at £6.50 per unit)	£58,000	
Units from stock (1,000 units at £3 per unit)	3,000	61,500
Gross margin		£38,500

The LIFO liquidation gain (the difference between the two gross margins) in this example is £3,500 – the £3.50 difference between the old and the current unit costs multiplied by 1,000 units. Just by ordering fewer replacement products, this business padded its gross margin – but in a very questionable way.

Of course, this business may have a good, legitimate reason for trimming stock by 1,000 units – to reduce the capital invested in that asset, for example, or to anticipate lower sales demand in the year ahead. LIFO liquidation gains may also occur when a business stops selling a product and that stock drops to zero. Still, we have to warn investors that when you see a financial statement reporting a dramatic decrease in stock and the business uses the LIFO method, you should be aware of the possible profit manipulation reasons behind the decrease.

Note: A business must disclose in the footnotes to its financial statements any substantial LIFO liquidation gains that occurred during the year. The outside auditor should make sure that the company includes this disclosure. (Book IV Chapter 6 discusses audits of financial statements by auditors.)

The average cost method

Although not nearly as popular as the FIFO and LIFO methods, the average cost method seems to offer the best of both worlds. The costs of many things in the business world fluctuate; business managers focus on the average product cost over a time period. Also, the averaging of product costs over a period of time has a desirable smoothing effect that prevents cost of goods sold from being overly dependent on wild swings of one or two purchases.

To many businesses, the compromise aspect of the method is its *worst* feature. Businesses may want to go one way or the other and avoid the middle ground. If they want to minimise taxable income, LIFO gives the best effect during times of rising prices. Why go only halfway with the average cost method? Or if the business wants its ending stock to be as near to current replacement costs as possible, FIFO is better than the average cost method. Even using computers to keep track of averages, which change every time product costs change, is a nuisance. No wonder the average cost method is not popular! But it *is* an acceptable method.

Identifying Stock Losses: Net Realisable Value

Regardless of which method you use to determine stock cost, you should make sure that your accountants apply the *net realisable value (NRV)* test to stock. (Just to confuse you, this test is sometimes called the *lower of cost or market (LCM)* test.) A business should go through the NRV routine at least once a year, usually near or at year-end. The process consists of comparing the cost of every product in stock – meaning the cost that's recorded for each product in the stock asset account according to the FIFO or LIFO method (or whichever method the company uses) – with two benchmark values:

✔ The product's *current replacement cost* (how much the business would pay to obtain the same product right now).

✔ The product's *net realisable value* (how much the business can sell the product for).

If a product's cost on the books is higher than either of these two benchmark values, your accountant should decrease product cost to the lower of the two. In other words, stock losses are recognised *now* rather than *later*, when the products are sold. The drop in the replacement cost or sales value of the product should be recorded now, on the theory that it's better to take your medicine now than to put it off. Also, the stock cost value on the balance sheet is more conservative because stock is reported at a lower cost value.

Buying and holding stock involves certain unavoidable risks. Asset write-downs, explained in the 'Decision-Making behind the Scenes in Profit and Loss Accounts' section of this chapter, are recorded to recognise the consequences of two of those risks – stock shrinkage and losses to natural disasters not fully covered by insurance. NRV records the losses from two other risks of holding stock:

- ✔ **Replacement cost risk:** After you purchase or manufacture a product, its replacement cost may drop permanently below the amount you paid (which usually also affects the amount you can charge customers for the products, because competitors will drop their prices).

- ✔ **Sales demand risk:** Demand for a product may drop off permanently, forcing you to sell the products below cost just to get rid of them.

Determining current replacement cost values for every product in your stock isn't easy! Applying the NRV test leaves much room for interpretation.

Keeping accurate track of your stock costs is important to your bottom line, both now and in the future, so don't fall into the trap of doing a quick NRV scan and making a snap judgement that you don't need a stock write-down.

Some shady characters abuse NRV to cheat on their company tax returns. They *write down* their ending stock cost value – decrease ending stock cost more than can be justified by the NRV test – to increase the deductible expenses on their tax returns and thus decrease taxable income. A product may have a proper cost value of £100, for example, but a shady character may invent some reason to lower it to £75 and thus record a £25 stock write-down expense in this period for each unit – which is not justified by the facts. But, even though the person can deduct more this year, she will have a lower stock cost to deduct in the future. Also, if the person is selected for an Inland Revenue audit and the tax inspectors discover an unjustified stock write-down, the person may end up being charged with tax evasion.

Most accounting software packages either support or have plug in modules that will allow you to run all these costing methods and compare their effect on your apparent financial performance. For example The Sage Pro Inventory Control module (`www.sageproerp.com/products/accounting/ic`) Supports LIFO, FIFO, average weighted, and standard cost inventory valuation methods.

Appreciating Depreciation Methods

In theory, depreciation expense accounting is straightforward enough: You divide the cost of a fixed asset among the number of years that the business expects to use the asset. In other words, instead of having a huge lump-sum expense in the year that you make the purchase, you charge a fraction of the cost to expense for each year of the asset's lifetime. Using this method is much easier on your bottom line in the year of purchase, of course.

But theories are rarely as simple in real life as they are on paper, and this one is no exception. Do you divide the cost *evenly* across the asset's lifetime, or do you charge more to certain years than others? Furthermore, when it eventually comes time to dispose of fixed assets, the assets may have some disposable, or *salvage*, value. Only cost minus the salvage value should be depreciated, right? Or, should salvage value estimates be ignored and the total cost of a fixed asset be depreciated? And how do you estimate how long an asset will last in the first place? Do you consult an accountant psychic hot line?

As it turns out, the Inland Revenue runs its own little psychic business on the side, with a crystal ball known as the Inland Revenue Code. The Inland Revenue Code doesn't give you predictions of how long your fixed assets will *last*; it only tells you what kind of timeline to use for income tax purposes, as well as how to divide the cost along that timeline. The Inland Revenue have a little help in their psychic predictions. They have a direct line to their boss, the Chancellor of the Exchequer, who varies these rules every year or so to stimulate capital spending by businesses. This is done by varying the *writing down allowance*, which is tax speak for the amount of depreciation expense you can get tax relief for. So if the Chancellor wants to encourage businesses to buy computers he can set a 100% writing down allowance for the first year, whereas the asset may well have an economic life of three years or more. Confused? Well at least you know what you are getting for your money when you hire a tax accountant.

Hundreds of books have been written on depreciation, but the only book that counts is the HM Revenue and Customs Code. Most businesses adopt the useful lives allowed by the income tax law for their financial statement accounting; they don't go to the trouble of keeping a second depreciation schedule for financial reporting. Why complicate things if you don't have to? Why keep one depreciation schedule for income tax and a second for preparing your financial statements? However, they do tell you what their policy is.

Tesco's 2002–2003 annual report contains this explanation of their depreciation policy:

Book IV

Managing the Finances

Depreciation is provided on a straight-line basis over the anticipated useful economic lives of the assets. The following rates applied for the Group and are consistent with the prior year:

- ✔ Land premiums paid in excess of the alternative use value – at 2.5% of cost.

- ✔ Freehold and leasehold buildings with greater than 40 years unexpired – at 2.5% of cost.

- ✔ Leasehold properties with less than 40 years unexpired are amortised by equal annual instalments over the unexpired period of the lease.

- ✔ Plant, equipment, fixtures and fittings, and motor vehicles – at rates varying from 10% to 33%.

By the way, keeping two depreciation schedules is an example of *keeping two sets of books*. In some situations a person using this term is referring to the illegal tactic of keeping one set of accounts for the actual amounts of sales revenue and expenses and keeping a second set of fictional accounts for income tax purposes. (We've never seen two sets of books in actual practice – although, we have seen cases of skimming sales revenue and inflating expenses on the books to minimise the taxable income of a business.)

Note: Taxation laws can change at any time and can get extremely technical. Please use the following information for a basic understanding of the procedures and *not* as tax advice. There are a number of annual income tax guides, such as *Tolley's Tax Guides*, published by Butterworths.

The Inland Revenue rules gives guidance on which of two depreciation methods to use for particular types of assets:

- ✔ **Straight-line depreciation method:** With this method, you divide the cost evenly among the years of the asset's estimated lifetime. So if a new building owned and used by a business costs £390,000 and its useful life is 39 years, the depreciation expense is £10,000 ($\frac{1}{39}$ of the cost) for each of the 39 years. (See the example of Tesco's above.) You must use straight-line depreciation for buildings and may choose to use it for other types of assets; once you start using this method for a particular asset, you can't change your mind and switch to another method later.

- ✔ **Accelerated depreciation method:** Actually, this term is a generic catch-all for several different kinds of methods. What they all have in common is that they're *front-loading* methods, meaning that you charge a larger amount of depreciation expense in the early years and a smaller amount in the later years. *Accelerated depreciation method* also refers to adopting useful lives that are shorter than realistic estimates (very few cars are useless after five years, for example, but they can be fully depreciated over five years).

One popular accelerated method is the *double-declining balance* (DDB) depreciation method. With this method, you calculate the straight-line depreciation rate and then you double that percentage. You apply that doubled percentage to the declining balance over the course of the asset's depreciation time line. After a certain number of years, you switch back to the straight-line method for the remainder of the asset's depreciation years to ensure that you depreciate the full cost by the end of the predetermined number of years. See the sidebar 'The double-declining balance depreciation method' for an example.

By the way, the salvage value of fixed assets (the estimated disposal values when the assets are taken to the junkyard or sold off at the end of their useful lives) is ignored in the calculation of depreciation for income tax. Put another way, if a fixed asset is held to the end of its entire depreciation life, then its original cost will be fully depreciated, and the fixed asset from that time forward will have a zero book value. (Recall that book value is equal to the cost minus the balance in the accumulated depreciation account.) Fully depreciated fixed assets are grouped with all other fixed assets in external balance sheets. All these long-term resources of a business are reported in one asset account called *property, plant, and equipment* (instead of fixed assets). If all its fixed assets were fully depreciated the balance sheet of a company would look rather peculiar – the cost of its fixed assets would be completely offset by its accumulated depreciation. We've never seen this, but it would be possible for a business that hasn't replaced any of its fixed assets for a long time.

The straight-line method has strong advantages: It's easy to understand and it stabilises the depreciation expense from year to year. But many business managers and accountants favour the accelerated depreciation method. Keep in mind, however, that the depreciation expense in the annual profit and loss account is higher in the early years when you use an accelerated depreciation method, and so bottom-line profit is lower until later years. Nevertheless, many accountants and businesses like accelerated depreciation because it paints a more conservative (a lower, or a more moderate) picture of profit performance in the early years. Who knows? Fixed assets may lose their economic usefulness to a business sooner than expected. If this happens, using the accelerated depreciation method would look good in hindsight.

Minimising taxable income and corporation tax in the early years to hang on to as much cash as possible is very important to many businesses, and they pay the price of reporting lower net income in order to defer paying corporation tax as long as possible. Or they may use the straight-line method in their financial statements even though they use an accelerated method in their annual tax returns, which complicates matters. (Refer to the section 'Reconciling Corporation Tax' for more information.)

The double-declining balance depreciation method

Suppose that a business pays £100,000 for a fixed asset that has a five-year useful life and for which the double-declining balance depreciation method is used. The annual depreciation expense by the straight-line method is ⅕, or 20%, of cost per year – which in this example would be £20,000 per year. With the DDB method, you double that percentage to 40%, which gives £40,000 depreciation for the first year. After the first year, however, the 40% rate of depreciation is applied to the declining balance of the fixed asset. For example, in the second year depreciation equals the £60,000 non-depreciated balance of the fixed asset (£100,000 cost less the £40,000 first year depreciation) multiplied by the 40% rate – which gives £24,000 depreciation for the second year. The third year's depreciation is 40% of £36,000 (£100,000 cost minus the £64,000 accumulated depreciation balance).

You then switch to the straight-line method on the remaining amount of non-depreciated cost for the last two years in this example (the exact number of years depends on the number of years in the asset's depreciation timeline) – meaning that you divide the remaining balance by the number of remaining years. In this example, you need to use the straight-line method after the third year because if you applied the 40% rate to the non-depreciated balance of the fixed asset at the start of the fourth year and again in the following year on the declining balance, the fixed asset's cost would not be completely depreciated by the end of five years.

Got all that? Good, because things get even more technical and complicated in company tax law. For example, businesses that buy fixed assets in the later part of a year must follow the *half-year* convention, which requires that the business use a midpoint date in the year that an asset is acquired and placed in service. We don't want to get into all the details here; suffice it to say that you need a good tax-law accountant to get the most out of your depreciation expense deduction.

Except for brand-new enterprises, a business typically has a mix of fixed assets – some in their early years of depreciation, some in their middle years, and some in their later years. So, the overall depreciation expense for the year may not be that different than if the business had been using straight-line depreciation for all its fixed assets. A business does *not* have to disclose in its external financial report what its depreciation expense would have been if it had been using an alternative method. Readers of the financial statements cannot tell how much difference the choice of depreciation method made in that year.

Collecting or Writing Off Bad Debts

A business that allows its customers to pay on credit granted by the business is always subject to *bad debts* – debts that some customers never pay off. You are allowed, provided that you demonstrate serious efforts to recover the money owed, to write the loss in value off against your tax bill. You may also recover any VAT paid in respect of the invoice concerned. Don't forget in your role as an unpaid tax collector you will have charged your defaulting customer Value-Added Tax, paid that over to HM Revenue and Customs as required, but failed to recover the loot from the said customer, along with the rest of the boodle owed.

Reconciling Corporation Tax

Corporation tax is a heavy influence on a business's choice of accounting methods. Many a business decides to minimise its current taxable income by recording the maximum amount of deductible expenses. Thus, taxable income is lower, corporation tax paid to the Treasury is lower, and the business's cash balance is higher. Using these expense maximisation methods to prepare the profit and loss account of the business has the obvious effect of minimising the profit that's reported to the owners of the business. So, you may ask whether you can use one accounting method for corporation tax but an alternative method for preparing your financial statements. Can a business eat its cake (minimise corporation tax), and have it too (report more profit in its profit and loss account)?

The answer is yes, you can. You may decide, however, that using two different accounting methods is not worth the time and effort. In other areas of accounting for profit, businesses use one method for income tax and an alternative method in the financial statements (but we don't want to go into the details here).

When recording an expense, either an asset is decreased or a liability is increased. In this example, a special type of liability is increased to record the full amount of corporation tax expense: *deferred tax payable*. This unique liability account recognises the special contingency hanging over the head of the business to anticipate the time in the future when the business exhausts the higher depreciation amounts deducted in the early years by accelerated depreciation, and moves into the later years when annual depreciation amounts are less than amounts by the straight-line depreciation method. This liability account does not bear interest. Be warned that the accounting for this liability can get very complicated. The business provides information

Book IV

Managing the Finances

about this liability in a footnote to its financial statements, as well as reconciling the amount of corporation tax expense reported in its profit and loss account with the tax owed the government based on its tax return for the year. These footnotes are a joy to read – just kidding.

Two Final Issues to Consider

We think that you have been assuming all along that *all* its expenses should be recorded by a business. Of course, you're correct on this score. Many accountants argue that two expenses, in fact, are not recorded by businesses, but should be. A good deal of controversy surrounds both items. Many think one or both expenses should be recognised in measuring profit and in presenting the financial statements of a business:

- **Share options:** As part of their compensation packages, many public companies award their high-level executives share options, which give them the right to buy a certain number of shares at fixed prices after certain conditions are satisfied (years of service and the like). If the market price of the company's shares in the future rises above the exercise (purchase) prices of the share options – assuming the other conditions of these contracts are satisfied – the executives use their share options to buy shares below the going market price of the shares.

  Should the difference between the going market price of the shares and the exercise prices paid for the shares by the executives be recognised as an expense? Generally accepted accounting principles (GAAP) do not require that such an expense be recorded (unless the exercise price was below the market price at the time of granting the share option). However, the business must present a footnote disclosing the number of shares and exercise prices of its stock options, the theoretical cost of the share options to the business, and the dilution effect on earnings per share that exercising the share options will have. But, this is a far cry from recording an expense in the profit and loss account. Many persons, including Warren Buffett, who is Chair of Berkshire Hathaway, Inc., are strongly opposed to share options – thinking that the better alternative is to pay the executives in cash and avoid diluting earnings per share, which depresses the market value of the shares.

  In brief, the cost to shareholders of share options is off the books. The dilution in the market value of the shares of the corporation caused by its share options is suffered by the shareholders, but does not flow through the profit and loss account of the business.

✔ **Purchasing power of pound loss caused by inflation:** Due to inflation, the purchasing power of one pound today is less than it was one year ago, two years ago, and so on back in time. Yet, accountants treat all pounds the same, regardless of when the pound amounts were recorded on the books. The cost balance in a fixed asset account (a building, for instance) may have been recorded 10 or 20 years ago; in contrast, the cost balance in a current asset account (stock, for instance) may have been recorded only one or two months ago (assuming the business uses the FIFO method). So, depreciation expense is based on very old pounds that had more purchasing power back then, and cost of goods sold expense is based on current pounds that have less purchasing power than in earlier years.

Stay tuned for what might develop in the future regarding these two expenses. If we had to hazard a prediction, we would say that the pressure for recording the expense of share options will continue and might conceivably succeed – although we would add that powerful interests oppose recording share options expense. On the other hand, the loss of purchasing power of the pound caused by inflation has become less important in an era signified by relatively low inflation rates around the world.; however an enormous increase in the rate of inflation would resurrect this argument, and with rates of 6% and more prevailing in some parts of emerging Europe, 5% in India, 10% in Russia and 8% in Turkey the beast is not quite as dead as economists would like us to believe.

Chapter 6

Professional Auditors and Advisers

In This Chapter

▶ Cutting the deck for a fair deal: Why audits are needed

▶ Interpreting the auditor's report

▶ Knowing what auditors catch and don't catch

▶ Growing beyond audits: Professional accountancy practices as advisers and consultants

▶ Questioning the independence of auditors

*I*f we'd written this chapter 50 years ago, we would have talked almost exclusively about the role of the professional chartered or certified accountant as the *auditor* of the financial statements and footnotes presented in a business's annual financial report to its owners and lenders. Back then, in the 'good old days', audits were a professional accountancy firm's bread-and-butter service – audit fees were a large share of these firms' annual revenue. Audits were the core function that accountants performed then. In addition to audits, accountants provided accounting and tax advice to their clients – and that was pretty much all they did.

Today, accountants do a lot more than auditing. In fact, the profession has shifted away from the expression *auditing* in favour of broader terms like *assurance* and *attest*. More importantly, accountants have moved into consulting and advising clients on matters other than accounting and tax matters. The movement into the consulting business while continuing to do audits – often for the same clients – has caused all sorts of problems, which this chapter looks at after discussing audits by accountants.

Why Audits?

When I (John) graduated from college, I went to work for a big national accountancy firm. The transition from textbook accounting theory to real-world accounting practice came as a shock. Some of our clients dabbled in window dressing, and more than a few used earnings management tactics.

A few of our clients were engaged in accounting fraud, but just a very few. I was surprised how many businesses cut corners to get things done. Sometimes they were close to acting illegally, and some went over the edge. I soon realised that I had been rather naive, and I came to tolerate most of the questionable practices in the rough and tumble world of business.

I mention my early experience in public accounting to remind you that the world of business is not like Sunday school. Not everything is pure and straight. Nevertheless, legal and ethical lines of conduct separate what is tolerated and what isn't. If you cross the lines, you are subject to legal sanctions and can be held liable to others. For instance, a business can deliberately deceive its investors and lenders with false or misleading numbers in its financial report. Instead of 'What You See Is What You Get' in its financial statements, you get a filtered and twisted version of the business's financial affairs – more of a 'What I Want You to See Is What You Get' version. That's where audits come in.

Audits are the best practical means for keeping fraudulent and misleading financial reporting to a minimum. A business having an independent accounting professional who comes in once a year to check up on its accounting system is like a person getting a physical exam once a year – the audit exam may uncover problems that the business was not aware of, and knowing that the auditors come in once a year to take a close look at things keeps the business on its toes.

The basic purpose of an annual financial statement audit is to make sure that a business has followed the accounting methods and disclosure requirements of generally accepted accounting principles (GAAP) – in other words, to make sure that the business has stayed in the ballpark of accounting rules. After completing an audit examination, the accountant prepares a short auditor's report stating that the business has prepared its financial statements according to GAAP – or has not, as the case may be. In this way, audits are an effective means of enforcing accounting standards.

An audit by an independent accountant provides assurance (but not an iron-clad guarantee) that the business's financial statements follow accepted accounting methods and provide adequate disclosure. This is the main reason why accountancy firms are paid to do annual audits of financial reports. The auditor must be *independent* of the business being audited. The auditor can have no financial stake in the business or any other relationship with the client that may compromise his objectivity. However, the independence of auditors has come under scrutiny of late. See the section 'From Audits to Advising' later in the chapter.

The core of a business's financial report is its three primary financial statements – the profit and loss account, the cash flow statement, and the balance sheet – and the necessary footnotes to these statements. A financial report may consist of just these statements and footnotes and nothing more. Usually, however, there's more – in some cases, a lot more.

The auditor's opinion covers the financial statements and the accompanying footnotes. The auditor, therefore, does not express an opinion of whether the chairman's letter to the shareholders is a good letter – although if the chairman's claims contradicted the financial statements, the auditor would comment on the inconsistency. In short, auditors audit the financial statements and their footnotes but do not ignore the additional information included in annual financial reports.

Although the large majority of audited financial statements are reliable, a few slip through the audit net. Auditor approval is not a 100 per cent guarantee that the financial statements contain no erroneous or fraudulent numbers or that the statements and their footnotes provide all required disclosures, as the all too frequent Enron-like events attest.

Who's Who in the World of Audits

To be a qualified accountant, a person usually has to hold a degree, has to pass a rigorous national exam, have audit experience, and satisfy continuing education requirements. Many accountants operate as sole practitioners, but many form partnerships (also called firms). An accountancy firm has to be large enough to assign enough staff auditors to the client so that all audit work can be completed in a relatively short period – financial reports are generally released about four to six weeks after the close of the fiscal year. Large businesses need large accountancy firms, and very large global business organisations need very large international accountancy firms. The public accounting profession consists of four very large international firms, several good-sized second-tier national firms, often with international network arrangements, many regional firms, small local firms, and sole practitioners.

All businesses whose ownership units (shares) are traded in public markets in the UK, the US, and most other countries with major stock markets are required to have annual audits by independent auditors. Every stock you see listed on the LSE (London Stock Exchange), the NYSE (New York Stock Exchange), NASDAQ (National Association of Securities Dealers Automated Quotations), and other stock-trading markets must be audited by an outside accountancy firm. The Big Four international accountancy firms are household names in the business world. (Big Five until Arthur Andersen sank in the wake of the Enron debacle.)

The Big Four are:

- ✔ **Ernst & Young**
- ✔ **PricewaterhouseCoopers** (all one word, with the C capitalised, being the result of the merger of two firms)

✔ **Deloitte & Touche**

✔ **KPMG** (the only one of the five firm names having only letters; the PM in the name derives from an earlier time when 'Peat Marwick' was part of the firm's name)

The next ten accountancy firms, in terms of size are:

✔ Grant Thornton

✔ BDO Stoy Hayward

✔ Baker Tilly

✔ Smith & Williamson

✔ PKF

✔ Tenon Group

✔ Moore Stephens

✔ Mazars

✔ Vantis

✔ Bentley Jennison

These guys bob up and down and on occasions even out of the top spots. Accountancy Age (www.accountancyage.com/resources/top50) keeps tabs on their movements each year.

Though these ten are pretty big bears, their combined fee income is less than that of Ernst & Young, the smallest of the Big Four.

The firms are legally organised as limited liability partnerships, so you see LLP after their names. The big four international Accountancy firms and a handful of those in the second tier audit almost all of the large, public corporations in the UK and the US. For these corporations the annual audit is a cost of doing business; it's the price they pay for going into public markets for their capital and for having their shares traded in a public marketplace – which provides liquidity for their shares.

Banks and other lenders to closely held businesses whose ownership shares are not traded in any public marketplace may insist on audited financial statements. We would say that the amount of a bank loan, generally speaking, has to be more than $5 million or $10 million before a lender will insist that the business pay for the cost of an audit. If outside, non-manager investors – for example venture capital providers or business angels – have much invested in a business, they will almost certainly insist on an annual audit to be carried out by a substantial firm such as those listed earlier.

Instead of an audit, which they couldn't realistically afford, many smaller businesses have an outside accountant come in regularly to look over their accounting methods and give advice on their financial reporting. Unless an accountant has done an audit, he has to be very careful not to express an opinion of the external financial statements. Without a careful examination of the evidence supporting the account balances, the accountant is in no position to give an opinion on the financial statements prepared from the accounts of the business.

In the grand scheme of things, most audits are a necessary evil that do not uncover anything seriously wrong with a business's accounting system and the accounting methods it uses to prepare its financial statements. Overall, the financial statements end up looking virtually the same as they would have looked without an audit. Still, an audit has certain side benefits. In the course of doing an audit, an accountant watches for business practices that could stand some improvement and is alert to potential problems. And fraudsters beware: Accountants may face legal action if they fail to report any dodgy dealings they discover.

The auditor usually recommends ways in which the client's *internal controls* can be strengthened. For example, an auditor may discover that accounting employees are not required to take holidays and let someone else do their jobs while they're gone. The auditor would recommend that the internal control requiring holidays away from the office be strictly enforced. Book II Chapter 1 explains that good internal controls are extremely important in an accounting system. Also, in many audits that we've worked on, we caught several technical errors that were corrected, and we suggested minor improvements that were made – the end result being that the financial statements were marginally better than they would have been without the audit.

What an Auditor Does Before Giving an Opinion

An auditor does two basic things: *examines evidence* and *gives an opinion* about the financial statements. The lion's share of audit time is spent on examining evidence supporting the transactions and accounts of the business. A very small part of the total audit time is spent on writing the auditor's report, in which the auditor expresses an opinion of the financial statements and footnotes.

This list gives you an idea of what the auditor does 'in the field' – that is, on the premises of the business being audited:

- ✔ Evaluates the design and operating dependability of the business's accounting system and procedures.
- ✔ Evaluates and tests the business's internal accounting controls that are established to deter and detect errors and fraud.
- ✔ Identifies and critically examines the business's accounting methods – especially whether the methods conform to generally accepted accounting principles (GAAP), which are the touchstones for all businesses.
- ✔ Inspects documentary and physical evidence for the business's revenues, expenses, assets, liabilities, and owners' equities – for example, the auditor counts products held in stock, observes the condition of those products, and confirms checking account balances directly with the banks.

The purpose of all the audit work (examining evidence) is to provide a convincing basis for expressing an opinion of the business's financial statements, attesting that the company's financial statements and footnotes (as well as any directly supporting tables and schedules) can be relied on – or not, in some cases. The auditor puts that opinion in the auditor's report.

The auditor's report is the only visible part of the audit process to financial statement readers – the tip of the iceberg. All the readers see is the auditor's one-page report (which is based on the evidence examined during the audit process, of course). For example, Deloitte & Touche spend thousands of hours auditing General Motors, but the only thing that GM's shareholders see is the final, one-page audit report.

What's in an Auditor's Report

The audit report, which is included in the financial report near the financial statements, serves two useful purposes:

- ✔ It reassures investors and creditors that the financial report can be relied upon or calls attention to any serious departures from established financial reporting standards and generally accepted accounting principles (GAAP).
- ✔ It prevents (in the large majority of cases, anyway) businesses from issuing sloppy or fraudulent financial reports. Knowing that your report will be subject to an independent audit really keeps you on your toes!

The large majority of audit reports on financial statements give the business a clean bill of health, or a *clean opinion*. At the other end of the spectrum, the auditor might state that the financial statements are misleading and should not be relied upon. This negative audit report is called an *adverse opinion*. That's the big stick that auditors carry: They have the power to give a company's financial statements an adverse opinion, and no business wants that. Notice that we say here that the audit firms 'have the power' to give an adverse opinion. In fact, the threat of an adverse opinion almost always motivates a business to give way to the auditor and change its accounting or disclosure in order to avoid getting the kiss of death of an adverse opinion. An adverse audit opinion, if it were actually given, states that the financial statements of the business are misleading, and by implication fraudulent. The LSE and the SEC do not tolerate adverse opinions; it would stop trading in the company's shares if the company received an adverse opinion from its auditor.

Between the two extremes of a clean opinion and an adverse opinion, an auditor's report may point out a flaw in the company's financial statements – but not a fatal flaw that would require an adverse opinion. These are called *qualified opinions*. The following section looks at the most common type of audit report: the clean opinion, in which the auditor certifies that the business's financial statements conform to GAAP and are presented fairly.

True and fair, a clean opinion

If the auditor finds no serious problems, the audit firm states that the accounts give a true and fair view of the state of affairs of the company. In the US the auditor gives the financial report an *unqualified opinion*, which is the correct technical name, but most people call it a *clean opinion*. This expression has started to make its way in UK accounting parlance as the auditing business becomes more international. The clean-opinion audit report runs about 100 words and three paragraphs, with enough defensive, legal language to make even a seasoned accountant blush. Figure 6-1 shows the audit report by PricewaterhouseCoopers on the financial statements of Tesco plc. This is a clean, or unqualified, opinion in the standard three-paragraph format:

In our opinion:

> *the financial statements give a true and fair view of the state of affairs of the company and the Group at 22 February 2008 and of the profit and cash flows of the Group for the year then ended;*

> *the financial statements have been properly prepared in accordance with the Companies Act 1985; and*

> *those parts of the Directors' remuneration report required by Part 3 of Schedule 7A to the Companies Act 1985 have been properly prepared in accordance with the Companies Act 1985.*

Book IV

Managing the Finances

Figure 6-1 presents a clean opinion but in a *one*-paragraph format – given by PricewaterhouseCoopers on Caterpillar's 1999 financial statements. For many years, Price Waterhouse (as it was known before its merger with Coopers) was well known for its maverick one-paragraph audit report.

REPORT OF INDEPENDENT ACCOUNTANTS

PRICEWATERHOUSECOOPERS

To the Board of Directors and Stockholders of Caterpillar Inc.: We have audited, in accordance with auditing standards generally accepted in the United States, the consolidated financial position of Caterpillar Inc. and its subsidiaries as of December 31, 1999, 1998 and 1997, and the related consolidated results of their operations and their consolidated cash flow for each of the three years in the period ended December 31, 1999, (not presented herein); and in our report dated January 21, 2000, we expressed an unqualified opinion on those consolidated financial statements.

In our opinion, the information set forth in the accompanying condensed consolidated financial statements is fairly stated, in all material respects, in relation to the consolidated financial statements from which it has been derived.

PricewaterhouseCoopers LLP

Peoria, Illinois
January 21, 2000

Figure 6-1:
A one-paragraph audit report.

The following summary cuts through the jargon and shows you what the audit report really says.

1st paragraph	We did the audit, but the financial statements are the responsibility of management; we just express an opinion of them.
2nd paragraph	We carried out audit procedures that provide us a reasonable basis for expressing our opinion, but we don't necessarily catch everything.
3rd paragraph	The company's financial statements conform to GAAP and are not misleading.

Other kinds of audit opinions

An audit report that does *not* give a clean opinion may look very similar to a clean-opinion audit report to the untrained eye. Some investors see the name of an audit firm next to the financial statements and assume that everything is okay – after all, if the auditor had seen a problem, the cops would have pounced on the business and put everyone in jail, right? Well, not exactly.

How do you know when an auditor's report may be something other than a straightforward, no-reservations clean opinion? *Look for a fourth paragraph*; that's the key. Many audits require the audit firm to add additional, explanatory language to the standard, unqualified (clean) opinion.

One modification to an auditor's report is very serious – when the audit firm expresses the view that it has substantial doubts about the capability of the business to continue as a going concern. A *going concern* is a business that has sufficient financial wherewithal and momentum to continue its normal operations into the foreseeable future and would be able to absorb a bad turn of events without having to default on its liabilities. A going concern does not face an imminent financial crisis or any pressing financial emergency. A business could be under some financial distress, but overall still be judged a going concern. Unless there is evidence to the contrary, the auditor assumes that the business is a going concern.

But in some cases, the auditor may see unmistakable signs that a business is in deep financial waters and may not be able to convince its creditors and lenders to give it time to work itself out of its present financial difficulties. The creditors and lenders may force the business into involuntary bankruptcy, or the business may make a pre-emptive move and take itself into voluntary bankruptcy. The equity owners (shareholders of a company) may end up holding an empty bag after the bankruptcy proceedings have concluded. (This in one of the risks that shareholders take.) If an auditor has serious concerns about whether the business is a going concern, these doubts are spelled out in the auditor's report.

Auditors also point out any accounting methods that are inconsistent from one year to the next, whether their opinion is based in part on work done by another audit firm, on limitations on the scope of their audit work, on departures from GAAP (if they're not serious enough to warrant an adverse opinion), or on one of several other more technical matters. Generally, businesses – and auditors, too – want to end up with a clean bill of health; anything less is bound to catch the attention of the people who read the financial statements. Every business wants to avoid that sort of attention if possible.

Do Audits Always Catch Fraud?

Business managers and investors should understand one thing: Having an audit of a business's financial statements does not guarantee that all fraud, embezzlement, theft, and dishonesty will be detected. Audits have to be cost-effective; auditors can't examine every transaction that occurred during the year. Instead, auditors carefully evaluate businesses' internal controls and rely on sampling – they examine only a relatively small portion of transactions closely and in depth. The sample may not include the transactions that would tip off the auditor that something is wrong, however. Perpetrators of fraud and embezzlement are usually clever in concealing their wrongdoing and often prepare fake evidence to cover their tracks.

Looking for errors and fraud

Auditors look in the high-risk areas where fraud and embezzlement are most likely to occur and in areas where the company's internal controls are weak. But again, auditors can't catch everything. High-level management fraud is extraordinarily difficult to detect because auditors rely a great deal on management explanations and assurances about the business. Top-level executives may lie to auditors, deliberately mislead them, and conceal things that they don't want auditors to find out about. Auditors have a particularly difficult time detecting management fraud.

Under tougher auditing standards adopted recently auditors have to develop a detailed and definite plan to search for indicators of fraud, and they have to document the search procedures and findings in their audit working papers. Searching is one thing, but actually finding fraud is quite another. There had been many cases in which high-level management fraud went on for some time before it was discovered, usually not by auditors. The new auditing standard was expected to lead to more effective audit procedures that would reduce undetected fraud.

Unfortunately, it does not appear that things have improved. Articles in the financial press since then have exposed many cases of accounting and management fraud that were not detected or, if known about, were not objected to by the auditors. This is most disturbing. It's difficult to understand how these audit failures and breakdowns happened. The trail of facts is hard to follow in each case, especially by just reading what's reported in the press. Nevertheless, we would say that two basic reasons explain why audits fail to find fraud.

First, business managers are aware that an audit relies on a very limited sampling from the large number of transactions. They know that there is only a needle-in-the-haystack chance of fraudulent transactions being selected for an in-depth examination by the auditor. Second, managers are in a position to cover their tracks – to conceal evidence and to fabricate false evidence. In short, well-designed and well-executed management fraud is extraordinarily difficult to uncover by ordinary audit procedures. Call this *audit evidence failure*; the auditor didn't know about the fraud.

In other situations, the auditor did know what was going on but didn't act on it – call this an *audit judgment failure*. In these cases, the auditor was overly tolerant of wrong accounting methods used by the client. The auditor may have had serious objections to the accounting methods, but the client persuaded the auditor to go along with the methods.

Take note of an article in *The Wall Street Journal* in late 1999, on the SEC's stepped-up activity in dealing with financial statement fraud. This article used the following terms: 'busted audits', 'bend the accounting rules', 'fake numbers', 'doctoring the books', 'weak-kneed auditors', and 'went soft on companies' books'. Even allowing for journalistic hype, these are rather harsh words for an article in such a respected newspaper as *The Wall Street Journal.* The tone of the article says a lot about the state of affairs in the world of auditing.

What happens when auditors spot fraud

In the course of doing an audit, the audit firm may make the following discoveries:

- ✔ **Errors in recording transactions:** These honest mistakes happen from time to time because of inexperienced bookkeepers, or poorly trained accountants, or simple failure to pay attention to details. No one is stealing money or other assets or defrauding the business. Management wants the errors corrected and wants to prevent them from happening again.

- ✔ **Theft, embezzlement, and fraud against the business:** This kind of dishonesty takes advantage of weak internal controls or involves the abuse of positions of authority in the organisation that top management did not know about and was not involved in. Management may take action against the guilty parties.

- ✔ **Accounting fraud (**also called **financial fraud** or **financial reporting fraud):** This refers to top-level managers who know about and approve the use of misleading and invalid accounting methods for the purpose of disguising the business's financial problems or artificially inflating profit. Often, managers benefit from these improper accounting methods – by propping up the market price of the company's shares to make their stock options more valuable, for example.

- ✔ **Management fraud:** In the broadest sense, this includes accounting fraud, but in a more focused sense, it refers to high-level business managers engaging in illegal schemes to line their pockets at the business's expense, or knowingly violating laws and regulations that put the business at risk of large criminal or civil penalties. A manager may conspire with competitors to fix prices or divide the market, for example. Accepting kickbacks or bribes from customers is an example of management fraud – although most management fraud is more sophisticated than taking under-the-table payments.

When the first two types of problems are discovered, the auditor's follow-up is straightforward. Errors are corrected, and the loss from the crime against the business is recorded. (Such a loss may be a problem if it were so large that the auditor thinks it should be disclosed separately in the financial report, but the business disagrees and does not want to call attention to the loss.) In contrast, the auditor is between a rock and a hard place when accounting or management fraud is uncovered.

When an auditor discovers accounting or management fraud, the business has to clean up the fraud mess as best it can – which often involves recording a loss. Of course, the business should make changes to prevent the fraud from occurring again. And it may request the resignations of those responsible or even take legal action against those employees. Assuming that the fraud loss is recorded and reported correctly in the financial statements, the auditor then issues a clean opinion on the financial statements. But auditors can withhold a clean opinion and threaten to issue a qualified or adverse opinion if the client does not deal with the matter in a satisfactory manner in its financial statements. That's the auditor's real clout.

The most serious type of accounting fraud occurs when profit is substantially overstated with the result that the market value of the corporation's shares was based on inflated profit numbers. Another type of accounting fraud occurs when a business is in deep financial trouble but its balance sheet disguises the trouble and makes things look more sound than they really are. The business may be on the verge of financial failure, but the balance sheet gives no clue. When the fraud comes out into the open, the market value takes a plunge, and the investors call their lawyers and sue the business and the auditor.

Investing money in a business or shares issued by a public business involves many risks. The risk of misleading financial statements is just one of many dangers that investors face. A business may have accurate and truthful financial statements but end up in the tank because of bad management, bad products, poor marketing, or just bad luck.

All in all, audited financial statements that carry a clean opinion (the best possible auditor's report) are reliable indicators for investors to use – especially because auditors are held accountable for their reports and can be sued for careless audit procedures. (In fact, accountancy firms have had to pay many millions of pounds in malpractice lawsuit damages over the past 30 years and Arthur Andersen was actually driven out of business.) Make sure that you don't overlook the audit report as a tool for judging the reliability of a business's financial statements. When you read the auditor's report on the annual financial statements from your pension fund manager, hopefully you'll be very reassured! That's your retirement money they're talking about, after all.

Auditors and GAAP

In the course of doing an audit, the accountant often catches certain accounting methods used by the client that violate GAAP, the approved and authoritative methods and standards that businesses must follow in preparing and reporting financial statements. All businesses are subject to these ground rules. An auditor calls to the attention of the business any departures from

GAAP, and he helps the business make adjustments to put its financial statements back on the GAAP track. Sometimes, a business may not want to make the changes that the auditor suggests because its profit numbers would be deflated. Professional standards demand that the auditor secure a change (assuming that the amount involved is material). If the client refuses to make a change to an acceptable accounting method, the accountant warns the financial report reader in the auditor's report.

Auditors do not allow their good names to be associated with financial reports that they know are misleading if they can possibly help it. Every now and then, we read in the financial press about an audit firm walking away from a client ('withdraws from the engagement' is the official terminology). As mentioned earlier in this chapter, everything the auditor learns in the course of an audit is confidential and cannot be divulged beyond top management and the board of directors of the business. A *confidential relationship* exists between the auditor and the client – although it is not equal to the privileged communication between lawyers and their clients.

If an auditor discovers a problem, he has the responsibility to move up the chain of command in the business organisation to make sure that one level higher than the source of the problem is informed of the problem. But the board of directors is the end of the line. The auditor does not inform the LSE, the SEC or another regulatory agency of any confidential information learned during the audit.

However, most outside observers will work on the 'no smoke without fire' principle. No firm, yet alone an accountancy partnership with their partnership profit share on the line, willingly gives up a lucrative client.

Auditors, on the other hand, are frequently being replaced, often for cost reasons – auditing is a negotiable deal too – but also because the firm being audited may have simply outgrown the auditor. This happens fairly frequently when a business is going for a public listing of its shares. The guy round the corner, who was cheap and competent, cuts no ice with the big wheels at the LSE and the placing houses that have to sell the shares. They want a big name auditor to help the PR push.

We can't exaggerate the importance of reliable financial statements that are prepared according to uniform standards and methods for measuring profit and putting values on assets, liabilities, and owners' equity. Not to put too fine a point on it, the flow of capital into businesses and the market prices of shares traded in the public markets (the London Stock Exchange, the New York Stock Exchange, and over the NASDAQ network) depend on the information reported in financial statements.

Book IV

Managing the Finances

Also, smaller, privately-owned businesses would have a difficult time raising capital from owners and borrowing money from banks if no one could trust their financial statements. Generally accepted accounting principles, in short, are the gold standard for financial reporting. Once financial reporting standards have been put into place, how are the standards enforced? To a large extent, the role of auditors is to do just that – to enforce GAAP. The main purpose of having annual audits, in other words, is to keep businesses on the straight-and-narrow path of GAAP and to prevent businesses from issuing misleading financial statements. Auditors are the guardians of the financial reporting rules. We think most business managers and investors agree that financial reporting would be in a sorry state of affairs if auditors weren't around.

From Audits to Advising

If Accountant Rip van Winkle woke up today after his 20-year sleep, he would be shocked to find that accountancy firms make most of their money not from doing audits but from advising clients. A recent advertisement by one of the Big Four international accountancy firms listed the following services: 'assurance, business consulting, corporate finance, eBusiness, human capital, legal services, outsourcing, risk consulting, and tax services'. (Now, if the firm could only help you with your back problems!) Do you see audits in this list? No? Well, it's under the first category – assurance. Why have accountancy firms moved so far beyond audits into many different fields of consulting?

We suspect that many businesses do not view audits as adding much value to their financial reports. True, having a clean opinion by an auditor on financial statements adds credibility to a financial report. At the same time, managers tend to view the audit as an intrusion, and an override on their prerogatives regarding how to account for profit and how to present the financial report of the business. Most audits, to be frank about it, involve a certain amount of tension between managers and the audit firm. After all, the essence of an audit is to second-guess the business's accounting methods and financial reporting decisions. So it's quite understandable that accountancy firms have looked to other types of services they can provide to clients that are more value-added and less adversarial – and that are more lucrative.

Nevertheless, many people argued that accountancy firms should get out of the consulting and advising business – at least to the same clients they audit. For the first years of this millennium things seem to be moving in this direction, and new legislation is gave them a none too gentle prod. Arthur Andersen only just split their consultancy business off before they went under themselves. Luckily they changed the name of the consulting business from

Andersen to Accenture, ditching a fair amount of the bad odour that attached itself to the accountancy practice's name. Now the pendulum is swinging back and big accountancy firms are pushing an integrated approach arguing that clients don't want to have to explain largely the same business facts to different teams of 'visiting firemen'. Although the big four are back in the consulting game figures from the Management Consultancies Association suggest that accountancy firms only have 16% of the market for consultancy services, right now at least.

Sometimes we take the pessimistic view that in the long run accountants will abandon audits and do only taxes and consulting. Who will do audits then? Well, a team of governmental auditors could take over the task – but we don't think this would be too popular.

Book IV

Managing the Finances

Book V
Employing Staff

After the FIFO method and the LIFO
method comes the **LILO** method.

In this book . . .

*U*nless you intend working on your own, you'll be involved in employing and motivating others to do what you want them to do. Even if you don't employ people full-time, or if you outsource some portion of your work to others, you'll have to choose who to give those tasks to, how to get the best out of them, and how to reward their achievements.

Employees are entitled to the National Minimum Wage, minimum periods of paid holiday, and statutory payments when they're off sick, on maternity leave, or are made redundant. You can stick to those legal minimum amounts – but you can be more generous, and that may help you attract better-qualified employees. Sometimes, it's the rest of the package, such as the pension scheme you offer, that encourages employees to stay with you.

Here are the contents of Book V at a glance:

Chapter 1

Working Out the Wages

In This Chapter

▶ Knowing who's entitled to what wages

▶ Complying with the law on the minimum wage – and the consequences of not doing so

▶ Considering the case for paying better wages

▶ Grasping the practicalities of payment

*I*f you employ a member of staff to work for you, it goes without saying that you have to pay her for her work. But you need to think about more than simply how and what you pay her. One of the first things to consider is what other companies are paying people in similar jobs in your area. You need to encourage people to apply for your jobs and you want to keep them once you have employed them, so make sure that they aren't going to leave you for better pay elsewhere. Money isn't the only thing that keeps workers motivated and happy in their jobs, but it can go a long way. But above all you must comply with the law as far as pay is concerned otherwise you can end up facing a claim at an Employment Tribunal. That means paying at least the national minimum wage, paying men and women equal pay for equal jobs, and avoiding discrimination.

Paying the Minimum Wage: Who's Entitled to What

Almost all workers in the UK are entitled to the National Minimum Wage. The only people this doesn't apply to are the self-employed, volunteers, prisoners, workers living as part of a family, and school children. Everybody else qualifies, including home workers, part-timers, agency workers, and casual workers.

Three different rates apply, depending on the employee's age:

- ✔ Anyone 22 or over must be paid at least £5.52 per hour from October 2007.
- ✔ 18–21-year-olds get at least £4.60 per hour from October 2007.
- ✔ Workers aged 16 and 17 who have reached the minimum school leaving age must be paid at least £3.40 an hour.
- ✔ Apprentices under 19 and those 19 and over in the first 12 months of their apprenticeship are not entitled to the National Minimum Wage.

If you don't pay the minimum wage employees can claim it through the civil courts or an Employment Tribunal. And if you dismiss an employee for claiming her rights to the minimum wage, the dismissal will be unfair and that's another case for an Employment Tribunal.

What counts as pay?

Not everything an employee gets in her wage packet counts towards the minimum wage. The following list shows the exemptions:

- ✔ Tips (unless you take employees' tips and use them to make up part of their salaries)
- ✔ Allowances, expenses, and 'on-the-job' travel costs
- ✔ Extra wages from overtime and shift work
- ✔ Most benefits in kind (such as the use of a company car, fuel, or meals)

Bonuses, incentive payments, and performance-related pay do count. If you provide an employee with accommodation, the total value of that doesn't count – only £4.30 a day counts towards the minimum wage. You also ignore loans and pension or redundancy payments.

What count as hours?

The number of hours for which you must pay an employee the minimum depends on the kind of work she does. Work is broken down into four legal categories:

- ✔ **Time workers** get paid for working a set number of hours.
- ✔ **Salaried-hours workers** are contracted to work a set number of hours each year for an annual salary paid in 12 equal monthly instalments.

✔ **Output work.** Paid according to the number of pieces of work produced.

✔ **Unmeasured work.** Paid to do specific tasks but without set hours.

You must pay an employee the minimum wage for her hours worked in a week or a month – whichever is the *pay reference period* (the period for which she is regularly paid – weekly or monthly) set out in her contract. A time worker paid to work a specific number of hours in a week must get at least the minimum wage for those hours. A salaried worker gets paid the minimum wage for each hour she works each week or month, and rest breaks, lunch breaks, sick leave, maternity, paternity, and adoption leave all count towards the minimum wage if they form part of the basic minimum hours. For output and unmeasured work it's a little more complicated.

You either have to pay an output worker the minimum wage for all of the hours she works or an amount for each piece of work, adding up to an effective minimum wage. So if a worker can make up two garments in an hour she should either be paid the current hourly minimum rate or £2.76 per garment she finishes.

If you hire someone to do certain jobs, such as a gardener who has no set hours but works when she's needed or when the work is available, you have to decide whether to pay her for every hour she works or to come to an agreement about the daily average hours she should work.

Keeping records of wage payments

You must keep records to prove that you've paid at least the minimum wage for all the necessary hours and you can be fined if you don't keep those records. You have to keep them for at least three years but you're advised to keep them for at least six years and employees can ask to see them. You have to give access within 14 days of a request or the employee can take a case against you at an Employment Tribunal.

If a dispute arises you'll need to prove that you have complied with the law. HMRC has responsibility for making sure that employers are toeing the line, so if a compliance officer asks to see your records you must produce them. No list exists of what records you have to keep, but you should probably have:

✔ Details of gross pay for each employee.

✔ Payments for overtime and shifts.

✔ Details of absences.

✔ Details of any agreements and contracts between you and your workers.

If you pay well above the minimum wage your company PAYE income tax records and National Insurance contribution records (see Book VI Chapter 1 for more on these) will be enough to prove that you're within the law.

Although you must keep your records for three years, an employee can bring a case against you in a civil court for up to six years after she says you failed to pay the minimum wage. So it's a wise move to keep your records for six years.

Penalties for not paying

An employee can bring a case against you at an Employment Tribunal or in a civil court for wages you haven't paid. Failing to pay the minimum wage is a criminal offence, meaning that you can also be prosecuted and fined.

If an HM Revenue & Customs compliance officer suspects that you aren't complying with the law she can pay you a visit. If she then sees your records and believes that you haven't been paying the right wage, she can serve you with an enforcement notice – which will require you to start making the correct payments and pay any back pay owed. If you ignore that notice you may get a penalty notice and ultimately a fine. Failing to pay minimum wage, in fact, puts you at risk for prosecution on six criminal charges:

- ✔ Refusal to pay the minimum wage
- ✔ Failure to keep sufficient records
- ✔ Keeping false records
- ✔ Producing false records or information
- ✔ Intentionally obstructing a compliance officer
- ✔ Refusing to give information to a compliance officer

In each case the maximum fine is £5,000.

Small business owners complain that they struggle because of the minimum wage, especially as it is now well above the £5 mark. In any case, if your business wants to attract the best employees, you can't afford to pay less than your competitors do.

Paying the Going Rate: Competing in the Market

You must pay your employees at least the minimum wage . . . but nothing stops you paying more than that. If you're thinking of taking on staff to do particular jobs and wondering how much to pay them, you need to take a look at what your competitors are paying and what the going rate for those types of jobs is in your area.

You want to attract the best possible people to work for you and although pay isn't the only factor that potential employees consider when deciding on what jobs to apply for, it is a fairly important one and can be a useful indicator of how good a business is to work for. You should pay people according to their qualifications and experience and if you don't offer good pay someone else will. Good pay is also important when it comes to keeping staff. Remember that if they leave you will have to go to all the trouble and expense of hiring someone new and possibly training her up again.

Look at what other employers in your area, in your industry, and your direct competitors are paying. This is called *benchmarking*. Use www.benchmark index.com to help you, and do a review of your pay rates once a year to make sure that you stay competitive.

Another issue to consider is what pay scheme you're going to use. Basically you have two choices, both systems with their pros and cons:

- ✔ **The basic rate system.** You pay a fixed amount on an hourly, weekly, or monthly basis. Basic pay is simple and straightforward, but offers no incentives for your employees to do better.

- ✔ **The incentive system.** Part of the pay is basic and part is based on performance and results. Incentive schemes can work out more expensive, are less transparent, and if you base them on the performance of a team you may get some people doing all the work and others not pulling their weight.

You need to work out what scheme or combination of schemes is best for your business. You may think about paying employees more the longer they work for you. That encourages people to stay on – but what about the younger ones you employ who have better qualifications? They may not be so happy.

On the other hand, you may decide to pay more for people with better qualifications and that system encourages them to take training courses to get better qualifications, but that additional expertise in turn makes them more attractive to other employers – who are possibly in a position to pay more.

Pay is important, but it isn't the only way to keep staff happy and make you the employer of first choice. A good work–life balance, flexible working, training opportunities, an employer who consults with staff, and good conditions in the workplace can be just as attractive to employees as money is.

Paying the Same for the Same Job

Under the *Equal Pay Act 1970* you must pay women and men equal pay for work of equal value. This applies to basic pay, hours of work, bonuses, and pension contributions. Your employees can ask you for information to help them work out whether or not they are getting equal pay and if not why not. They can also get advice from the Equality and Human Rights Commission – see the Web site at www.equalityhumanrights.com or call 0845-604 6610 in England, 0845 604 8810 in Wales, or 0845 604 5510 in Scotland and obtain a questionnaire to submit to you for that information. Employees in Northern Ireland can contact the Equality Commission for Northern Ireland through the Web site at www.equalityni.org or by phone at 02890 890 890. Just as you can't discriminate against people, harass them, or victimise them in any aspect of their working conditions, you must be equally fair about pay.

An employee's contract of employment implies an equality clause even if one doesn't actually exist. As women bring the majority of the cases against employers under the Equal Pay Act, this example uses a woman's perspective, but it applies equally to men. A woman can compare herself with a man employed by you if:

✔ She does 'like work'.

✔ A job evaluation scheme has rated her work as equivalent.

✔ Her job is of equal value.

A woman is employed on *like work* if her work and that of a man are broadly similar and any difference between the two roles isn't of practical importance. Job titles carry far less importance in this situation than job descriptions.

You don't have to carry out a job evaluation, but if you do and a woman's job is rated as equivalent to a man's when it comes to effort, skill, qualification, and responsibilities, make sure that the pay is equal too. A woman can bring a claim against you for equal pay if she can show that her work is of equal value to a man's – again taking into account effort, skills, qualifications, and responsibilities – so a job evaluation may well be worth your time!

If an employee wants to make a claim for equal pay, she can do it at any time you employ her or within six months of the date she leaves. The Tribunal can make you pay up to six years' arrears up to the date the employee started proceedings (five years in Scotland).

Interestingly, a woman can't bring a claim for equal pay if the job she's doing has more responsibility or requires more skill than a man's but is less well paid – although recent cases suggest that she can claim if the work she's doing is of greater value than a male counterpart's.

You are on fairly safe ground if you pay one employee more because of something that has nothing to do with gender. For example, if a man and a woman are doing similar jobs but the woman earns more because she earns a bigger sales-related bonus that will be fair, or if the man gets more because he's been in the job longer and you pay more for longer service that will also be OK.

Paying Extras

On top of basic pay you may have a system for paying extras to your employees. Perhaps you offer the opportunity to work more hours than the normal working week and pay for that overtime, or maybe you pay bonuses or commission. In some businesses such as restaurants and hotels tips and gratuities boost staff wages. This section gives you the low-down on these little extras.

Overtime

When employees work extra hours, you have to pay them at the rate set out in their contract. The contract can spell out any rate for overtime you want (provided you pay at least the national minimum wage, of course). You may simply pay the same for an hour of *overtime* as you do for a normal hour of work. But if you want to give employees an incentive to do any extra work as and when you need it done you may pay a little extra – perhaps one-and-a-half times the normal rate or even twice or three times the usual hourly rate.

Bonuses

You pay *bonuses* on top of basic wages and salary, and usually link them in some way to the performance of the business. The general idea is that a flourishing business benefits everyone, and that an employee who contributes to that business performance can expect a bonus that in turn acts as an incentive to her to work that bit harder. But you need to be careful that bonuses really do act as incentives and don't cause destructive rivalries. Bonuses can be counted towards the minimum wage.

Commission

Commission is a payment on top of basic salary based on performance – of the whole team or an individual. Commission is different to a bonus because it's based on the individual or team performance rather than the performance of the business. Commission counts towards the minimum wage.

Commission is common for people like sales workers, who often have lower basic salaries than other employees. Their total wage can be made up partly of a basic salary and partly of a certain amount of commission on every sale made.

The more dependent your employees are on commission to give them a decent wage, the more anxious they will be to make sales. That may be good for your business, but it can also lead to poor sales practices such as pressurising people into buying or selling customers products that aren't right for them. So pushy sales people may not do your firm's reputation much good and can be bad for business in the long run. It's important to get the balance right.

Tips and gratuities

If you let your employees keep any tips and gratuities your customers leave, they don't count towards the minimum wage. But many employers operate different ways of dividing gratuities up. Some insist that employees put all such money into a communal pot and share it out equally, and some collect all of it and pay out a share to each employee through the payroll.

If tips and gratuities go through the payroll they count towards the minimum wage.

Expenses

A member of staff has the right to recover any expenses she's run up while doing work for you. You'll need to have a system in place for dealing with expenses claims. Some employers expect employees to pay out of their own pockets and then claim the money back; others book travel tickets, hire cars, and accommodation – the bigger expenses – and pay those direct, leaving only the smaller ones for staff to pay and claim back. If you have a deadline by which employees have to claim expenses you can spread the expense more evenly through the year. Without a deadline employees are very good at forgetting to do their expenses and end up claiming a whole year's worth at once.

Make it clear what employees can and can't claim. If, for example, you will pay for meals while employees are away from their usual workplace, decide whether you want to pay the price of the meal that's eaten or want to place a limit on the amount that can be claimed for each meal. Make sure your employees know this before they order another bottle of expensive wine to wash their expenses account away with.

Paying: The Practicalities

There was a time when manual workers had the right to be paid in cash, but now the way you pay your employees is wholly a matter between you and them. Another main issue to sort out with employees is when and how often you pay them. Most employers will pay monthly rather than weekly, but the details should be set out in the contract with the date each month that payments are due. Some employers pay monthly at the end of the month in which the work has been done. Others pay in the middle of the month, when they are effectively paying two weeks in arrears and two weeks in advance. It's important to be clear how your system works to avoid confusion about what you owe when employees leave your firm. You also need to be clear about how you pay bonuses, commission, tips, overtime and any other payments due. For example, a bonus may only be paid once a year instead of monthly.

On time

Whatever system you use, always pay on the day you've said you will pay. If you don't employees may have nothing to live on until you do pay and may get into financial trouble through going overdrawn or having direct debits and standing orders cancelled and cheques bounced. You also need to let your staff know what will happen if the normal date of payment falls on a Sunday or a bank holiday. Can they expect their wages to be in the bank the day before or will they have to wait a day longer?

Into bank accounts

Employers still pay many people in cash, especially if they pay them weekly, but payment by credit transfer into your employees' bank accounts is more common. To do that you need bank account details from your employees; if an employee doesn't have a bank account and prefers not to have one, you may need to come to an agreement about an alternative means of payment (such as cash or cheque).

Make sure you keep employees' bank details safe. To do this, keep them locked up in a filing cabinet or in password-protected computer files. Make sure only the people who need to access them can.

In cash

If you pay your employees in cash and decide to change to another method of payment without their agreement, you are in breach of contract. But the courts only award nominal compensation if employees bring cases in such circumstances, so there seems to be little to stop you so long as you give reasonable notice and have a good business reason – such as increasing efficiency or security by changing over to a cashless payment system. But in the interests of workplace harmony it's best to get everyone's agreement before you go ahead. Some people are very keen to be paid in cash and some still don't have bank accounts and so will have trouble cashing a cheque.

In euros

Occasionally people want their wages in euros. They can open a euro account into which you can transfer their wages as usual and the bank will convert the money to euros and hold it in that currency.

Tax Credits

Tax credits are the way that the government provides extra income for parents and low-paid workers. Child Tax Credits support families with children whether or not any of the adults has a paid job, and Working Tax Credits help low-paid workers without children. If your employees qualify for tax credits, these are processed by HM Revenue & Customs and paid directly. You don't have to do anything and they won't affect how much you pay in wages.

Laying Off Staff: Guarantee Payments

If you decide to lay employees off temporarily, employees who you've employed for at least a month have a right to *guarantee pay* (payment to make up for some of the work they're missing out on). This means that you must pay them for up to five days' pay in any period of three months. The maximum amount you have to pay is £19.60 for any one day, and you can only pay less than that if the employee will normally earn less than that in a day.

You don't have to pay guarantee pay if:

Book V

Employing Staff

- ✔ The employee's contract is for three months or less.
- ✔ She isn't available for work.
- ✔ You offer her suitable alternative work and she refuses.
- ✔ She's on strike or can't work because of a strike.
- ✔ Her contract of employment doesn't require her to accept work that you offer her.
- ✔ You have a collective agreement covering guarantee payments.

Going Bust

Going out of business isn't a nice prospect to contemplate, but it can happen. If it does, the chances are that you will owe your employees some outstanding pay. Your assets are sold off and any money made is given to your creditors in order of priority. Your employees are preferred creditors, so they will be entitled to any money left after your *secured creditors* (those who have some kind of security such as a mortgage on the business property, equipment, or assets) have been paid. Your employees are entitled to all wages and salary for up to four months before the company went bust and to all their holiday entitlement.

If no money is available to pay employees, the state will pick up the bills for:

- ✔ Pay arrears for up to eight weeks at a maximum of £330 a week.
- ✔ Holiday entitlement for up to six weeks at the same maximum weekly amount.
- ✔ The statutory minimum notice period at a maximum of £330 a week.
- ✔ Any statutory maternity pay owed.
- ✔ Redundancy payments.

These payments are made by the Redundancy Payments Offices. Employees can call the Redundancy Payments Helpline on 0845-1450004 or go to www. insolvency.gov.uk to download the leaflet *Redundancy and Insolvency – a Guide for Employees*. They need to fill in form RP1 which is in the back of that leaflet and send it to the Redundancy Payments Office which deals with the area they live in. The addresses for these are listed in the leaflet.

Chapter 2

Employee Payroll and Benefits

*U*nless your business employs just one person (you, the owner), you probably need to hire employees, and that means you have to pay them, offer benefits, and manage a payroll.

Responsibilities for hiring and paying employees are usually shared between the human resources staff and the bookkeeping staff. As the bookkeeper, you must make sure that all HM Revenue & Customs tax-related forms are completed, and you need to manage all payroll responsibilities including paying employees, collecting and paying employee taxes, collecting and managing employee benefit contributions, and paying benefit providers.

Before you proceed any further, log onto the HM Revenue & Customs Web site at www.hmrc.gov.uk, and click on the New employers link in the Employers section to get to the help area for new employers. Alternatively, phone the New Employer Hotline on 0845 607 0143 and let them talk you through the process. You may be surprised how helpful the people working there are.

This chapter examines the various employee staffing issues that bookkeepers need to be able to manage.

Staffing Your Business

After you decide that you want to hire employees for your business, you must be ready to deal with a lot of official paperwork. In addition to paperwork, you're faced with many decisions about how employees are to be paid and who's going to be responsible for maintaining the paperwork that HM Revenue & Customs requires.

Knowing what needs to be done to satisfy these officials isn't the only issue you must consider before the first person is hired; you also need to decide how frequently you're going to pay employees and what type of wage and salary scales you want to set up.

Completing new starter forms

Even before you pay your first employee, you need to start completing the HM Revenue & Customs forms related to hiring. If you plan to hire staff, you must first make sure that they have a National Insurance number. HM Revenue & Customs uses this number to track your employees, the money you pay them, as well as any PAYE (Pay As You Earn) tax and NICs (National Insurance Contributions) collected and paid on their behalf.

The following sections explain how to deal with each of these situations.

Obtaining an Employer's PAYE Reference

Every business must have an Employer's PAYE Reference in order to hire employees. Without this Reference you can't legally pay staff and deduct PAYE tax and NICS.

Luckily, HM Revenue & Customs makes it very straightforward to obtain an Employer's PAYE Reference, which is typically a three-digit number (to identify the tax office) followed by four alpha characters (to identify the employer). The fastest way is to call HM Revenue & Customs New Employer Hotline on 0845 607 0143 and complete the form by telephone. Be prepared to provide the following information:

- ✔ **General business information:** Business name, trading address, name and address of employer, National Insurance number and Unique Taxpayer Reference of employer, contact telephone number, contact e-mail address if registering using e-mail, nature of business.

- ✔ **Employee information:** The date you took on (or intend to take on) your first employee(s), how many employees you intend to have, the date you intend to pay them for the first time, how often you intend to pay them.

If your business is a partnership or a limited company, you need to give additional information:

- ✔ **Partnership:** Names and addresses of any business partners, National Insurance numbers and Unique Taxpayer References of any business partners, and your LLP number if you are a Limited Liability Partnership (LLP).
- ✔ **Limited company:** The company's registered address, company registration number and date of incorporation, the names, addresses, private telephone numbers, National Insurance numbers and Unique Taxpayer References of the company directors.

After obtaining your Employer's PAYE Reference, you can start to pay your employees legally.

In addition to your Employer's PAYE Reference you receive a New Employer's Guide, which includes a CD-ROM with online help and a payroll Tax and National Insurance Calculator, which makes your life so much easier. This guide also includes some samples of the forms you need, which are covered later in this chapter.

As well as tracking pay and taxes, HM Revenue & Customs uses your PAYE Reference to track the payment of PAYE tax and NICs, both of which the employer must pay.

If you try to pay staff without an Employer's PAYE Reference, HM Revenue & Customs doesn't have a record of these deductions. In the worst case scenario the employee may have to pay his tax again and lose pension and unemployment rights when the business doesn't pass these deductions over to HM Revenue & Customs.

Collecting P45s

Every person you hire must bring a P45 from his previous employer. The *P45* is a record of the employee's taxable earnings, PAYE deducted, and tax code for the current tax year.

This form, shown in Figure 2-1, gives you the information you need as the new employer to make sure that you can deduct the correct amount of PAYE and National Insurance from the new employee.

Ask a new employee right from the start if he has a P45 from a previous employer. If an employee doesn't have a P45, you must deduct income tax out of his wage as if it is all taxable. We talk more about deducting taxes in the section 'Collecting Employee Taxes', later in this chapter.

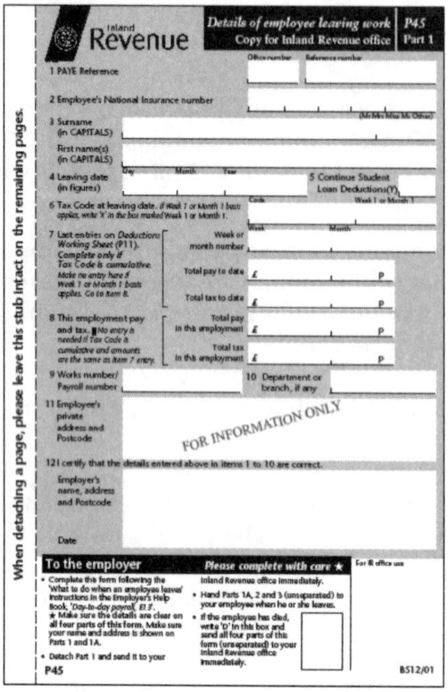

Inland Revenue

Details of employee leaving work
Copy for Inland Revenue office

P45
Part 1

Office number / Reference number

1 PAYE Reference

2 Employee's National Insurance number

3 Surname (in CAPITALS) (Mr Mrs Miss Ms Other)

First name(s) (in CAPITALS)

4 Leaving date (in figures) Day Month Year

5 Continue Student Loan Deductions(Y)

6 Tax Code at leaving date. *If Week 1 or Month 1 basis applies, write 'X' in the box marked Week 1 or Month 1.* Code / Week 1 or Month 1

7 Last entries on *Deductions Working Sheet* (P11). *Complete only if Tax Code is cumulative. Make no entry here if Week 1 or Month 1 basis applies. Go to item 8.*
Week or month number — Week / Month
Total pay to date £ p
Total tax to date £ p

8 This employment pay and tax. *No entry is needed if Tax Code is cumulative and amounts are the same as item 7 entry.*
Total pay in this employment £ p
Total tax in this employment £ p

9 Works number/ Payroll number

10 Department or branch, if any

11 Employee's private address and Postcode

FOR INFORMATION ONLY

12 I certify that the details entered above in items 1 to 10 are correct.

Employer's name, address and Postcode

Date

When detaching a page, please leave this stub intact on the remaining pages.

To the employer *Please complete with care ★*

- Complete this form following the 'What to do when an employee leaves' instructions in the Employer's Help Book, *'Day-to-day payroll', E13*.
  ★ Make sure the details are clear on all four parts of this form. Make sure your name and address is shown on Parts 1 and 1A.
- Detach Part 1 and send it to your Inland Revenue office immediately.
- Hand Parts 1A, 2 and 3 (unseparated) to your employee when he or she leaves.
- If the employee has died, write 'D' in this box and send all four parts of this form (unseparated) to your Inland Revenue office immediately.

For IR office use

P45

BS12/01

Figure 2-1: All new employees bring form P45 so that you know how much to take out of their wages for PAYE and National Insurance.

The P45 is a four-part carbon form:

- **Part 1** shows details of employee leaving work. The previous employer sends Part 1 to its tax office. This process keeps HM Revenue & Customs informed that the employee has left his old job.
- **Part 1A** is an exact copy of Part 1 that the employee keeps for his records.
- **Part 2** contains the information that you (as the new employer) need to have to ensure that you deduct the correct amount for PAYE tax and National Insurance. Keep this part in your records system. The information you need to answer the seven questions here is already filled in as a result of Part 1 being completed – so you have nothing to complete, just keep it.
- **Part 3** is filled in by you as the new employer. Again questions 1 to 7 are already completed for you as a result of Part 1 being completed. You complete the bottom half of the P45 – boxes 8 to 16 – sign the declaration in box 17, and send it on to your local HM Revenue & Customs Office. Fortunately this process is very straightforward. The questions you need to answer are:
  - Q8: Enter your PAYE Reference.
  - Q9: Enter the date the new employee started working for you.

- Q10: Enter details of the new employee's works/payroll number, branch or depot, and tick if you want these details shown on any tax code notifications.

- Q11: Enter P if the employee will not be paid by you between the employment start date and the next 5 April.

- Q12: Enter the tax code in use if different to code at Q6.

- Q13: If the tax figure you are entering on form P11 differs from item shown in Q7 enter your figure.

- Q14: Enter the employee's private address.

- Q15: Enter the employee's date of birth.

- Q16: Enter the employee's job title or description.

Starting fresh with employees without a P45

If a worker is new to the job market, he must have a National Insurance number. In some cases, however, a new employee may not have a National Insurance number or a P45.

Many new employees don't have P45s, perhaps because they've lost it, or this is their first job, or maybe they are keeping another job as well as working for you. In these cases your new employee must complete a P46. Essentially, the P46 is a substitute for the P45. The new employee must complete Section 1, shown in Figure 2-2, and the new employer (that's you) completes Section 2, shown in Figure 2-3. You then send the completed form to your local tax office on the employee's first pay day.

The end result of using a P46 is that the new employee initially pays too much tax and National Insurance until the local HM Revenue & Customs office sends you the correct tax code and cumulative taxable pay and tax paid information. In effect the HM Revenue & Customs office provides you with what would have been on the P45.

Completing forms for foreign workers

As an employer in the UK, it is your responsibility to verify that any person you hire is a UK citizen or has the right to work in the United Kingdom – you can't just accept his word. If you have any doubts ask to see his passport and Home Office Work Permit. Of course some foreign workers, namely those from the European countries that make up the European Economic Area (EEA), don't need a work permit.

The EU has an agreement with Norway, Iceland, and Liechtenstein (countries within the European Economic Area or EEA) and a separate agreement with Switzerland, which confer rights similar to those of EU nationals on nationals of those countries.

HM Revenue & Customs

P46: Employee without a Form P45

Section one To be completed by the employee

Please complete section one and then hand back the form to your present employer.
If you later receive a form P45 from your previous employer, please hand it to your present employer.

Your details Please use capitals

National Insurance number
This is very important in getting your tax and benefits right.

Date of birth
D D M M Y Y Y Y

Name
Title – enter MR, MRS, MISS, MS or other title

Address
Postcode

Surname or family name

House or flat number

First or given name(s)

Rest of address including house name or flat name

Are you male or female?
Male ☐ Female ☐

Your present circumstances

Please read all the following statements carefully and tick **the one** that applies to you.

A - This is my first job since last 6 April and **I have not** been receiving taxable Jobseeker's Allowance or taxable Incapacity Benefit or a state or occupational pension. ☐ A

OR

B - This is now my only job, but since last 6 April I **have** had another job, or have received taxable Jobseeker's Allowance or Incapacity Benefit. I do not receive a state or occupational pension. ☐ B

OR

C - I have another job or receive a state or occupational pension. ☐ C

Student Loans

If you left a course of Higher Education before last 6 April and received your first Student Loan instalment on or after 1 September 1998 and you have not fully repaid your student loan, tick box D. *(If you are required to repay your Student Loan through your bank or building society account do **not** tick box D.)* ☐ D

Signature and date

I can confirm that this information is correct

Signature

Date
D D M M Y Y Y Y

P46(2006) Page 1 HMRC 11/05

Figure 2-2:
Section 1 of the P46 that a new employee must complete if he doesn't have a P45.

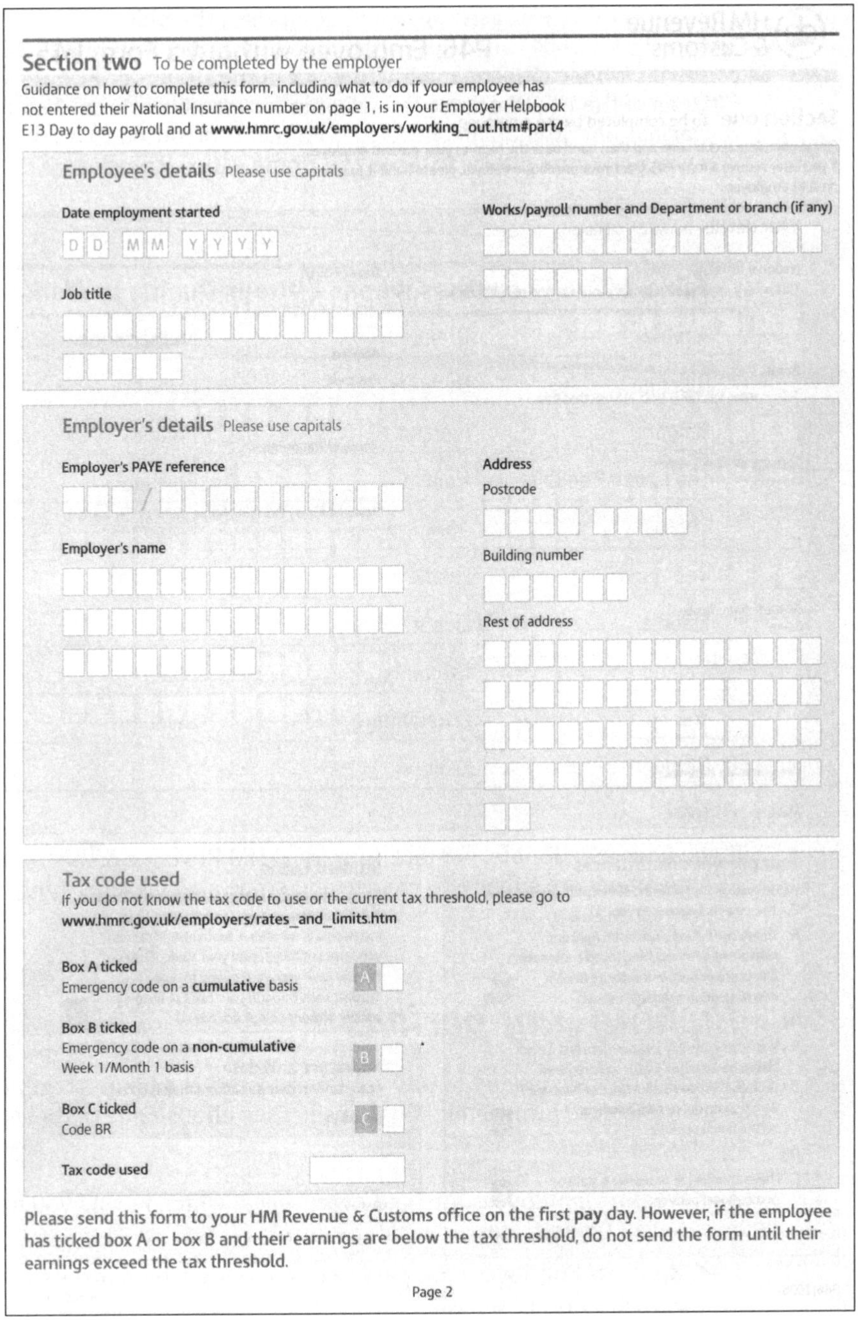

Section two   To be completed by the employer

Guidance on how to complete this form, including what to do if your employee has not entered their National Insurance number on page 1, is in your Employer Helpbook E13 Day to day payroll and at **www.hmrc.gov.uk/employers/working_out.htm#part4**

Employee's details   Please use capitals

Date employment started

D D   M M   Y Y Y Y

Job title

Works/payroll number and Department or branch (if any)

Employer's details   Please use capitals

Employer's PAYE reference

/

Employer's name

Address

Postcode

Building number

Rest of address

Tax code used

If you do not know the tax code to use or the current tax threshold, please go to **www.hmrc.gov.uk/employers/rates_and_limits.htm**

Box A ticked
Emergency code on a **cumulative** basis

A

Box B ticked
Emergency code on a **non-cumulative**
Week 1/Month 1 basis

B

Box C ticked
Code BR

C

Tax code used

Please send this form to your HM Revenue & Customs office on the first **pay** day. However, if the employee has ticked box A or box B and their earnings are below the tax threshold, do not send the form until their earnings exceed the tax threshold.

Page 2

Figure 2-3:
Section 2 of the P46 that a new employer must complete if he doesn't have a P45.

The EEA is quite extensive now and comprises the older member states (before 1 May 2004) and those that joined on 1 May 2004. Table 2-1 shows the countries whose citizens qualify to work in the UK under EEA residence rules. Citizens of the UK, of course, are eligible for jobs here. From January 2007, Bulgarians and Romanians need to obtain authorisation to work in the UK. You can find more information on the Home Office Web site `www.bia.home-office.gov.uk`.

Table 2-1	Countries whose Citizens Qualify to Work in the UK	
Austria	Greece	Netherlands
Belgium	Hungary	Norway
Bulgaria	Iceland	Poland
The Czech Republic	Ireland	Portugal
Cyprus	Italy	Romania
Denmark	Latvia	Slovakia
Estonia	Liechtenstein	Slovenia
Finland	Lithuania	Spain
France	Luxembourg	Sweden
Germany	Malta	

If you have any doubts, contact your local HM Revenue & Customs office: EEA members are subject to change and some special rules apply to some of the newer signatories.

Picking pay periods

Deciding how frequently to pay your employees is an important point to work out before hiring staff. Most businesses choose one of these two pay periods:

- **Weekly:** Employees are paid every week, which means you must do payroll 52 times a year.

- **Monthly:** Employees are paid once a month, which means you must do payroll 12 times a year.

Keeping time with time sheets

For each hourly paid employee, you need to have some sort of time sheet to keep track of his work hours. These time sheets are usually completed by the employees and approved by their managers. Completed and approved time sheets are then sent to the bookkeeper so that wages can be calculated based on the exact number of hours worked.

You can choose to use either pay period, and you may even decide to use more than one type. For example, some businesses pay hourly employees (employees paid by the hour) weekly and pay salaried employees (employees paid by a set salary regardless of how many hours they work) monthly. Whatever your choice, decide on a consistent pay period policy and be sure to make it clear to employees when they're hired.

Determining wage and salary scales

You have a lot of leeway regarding the level of wages and salary that you pay your employees, but you still have to follow some rules laid out by the government. Under the National Minimum Wage Regulations, employers must pay workers a minimum amount as defined by law. These rules apply to businesses of all sizes and in all industries.

The three levels of minimum wage rates from 1 October 2007 are:

- £5.52 per hour for workers aged 22 years and older.

- £4.60 per hour for workers aged 18 to 21 years, and workers aged 22 years and above who fall under a development rate for workers starting a new job with a new employer and doing an accredited training.

  Accredited training is defined as a course approved by the UK government to obtain a vocational qualification.

- £3.40 per hour for workers under the age of 18 who are no longer of compulsory school age.

  The compulsory school age in the UK is generally 16 but depends when the person's birthday falls in relation to the last day of the school year.

  Don't assume that the minimum wage isn't going to change though, and check the HM Revenue & Customs Web site periodically to get the current wage rates.

Making statutory payments

As well as guaranteeing minimum wage payments for workers, government statutes provide other benefits:

- ✔ **Sick pay:** Employees who are off sick for more than four consecutive work days are entitled to receive Statutory Sick Pay (SSP). Of course, a sick employee must inform you as soon as possible and supply you with evidence of his sickness.

  In many cases the business continues to pay employees for short periods of sickness as part of good employment practice. However, if you don't pay employees when they are off sick for more than four days, they can claim SSP, which is based on their average earnings. As an employer you may be able to recover some of the SSP you have paid against your NIC amounts.

  The first three days that the employee is away from work are called *waiting days* and don't qualify for SSP.

- ✔ **Parental pay:** Mothers whose baby was due on or after 1 April 2007 are entitled to receive Statutory Maternity Pay (SMP) for up to 39 weeks while away from work, if they meet certain conditions. For the first six weeks an employee is entitled to 90 per cent of her average wage. For the remaining 33 weeks she is entitled to up to £112.75 per week.

  New dads are entitled to Statutory Paternity Pay (SPP) for one or two weeks, calculated in much the same way as SMP.

  Most employees who adopt children are entitled to Statutory Adoption Pay (SAP) which is payable for up to 39 weeks at the lower rate of £112.75 per week or 90 per cent of average weekly wages if this is less.

All these statutory payments are offset against the NICs, which the business has to pay over each month. For example, if the business was due to pay over £1,000 in NICs but paid out recoverable SSP of £112.75, it makes a net payment of £887.25. The payslip has room for you to show this adjustment.

Dealing with the Payroll Administration

Before you start to take on and pay any employees you need to be up to speed on all the forms you need. Day-to-day payroll involves forms and more forms. The following list gives you an idea of the typical range of HM Revenue & Customs forms you have to deal with during the tax year:

✔ **P45:** You complete this form for each employee who leaves at any time during the tax year and for all new employees starting work for your business. The P45 gives details of earnings, Pay As You Earn (PAYE), National Insurance Contributions (NICs), and the tax code for the tax year.

✔ **P46:** You complete this form for any new start employees who don't have a P45.

✔ **P46 (Car):** You use this form to notify HM Revenue & Customs when an employee is first provided with a company car or any change occurs to this benefit.

✔ **P6:** Notification from HM Revenue & Customs of a new tax code for an employee. This form is your authority to change an employee's tax code.

✔ **P11 (Deductions Working Sheet):** This form is the record of each individual employee's NICs, earnings, statutory payments, PAYE deductions, and student loans.

✔ **P32 (Employers Payment Record):** Use this form to record details of the total deductions for all employees including PAYE, student loans, NICs, Statutory Sick Pay (SSP), Statutory Maternity Pay (SMP), Statutory Paternity Pay (SPP), Statutory Adoption Pay (SAP), and the reclaims you have received for SSP, SMP, SPP, and SAP.

✔ **CA6855:** Use this form to trace a National Insurance number (NINO) if a new employee can't provide one.

✔ **TC711-03 (Tax Credit funding application form):** Complete this form if you have to pay out more in statutory payments (SSP, SMP, SPP, SAP, and so on) than you have deducted in PAYE and NICs and you need some help with funding.

A whole range of guides is available from HM Revenue & Customs (www.hmrc.gov.uk) to help you. Here are just a few:

✔ **New Employer Guide Pack:** This pack is an absolute must for any new employer. The pack contains sample P45, P46, and P11 forms, and also a CD-ROM with tutorials and the excellent P11 Calculator, which calculates and records PAYE and NICs.

✔ **P49 (Paying someone for the first time):** The current guide on how to get your payroll started.

✔ **E13 (Day-to-day payroll):** Similar to P49 but with additional useful information and easier to understand.

✔ **E3 (NE) (2007) (Order form):** This form lists all the forms and guides you can possibly want, and you can use it to order each one.

Collecting Employee Taxes

As the bookkeeper you must be familiar with how to calculate the Pay As You Earn (PAYE) tax and National Insurance Contributions (NICs) that you must deduct from each employee's wage or salary.

Although you can run a manual payroll, the calculation of PAYE and NICs is a monumental nightmare, demanding the most accurate and methodical approach to using the tables that HM Revenue & Customs provides each tax year. As well as getting the calculations correct you have to record this information on a Deductions Working Sheet for each employee, which is very time consuming.

Save yourself a lot of grief and use a payroll bureau to run your weekly and monthly payroll and end-of-tax-year returns. If you employ more than 30 employees this method saves you a lot of time and the cost isn't all that high. If you employ less than 30 employees and have the time to spare, use the P11 Calculator that HM Revenue & Customs gives you as part of the New Employer Guide, or buy an off-the-shelf payroll package.

Sorting out National Insurance Contributions

The easiest and quickest way to work out the National Insurance Contributions (NICs) is to use the NICs Calculator on the Employer CD-ROM you receive when you first become an employer, and which is updated each time NICs are changed. However, for those of you who are feeling masochistic or want to know the principles behind the NICs, this section gives a broad outline.

NICs are made up of two elements:

✔ Employee contributions, which you deduct from your employees' pay.

✔ Employer's contributions, which your business must pay.

Several different categories of NICs exist depending on the employee's age and sex. For most men aged 16 to 64 and most women aged 16 to 59 you use Category A, which is referred to later as Table A. If you are unsure about which category your employee falls under, contact your local HM Revenue & Customs or go on to its Web site at www.hmrc.gov.uk.

To calculate Category A NICs you need booklet *CA38 National Insurance Contributions Tables A & J* from HM Revenue & Customs. Make sure that the tables you have are for the correct year. Start at page 8 of Table A if you are doing weekly pay and page 20 for monthly pay.

The next challenge is using Table A correctly. Look up the employee's gross pay in the left hand column of the table 'Employee's Earnings up to and including the UEL (Upper Earnings Limit)'. If the exact amount isn't shown in the table, use the next smaller figure. We show an example of both weekly and monthly NICs in the following sections.

If your employee earns more than £87 per week or £377 per month you must keep a record of his earnings even if no NICs are due.

A weekly pay example

In this example an employee is paid £201.92 on 1 June 2007, for the week. According to Table A, the week is number 8 (based on the fact that this is the eighth week after the start of the tax year, which starts on 6 April). Look at Weekly Table A to find the next smaller figure than the amount being paid, which in this example is £201. Copy the figures from columns 1a to 1e of Weekly Table A to columns 1a to 1e of form P11 (the Deductions Working Sheet). Figure 2-4 shows an extract from Table A as well as where to enter information on form P11.

Each year HM Revenue & Customs sets new Lower Earnings Limits (LEL) below which no NICs are payable by an employee. It also sets an Upper Earnings Limit (UEL) above which no more NICs are payable. There is an Earnings Threshold (ET), below which lower NICs are due and above which higher NICs are due. These are shown above the columns on P11 in Figures 2-4 and 2-5.

A monthly pay example

In this example, an employee is paid £450.50 on 31 May 2007, for the month. According to Table A the month is number 2 (based on the number of months from the start of the tax year in April). Look at Monthly Table A to find the next smaller figure, which in this example is £449. Copy the figures from columns 1a to 1e of Monthly Table A to columns 1a to 1e of form P11 (the Deductions Working Sheet). Figure 2-5 shows how this information appears.

Figuring out Pay As You Earn tax

Deducting Pay As You Earn (PAYE) tax is a much more complex task for bookkeepers than deducting NICs. You have to worry about an employee's tax code (of which numerous permutations exist) as well as using Table A to calculate the final tax figure to deduct.

Extract from Weekly Table A

Employee's Earnings up to and including the UEL	Earnings at the LEL (where earnings are equal to or exceed the LEL)	Earnings above the LEL, up to and including the ET	Earnings above the ET, up to and including the UEL	Total of employee's and employer's contributions	Employee's contributions payable on all earnings above the ET	Employer's contributions
	1a	1b	1c	1d	1e	
£	£	£ P	£ P	£ P	£ P	£ P
200	87	13.00	100.00	23.91	11.05	12.86
201	87	13.00	101.00	24.15	11.16	12.99

Extract from P11

Figure 2-4: Extract from Table A showing the NICs due and how to enter the numbers on form P11 for a weekly paid employee.

Deductions Working Sheet P11   **Year to 5 April 2008**   Employee's details in CAPITALS

Box A Employer's name

Box B HM Revenue & Customs office name   Employer PAYE reference

Box C Surname

Box D First two forenames

Note 1   For guidance on preparing the P11 see Employer Helpbook E11 'Starting... out and recovering tax and NICs on the P11, see Employer Helpbook E13... and on finishing off the P11 see Employer Helpbook E10 'Finishing the tax year'. For guidance on Statutory Sick Pay, see Employer Helpbook E14 'What to do if your employ... Statutory Maternity Pay and Statutory Paternity Pay, see Employer Helpbook E15 'Pay and... parents'; and for Statutory Adoption Pay see Employer Helpbook E16 'Pay and time off work... If you need further assistance, please contact the Employer Helpline on 0845 7 143 143.

Using the P11 Calculator on your Employer CD-ROM will make it easier and quicker for you to work out and record PAYE and NICs.

National Insurance contributions   Note: LEL = Lower Earnings Limit; ET = Earnings Threshold; UEL = Upper Earnings Limit   Statutory pay

Month number	Week number	For Employer's use	Earnings at the LEL (where earnings are equal to or exceed the LEL) 1a £	Earnings above the LEL up to and including the ET 1b £ p	Earnings above the ET, up to and including the UEL 1c £ p	Total of employee's and employer's contributions -mark minus amounts 'R' 1d £ p	Employee's contributions due on all earnings above the ET 1e £ p	Statutory Sick Pay (SSP) paid to employee in the week or month included in column 2 1f £
1	1							
	2							
	3							
	4							
	5							
	6							
	7							
2	8		87	1300	10100	2415	1116	
	9							
	10							
	11							
	12							
3	13							
	14							

Extract from Monthly Table A

▼ Employee's earnings up to and including the UEL	Earnings at the LEL (where earnings are equal to or exceed the LEL)	Earnings above the LEL, up to and including the ET	Earnings above the ET, up to and including the UEL	Total of employee's and employer's contributions	Employee's contributions payable on all earnings above the ET	▼ Employer's contributions
		1a	**1b**	**1c**	**1d**	**1e**	
£	£	£ P	£ P	£ P	£ P	£ P
445	377	58.00	10.00	2.86	1.32	1.54
449	377	58.00	14.00	3.81	1.76	2.05

Extract from P11

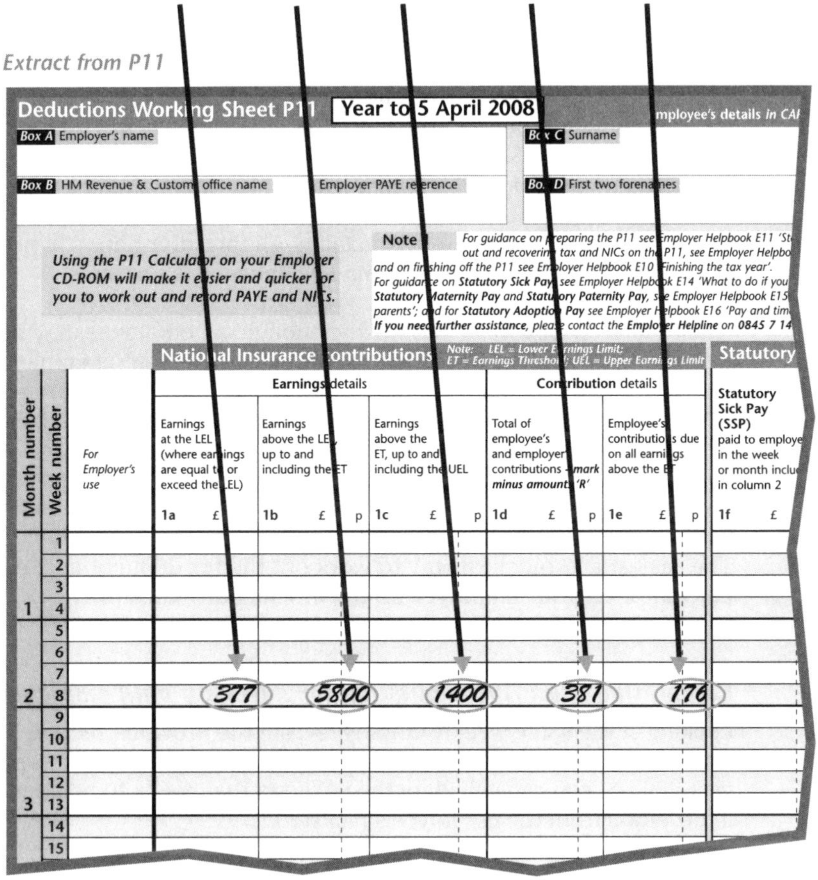

Deductions Working Sheet P11 | **Year to 5 April 2008** | Employee's details *In CA*

Box A Employer's name

Box C Surname

Box B HM Revenue & Customs office name | Employer PAYE reference

Box D First two forenames

Using the P11 Calculator on your Employer CD-ROM will make it easier and quicker for you to work out and record PAYE and NICs.

Note For guidance on preparing the P11 see Employer Helpbook E11 'St... out and recovering tax and NICs on the P11, see Employer Helpbo... and on finishing off the P11 see Employer Helpbook E10 'Finishing the tax year'. For guidance on **Statutory Sick Pay** see Employer Helpbook E14 'What to do if you... **Statutory Maternity Pay** and **Statutory Paternity Pay**, see Employer Helpbook E15... parents'; and for **Statutory Adoption Pay** see Employer Helpbook E16 'Pay and tim... If you need further assistance, please contact the Employer Helpline on 0845 7 14...

National Insurance Contributions | Note: LEL = Lower Earnings Limit; ET = Earnings Threshold; UEL = Upper Earnings Limit | **Statutory**

			Earnings details			Contribution details		Statutory
Month number	Week number	For Employer's use	Earnings at the LEL (where earnings are equal to or exceed the LEL) 1a £	Earnings above the LEL up to and including the ET 1b £ p	Earnings above the ET, up to and including the UEL 1c £ p	Total of employee's and employer contributions - mark minus amount 'R' 1d £ p	Employee's contributions due on all earnings above the ET 1e £ p	Statutory Sick Pay (SSP) paid to employee in the week or month includ in column 2 1f £

The monthly rows show: Month number 1 (weeks 1–5), Month number 2 (weeks 6–9), Month number 3 (weeks 10–15).

On week 8 (month 2) row the entries are: **377** | **5800** | **1400** | **381** | **176**

Figure 2-5: Extract from Table A showing the NICs due and how to enter the details on form P11 for a monthly paid employee.

© *Crown Copyright.*

Considering the tax codes

A tax code is usually made up of one or more numbers followed by a letter. The number indicates the amount of pay an employee is allowed to earn in a tax year before tax becomes payable. For example, an employee with a tax code of 300L can earn £3,000 in the current tax year before becoming liable to pay any tax at all.

A letter follows the number part of the tax code: L, P, T, V, or Y. The letters show how the tax code is adjusted to take account of any budget changes.

If the tax code is followed by week 1/month 1, or an X, instead of keeping a running total of the pay to date, you treat each pay day for that employee as if it is the first week or month of the tax year. For regular employees, you work on a running total basis of 'total pay to date' at each pay day.

Tax codes work on an annual cumulative tax allowance. For example, a tax code of 510L means an employee can earn £5,100 tax free in a complete tax year (52 weeks or 12 months). If he is paid weekly, this tax free sum adds up as the weeks go by. In this example, in week 1 the employee can earn £98.07 total pay without paying any tax (£5,100 ÷ 52). By week 8, that employee could have earned £784.61 total pay to date that year without paying any tax. Assuming that he has been paid in each of the intervening weeks (1 to 7), these sums earned are deducted from the total year to date tax free earnings figure to calculate how much is taxable. All this information is provided in the tax tables that you can obtain from HM Revenue & Customs.

Finally, as if all this wasn't confusing enough, an employee may have a totally different BR tax code, which stands for Basic Rate. For an employee with a BR tax code you must deduct tax from all the pay at the basic rate – 20 per cent from April 2008. The BR code can also be followed by a week 1/month 1 or X, which indicates that you operate the code on a 'non-cumulative' basis. Of course, if week 1/month 1 or X aren't indicated, you work on a running total basis of 'total pay to date' at each pay day.

The easiest and quickest way to work out the tax deduction is to use the Tax Calculator on your Employer CD-ROM. This Calculator provides you with the figures you need for columns 2 to 8 of the P11.

Calculating the PAYE deduction for a weekly paid employee

Looking at the same weekly employee from the previous section 'A weekly pay example', who earned £201.92 in his new employment for tax week 8 in the tax year 2007–8, you can calculate the PAYE tax that needs to be deducted. The information from the employee's P45 states:

- ✔ Tax code is 510L
- ✔ Total pay to date is £1,546.15
- ✔ Total tax to date is £152.73

Figure 2-6 shows the entries on the form P11 (Deduction Working Sheet).

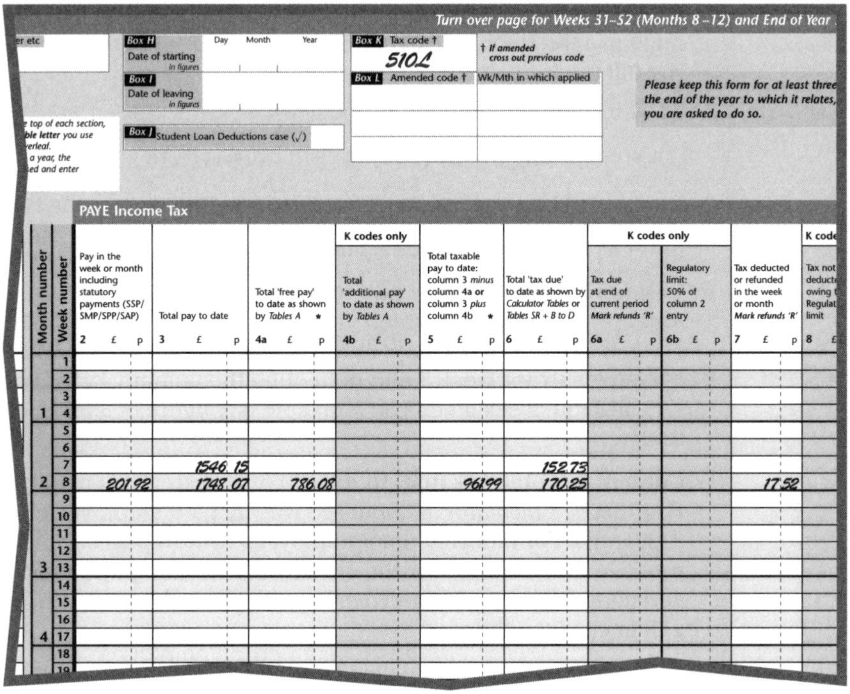

Figure 2-6:
PAYE entries on form P11 for a weekly paid employee.

© Crown Copyright.

The following list explains how the numbers in Figure 2-6 are calculated:

- **Column 2 (Pay in the week or month):** Enter here the pay that the employee earned in the current week, which is week 8.

- **Column 3 (Total pay to date):** This column includes pay from any previous employment during the current tax year. The employee's P45 indicates that this amount is £1,546.15 for week 7 – the week before the current pay week.

  As PAYE works on a cumulative basis, you then add the current week's pay – £201.92 – to this figure to get the cumulative or 'Total pay to date' figure, which is £1,748.07. You enter that total on the line for week 8, just below the previous 'Total pay to date' figure.

- **Column 4a (Total 'free pay' to date):** Find the page in Table A for the week that includes the pay date (week 8). Next, find your employee's tax code, which in the example is 510L, and read off the table the amount of tax free pay. In the example (and you have to take our word for this) code 510L gives free pay of £786.08 at week 8, made up of two elements

(£769.28 + £16.80), shown in the following list. For codes over 500 you must use the further instructions at the bottom of the page to calculate the full tax free pay to date:

- Week 8 figure for code 500 is £769.28
- Week 8 figure for code 10 (510 − 500) is £16.80
- Total free pay for week 8 is £786.08 – the sum of the two figures

Enter £786.08 on the week 8 line in column 4a.

✔ **Column 5 (Total taxable pay to date):** This column features a straight-forward calculation in which you deduct the column 4a figure from the column 3 figure to see how much pay is taxable. In this example, column 3 is £1,748.07 for week 8 and deducting the column 4a figure of £786.08 for the same week gives you a taxable pay figure of £961.99 for the year to date.

✔ **Column 6 (Total 'tax due' to date):** For this step you need your *Taxable Pay Tables, Calculator Method.* For weekly paid employees turn to pages 2, 3, and 4. For monthly paid employees turn to pages 5 and 6. Find the week, in this example for the employee's taxable pay period (week 8), and go to Section A of the Weekly paid – Calculator Tables. Follow the guidance given there.

You can obtain these booklets from HM Revenue & Customs and you definitely need them prior to paying anybody. If you hate using tables then use the CD-Rom that HM Revenue & Customs send out with the New Employer pack.

In the example, the £961.99 taxable pay figure is rounded down to £961 on which tax is due at 22 per cent (the standard rate up to 5 April 2008), amounting to £211.42 for the year to date. However, because the employee is new, deduct the Starting Rate Relief (Week 8) figure (£41.17), which reduces the figure to £170.25 (£211.42 − £41.17). Enter this figure in column 6 against the week 8 line.

✔ **Column 7 (Tax deducted or refunded):** Assuming that the 'Total tax to date' figure from the P45 is correct – you can check this by following the instructions on page 5 of the tables – you can move on to the final stage. If the figure in column 6 against week 8 (£170.25) is greater than the figure in column 6 week 7 (£152.73), the difference – £17.52 – is tax to be deducted, which you enter in column 7 against week 8.

As a point of interest, if the figure in column 7 for week 8 is the same as in week 7, no tax is deductable. Also, if the figure in column 7 for week 8 is less than in week 7, a tax refund is due to the employee.

After you work out how much PAYE tax and NICs to deduct from your employees' pay, and record the amounts on their P11s, you need to work out how much pay to give your employees – the next section tells you how. In fact by law all your employees are entitled to receive a statement (usually a payslip), which shows the deductions you have made from their pay. The statement must show: gross pay, NICs deducted, and tax deducted. At the end of the year you must give all your employees a record showing the details for the whole year. (This record, the P60, is covered in Book V Chapter 3.)

Determining Net Pay

Net pay is the amount a person is paid after subtracting all tax and benefit deductions from his gross pay.

After you figure out all the necessary PAYE and NICs to be taken from an employee's wage or salary (see the preceding sections), you can calculate the pay amount, which is shown on his payslip. The equation you use is pretty straightforward:

Gross pay – (PAYE + NICs) = Net pay

This formula when used for a sample employee may look like this:

Gross pay = £201.92

Less: PAYE tax deducted – £17.52

Less: Employee NICs – £11.16

Net pay = £173.24

 This net pay calculation doesn't include any deductions for benefits. Many businesses offer their employees health, pensions, company cars, and other benefits but expect the employees to share a portion of some of those costs. Most benefits are liable to PAYE tax and NICs, whereas employee contributions to pensions and some other benefits are tax deductible. To get full details on which benefits are taxable and which are not, visit the HM Revenue & Customs Web site (www.hmrc.gov.uk) or ask your tax adviser.

Taxing Benefits

Many businesses offer their employees a range of benefits as well as their wage or salary. These benefits may include perks like a company car, all fuel paid for, health insurance, and a business pension scheme. However, most benefits are taxable, so the employee has to pay tax on the money on the value of the benefits received. Very few benefits are non-taxable.

Fortunately the process of collecting this tax on benefits is very straightforward. Your business informs HM Revenue & Customs what benefits each employee receives each tax year and it adjusts the employee tax code to ensure that you collect the tax due through the payroll.

However, two benefits – company cars and fuel benefits – involve some additional work for you if you're involved in the payroll.

The quickest and simplest way to calculate the value of these benefits is to use the Car and Car Fuel Benefit Calculator, which comes with the New Employer Guide from HM Revenue & Customs. The calculator guides you through the whole process. Also, all the monthly car magazines include the taxable benefit figures in their rating for each car reviewed.

You're responsible for working out the value of the company car benefit and telling HM Revenue & Customs. In simple terms the car benefit charge is obtained by multiplying the list price of the car plus accessories less any capital contribution by the employee by the appropriate percentage. The *appropriate percentage* is based on the car's approved CO_2 emissions figure. The maximum appropriate percentage is 35 per cent but this amount can be reduced to just 9 per cent for electric-only cars. However, just to complicate matters, older cars registered prior to 1 January 1998 don't have an approved CO_2 emissions figure, and so their engine size determines the approved percentage.

If an employer pays for all the fuel for company car users, they can claim an additional taxable benefit called a fuel benefit charge for the non-business fuel used. Fortunately, this is even simpler to calculate. Since April 2008 the fuel benefit charge has been a fixed sum of £16,900, to which you apply the appropriate percentage used to calculate the car benefit. So if your car had an appropriate percentage (based on CO_2 emissions) of 24 per cent, for example, then your taxable fuel benefit charge would be £4,056 (£16,900 × 24 per cent).

When you have calculated the taxable value of the company car and fuel benefit, you must inform HM Revenue & Customs so that it can issue you with a revised tax code for that employee to collect the extra PAYE and NICs due each month. You use form P46 (Car) to notify HM Revenue & Customs of any new company cars and fuel benefits, or any changes to these benefits.

Preparing and Posting Payroll

After you deal with deductions and taxes, you have to figure out your employee's gross and net pay and post all the amounts in your journals.

Calculating payroll for hourly employees

When you're ready to prepare payroll for your hourly paid employees, the first thing you need to do is collect time records from each person being paid hourly. Some businesses use time clocks, and some use time sheets to produce the required time records, but whatever the method used, usually the manager of each department reviews the time records for each employee that he supervises and then sends those time records to you, the bookkeeper.

With time records in hand, you have to calculate gross pay for each employee. For example, if an employee worked 45 hours and is paid £12 an hour, you calculate gross pay as follows:

40 standard hours × £12 per hour = £480

5 overtime hours × £12 per hour × 1.5 overtime rate = £90

£480 + £90 = £570

Doling out funds to salaried employees

You also must prepare payroll for salaried employees. Payments for salaried employees are relatively easy to calculate – all you need to know are their base salaries and pay period calculations. For example, if a salaried employee is paid £15,000 per year and is paid monthly (totalling 12 pay periods), that employee's gross pay is £1,250 for each pay period (£15,000 ÷ 12).

Totalling up for commission payments

Running payroll for employees who are paid based on commission can involve complex calculations. To show you a number of variables, in this section we calculate a commission payment based on a salesperson who sells £60,000 worth of products during one month.

For a salesperson on a straight commission of 10 per cent, you calculate pay using this formula:

Total amount sold × Commission percentage = Gross pay

£60,000 × 0.10 = £6,000

For a salesperson with a guaranteed base salary of £2,000 plus an additional 5 per cent commission on all products sold, you calculate pay using this formula:

Base salary + (Total amount sold × Commission percentage) = Gross pay

£2,000 + (£60,000 × 0.05) = £5,000

Although this salesperson may be happier with a base salary that he can count on each month, in this scenario he actually makes less with a base salary because the commission rate is so much lower. The salesperson makes only £3,000 in commission at 5 per cent if he sells £60,000 worth of products. Without the base pay, he would have made 10 per cent on the £60,000, or £6,000. Therefore, taking into account his base salary of £2,000, he actually receives £1,000 less with a base pay structure that includes a lower commission pay rate.

If a salesperson has a slow sales month of just £30,000 worth of products sold, the pay is:

£30,000 × 0.10 = £3,000 on straight commission of 10 per cent

and

£30,000 × 0.05 = £1,500 plus £2,000 base salary, or £3,500

For a slow month, the salesperson makes more money with the base salary rather than the higher commission rate.

You can calculate commissions in many other ways. One common way is to offer higher commissions on higher levels of sales. Using the figures in this example, this type of pay system encourages salespeople to keep their sales levels over a threshold amount to get the best commission rate.

With a graduated commission scale, a salesperson can make a straight commission of 5 per cent on the first £10,000 in sales, 7 per cent on the next £20,000, and 10 per cent on anything over £30,000. Here's what this salesperson's gross pay calculation looks like using this commission pay scale:

(£10,000 × 0.05) + (£20,000 × 0.07) + (£30,000 × 0.10) = £4,900 Gross pay

One other type of commission pay system involves a base salary plus tips. This method is common in restaurant settings in which servers receive between £2.50 and £5 per hour plus tips.

Businesses that pay less than minimum wage must prove that their employees make at least minimum wage when tips are accounted for. Today, that's relatively easy to prove because most people pay their bills with credit cards and include tips on their bills. Businesses can then come up with an average tip rate using that credit card data.

As an employer, you must report an employee's gross taxable wages based on salary plus tips. Here's how you calculate gross taxable wages for an employee whose earnings are based on tips and wages:

Base wage + Tips = Gross taxable wages

(£3 × 40 hours per week) + £300 = £420

If your employees are paid using a combination of base wage plus tips, you must be sure that they're earning at least the minimum wage rate appropriate to them (generally £5.05 per hour). Checking this employee's gross wages, the hourly rate earned is £10.50 per hour.

Hourly wage = £10.50 (£420 ÷ 40)

PAYE and NICs are calculated on the base wage plus tips, so the net payment you prepare for the employee in this example is for the total gross wage minus any taxes due.

After calculating the take home pay for all your employees, you prepare the payroll, make the payments, and post the payroll to the books. In addition to Cash, payroll impacts many accounts, including:

- ✔ **Accrued Pay As You Earn (PAYE) Payable,** which is where you record the liability for tax payments.
- ✔ **Accrued National Insurance Contributions (NICs) Payable,** which is where you record the liability for NICs payments.

When you post the payroll entry, you indicate the withdrawal of money from the Cash account and record liabilities for future cash payments that are due for PAYE and NICS payments. To give you an example of the proper setup for a payroll journal entry, we assume the total payroll is £10,000 with £1,000 each set aside for PAYE and NICs payable. In reality, your numbers are sure to be very different, and your payments are likely to never all be the same. Table 2-2 shows what your journal entry for posting payroll looks like.

Table 2-2	Payroll Journal Entry for 30 May 2008	
	Debit	*Credit*
Gross Salaries and Wages Expense	£10,000	
Accrued PAYE Payable		£1,000
Accrued NICs Payable		£1,000
Cash (Net Payment)		£8,000

Table 2-2 shows only the entries that affect the take home pay of the employees. The business must also make Employer's National Insurance Contributions payments. Use the manual tables or the P11 Calculator on the New Employers Guide CD-ROM to calculate this amount. The Employer's NIC is a cost of employment and therefore must be treated in the books in exactly the same way as Gross Salaries and Wages. Table 2-3 shows the journal entry to record Employer NICs payments.

Table 2-3	Employer NICs Expenses for May	
	Debit	Credit
Employer's NICs Expense	£1,100	
Accrued Employer's NICs Payable		£1,100

In this entry, you increase the Expense account for salaries and wages as well as all the accounts in which you accrue future obligations for PAYE and employee NICs payments. You decrease the amount of the Cash account; when cash payments are made for the PAYE and NICs payments in the future, you post those payments in the books. Table 2-4 shows an example of the entry posted to the books after making the PAYE withholding tax payment.

Table 2-4	Recording PAYE Payments for May	
	Debit	Credit
Accrued PAYE and NICs Payable	£3,100	
Current Account		£3,100

Settling Up with HM Revenue & Customs

Every month you need to pay over to HM Revenue & Customs all the PAYE and NIC amounts you deduct from your employees. To work out what you have to pay HM Revenue & Customs, add together:

✔ Employee NICs

✔ Employer NICs

✔ PAYE tax

✔ Student loan repayments

Of course against these items you can offset any tax refunds that you paid out to employees and any of the statutory payments you made for sickness, maternity, paternity, and adoption.

These payments must be made to HM Revenue & Customs by the 19th of the following month if paying by cheque, or on the 22nd of the following month if paying electronically. If you employ more than 250 employees, you must make monthly electronic payments. Contact the HM Revenue & Customs Contact Centre on 0845 366 7816 for further help on setting up this facility. A special concession exists for small businesses to pay quarterly (5 July, 5 October, 5 January, and 5 April) if the average monthly payment of PAYE and NICs is less than £1,500.

To help you keep track of these payments HM Revenue & Customs sends you a payslip booklet in which you record details of your total payments. In addition you're sent a P32 Employment Record to work out and record your total monthly payments.

Outsourcing Payroll and Benefits Work

Given everything that's required of you to prepare the payroll, you may think that outsourcing the work of payroll and benefits for your small business is a good idea. We don't disagree. Many businesses outsource the work because this area is so specialised and requires extensive software to manage both payroll and benefits.

If you don't want to take on payroll and benefits, you can pay for a monthly payroll service from the software company that provides your accounting software. For example, Sage provides various levels of payroll services. The Sage payroll features include calculating earnings and deductions, printing cheques or making direct deposits, providing updates to the tax tables, and supplying the data needed to complete all HM Revenue & Customs forms related to payroll. The advantage of doing payroll in-house in this manner is that you can more easily integrate payroll into the business's books.

Book V

Employing Staff

Chapter 3

Completing Year-End Payroll and Reports

*E*ven when you keep diligently up to date with everything concerning your employee payroll and benefits, you still have some paperwork to complete at the end of the year. You need to submit forms for each of your employees as well as some summary reports.

Yes, you guessed it. End-of-the-year HM Revenue & Customs paperwork takes some time. To help make the process as painless as possible, this chapter reviews the forms you need to complete, the information you need for each form, and the process for filing your business's payroll information with HM Revenue & Customs. We dealt with some of the payroll basics in Book V Chapter 2.

Reporting on Employees

You may think that you've done a lot of paperwork relating to your payroll throughout the year, but the job isn't yet complete. Although you keep individual records for deduction of PAYE tax and National Insurance for each employee, and make payments to HM Revenue & Customs throughout the year, at the end of the tax year on 5 April, HM Revenue & Customs wants more information, to be sure that you haven't missed out on any PAYE tax and National Insurance Contributions (NICs).

We cover the forms you need to submit in some detail in the following sections in the order in which they need to be submitted – so you know when to panic!

HM Revenue & Customs publishes an *Employer Helpbook E10* each year that covers finishing the tax year. You can obtain this from their Web site at http://www.hmrc.gov.uk/ and find examples of the forms we discuss at http://www.hmrc.gov.uk/employers/fgcat-finishtaxyear.shtml.

Form P14

As far as forms go, the P14 is pretty straightforward. In essence the P14 is a summary of each employee's P11 that you have been working with all tax year, and you don't need any more information than what you already have on the employee's P11. We covered P11 in Book V Chapter 2. Please remember that if you do not send a P14 to HM Revenue & Customs for every employee each tax year they will not have a record of that person's PAYE, NICs, and other deductions record. Also, if you have more than one employee please ensure that you send these to HM Revenue & Customs in alphabetical order. Table 3-1 tells you what to put in each section.

The P14 is due mid-May; check with HM Revenue & Customs for the exact date for the current year.

With this form, and all the end-of-the-year employee-related forms, the keyword is accuracy – take care and complete the form slowly. Make sure that you are picking up the correct tax year details.

Table 3-1	Sections of Form P14
Section	*What to Do*
Employer's name and address	Show your full address, including the postcode.
Inland Revenue office name and Employer's PAYE reference	Enter your Inland Revenue office name and Employer's PAYE reference from the front of form P35. You can also find this on your payslip booklet.
Tax year to 5 April 2006	Usually pre-printed on the form. Take care to submit the correct year's figures!
Employee's details	
National Insurance number	Copy this from the front of form P11.
Date of birth	Enter the day and month as well as all four numbers of the year.

Section	What to Do
Surname and first two forenames	If you don't know all the employee's forenames, put initials. Don't put titles (Mr, Mrs, Miss, and so on).
National Insurance contributions in this employment	
NIC (National Insurance Contribution) Table letter	Copy from the End of Year Summary section on the back of form P11.
Columns 1a to 1c	Copy these amounts from the End of Year Summary of form P11. Make entries in whole pounds and right justify the figures. If an entry exists in column 1a you must still send in form P14 even though no NICs may be payable.
Columns 1d and 1e	Copy these amounts from the End of Year Summary of form P11. Make entries in pounds and pence. Where you operate a contracted-out pension scheme and the column 1d total to be carried forward from the P11 is a minus figure, enter 'R' in the corresponding box immediately to the right of the column of the column 1d total boxes on the P14.
Statutory payments in this employment	
Box 1f	Insert the total amount of Statutory Sick Pay (SSP) paid in those months for which an amount has been recovered under the Percentage Threshold Scheme.
Boxes 1g to 1i	Copy these amounts from the corresponding columns on form P11.
Scheme Contracted-Out number	Complete this only if the employee is a member of a Contracted-Out Money Purchase (COMP) scheme, COMP Stakeholder Pension (COMPSHP) scheme, or the COMP part of the Contracted-Out Mixed Benefit (COMB) scheme you operate.

(continued)

Table 3-1 *(continued)*

Section	What to Do
	Members of these schemes only receive their Age Related Rebate (ARR) if this part is entered correctly.4
Student loan deductions	Copy this amount from the totals box at the bottom of column 1j on form P11. Enter whole pounds only.
Tax credits	Copy this amount from the totals box below the bottom of column 9 on form P11. If an entry exists in this box you must still send in form P14 even though no NICs may be payable.
Date of starting and date of leaving	Make entries if an employee starts and/or leaves your employment during the tax year (2005/6 in this example). Enter date as figures: 09 05 2006, for example.
Pay and income tax details	
In previous employment(s)	Copy these amounts from the End of Year Summary of form P11.
In this employment	Copy these amounts from the End of Year Summary of form P11.
Total for year	Copy these amounts from the End of Year Summary of form P11. Fill in these boxes only if the employee was still working for you at 5 April.
Employee's Widows and Orphans/Life Assurance contributions in this employment	Applies where an employee is legally obliged to pay contributions that qualify for tax relief but are not authorised under 'net pay arrangements' for tax relief. See *CWG2 Employers Further Guide to PAYE and NICs* for more information.
Final tax code	Fill in boxes from the left-hand side. Always show the last tax code you were using at the 5 April date.

Section	What to Do
Payment in week 53	Use only if Week 53 is included in the Pay and Tax totals, and then put one of the following in this box:
	'53' if 53 weekly pay days were in the year
	'54' if 27 fortnightly pay days were in the year
	'56' if 14 four-weekly pay days were in the year.

HM Revenue & Customs ask that you submit your P14 forms in alphabetical order.

The last part of form P14 is the P60 but the form is blue (instead of orange). You don't send this to HM Revenue & Customs. Instead, you give each employee her own copy, which summarises pay, tax, NICs deductions, and so on made during the year.

Don't give a P60 to employees who were no longer with the business at the end of the tax year.

Detailing benefits

Fortunately, you don't need these forms for the majority of your employees in the typical small business. Basically, these forms are used to report back to HM Revenue & Customs the various benefits in kind that employees received during the year.

The forms and the circumstances they address are as follows:

- ✔ Use the fairly simple form P9D if the employee in question earned at the rate of £8,500 per annum or less. Earnings includes all bonuses, tips, and benefits.

- ✔ Use the significantly more complicated form P11D for employees who earned at the rate of £8,500 or more and for all directors regardless of earnings.

- ✔ Use form P11D(b) to

  - Confirm that by 6 July all forms P11D have been completed and sent to your HM Revenue & Customs office.

  - Declare the total amount of Class 1A NICs you are due to pay. *Class 1A* contributions are the extra NICs that may be due on taxable benefits that you provide to your employees.

HM Revenue & Customs produces a series of guides to help you get this area of reporting right. Look for the publication for the current tax year:

- *480 Expenses and Benefits – A Tax Guide:* This guide runs to some 100 pages and is the definitive guide.
- *CWG2 Employer Further Guide to PAYE and NICs.*
- *CWG5 Class 1A NICs on benefits in kind.*
- *P11D Guide*: This guide is a four-page overview, which makes reference to the *480* guide for more detail.

Within the confines of this book, we can't possibly hope to do justice to the whole detail of benefit in kind reporting. However, the following list gives you a brief outline of the kind of things that are deemed to be benefits in kind and need to be included on the P9D or P11D:

- Assets transferred (cars, property, goods, or other assets)
- Payments made on behalf of the employee
- Vouchers and credit cards
- Living accommodation
- Mileage allowance payments/passenger miles
- Cars, vans, and car fuel
- Interest-free, low interest, and notional loans
- Private medical treatment or insurance
- Qualifying relocation expenses payments and benefits
- Services supplied
- Assets placed at employees' disposal
- Computer equipment
- Other items – subscriptions, educational assistance, non-qualifying relocation benefits and expenses payments, incidental overnight expenses
- Employer-provided childcare
- Expenses payments made to, or on behalf of, the director or employee – general expenses for business travel, travel and subsistence, entertainment, home telephone, other non-qualifying relocation expenses

The list seems to go on and on.

Reporting PAYE-free earnings

Forms P38 and P38A ask you to report payments made to employees from whom you haven't deducted PAYE – such as part-time casual staff. Form P38 (S) applies to students. The following subsections show the type of payments that you need to include or omit on forms P38 or P38A.

Section A

In this section, you

> ✔ Include payments above the PAYE threshold.
>
> ✔ Include payments to employees who have not produced a P45 and were engaged for more than one week, if both of the following conditions are met:
>
>> • The rate of pay was above £1 per week or £4 per month.
>>
>> • The employee failed to complete certificate A or B on form P46.
>
> ✔ Exclude payments included on form P14.

Section B

In this section, you

> ✔ Include payments that total over £100 made to any employee including casuals during this tax year.
>
> ✔ Exclude those included on forms P14, those in section A (above), those payments to employees with completed P46 certificates A and B, and payments returned on forms P38(S).

P38 (S)

P38(S) is the appropriate return for students who work for you solely during a holiday. You don't need to deduct tax from a student as long as

> ✔ She fills in the student's declaration, *and*
>
> ✔ The student's pay in your employment doesn't exceed £5,435 during the tax year.
>
> If a student's pay in your employment exceeds this figure you must deduct tax using code 'OT week 1/month 1' in accordance with paragraphs 110 and 111 of the booklet *CWG2 Employers' Further Guide to PAYE and NICs*.

Submitting Summary Information

Form P35 is a four-part monster of a form. In essence it lists every employee, including directors (who must be shown first with an asterisk by their names), NIC amounts, and income tax you deducted from their pay. If you have more than ten employees, you need one or more continuation sheets (form P35CS).

Also, as per the P14, you need to list employees in alphabetical order.

- ✔ Page 1 tells you what your obligations are and where to get further help: Nothing to complete here.

- ✔ Pages 2 and 3 require you to list the details of your employees and summarise your payments of NICs, PAYE tax, SSP, SMP, and SAP for the year.

- ✔ Page 4 contains several 'tick box' questions for you to complete before signing and dating the form.

Boxing out Parts 1 and 2

You can get much of the information you need to complete Parts 1 and 2 of form P35 from the P11 forms you have for each person to which you pay money:

- ✔ The total of each employee's and the employer's NICs are in column 1d of the End of Year Summary.

- ✔ The total tax deducted or refunded is in the 'In this employment' box at the foot of column 6.

Completing Parts 1 and 2 makes you check that your payments to the accounts office are correct. If this form shows that you should have paid over more to HM Revenue & Customs during the year, you need to make an additional payment.

Okay, we can't put it off any longer; Table 3-2 ploughs through the 32 boxes of form P35.

Table 3-2	Boxes of Form P35
Box Number	*What to Do*
1	Add up all the entries from the NICs columns on the form.
2	If you have any continuation sheets (P35CS), add these up and put the total for all continuation sheets in this box.
3	Add boxes 1 and 2 together. If the figure is a refund, mark 'R'.
4	Add up the entries from the income tax column on the form.

Box Number	What to Do
5	If you have any continuation sheets (P35CS), add these up and put the total for all continuation sheets in this box.
6	Add boxes 4 and 5 together. If the figure is a refund, mark 'R'.
7	Use this box only if the business has asked your accounts office for an advance; if so, enter that amount here.
8	Use this box only if you deducted tax from subcontractors during the year. Refer to *CIS36, Contractor's Annual Return.* Copy the amount from box F of the CIS36 to box 8 of the P35.
9	Add boxes 6, 7, and 8 and enter the total here.
10	Add box 3 to box 9 and enter the total here.
11	Fill in this box only if you made student loan deductions this year. Pick up the total of all the boxes at the bottom of column 1j on each of the form P11s and put the total here (whole pounds only).
12	Add boxes 10 and 11 and enter the total here.
	This gives the total deductions made for NICs, income tax, and student loan deductions.
13	If you have paid any Statutory Sick Pay (SSP) to employees, enter the amount you are entitled to recover under the Percentage Threshold Scheme (PTS) in this box. Include any payments you received directly from your accounts office to cover recovery of SSP, which you show in box 21. For further details see the *Employer Helpbook E14, What to do if your employee is sick.*
14	If you paid any SMP (Statutory Maternity Pay) to employees, enter in this box the amount you are entitled to. Include any payments you received directly from your accounts office to cover recovery of SMP, which you show in box 21. For further details see the *Employer Helpbook E15, Pay and time off work for parents.*
15	Enter here any compensation you are entitled to claim in addition to the SMP recovered. For further details see the *Employer Helpbook E15, Pay and time off work for parents.*
16	Enter here any SPP (Statutory Paternity Pay) you have paid to employees and are entitled to recover. For further details see the *Employer Helpbook E15, Pay and time off work for parents.*

(continued)

Table 3-2 *(continued)*

Box Number	What to Do
17	Enter here any compensation you are entitled to claim in addition to the SPP recovered.
	For further details see the *Employer Helpbook E15, Pay and time off work for parents.*
18	Enter here any SAP (Statutory Adoption Pay) paid to employees that you are entitled to recover. Include any payments received directly from your accounts office to cover the recovery of SAP, also shown in box 21.
	For further details see the *Employer Helpbook E16, Pay and time off work for adoptive parents.*
19	Enter here any compensation you are entitled to claim in addition to the SAP recovered.
	For further details see the *Employer Helpbook E16, Pay and time off work for adoptive parents.*
20	Add all boxes from 13 to 19 and enter the total in box 20.
21	Use this box only if you received funding from your accounts office to pay SSP/SMP/SPP/SAP. Enter here the amount you received in funding.
22	Calculate box 20 minus box 21 and enter the total here.
23	Use this box only if you received form *TC700, Employer notification to start paying tax credits to your employees.* Add together all amounts shown in column 9 on all forms P11 and enter the total here.
24	Use this box only if the business received funding from its accounts office to pay tax credits. Enter here the total funding received.
	Refer to your final form *TC712, Tax credits – Funding Notice,* for this year.
25	Calculate box 23 minus box 24 and enter the total here.
26	Add box 22 to box 25 and enter this total here.
27	You need to apply a logic check here to get this amount right: Calculate box 12 minus box 26, but if box 26 is a minus figure, add box 26 to box 12.
28	Enter here the total of NICs and tax paid over so far for the tax year.
29	Enter here any amount credited to the business's PAYE payment record for tax-free incentives for sending in its return electronically the previous year.

Box Number	What to Do
30	Calculate box 27 minus boxes 28 and 29.
	If the total of boxes 28 and 29 is less than the amount in box 27, the amount in box 30 is the amount still to be paid to HM Revenue & Customs.
	Send the balance due immediately to the accounts office. Interest is charged if the balance is paid after 19 April.
	Of course, if boxes 28 and 29 total more than the figure in box 27, you may have overpaid and need to enter the amount in box 30 with a 'M' for minus in front. You then get a refund in due course.

The following boxes are only for limited companies that deducted CIS (Construction Industry Scheme) deductions from payments

31	CIS deductions are recorded on forms CIS25 (for each employee). Refer to form CIS132 (which summarises all employees), column E, for the total deductions suffered and copy this amount here.
32	Calculate box 30 minus box 31.
	Apply the same test as at per box 30.

Ticking off the Part 3 checklist

Page 4 of the form has three sections – Parts 3, 4, and 5. Part 3 has no numbers, just a checklist of questions to answer:

- ✔ **Question 1:** If you had any employees for whom you didn't complete a form P14 or P38(S), tick 'No'.

  These employees are likely to be part-time or casual staff. If you tick 'No' you must complete a *P38A, Employer Supplementary Return*.

- ✔ **Question 2:** Did you make any 'free-of-tax' payments to an employee? A free-of-tax payment is one where the employer bears any tax due.

- ✔ **Question 3:** Has anyone other than the employer paid expenses or provided benefits to any of your employees during the year as part of their employment with you?

- ✔ **Question 4:** This question is in two parts. If the answer to the first part is 'Yes' you have to complete a form P14 for each employee concerned.

- ✔ **Question 5:** This question asks if you have paid any part of an employee's pay direct to anyone else, for example, paying school fees direct to a school. If you did, you need to report whether the payment was included in the employee's pay for tax and NICs purposes and in the pay shown on form P14.

This question doesn't include attachment of earnings orders or payments to the Child Support Agency.

✔ **Question 6:** This question covers IR35 under which HM Revenue & Customs has restricted workers' ability to form services companies or partnerships through which they sell their services. Your best bet is to find out more about IR35 at www.hmrc.gov.uk/ir35, to make sure that you comply. If, for example, you don't deduct tax and NICs when you need to, you may become liable for any non-payment of tax and NICs by the person employed.

If you included PAYE and NICs from workers who you deemed to be employees, tick the second box 'Yes'. If you tick the second box 'Yes' but the amount of the deemed payment is provisional, confirm on a separate sheet and send it with the form P35.

Computerised systems

If you use a computerised payroll system, you can save a lot of grief because most of the year-end reports (certainly P14, P35, and P60) are done automatically.

Also, if you use the HM Revenue & Customs payroll CD-ROM that comes with the New Employer Pack you can enjoy the same benefits of a computerised payroll system and all the online HM Revenue & Customs guides.

Chapter 4

Adding Up the Bill for Time Off

*E*mployees do take time off work, whether they're on holiday, parental leave, or sometimes unwell. You have to pay for some of this time off out of your business profits and some of it you can recover from HM Revenue and Customs, the new department which combines the work of the Inland Revenue and Customs and Excise.

Paying for Holidays

Most employers accept that there's a good business case for allowing members of staff to take time off to recharge their batteries. The law now says that employers must pay most people for a certain minimum amount of time off each year, although a few employment exceptions do still exist.

To keep matters clear for everyone, set out policies on how much annual leave your employees are entitled to, the dates your company's holiday year runs from and to, and your policy on public holidays.

Annual leave

Spell out the details of annual leave entitlement in your employees' contracts. The law entitles employees to at least 4.8 weeks' paid leave, but you may be more generous than that. You can count bank and public holidays as part of those 4.8 weeks, but again you may decide to give employees those days off on top. You can also increase the amount of annual leave depending on how long people work for you. Whatever you decide, you can't give your employees less than the legal minimum. So if someone works 5 days a week he should get 24 days off. If he works 6 days a week he should get 28.8 (go on, make it the full 29!) days off, and if he works fewer days a week he should get 4.8 times what he works on average (so someone who works a 3-day week should get 14.4 days' holiday).

Holiday entitlement goes up again on 1 April 2009 to 5.6 weeks' paid leave. You can find an easy calculator on the Business Link Web site at www.business link.gov.uk to help you work out your employees' holiday entitlement.

The holiday year

For the sake of your payroll it's a good idea to make sure that all your staff have the same holiday year regardless of when they joined you. Otherwise calculating all their different entitlements and holiday pay will be a nightmare. Most bosses opt for a holiday year running from 1 January to 31 December, from 6 April to 5 April the following year, or a year that coincides with their accounting year.

If, for the sake of argument, your holiday year runs from 1 January to 31 December, someone who starts working for you on 1 January and stays with you for six months will only be entitled to half of his annual holiday entitlement by the time he leaves. If he works from 1 January through to the end of December he should have taken his full year's entitlement and be starting again from 1 January. If he joins you on 1 September and your holiday year runs from 1 January to 31 December, then by 31 December he will only be entitled to a quarter of a total year's holiday.

Public and bank holidays

There are eight bank and public holidays in England, Wales, and Scotland and ten in Northern Ireland. If you count them as part of your employees' total holiday entitlement you simply have to allow employees 4.8 weeks off a year and pay them for that time. They don't have to have those actual public holidays off. People assume that they are entitled to have those particular days off or to receive more than their normal pay if they work on those days, but that's only the case if that's what it says in their contracts.

Calculating Holiday Pay

If your employees work the same hours each week and get the same pay per hour, then when they take any holiday they simply get their usual week's wage, even though they're not at their desks. If they would normally get bonuses, shift payments, or guaranteed overtime payments, you should include these in their holiday pay. You basically pay them for 52 weeks a year but they only work for 47.2 of them.

If employees' hours and wages vary, as they do for *piece workers,* or output workers who are paid for each unit of work they do – for example each garment they stitch together – then on a week that they are on holiday, you should pay them an amount calculated by taking the average of the pay they took home in the previous 12 weeks. Again, that should include the extra wages like bonuses, commissions, and guaranteed overtime.

If you do give your employees more than the statutory 4.8 weeks' minimum holiday, the rate of pay for the days over and above the 4.8 weeks can be whatever you agree with your employees in their contract.

When you're thinking about how much holiday pay to give, think about what your competitors are up to. If you offer less annual leave and lower rates of pay than those being paid in the rest of the market, you may not get or keep the best staff.

Paying in lieu of holiday

You have to make it possible for employees to take their holidays, but if they choose not to take them all by the end of the holiday year you aren't under any obligation to allow them to carry the untaken days forward or to pay extra for days lost. The only time you have to pay in lieu of employees taking holiday is when they leave and haven't taken the full proportion of annual leave they're entitled to.

Paying while sick on holiday

If an employee is off sick their future holiday entitlement continues to build up unless the illness becomes long-term. If they get sick when they're off on holiday, they may qualify for Statutory Sick Pay. They should notify you that they're sick in the same way as you expect them to notify you that they're sick on a work day. Because in most cases the employee won't be entitled to any payment for the first three days off sick, they may prefer to carry on taking their paid holiday.

Paying when changing jobs

It's possible that an employee leaves you in the middle of the holiday year but hasn't taken all of his holiday entitlement up to that date. If you can't let him take the remaining days off between handing in his notice and actually leaving, then you have to add those days' pay into his final pay packet. If an employee has already taken more days off than he is entitled to at the time he leaves, you will be within your rights to deduct that money from his final pay, but only if this is stated in the employee's contract.

Rolling up holiday pay

There is another way of paying holiday pay. Some employers give employees their basic pay plus an amount for holiday pay each week. They then expect employees to save up the holiday pay element throughout the year and use that to pay for their weeks off. If you do roll up holiday pay you have to set out the details of the holiday pay in employees' contracts and it has to be a genuine additional amount on top of basic pay. The details need to be stated on the employee's wage slip.

Rolling up holiday pay in this way is illegal in Scotland because of the outcome of a court dispute over the issue, but not in the rest of the UK.

Paying While off Sick

The most common reason for having to pay someone while he's not at work is because he's sick. Apart from the first few days of any period of sickness, employees can usually expect that you will pay them.

The minimum amount of pay an ill employee is entitled to is set down by law, and is known as Statutory Sick Pay (SSP). In many cases employers pay well over the SSP amounts and sometimes even give full pay for at least the first few weeks of a period of illness.

Statutory sick pay

In smaller firms most employees depend on Statutory Sick Pay to tide them over an illness. But employees aren't all entitled to SSP; the following employees can't get it:

- Employees who haven't yet done any work for you under their contract of employment.
- Employees who are sick for less than four days in a row.
- People working for you on a freelance or self-employed basis.
- Employees who are under 16 or over 65 on the first day of their sickness.

✔ Employees who earn less than the Lower Earnings Limit for National Insurance (£90).

✔ Employees who have claimed incapacity benefit or severe disablement allowance from the state within the last eight weeks.

✔ Employees who are pregnant and go off sick during the maternity pay period (Statutory Maternity Pay starts immediately instead; see the section 'Paying mum' for more details).

✔ Employees who are off sick during a stoppage at work due to a trade dispute – on strike – unless they can prove that at no time did they have a direct interest in that dispute.

✔ Employees who are in police custody on the first day they're sick.

✔ Employees who have already had 28 weeks of SSP from you in any one period of incapacity for work or in any two periods of illness separated by eight weeks or less in a period of three years.

✔ Employees who are outside the European Economic Area.

✔ Employees who have already had 28 weeks of SSP from a previous employer and, having moved to your firm go off sick again within eight weeks or less.

To qualify for SSP employees must:

✔ Have four or more consecutive days off sick on which they would normally work (including weekends, non-work days, and holidays). These are the *qualifying days*.

✔ Notify you of their absence as soon as possible and in accordance with your company's rules.

✔ Supply you with evidence that they are too sick to work – such as a self-certificate for the first seven days and a doctor's sick note for the eighth day onwards.

Unless you've allowed for it in their contracts your employees won't be entitled to any pay for the first three days they're off sick. The first three days are the *waiting days* and a period of sickness of four days or more is known as a *Period of Incapacity for Work* (or PIW), during which you pay SSP if the employee qualifies from the information shown in the bulleted lists.

You may be able to claim back some of the SSP you pay out to your employees through the income tax and National Insurance Contributions you pay to HM Revenue and Customs (formerly the Inland Revenue). If your total SSP payments in a month are more than 13 per cent of the total Class 1 National Insurance liability (see Book V Chapter 2) for your whole company for that same tax month, you can get the difference back. You do the calculations yourself and deduct the amount you are reclaiming from the amount you are due to pay over to HMRC. You can get help with this from HMRC. There is a lot of information for employers on its Web site www.hmrc.gov.uk including a section called 'What to do if your employee is sick'; you can pick up relevant leaflets from your local HMRC office or call the HMRC Employer's Helpline on 0845-7143143.

If an employee goes off work sick for four days or more, comes back to work, and goes off sick again within eight weeks for another four days or more, SSP will start immediately on the second occasion – without a second period of three waiting days.

SSP is paid for up to a maximum of 28 weeks. To qualify employees have to have been earning more than the Lower Earnings Limit for National Insurance Contributions over the eight weeks before the illness (£90 per week). SSP is £72.55 per week.

If an employee has used up his entitlement to the maximum 28 weeks SSP and you don't have any contractual agreement to pay him for longer, he will have to apply through the benefits system via his local Benefit Agency office or Job Centre Plus for Sick Benefit from the State. The same applies if he's not eligible for SSP in the first place.

If you don't pay SSP when one of your employees qualifies for it he can complain to an HM Revenue and Customs (formerly Inland Revenue) adjudication officer, leading to a decision as to whether or not you must pay. However, you can decide not to pay SSP if you believe that the employee isn't really ill or he doesn't notify you in accordance with the rules you operate on notification of sickness.

You have to keep records for at least three years of any SSP you pay and of the dates of any periods of sickness lasting at least four days in a row.

Contractual sick pay

If your employees' contracts state that they get better sick pay than the SSP rates, you have to stick to those contractual amounts or be in breach of the contract. Some employers pay their employees their full salary for up to six months of sick leave and then half their normal pay for another six months. Some have contractual agreements where people can be off sick long term and still get some pay from the company. In most cases these contracts have been negotiated between the employer and a recognised union. You can't claim back any amounts you pay over and above Statutory Sick Pay.

Paying Parents

Employees who are about to become parents, whether because they're pregnant, soon to be a father, or adopting a child, will be entitled to leave and will usually be entitled to be paid for some or all of that leave. HM Revenue and Customs produces leaflets that explain all the procedures for paying Statutory Maternity, Paternity and Adoption Pay. Visit the Web site at www.hmrc.gov.uk, call the employers' helpline on 0845-7143143, contact the HMRC office that deals with your business accounts or call into the local office to pick up leaflets.

Paying mum

All pregnant employees are entitled to 52 weeks of maternity leave regardless of how long they've been employed by you. Your pregnant employee may be entitled to Statutory Maternity Pay (the minimum amount set out in law). To qualify for Statutory Maternity Pay (SMP) a pregnant employee:

- ✔ Has to have worked for you continuously for at least 26 weeks by the Qualifying Week (the fifteenth week before the expected week of the birth).

- ✔ Has to earn more than the Lower Earnings Limit for National Insurance Contributions (which is £90 a week).

- ✔ Must still be pregnant or have given birth at the beginning of the eleventh week before the expected week of childbirth.

- ✔ Has to give you proper notification.

- ✔ Must provide you with medical evidence (a MAT B1 form) of the expected week of the birth.

Statutory Maternity Pay lasts for 39 weeks. If an employee chooses to stay off longer than the ordinary maternity leave period of 39 weeks, Statutory Maternity Pay doesn't cover the additional maternity leave between 39 and 52 weeks. You may of course have made more generous provisions for paying for maternity leave in your employees' contracts. The HMRC Web site at www.hmrc.gov.uk has all the information you need and you should check the site each time an employee informs you that she's pregnant.

For the first six weeks of Statutory Maternity Pay, an employee's entitled to nine-tenths of her average earnings (averaged for the last eight weeks up to and including the Qualifying Week). Shift allowances, overtime payments, bonuses, and commission are included. For the other 33 weeks, she's entitled to either the £112.75 set by the Government or 90 per cent of her average earnings – whichever is the lower amount.

An employee doesn't have to intend to come back to work in order to get SMP. You have to keep on paying SMP for the full 39 weeks even if she leaves your employment after she qualifies for the money. Payment of SMP can begin on any day of the week, so payments can start on the day the employee leaves work to start her maternity leave, and can start at any time from the start of the eleventh week before the expected week of childbirth. But if she decides to work right up until the baby is born, the maternity pay starts the day after she leaves. Your employee can work for you for 10 days – Keep In Touch days – while on SMP without losing her entitlement. If your employee decides to come back to work before the end of the 39 weeks of SMP, her SMP stops. From the point of view of income tax and National Insurance, SMP is regarded as earnings. She must give you eight weeks' notice that she intends to return to work before the SMP period is up.

If you don't pay SMP when an employee is entitled to it she can apply to HM Revenue and Customs for a formal decision. If HM Revenue & Customs decides that you should be paying SMP and you still don't pay up within the time allowed, you can be fined up to £1,000.

Getting help with SMP

The good news is that employers do get some help from the government to pay SMP bills. You can usually get a refund of 92 per cent of the SMP for any employee by taking money back through the National Insurance Contributions system (see Book V Chapter 2). If you're a small employer whose total National Insurance Contributions are under £45,000 a year, you can recover the full amount of SMP paid out plus 4.5 per cent compensation. As with Statutory Sick Pay you calculate how much you should be entitled to reclaim and deduct that from the amount of Income Tax and National Insurance you are due to pay over to HM Revenue and Customs each month.

If your finances are a bit tight and you can't afford to pay an employee's SMP, you may be able to claim funding in advance from HM Revenue and Customs. Contact the HMRC office that deals with your Income tax and National Insurance accounts.

Contractual maternity payments

After the 39 weeks of Statutory Maternity Pay are finished, nothing in law accounts for payments for any further maternity leave. But some employers do give their employees better terms for both maternity leave and pay. If you have written better terms into your contracts and don't deliver you can be sued for breach of contract.

Paying dad

New dads are entitled to two weeks' paid leave to help care for their child and the mother. To be eligible the employee must have responsibility for the child's upbringing, be the father of the baby or the mother's husband or partner, and have worked for you continuously for 26 weeks as at the fifteenth week before the baby is due. He is entitled to take either one week or two consecutive weeks off, but can't take the time off in odd days here and there. He is entitled to Statutory Paternity Pay (SPP) for the time off if he earns more than the Lower Earnings Limit for National Insurance (£90 a week). SPP is £112.75 a week or 90 per cent of his average weekly wage if that's a lower amount.

As with SMP, if you have to pay fathers' paternity pay you'll be able to recover most of it through National Insurance payments in the same way. See the section on 'Paying Mum' above for more details.

Adopting

Most employees who adopt children are entitled to adoption leave for up to 52 weeks and to Statutory Adoption Pay (SAP) for 39 weeks. It's very similar to Statutory Maternity Pay. To qualify, your employee has to have worked for you continuously for at least 26 weeks by the date she is notified that she has been matched with a child for adoption.

Individuals who adopt, or one partner of a couple who adopt jointly, can qualify for adoption leave and SAP. The other partner of an adopting couple may be eligible for paternity leave and pay. Step-parents adopting their partner's children don't qualify for adoption leave or SAP.

SAP is the same amount as SPP: £112.75 a week for up to 39 weeks or 90 per cent of average weekly earnings if that's a lower amount. Adopters who earn less than the Lower Earnings Limit for National Insurance Contributions (£90 a week) don't qualify.

If you do have to pay out for SAP you can claim it back in the same way as SMP and SPP. See the section on 'Paying Mum' for more details.

Parental leave

Parents have a right to take time off to look after children or to make arrangements for their welfare. But although each parent can take up to thirteen weeks off work in the first five years of each child's life, it is unpaid leave and you're under no obligation to pay for that time off unless you've written better terms into your employees' contract.

Paying Part-Timers

The rules are the same for part-timers as full-timers. If an employee works a three-day week and you've given him the statutory holiday entitlement of four weeks, he's entitled to four times three days off in the year. If he works different hours each week he is entitled to four times the average number of hours he works.

Part-time employees are entitled to Statutory Sick, maternity, paternity, and adoption pay in the same way as full-time employees. The same rules apply.

Unpaid Leave

Sometimes no matter how generous you are with holiday allowances, an employee needs a bit more time off to get over a domestic crisis or to sort his life out. If he has no paid leave left he may ask you to agree to unpaid leave. If you agree you don't pay him for the time he takes off so there are no Income Tax, National Insurance, or other usual deductions to be made. Because he isn't leaving and you aren't dismissing him all his employment rights under the terms and conditions of his contract continue unless you both agree otherwise. So he'll still be building up holiday entitlement, have the same rights to private health care if you make that available to your employees, and the same right to a redundancy payment if you have to make him redundant in future.

Whether or not you can grant his wish depends on what effect his absence will have on your business – but if you can afford to let him take the time away you may be rewarded with a more productive and loyal employee when he comes back.

Chapter 5

Figuring Out Final Payments

. . . .

In This Chapter

▶ Adding up final payments and deductions for departing employees

▶ Working out payments in lieu of notice, for unused holidays, and pensions payments

▶ Calculating redundancy payments

. . . .

*W*hen an employee leaves your firm, for whatever reason, you'll have to work out what should be in her final pay packet. A few people move on each year from most businesses, so this is something you may find you get a lot of practice at!

Some employees choose to leave to go to another job, and others leave to retire. You may have to let others go because you have to reduce your workforce or because you have reason to sack someone. Whatever the situation, handle it as well as you possibly can, because people do talk afterwards and your reputation as an employer can be affected.

If someone resigns, don't take it personally! She may have picked up skills and experience with you and want to move on to learn new skills and take on new responsibilities. Or she may simply want an easier life with fewer responsibilities. And no matter how tempting, don't jump up and down with glee because you can't wait to get rid of her. Organise a leaving party and a present so that everyone feels good about the event. Use your employee's exit to take another look at your workforce and see if you need to make changes in its structure.

Give the person who's leaving the opportunity to have a final interview with you. You may learn something valuable from what she has to say about the way you run the company.

If you have to sack an employee, make sure you are doing so for a fair reason and that you follow all the correct dismissal and dispute resolution procedures. If you have to make people redundant, don't select them unfairly for redundancy or discriminate against anyone, and remember that those left will feel vulnerable and need to be kept informed.

Above all – get the final wages right! The last thing you want is a dispute over money that ends up at an Employment Tribunal and drags on well after the employee has left.

Working Out What's Owed When Staff Leave You

An employee's last wage packet should have all the money in it that your employee is entitled to up to the date she leaves. This includes:

- ✔ Wages up to the employee's final day.
- ✔ Any bonuses, commission, shift pay, overtime, or share of tips.
- ✔ Any money in lieu of notice.
- ✔ Any holiday pay the employee's entitled to for days that she was entitled to take off but wasn't able to.
- ✔ Any redundancy payments.
- ✔ Any sick, maternity, paternity, or adoption pay due.
- ✔ Any guarantee payments which are due for a period when the employee has been laid off (see Book V Chapter 1 for more details).

See the section 'Paying Redundancy Money' for more details about redundancy pay. Book V Chapter 1 gives more details about wages, and Book V Chapter 4 provides information on holiday pay, sick pay, and payments for new parents.

After you know exactly how much you owe in the employee's final pay packet, any income tax and National Insurance has to be deducted along with any other deductions that you normally make (such as student loan repayments, Attachment of Earnings Orders, or union dues). The final pay packet is the last time you can make those deductions, so you need to make sure that you let everyone know that your employee is no longer working for you and that you will be making no more of those deductions. The people you need to inform include HM Revenue & Customs and other organisations who need to know about changes to salary deductions – student loan companies, for instance.

The employee may owe you some money too, such as an outstanding loan, advances, overpayments of wages, or money for shortfalls in the till or stock. You're entitled to take any overpayments and shortfalls out of the employee's final pay packet, and will probably be entitled to take any advances of wages and remaining loan repayments too – if that's the agreement you drew up when you gave your member of staff the money. If you didn't make an agreement that anything still to be paid on a loan can come out of final wages but that the employee will repay it at a certain amount over a particular period of time, then that agreement still stands. Such agreements are separate to employment contracts and have their own terms and conditions.

An employee is entitled to a final wage slip detailing all the payments and deductions you've made, and a P45 showing how much tax and National Insurance you have deducted for the year to date. There's more on P45s in Book V Chapter 2.

Paying Redundancy Money

Regardless of your financial situation, most employees you make redundant are entitled to a redundancy payment as compensation for losing their jobs and to tide them over until they get back into work.

A departing employee may already have a new job to go to before she leaves or she may find a new job straight away, but she's still entitled to her redundancy payment.

Knowing who's entitled to redundancy payments

The law entitles most people who've been employed by you for two years or more to a *statutory redundancy payment* (the minimum amount that the law says you have to pay an employee when you make her redundant – there's more in the section 'Payments the law says you must give'). To qualify, an employee has to have been employed by you for two years continuously and to have been dismissed by you because of redundancy.

Employees aren't entitled to a redundancy payment if they:

- ✔ Have their fixed-term contract renewed.
- ✔ Have their contract renewed with a break of less than four weeks.
- ✔ Accept an alternative job offer from you.
- ✔ Resign before the redundancy notices were issued.
- ✔ Unreasonably turn down a suitable alternative job offer from you.

An employee aged 65 or more when she's made redundant qualifies for a redundancy payment since the new age discrimination legislation came into force in 2006.

If you've given your employees redundancy notices but don't pay redundancy money, they can apply to an Employment Tribunal to decide whether you owe them money and how much. Anyone who doesn't claim within six months of leaving loses her entitlement.

Payments the law says you must give

No flat rate covers all statutory redundancy payments. The amount you have to pay each employee depends on how long she's worked for you, how old she is, and how much she earns. The best way to work out the exact entitlement is to use Table 5-1.

A *week's pay* means the employee's gross wage for the week in which you hand out the redundancy notices. If your employees get a fixed amount each week, use that in the calculation; if their pay varies from week to week, take the average over the previous 12 weeks. A limit to what constitutes a week's wages is in place for redundancy calculations; you calculate the payment using your employees' normal week's wages up to a maximum of £330 a week and anything they earn over £330 doesn't count. The calculation is made starting at the date of redundancy and working backwards to take into account the years of service that give the greatest entitlement. The table below shows you how many weeks money you have to pay out depending on age and total number of years worked.

Table 5-1   **Calculating Redundancy Pay from Years of Service**

Age	Service (Years)																		
	2	3	4	5	6	7	8	9	10	11	12	13	14	15	16	17	18	19	20
17*	1																		
18	1	1½																	
19	1	1½	2																
20	1	1½	2	2½	-														
21	1	1½	2	2½	3	-													
22	1	1½	2	2½	3	3½	-												
23	1½	2	2½	3	3½	4	4½	-											
24	2	2½	3	3½	4	4½	5	5½	-										
25	2	3	3½	4	4½	5	5½	6	6½	-									
26	2	3	4	4½	5	5½	6	6½	7	7½	-								
27	2	3	4	5	5½	6	6½	7	7½	8	8½	-							
28	2	3	4	5	6	6½	7	7½	8	8½	9	9½	-						
29	2	3	4	5	6	7	7½	8	8½	9	9½	10	10½	-					
30	2	3	4	5	6	7	8	8½	9	9½	10	10½	11	11½	-				
31	2	3	4	5	6	7	8	9	9½	10	10½	11	11½	12	12½	-			
32	2	3	4	5	6	7	8	9	10	10½	11	11½	12	12½	13	13½	-		
33	2	3	4	5	6	7	8	9	10	11	11½	12	12½	13	13½	14	14½	-	

Table 5-1 (continued)

(continued)

Age	2	3	4	5	6	7	8	9	10	11	12	13	14	15	16	17	18	19	20
34	2	3	4	5	6	7	8	9	10	11	12	12½	13	13½	14	14½	15	15½	-
35	2	3	4	5	6	7	8	9	10	11	12	13	13½	14	14½	15	15½	16	16½
36	2	3	4	5	6	7	8	9	10	11	12	13	14	14½	15	15½	16	16½	17
37	2	3	4	5	6	7	8	9	10	11	12	13	14	15	15½	16	16½	17	17½
38	2	3	4	5	6	7	8	9	10	11	12	13	14	15	16	16½	17	17½	18
39	2	3	4	5	6	7	8	9	10	11	12	13	14	15	16	17	17½	18	18½
40	2	3	4	5	6	7	8	9	10	11	12	13	14	15	16	17	18	18½	19
41	2	3	4	5	6	7	8	9	10	11	12	13	14	15	16	17	18	19	19½
42	2½	3½	4½	5½	6½	7½	8½	9½	10½	11½	12½	13½	14½	15½	16½	17½	18½	19½	20½
43	3	4	5	6	7	8	9	10	11	12	13	14	15	16	17	18	19	20	21
44	3	4½	5½	6½	7½	8½	9½	10½	11½	12½	13½	14½	15½	16½	17½	18½	19½	20½	21½
45	3	4½	6	7	8	9	10	11	12	13	14	15	16	17	18	19	20	21	22
46	3	4½	6	7½	8½	9½	10½	11½	12½	13½	14½	15½	16½	17½	18½	19½	20½	21½	22½
47	3	4½	6	7½	9	10	11	12	13	14	15	16	17	18	19	20	21	22	23
48	3	4½	6	7½	9	10½	11½	12½	13½	14½	15½	16½	17½	18½	19½	20½	21½	22½	23½
49	3	4½	6	7½	9	10½	12	13	14	15	16	17	18	19	20	21	22	23	24
50	3	4½	6	7½	9	10½	12	13½	14½	15½	16½	17½	18½	19½	20½	21½	22½	23½	24½

Age																		
51	3	4½	6	7½	9	10½	12	13½	15	16	17	18	19	20	21	22	23	24	25
52	3	4½	6	7½	9	10½	12	13½	15	16½	17½	18½	19½	20½	21½	22½	23½	24½	25½
53	3	4½	6	7½	9	10½	12	13½	15	16½	18	19	20	21	22	23	24	25	26
54	3	4½	6	7½	9	10½	12	13½	15	16½	18	19½	20½	21½	22½	23½	24½	25½	26½
55	3	4½	6	7½	9	10½	12	13½	15	16½	18	19½	21	22	23	24	25	26	27
56	3	4½	6	7½	9	10½	12	13½	15	16½	18	19½	21	22½	23½	24½	25½	26½	27½
57	3	4½	6	7½	9	10½	12	13½	15	16½	18	19½	21	22½	24	25	26	27	28
58	3	4½	6	7½	9	10½	12	13½	15	16½	18	19½	21	22½	24	25½	26½	27½	28½
59	3	4½	6	7½	9	10½	12	13½	15	16½	18	19½	21	22½	24	25½	27	28	29
60	3	4½	6	7½	9	10½	12	13½	15	16½	18	19½	21	22½	24	25½	27	28½	29½
61+	3	4½	6	7½	9	10½	12	13½	15	16½	18	19½	21	22½	24	25½	27	28½	30

The maximum number of weeks' pay the law says you have to pay is 30. That would be due to a member of staff aged 61. For employees aged 61 and over the payment remains the same as for employees aged 61.

Paying what the contract says

As with any payment where the law lays down a minimum, you can pay more if you choose to. Although some firms do make enhanced payments, most small employers don't exceed the letter of the law. But if you have in the past made people redundant with enhanced redundancy payments and nothing in your current employees' contracts states otherwise, your staff may interpret those enhanced payments as 'custom and practice' that have become part of their contracts. So you need to make clear in employees' contracts what your terms will be if you have to make people redundant.

On the other hand, some employers try to wriggle out of making redundancy payments by making employees contract themselves out of their rights to payments. You can't force employees to waive their rights to redundancy payments. Such contracting-out agreements are void unless the employee:

- ✔ Was on a fixed-term contract of two years or more made before the Fixed Term (Prevention of Less Favourable Treatment) Regulations 2002 came into force.
- ✔ Agreed in writing, before she started work, to waive her rights to redundancy payments at the end of the contract.

Taxing redundancy payments

No one pays tax or National Insurance contributions on statutory redundancy payments. But if you're paying out enhanced redundancy payments there may be tax to consider. The payments are tax free up to £30,000. If the redundancy plus any other amounts that have to be paid to someone who's leaving come to more than £30,000, income tax has to be paid on the amount over £30,000.

You can find details about redundancy pay at the Department for Business, Enterprise, and Regulatory Reform Web site (www.berr.gov.uk) or talk to your local Business Link office. You can find details in the phone book, or call 0845 6009006.

Lay-offs and short-time working

Some situations allow an employee to claim a redundancy payment without being dismissed. The Redundancy Payments Scheme prevents dodgy bosses from deliberately laying off a worker or putting her on *short-time work* (where an employee has less than half a normal weeks work and pay during any week in which she has a contract of employment with you) instead of dismissing her when little work is available, avoiding having to give a redundancy payment.

An employee who's worked for you continuously for two years, whose pay is directly linked to the number of hours she works or her output, may be entitled to a redundancy payment even though you don't dismiss her. An employee can resign and claim a redundancy payment within four weeks of the last day of lay-off or short-time working if she has:

✔ Been laid off or put on short time for at least four consecutive weeks.

✔ Been laid off or put on short time for six weeks or more in a total of thirteen weeks.

If an employee in this situation claims a redundancy payment, you can give her notice in writing within seven days that you fully expect to give her full-time working for at least thirteen weeks, starting within the next four weeks. If she doesn't accept that offer she can resign – giving you the correct period of notice – and ask a tribunal to settle the argument.

Getting on the wrong side of the law

If you aren't careful, you can commit various offences when it comes to redundancy payments, and the consequences can be fairly severe. Here are a few key offences to be aware of:

✔ If you don't make redundancy payments when you should, an employee can make a claim against you at an Employment Tribunal or can claim from the National Insurance Fund.

✔ If you fail to hand over any information the National Insurance Fund adjudication officer asks for to help decide whether a payment should be made.

✔ If you don't give an employee written details of the calculation of her redundancy payment she can bring a claim to an Employment Tribunal.

✔ If you're making multiple redundancies (20 or more), you must notify the Secretary of State – through the Department for Business, Enterprise, and Regulatory Reform – by letter, or fill in form HR1. You can download this from the BERR Web site (www.berr.gov.uk) or get it from your local Job Centre Plus or through the Redundancy Payments Helpline – 0845 145 0004. If you don't notify the Secretary of State you can be fined up to £5,000.

Money Instead of Notice

Whether an employee's leaving you voluntarily, you have sacked her, or made her redundant, the question of notice periods must raise its head. Normally an employee works until the end of her notice period, but sometimes you may want to let her go immediately or before the end of the notice period. For example, if you are letting go someone who has access to sensitive materials and for any reason think she may do something irresponsible with those materials, you probably don't want the person coming into work during the notice period, even if she's been a trustworthy employee to this point.

Likewise, sometimes the employee is giving you notice of a change of jobs, but is really hoping you'll offer the money instead of asking her to come in the next couple of weeks because she'd rather have the time off before starting her next job. However, if your employee wants to leave before the end of the notice period by her own choice, she's not entitled to money in lieu. For example, if you really need her expertise to make sure she has time to pass along what she knows to the next person to fill her slot, you don't have to let her go early.

If you do let an employee go before the end of her notice period, you have to pay her for those weeks even though she's no longer working for you. Otherwise she can bring a case against you for the money on the grounds of wrongful dismissal. If your employee wants to leave before the end of the notice period by her own choice, she's not entitled to money in lieu.

When it comes to paying money in lieu of notice, there's no limit on what constitutes a week's wages (unlike the caps placed on redundancy payments). You will have to pay the employee's normal week's wages or, if the pay and hours vary, a week's wages are calculated as the average of the last 12 weeks immediately preceding the first day of the notice period.

If you've given your employee notice and she gets sick during that notice period, she is still entitled to be paid her notice weeks at her normal weekly wage. If you have given her more notice in her contract than the statutory amount, the extra weeks can be paid at the Statutory Sick Pay rates (see Book V Chapter 4 for more on sick pay).

Retiring Staff

You have to work out final payments for a member of staff when she's retiring. You can't make anyone retire earlier than 65. You may set a retirement age for your company that is over 65, but if you don't set one at all 65 is regarded as the default age at which employees will expect to retire.

Employees can still ask to go on working after 65, or after the age you set, and you must consider that request. This arrangement will be reviewed again by the Government in 2011. If you want any advice on issues related to the age of your employees you can call the Advisory, Conciliation, and Arbitration Service (ACAS) on 0845 7474747 or check out the Web site at www.acas.org.uk. You need to work out what exactly you owe her and anything she owes you, make the necessary deductions, and then pay her what's left. Retirement and pensions are covered more in Book V Chapter 6.

Paying Up if You're Going Bust

If you've totted up final payments but can't pay them, you're likely to be at the point of having to wind up your business or go into liquidation. In this situation, your employees are creditors of your business and as such are entitled to what's owed to them if there's enough money in the pot. They are *preferred creditors* and should get their money after your *secured creditors*, who have security such as a mortgage. You need to keep employees informed of what's going on and make sure they know that if you can't pay, the state, through the National Insurance Fund, will pick up at least some of the bills.

It can be a long process. If you are formally insolvent and an insolvency practitioner or official receiver has been appointed to deal with your business affairs your employees can contact the Redundancy Payments helpline on 08451450004 for help to make a claim. If you simply stop trading and aren't formally insolvent but can't pay what you owe them, your employees have to claim through an Employment Tribunal and if you still can't pay they can then apply to the fund. They may not get all the pay or notice pay they're entitled to – a week's wage is calculated up to a maximum of £330 – but they will be paid the amount of statutory redundancy payment they're entitled to. Book V Chapter 1 has more information on this situation.

If your business is about to go 'pop', you need to try to keep all employees on your side, especially your finance and payroll people, while you're going through the process.

Chapter 6

Making Provision for Life after Work

*I*n an ironic twist of the business world, to attract and keep the best employees in your business, you may need to look at what you offer them when they are ready to stop working – namely, your pension or retirement plan. There *is* life after work . . . and a whole generation of retirees out there on golf courses and foreign beaches can prove it. But many employees work on beyond the *state pension age* of 60 for women born on or before 6th April 1955 (by 2020 it will be 65 for women) or 65 for men. Nothing in the law stops people working as long as they like or are able to, as long as their employer is willing to keep them on or they can find another job. As well as the people who've had to keep working because they don't have sufficient pensions to retire on, for some people the prospect of not working is a nightmare, whether they have money or not. They may leave their careers and move into less pressurised, less lucrative jobs, but they want to carry on working to keep themselves busy.

You need to plan ahead to make sure that your staff have as easy a transition into retirement as possible and are as well taken care of financially as you'd like to be yourself – so this chapter also helps you think through the pensions options to offer staff. If you don't, you may find that you aren't getting the best staff because they're going to employers who offer better working conditions and pensions.

In 2006 age discrimination legislation came in to force stopping employers using age as a reason for getting rid of employees.

Retiring Your Workforce

You can't make any of your employees retire before the age of 65. If you have set a retirement age for your employees it should be 65 or over and stated in their contract. Most employers set a retirement age that's the same for most of their industry. If you haven't set one it will be the default age for retirement – set by the Government at 65. This will be reviewed in 2011. However anyone has the right to ask to be allowed to carry on working after your set retirement age or over 65, and you must consider their request. Of course anyone who wants to retire earlier has the right to resign.

If the contract states a clear retirement age, once employees reach that age you don't have to do anything other than make sure that they get all their final payments and give them a nice send-off, but you'll have to consider their request if they ask to be allowed to carry on working. If you don't specify an age in the contract then you have to give the correct notice period.

You have to make plans to replace an employee who's retiring and who's handing over his work to a new person. Think about whether or not the outgoing and the incoming employees need to work together for a while to smooth the transition. You might also want to include your retiring employee in the recruitment process. After all, he's been doing the job and probably knows more about it than you do.

Exit interviews with departing employees can be very useful to both parties. An *exit interview* gives the employee the opportunity to have his say about how the place is run and anything he's not been happy about during his employment. You're losing an employee with a lot of knowledge of your business and with the best will in the world not everything he knows can be written down, put in files or databases, and left behind. An exit interview gives you the chance to gain useful insights, from your soon-to-be-departing employee, into the running of your business. And the fact that you listen will enhance your reputation no end.

Easing employees into retirement

Many people are very excited about retiring. They have plans or are motivated to find new ways to fill their time. How often do you hear retired people say 'I have no idea how I ever found time to work'? But retirement can look like a big black void to others. The gloom hanging over them can affect their work for a long time before they leave and can rub off on everybody else, especially if you have a small staff. Think about what you can do to help lift the gloom.

Retiring (but maybe not so shy)

Big companies can afford to send their people on retirement courses that spell out all the details of pensions, benefits, financial planning, work opportunities, or voluntary work and so on. One retiring friend even had advice on exercise for the over-60s. You probably can't afford to do all that, but you can let an employee have time off to make appointments with a pensions adviser or the local Citizen's Advice Bureau if he's worried about living on less money. He can talk to various organisations locally about any voluntary work available if he's worried about having too much time on his hands and becoming isolated at home. And maybe you can encourage him to use your work computers to look for courses or classes he'd like to do. The Life Academy that used to be the Pre-Retirement Association and the University of the Third Age are just a couple of organisations to contact. The Life Academy can be contacted on 01483-301177 or at `www.life-academy.co.uk` and the University of The Third Age is on 0208-4666139 or at `www.u3a.org.uk`.

Talk to staff well before retirement about how they feel about it and what concerns they have and try, together, to come up with ways of making it easier. Sometimes information is all that's needed. Sometimes it's something practical such as having a computer at home when you've been used to having one at work. You may even have an old one you don't need or stretch to one for a leaving present.

You can pay for your employees to take advice on pensions as an employee benefit. It's not a taxable benefit as long as the advice or information is offered to all employees and costs you less than £150 per employee per year. Your local Business Link can give you more information and you'll find their details in the phone book or on the Web site `www.businesslink.gov.uk`.

If a member of staff looks forward to retirement he'll be a valuable member of staff right up until the last day and remain loyal to you after he's left. And the remaining staff are likely to recognise that you're a good employer and do their best to earn their own comfortable retirements. You know it makes sense!

Offering early retirement

An employee who doesn't want to carry on working up to retirement age always has the option simply to hand in his notice and leave. But if you want an employee to go early you'll have to:

- ✔ Have a reason to dismiss him
- ✔ Make him redundant if you genuinely have to cut jobs
- ✔ Offer employees who retire early an incentive package

The last is an option open to employers who have occupational pension schemes (explained in the section 'Offering an occupational pension', later in this chapter). Depending on the particular scheme there may be enough money in the pot to allow you to offer an employee a retirement package that encourages him to go before his normal retirement age.

As in any situation where someone leaves of his own volition, you give him the pay due to him and his P45. There may be no pension payments involved unless he is old enough to start taking his occupational pension if there is one in place.

Managing older employees

Current employment trends see employees working on to a greater age than used to be the case. Some employers have dropped retirement ages completely and encourage employees to stay on. And as with any employees you have a duty of care for their welfare, meaning that bosses have to pay more attention to the health and safety of older workers. For example, older workers may need more help to make sure that their workstations are ergonomically set up. They may have more problems with viewing computer screens. Simple things like more *screen breaks* (working away from the computer), more opportunities to walk around, and bigger text size on computer screens don't need to cost much but can make a big difference.

You need to talk to all employees about any problems they're having around the workplace and that's probably even more true as they get older. The best way of doing this is to incorporate frequent, brief informal chats into the general running of the workplace so that employees feel you care without being intrusive. If problems do crop up deal with them quickly and involve your employees in coming up with solutions. They've probably all got older relatives and may have some useful ideas.

Encourage your older and younger staff to work together – they can all learn from each other. Some older staff think that just because they've always done something in one particular way that's the only way to do it. They can learn new tricks from younger dogs, who in turn will benefit from older employees' experience and knowledge.

Many people don't want to retire or would like to retire gradually rather than being in work one day and out of it the next. If your employee has been good at his job it's worth thinking about whether or not he'd still be useful to have around in another capacity. Perhaps he can work fewer hours and reduce his hours over a period of time to ease him into retirement. Maybe he can continue working for you as a consultant on a self-employed basis after he leaves. You're not only looking after his welfare but making sure that you don't lose all his knowledge and expertise at once.

If you want to keep an employee, and he wants to stay on there's nothing to stop you keeping him on the payroll past the normal retirement age for your company – or 65 if there isn't one. Age discrimination legislation also applies to occupational pension schemes so any scheme you run can't require employees to retire before 65.

Avoiding discrimination

Employers are becoming increasingly dependent on older workers as demographics shift and the pool of younger people becomes smaller. But some employers feel that older people are more trouble around the workplace and because they've worked their way up are probably more expensive than younger replacements would be. So the temptation exists to get rid of older employees if the opportunity arises or not to hire them in the first place but older workers have the same rights as younger ones.

The Advisory, Conciliation, and Arbitration Service (ACAS) has been designated as the organisation to deal with issues about employment and age. You can contact ACAS on the helpline 0845 7474747 or through their Web site at `www.acas.org.uk`.

Pensioning Off Your Employees

Pension planning is important. Even young people see pension provision as an increasingly important part of the whole employment and pay package that prospective employers offer. More paranoia exists now about pensions than there has been for decades. People are worried about changing jobs in case their new employer's pension scheme is worth less than their existing one. Where people used to say 'I've just got a couple of years until I get my pension – much as I hate my job I'm going to stay put', they're now saying the same with six or eight years to go. So you need to understand the pension system.

Pensions broadly break down into four categories:

- ✔ **State pensions.** The basic state pension, the state second pension and SERPS. State pensions are available to all workers who've paid the right National Insurance Contributions.

- ✔ **Occupational pensions.** Including final salary, money purchase, and group personal pensions; occupational pensions are organised privately by employers.

✔ **Stakeholder pensions.** Like occupational pensions, stakeholder pensions are private pensions, but are available to self-employed workers too and people who aren't working but can afford them.

✔ **Personal pensions**. These are private plans that people arrange for themselves.

If you employ five or more workers you have to offer an occupational scheme, or a stakeholder scheme, or pay contributions worth at least 3 per cent of your employees' wages into your employees' private schemes.

An employee may already have his own (non-employment-related) personal pension plan when he joins you and not want to join whatever scheme you offer for some reason. That may not be the most sensible decision and you should advise him to talk to a financial adviser: If employees don't have access to an occupational scheme and don't save into a personal pension or a stakeholder scheme, they're dependent on the state pension.

You should encourage your employees to apply for *combined pension fore-casts* from the Pension Service – allowing them to see forecasts of their state, private, and occupational pension provisions together. If they have that information they can plan better for their retirement. The Pension Service Web site is at www.thepensionservice.gov.uk or on 0845-6060265. Employees in Northern Ireland can contact the Department for Social Development at www.dsdni.gov.uk/ssa_pension_information or call 0845 603 3332.

Depending on the State

A *state pension* is the sum of money paid to all retired workers by the government; everyone who works saves for their future by paying National Insurance Contributions (NICs), which contribute to their final pension. As an employer, you're responsible for collecting these NICs (see Book V Chapter 2 for more about this).

Several types of state pension exist, and which one retired workers qualify for depends on their circumstances. As an employer you need to be familiar with the state scheme and encourage your employees to find out how much they can expect when they retire. They'll be entitled to some or all of the elements explained in this section and they can ask for a pension forecast from the Pension Service so that they know how much to expect from the state on retirement. Call the Pensions Service on 0845 3000168 for a State Pension forecast or visit the website (details above).

The state of state pensions

People are often very shocked when they find out how little they can expect from their state pension. Newspaper headlines for years were full of stories of well-off pensioners indulging their every whim and the importance of their spending power to the economy. As a result, an expectation arose among employees approaching retirement age that all pensioners can expect to be well off.

The reality is that unless they can afford to save money into an occupational pension provided by an employer, or into a private pension that they arrange themselves, retired workers are unlikely to be able to live the high-life as pensioners. In 1975 the full state pension was worth around 22 per cent of the average wage. Now it's worth about 16 per cent . . . and falling.

Basic state pension

The *basic state pension* is for people who've reached state pension age. At the time of writing, that's 60 for women and 65 for men. From 2010 women will have to retire later and by 2020 the state pension age will be 65 for both sexes. Remember that the state pension age is the age people qualify for the state pension – not the retirement age.

The amount paid by the basic state pension depends on the number of years an employee has paid National Insurance Contributions – NICs – during his working life. *Working life* is 49 years for men and 44 for women, starting at the age of 16. If an employee has paid enough NICs during his working life, he gets the full amount (for example, £87.30 per week in April 2007/2008).

Employees who haven't paid enough can add voluntary Class 3 contributions to make up the difference. They pay these direct to HM Revenue and Customs (formerly the Inland Revenue). If that's not an option the amount the employee gets will be reduced. If he hasn't worked he can claim on his spouse's contributions and will get £52.30 (that applies for both men and women). If the two members of a couple have both paid enough NICs they will both be entitled to a full pension.

People who have been out of work looking after children and getting child benefit are protected and have to pay fewer years' NICs to qualify for a full basic pension. Additional amounts are available for adult and child dependants. If you or your employees want to know more, go to the Pension Service Web site (www.thepensionservice.gov.uk) for a full explanation.

State second pension

The *state second pension*, sometimes known as an *additional state pension*, is for low and moderate earners. Employees earning up to £26,600 can get the second state pension on top of the basic state pension. It replaced SERPS (see the next section) in April 2002 and the government claims that the second state pension gives people earning up to £26,600 a better second pension than SERPS did.

Employees can leave, or *contract out* of, the additional state pension as long as they join a personal scheme, their employer's contracted-out occupational scheme, or a stakeholder scheme (all explained in the following sections). If they do choose to opt out and pay into your occupational scheme instead, you and they will both pay smaller NICs. If they contract out with a stakeholder or personal pension the NICs aren't reduced, but once a year the Inland Revenue rebates some NICs directly into their scheme.

SERPS – State Earnings Related Pension Scheme

The *State Earnings Related Pension Scheme* (SERPS) was the second state pension until April 2002, although employees who qualified for SERPS still accumulate a pension through the scheme. It started in 1978 and anyone who earned more than the lower earnings limit for National Insurance Contributions (see Book V Chapter 2) built up an entitlement to a SERPS. The amount contributed to SERPS increased the more you earned.

Working out SERPS is complicated and employees can fill in form BR19 (available from the local Benefits Agency or Job Centre Plus) and send it to the Pension Service or visit the Web site at www.thepensionservice.gov.uk or call 0845-3000168 for a forecast of how much they'll get on retirement.

Graduated pensions

Anyone who worked between 1961 and 1975 may be entitled to a graduated pension. Lots of people coming up to retirement age in the early twenty-first century fall into that category. They would have to have paid Graduated National Insurance Contributions to qualify and the amounts paid out are very small. A state pension forecast from the Pensions Service will tell employees about any graduated pension they are entitled to and it will be paid to them with their state pension payments.

Offering an occupational pension

The government offers tax relief on contributions paid into personal, stakeholder, or employer's pension schemes. *Occupational pensions* are run by private financial companies rather than the government, and allow workers and employers (if they choose to – many typically pay around 3 per cent of an employee's earnings) to contribute to their own pension scheme.

Two types of occupational pension schemes are available:

- ✔ **Final salary schemes.** Salary-related schemes promise to pay an employee a pension of a certain percentage of his final salary or an average over his total employment.

  You pay contributions for each of your employees who join the scheme and your employees pay contributions at a certain percentage of their salary. As their salary goes up so the contributions increase and what's in the pot when they retire is dependent on their earnings and how long they've been a member. All the money paid into the fund is invested by the fund managers and if the investments do well everybody wins. If the investments do badly your contributions have to increase.

  You take all the risk with a scheme of this sort, so fewer employers are setting them up and some who are already operating them are closing them to new members because they say they're too expensive to run.

  In some cases firms have gone bust and there hasn't been enough money in the pot to pay out the pension obligations.

- ✔ **Money purchase schemes.** These operate in a similar way to final salary schemes – up to a point. Each member pays contributions into the scheme and builds up his own pot. The size of the pot will depend on how much employers and employees contribute and how the pension fund has been invested. When an employee retires his money is used to purchase an annuity. An *annuity* is an investment product sold by a range of insurance companies, and pays out regular payments to the employee after retirement until he dies.

- ✔ No guarantees are made about how much an employee will get after he retires because this depends on how the money in the annuity is invested and how well it does. Another problem for the employee when he retires is that he has a pension fund but he has to use it to buy an annuity – and a big choice of annuities exists. Getting it right is a gamble.

- ✔ More employers are opting to set up money purchase schemes and some are using them to replace final salary schemes.

The Pensions Regulator regulates pension schemes as the name suggests. That's the place to start for advice and information on your role as an employer. The Web site is at www.thepensionsregulator.gov.uk or you can call 0870 6063636. The Pensions Service and your local Business Link can also help. Details for both are given earlier in this chapter. The Office of the Pensions Advisory Service has a wealth of general information on the whole range of pension schemes. The Web site is at www.pensionsadvisory service.org.uk or you can call 0845-6012923.

You can't force employees to join an occupational pension scheme just because you offer it, but by not joining they miss out on the contributions you may choose to make to the scheme on their behalf. Most schemes will also provide for employees who have to retire early on the grounds of ill health and have a life insurance element so that their dependants get a lump sum if they die while they're a scheme member.

If you don't offer an occupational pension scheme or offer to make contributions worth at least 3 per cent of your employees' wages into their personal schemes, you will have to provide access to a stakeholder scheme (see 'Offering a stakeholder pension', later in this chapter).

If you do decide to go ahead with an occupational pension, you have to follow all the rules and regulations in place to protect the members, your employees. HM Revenue and Customs (Inland Revenue) approved occupational pension schemes give tax relief on contributions, allow members to take part of their eventual benefits as a tax-free lump sum, and allow members to contract out of the state second pension in return for a reduction in, or a rebate of, National Insurance Contributions (see 'State second pension', earlier in this chapter).

You don't have to set up and run an employer's or occupational scheme, but if you don't you may miss out on all the best recruits. Check out what your competition is offering and what the situation is throughout your industry. You may think you can't afford to run a pension scheme, but maybe you can't afford not to.

Running an occupational pension scheme

If you're thinking of running an occupational pension scheme you'll need a *pension provider* – one of the companies that sells and designs pension schemes – to set up and operate the scheme on a day-to-day basis, investing the money and administering it with the trustees who make the decisions. The scheme has to be registered with the Pensions Regulator (see above) and the pension provider usually does that.

Your scheme must have a qualified scheme auditor and, if it's a salary-related scheme, a qualified scheme actuary. Trustees have to be appointed to run the scheme and they have to be trained. The scheme has to be run in the interests of the people who will benefit from it, not in the interest of your business, and its assets and money have to be kept separate from those of your business.

Fulfilling your duties

Your role is to give employees access to the scheme and information about it, and to make contributions to their pensions. Employees should have:

 ✔ A booklet explaining the scheme

 ✔ An annual benefits statement showing how their pension is doing

 ✔ The trustees' report and accounts

 ✔ Information about their options if they leave the scheme

You have to get your employees' agreement when they join the scheme that you can take their contributions out of their wages. You have to send those contributions and your own contributions if you make any to the pension provider by the 19th of each month and you can be fined if you don't. You need a system for making deductions, paying them, and keeping records. Book V Chapter 2 gives advice on these areas.

Appointing trustees

You have to appoint *trustees* to hold and make decisions about your scheme's assets for the people who will eventually receive pensions from it. Trustees have to act separately from you for the benefit of the scheme members, and their powers are set out in the trust deed – the legal document detailing their duties and responsibilities – and the scheme's rules.

The Pensions Act 2004 (which took effect from April 2005) requires trustees to be trained so they know exactly what they're taking on and what they have to do.

The Trust Deed sets out how new trustees are to be appointed. Members of the scheme have the right to elect or appoint at least half the trustees, and normally other trustees are appointed by you or by the existing trustees. One third of trustees should be Member Nominated Trustees (but the rules are very complicated. You can't remove trustees yourself; only the other trustees, the regulatory authority – The Pensions Regulator – and a court have the power to do so. As long as they are over 18 trustees can be:

 ✔ A scheme member

 ✔ An employee

 ✔ A professional trustee or trustee company

 ✔ You, the employer

 ✔ A business associated with the scheme

Becoming a trustee of your own scheme creates the potential for a conflict of interests: You have to act in the best interests of the members not your own business.

Trustees have a legal duty to:

✔ Register a scheme, pay the annual levy, and take decisions for example about investments

✔ Take and keep records of meetings, decisions, and transactions

✔ Keep financial and member records

✔ Keep scheme assets separate from business assets

✔ Appoint professional advisers

✔ Get auditor's statements and actuarial certificates

✔ Approve and file the annual report

✔ Take investment decisions and appoint advisers

✔ Provide information for members, beneficiaries, and prospective members

✔ Sort out disputes for example where members complain about the scheme

Being a trustee isn't easy, and you should give employees time off to carry out their duties as trustees. They can be personally and jointly liable for scheme losses and be fined by OPRA if they don't comply with legislation. Your trustees do a very important job, so they need to be chosen carefully.

Making employer contributions

You don't have to make contributions to occupational pensions for your employees. Some employers pay all the contributions and don't expect their employees to make any from their salaries; on the other hand, sometimes the contributions the employer makes aren't big enough to provide a decent pension. Some employers have been cutting their contributions to salary-related schemes because they're no longer willing to carry so much of the risk.

Another option is to make contributions to your employees' private pensions. If you contribute at least 3 per cent to private pensions, you won't need to provide employees with access to a stakeholder or occupational scheme.

Overseeing workers' contributions

Some employers run schemes where employees don't have to make any contributions, but such generosity is rare. Usually employees join a scheme where the percentage of salary they're expected to contribute is already set.

Employees don't have to join any scheme you offer. They can make their own arrangements or decide they can't afford to pay into a pension at all. So far it's not compulsory.

If you do provide a salary-related scheme, you also have to give employees the opportunity to build up extra savings through *Additional Voluntary Contributions* (AVCs) which do what they say on the tin and allow employees to make extra contributions to enhance their pensions. You might choose to have the same company provide your AVC scheme that operates your occupational scheme or choose a different one.

Making contributions to group personal pensions

One other type of occupational pension you can consider offering is the group personal pension, a variation on personal (non-employment-related) pensions. *Group personal pensions* are arranged by individual employees, each having their own individual plan. However as the employer, you choose the plan for your employees. These pensions are money purchase schemes (see 'Money purchase schemes', earlier in this chapter) but are cheaper in terms of charges than the other occupational schemes due to group discounts.

Changing jobs

If an employee has been with you for less than two years and leaves, he's entitled to a refund of the pension contributions he's made into an occupational scheme, minus tax. If he's contributed to it for at least two years he can leave the money in your scheme where it remains invested and grows (with luck) and provides him with a preserved pension when he reaches the retirement age set down by that scheme. Alternatively, he may be able to transfer the value of what he has built up so far into his new employer's scheme. He may want to do that so he doesn't have to keep track of more than one pension, or it may be that the new scheme seems a better prospect. You should advise him to get financial advice.

The employee will carry on making NICs towards his state pension through his new employer.

Offering a stakeholder pension

Stakeholder pensions are a way for your employees to save for their retirement, but they can also be used by people who aren't employed. These low-cost schemes are intended for people who don't have access to an occupational or personal pension. They must have low charges, flexibility, and security. Minimum contributions should be £20 or less.

You have to provide your employees with access to a stakeholder pension if you have five or more employees and:

 ✔ You don't offer an occupational pension.

 ✔ You don't pay an amount equal to at least 3 per cent of your employees' wages into all private pensions for all your employees who are 18 or over.

Stakeholder pensions are chosen from a range offered by financial services companies. Take a look at several of the schemes, all of which must be registered with the Pensions Regulator (contact details earlier in this chapter), get all the information so that you can compare them, discuss the options with your employees, and together choose which one they should access. Giving employees *access* to a stakeholder pension scheme means:

 ✔ Giving them all the details of the scheme and the stakeholder provider.

 ✔ Consulting them about deducting their payments directly from their wages.

 ✔ Collecting their contributions and sending them to the stakeholder provider by the deadlines if that's what they want.

 ✔ Keeping records of all the payments you make.

You don't have to make employer contributions to the stakeholder pension if you choose not to.

Carrying on working and pensions

Nothing stops people going on working as long as they like, provided they can find the work. Occupational pension schemes may allow them to start taking their pension at 60 – and perhaps they can take the pension and carry on working or find another job as well. Depending on the type of scheme, workers may be able to defer taking their pension until they do decide to retire, or take money out in stages to provide some income to top up earnings and take the remainder at 75.

Since December 2006, new rules have made occupational pension schemes more flexible. If your scheme has adopted the new rules, you may be able to keep someone on your payroll and allow him to receive his occupational pension, or to work part time and claim some pension payments to augment his salary at the same time.

Employees can receive the state pension and carry on working, or delay receiving it until they've retired fully. If they do carry on working after state pension age, they won't need to make any more NICs. Workers can defer taking the state pension as long as they like, and if an employee carries on working and wants to have a bigger state pension later he'll earn an extra state pension worth around 7.5 per cent of pay for every year he defers.

All pension payments are taxable.

Spouses, unmarried partners, and same-sex partners

State pensions and additional state pensions have regulated amounts that can be passed on to spouses, widows, and widowers, but similar payments from occupational pensions are determined entirely by the trustees.

You can write into the provisions of the scheme that unmarried partners and same-sex partners should be treated in the same way as spouses. These days when more people do live together without marrying or in same-sex partnerships, that's something that you should consider and discuss with your employees and trustees.

Book VI
Keeping On Top of Tax

'Under gifts, you seem to have made several large donations to the poor starving bank managers of the Cayman Islands.'

In this book . . .

*I*n business, you need to stay informed about tax – not just to ensure that the taxman gets no more than his fair share, but also to keep up to speed with the rules and regulations that you need to abide by to stay in the taxman's good books. From tax statuses and business types through to tax investigations and VAT, this Book tells you what you need to know.

Here are the contents of Book VI at a glance:

Chapter 1

Working for Yourself

*A*ccording to the Federation of Small Businesses, around four million people in the UK work for themselves. But whatever the exact head-count, the Inland Revenue taxes all these businesspeople. This chapter looks at dealing with the tax authorities as the owner of your own business instead of as an employee in someone else's.

Doing your taxes correctly can put your new firm on the road to success; messing them up is a sure-fire road to commercial oblivion or even bank-ruptcy. In this chapter we show you the tax advantages of self-employment and steer you away from some of the dangerous pitfalls.

Defining the Terms

Most people who strike out on their own, even if they go on to become multi-billionaires, often start as sole traders – the technical term for working for yourself, being a one-person band, or working as a freelancer.

For some, being self-employed means running a full-time business complete with commercial plans, business bank loans, staff, and public-liability insur-ance. If that's you, then, one day, you may hope to be a really big company and even float the company on the stock market. Lots of quoted companies started off as ventures run from an entrepreneur's dining room table.

Some sole traders offer the skills they have, such as plumbing, management consultancy, car mechanics, or writing books about business, directly to the client or end-user. Most of these businesspeople will never be big firms but they enjoy the freedom (as well as the responsibilities) of self-employment.

And for a growing number, it's all about part-time boosts to their earnings from a paying job that can be anything from regular wheeling and dealing on online auction sites to being a buy-to-let landlord.

Whatever category you are in, you are in business. And that puts you firmly into the tax-paying net even if you already pay income tax because you work full-time for an employer.

Some small businesses decide to become companies rather than sole traders. The advantages, and tax implications, of limited company status are dealt with in the next chapter.

Meeting HMRC's standards for self-employment

HMRC applies basic tests to determine whether you are really self-employed rather than working for someone else. Pass them and you can be on the way to tax savings! The standards are that:

- ✔ You work for more than one customer – and preferably several.

- ✔ You work from your own premises, or, if you don't, you work from several locations. If you're a writer, for example, you probably work from your home; however, if you're a plumber, you travel to your customers' premises.

- ✔ You're in control of what you do and the hours you work. You must be able to turn down work you do not fancy, and you should set your own prices.

- ✔ You have a business address – often your home – from which you carry out some business functions, if only message taking.

- ✔ You supply and maintain your own vehicles, tools, computers, and/or other items of equipment needed for your trade or profession.

- ✔ You correct bad work in your own time and at your own expense.

- ✔ You are legally liable for your mistakes.

Some businesses have acquired a reputation for turning people whose main function is selling their labour into self-employed workers when they should be employed under PAYE. Some examples are computer consultants who work for one company, sub-contract builders who work for others on sites, and hairdressers who rent the chair and basin space in the salon. HMRC makes big (and usually successful) efforts to deny such people self-employed status and the tax savings that can go with it.

Delving into the grey area

Most know when they start as a sole trader. They do work for customers in return for a commercial rate of reward. But there is a grey area where you may not know if you are trading or simply selling something.

One activity HMRC is targeting is selling via online auction. Proceeds from these sales are not, as some believe, always outside the tax net. Nor are car boot sales. Tax inspectors look for evidence of trading.

If you buy goods, either from wholesalers, or from other auctions, or from junk or charity shops with the intention of selling these things on at a profit, you are trading and so face a potential tax bill.

If you're clearing out the loft or spare room and have a one-off sale as an alternative to carting the lot to the charity shop or dump, then you are not trading, so there are no tax hassles. Although, should you find a Picasso in your loft and sell it for wads of money, you can face a Capital Gains Tax bill on the proceeds!

It is your responsibility to register, so find out about your status if you are in doubt. You cannot argue against a fine or penalty by saying you did not know or that you were waiting for HMRC to contact you.

Testing your wings while staying employed

These days, HMRC insists that the newly self-employed register within three months of starting up their activity. But, in practice, someone on PAYE who earns a one-off payment, perhaps for contributing to a publication or a one-off consultancy payment, does not need to register as self-employed although the remuneration she receives for this must be declared for tax. No absolute rules govern this – if you're unsure of your status, make sure you register with HMRC, just to be safe.

Book VI

Keeping On Top of Tax

Formalising Your Status

Just as no job is complete until the paperwork is done, neither can you start a business without filing forms with HMRC and deciding when your tax year runs. The following sections tell you what you need to do.

Registering your new business

The self-employed have to register as such with HMRC. This procedure includes making arrangements to pay national insurance contributions, which you will probably have to make. The upcoming 'Scanning National Insurance' section covers this issue.

You can register by:

- Calling a special helpline on 0845 915 4515. It's open between 8.00 a.m. and 8.00 p.m. seven days a week (except Christmas Day and one or two bank holidays).

- Filing form CWF1. Find it in HMRC leaflet PSE1 Thinking of working for yourself? Or download it online at www.hmrc.gov.uk/forms/cwf1.pdf or register online at www.hmrc.gov.uk/startingup/register.htm.

Failing to register within three months of starting self-employment can bring a £100 penalty. In some cases, the business's exact start date may be debatable, so it is best to register as soon as you can.

Larger penalties can be imposed if tax is paid late because an unincorporated business failed to register by 5 October of the following tax year in which it was set up.

Choosing your tax year carefully

Most businesses have an accounting year that runs alongside the tax year from 6 April to 5 April, though you may find it more convenient to use 31 March as the end date for your tax year. If you use 5 April or 31 March as the last day of your year, you're opting for fiscal accounting, so-called because your business year is the same as the tax, or fiscal, year. Fiscal year users account for tax by the 31 January following the end of their year.

You can use any other date for your year-end. Choosing a different date can give you longer to file and more time to keep the tax earning interest in the bank, which sounds like a great tax-saving idea. However, while many accountants still recommend choosing a different date, there are drawbacks.

Filing your first two returns

If you don't opt for a fiscal year-end, you have to meet extra requirements when filing tax returns for your first two years of operation. Your first year's tax bill is based on profits, if any, from the start of trading until the next 5 April – even though that's not the year-end date you chose. So, depending on when you start your business, your first tax bill may cover a matter of a few days or virtually a whole year.

Taxes for the second year are based on either the 12 months trading that ends on the date you chose in that year or your first 12 months of trading. You have to use the second option if the selected year-end date is less than 12 months after the start of the business.

Jessica starts her business on 1 August 2007 and decides on a 31 July year end. She makes a regular £2,000 a month profit. Under the start-up rules for the first two years, she has to account for her business from her 1 August 2007 start-date to 5 April 2008 on her 2007–8 tax return due in by 31 January 2009. She has to declare profits of £16,000 for these eight months because her selected year-end date is less than 12 months from the start of her business.

So far, so good. But her second year-end date is after her first 12 months of trading, so she has to account for the full 12 months from 1 August 2007 to 31 July 2008. Her profits here will be £24,000. Now for the really bad bit, which sounds like something out of Alice in Wonderland.

Even though Jessica has had to pay tax on her first eight months, she also has to pay tax on the first year. Now these overlap to a big extent. So, although she has only 12 months of trading to earn her money, she is assessed for 20 months of tax payments. On her £2,000 a month profits, she has earned £24,000 but she has to pay as though she has earned £40,000 (that's 20 months or 12 months plus eight months).

Of course, no one who is self-employed has exact months like that all the time. But we selected the same amount each month to make a complicated overlap a little simpler.

Lessening the effects of overlap

Having to pay tax on profits you haven't yet made is known in the tax trade as overlap. And you ignore it at your peril. For most small businesses, overlap is something to avoid. The answer is to align your business year with the tax year.

You can change your accounting year-end during the life of your business to lessen the effect of overlap if you need to. You can elect for a year-end change by notifying HMRC on a self assessment form or sending your tax inspector a letter.

If you don't cure your overlap while you are in self-employment, you only get your excess tax payment back when you cease trading. Such an event can be many years in the future, and the overpayments you made on starting will not be adjusted for inflation or changing tax rates.

If you have to borrow extra cash because paying overlap tax takes cash out of your business, you can claim the interest against a future tax bill.

Those setting up a business where the costs of the first year or so of trading are likely to be greater than their earnings obviously need have less fear of overlap as there will be no profits to tax.

Signing on for VAT

Whether you are a self-employed sole trader, a partnership, or a limited company, you have to register for VAT once your annual sales top a threshold amount ($64,000 in 2007–08) determined by the Chancellor of the Exchequer. This threshold tends to rise each year roughly in line with inflation. (For the current VAT threshold, go to HMRC Web site at www.hmrc.gov.uk.)You also need to register if your earnings in any one quarter are such that, multiplied by four, they would exceed the threshold. (See Book VI Chapter 4 for more on this.)

Keeping Accounts to Keep Everyone Happy

Here's a scary thought: The biggest single cheque you'll ever write out may well be to HMRC. In this section, we show you how to minimise your tax bite legally. And, in keeping with this book's theme of making sure that you don't give up all the tax you've saved by sending it all back, and, even worse, paying penalties, we focus on how to stick to the rules.

You have to keep records of your business for five years following the final filing date for your trading year. Someone with a trading year ending on 31 March 2008 will file by 31 January 2009 and needs to keep the paperwork (or computer records) until 31 January 2014.

Filling out Schedule D can pay dividends

Self-employed people have to fill in the basic self assessment tax form and also the self-employment pages (downloadable from the Inland Revenue Web site at www.hmrc.gov.uk/sa/index.htm or available via the HMRC helpline on 0845 9000444).

If you are self-employed, you will end up being taxed under what the taxman and accountants used to call Schedule D (which we'll still use as shorthand). Being on Schedule D can make your personal bank balance happier, most importantly because you can claim many expenses against what you earn. (See the following section.)

Those who work for someone else on PAYE can claim business expenses against tax only if those expenses are 'wholly, exclusively, and necessarily' incurred in carrying out their contract of employment. That definition is really tough to meet. But when you are on Schedule D, the 'necessarily' part of the PAYE definition goes. The reason? No outsider can define 'necessity'. Do you actually need to advertise your services in one particular way? Do you necessarily need a new vehicle when you can do the work using a clapped-out pushbike? Is your computer over-specified and do you need one at all?

All these choices are open to big companies and small firms alike and all the expenses can be set against the company's tax or your personal self-assessment form.

Book VI

Keeping On
Top of Tax

Counting your credits

You have a lot of freedom as a self-employed person. You can choose how you'll carry out your business and money spent wholly and exclusively for your business can be set against your earnings.

The tax authorities are not idiots. Don't try putting the costs of a Rolls-Royce down against tax, claiming it is a vehicle you use 'wholly and exclusively' for your business – unless, of course, you run a wedding limousine hire firm.

HMRC is always on the lookout for exaggerated expenses, but you don't have to exaggerate to minimise your tax bill. Just make sure you deduct everything you're legally allowed to, including:

✔ The administrative cost of running the business against your earnings from it. This sounds elementary, but many people with start-ups or those who have a small business on the side still have the mindset of working for an employer who picks up all the costs of running the business. All those little items such as postage stamps, fuel, mobile and fixed telephone charges, and even heating and lighting for your workplace add up over a year and are legally deductible.

✔ The cost of equipment including computers, machinery, and other big items. We explain how to deal with big items in the next section. Cars have rules of their own and are covered in the next section.

✔ Bank charges on business accounts and interest on loans for your business.

✔ A proportion of the costs of running your home if you use part of your property as a base. There are no specific rules for this. It's a question of common sense. If you have a house with six rooms and use one fairly regularly for your business, then look at your domestic bills and take a sixth part.

Obviously, if you use other premises solely for business, then you can deduct all the costs.

Always make sure you say the rooms you use are 'non-exclusive' and don't claim mortgage interest or council tax for that portion of your property otherwise you could run into Capital Gains Tax problems when you sell the home and incur a business rate from the local council.

✔ Accountancy and legal fees and the costs of debt collection.

✔ Pension contributions can count against self-employment earnings.

✔ Publications, stationery, postage, wages and other costs of employing people, insurance, travel, subsistence, gas, electricity, water – all the way down to the batteries in your calculator.

Accounting for big business items

Big expenditure items such as plant and machinery, cars, and computers are not counted against your profits in the same way as the goods and services you buy in to make your business work. With these big items, you can claim capital allowances against your profits. A capital allowance is a proportion of the purchase cost that you can set against profits each year as long as you own the item. The result is that tax relief against the expenditure made on these items can be spread out over several years.

The following list explains capital allowances for major items:

- From April 2008, the old first-year capital allowances applicable to small and medium businesses are replaced by a new Annual Investment Allowance of £50,000 for all businesses, whether they are self-employed or incorporated, and regardless of their size. That means that in the year in which the purchase was made, 100 per cent of expenditure, up to £50,000, on general plant and machinery other than cars can be offset against taxable profits.

- The annual *writing down* allowance, applied to the written-down value of equipment brought forward from earlier years (in other words, over the first year allowance) is reduced from 25 per cent to 20 per cent from April 2008. So if you buy an item costing £60,000, then £50,000 of that can be offset against tax in the first year; 20 per cent of the balance of £10,000 (£2,000) can be offset in the second year, 20 per cent of the remaining £8,000 (£1,600) in the third, and so on. You never get to zero!

- Cars qualify for a 25 per cent capital allowance each year with a limit of £12,000 on the value of the car. Using this ceiling, the maximum allowance in the first year is £3,000, then 25 per cent of the remaining £9,000 (£2,250), and so on.

Low-emission vehicles benefit from a 100 per cent allowance for the first year. The vehicle manufacturer will tell you if your vehicle qualifies as less noxious – printing the rules in full would take up a large part of this book.

Book VI

Keeping On Top of Tax

Capital allowances are available against the actual cost of the asset. You set the costs of any bank loan or other financing against business expenses.

You cannot claim capital allowances greater than your profits. But there is nothing to stop you claiming less than your maximum and then carrying the remaining amounts into a subsequent year.

Claiming extra help as you start up

Money you spend before you start can be counted against your profits once you set up. This expenditure may include the money you paid for a computer and other machinery you already possess and the cost of feasibility studies into your hoped-for business. These sums will normally be counted against your first year's profits. But if you make a loss, you can count them against the next year (and so on, for a total of four years if you fail to make a profit).

Accounting for loss-making

With the best will in the world, your self-employment could result in a loss. In such a case, you have two tax options, which we explore in the next two sections.

Deducting the loss from other taxable sums

Provided you have earnings from a PAYE job, a pension, from dividends or interest, or from taxable capital gains, you could set your loss off against these amounts. This is a good route for a self-employed person whose business is part-time. Someone earning £20,000 from a PAYE post, and losing £2,000 on her business would end up with a tax bill based on £18,000.

If you make a loss in any of the first four years of a new business, you can offset this loss against tax on your salary in the three years preceding the establishment of your business. You may have to prove you intended to make profits during this period: Tax inspectors look out for loss-making 'hobbies' whose main function is to dodge tax.

You have to inform the tax inspector within 12 months following the 31 January after the end of your loss-making business year.

Subtracting the loss from future earnings

If your losses exceed your taxable sums, you can carry forward the loss against future profits. You can do this for as many years as you need – there is no limit. But you have to tell the Inland Revenue within five years of the 31 January following the end of the tax year in which your personal accounted year finished.

In most cases, it makes sense to offset your losses against earnings, dividends, interest, and capital gains from elsewhere. But if you expect your self-run business to be very remunerative in the future and take you into the top tax band, then consider subtracting early losses from future earnings.

Scanning National Insurance

As a self-employed person, profits you make from your business are added to other earnings, pensions, dividends, and interest for income tax. National insurance is different. There are special rules for the self-employed and two sets of payments you may have to make.

Complicating the classes

National insurance comes in four classes, numbered one to four. Class 1 is for employed persons. The self-employed have to look at Classes 2 and 4, which we do in the next sections. And in case you're wondering, Class 3 is voluntary – it's paid by people who do not work but who wish to keep up their record to qualify for the state retirement pension and other benefits.

Class 4 is collected through the annual self assessment return. It is the only national insurance to be collected in this way. Most people pay Class 1 via their salary packet, while Class 2 and Class 3 are paid usually with a direct debit.

Paying Class 2

As a self-employed person you have to pay a fixed £2.30 a week (in 2008–9) in national insurance. This maintains your payment record for the state pension and health-related benefits – but not jobseeker's allowance.

If your earnings from all self-employment are below the Class 2 threshold (£4,825 in 2008–9), you are exempt from Class 2.

Paying Class 4

Class 4 national insurance is effectively an additional tax on the self-employed. It does not provide any benefits, but that doesn't mean you don't have to pay it if your profits (what you take in less your costs) are at least £5,435 in a year. If your profits are below that figure, you don't have to worry about Class 4.

But if you do have to pay, it is currently (2008–9) charged at 8 per cent of your taxable profits from £5,435 a year to £40,040. The 8 per cent stops there. But there's a 1 per cent surcharge on all sums above that. So if your profits were £50,040, you would pay 1 per cent on the £10,000 above the upper profits level.

Putting a cap on National Insurance

Someone with a mix of self-employment and employment could end up paying Class 1, Class 2, and Class 4. The bad news is that many pay more in national insurance for the same amount of income if it comes from a variety of sources, such as self-employment and employment, than they would if it all came from one source. The good news is that there are ceilings on payments.

Book VI

Keeping On
Top of Tax

If all your income comes from being self-employed, then you cannot pay more than £2,888 (in tax year 2008@'nd9) in Class 2 and Class 4 together. The HMRC Web site (www.hmrc.gov.uk) or your local tax office can give details of future rates. And if you have earnings from employment as well, there is a chance you have paid a lot more than you should when you add up all the sums from your job and your self-employment. Check with HMRC if you think you may have overpaid.

This limit does not include the 1 per cent national insurance surcharge on earnings over £40,040.

If you know, or reasonably suspect, that you will hit the overall national insurance limit, you can apply for Class 2 and/or Class 4 payments to be deferred until you know the outcome of the year's earnings pattern. You should do this before the start of the tax year, but HMRC, which runs the national insurance collection, often allows later applications.

Hiring Helpers

Being a sole trader doesn't mean you have to work on your own. It's a tax definition, after all. You may need to pay for help on a part- or full-time basis or to hire someone to help out every now and again. If you have family, you may want to make the most of the tax advantages you can reap by employing them. The next sections tell you how to look at employees as ways to lower your tax.

Employing your family

You can employ your family in the business and thereby take advantage of the lower tax rates your spouse or children fall under to reduce your household's overall tax bill.

You do have to keep a few rules in mind, though:

- ✔ You have to hire your relative to do real work at commercial wage rates. You cannot get away with paying a small child £100 an hour for taking telephone messages!
- ✔ Local authorities have rules on children working. This will not apply to a few hours working in the home. But if you want to employ a child under 16 in other circumstances, always check with the council first.

✔ Family members who earn more than £105 (in 2008–9) in any week are liable for national insurance payments. As the employer, you also have to pay national insurance on their behalf. This is called the national insurance earnings threshold.

✔ Your teenage children might have no income to offset against their personal allowance. Or you might be a top-rate tax-payer and have a partner whose maximum is at the basic or lower rate.

You set up a computer repair service working from a small shop. Your 16-year-old helps you at your premises for four hours a week at £5 an hour. That's £20 a week – say £1,000 a year, allowing for holidays and some overtime. You can offset the £1,000 against your profits. And, if your teenager has no other income, he or she does not have to pay tax at all as the £1,000 is well within the personal allowance limit. Had you done the work yourself and not used your child, the £1,000 would have been taxable as profits at up to 40 per cent, so the household would only have £600 instead of the full £1,000.

You have to pay the money for real, of course. The taxman can ask for the audit trail to see how the payment goes from your business to the family member concerned.

Book VI

Keeping On Top of Tax

Establishing a partnership with your partner

If you and your spouse or partner are both involved in running a business, it could be worth exploring a partnership structure. There are legal concerns such as each partner being liable for debts incurred by other partners. For tax reasons, it is best to have a partnership contract which sets out how profits will be shared.

Starting a Business For Dummies by Colin Barrow (Wiley) sets out who should and who should not set up as partners. You need to work out whether you are better off with a partnership but, more importantly, whether your relationship could stand it.

HMRC is on the lookout for phoney partnerships, established solely with the aim of reducing a couple's overall tax bill. If you have a business partnership with your spouse, you may have to show that both work in the firm and both contribute work according to the proportion of the profits you each earn. This is a measure to prevent couples sharing profits on a 50-50 basis to use up tax allowances of the non-worker when only one works.

Paying employees

If you hire employees, you are in the same situation as any other employer. You have to sort out any PAYE tax and national insurance contributions they owe. (See Book V Chapter 2 for information on employees' tax and national insurance contributions.)

Giving Up Work

Stopping work is easier than starting. You should inform the Inland Revenue if you intend to stop working in your business. And if you were caught by overlap, now is the time to claim it back. Your final accounts can also take care of what happens when you sell plant, machinery, vehicles, or stock.

The reality of self-employment is that most businesses cease entirely when the self-employed person retires or goes back to working for someone else. A few businesses have a future value. (See the section Selling Up and Tax Rules in Book VI Chapter 2.)

Chapter 2

Considering Your Company's Status

*P*aying taxes and reporting income for your business are very important jobs, and the way in which you complete these tasks properly depends on your business's legal structure. From sole traders (self-employment) to limited companies and everything in between, this chapter briefly reviews business types and explains how taxes are handled for each type.

Finding the Right Business Type

Business type and tax preparation and reporting go hand in hand. If you work as a bookkeeper for a small business, you need to know the business's legal structure before you can proceed with reporting and paying tax on the business income. Not all businesses have the same legal structure, so they don't all pay tax on the profits they make in the same way.

Sole trader

The simplest legal structure for a business is the *sole trader,* a business owned by one individual. Most new businesses with only one owner start out as sole traders, and some never change this status. Others, however, grow by adding partners and become *partnerships*. Some businesses add lots of staff and want to protect themselves from lawsuits, so they become *Limited Liability Partnerships (LLPs)*. Those seeking the greatest protection from individual lawsuits, whether they have employees or are simply single-owner companies without employees, become limited companies. We cover these other structures in Book VI Chapter 1.

Partnership

HM Revenue & Customs considers any unincorporated business owned by more than one person to be a *partnership*. The partnership is the most flexible type of business structure involving more than one owner. Each partner in the business is equally liable for the activities of the business. This structure is slightly more complicated than a sole trader (see the preceding 'Sole trader' section), and partners need to work out certain key issues before the business opens its doors. These issues include:

✔ How are the partners going to divide the profits?

✔ How does each partner sell his share of the business, if he so chooses?

✔ What happens to each partner's share if a partner becomes sick or dies?

✔ How is the partnership going to be dissolved if one of the partners wants out?

Partners in a partnership don't always have to share equal risks. A partnership may have two different types of partners: general and limited. The general partner runs the day-to-day business and is held personally responsible for all activities of the business, no matter how much he has personally invested. Limited partners, on the other hand, are passive owners of the business and not involved in day-to-day operations. If a claim is filed against the business, the limited partners can be held personally liable only for the amount of money they individually invested in the business.

Filing tax forms for partnerships

If your business is structured as a partnership (meaning it has more than one owner) and is not a limited liability company, your business doesn't pay taxes. Instead, all money earned by the business is split up among the partners and they pay the tax due between them very much as if they were sole traders. However, a partnership is required to complete a partnership tax return to aid the assessment of the members of the partnership. Essentially, the partnership tax return is sent out to the nominated partner and he completes the partnership tax return in a manner similar to the sole trader tax return explained in the preceding sections. That partner states what profit share is attributable to each partner and each partner is responsible for showing this profit figure in his own personal tax return.

Don't be tempted to forget to include partnership profits (or any other source of income for that matter), because HM Revenue & Customs knows from the partnership tax return what you earned in that tax year.

Limited Liability Partnership

The *Limited Liability Partnership,* or LLP, is a structure that provides the owners of partnerships with some protection from being held personally liable for their businesses' activities. This business structure is somewhere between a partnership and a limited company: The business ownership and tax rules are similar to those of a partnership, but like a limited company, if the business is sued, the owners aren't held personally liable.

Rather like forming a limited company, an LLP is formed by filing the appropriate forms with Companies House. On receipt of these forms the Registrar of Companies issues a Certificate of Incorporation.

Both for business and practical reasons, we recommend drawing up an agreement to establish the rights, responsibilities, and duties of the partners to each other, and to outline how the business is going to be run, because few provisions are contained within the act governing these relationships.

Growth of the LLP

Limited Liability Partnerships are the latest business vehicle and were introduced on 6 April 2001 after the Limited Liability Partnerships Act 2000 received royal assent on 20 July 2000. Many law firms and accounting firms are set up as LLPs. More and more small business owners are choosing this structure rather than a limited company because the LLP's easier and cheaper to maintain (it involves a lot less paperwork plus less legal and accounting fees), and yet still provides personal protection from legal entanglements.

Limited company

If your business faces a great risk of being sued, the safest business structure for you is the *limited company*. Courts in the UK have clearly determined that a limited company is a separate legal entity (Saloman v Saloman 1897) and that its owners' personal assets are protected from claims against the company. Essentially, an owner or shareholder in a company can't be sued or face collections because of actions taken by the company. This veil of protection is the reason many small business owners choose to incorporate even though it involves a lot of expense (both for lawyers and accountants) and paperwork.

Being incorporated is not as scary as it sounds. Incorporation is when you decide on the legal (and therefore tax) framework of a limited company. It's essential for a firm that is going places big time. But it can turn out to be a bad deal for you in your early trading days, or if you never intend growing past the status of a one-man or a one-woman band.

Looking at reasons to reject the company route

Company status can be a really bad option for many small businesses. So start with looking at some negatives to see if corporate life rather than self-employment is really such a good idea. If you tick two or more of the disadvantages in the following list, you may be better off staying unincorporated. Go back to Book VI Chapter 1 on self-employment status, and use the time you would have spent reading this chapter on growing your business instead!

It may sound great to have Co Ltd after your firm's name; and to be able to put up a brass plate. But here are some pointers as to why it can be a bad idea:

- There can be complications where your personal tax dealings and those of your company interface.
- You generally have more flexibility in dealing with the tax authorities over income tax and national insurance as a self-employed individual than you do as a company director.
- The additional legal and regulatory costs involved with incorporating and complying with company law may outweigh tax savings.
- It can be difficult to escape paying accountancy fees to audit the accounts you have to file with the Inland Revenue.

✔ You have to file details of your business once a year with Companies House. These details such as share ownership, home addresses, and some financial details are available to the public so your competitors (or even nosy neighbours) can find out some things about your business affairs. However, small companies do not have to file full accounts.

✔ You have to make national insurance payments as both an employer and an employee. If you are self-employed, you make only one set of payments.

✔ Tax rules make some company pension plans less flexible – and often more expensive to administer.

✔ HMRC is clamping down on what it considers to be the abuses of the company structure by what are essentially one-person, personal service businesses (see 'Steering clear of the big tax clampdown' later in this chapter). If you are caught by this, you can get the worst of both company and self-employed status.

Book VI

Keeping On Top of Tax

Taking advantage of company status

Incorporating can appear to be a no-brainer option. There's lower tax levels compared to working as a self-employed person as the company grows. And there's the glamour of the brass plate outside your premises proclaiming your existence.

Some reasons you may want to turn your small business into a limited company are:

✔ You have the ability to plan where profits go. This can bring big tax benefits to a growing company.

✔ You only need two shareholders with one share each – the minimum per share investment is £1.

✔ You can repay people who back your venture, but who do not have any part in the operation of the business, by giving them dividends (payments once or twice a year decided by the directors which depend on profits).

✔ Selling or passing on an incorporated business when you retire or die is often less complicated tax-wise than the same procedure for an unincorporated business.

✔ You may be able to raise money for your business through the Enterprise Investment Scheme (EIS), which gives a number of tax-saving deals to those who put their cash into your firm via a share issue. The EIS is complicated, so take advice from a stockbroker and accountant.

Oddly enough, the list of reasons for becoming a company is shorter than the list for not going for incorporation. But don't worry. The tax and other plus points in favour of company status are powerful even if they are not too long!

Setting Up a Limited Company

In a limited company, each share represents a portion of ownership, and profits must be split based on share ownership. You don't have to sell shares on the public stock markets in order to be a limited company, though. In fact, most limited companies are private entities that sell their shares privately among friends and investors.

Roles and responsibilities of the limited company board

Limited companies provide a veil of protection for company owners, but in order to maintain that protection, the owners must comply with many rules unique to corporations. The *board of directors* takes on the key role of complying with these rules, and it must maintain a record of meeting minutes that prove the board is following key operating procedures, such as:

- Establishment of records of banking associations and any changes to those arrangements

- Tracking of loans from shareholders or third parties

- Selling or redeeming shares

- Payment of dividends

- Authorisation of salaries or bonuses for officers and key executives

- Undertaking of any purchases, sales, or leases of corporate assets

- Buying another company

- Merging with another company

- Making changes to the Articles of Incorporation

- Election of corporate officers and directors

Corporate board minutes are considered official and must be available for review by HM Revenue & Customs and the courts. If a company's owners want to invoke the veil of protection that corporate status provides, they must prove that the board has met its obligations and that the company operated as a limited company. In other words, you can't form a board and have no proof that it ever met and managed these key functions.

Minimising tax on death

Provided you owned your business in whole or in part for at least two years, your heirs can deduct 100 per cent of its value from the value of other assets you leave behind when you die.

This does not apply to companies that are set up for dealing in shares or other securities, or for dealing in property. And the assets have to be real business assets. You can't stuff the valuable jewellery and priceless works of art that you intend leaving behind into your bike repair company.

If you're a small business owner who wants to incorporate, first you must form a *board of directors* (see the sidebar 'Roles and responsibilities of the limited company board'). Boards can be made up of owners of the company as well as non-owners. You can even have your spouse and children on the board – we bet those board meetings are interesting.

Setting up a limited company is easy. You can do it yourself with forms from Companies House (www.companieshouse.gov.uk), the organisation that controls all of Britain's 1.8 million companies. But most people buy an off-the-shelf company from a firm specialising in company formations at a cost of around £100 to £200. An off-the-shelf company essentially gives you the go-ahead for company status. You can change the name of this company and take off the original directors and replace them with names of your choice. It's quicker than having a company set-up specialist establishing a company just for you.

However you set up a company, don't forget that the initial setting-up costs involved, as well as the continuing costs such as the £15 annual filing fee with the Registrar of Companies and accounting and auditing fees, can all be set off against your profits and so reduce the business's tax bill.

As a company, you can give as much as you like to your favourite charity! The amount is tax-deductible from the firm's profits so it's free of corporation tax. But your company must not derive any significant benefit from the donation. The glow of doing good is fine but insisting that your generosity appears plastered all over town as an advert is not.

And don't forget a company can always cease trading and the owners revert to the self-employment option in some circumstances.

Steering clear of the big tax clampdown

The taxman is determined not to allow small businesses to choose between self-employment and company structure just to reduce income tax and national insurance. Its first move was against personal service companies, the technical name for one-person firms (plus one other shareholder, usually a spouse or partner) that supply nothing other than labour.

Most personal service companies work in the information technology business. The proprietors became limited companies employing themselves because many did not qualify for self-employment status as they worked full-time for one employer. Becoming companies, and having a supply contract with a big company whose computers they looked after, resulted in them paying less tax and national insurance than being employed by those companies.

HMRC's argument is that most of these firms do nothing more than work for bigger companies on a series of fixed-term contracts. So the company structure is an artificial means of dodging tax. IR35 people (named after the number of the Inland Revenue circular that authorises the crackdown on these companies) do not use their own materials, nor work from their own premises, nor are they able to set their own hours or other terms of work – all signs of business independence. So the taxman says they should be treated as employees and be on PAYE.

But not all IT contractors are caught by IR35. Those who genuinely work for a number of people, have invested in their own equipment, can control their own working hours, and risk making a loss continue to qualify as companies.

Making use of family to lessen the tax bite

You can use members of your family in your business to help reduce the overall tax bill of your household.

As the director of a company, you have control of your business. As a taxpayer, you can manage your takings from your company to lessen your tax bite.

Transferring money to your spouse is a well-known and perfectly legal method to minimise the tax your family pays. You can pay family members dividends or hire them to work for your company (I talk about the issues related to hiring family in Book VI Chapter 1). In this section, we give you some hints on how to make the most of your earnings by paying the least possible in tax.

Suppose a company owner wants (and can afford) to take £50,000 a year from the firm. This is well over the top-rate threshold so whether it is paid as salary or a dividend, there will be a 40 per cent tax bill on the top slice of this money.

But if the owner has a spouse who earns very little, and the company is structured in such a way that the low-earning spouse owns 99 per cent of the shares and hence gets 99 per cent of the dividend payouts, the £50,000 can be divided up so the owner gets £30,000 in salary, putting this person easily into the basic-tax band.

The other £20,000 from the £50,000 is paid in dividends. This would divide up as £200 (1 per cent) for the owner and £19,800 (99 per cent) for the spouse. So neither would pay top-rate tax. The dividend tax would be 19 per cent (£3,800 on the £20,000), but that's a lot better than paying up to 40 per cent.

Book VI

Keeping On Top of Tax

An alternative would be to pay the spouse £20,000, declaring no dividend or just a tiny one. This would work out at a combined income tax and national insurance take of £4,734, more than the dividend route but still saving a good few thousand compared with the working spouse earning £50,000.

HMRC is increasingly questioning these 'husband and wife' company arrangements. It checks to see if a paid spouse really does work to the value of the salary – doing one hour a week for £20,000 a year won't wash if that's far less than the commercial rate of employing someone else.

In 2007 HMRC lost a legal test case on this point in the House of Lords. However, the Treasury intends to clamp down on so-called 'income splitting' one way or another. It is introducing legislation in April 2009 that will require all small businesses paying out dividends or partnership profits to calculate whether the recipients receive a market rate for their contributions to the success of the business.

Deciding How Best to Pay Yourself

Once you set up as a limited company, you still have to work out your profits in just the same way as you did when you were just a self-employed person – by taking costs away from your earnings from customers. So if your customers paid you £40,000 and your total expenditure was £10,000, you end up with £30,000 in profit.

It's what you then do with your profit that matters. These profits can be distributed in three different ways, all with their own set of tax rules:

- ✔ Keep profits within the company: Cash you keep within the company to fund further expansion; research or marketing is subject to corporation tax.

- ✔ Pay salaries: In most small companies, the directors and their family or friends are likely to be the only employees. Profits paid as salaries are subject to PAYE income tax and national insurance.

- ✔ Distribute dividends: This does not attract national insurance payments and once the company itself has paid corporation tax on it, there is no further tax to pay for basic-rate tax-payers.

This three-way split gives companies a number of tax planning opportunities as well as a number of tax disasters. Directors can, for instance, decide between keeping money in the company to fund the future and raising a bank loan. And, more importantly for tax saving, they can decide between paying themselves a salary or paying themselves through dividends.

Paying yourself a salary out of the profits

Paying yourself (or other directors) a regular salary means accounting for the PAYE and National Insurance, too. Despite this, a regular salary does have advantages – you need to have a regular salary if you apply for many types of personal loan, including most mortgages. Until new rules kicked in (in April 2006), the amount you could pay into a pension plan was also governed by your salary. Now, only the tax relief has a ceiling. You can make tax-efficient contributions of up to £235,000 in any one tax year, with a lifetime cap of £1.65 million on your pension pot (2008–9 limits).

However, the biggest advantage of paying yourself a regular salary is that the Inland Revenue will not question these arrangements, as salaries represent the biggest possible take for the tax inspector.

Taking dividends vs. salary

The main advantage of taking dividends instead of a salary is that dividends are not liable to national insurance payments. Not paying national insurance can save the company 12.8 per cent and the recipient up to 11 per cent. And basic rate taxpayers who receive dividends pay only 10 per cent tax on them, rather than the standard income tax rate of 20 per cent (from April 2008).

The disadvantages to paying yourself with dividends are that you have less money on which to base pension contributions and a lower salary for purposes such as impressing the bank or building society when you want to take out a mortgage.

How it all works

When you set up your new business for real, you need to decide how to structure it. You have a choice of:

✔ Staying self-employed and not bothering with a company structure.

✔ Establishing a limited company and paying yourself a salary out of the profits.

✔ Going down the limited company route, but paying yourself mostly through a dividend.

Each has its own set of tax rules; and each produces quite different amounts of cash for the firm's owner, especially in the early years.

I can't pretend the choice is easy. It's not. Or that understanding the rules is a piece of cake. It's not. But if you take your future business seriously, you'll need to make up your mind, although it's always possible, if costly, to change your decision later on.

So bear with me and look at how Ali, Ben, and Charlotte's big ideas progress. These are just outlines, but they should give you enough information to help you in coming up with the business plan your bank manager or other advisers will demand to see.

Ali, Ben and Charlotte all set out in business on the same day. All three are interior decorators and designers with ambition. All three need £115,000 to kick-start their businesses. And all three turn out to have the same earnings from customers and the same outlay on materials and other expenses (hey, this is just an example, after all!). They make just £1,500 profits each in their difficult first year; and £20,000 profits in their second year when they are more confident. So are they all equal? Absolutely not:

✔ Ali stays self-employed, and is technically a sole trader.

✔ Ben has a limited company but largely pays himself through dividends from his profits, with the balance as a salary.

✔ Charlotte will take all her future earnings from her limited company as a salary.

So read on and see how they progress from start-up to long term going concern. We round the sums of money so you can see how it works without worrying about slight changes of tax rates each year. The gaps between the three are gigantic, anyway.

Ali's Alluring Interiors

Ali is self-employed. He borrows £100,000 from the bank at 6% to start his business and puts in £15,000 from his own savings.

In his first year, Ali makes £1,500 from customers but after paying his £6,000 bank interest he loses £4,500. He can claim this loss against his other income either in the current year or in preceding years. He does not have to pay national insurance because he does not earn enough.

In year 2, his business earns £20,000 after costs. This all goes down on his tax form so he ends up with around £15,600 to take home after tax and national insurance.

In year 3, he expands. He can now offset part of the money he spends on his new premises against his earnings.

Many years later, he decides to sell up. He will be liable to capital gains tax on any profit he makes but at the business asset rate so he could get away with a 10 per cent rate.

Ben's Beautiful Homes

Ben borrows £100,000 from the bank but uses his £15,000 to create shares in his limited company. He decides on a minimal £5,000 a year salary and to take the rest in dividends when his profits grow.

The first year is poor and he makes just £1,500. And after paying himself £5,000 and bank interest of £6,000, he makes a £9,500 loss. He can't offset this against any other earnings present or past. So he has to wait until the company does better. He has very little tax or national insurance to pay so he can take home just over £5,040.

In year 2, he makes £20,000. He still takes £5,000 as a salary. Now, because it's profitable, his company has to pay corporation tax – around £2,550. The balance of around £12,450 is paid to Ben as a dividend. As this has already been taxed through corporation tax, and as Ben is a basic rate taxpayer, he has no more income tax to pay on his dividend. So his take home is roughly £17,450.

Looking further ahead, Ben will be able to claim allowances against profits for capital spending and by doing so cuts his corporation tax bill. But he must not forget that dividends can only be earned from taxed profits. And dividends do not count for pensions, or for most mortgage loan applications.

When Ben decides to sell up, he faces capital gains tax on the increased value of the shares at the business rate. But this future change of ownership has no effect on the company itself.

Charlotte's Classy Décor

Charlotte borrows £100,000 from the bank and then adds her own £15,000 to turn the whole £115,000 into shares. She wants a steady income as a salary from her company.

She has a tax-saving idea. Because her company has five or fewer shareholders, it's what accountants call a close company. This allows her to offset the £6,000 bank interest against her earnings. So her £20,000 taxable pay is cut to around £12,500 after national insurance and the loan interest deduction. The company, however, loses £18,500 in its first year because it pays her £20,000 salary but only earns £1,500 from customers. This loss can be offset against future profits.

In year 2, the £20,000 profit has to pay not just her salary but also the employer's national insurance contribution of around £1,725. She has to pay national insurance and income tax on the £18,275 over giving her a take home pay of around £14,100.

As she becomes more successful, she will have to juggle raising her salary and not having enough profits to offset against her spending on expansion, or restraining her salary, and having enough profits to set against tax. She will also have to weigh up the pros and cons of paying corporation tax on profits against income tax and national insurance on her salary. She might then start to take part of her money in salary and part in dividend.

When she wants to quit, she does not sell the company. Instead, she decides that selling the assets is a better idea. This way, she pays corporation tax on the profits, possibly a better deal than the capital gains tax she might have had to pay. She may, of course, pay no corporation tax as she might still have losses from previous years to set against the amount she gets for the firm's assets.

Setting Up Special Pension Plans

As a director of a limited company, you can use the tax saving on paying into a pension plan to reduce the amount of your hard-earned cash that the HMRC takes. Pensions qualify for tax relief on the contribution at your top rate, grow in a tax-free fund, and offer a tax-free lump sum when you decide to retire.

Directors can set up personal pension schemes (like the self-employed) or contribute to stakeholder plans (again like the self-employed). For many, one of these options is the easiest route. You can pay in up to the lifetime pension fund limit.

You can subtract the costs of setting up and maintaining a company pension plan from your profits.

Starting your very own company scheme

You can set up your very own company pension scheme, just like those operated by really big companies. But you can limit it to yourself, or to yourself and fellow directors, if you don't want to extend it to any staff you hire.

One big advantage is that money spent on pensions for directors and other staff comes off your profits so there is no corporation tax to pay. And to top that with another bonus, employers do not pay national insurance on company pension contributions.

You cannot count money you receive as dividends for your own pension purposes. But the tax rules say you can use it to pay up to £3,600 before tax relief (£2,808 net) into a stakeholder pension for someone in your family.

Looking at limits on how much you can pay in

Your pension scheme will probably invest in a fund, just like those on offer to personal pension plan purchasers. Putting on your other hat as a controlling director, you can invest really large sums into the pension as an employer contribution.

On 6 April 2006 the previous complex restrictions on pension scheme contributions were removed. Under the new rules, each scheme member can now contribute up to 100 per cent of their earnings for the tax year. The combined total of employee and employer contributions must not exceed the annual allowance (£235,000 in the 2008–9 tax year).

If you're offering a pension scheme for employees then you must make a significant contribution in order for HMRC to approve the scheme (at least 10 per cent of total contributions).

By balancing the sums you pay yourself as a salary and the amount of your profit, your firm can save a fortune in national insurance and you can save personal tax and national insurance as well.

You start your new company when you are 50. Instead of paying yourself the £60,000 you can afford as a salary, you decide to earn £30,000 and get the company to pay in a £30,000 contribution to the company pension plan on your behalf. The result is your firm only pays employer's national insurance on £30,000 and not £60,000. This saves £3,840 (£30,000 times the 12.8 per cent national insurance rate). As an employee, you save 11 per cent national insurance on the slice between £30,000 and £40,040, which is worth £1,104 (£10,040 times 11 per cent), and you save 1 per cent on the £19,960 balance – another £199. And you can also put in your salary as your own personal contribution and keep that out of the tax net as well! Or at least you could in theory. Very few people put in their entire annual salary.

Book VI

Keeping On Top of Tax

Some small company pension plans known as Small Self Administered Pension Schemes let you choose the investments yourself. In some circumstances, you can sell your company premises to the scheme as a contribution and then pay your plan a commercial rent. Because this is a pension plan, that rent will not be taxed. Make sure you know what you're doing, though, as these plans can be costly and complex. They are not for DIY pension buyers!

Selling Up and Tax Rules

Stopping your business can have as many tax implications as starting it. There are a number of options, which we lay out here. But before you read them, a word of advice. No two companies or two people are the same, so it is always worthwhile seeking individual help from an accountant before acting. However, we can give you some general advice.

One route when you decide you want to cash in on your company is selling the shares in your business to another person. This is worthwhile if the company's business and reputation have a value.

In general, you'll be liable for Capital Gains Tax (CGT) on the difference between what you paid for the shares (or what they were worth when the company started) and what you get for them. The complex rules for Capital Gains Tax have been overhauled with effect from April 2008: Taper relief (which meant that the amount of CGT payable dropped to 10 per cent if a business asset was held for more than two years) has been removed, and a single flat rate of 18 per cent now applies to both business and personal assets. However, the Chancellor made an 'entrepreneurs' concession' with a 10 per cent rate for gains of up to £1 million.

Or you can sell the assets and shut the company. This can be more complicated, involving corporation tax on any gains plus tax when you take out the money from the company to pay it to yourself.

If your company is worth something, then it is worth hiring an accountant to tell you the best way of disposing of it. In some cases, you might consider stretching the sale over more than one tax year.

Chapter 3

Taxes, Taxes, and More Taxes

. . . .

In This Chapter

▶ Paying taxes as an employer and a property owner

▶ Putting on your tax collector hat and collecting value added tax (VAT)

▶ Filing taxes for limited companies

▶ What happens if you face a tax investigation

. . . .

*A*s an employer, a business pays taxes. As a property owner or occupier, a business pays taxes. As a seller of goods and services, a business collects value-added-taxes paid by customers and remits the amounts to the government's Customs and Excise Department. And, of course, a business, or its owners, must pay corporate income tax. Yikes! Is there no escaping the tax millstone?

Nope, afraid not (short of resorting to illegal activity or a sly move to another country – you'll have to find another book to tell you about those options). But you can take advantage of the many options in tax laws that can minimise how much you pay and delay your payment (a perfectly legal strategy known as *tax avoidance*). This chapter starts you on your way by explaining the various types of taxation that a business faces.

We say that this chapter '*starts* you on your way' because we can't possibly provide you with exhaustive detail in one chapter. And besides, no one can give you good tax advice without first looking at your specific situation – consult a professional tax expert for that.

Taxing Wages and Property

Even if you don't earn a profit in your business, you still have to pay certain taxes. Unlike corporation tax, which is a *contingent* or *conditional* tax that depends on whether a business earns taxable income for the year, the two major types of non-income taxes – *employer payroll taxes* and *business rates* – always have to be paid. (See 'Taxing your bottom line' later in this chapter, for more about income tax.)

Putting the government on the payroll

In addition to deducting income tax from employees' wages and remitting those amounts to the proper government agencies, businesses need to pay National Insurance for all employees, yourself included. (Actually, National Insurance isn't really a tax, but we won't get technical.)

National Insurance

Most people don't realise that they usually pay less than half of their National Insurance bill – the employer picks up the rest of the tab. The idea is that the burden should be shared almost evenly, but with the employer generally picking up a little more of the tab.

We don't want to get into a debate about the National Insurance system and the financial problems it's facing; we'll just say that the amount you'll pay in National Insurance almost certainly won't diminish in the future. Here's an idea of what a business pays in National Insurance: In 2008–9, the first £5,435 of annual wages were exempt from any National Insurance charges. Then up to a ceiling of £ 40,040 the employer pays 12.8% and the employee pays 11%. Above £40,040 comes the big divide. The employee now only pays 1% National Insurance, whilst the employer still keeps shelling out at the 12.8% level.

That is, for every £100.00 paid to an employee above the basic level of £100 per week, the employer's total cost is £112.80. (Tell *that* to Nigel in Marketing the next time he gripes about the tax deductions in his pay cheque!)

Employment tax

Employing people requires you to manage a PAYE (Pay As You Earn) system. If your business is a limited company, the owner (you) is also liable for PAYE. You will also have to deduct National Insurance. Both these tasks will involve some additional record keeping as once again owner managers are being asked to be unpaid tax collectors. There are serious penalties for getting it wrong.

PAYE

Income tax is collected from employees through the PAYE system, or Pay As You Earn. The employee's liability to income tax is collected as it is earned instead of by tax assessment at some later date. If the business is run as a limited company then the directors of the company are employees. PAYE must be operated on all salaries and bonuses paid to them, yourself included.

Book VI

Keeping On Top of Tax

The way to an employee's heart is through the payroll department

Remember the first time you received a real pay cheque? Your jaw dropped when you compared the *gross wages* (the amount before deductions) and the *net,* or *take-home pay* (the amount you actually received), right? A business's accountants need to track how much of the following, by law, to deduct from employees' pay cheques:

✔ National Insurance.

✔ Pay As You Earn (PAYE) taxes on income which go to the Government.

✔ Other, non-tax-related withholdings that the employee agrees to (such as union dues, pension plan contributions and health insurance costs paid by the employee).

✔ Other non-tax-related withholdings required by a court order (for example, a business may be ordered to withhold part or all of an employee's wages and remit the amount to a legal agency or a creditor to which the employee owes money).

For all these deductions, a business serves as a collection agent and remits the appropriate amount of wages to the appropriate party. As you can imagine, this task requires lots of additional accounting and record-keeping.

HM Revenue and Customs now issues booklets in reasonably plain English, explaining how PAYE works. The main documents you need to operate PAYE are:

✔ **Form P11,** a deduction working sheet for each employee.

✔ **The PAYE Tables.** There are two books of tax tables in general use, which are updated in line with the prevailing tax rates.

  • Pay Adjustment Tables show the amount that an employee can earn in any particular week or month before the payment of tax.

  • Taxable Pay Tables show the tax due on an employee's taxable pay.

✔ **Form P45,** which is given to an employee when transferring from one employment to another.

✔ **Form P46,** which is used when a new employee does not have a P45 from a previous employment (e.g., a school-leaver starting work for the first time).

✔ **Form P60,** which is used so that the employer can certify an employee's pay at the end of the income tax year in April.

✔ **Form P35,** the year-end declaration and certificate. This is used to summarise all the tax and National Insurance deductions from employees for the tax year.

✔ **Form P6,** the tax codes advice notice issued by the Inspector of Taxes telling you which tax code number to use for each employee.

HM Revenue and Customs (www.hmrc.gov.uk/employers/employers-pack.htm) provides tables giving details of PAYE and NIC rates and limits for the current tax year, for every conceivable category.

Taxing everything you can put your hands on: Property taxes

Businesses and other occupiers of non-domestic properties pay Non-Domestic Rates (also know as Business Rates) to directly contribute towards the costs of local authority services. Non-domestic properties are business properties such as shops, offices, warehouses and factories, and any other property that is not classed as domestic property. In some cases, properties may be used for both domestic and non-domestic purposes (for example, a shop with a flat above it) in which case both council tax, the tax charged on personal properties, and Business Rates will be charged.

Apart from the few lucky properties such as churches, agricultural land, sewers, public parks, certain property used for disabled people and swinging moorings for boats, which are all exempt from Business Rates, each non-domestic property has a rateable value. The valuation officers of the Valuation Office Agency (VOA) set the rateable values. The VOA is a part of the Inland Revenue. It draws up and maintains a full list of all rateable values.

The Valuation Office Agency carries out a revaluation every five years so that the values in the rating lists can be kept up-to-date. The total amount of Business Rates collected does not change except to reflect inflation, but revaluations make sure that this is spread fairly between ratepayers. The most recent revaluation was in April 2005.

The rateable value broadly represents the yearly rent the property could have been let for on the open market on a particular date. Your local council works out your Business Rates bill by multiplying your rateable value by the multiplier or 'poundage' which the Government sets from 1 April each year for the whole of England. For example if the multiplier (which is often called the uniform business rate or UBR) was set at 44.4p and your rateable value was £10,000, the local authority would multiply this by 44.4p and your 'property tax' bill for the year would be £4,440.

Your property may qualify for exemption under various national and local regulations or may be eligible for special reductions.

You may be able to get relief if one of the following applies to you:

✔ Your business is small. In this case a UBR of 44.1p will apply to certain businesses with rateable values of below £5,000. In fact the rules are complex and operate on a slicing scale.

✔ Your property is empty and unused. In general, there will be no Business Rates to pay for the first three months that the property is empty. Prior to April 2008, a 50 per cent rate was charged on properties that had been empty for more than three months. From April 2008 onwards, properties that are empty for three months or more are subject to the full business rate

✔ Your business is in a rural village with a population below 3,000. The types of business that qualify for this relief are:

- The only village general store or post office as long as it has a rateable value of up to £7,000

- A food shop with a rateable value of up to £7,000

- The only village pub and the only petrol station as long as it has a rateable value of up to £10,500

These premises are entitled to a 50% reduction in the Business Rates bill, or more if the council believes you need it.

If you're a business in a qualifying rural village with a rateable value of up to £14,000, your local council may decide to give you up to 100% relief, as long as your business is of benefit to the community.

✔ You are suffering severe hardship and cannot pay your Business Rates bill. Your local council may decide to give you up to 100% relief – the decision is up to them. They normally only do this in extreme cases of hardship and for businesses which are particularly important to the local community. This takes account of the fact that local Council Tax payers will cover part of the cost of the relief.

If you think you may qualify for any of these types of relief, you should contact the Business Rates Section of your local council for more information and advice on how to apply.

Working from home

If you work from home, your local council may charge Business Rates for the part of the property used for work, and you will have to pay council tax for the rest of the property (although your property's valuation band may change). It will depend on the circumstances of each case and you should ask your local Valuation Office Agency office for advice.

Book VI

Keeping On Top of Tax

Property taxes can take a big chunk out of a business's profit. In large organisations, an in-house accountant who deals with property taxes and knows the tax law language and methods is responsible for developing strategies to minimise property taxes. Small-business owners may want to consult a rating adviser. Members of the Royal Institution of Chartered Surveyors (RICS) and the Institute of Revenues Rating and Valuation (IRRV) are qualified and are regulated by rules of professional conduct designed to protect the public from misconduct.

You can find details of these organisations and their members on their Web sites:

- RICS – `http://www.rics.org`
- IRRV – `www.irrv.net`

Also you will find the latest information on business rates on the Governments official Web site (`www.mybusinessrates.gov.uk`).

Before you employ a rating adviser, you should check that she has the necessary knowledge and expertise, as well as appropriate indemnity insurance. You should also be wary of false or misleading claims.

'Cause I'm the Tax Man: Value Added Tax

Most governments, and the UK Government is no exception, levy *sales taxes* on certain products and services sold within their jurisdictions. In the UK this tax is known as the Value Added Tax (VAT). The final consumer of the product or service pays the VAT – in other words the tax is tacked onto the product's price tag at the very end of the economic chain. The business that is selling the product or service collects the VAT and remits it to the appropriate tax agency (Customs and Excise in the UK). Businesses that operate earlier in the economic chain (that is, those that sell products to other businesses that in turn resell the products) generally do not end up paying VAT but simply collect it and pass it on. (For the lowdown on VAT, see Book VI Chapter 4).

Paying Taxes for Limited Companies

Limited companies are more complex than sole traders and partnerships. Although many aspects of their accounting and taxation are similar, their accounts are open to public scrutiny because each year a limited company must file its accounts at Companies House, the UK government organisation responsible for tracking information about all UK limited companies. This means that although only HM Revenue & Customs knows the full details of a sole trader or partnership, the whole world has access (for a fee) to a limited company's accounts.

Companies make a separate tax return, known as a CT600, to HM Revenue & Customs, in which they detail their financial affairs. As a result the limited company pays corporation tax on its earnings (profit) as well as tax on any dividends paid out to its shareholders. This means that its shareholders receive dividends net of basic rate of income tax because the company has already paid it for them.

Two forms of CT600 exist: A short version, only four pages, is sufficient for companies with straightforward tax affairs, but more complicated companies, as designated by HM Revenue & Customs, must complete the eight-page return (for full details look at the publication *Company tax return form guide (2007) to form CT600 version 2*). The following (among others) must file the eight-page return:

✔ Any company that owns 25 per cent of another non-UK company

✔ Any insurance company (or friendly society) having business treated as overseas life assurance business

✔ Any company liable to pay its corporation tax in instalments (profit in excess of £1.5m)

Taxing Your Bottom Line

Every business must determine its annual *taxable income*, which is the amount of profit subject to corporate tax, or income tax if the business is not a limited company. To determine annual *taxable income*, you deduct certain allowed expenses from gross income. Corporation tax law rests very roughly on the premise that all income is taxable unless expressly exempted, and nothing can be deducted unless expressly allowed.

When you read a profit-and-loss account that summarises a business's sales revenue and expenses for a period and ends with bottom-line profit, keep in mind that the accrual basis of accounting has been used to record sales revenue and expenses. The accrual basis gives a more trustworthy and meaningful profit number. But accrual-based sales revenue and expense numbers are not cash inflows and outflows during the period. So the bottom-line profit does not tell you the impact on cash from the profit-making activities of the business. You have to convert the revenue and expense amounts reported in the profit-and-loss account to a cash basis in order to determine the net cash increase or decrease. Well, actually, you don't have to do this – the cash flow statement does this for you, which Book III Chapter 3 explains.

Although you determine your business's taxable income as an annual amount, you don't wait until you file your tax return to make that calculation and payment. Instead, corporation tax law requires you to estimate your corporation income tax for the year and, based on your estimate, to make two half-yearly instalment payments on your corporation tax during the year, one at the end of January and one at the end of July. Rather than calculating the tax due yourself, you can rely on the Inland Revenue to do the sums for you if you send in a completed tax return before the 30 September for the year in question. When you file the final tax return – with the official, rather than the estimated, taxable income amount – after the close of the year, you pay any remaining amount of tax you owe or claim a refund if you have overpaid your corporation tax during the year. If you grossly underestimate your taxable income for the year and thus end up having to pay a large amount of tax after the end of the year, you probably will owe a late payment penalty. After your first year in business, the tax you have to pay will be based on your profits for the previous tax year. A tax year runs from 6 April to 5 April.

You must keep adequate accounting records to determine your business's annual taxable income. If you report the wrong taxable income amount, you can't plead that the bookkeeper was incompetent or that your accounting records were inadequate or poorly organised – in fact, the good old Tax Man may decide that your poor accounting was intentional and is evidence of income tax evasion. If you under-report your taxable income by too much, you may have to pay interest and penalties in addition to the tax that you owe.

When we talk about adequate accounting records, we're not talking about the accounting *methods* that you select to determine annual taxable income – Book IV Chapter 5 discusses choosing among alternative accounting methods for certain expenses. After you've selected which accounting methods you'll use for these expenses, your bookkeeping procedures must follow these methods faithfully. Choose the accounting methods that minimise your current year's taxable income – but make sure that your bookkeeping is done accurately and on time and that your accounting records are complete. If your business's income tax return is audited, the Inland Revenue agents first look at your accounting records and bookkeeping system.

Furthermore, you must stand ready to present evidence for expense deductions. Be sure to hold on to receipts and other relevant documents. In an Inland Revenue audit, the burden of proof is on *you*. The Inland Revenue doesn't have to disprove a deduction; you have to prove that you were entitled to the deduction. *No evidence, no deduction* is the rule to keep in mind.

The following sections paint a rough sketch of the main topics of business income taxation. (We *don't* go into the many technical details of determining taxable income, however.)

Different tax rates

Corporation tax rates vary according to how much taxable profit the company makes. Although starting rates are low for a limited company, they soon escalate to the higher (main) rate. Current corporation tax rates on profits are shown in Table 3-1.

Table 3-1	Corporation Tax Rates	
Taxable Profits	*Tax Rate 2007–8*	*Tax rate 2008–9*
0–£300,000	20%	21%
£300,001–£1.5 million	Marginal relief	Marginal relief
1.5 million or more	30%	28%

In years past, corporate income tax rates were considerably higher, and the rates could always go up in the future – although most experts don't predict any increase. The Chancellor of the Exchequer looks at the income tax law every year and makes some changes virtually every year. Many changes have to do with the accounting methods allowed to determine annual taxable income. For instance, the methods for computing annual *writing down expense*, which recognises the wear and tear on a business's long-lived operating assets, have been changed back and forth by chancellors over the years. Check with HM Revenue and Customs for the latest rules at www.hmrc.gov.uk/businesses/tmacorporate-tax.shtml.

Businesses pay tax on income at one or two rates dependent on their size. But any capital gains, made say when part of a business is sold, or when owners cash in, used to be taxed at 10% if the asset concerned had been owned for two years or more, then on a sliding scale up to 40% for some assets and some time periods. However there were also some fiendishly complicated 'taper reliefs' which made it hard to understand the true tax position. From 2008, all capital gains are taxed at a single rate of 18%, although gains of less than £1 million are taxed at 10%. The simplification does mean some tax payers, in particular entrepreneurs making large sales, face a tax hike of 80% (from 10% up to 18%).

Profit accounting and taxable income accounting

You're probably thinking that this section of the chapter is about how a business's bottom-line profit – its net income – drives its taxable income amount. Actually, we want to show you the exact opposite: how income tax law drives a business's profit accounting. That's right: Tax law plays a large role in how a business determines its profit figure, or more precisely the accounting methods used to record revenue and expenses.

Before you explore that paradox, you need to understand something about the accounting methods for recording profit. For measuring and recording many expenses (and some types of revenue), no single accounting method emerges as the one and only dominant method. Accountants have a certain amount of legitimate leeway in measuring and reporting the revenue and expenses that drive the profit figure. (See Book IV Chapter 5 for further discussion of alternative accounting methods.) Therefore, two different accountants, recording the same profit-making activities for the same period, would most likely come up with two different profit figures – the numbers would be off by at least a little, and perhaps by a lot.

And that inconsistency is fine – as long as the differences are due to legitimate reasons. We'd like to be able to report to you that in measuring profit, accountants always aim right at the bull's-eye, the dead centre of the profit target. One commandment in the accountants' bible is that annual profit should be as close to the truth as can be measured; accounting methods should be objective and fair. But in the real world, profit accounting doesn't quite live up to this ideal.

Be aware that a business may be tempted to deliberately *overstate* or *understate* its profit. When a business overstates its profit in its profit and loss account, some amount of its sales revenue has been recorded too soon and/ or some amount of its expenses has not yet been recorded (but will be later). Overstating profit is a dangerous game to play because it deceives investors and other interested parties into thinking that the business is doing better than it really is. Audits of financial reports by chartered accountants (as discussed in Book IV Chapter 6) keep such financial reporting fraud to a minimum but don't necessarily catch every case.

More to the point of this chapter is the fact that most businesses are under some pressure to *understate* the profit reported in their annual income statements. Businesses generally record sales revenue correctly (with some notable exceptions), but they may record some expenses sooner than these costs should be deducted from sales revenue. Why? Businesses are preoccupied with minimising income tax, which means minimising *taxable income*. To minimise taxable income, a business chooses accounting methods that record expenses as soon as possible. Keeping two sets of books (accounting records) – one for tax returns and one for internal profit accounting reports to managers – is not very practical, so the business uses the accounting methods kept for tax purposes for other purposes as well. And that's why tax concerns can drive down a business's profit figure.

In short, the income tax law permits fairly conservative expense accounting methods – expense amounts can be *front-loaded,* or deducted sooner rather than later. The reason is to give a business the option to minimise its current taxable income (even though this course has a reverse effect in later years). Many businesses select these conservative expense methods – both for their income tax returns and for their financial statements reported to managers and to outside investors and lenders. Thus financial statements of many businesses tilt to the conservative, or understated, side.

Of course, a business should report an accurate figure as its net profit, with no deliberate fudging. If you can't trust that figure, who knows for sure exactly how the company is doing? Not the owners, the value of whose investment in the business depends mostly on profit performance, and not even the business's managers, whose business decisions depend on recorded profit performance. Every business needs a reliable profit compass to navigate its way through the competitive environment of the business world – that's just common sense and doesn't even begin to address ethical issues.

Book VI

Keeping On Top of Tax

Other reasons for understating profit

Minimising taxable income is a strong motive for understating profit, but businesses have other reasons as well. Imagine for the moment that business profit isn't subject to income tax (you wish!). Even in this hypothetical, no-tax world, many businesses probably would select accounting methods that measure their profit on the low side rather than the high side. Two possible reasons are behind this decision:

✔ **Don't count your chickens before they hatch philosophy:** Many business managers and owners tend to be financially conservative; they prefer to err on the low side of profit measurement rather than on the high side.

✔ **Save for a rainy day philosophy:** A business may want to keep some profit in reserve so that during a future downturn, it has a profit cushion to soften the blow.

The people who think this way tend to view *overstating profit* as a form of defrauding investors but view *understating profit* as simply being prudent. Frankly, we think that putting your thumb on either side of the profit scale (revenue being one side and expenses the other) is not a good idea. *Let the chips fall where they may* is our philosophy. Adopt the accounting methods that you think best reflect how you operate the business. The income tax law has put too much downward pressure on profit measurement, in our opinion.

We should say that many businesses do report their annual profit correctly – sales revenue and expenses are recorded properly and without any attempt to manipulate either side of the profit equation.

Refer to Book IV Chapter 5 for more about how choosing one expense accounting method over another method impacts profit. (***Note:*** The following sections, which discuss expenses and income that are not deductible or are only partially deductible, have nothing to do with choosing accounting methods.)

Deductible expenses

What expenses can you claim when you are self-employed? Expenditure can be split into two main categories, 'Capital' and 'Revenue'.

Capital Expenditure: Capital expenditure is expenditure on such items as the purchase or alteration of business premises, purchase of plant, machinery, and vehicles, or the initial cost of tools. You cannot deduct 'Capital expenditure' in working out your taxable profits, but some relief may be due on this type of expenditure in the form of Capital Allowances. Your Tax Office can give further advice on these allowances.

Revenue Expenditure: It is impossible to list all the expenses that can be deducted but, generally speaking, allowable expenditure relates to day to day running costs of your business. It includes such items as wages, rent, lighting and heating of business premises, running costs of vehicles used in the business, purchase of goods for resale, and the cost of replacing tools used in the business.

Non-deductible expenses

To be deductible, business expenses must be *ordinary and necessary* – that is, regular, routine stuff that you need to do to run your business. You're probably thinking that you can make an argument that *any* of your expenses meet the ordinary and necessary test. And you're mostly right – almost all business expenses meet this twofold test.

However, the HMRC considers certain business expenses to be anything but ordinary and necessary; you can argue about them until you're blue in the face, and it won't make any difference. Examples of non-allowable expenditure are your own wages, premiums on personal insurance policies, and income tax and National Insurance contributions. Where expenditure relates to both business and private use, only the part that relates to the business will be allowed; examples are lighting, heating, and telephone expenditure. If a vehicle is used for both business and private purposes then the capital allowances and the total running expenses will be split in proportion to the business and private mileage. You will need to keep records of your total mileage and the number of miles travelled on business to calculate the correct split.

Here's a list of expenses that are *not* deductible or are only partially deductible when determining annual taxable income:

- **Customer entertainment expenses:** Definitely a no go area. For a while entertaining overseas customers were an allowable tax expense until the Revenue became suspicious of the amazing number of people being entertained by businesses with no export activity whatsoever.

- **Bribes, kickbacks, fines, and penalties:** Oh, come on, did you really think that you could get rewarded for doing stuff that's illegal or, at best, undesirable? If you were allowed to deduct these costs, that would be tantamount to the Inland Revenue encouraging such behaviour – a policy that wouldn't sit too well with the general public.

- **Lobbying costs:** You can't deduct payments made to influence legislation. Sorry, but you can't deduct the expenses you ran up to persuade Minister Hardnose to give your bicycle business special tax credits because riding bicycles is good exercise for people.

- **Start-up costs:** You can't just deduct the cost of everything needed to start a business in year one. Some assets such as cars and equipment or machinery has to be written down over a number of future years. This area of the tax law can get a little hairy. If you have just started a new business, you may be wise to consult a tax professional on this question, especially if your start-up costs are rather large.

- **Working from home**: If you use part of your home for work, you will need to keep sufficient records to back up the proportion of heating and lighting costs that relate to your business and your private use. Sometimes you may not get evidence, such as a receipt, for cash expenses, especially where the amounts are small. If this happens, make a brief note as soon as you can of the amount you spent, when you spent it, and what it was for. The Inland Revenue doesn't expect you to keep photocopies of bills, although you may find them useful.

- **Life insurance premiums:** A business may buy life insurance coverage on key officers and executives, but if the business is the beneficiary, the premiums are not deductible. The proceeds from a life insurance policy are not taxable income to the business if the insured person dies, because the cost of the premiums was not deductible. In short, premiums are not deductible, and proceeds upon death are excluded from taxable income.

Book VI

Keeping On Top of Tax

✔ **Travel and convention attendance expenses:** Some businesses pay for rather lavish conventions for their managers and spend rather freely for special meetings at attractive locations that their customers attend for free. The Inland Revenue takes a dim view of such extravagant expenditures and may not allow a full deduction for these types of expenses. The Inland Revenue holds that such conventions and meetings could have been just as effective for a much more reasonable cost. In short, a business may not get a 100% deduction for its travel and convention expenses if the Inland Revenue audits these expenditures.

✔ **Transactions with related parties:** Income tax law takes a special interest in transactions where the two parties are related in some way. For example, a business may rent space in a building owned by the same people who have money invested in the business; the rent may be artificially high or low in an attempt to shift income and expenses between the two tax entities or individuals. In other words, these transactions may not be based on what's known as *arm's-length bargaining*. A business that deals with a related party must be ready to show that the price paid or received is consistent with what the price would be for an unrelated party.

bytestart.co.uk, a small business portal, has a useful Business Expenses Guide (go to www.bytestart.co.uk and click on 'Tax and Accounting' and 'Business Expenses Guide').

Equity capital disguised as debt

The general term *debt* refers to money borrowed from lenders who require that the money be paid back by a certain date, and who require that interest be paid on the debt until it is repaid. *Equity* is money invested by owners (such as shareholders) in a business in return for hoped-for, but not guaranteed, profit returns. Interest is deductible, but cash dividends paid to shareholders are not – which gives debt capital a big edge over equity capital at tax time.

Not surprisingly, some businesses try to pass off equity capital as debt on their tax returns so that they can deduct the payments to the equity sources as interest expense to determine taxable income. Don't think that the Inland Revenue is ignorant of these tactics: Everything that you declare as interest on debt may be examined carefully, and if the Inland Revenue determines that what you're calling debt is really equity capital, it disallows the interest deduction. The business can make payments to its sources of capital that it calls and treats as interest – but this does not mean that the Inland Revenue will automatically believe that the payments are in fact interest. The Inland

Revenue follows the general principle of substance over form. If the so-called debt has too many characteristics of equity capital, the Inland Revenue treats the payments not as interest but rather as dividend distributions from profit to the equity sources of capital.

In summary, debt must really be debt and must have few or none of the characteristics of equity. Drawing a clear-cut line between debt and equity has been a vexing problem for the Inland Revenue, and the rules are complex. You'll probably have to consult a tax professional if you have a question about this issue. Be warned that if you attempt to disguise equity capital as debt, your charade may not work – and the Inland Revenue may disallow any 'interest' payments you have made.

Surviving a Tax Investigation

Hopefully with good bookkeeping and accounting systems you can avoid any disputes over tax and other matters. Complete records are vital if you are to successfully defend yourself from mistaken allegations of wrongdoing. Reading the following sections may help you understand more about how tax enquiries get started and what may happen if you face one.

Rationalising the reasons

HM Revenue & Customs gets its information from three sources. Its own investigations and tips from the public account for the vast majority of information received. However, an increasingly effective third measure is to ask people to inform on themselves. Self-employed people who have strayed across the boundary between tax avoidance and tax evasion can contact the tax authorities anonymously and get confidential advice on how to sort themselves out.

Sometimes the tax authorities look closely at whole industries. In recent years, they have looked at the amusement arcade business, construction, betting and gaming, commodities dealing, and some doctors and dentists.

Tax inspectors may also do any of the following:

- ✔ Drive around exclusive residential areas and look carefully at any expensive-looking renovation work.
- ✔ Use the services of pubs, restaurants, hotels, copy shops, and other cash businesses, looking carefully at the businesses' cost structures.

- ✔ Read local newspapers and use press-cutting agencies to cross-check a person's claimed lifestyle with their actual one.

- ✔ Access company databases and online records from Companies House.

- ✔ Check up on local authority parking permits in certain areas.

- ✔ Examine the land registry to monitor house purchases and property prices and sales, and keep an eye on the yachting register.

HM Revenue & Customs puts all the information that it gathers into its computers and cross-correlates all these sources of data. A skilled project team looks specifically at the uses of information technology for tax investigations and they can usually uncover anything that does not look quite right. For example, if someone is claiming to make no profit from her business, but owns a yacht, has a residence parking permit for inner-city parking in an area she doesn't appear to live in, and is having a new swimming pool installed, alarm bells ring.

What is more likely is that someone tips the tax inspectors off. Informers are often aggrieved spouses or employees, competitors, jealous neighbours, or jilted lovers. Some people like to brag about how they load their expenses, or take cash payments that they don't enter in the books, so not surprisingly gossip spreads. If that gossip reaches the wrong ears, then it may trigger an investigation.

The duration of an investigation varies according to the complexity of the case and the availability of information. It is surprising if most cases – from beginning to end – aren't cleared within 18 months. A technically based case, however, can take much longer – if, for example, both sides need to seek tax counsel's advice. When parts have to be taken to the General Commissioners of Income Tax (www.generalcommissioners.gov.uk), who hear appeals against HMRC decisions on taxation, a case can last for years.

Recognising the signs that you're under scrutiny

Becoming aware that a tax investigation is underway is not difficult. You're likely to get a standard letter from the Special Compliance Office, or your accountant may. This letter states that enquiries have begun under Code of Practice 8 for less serious matters and Code of Practice 9 for serious matters. Booklets accompany the letter, to explain the procedure. By this stage you can be sure that the authorities have already gathered a lot of information.

Anticipating the worst that can happen

HM Revenue & Customs has sweeping powers to demand documents from the taxpayer and from third parties under section 20 or section 745 of the Taxes Management Act. It is always entitled to obtain papers and documents and they can go back 20 years into a person's affairs in cases of suspected fraud. That is way beyond the six years for which you are required to keep your own accounting records. So if you have stuck strictly to the six-year rule, you may be at something of a disadvantage in a tax enquiry.

What HM Revenue & Customs is not entitled to do is to insist on an interview with the taxpayer or third parties. It cannot force people to speak. HM Revenue and Customs is allowed to search premises and remove documents if it has a warrant. If its staff raid your premises, don't obstruct them. But do follow a few simple rules:

- ✔ Make sure that your professional adviser gets round to the premises as fast as possible.

- ✔ Read the warrant and make sure that you understand it.

- ✔ Remember that you are under no legal obligation to talk.

- ✔ Inform your staff that they are under no legal obligation to talk.

- ✔ Ask for the purpose of the search.

- ✔ Obtain a receipt for any materials that the investigators take away.

- ✔ Get the name and office of the investigator in charge.

HM Revenue & Customs understands the real world and that people in it have complex financial, commercial, and personal lives. It goes to great lengths to protect confidences and save embarrassment. This means in practice that you can make disclosures on a managed basis. Two spouses, say, can go through one joint disclosure as appropriate, and then have separate meetings with HM Revenue & Customs in which they can make disclosures of which the other is unaware. Likewise, directors of a business can make disclosures of which fellow directors remain ignorant.

Negotiating around penalties

The penalties as a result of tax investigations can theoretically be as high as 100 per cent of the unpaid tax; in practice they are nearly always dwarfed by the amount of tax to be paid and in the worst case you may go to jail. But in practice, HM Revenue & Customs prosecutes very rarely, so the number of investigations that end up with someone in prison is relatively small.

If HM Revenue & Customs says that it is going to prosecute you, the consequences can be serious. You must seek professional advice immediately.

Bargaining is inevitable in most cases. HM Revenue & Customs' main aim is to ensure that taxpayers pay the right amount of tax. But what the right amount of tax is is open to discussion. Investigators are also concerned with hitting their own 'sales' targets in an efficient manner. They have goals for how much unpaid tax they have to collect each year and deadlines to meet along the way. Anyone with a goal and a deadline can be negotiated with.

Insuring against loss

Tax investigations can be costly. Apart from any fine, you have to bear the cost of your own advisers answering the tax inspector's questions. Even if you win, you don't get those costs back. You can protect yourself from some problems by getting insurance against a tax, VAT, or NI investigation, which ensures that you get good, timely advice at no additional cost. The Association of British Insurers (www.abi.org.uk) can put you in contact with a source of such insurance as well as advice.

Tax Café (www.taxcafe.co.uk) publishes a range of regularly updated tax advice guides aimed at anyone wanting to find out how to pay less tax legally. It also offers an online tax advice service, where you can ask experts complex business tax questions. Responses in three to five working days cost £89.95. The Express service, where questions asked before 12 noon on a working day are answered the same day, costs £129.95.

Chapter 4

Adding the Cost of VAT

. . . .

In This Chapter

▶ Examining the nuts and bolts of VAT

▶ Setting up for VAT

▶ Getting the return right

▶ Paying and reclaiming VAT

▶ If you want to deregister

. . . .

A lot of mystery and tales of horror surround the subject of VAT (Value Added Tax). Now that HM Revenue & Customs administers both tax and VAT, the average business person is facing an even more powerful organisation with a right to know even more about your business.

The rules governing which goods and services are subject to VAT and which items of VAT are reclaimable can be quite complex. This chapter can only scratch the surface and give a broad understanding. Contact both HM Revenue & Customs and your accountant/auditor at an early stage to find out whether all your sales are subject to VAT and how you can ensure that you are only reclaiming allowable VAT. Remember the following – get it right from the beginning.

Looking into VAT

VAT (Value Added Tax) is a tax charged on most business transactions made in the UK or the Isle of Man. VAT is also charged on goods and some services imported from certain places outside the European Union and on some goods and services coming into the UK from other EU countries. VAT applies to all businesses – sole traders, partnerships, limited companies, charities, and so on. In simple terms all VAT-registered businesses act as unpaid collectors of VAT for HM Revenue & Customs.

Examples of taxable transactions are:

- ✔ Selling new and used goods, including hire purchase
- ✔ Renting and hiring out goods
- ✔ Using business stock for private purposes
- ✔ Providing a service, for example plumbing or manicure
- ✔ Charging admission to enter into buildings

As you can see this list covers most business activities.

Certain services are exempt from VAT, including money lending, some property transactions, insurance, and certain types of education and training. Supplies exempt from VAT don't form part of your turnover for VAT purposes.

As the name suggests, Value Added Tax is a tax on the difference between what you buy (inputs) and what you sell (outputs), as long as these items fall within the definition of taxable transactions (see the next sections). At the end of a VAT reporting period, you pay over to HM Revenue & Customs the difference between all your output tax and input tax.

- ✔ **Input tax** is the VAT you pay out to your suppliers for goods and services you purchase for your business. You can reclaim the VAT on these goods or services coming *in* to your business. (See 'Getting VAT back', later in this chapter.) It is in effect a tax added to all your purchases.
- ✔ **Output tax** is the VAT that you must charge on your goods and services when you make each sale. You collect output tax from your customers on each sale you make of items or services going *out* of your business. It is in effect a tax added to all your sales.

Notice 700: The VAT Guide needs to be your bible in determining how much you need to pay and what you can reclaim.

Knowing what to charge

In addition to the obvious trading activities, you need to charge VAT on a whole range of other activities, including the following:

- ✔ **Business assets:** If you sell off any unneeded business assets, such as office equipment, commercial vehicles, and so on, you must charge VAT.
- ✔ **Sales to staff:** Sales to staff are treated no differently than sales to other customers. Therefore you must charge VAT on sales such as canteen meals, goods at reduced prices, vending machines, and so on.

✔ **Hire or loans:** If you make a charge for the use of a business asset, this amount must incur VAT.

✔ **Gifts:** If you give away goods that cost more than £50, you must add VAT. Treat gifts as if they are a sale for your VAT records.

✔ **Goods for own use:** Anything you or your family take out of the business must go on the VAT return. HM Revenue & Customs doesn't let you reclaim the VAT on goods or services that aren't used for the complete benefit of the business.

HM Revenue & Customs is really hot on using business stock for your own use, which is very common in restaurants, for example. HM Revenue & Customs knows you do it and has statistics to show how much on average businesses 'take out' this way. If you don't declare this item when you've used business stock be prepared to have HM Revenue & Customs jump on you from a great height.

✔ **Commission earned:** If you sell someone else's goods or services and get paid by means of a commission, you must include VAT on this income.

✔ **Bartered goods:** If you swap your goods or services for someone else's goods or services, you must account for VAT on the full value of your goods or services that are part of this arrangement.

✔ **Advance payments:** If a customer gives you any sum of money, you must account for VAT on this amount and the balance when he collects the goods. If, for example, you accept payment by instalments, you collect VAT on each instalment.

✔ **Credit notes:** These items are treated exactly like negative sales invoices, and so make sure that you include VAT so you can effectively reclaim the VAT on the output that you're going to, or may have already, paid.

In general you don't have to charge VAT on goods you sell to a VAT registered business in another European Community (EC) member state. However, you must charge UK VAT if you sell goods to private individuals.

Knowing how much to charge

The rate of VAT applicable to any transaction is determined by the nature of that transaction. The 17.5 per cent rate applies to most transactions. The type of business (size or sector) generally has no bearing on the VAT rates. Three rates of VAT currently exist in the UK:

Book VI

Keeping On Top of Tax

✔ A standard rate, currently 17.5 per cent. This is the rate at which most businesses should add VAT to products and services that they sell.

✔ A reduced rate, currently 5 per cent. Some products and services have a lower rate of VAT, including domestic fuel, energy-saving installations, and the renovation of dwellings.

✔ A zero per cent rate. Many products and services are given a zero rating, including some foods, books, and children's clothing. A zero rating for a product or service is not the same as a total exemption.

You can view a list of business areas where sales are reduced-rated or zero-rated in *Notice 700,* which you can download from www.hmrc.gov.uk. You can call the National Advice Service on 0845 010 9000 if you have queries about the list.

Registering for VAT

The starting point is registering for VAT so that you can charge VAT on your sales and reclaim VAT on your purchases.

The current VAT registration threshold is £67,000, from April 2008 (this changes each year, so check with HM Revenue & Customs for the current threshold). So, if your annual turnover (sales, not profit) is less than this figure you don't have to register for VAT.

You may find it advantageous to register for VAT even though your sales fall below the VAT registration threshold (and may never exceed it). Registering for VAT gives your business increased credibility – if your customers are large businesses, they expect their suppliers to be VAT registered. Also, you can't reclaim VAT if you're not registered. If your business makes zero-rated supplies but buys in goods and services on which you pay VAT, you want to be able to reclaim this VAT.

As your business grows, it may be difficult to know whether you have broken through the VAT registration threshold. HM Revenue & Customs states that you must register for VAT if:

✔ At the end of any month the total value of the sales you made in the past 12 months (or less) is more than the current threshold.

✔ At any time you have reasonable ground to expect your sales to be more that the threshold in the next 30 days.

After you register for VAT you're on the VAT treadmill and have to account for output tax on all your sales, keep proper VAT records and accounts, and send in VAT returns regularly.

Paying and Reclaiming VAT

HM Revenue & Customs adopts a very simple process, laying down and policing the rules in two ways:

✔ Businesses must file periodic returns to the VAT Central Unit (see 'Completing Your VAT Return', later in this chapter, for when to file VAT payments).

✔ Businesses receive periodic enquiries and visits from HM Revenue & Customs to verify that these returns are correct.

Book VI

Keeping On Top of Tax

VAT returns must be posted to arrive at the VAT Central Unit by the due date, which is shown on the form, and is usually one month after the period covered by the return. Yes, this schedule means that you have one month to complete your VAT return. Any payment due to HM Revenue & Customs must be sent with the VAT return.

As long as you complete your VAT return on time and don't arouse the suspicions of HM Revenue & Customs, you may not meet the staff for many years.

You face a financial penalty if your return is late and/or seriously inaccurate. HM Revenue & Customs can and does impose hefty fines on businesses that transgress. Also, offenders who previously had the luxury of quarterly VAT returns often find themselves having to complete monthly VAT returns. Don't mess around with HM Revenue & Customs!

HM Revenue & Customs targets some business sectors. In general, businesses structured in a complex manner (such as offshore companies) that involve a lot of cash are likely to come in for extra scrutiny. Experience tells HM Revenue & Customs that looking closely at certain types of businesses often yields extra revenues. Also, businesses that submit VAT returns late on a regular basis attract fines and may be forced to submit monthly VAT returns together with payments on account.

Choosing paper or ether

You can file your VAT return by post or via the Internet. You must meet the stated deadline no matter which method you choose and include any payment due. Of course, if you complete your VAT return electronically you need to pay electronically as well. Visit the HM Revenue & Customs Web site at www.hmrc.gov.uk and click VAT Online Services to find out about doing your VAT return online.

Your paper-based VAT return comes with a pre-addressed envelope in which you need to send your return. If you lose this envelope, send your return to

> VAT Central Unit
>
> Alexander House
>
> Southend-on-Sea
>
> Essex
>
> SS99 1AA

What to look out for on your paper VAT return

Fill in boxes 1 to 9, but complete boxes 8 and 9 only if you trade in goods with other EC member states. Write one amount in each box or put 'NONE' if appropriate.

- ✔ Correct any mistakes by crossing out, writing in the correct figure, and initialling the amendment.
- ✔ Enclose negative figures in brackets.
- ✔ Write your VAT registration number on the back of all cheques.
- ✔ Inform your local HM Revenue & Customs office if any of the details printed on the return are incorrect. Don't make any alterations on the return but write a separate letter to your local VAT Business Advice Centre.
- ✔ Leave blank boxes or areas labelled 'For Official Use'.
- ✔ Send *only* cheques or crossed postal orders with your return.
- ✔ Do *not* send post-dated cheques.

What to look out for on your electronic VAT return

Fill in the appropriate boxes, using 0.00 for nil amounts.

- ✔ Make any payment due by electronic methods (BACS, CHAPS, or bank giro).
- ✔ Wait for the acknowledgement that your electronic return was received.
- ✔ Keep a copy of the electronic acknowledgement page for your records.

Meeting deadlines for small businesses

Most businesses pay VAT quarterly regardless of size. Return forms are sent out in advance by post. Generally, you get your next VAT return about a month in advance of when you need to send it in. If your next VAT return doesn't arrive within this time scale, call your local HM Revenue & Customs office and ask for another. Remember that you're responsible for completing a VAT return even if you don't receive a form!

HM Revenue & Customs has introduced some arrangements to make VAT accounting easier for small businesses. The accounting method that your business uses determines when you pay VAT:

Book VI

Keeping On
Top of Tax

- ✔ **Annual Accounting:** If you use the Annual Accounting scheme, you pay monthly or quarterly installments towards an estimated annual VAT bill. This arrangement evens out VAT payments and helps to smooth cash flow. At the end of the year you submit a single annual return and settle up for any balance due (or maybe receive a cheque back from HM Revenue & Customs). In effect you complete one annual VAT return at the end of the year but make either monthly or quarterly payments on account (you agree with HM Revenue & Customs which you want).

  This arrangement may suit the disorganised business that struggles to complete the more traditional four quarterly VAT returns.

  You can use this scheme if your annual sales (excluding VAT) aren't expected to exceed £1,350,000 and continue until your annual sales exceed £1,600,000.

  The range is based on estimates of your total sales. If your sales have a boost and exceed £1,350,000, you can stay on this scheme just as long as sales don't go beyond £1,600,000. If sales exceed £1,600,000 you must come off this scheme.

- ✔ **Cash Accounting:** If you use the Cash Accounting scheme, your business accounts for income and expenses when they're actually incurred. Therefore, you don't pay HM Revenue & Customs VAT until your customers pay you. This arrangement may suit a business that has regular slow paying customers.

- ✔ **Flat Rate Scheme:** This arrangement makes VAT much simpler by allowing you to calculate your VAT payment as a flat percentage of your turnover. The percentage is determined according to the trade sector in which your business operates.

  Under this scheme you can't reclaim any VAT on your actual purchases, which may mean you lose out if your business is significantly different to the business model HM Revenue & Customs applies to you. Also, if your business undertakes a large capital spend, which has a lot of VAT on it, you are unlikely to get the entire amount back under this scheme.

A word on cash basis accounting for Value Added Tax

Cash basis accounting (also known as *cheque-book accounting*) isn't generally acceptable in the world of business, but is permitted by Value Added tax law for some businesses. To use cash basis VAT accounting, a business must keep these factors in mind:

✔ Cash accounting is open to you if you are a registered trader with an expected turnover not exceeding **£1,350,000** in the next 12 months. There is a 25% tolerance built into the scheme. This means that once you are using cash accounting, you can normally continue to use it until the annual value of your taxable supplies reaches **£1,600,000**.

✔ The main accounting record you must keep will be a cash book summarising all payments made and received, with a separate column for the relevant VAT. You will also need to keep the corresponding tax invoices and ensure that there is a satisfactory system of cross-referencing.

✔ These VAT records must be kept for six years, unless you have agreed upon a shorter period with your local VAT office.

✔ The longer the time lag between your issuing sales invoices and receiving payment from your customers, the more benefit cash accounting is likely to be to you. If you are usually paid as soon as you make a sale (e.g. if you use a retail scheme) you will normally be worse off under cash accounting. The same applies to the situation where you

regularly receive re-payments of VAT (e.g. because you make zero-rated supplies).

✔ One major advantage of the scheme is that it simplifies your bookkeeping requirements, and many businesses can be controlled simply by using an appropriately analysed cash book.

For the great majority of businesses, cash basis accounting is not acceptable, neither for reporting to the Inland Revenue nor for preparing financial statements. So this last advantage of cash-based VAT accounting is illusory. This method falls short of the information needed for even a relatively small business. Accrual basis accounting, described in Book II Chapter 1 and Book III Chapter 1, is the only real option for most businesses. Even small businesses that don't sell products should carefully consider whether cash basis is adequate for:

✔ Preparing external financial statements for borrowing money and reporting to owners.

✔ Dividing profit among owners.

For all practical purposes, only sole proprietorships (one-owner businesses) that sell just services and no products can use cash basis VAT accounting. Other businesses must use the accrual basis – which provides a much better income statement for management control and decision-making, and a much more complete picture of the business's financial condition.

You can use this scheme if your annual sales (excluding VAT) aren't expected to exceed £150,000 or £187,500 including VAT.

✔ **Retail Schemes:** If you make lots of quite small sales to the public, you may find it difficult to issue a VAT invoice for each sale. Several available retail schemes may help. For example, you can use a simpler receipt that a till can print out.

To find out more about the numerous retail schemes, log onto the HM Revenue & Customs Web site `www.hmrc.gov.uk` and click the link to VAT, under Businesses and Corporations. You then need to click on the link to Information and Guides and select Special Schemes & Options. You will find a link to detailed information about retail schemes on the next page.

Getting VAT back

When you are completing your VAT return, you want to reclaim the VAT on every legitimate business purchase. However, you must make sure that you only reclaim legitimate business purchases. The following is the guidance that HM Revenue & Customs gives:

- ✔ **Business purchases:** You can reclaim the VAT on all business purchases and expenses, not just on the raw materials and goods you buy for resale. These purchases include things like business equipment, telephone and utility bills, and payments for other services such as accountants and solicitors' fees.

    You can't deduct your input tax for certain purchases, including cars, business entertainment, and second-hand goods that you bought under one of the VAT second-hand schemes.

- ✔ **Business/private use:** If you use services for both business and private purposes, such as your telephone, you can reclaim VAT only on the business use. No hard and fast rules exist on how you split the bill – your local HM Revenue & Customs office is likely to consider any reasonable method.

- ✔ **Pro-forma invoice:** If a supplier issues a pro-forma invoice, which includes VAT that you have to pay before you are supplied with the goods or service, you can't deduct this amount from your VAT bill on your next return. You can only deduct VAT when you get the proper invoice.

- ✔ **Private motoring:** If you use a business car for both business and private use, you can reclaim all the VAT as input tax, but you have to account for tax on any private motoring using a scale charge (see 'Using fuel for private motoring', later in this chapter).

- ✔ **Lost invoices:** You can't reclaim any VAT on non-existent invoices. If you do and you get a VAT visit you're in for the high jump!

- ✔ **Bad debt relief:** Occasionally customers don't pay you, and if you have already paid over to HM Revenue & Customs the output VAT on this sale you're going to be doubly annoyed. Fortunately HM Revenue & Customs isn't totally heartless – you can reclaim this VAT on a later VAT return.

Completing Your VAT Return

You can complete a paper-based return or an electronic one via the Internet.

Letting your accounting software complete your VAT return is the easiest method. Sage 50 Accounts does VAT returns as a matter of routine, picking up all the necessary information automatically. You just need to tell the program when to start and when to stop picking up the invoice information. Sage 50 Accounts even prints out the VAT return in a format very similar to HM Revenue & Customs' own VAT return form. Figure 4-1 shows Sage 50 Accounts' VAT return.

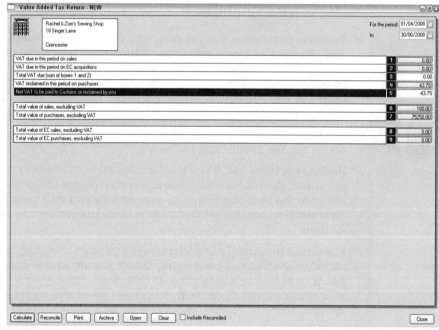

Figure 4-1:
The Sage 50 Accounts' VAT return; as close as you're going to get to a real life VAT return without being VAT registered.

VAT returns are a controlled document and are issued only with a business name and VAT registration number pre-printed on the form – so we can't show you a specimen form.

Filling in the boxes

At last we come to nitty-gritty of what figures go into each of the nine boxes on the VAT return. Table 4-1 helps keep the process simple.

Table 4-1	VAT Return Boxes
Box	**Information Required**
1	VAT due on sales and other outputs in the period. *Notice 700: The VAT Guide* gives further help.
2	VAT due from you on acquisitions of goods from other EC Member States. *Notice 725 VAT: The Single Market* gives further help.
3	For paper returns, enter the sum of boxes 1 and 2. The electronic form handles all the maths needed in completing the form.
4	The input tax you are entitled to claim for the period.
5	The difference between the figures from boxes 3 and 4. Deduct the smaller from the larger. If the figure in box 3 is more than the figure in box 4, **you owe** this amount to HM Revenue & Customs.
	If the figure in box 3 is less than the figure in box 4, HM Revenue & Customs **owes you** this amount.
6	Your total sales/outputs excluding any VAT.
7	Your total purchases/inputs excluding any VAT.
8	Complete this box only if you supplied goods to another EC member state. Put in this box the total value of all supplies of goods (sales) to other member states.
	Note: If you include anything in box 8, make sure that you include the amount in the box 6 total.
9	Complete this box only if you acquired goods from another EC member state. Put in this box the total value of all goods acquired (purchases) from other member states.
	Note: If you include anything in box 9 make sure that you include the amount in the box 7 total.

We deliberately keep this process simple, but remember that behind every box is a multitude of traps set to ensnare you.

Glancing at some problem areas

Not all businesses are entirely straightforward for VAT purposes. Some business activities have their own unique rules and regulations. The list below outlines the exceptions to the rule:

- **Building developer:** See *VAT Notice 708: Buildings and construction* about non-deductible input tax on fixtures and fittings.

- **Tour operator:** See *VAT Notice 709/5: Tour operators' margin scheme* about VAT you can't reclaim on margin scheme supplies.

- **Second-hand dealer:** See *VAT Notice 718: margin schemes for second-hand goods, works of art, antiques, and collectors' items* about VAT you can't reclaim on second-hand dealing.

Using fuel for private motoring

If your business pays for non-business fuel for company car users you must reduce the amount of VAT you reclaim on fuel by means of the scale charge, shown in Table 4-2.

Notice 700/64: Motoring expenses gives full details. If you use the scale charge, you can recover all the VAT charged on road fuel without having to split your mileage between business and private use. Until 2007 the charge was based on engine size and the type of fuel used, but with effect from the 2007 Budget the charge is based on carbon dioxide emissions. If your vehicle is registered since 2001, its carbon dioxide emissions figure appears on the Vehicle Registration Certificate (VC5). If your vehicle was registered before 2001, you can get the carbon dioxide emissions figure from the Society of Motor Manufacturers and Traders Ltd Web site (www.smmt.co.uk).

Table 4-2	Fuel Charge Table for Quarterly Periods		
CO_2 Band	*Scale Charge (£)*	*VAT Due per Car (£)*	*Net Amount*
140 or below	182.00	27.11	154.89
145	195.00	29.04	165.96
150	207.00	30.83	176.17
155	219.00	32.62	186.38
160	231.00	34.40	196.60

CO_2 Band	Scale Charge (£)	VAT Due per Car (£)	Net Amount
165	243.00	36.19	206.81
170	256.00	38.13	217.87
175	268.00	39.91	228.09
180	280.00	41.70	238.30
185	292.00	43.49	248.51
190	304.00	45.28	258.72
195	317.00	47.21	269.79
200	329.00	49.00	280.00
205	341.00	50.79	290.21
210	353.00	52.57	300.43
215	365.00	54.36	310.64
220	378.00	56.30	321.70
225	390.00	58.09	331.91
230	402.00	59.87	342.13
235	414.00	61.66	352.34
240 or above	426.00	63.45	362.55

Book VI

Keeping On Top of Tax

Therefore, if you provide free fuel for personal use to an employee who drives a vehicle in carbon dioxide band 160 (regardless of how much fuel the person uses), you can't claim the input tax for £34.40 on that person's fuel bills. In effect you have to deduct £34.40 from box 4 and £196.60 from box 7 in this case.

Leasing a motor car

You may find that you are able to claim only 50 per cent of the input tax on contract hire rentals in certain situations. If you lease a car for business purposes, you normally can't recover 50 per cent of the VAT charged. The 50 per cent block is to cover the private use of the car. You can reclaim the remaining 50 per cent of the VAT charged. If you lease a qualifying car that is used exclusively for business purposes and not available for private use, you can recover the input tax in full.

Filing under special circumstances

If you're filing your first VAT return, your final return, or a return with no payment, bear a few things in mind:

TIP

- ✓ **First return:** On your first return you may want to reclaim VAT on money you spent prior to the period covered by your first VAT return. In general, you can recover VAT on capital and pre-start up costs and expenses incurred before you registered for VAT as long as they are VAT qualifying. For further help on this, refer to *Notice 700: The VAT Guide,* available from HM Revenue & Customs.

  If you're completing a VAT return for the first time, go onto the HM Revenue & Customs Web site for help (www.hmrc.gov.uk) and/or speak with your accountant. You may be missing a trick in not reclaiming VAT on something you bought but didn't reclaim the VAT on. More importantly, you may be reclaiming VAT on something that you aren't permitted to reclaim.

- ✓ **Final return:** For help with your final return read *Notice 700/11: Cancelling your registration.* If you have any business assets, such as equipment, vehicles, or stock on which you previously reclaimed VAT, you must include these items in your final VAT return. In effect HM Revenue & Customs wants to recover this VAT (unless the amount is less than £1,000) in your last return. Note that even if you previously completed electronic returns you must complete a paper-based return for this final return.

- ✓ **Nil return:** You can file a Nil return if you

  - Have not traded in the period covered by the VAT return *and*

  - No VAT exists on purchases (inputs) to recover *or*

  - No VAT exists on sales (outputs) to declare.

  Complete all boxes on the return as 'None' on your paper-based return or '0.00' on your electronic return.

Correcting mistakes

If you make a small mistake (£2,000 or less) on a previous return you can adjust your VAT account and include the value of that adjustment on your current VAT return. If the amount is payable to HM Revenue & Customs, include it in the total for box 1 or box 2 (acquisitions). If the amount is repayable to you, include it in the total for box 4.

If you make a bigger mistake (more than £2,000), *do not* include the amount on your current return. Inform your local VAT Business Advice Centre by letter or on form *VAT 652: Voluntary disclosure of errors on VAT returns*. A Notice of Voluntary Disclosure is then issued showing only the corrections to the period in question, and you become liable to the under-declared VAT and interest. Under these circumstances no mis-declaration penalty is applied. Form *Notice 700/45: How to correct VAT errors and make adjustments or claims* helps you.

Pursuing Payments and Repayments

Your completed VAT return results in one of two outcomes: You owe HM Revenue & Customs money or it owes you money – unless of course you complete a Nil return, in which case you and HM Revenue & Customs are quits.

If you owe VAT but can't afford to pay by the due date, still send in your completed VAT return and write a separate letter to your local VAT Business Advice Centre explaining why you can't pay *(see Notice 930: What if I don't pay?)*. Don't send post-dated cheques.

If you're making payments on account, don't adjust any of the figures in the boxes on your VAT return. Pay the net liability (shown in box 5) less any payments on account already made for that period.

If you are owed money, you should receive a repayment about two weeks after you submit your VAT return. If after three weeks you haven't received your repayment, contact the Customs and Excise National Advice Service on 0845 010 9000.

If your business is due a repayment of VAT on a regular basis and you are on quarterly VAT returns, switch to monthly VAT returns at the earliest opportunity. Under a monthly system you wait only two weeks for your VAT repayment rather than an additional two months.

If for any reason you receive a 'Notice of assessment and/or over-declaration' as a result of a mistake found by a visiting officer, don't wait until your next VAT return to rectify the issue. If you owe VAT, send your payment and the remittance advice in the envelope provided. If you're owed, suppress a large smile and pay in the cheque, or check your bank account if you normally pay electronically.

Deregistering for VAT

If your sales fall to below the VAT threshold (£62,000 in 2008–9) you can opt to deregister. This drop takes you out of the VAT net. But you don't have to deregister.

If you anticipate that your business downturn is temporary and if charging VAT does not harm your relationships with customers, stick with it if you can stand the paperwork as you'll only have to reregister when your sales go up again. And keeping a VAT number means you can continue to offset all the VAT on goods and services you buy in.

Index

Notes

Notes

Notes

FOR DUMMIES®

Do Anything. Just Add Dummies

UK editions

SELF HELP

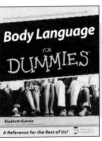
978-0-470-51291-3

978-0-470-03135-3

978-0-470-51501-3

BUSINESS

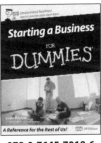
978-0-7645-7018-6

978-0-7645-7056-8

978-0-7645-7026-1

PERSONAL FINANCE

978-0-7645-7023-0

978-0-470-51510-5

978-0-470-05815-2

Answering Tough Interview
Questions For Dummies
(978-0-470-01903-0)

Being the Best Man
For Dummies
(978-0-470-02657-1)

British History
For Dummies
(978-0-470-03536-8)

Buying a Home on a Budget
For Dummies
(978-0-7645-7035-3)

Buying a Property in Spain
For Dummies
(978-0-470-51235-77)

Buying & Selling a Home For
Dummies
(978-0-7645-7027-8)

Buying a Property in Eastern
Europe For Dummies
(978-0-7645-7047-6)

Cognitive Behavioural Therapy
For Dummies
(978-0-470-01838-5)

Cricket For Dummies
(978-0-470-03454-5)

CVs For Dummies
(978-0-7645-7017-9)

Detox For Dummies
(978-0-470-01908-5)

Diabetes For Dummies
(978-0-470-05810-7)

Divorce For Dummies
(978-0-7645-7030-8)

DJing For Dummies
(978-0-470-03275-6)

eBay.co.uk For Dummies
(978-0-7645-7059-9)

Economics For Dummies
(978-0-470-05795-7)

English Grammar For Dummies
(978-0-470-05752-0)

Gardening For Dummies
(978-0-470-01843-9)

Genealogy Online
For Dummies
(978-0-7645-7061-2)

Green Living For Dummies
(978-0-470-06038-4)

Hypnotherapy For Dummies
(978-0-470-01930-6)

Neuro-linguistic Programming
For Dummies
(978-0-7645-7028-5)

Parenting For Dummies
(978-0-470-02714-1)

Pregnancy For Dummies
(978-0-7645-7042-1)

Renting out your Property
For Dummies
(978-0-470-02921-3)

Retiring Wealthy For Dummies
(978-0-470-02632-8)

Self Build and Renovation
For Dummies
(978-0-470-02586-4)

Selling For Dummies
(978-0-470-51259-3)

Sorting Out Your Finances
For Dummies
(978-0-7645-7039-1)

Starting a Business on
eBay.co.uk For Dummies
(978-0-470-02666-3)

Starting and Running an Online
Business For Dummies
(978-0-470-05768-1)

The Romans For Dummies
(978-0-470-03077-6)

UK Law and Your Rights
For Dummies
(978-0-470-02796-7)

Writing a Novel & Getting
Published For Dummies
(978-0-470-05910-4)

FOR DUMMIES®

Do Anything. Just Add Dummies

HOBBIES

978-0-7645-5232-8

978-0-7645-5395-0

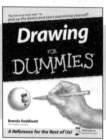

978-0-7645-5476-6

Also available:

Art For Dummies
(978-0-7645-5104-8)

Aromatherapy For Dummies
(978-0-7645-5171-0)

Bridge For Dummies
(978-0-471-92426-5)

Card Games For Dummies
(978-0-7645-9910-1)

Chess For Dummies
(978-0-7645-8404-6)

Improving Your Memory
For Dummies
(978-0-7645-5435-3)

Massage For Dummies
(978-0-7645-5172-7)

Meditation For Dummies
(978-0-471-77774-8)

Photography For Dummies
(978-0-7645-4116-2)

Quilting For Dummies
(978-0-7645-9799-2)

EDUCATION

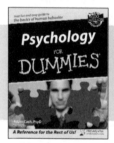

978-0-7645-5434-6

978-0-7645-5581-7

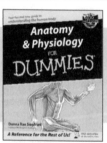

978-0-7645-5422-3

Also available:

Algebra For Dummies
(978-0-7645-5325-7)

Astronomy For Dummies
(978-0-7645-8465-7)

Buddhism For Dummies
(978-0-7645-5359-2)

Calculus For Dummies
(978-0-7645-2498-1)

Cooking Basics For Dummies
(978-0-7645-7206-7)

Forensics For Dummies
(978-0-7645-5580-0)

Islam For Dummies
(978-0-7645-5503-9)

Philosophy For Dummies
(978-0-7645-5153-6)

Religion For Dummies
(978-0-7645-5264-9)

Trigonometry For Dummies
(978-0-7645-6903-6)

PETS

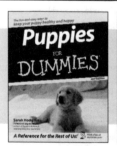

978-0-470-03717-1

978-0-7645-8418-3

978-0-7645-5275-5

Also available:

Aquariums For Dummies
(978-0-7645-5156-7)

Birds For Dummies
(978-0-7645-5139-0)

Dogs For Dummies
(978-0-7645-5274-8)

Ferrets For Dummies
(978-0-7645-5259-5)

Golden Retrievers
For Dummies
(978-0-7645-5267-0)

Horses For Dummies
(978-0-7645-9797-8)

Jack Russell Terriers
For Dummies
(978-0-7645-5268-7)

Labrador Retrievers
For Dummies
(978-0-7645-5281-6)

Puppies Raising & Training
Diary For Dummies
(978-0-7645-0876-9)

FOR DUMMIES®

The easy way to get more done and have more fun

LANGUAGES

Speak Spanish — the fun and easy way!

Spanish FOR DUMMIES

A Reference for the Rest of Us!

978-0-7645-5193-2

Speak French — the fun and easy way!

French FOR DUMMIES

A Reference for the Rest of Us!

978-0-7645-5193-2

Start speaking Italian

Italian FOR DUMMIES

A Reference for the Rest of Us!

978-0-7645-5196-3

Also available:

Chinese For Dummies
(978-0-471-78897-3)

Chinese Phrases
For Dummies
(978-0-7645-8477-0)

French Phrases For Dummies
(978-0-7645-7202-9)

German For Dummies
(978-0-7645-5195-6)

Hebrew For Dummies
(978-0-7645-5489-6)

Italian Phrases For Dummies
(978-0-7645-7203-6)

Japanese For Dummies
(978-0-7645-5429-2)

Latin For Dummies
(978-0-7645-5431-5)

Spanish Phrases
For Dummies
(978-0-7645-7204-3)

Spanish Verbs For Dummies
(978-0-471-76872-2)

MUSIC AND FILM

The bestselling guide, now updated!

Guitar FOR DUMMIES

A Reference for the Rest of Us!

978-0-7645-9904-0

Filmmaking FOR DUMMIES

A Reference for the Rest of Us!

978-0-7645-2476-9

Play-along audio CD included!

Piano FOR DUMMIES

A Reference for the Rest of Us!

978-0-7645-5105-5

Also available:

Bass Guitar For Dummies
(978-0-7645-2487-5)

Blues For Dummies
(978-0-7645-5080-5)

Classical Music For Dummies
(978-0-7645-5009-6)

Drums For Dummies
(978-0-471-79411-0)

Jazz For Dummies
(978-0-471-76844-9)

Opera For Dummies
(978-0-7645-5010-2)

Rock Guitar For Dummies
(978-0-7645-5356-1)

Screenwriting For Dummies
(978-0-7645-5486-5)

Singing For Dummies
(978-0-7645-2475-2)

Songwriting For Dummies
(978-0-7645-5404-9)

HEALTH, SPORTS & FITNESS

Fitness FOR DUMMIES

A Reference for the Rest of Us!

978-0-7645-7851-9

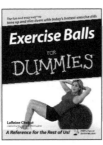

The fun and easy way to tone up and slim down with today's hottest exercise aids

Exercise Balls FOR DUMMIES

A Reference for the Rest of Us!

978-0-7645-5623-4

Asthma FOR DUMMIES

A Reference for the Rest of Us!

978-0-7645-4233-6

Also available:

Controlling Cholesterol
For Dummies
(978-0-7645-5440-7)

Diabetes For Dummies
(978-0-470-05810-7)

High Blood Pressure
For Dummies
(978-0-7645-5424-7)

Martial Arts For Dummies
(978-0-7645-5358-5)

Menopause FD
(978-0-470-061008)

Pilates For Dummies
(978-0-7645-5397-4)

Weight Training
For Dummies
(978-0-471-76845-6)

Yoga For Dummies
(978-0-7645-5117-8)

FOR DUMMIES®

Helping you expand your horizons and achieve your potential

INTERNET

978-0-470-12174-0

978-0-471-97998-2

978-0-470-08030-6

Also available:

Blogging For Dummies
For Dummies, 2nd Edition
(978-0-470-23017-6)

Building a Web Site For
Dummies, 3rd Edition
(978-0-470-14928-7)

Creating Web Pages
All-in-One Desk Reference
For Dummies, 3rd Edition
(978-0-470-09629-1)

eBay.co.uk
For Dummies
(978-0-7645-7059-9)

Video Blogging FD
(978-0-471-97177-1)

Web Analysis For Dummies
(978-0-470-09824-0)

Web Design For Dummies,
2nd Edition
(978-0-471-78117-2)

DIGITAL MEDIA

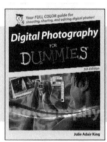

978-0-7645-9802-9

978-0-470-17474-6

978-0-470-14927-0

Also available:

BlackBerry For Dummies,
2nd Edition
(978-0-470-18079-2)

Digital Photography
All-in-One Desk Reference
For Dummies, 3rd Edition
(978-0-470-03743-0)

Digital Photo Projects
For Dummies
(978-0-470-12101-6)

iPhone For Dummies
(978-0-470-17469-2)

Photoshop CS3 For Dummi
(978-0-470-11193-2)

Podcasting For Dummies
(978-0-471-74898-4)

COMPUTER BASICS

978-0-470-13728-4

978-0-470-05432-1

978-0-471-74941-7

Also available:

Macs For Dummies,
9th Edition
(978-0-470-04849-8)

Office 2007 All-in-One Desk
Reference For Dummies
(978-0-471-78279-7)

PCs All-in-One Desk
Reference For Dummies,
4th Edition
(978-0-470-22338-3)

Upgrading & Fixing PCs
For Dummies, 7th Edition
(978-0-470-12102-3)

Windows XP For Dummies,
2nd Edition
(978-0-7645-7326-2)